Understanding FORTRAN 77
Second Edition

Understanding FORTRAN 77
with Structured Problem Solving

Second Edition

Michel Boillot
Pensacola Junior College

WEST PUBLISHING COMPANY
St.Paul/New York/Los Angeles/San Francisco

Copyediting: Pamela S. McMurry
Composition: Carlisle Graphics
Cover and interior design: Lois Stanfield
Cover photo: Steven Hunt/The Image Bank

Library of Congress Cataloging-in-Publication Data

Boillot, Michel H.
     Understanding FORTRAN 77 with structured problem
solving.

     Includes index.
     1. FORTRAN (Computer program language)   2. Structured
programming.   I. Title.
QA76.73.F25B643   1987   005.13'3   86-26662
ISBN 0-314-27031-0

Contents

Preface to Second Edition

The focus of this second edition is on a disciplined approach to program structure through the sequence, the decision (IF THEN/ELSE) and the loop structures (WHILE DO/ENDWHILE and DO CONTINUE). The GO TO statement is practically never used except in the following situations:

1. To simulate the nonstandard FORTRAN WHILE DO/ENDWHILE construct which is only available on certain FORTRAN 77 compilers. The FORTRAN WHILE DO and its simulated code is:

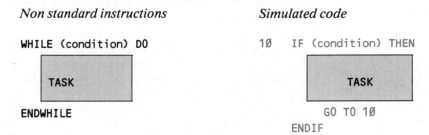

Non standard instructions

```
WHILE (condition) DO

        TASK

ENDWHILE
```

Simulated code

```
10    IF (condition) THEN

           TASK

      GO TO 10
ENDIF
```

The WHILE DO simulated code is shown in red type wherever it occurs in the text, to remind the reader that the task under consideration is under the control of the WHILE DO structure.

2. To read an input file using the END = option:

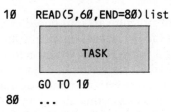

```
10    READ(5,60,END=80) list

           TASK

      GO TO 10
80    ...
```

The logical IF/GO TO statement is practically no longer used in any of the programming problems and examples since in most instances it encourages nonsequential execution of tasks. To allow for such a practice would run contrary to the underlying theme of the text which stresses sequential execution of tasks. Thus the IF/GO TO, the computed GO/TO and the arithmetic IF statements are presented in Appendix A.

The major goal of this text is to convince the student that a program is not just a "bunch" of instructions put together insouciantly which somehow manages to solve a particular problem, but that a program is the result of a carefully planned decomposition of a problem into one or more well defined independent tasks, which when executed sequentially yields the solution to a given problem. Such a resulting task structure requires that each task have one and only one entry point and one and only one exit point, for only in this way can tasks be executed sequentially. Thus the continued emphasis throughout the text on the three above mentioned control structures.

Some reviewers have argued that program modularization should be stressed early on in the first chapters to underscore the importance of a design where tasks are no longer local in nature but generalized and independent. The metamorphosis of a local task into an independent module that can be activated more than once from any other module is made possible through the use of subprograms. Section 8.8.1 on program modularity (subroutines and function subprograms) has been totally rewritten to allow inclusion of that section in chapters 3 and/or 4. The initial chapter sequence could then be: chapter 1, chapter 2, chapter 3, [section 8.8.1], chapter 4, [section 8.8.1] etc.

Other reviewers have argued that formatted input output should appear in the very first few chapters of the book rather than in later chapters (chapter 5 in this edition). This can still be done by bringing section 5.1 on formats into the discussion of input/output in chapters 3 and 4. Section 5.1 is modular and can thus be treated independently of all other chapters.

Because support for substring processing is not available on most FORTRAN 77 compilers, materials on substrings including the DO IT NOW, self-test, programming problems and programming exercises have been pulled together into Appendix B.

On the subject of preferred chapter order, I would like to share with other instructors a happy discovery. Traditionally, the treatment of file processing involving random access of records has been relegated to the very last chapters of a FORTRAN textbook—with the result that very few instructors ever get the time to expose students to file access techniques. This last semester, I decided to cover chapter 6 on arrays simultaneously with direct access files (using section 9–4 of chapter 9). This was a first experience for me in a FORTRAN class. The result was remarkable. Working with microcomputers in an interactive environment, the students really took on to files. Every problem became more relevant, more interesting and more real. The consensus of the class was that direct access files made programming more exciting and meaningful.

The list below delineates the main differences between this edition and the preceding one.

The concepts of structure are introduced in Chapter 1; these are then systematically expanded upon in each successive chapter. Chapter 2 introduces the IF THEN/ELSE structure, chapter 3 the WHILE/DO structure and chapter 5 the DO/CONTINUE structure. Such gradual presentation of structures allows the student to bridge the conceptual to the applied with minimum trauma. Meanwhile this spiral approach to program design enforces a lasting discipline of structure upon the reader.

Format-less input/output is used throughout the first four chapters. Formatted input/output is covered in Chapter 5.

Chapters 3 and 4 of the first edition has been combined into chapter 4 of the second edition. Thus counting and accumulating are treated at the same time.

Chapters 9 and 10 of the original edition have been combined into one chapter on subprograms (Chapter 8).

Flowcharts have essentially been replaced with pseudo code.

Commonly used mathematical functions have been introduced in Chapter 2.

Many nonessential FORTRAN statements have been relegated to appendices.

More scientific problems have been used in chapter problem illustrations as well as in the programming exercise sections.

All programs have been rewritten to emphasize better program structure.

Acknowledgments

Few successful textbooks are ever produced without the assistance and better judgment of reviewers. In that perspective I would like to thank the reviewers listed below for their active participation in this second edition.

Michael Albright, Union College
Felipe de la Garza, San Antonio College
Ed Dionne, San Jose State University
Henry Etlinger, Rochester Institute of Technology
Joe Jones, University of Arkansas
Eileen Lopp, Guilford Technical Community College
Paul Lou, Diablo Valley College
Earl McCullough, University of Wisconsin—Platteville
William Mayo, Rutgers University
Thomas Murtagh, San Jacinto College—South
Linda Ottenstein, Michigan Technological University
Carol Peterson, Bellevue Community College
Tom Thomasma, University of Michigan
Henry Todd, Brigham Young University
Kenneth Walter, Weber State College
Donald Whitt, Houston Community College

Once again, I am greatly indebted to David Whitney of San Francisco State University for his powerful reviews. David is always there to remind me of my *faiblesses humaines* when it comes to syntax and logic. His salient remarks and constructive criticisms (an over-used expression, but right on the mark in this case) have contributed significantly to the improvement of this second edition. David has also authored the first and second edition of the Instructor's Manual of UNDERSTANDING FORTRAN 77.

I also want to thank Paul Calter and McGraw Hill, Inc., Gregg Division for allowing us to use certain material from PROBLEM SOLVING WITH COMPUTERS, 1st ed. © 1973. These are Figure 4-6 on page 163, exercise #17 on page 128, #25 on page 131, #16, #17, and #18 on page 188, #20 on page 190, and #6 on page 338.

Other people who have helped shape this book into existence are Donna Healy, Kathy Theis, Marty Ploessl and Louise March. Thank you all for the hard work. Not to be forgotten in the production phase of this text is John Carlisle and his group who, in conjunction with Tad Bornhoft of West, have worked feverishly to metamorphose a sorry looking manuscript into an attractively designed text.

Finally I would like to thank Peter Marshall, executive editor, and Marlene Bates, developmental editor, for their encouragement, understanding, patience and support during this eighteen-month-long adventure.

Preface to First Edition

This text presents a unique approach to teaching and learning FORTRAN. Each chapter begins with a completely defined problem and a programmed solution to the problem. This program introduces the new language features and syntax that will be discussed in the chapter. Displaying a complete program before discussing the material in the chapter is intended to stimulate the student's curiosity by confronting him or her with a conceptual whole. The student can capture the essence of the program without much difficulty, and he or she is warned not to spend too much time on the introductory programming example. Subsequent sections will clarify the details of the program; at this point, they are unimportant.

The remaining sections of each chapter also have a specific purpose. The second and third sections explain new features, syntax, and programming techniques. Numerous short, illustrative examples are included to show both correct and incorrect coding and applications of programming techniques.

Another section of each chapter contains two or three worked-out problems that apply the language features and programming techniques covered in the preceding sections. All programs contain a data dictionary of variables, and the input and output (results) files are displayed along with the FORTRAN code.

Many chapters have an optional section containing material that is included for the sake of complete presentation of the FORTRAN language, but that is not necessarily essential to all students. Each instructor can decide whether to include or omit these sections.

A section entitled "You Might Want to Know" is in question-and-answer format. It attempts to anticipate commonly asked questions and provides informally phrased answers. Many of the questions point out predictable pitfalls for novice programmers.

Interspersed in the chapter are many "Do It Now" exercises and coding problems, which let students test their understanding of the material just covered. Answers to these exercises, including partial program code, are provided for immediate feedback.

All chapters conclude with exercises. The first section, "Test Yourself" lets the reader test his or her understanding of the material covered in the chapter and practice writing short FORTRAN coding segments covering important programming techniques. Answers to "Test Yourself" are provided at the end of each chapter. The following section contains programming exercises, an extensive collection of problems ranging over a wide variety of subject areas and levels of difficulty. Problems are generally presented in graduated order of difficulty. The instructors or students should be able to find problems that relate to their own areas of interest.

There are some "fun" problems dealing with the simulation of processes or environments (a random number generator function is supplied in chapter 9 for use in these problems), "total" problems requiring the student to design a complete system, and, of course, more traditional problems. Some instructors may wish to present one of these problems as the first programming example of the chapter. In any event, the abundance of problems will allow the instructor to assign different problems semester after semester.

Understanding FORTRAN 77
Second Edition

1 Computers and Programming Concepts

1.1 COMPUTERS—WHAT ARE THEY?

Computers are automatic electronic machines that can:

1. Accept (read) data.
2. Store the accepted data in memory.
3. Manipulate the data according to instructions stored in the computer's memory.
4. Produce intelligible reports (results) from the manipulated data.

1.1.1 Data, Instructions, and Information

The objective of computer data processing is to convert raw data into information that can be used for decision making. *Data* refers to raw facts that have been collected from various sources. Consider, for example, the number 2909. Is that number someone's street address, or is it the balance in his/her checking account? The number 2909 is data, but once it has meaning it becomes information. *Data* can be defined as unprocessed facts, while *information* is the result of organizing unprocessed facts into a meaningful arrangement.

Data is generally fed to a computer to produce information, i.e., data is input to the computer and information is output from the computer (see Figure 1.1). Instructions tell the computer how to process the data. A *program* is a set of instructions written to solve a particular problem.

The computer can accept:

1. The set of instructions (program) that tell it what to do, i.e., how to solve the particular problem.
2. The specific data to be processed by the program to produce the desired information.

Thus, the program and the data are clearly independent entities. For example, a program might consist of the set of instructions telling the computer how to sort a list of names in alphabetical order, while the data could be any list of names. The program would be general enough to process different lists containing various numbers of names.

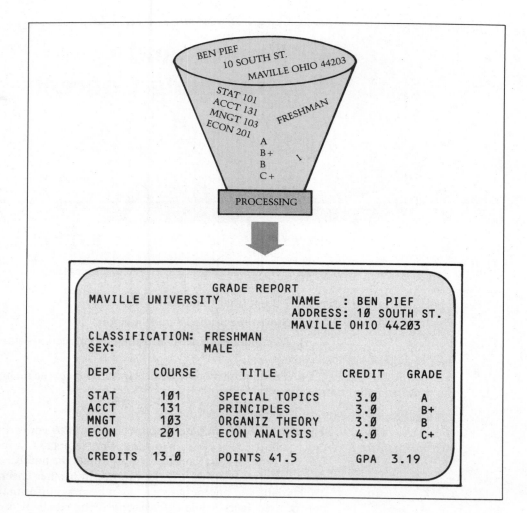

FIGURE 1.1
*DATA VERSUS
INFORMATION*

1.1.2 Computer Hardware and Software

The term *hardware* refers to the physical components of the computer. The term *software* refers to programs or systems of programs written to accomplish specific tasks.

Computers accept (read) programs and data from a variety of input devices. Terminals allow the user to enter programs and data directly on the computer using either a visual screen (cathode ray tube (CRT)) or a hard copy terminal (paper display typewriters). Flexible magnetic disks, called *diskettes* or *floppy disks,* are another medium for data entry. The diskette is inserted into a slot (disk drive) on the terminal and then the keyboard is used to write the input data and programs onto the diskette (see Figure 1.2). These programs and data can then be read and processed by the computer at any convenient time. Such systems are widely used in schools to provide economical and easy computer access for students. In industry and in any large data processing center, data and programs are usually stored on mass storage devices such as magnetic tape and magnetic disks (see Figure 1.3).

FIGURE 1.2
MICROCOMPUTER HARDWARE AND STORAGE DEVICES

FIGURE 1.3
A MAINFRAME SYSTEM WITH MASS STORAGE DEVICES

Before a program can be executed by a computer, it must first be loaded into the computer's memory, which consists of many cells (locations) into which data and program instructions can be stored. This memory is often referred to as *primary storage*.

Once the program is stored in memory, the central processing unit (CPU) of the computer carries out (executes) the instructions one by one. Executing an instruction may mean adding or multiplying numbers or comparing two numbers to determine the larger of the two. It can also involve input/output operations such as reading data into storage or printing results onto a terminal, a printer, or some other type of storage device such as a magnetic disk. Storage media such as magnetic disk drives, which are not part of memory, are referred to as *secondary storage* devices.

From this discussion, we can see that a typical computer system consists of input and output devices and a processing unit (see Figure 1.4); the processing unit is generally composed of the following units:

1. *Memory*   Programs and data are stored in memory locations.

2. *Arithmetic/Logic*   This unit can add, subtract, multiply, divide, and raise to a power. It can also compare numbers algebraically and compare words (one character at a time).

3. *Control*   The control unit fetches program instructions or data in memory and executes each instruction in conjunction with the arithmetic/logic unit.

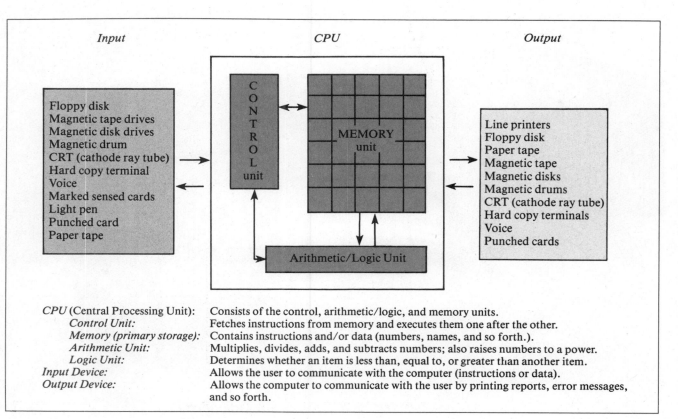

CPU (Central Processing Unit):	Consists of the control, arithmetic/logic, and memory units.
Control Unit:	Fetches instructions from memory and executes them one after the other.
Memory (primary storage):	Contains instructions and/or data (numbers, names, and so forth.).
Arithmetic Unit:	Multiplies, divides, adds, and subtracts numbers; also raises numbers to a power.
Logic Unit:	Determines whether an item is less than, equal to, or greater than another item.
Input Device:	Allows the user to communicate with the computer (instructions or data).
Output Device:	Allows the computer to communicate with the user by printing reports, error messages, and so forth.

FIGURE 1.4
FUNCTIONAL UNITS OF A COMPUTER

In Figure 1.5 the problem of alphabetizing a list of names is illustrated in terms of program instructions, input of data, output of information, and hardware requirements. Notice the relationship between program execution and input/output and the role of the hardware in each step.

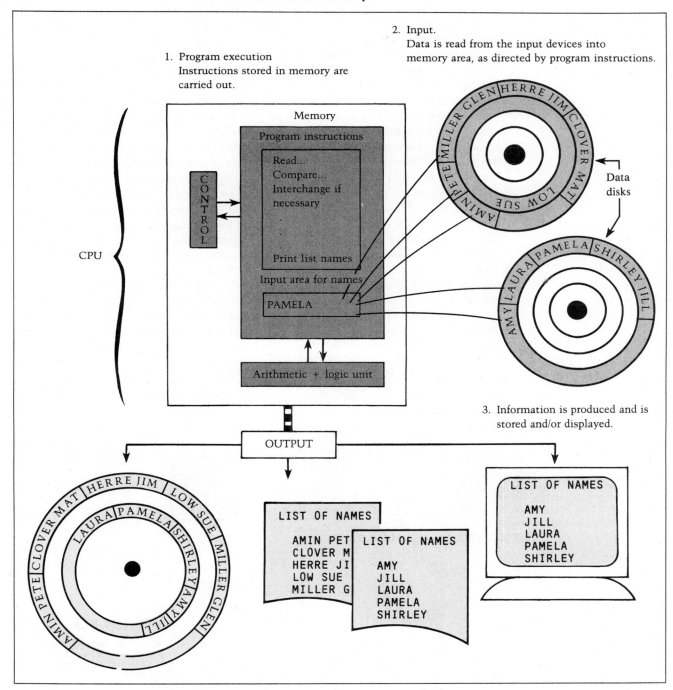

FIGURE 1.5
INPUT, PROCESSING, AND OUTPUT

1.2 COMPUTER LANGUAGES AND PSEUDO CODE

1.2.1 High-Level Languages

A program can be executed (processed) by the computer only when it is stored in the computer's memory and is in binary code (machine language code). Machine language is the only language the central processing unit can understand. In machine language, all operations are represented by machine-recognizable numeric codes, and memory locations containing data and program instructions are represented by numeric addresses. Machine language programs are very detailed, time-consuming, and difficult to write. Machine languages vary from one computer manufacturer to another; they are machine-specific, reflecting the design of each computer.

High-level languages such as FORTRAN have been developed to allow the user to formulate problems more conveniently. (Programs written in a high-level language can be run on any type of digital computer; such programs are called *portable*. Machine language programs are not portable.) FORTRAN (FORmula TRANslation) is most often used by engineers and scientists. It allows them to write computer instructions in an English-like language that parallels the way in which engineers and scientists express and solve problems. A special program called the FORTRAN *compiler* is used by the computer to translate FORTRAN instructions (often referred to as *source code*) into machine code (often referred to as *object code*).

The process of creating, translating, and executing a FORTRAN program is illustrated in the three time frames of Figure 1.6 (the same computer is shown in each time frame). On some systems the compiler, the source code, the object code, and the input data all reside on the same disk. On other systems the compiler is stored on a separate disk while the source code, object code, and input data are on some other disk(s).

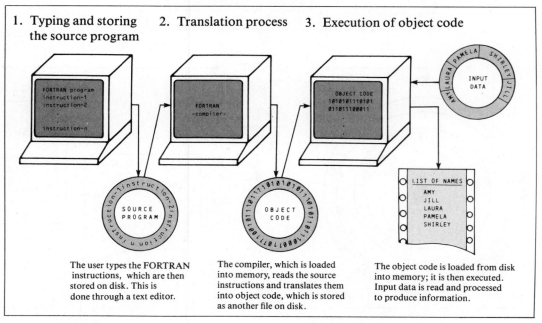

FIGURE 1.6
SOURCE PROGRAM/COMPILATION/EXECUTION

1.2.2 Pseudo Code and Flowcharts

Computers are problem-solving tools, but they are useful only when we can provide them with the step-by-step description of the method for solving a given problem. The description of how we proceed from one step to the next in order to solve a problem is called the *logic* of a problem.

Pseudo code is a very practical tool for expressing the logic of a problem. It uses the English language in an informal, abbreviated form to describe each step of the problem-solving process. Pseudo code is not subject to the strict grammatical rules of the FORTRAN language, thus the writer can concentrate on developing the proper structure of the logic without worrying about the details of a programming language. Pseudo code statements are typically written one per line; occasionally they are indented for readability and clarity. In the next section, we will see how pseudo code is used to develop the structure of a program.

Flowcharts are one of the earliest tools adopted by programmers for describing the logic (or *algorithm*) of a program. A flowchart is a graphical representation of an algorithm. It illustrates the sequence of steps that are to be carried out in order to solve a particular problem. As an example, consider the flowchart in Figure 1.7, which a rather narrow-minded student might use for selecting a course. The various block shapes represent the standard types of operations that are used in an algorithm,

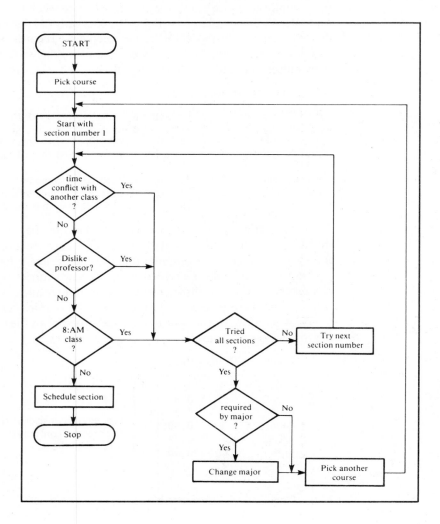

FIGURE 1.7
*ALGORITHM FOR
SELECTING COURSE
SELECTION*

such as processing (arithmetic calculations, data movement, and so forth), decisions, and input/output operations. English descriptions or algebraic expressions are placed inside the boxes to describe what actions are to be performed in each step of the algorithm. The lines connecting the boxes are called *flow lines;* they show the order in which steps are to be carried out.

The use of flowcharts is less prevalent today than in the past, although they are still used occasionally to illustrate a particular component of a program.

1.3 PROGRAM DESIGN AND STRUCTURE

1.3.1 A First Attempt at Program Development

Consider the following problem:

You, your two brothers, and your sister own a small company. As executive officers of the company, you are paid at the fixed rate of $20 per hour, while your part-time employees (who may vary in number from week to week) are paid $4 or $5 per hour, depending on their position in the company ($5 per hour for pay code 1, and $4 dollars per hour for pay code 2). You keep daily records of the hours worked by everyone. At the end of the week, you summarize the work activities of the four company officers and the part-timers as follows:

Name	Hours	Code
JONES M	2	
JONES L	5	
JONES S	0	
JONES T	4	
HUNT L	30	1
LARD S	35	2

The summary always starts with the four records of the officers of the company.
Each record consists of two entries: name and hours.
Officers are paid at a fixed rate of $20 per hour.

Part-time work force. Assume at least one part-time record.
Each record consists of three entries: name, hours, and pay code.
The special symbol ■ identifies the end of the weekly summary.

Such a collection of related records is called a *file.* To physically identify the end of the file, the symbol ■ is placed after the last record. In a computerized environment, this symbol informs the computer that the end of the file has been reached.

Note that each officer's record consists of two entries, while each part-time worker's record consists of three entries (name, hours, and position code). Such entries within records are generally referred to as *fields* or *data items.*

We will now write the logic to read and process this file (our input data) to produce the following pay report:

Name	Hours	Pay
JONES M	2	40.00
JONES L	5	100.00
JONES S	0	0.00
JONES T	4	80.00
HUNT L	30	150.00
LARD S	35	140.00

This report consists of six records (output lines). Each record contains three fields: the name, the hours, and the pay.

1.3.2 Decomposition of a Program into Tasks

The objective of the program development process is to produce code that will (obviously) solve the intended problem and that will also be easy to read, easy to understand, and easy to maintain (i.e., correct or change if the need arises). One way to achieve this goal is to decompose the logic of the program into separate tasks that are clearly defined and independent of one another.

Breaking down a problem into smaller pieces allows the programmer to focus more easily on a particular part of the problem without having to worry about the overall problem. The individual tasks are easier to program and are much more manageable since each performs a specific function. Of course, some of these tasks may need to be further broken down into smaller subtasks, each reflecting decreased levels of responsibility.

Thus a hierarchy of tasks is created: each task can be respecified into a sequence of subtasks describing what is to be performed at an increasing level of detail. This technique of expanding a program plan into several levels of detail is sometimes referred to as a *stepwise refinement* process.

1.3.3 Pseudo Code Solution to Problem

The decomposition of a problem into tasks is made possible by the following three control structures:

1. The sequence structure.
2. The decision structure using the IF THEN ELSE/ENDIF structure.
3. The loop structure using the WHILE DO/END WHILE and the DO/CONTINUE LOOP structures.

The use of these structures is illustrated in Figure 1.8, which displays the pseudo code solution to the pay report problem. The control structures are discussed further in section 1.3.4.

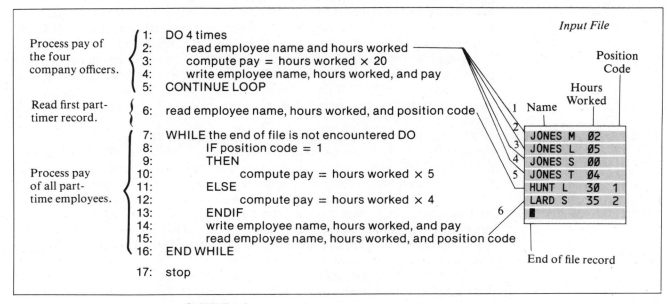

FIGURE 1.8
DECOMPOSITION OF A PROBLEM INTO TASKS

The pseudo code in Figure 1.8 is broken down into three tasks: the first one processes the pay for the four company officers (lines 1–5); the second one reads the first part-time employee record (line 6); and the third one processes the pay for all part-time employees (lines 7–16). Note that these three tasks are carried out sequentially.

The DO/CONTINUE LOOP structure causes instructions 2, 3, and 4 to be carried out four times; it is an example of a *loop* structure. The first *read* instruction captures the employee name and hours worked (JONES M and 2) and the corresponding pay is calculated at line 3 ($40.00) and printed at line 4. The same process is repeated for the remaining three company officers, after which the DO structure automatically passes control to line 6.

The *read* instruction at line 6 then reads the fifth record, which is actually the first part-timer record. The employee name is HUNT L, the hours worked is 30, and the position code is 1.

The WHILE DO/END WHILE (lines 7–16) is an example of a different type of loop structure. Instead of carrying out a task a fixed number of times as in the DO/CONTINUE LOOP, the task is repeated until a specified condition is satisfied. In our example, lines 8 through 15 are carried out until the end-of-file record is read. The WHILE statement at line 7 first determines whether the condition stated is satisfied; i.e., has the end-of-file record been read? If the end of file has *not* been read, *then* lines 8 through 15 are carried out; if the end of file has been read, lines 8 through 15 are skipped and control is passed to line 17. The first time through the WHILE DO structure, the end of file has *not* been encountered, since the most recent record read is that of HUNT L (the first part-timer record).

The IF structure (lines 8–13) asks whether the position code is 1. If it is, the instruction specified by the THEN statement is carried out (line 10); otherwise (position code not equal to 1), the instruction(s) between the ELSE and ENDIF statements (line 12) is carried out. The first time line 8 is carried out, position code is 1, so we compute pay = 30 × 5 = 150. Control is then passed to line 14, where the pay for HUNT is printed. A new record is then read at line 15: LARD S 35 2. At this point, the end of the WHILE DO structure is reached and control is passed back to the WHILE DO statement at line 7. Since the end-of-file condition is not satisfied, the WHILE DO structure is carried out one more time. This time the position code is 2, so LARD's pay is computed at line 12. The output line for LARD is then printed out and the next record is read. This record turns out to be the end-of-file marker ∎. Control is then passed again to the WHILE DO statement at line 7, where, this time, the end-of-file condition is satisfied. Thus lines 8 through 16 are skipped and the program terminates at line 17.

One reason for including a separate *read* statement at line 6 is to ensure that the employee name, the hours worked, and the position code are well defined the first time through the WHILE DO structure. This *read* statement is carried out only once. All other records are read by the *read* instruction at line 15. Every time a record is read at line 15, it is immediately processed at lines 8–14. When the end-of-file record is encountered, exit is made from the structure. Note that if there were no part-timer records in the input file, the *read* statement at line 6 would read the end-of-file symbol ∎. Then, since the end-of-file condition would be satisfied at line 7, the program would stop (control is passed directly to line 17).

The code in Figure 1.8 will not "work" as intended if the input data is faulty, i.e., if the position code is neither 1 or 2 or if one company officer's record has been mistakenly omitted. It is very important that input data *always* be validated to ensure that "tainted" data not be processed alongside valid data. Later chapters will address this crucial issue.

The step-by-step execution of the pseudo code is shown in Figure 1.9. Lines 2, 3, and 4 (DO structure) are carried out four times, and lines 8 through 15 (WHILE DO structure) are carried out twice.

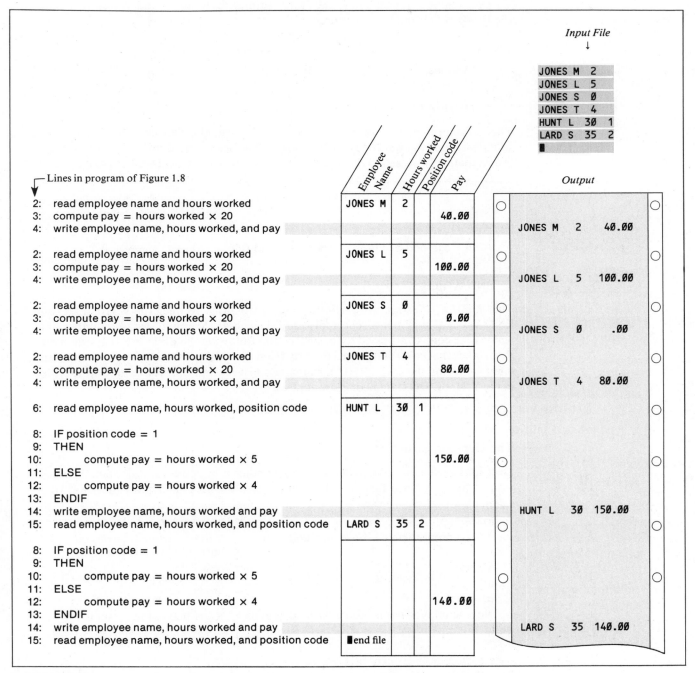

FIGURE 1.9
STEP-BY-STEP EXECUTION OF THE PSEUDO CODE IN FIGURE 1.8

1.3.4 Tools
For Structure

As illustrated in the pseudo code of Figure 1.8, the decomposition of a problem into a well-designed task structure is made possible by the sequence, decision, and looping control structures.

The Loop Structure

To loop means to repeat a task one or more times. Looping is made possible through the WHILE DO and DO structures.

EXAMPLE 1

```
DO 4 times              (line 1, Figure 1.8)
  .
  .
CONTINUE LOOP           (line 5)
```

This structure carries out the instructions between the DO and the CONTINUE LOOP statements four times. After this task has been carried out four times, control is automatically passed to the instruction following the CONTINUE LOOP.

EXAMPLE 2

```
WHILE the end of file is not encountered DO    (line 7, Figure 1.8)
  .
  .
END WHILE                                       (line 16)
```

This WHILE DO structure carries out the instructions between the WHILE DO and END WHILE statements repeatedly until the end of the input file is encountered, at which time control is passed to the instruction following the END WHILE statement. **Remember that control is passed directly from the WHILE DO statement to the statement following the END WHILE statement the very first time the condition specified in the WHILE DO statement ceases to be true.**

The Decision Structure

Decisions are based on whether a certain condition or conditions are met. The decision structure is illustrated in the computation of the part timer's pay (lines 8–13):

```
IF position code = 1         Question is asked
THEN
      compute pay = hours-worked × 5     This instruction is carried out if the
                                         answer to the question is yes.
ELSE
      compute pay = hours-worked × 4     This instruction is carried out if the
                                         answer is no.
ENDIF
write employee name, hours worked, and pay    Regardless of the answer to the
                                              question, this instruction is always
                                              carried out, since it follows the
                                              ENDIF.
```

The ENDIF is a visual marker that defines the "reach" of the IF structure.

The Sequence Structure

The sequence structure is illustrated within each task as instructions are executed one after the other; it is also inherently present in the program design, as each task is carried out sequentially.

1.3.5 Characteristics of a Well-Structured Design

In terms of structure, all program designs should adhere to the following rules:

1. The only valid "building blocks" that can be used in writing a program or pseudo code are the three control structures discussed in the preceding section: the sequence, the decision, and the loop structures.

2. Each structure should have *one and only one* entry point (DO, WHILE, and IF) and *one and only one* terminal point (CONTINUE LOOP, END WHILE, and ENDIF). Thus each structure is a self-contained entity that can be activated only at its entry point and which can terminate only at the terminal point, i.e., no entry into a structure can be made other than at the entry point, and no exit out of a structure can be made other than through the terminal point. Such an orderly control of entry and exit points ensures a sequential flow of tasks.

Program designs that do not conform to these rules inevitably lead to "spaghetti" designs, where multiple entries and exits into and out of tasks make it almost impossible for the reader to know where he/she is coming from and where he/she is going!

1.3.6 Data Description

The idea of structure goes beyond the area of program logic and into the area of data definition and description. Input and output data and logic are inseparable entities—logic needs input data to produce output (information).

The FORTRAN READ instruction will generally read one input record at a time. This record will most often consist of several distinct items (a name, a number of hours worked, etcetera). Similarly, the WRITE statement produces a line of output that usually consists of different types of items (name, hours worked, pay, etcetera) placed at particular positions on the output line. In a real-life programming situation, both input and output records have predesignated layouts or formats. Information processing managers will typically insist on a particular type of format for a report, while the layout of the input record may or may not be determined by the programmer.

The pseudo code in Figure 1.10 describes the record layouts by giving the format for each of the various READ/WRITE instructions. These formats specify the order, the type, and the length of each item that is to be read or written. Thus each READ or WRITE statement has a corresponding format that tells the system how to read or print the various items.

In addition to the input and output formats, the programmer generally needs to specify the names and types of all items used or referred to in the code. The type specifies whether the items in question are numeric or alphanumeric. Numeric items can be processed algebraically, i.e., they can be compared to one another as signed numbers and can be added, subtracted, and so forth. Alphanumeric items (referred to as character data in FORTRAN) cannot be processed arithmetically (for example, you can't add names!), but they can be compared to one another, just like numeric data.

Figure 1.10 contains both the pseudo code and the data definition and description for the problem of Figure 1.8. Note that numeric data has been further classified as

```
*Purpose of program is to compute company payroll
***********************************************************************
*       Data definition and description
*           REAL hours worked, pay
*           INTEGER position code
*           CHARACTER employee name
*       Input and output formats
*       Input format for Read (line 2 of Figure 1.8)
*           FORMAT (8 character positions, 2 numeric digits)
*       Input format for Read at lines 6 and 15
*           FORMAT (8 character positions, 2 numeric digits, 1 numeric digit)
*       Output format for the Write at lines 4 and 14
*           FORMAT (8 character positions, 2 numeric digits, 4 numeric digits)
***********************************************************************
*       Program development
*       Compute pay for the company officers
            DO 4 times
                read employee name and hours worked
                compute pay = hours worked × 20
                write employee name, hours worked, and pay
            CONTINUE LOOP
*       Read the first part-timer record
        read employee name, hours worked, and position code
*       Compute pay for part timers
            WHILE the end of file is not encountered DO
*           Check position code
            IF position code = 1
            THEN
                compute pay = hours worked × 5
            ELSE
                compute pay = hours worked × 4
            ENDIF
            write employee name, hours worked, and pay
*           Read the next employee record
            read employee name, hours worked, and position code
        END WHILE
        stop
```

FIGURE 1.10
*THE COMPLETE
PSEUDO CODE*

REAL numbers (numbers with decimal points) and INTEGER numbers (numbers without decimal points). It is not actually necessary to include the data definition and description when writing pseudo code, but their presence documents the data used by the logic and thus ties the data and the logic into a complete structure. In a complete FORTRAN program, however, both data description and formats will be required.

*1.3.7 Readability and
Documentation*

Although pseudo code is an informal language with no grammatical rules, there are a few guidelines for writing pseudo code that will be readable, meaningful, and easy to understand.

In the pseudo code of Figure 1.8, we could have written the IF structure or, for that matter, the entire compute part timer pay task as follows:

IF position code = 1 THEN *compute* pay = hours worked × 5 ELSE compute pay = hours worked × 4 ENDIF write employee name, hours worked, and pay read employee name, hours worked, and position code

But this arrangement is difficult to read and understand, so we usually write one instruction per line, as is done in FORTRAN. In the IF structure, we also use indentation to emphasize visually what actions are to be carried out if the answer to the question asked is true or false.

Item names, which are called *variables* in FORTRAN, should be meaningful, i.e., they should somehow describe the nature of the item in question. With meaningful variable names, pseudo code instructions resemble English sentences and can be understood by all. Beginning FORTRAN students sometimes tend to use short, secretive names for variables because it takes less time and effort to write them. Instructions such as $P = H \times R + B$ are often written to compute a pay. However a better documented and more meaningful instruction might be *pay = hours worked × rate + bonus*. Think of looking at these two formulas two months later—which version would be easier to understand? The additional time required to write this instruction now will be much less trouble than the headaches and hours of lost time that might result later from the more telegraphic form of expression.

Although pseudo code is very descriptive, there may still be a need to explain or summarize the function of groups of statements and describe how they relate to the entire logic. Lines that begin with an asterisk (∗) are *comments* (see Figure 1.10 for examples); comments can be interspersed at any point in the pseudo code. These comments serve as internal documentation and are an important part of the program development phase. Because the program must be understandable to others and because it may need to be revised, updated, or expanded, it is very important that the program be self-documenting and that it contain explanations and comments to help the reader understand its nature and purpose. Remember comments are **not** instructions—they are not executed by the computer, they are merely observations or explanations to help the reader better understand the program or logic.

The wording of pseudo code instructions is a matter of personal judgment. For example, in the part-time pay computation of Figure 1.10, the programmer might initially write *compute $5 pay* instead of *compute pay = hours-worked × 5;* this form of abbreviation especially makes sense in programs that include typing long and complex operations or formulas, which must eventually be coded into FORTRAN anyhow! If the programmer feels more comfortable with the statement like *compute overtime pay* instead of spelling out the many individual sentences to compute an overtime pay, this is certainly his/her prerogative.

1.3.8 Do It Now

1. What results would be produced by the pseudo code of Figure 1.8 if:
    a. The position code is neither 1 or 2.
    b. One of the officer input records is missing from the input file.
    c. One of the hours entries has been mistakenly typed as a negative number.

2. Would the logic outlined in Figure 1.8 take care of not just two part-timers but an unknown number of part-timers?

3. Suppose the *read* instruction at line 6 of Figure 1.8 had been omitted. What consequences would this omission have on the results and the logic? Explain exactly what happens.

4. Suppose that the very last *read* instruction (line 15) in Figure 1.8 had been omitted. What consequences would this omission have on the logic of the program? Explain what happens.

5. Consider the following code, which is almost identical to the one shown in Figure 1.8. How would this code affect the output of the program?

```
 1:  DO 4 times
 2:      read employee name and hours worked
 3:      compute pay = hours worked × 20
 4:      write employee name, hours worked, and pay
 5:  WHILE the end of file is not encountered DO
 6:      read the employee name, hours worked, and position code
 7:      IF position code = 1
 8:      THEN
 9:          compute pay = hours worked × 5
10:      ELSE
11:          compute pay = hours worked × 4
12:      ENDIF
13:      write employee name, hours worked, and pay
14:  END WHILE
15:  stop
```

6. Suppose there were a variable number of company officers in the input file, with a special record containing a dummy name and a negative entry for the hours field separating the company officer records from the part-time records. For example:

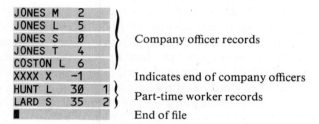

How would you write the code to compute the company payroll?
[*Hint:* Use the WHILE/DO instead of the DO structure to process the company officer records.]

Answers

1. a. The pay will be computed at $4.00 per hour at line 12.

   b. The first part-timer record will be treated as a company officer record.

   c. A negative pay will be computed.

2. Yes

3. The pay for T. JONES is processed twice. The last record read before the WHILE DO statement at line 7 is that of T. JONES, who worked 4 hours. Hence the first time the WHILE DO task is carried out, the position code is undefined (no position code is stated for company officer T. JONES). Since the position code is not equal to 1, the ELSE clause is executed, yielding $16.00. The records of the part-time employees would then be read by line 15, and their pays would be computed correctly.

4. The WHILE DO task (lines 8–14) would be carried out indefinitely using the first part-time employee record, since the end-of-file record would never be encountered.

5. Reading the end of file record at line 6 does not change the contents (values) of employee name, hours worked and position code. Thus, after the end of file record is read, lines 7 through 13 are carried out one more time, and line 13 causes the output line LARD S 35 140.00 to be printed a second time.

1.4 YOU MIGHT WANT TO KNOW

1. What is the history of FORTRAN?

Answer:

■ November 10, 1954. An IBM Programming Research Group sets a goal of producing a Formulation Translation system that will allow programs written in a language other than machine language to be run on an IBM 704.

■ March 15, 1957. Release of FORTRAN for the IBM 704.

■ June 1958. FORTRAN II (a newer version) is released for the IBM 704.

■ March 1966. FORTRAN IV.

■ February 1978. FORTRAN 77. Among many other differences with prior FORTRANs, the IF THEN ELSE statement becomes a standard construct and certain versions of FORTRAN 77 feature the WHILE DO control structure.

2. What is the history of structured programming?

Answer: In 1966 the *Communications of the ACM* (a publication of the Association for Computing Machinery) published a paper by E. Boehm and G. Jacopini that was presented two years earlier during an international colloquium of algebraic linguistics. In essence, the paper demonstrated that a program with one entry and one exit could be written using only three control structures: the sequence, the decision, and the loop structures.

In 1968 Mr. E. Dijkstra of the Netherlands proposed that program code could be written without using the GO TO statement. Mr. Dijkstra considered the GO TO statement harmful and stated, "I discovered why the use of the GO TO statement has such disastrous effects, and I became convinced that the GO TO statement should be abolished from all higher level programming languages. . . ."

Subsequently, Dr. Mills of the IBM Corporation wrote an article on the mathematical foundation of structured programming. With Mr. Baker of IBM, the "New York Times" project was developed using sturctured program concepts.

From 1971 on, structured programming has been a replacement for the previous program development methods, which have practically disappeared from the programming scene.

3. What other high-level languages are there besides FORTRAN?

Answer: One survey reported 600 computer languages in more or less widespread use. Among these are COBOL (Common Oriented Business Language), RPG (Report Program Generator—for small shops), Algol (scientific and system language), BASIC (Beginners All-purpose Symbolic Instruction Code), PL/1 (combining both FORTRAN and COBOL capabilities, well suited for business and for scientific problems), and Pascal.

4. Just how fast do computers operate?

Answer: The latest model computers operate at speeds measured in *nanoseconds* (1 nanosecond = 1 billionth of a second). For example, the Cray 2 computer is capable of executing 100 to 200 million instructions per second; that is, one instruction takes 5 to 10 nanoseconds to execute.

5. I cannot conceive of how fast a nanosecond is. Can you help me?

Answer: Perhaps. One nanosecond is to 1 second as 1 second is to 32 years (in other words, there are approximately 1 billion seconds in 32 years). One nanosecond is the approximate time required for light to travel 1 foot.

6. Is there any limit to the internal speeds of a computer?

Answer: Electrical signals are propagated at speeds approaching the speed of light (1 foot/nanosecond). Integrated circuits packing many thousands of transistors per square inch have been designed to minimize the length of interconnections through which electrical signals are propagated, thereby reducing the time it takes a signal to travel from one transistor to another in that circuit. Figure 1.11 illustrates the density of an integrated circuit "chip."

7. What is an operating system?

Answer: An operation system is a collection of programs usually supplied by the computer manufacturer to assist in the overall operation of the computer system. They are used to regulate and supervise the sequence of activities going on at any time in the system. These programs minimize operator intervention in the actual operation of the computer and ensure a smooth, fast, and efficient transition among the various tasks performed by the system. Other operating system programs such as utility and library programs aid the programmer in his/her work. The following functions are performed by operating system programs:

1. Load programs into memory from mass storage.

2. Print messages for the operator and the programmer regarding the status of the program.

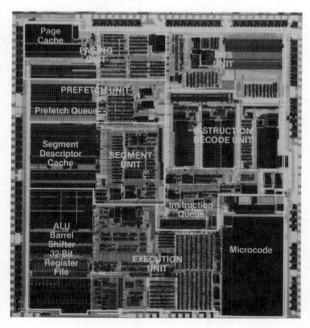

FIGURE 1.11
MAGNIFIED VIEW OF THE INTEL 80386 SINGLE CHIP MICROCOMPUTER (COURTESY INTEL CORPORATION)

3. Perform job accounting by keeping track of who uses the computer and for how long.

4. Handle requests for input/output from executing programs.

5. Handle the collection of data from telecommunication lines (in a time-sharing system).

6. Schedule the slice of time to be allocated to each user's program (in a time-sharing or multiprogramming system).

7. Perform some routine processing of data, such as sorting and copying the contents of one data set onto a specified device.

8. Maintain the store of programs on the mass storage device—adding programs to the store, deleting those no longer needed, and so forth.

9. Attempt to recover from and/or correct errors that may occur in any segment of the computing system.

10. Interpret the job set-up and job control instructions specified by the programmer.

At the heart of most operating systems is a program variously called the *supervisor,* the *executive,* or the *monitor.* This program is usually resident in memory at all times and performs many essential tasks such as program loading and error checking. This resident portion of the operating system loads other less frequently used routines as they are required.

8. What are the different symbols used in a flowchart?

Answer:

	Symbols (blocks)	Meaning
	Terminal (oval):	Identifies start and end of program instructions.
	Input/Output (parrallellogram):	Reserved for input/output instructions.
	Processing (rectangle):	Calculations are performed in this block.
No / Yes	Decisions (diamond):	Allows for a two-way transfer.
	Task	A task is to be processed. The task is detailed elsewhere.
	Flowlines	The sequence of instructions is shown with arrow lines. The direction of flow is always in the direction indicated by the arrowhead.

EXAMPLE

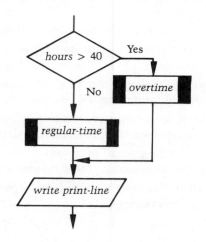

If hours > 40 carry out overtime and write the results.
If hours ≤ 40 carry out regular time and write the results.

1.5 EXERCISES

1.5.1 Test Yourself

1. Define the following words:
   a. Computer
   b. Data
   c. Instruction
   d. Information
   e. Memory
   f. Central processing unit
   g. Input/output devices
   h. Hardware/software
   i. High-level language

2. List the five components of a computer system. Explain the function of each.

3. Are the following statements true or false?

   a. A compiler is a program that translates machine code into a high-level language.

   b. Computer hardware consists of all the physical components that make up a computer system.

   c. High-level languages are machine-independent.

   d. The term *software* refers to such material as diskettes, paper/magnetic tapes, and so forth.

   e. Pseudo code is a language that can be processed by a computer.

4. An input file consists of exactly five records, each containing an employee-name and a number of hours worked. Write the pseudo code to read these five records and compute each employee's pay as follows: The rate of pay for the first 40 hours is $3.76 per hour, while the rate of pay for hours beyond 40 is $5.00 per hour. Print the name, the number of hours worked, the number of overtime hours, the overtime pay, the gross pay, and the net pay (the net pay is 80% of gross). First use the DO structure to write the code, then use the WHILE DO structure with a sixth record containing an end of file.

1. **a. Computer**   A machine that can perform arithmetic operations and make decisions based on comparisons by following a set of instructions stored in its memory.

   b. Data   Raw facts.

   c. Instruction   A statement specifying one or more operations to be performed.

   d. Information   Data that has been organized and processed so that it is meaningful.

   e. Memory   Physical component of a computer that stores instructions and data.

   f. Central Processing Unit   Brain headquarters of a computer, consisting of memory, arithmetic and logic unit, and control unit.

   g. Input/Output Devices   Devices from which the computer can accept data and information and onto which it can write or store data/information.

   h. Hardware   Physical components of a computing system.

   i. High-Level Language   A language that can be used to communicate with computers in a semi-English written language.

2. Input, output, memory, arithmetic/logic and control.

3. **a.** F   **b.** T   **c.** T   **d.** F   **e.** F

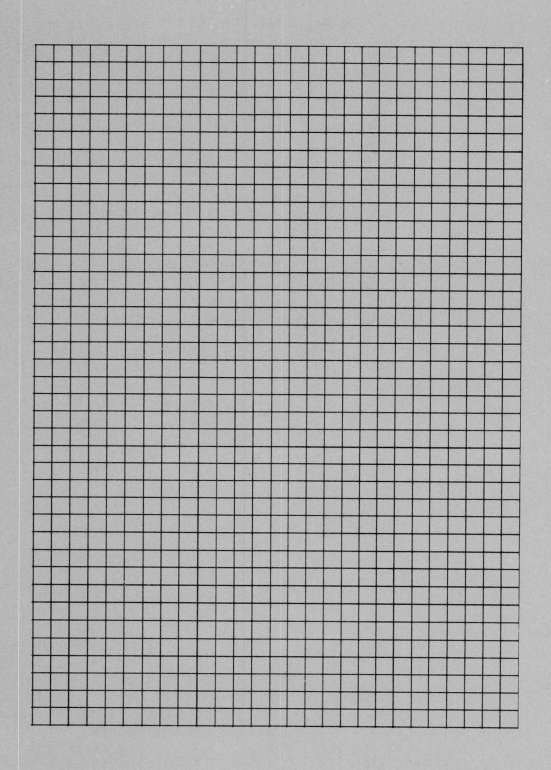

Variables, Replacement Statements, List-Directed Output, Errors

2.1 PROGRAMMING EXAMPLE

Problem Specification. Mr. Rancher owns a 198.6- by 301.5-foot rectangular plot of land in the city and some acreage in the county, the latter in the form of a circle (radius 300 feet). The city lot is taxed at the rate of $0.043 per square foot, while the county land is taxed at $0.019 per square foot.

Write a FORTRAN program to print the following:

- The area of each lot.
- The tax to be paid for each lot.
- The total combined taxes.

A FORTRAN program to solve this problem is shown in Figure 2.1, which contains the listing of the FORTRAN code and the results (output) produced by the program. Note the following types of FORTRAN statements:

1. The comment statements throughout the program. Comments start with an asterisk in column position 1 and are used for documentation.

2. The REAL statements (lines 3–5), which list all the numeric items used in the program.

3. The PARAMETER statement (line 6), which is used to associate a particular value with a symbolic name.

4. The OPEN statement (line 8), which may or may not be needed on your system. This statement is used to select a particular output device—a printer in this case.

5. The replacement statement, which is used for calculations, for example CITYA = CITYLN * CITYW (line 11).

6. The WRITE statement (line 18), which specifies the values to be printed. Note that alphabetic captions are enclosed in single quotation marks.

7. The STOP statement (line 24), which terminates the execution of the program.

8. The END statement (line 25), which must be the last statement in the program.

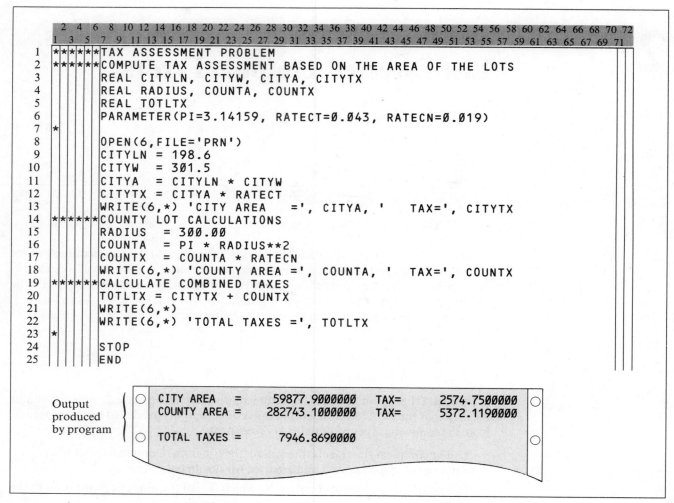

```
    2  4  6  8 10 12 14 16 18 20 22 24 26 28 30 32 34 36 38 40 42 44 46 48 50 52 54 56 58 60 62 64 66 68 70 72
  1  3  5  7  9 11 13 15 17 19 21 23 25 27 29 31 33 35 37 39 41 43 45 47 49 51 53 55 57 59 61 63 65 67 69 71
 1 ******TAX ASSESSMENT PROBLEM
 2 ******COMPUTE TAX ASSESSMENT BASED ON THE AREA OF THE LOTS
 3       REAL CITYLN, CITYW, CITYA, CITYTX
 4       REAL RADIUS, COUNTA, COUNTX
 5       REAL TOTLTX
 6       PARAMETER(PI=3.14159, RATECT=0.043, RATECN=0.019)
 7 *
 8       OPEN(6,FILE='PRN')
 9       CITYLN = 198.6
10       CITYW  = 301.5
11       CITYA  = CITYLN * CITYW
12       CITYTX = CITYA * RATECT
13       WRITE(6,*) 'CITY AREA   =', CITYA, '   TAX=', CITYTX
14 ******COUNTY LOT CALCULATIONS
15       RADIUS  = 300.00
16       COUNTA  = PI * RADIUS**2
17       COUNTX  = COUNTA * RATECN
18       WRITE(6,*) 'COUNTY AREA =', COUNTA, ' TAX=', COUNTX
19 ******CALCULATE COMBINED TAXES
20       TOTLTX = CITYTX + COUNTX
21       WRITE(6,*)
22       WRITE(6,*) 'TOTAL TAXES =', TOTLTX
23 *
24       STOP
25       END
```

Output
produced
by program
```
CITY AREA   =     59877.9000000    TAX=      2574.7500000
COUNTY AREA =    282743.1000000    TAX=      5372.1190000

TOTAL TAXES =      7946.8690000
```

FIGURE 2.1
A LAND TAX ASSESSMENT PROBLEM

2.2 HOW AND WHERE TO START

*2.2.1 Practical
Considerations:
Communicating with
Your System*

Because of the many types of operating systems and the wide variety of computers (ranging from the microcomputers to large mainframe computers), the ways in which programs are typed, stored on disk, and then submitted for processing vary considerably from one system or installation to another. Specific information regarding access to your particular system is not discussed in this chapter; it is available from your instructor, computer lab assistants, or appropriate technical reference manuals. Section 2.2.4 is left open for you to record this information.

2.2.2 Text Editors

The source file (FORTRAN program) consists of lines of text that must be typed and recorded on some device (usually a disk) before they can be processed by the computer. Text editors are used for this purpose. Text editors are essentially unsophisticated word processors that allow you to type lines of text and display the text on screens or hard copy terminals. Such lines can then be *edited* at will, i.e., lines can be deleted or added, and text within a line can be changed. The resulting lines of text can then be stored (saved) on disk under a particular file name (catalogued).

Text editors have their own commands or instructions for the various editing functions. Keep in mind that these text editing commands have *nothing* to do with the FORTRAN language! The text editor is used solely to create and edit files—you could even use it to write letters or essays!

Typically, each line of text is automatically numbered by the editor; this makes it possible for you to refer to the particular line number that you wish to edit. Even though the line numbers appear on the screen or on your hard copy terminal, these line numbers are ignored by FORTRAN when the computer reads the FORTRAN source file or the data file, i.e., as far as FORTRAN is concerned, position 1 starts after the numeric label provided by the text editor (on screens, at the beginning cursor position).

Figure 2.2 shows text processed by two different types of text editors.

Once the input or source file has been typed, a text editor command is used to save that file on disk. The user gives the file a name so that it can be catalogued on disk for subsequent retrieval. The user-chosen file name is added to the directory of the disk, which contains the names of all the files currently on the disk.

Use the open space provided in section 2.2.4 to record:

1. The necessary instructions to load (call) your text editor.

2. The text editor commands that you are likely to use, i.e., those to insert, delete, and change lines of text.

3. The instructions to save a file and give it a name.

4. The instructions to print the text file and to access the disk directory in case you forget the names of your files.

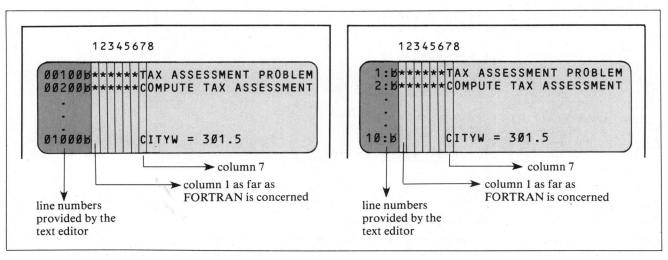

FIGURE 2.2
TYPICAL TEXT EDITOR SCREENS

2.2.3 Typing Your
FORTRAN Program:
Practical
Considerations

Now, using your text editor, type the FORTRAN program shown in Figure 2.1:

1. Note that comment statements start with an asterisk (∗) in column 1 and that all other statements start in column 7.

2. Determine whether your FORTRAN system supports the PARAMETER feature at line 6. If it does not, insert three replacement statements between lines 8 and 9 setting PI, RATE1, and RATE2 to their respective values; use the form shown in line 9.

3. Check with your instructor to determine whether the OPEN statement at line 8 is needed.

4. In many systems PRINT∗, can be used instead of WRITE(6,∗). Check with your instructor or your technical reference manual.

When you have finished, your screen should be similar to the example in Figure 2.3; remember that your text editor may generate a different type of line numbers than the ones shown in Figure 2.2.

5. Once you have typed your program, save it on disk. On most microcomputing systems you will need to give your program file a name so that it can be catalogued. Let us give it the name AREATX.

At this point your program file should be stored on disk and the disk directory should show the entry AREATX (see Figure 2.4).

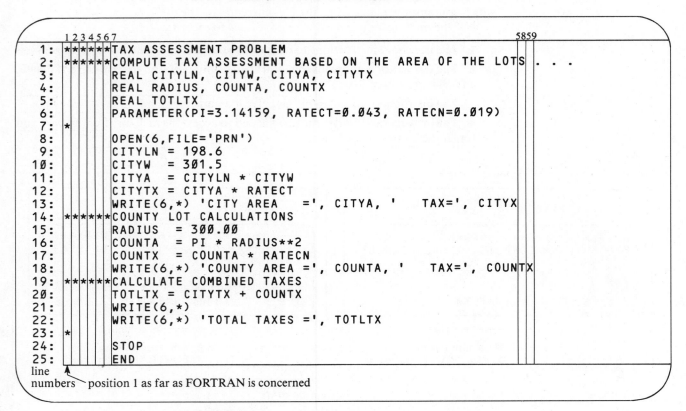

```
      1234567                                                5859
 1: ******TAX ASSESSMENT PROBLEM
 2: ******COMPUTE TAX ASSESSMENT BASED ON THE AREA OF THE LOTS . . .
 3:       REAL CITYLN, CITYW, CITYA, CITYTX
 4:       REAL RADIUS, COUNTA, COUNTX
 5:       REAL TOTLTX
 6:       PARAMETER(PI=3.14159, RATECT=0.043, RATECN=0.019)
 7: *
 8:       OPEN(6,FILE='PRN')
 9:       CITYLN = 198.6
10:       CITYW  = 301.5
11:       CITYA  = CITYLN * CITYW
12:       CITYTX = CITYA * RATECT
13:       WRITE(6,*) 'CITY AREA   =', CITYA, '   TAX=', CITYX
14: ******COUNTY LOT CALCULATIONS
15:       RADIUS  = 300.00
16:       COUNTA  = PI * RADIUS**2
17:       COUNTX  = COUNTA * RATECN
18:       WRITE(6,*) 'COUNTY AREA =', COUNTA, '   TAX=', COUNTX
19: ******CALCULATE COMBINED TAXES
20:       TOTLTX = CITYTX + COUNTX
21:       WRITE(6,*)
22:       WRITE(6,*) 'TOTAL TAXES =', TOTLTX
23: *
24:       STOP
25:       END
line
numbers    position 1 as far as FORTRAN is concerned
```

FIGURE 2.3
TYPING A FORTRAN PROGRAM ON A SCREEN

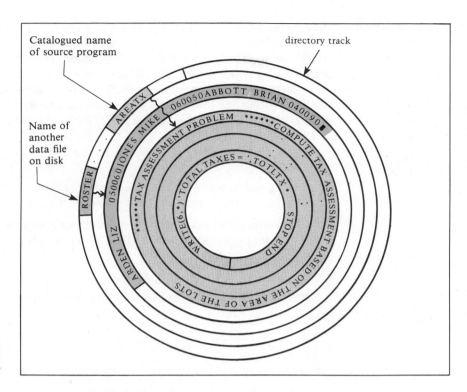

Catalogued name
of source program

directory track

Name of
another
data file
on disk

FIGURE 2.4
DISK CONTAINING
FORTRAN PROGRAM AND
DATA FILE

2.2.4 My System is Different

In this section record the various text editor commands that you will use, as well as any system or FORTRAN statements that need to be changed or added so that your program will run on your system.

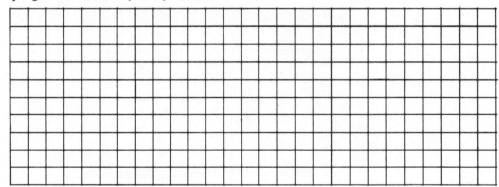

2.2.5 Compiling Your Program

Now that the FORTRAN program is stored on disk under the name **AREATX**, it must be translated into machine language (object code) before it can be executed by the central processing unit. Special system commands such as COMPILE *program name* (COMPILE AREATX) or other types of job control instructions are used to initiate the compilation process. Record the instructions for your system in section 2.2.4.

If you have introduced errors while typing your FORTRAN statements (forgotten parentheses, incorrect spelling, and so forth), the compiler will not be able to translate the corresponding FORTRAN entries into object code. Your errors will be listed by line number. They must be corrected by loading the text editor and going through the editing process described in section 2.2.2.

2.2.6 Running Your Program

If no errors occurred during the compilation process, the resulting object code is now ready to be executed. Special system instructions such as RUN *program name* (RUN AREATX) or some other job control instructions are used to initiate this process. The program should then produce the desired results. If these results are incorrect (for example, if there is only one line of output when more are expected), analyze your logic carefully and correct the instructions that generated the errors. The entire process of text editing, compiling, and running your FORTRAN program is illustrated in Figure 2.5.

2.3 THE FORTRAN CODING SHEET

Rules governing the positioning of the various components of a FORTRAN statement are very important. The FORTRAN coding form shown in Figure 2.6 is broken down into four areas:

- column 1:   Comment field
- columns 1–5:   FORTRAN statement number

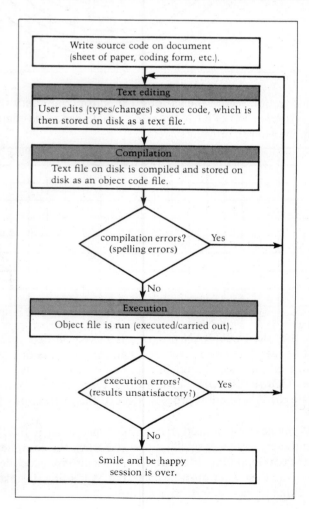

FIGURE 2.5
PROGRAM SUBMISSION PROCESS

■ column 6:   Continuation column
■ columns 7–72:   FORTRAN statement
■ columns 73–80:   Identification

Column 1

As we discussed in chapter 1, it is very important that a FORTRAN program be self-documenting and that it contain explanations and comments to help the reader understand its nature and purpose. For this reason, FORTRAN allows the programmer to intersperse comments throughout the FORTRAN code. Comment lines can be inserted anywhere in a program by entering an asterisk or the character C in column 1. When the compiler reads the C or the asterisk in position 1, it realizes that the information in that statement is just for the programmer and does not view the statement as a FORTRAN instruction.

Columns 1–5

A statement number is an unsigned integer number (no decimal point) that identifies a particular FORTRAN statement. Statement numbers can be from one to five digits long; the digits should be entered in consecutive columns. Statement numbers need not be sequential and are required only when a statement is to be referred to by another FORTRAN statement in the program. Many programmers number their statements sequentially to make it easier to locate statements in the program.

Column 6

If a FORTRAN statement is too long to fit in columns 7–72, the statement can be continued onto one (or more) succeeding lines by typing any character (other than a blank or zero) in column 6 of the second (or any following) line. For example:

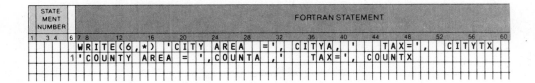

Character constants enclosed in quotation marks can be carried over from one line to the next if the enclosed text is typed continuously through column 72 before moving to the next line. No such stradling is necessary in the above example, however, where 'COUNTY AREA =' has been typed entirely on the next line.

Columns 7–72

The FORTRAN statement itself can be entered anywhere in positions 7–72. For program readability, the beginning programmer may wish to start most statements in position 7. Statements within the decision and loop structures are generally indented.

Columns 73–80

These columns are generally left blank. They can be used for author/program identification or for sequencing purposes.

FORTRAN Coding Form

SYSTEM		PUNCHING INSTRUCTIONS	PAGE 1 OF 1
PROGRAM CALCULATION OF THE AREA OF TWO LOTS	GRAPHIC		CARD FORM =
PROGRAMMER MICHAEL H. BOILLOT DATE JAN. 1987	PUNCH		

```
STATEMENT                           FORTRAN STATEMENT                        IDENTIFICATION
NUMBER
*****  TAX ASSESSMENT PROBLEM
*****  COMPUTE TAX ASSESSMENT BASED ON THE AREA OF THE LOTS
       REAL CITYLN, CITYW, CITYA, CITYTX
       REAL RADIUS, COUNTA, COUNTX
       REAL TOTLTX
       PARAMETER(PI=3.14159, RATECT=0.043, RATECN=0.019)
*
       OPEN(6,FILE='PRN')
       CITYLN = 198.6
       CITYW = 301.5
       CITYA = CITYLN * CITYW
       CITYTX = CITYA * RATECT
       WRITE(6,*) 'CITY AREA  =', CITYA, '  TAX=', CITYTX
*****  COUNTY LOT CALCULATIONS
       RADIUS = 300.00
       COUNTA = PI * RADIUS**2
       COUNTX = COUNTA * RATECN
       WRITE(6,*) 'COUNTY AREA  =', COUNTA, '  TAX=', COUNTX
*****  CALCULATE COMBINED TAXES
       TOTLTX = CITYTX + COUNTX
       WRITE(6,*)
       WRITE(6,*) 'TOTAL TAXES =', TOTLTX
*
       STOP
       END
```

FORTRAN   continuation   FORTRAN statement   Identification
statement   field
numbers

FIGURE 2.6
A FORTRAN CODING FORM

2.4 ELEMENTS OF FORTRAN SYNTAX

In general, FORTRAN statements consist of certain elements (key words, constants, variables, and special characters) strung together according to strict grammatical rules. The following example illustrates the various grammatical components of a FORTRAN replacement statement.

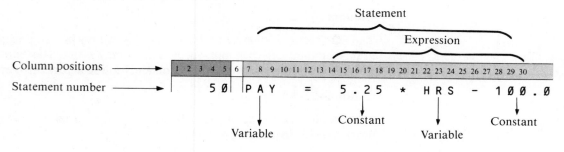

2.4.1 The Character Set   The characters used in FORTRAN are grouped into three classes:

- alphabetic characters: ƀ(blank), A through Z and on many systems a through z
- numeric characters: 0 through 9
- special characters: + − * / = . ' ( ) ,

In addition, text enclosed within single quotation marks (character constants) can include any of the keyboard characters.

2.4.2 Numeric Constants   A constant is a fixed numerical value that is explicitly stated; in other words, it is a number. A constant can be expressed in *integer* mode or *real* mode. An integer constant is always written without a decimal point; a real constant is always written with a decimal point. Either type may be preceded by a sign. If the number is negative, a minus sign must be used; if the number is positive, the plus sign is optional. No characters other than the digits 0 through 9, the + and − symbols, the E and D symbols for exponentiation (discussed in chapter 5), and the decimal point can be used in a constant.

Generally (depending on the system), a constant can have no more than seven or eight digits. Number magnitudes and significant digits are discussed in chapter 5.

EXAMPLE 1

300	− 2	63247	+ 4	0	are integer constants.
6.32	− 3.21	.0005	+ 63.04	0.	are real constants.

Imbedded blanks (blanks between the first and last digit) in a constant have no effect on the value of the constant.

EXAMPLE 2   The following integer constants have the same value:

```
6    32
632
6    3    2
```

EXAMPLE 3   The following constants are invalid:

632,000	No commas are allowed.
23.34.	Only one decimal point is permitted.
$30.50	Special character $ is invalid.
111-333-444	Special character - is invalid.

2.4.3 Character Constants   Character constants can consist of any sequence of characters available on your keyboard. They must be enclosed in single quotes (')—not double quotes ("). The single quotes are not part of the string; they simply identify the start and the end of the string.

Most FORTRAN versions allow character constants up to 127 characters.

EXAMPLES

Constant	Number of Characters
'CALCULUS '	10 (includes two trailing blanks)
'3210 NORTH 10TH ST.'	19
'$23.45'	6
'111-21-8444'	11
'33'	2
'HE SAID "FORGET IT SAM"'	23

Note that character constants cannot be processed arithmetically. For example, '1' * '4' is invalid and so is 2 * '3'.

To include an apostrophe in a character constant, use two apostrophes instead of one, as in

'MONA''S CAT'   to mean   MONA'S CAT
''''   to mean   '

2.4.4 Variables

A variable is a symbolic name given to a memory locaton into which data is to be stored. The rules for forming variable names are as follows:

1. Composition: 1 to 6 characters $\begin{cases} \text{letters of the alphabet A–Z and a–z} \\ \text{numerical digits 0–9} \\ \text{Imbedded blanks are ignored.} \end{cases}$

2. Restrictions: first character must be alphabetic.

Obscure or secretive names such as X or P3 should be avoided. The little extra effort to think of a descriptive name is well worth your time in terms of readability and code documentation.

EXAMPLES

Valid Names	Invalid	Reason	Change
X	AMT-IN	– sign not permitted	AMTIN
Q12345	1RATE	first character must be alphabetic	RATE1
COUNT	SUM.	period not permitted	SUM
WRITE	VECTORS	more than 6 characters	VECTRS
Sum (same as) SUM	$RATE	$ sign not allowable character	RATE

2.4.5 Type Specification Statements

Since variables represent memory locations and since memory locations can contain integer, real, or character constants, how does one know by looking at a variable whether the variable represents an integer or a real or a character value?

The *type* of a variable can be explicitly specified by the user through the FORTRAN specification statements INTEGER, REAL, and CHARACTER. If a variable is *not* declared by means of specification statements, the type of the variable is implicitly defined by the variable's name: **If the first letter of the variable is I, J, K, L, M, or N, the variable is integer; otherwise the variable is real.** Thus, ISAM and KLM are integer variables, while HIM and SOCSEC are real variables.

It is becoming a common practice to declare all variables used in a program as INTEGER, CHARACTER, or REAL (see IMPLICIT typing in Appendix A). This practice provides better program documentation by accounting for all variables used in a program and it informs the reader of the way in which each variable is treated.

REAL and INTEGER Type Declarations

To declare SUM, K, and FICA as integers, use one or more statements:

```
INTEGER SUM,K,FICA    or    INTEGER SUM
                            INTEGER K
                            INTEGER FICA
```

To declare PAY, JET, and LENGTH as reals, use

```
REAL PAY, JET, LENGTH
```

CHARACTER Type Declaration

All character variables *must* be declared using one of the two forms of the CHARACTER specification statement:

> 1. CHARACTER*n variable-1, variable-2, ...
> 2. CHARACTER   variable-1*a, variable-2*b, ...

In case 1 all variables in the list are *n* characters long. In case 2 *variable-1* is *a* characters long and *variable-2* is *b* characters long. If *a* or *b* is omitted in case 2, the variable is then one character long. On most systems *n, a* and *b* must be less than or equal to 127.

EXAMPLES

```
CHARACTER MESSG*10,ERROR*4,X
or
 CHARACTER MESSG*10
 CHARACTER ERROR*4
 CHARACTER X

 CHARACTER*10 X,Y,Z

 CHARACTER*5 A,B,C*10
```

Variable MESSG can contain up to 10 characters. Variable ERROR can contain up to 4 characters. Since the * is omitted, only 1 character is reserved for X.

X, Y, and Z can each contain up to 10 characters. Note the position of the asterisk.

A and B are 5 characters long while C is 10 characters long.

Specification statements are usually placed at the very beginning of the program (see section 2.4.14).

2.4.6 Do It Now

1. Classify each of the following as a valid or invalid constant. For valid constants, specify the mode (type). If invalid, explain why.

a.	$25	d.	1432	g.	23.24.
b.	23,672	e.	− .1270	h.	'111-22-111'
c.	− 1.2	f.	4A	i.	''''

2. Classify each of the following as a valid or invalid variable name. For valid variable names, specify the mode (type). If invalid, explain why.

a.	JJ2	d.	BETAMAX	g.	A$
b.	A4	e.	KORN	h.	'MODULE'
c.	4A	f.	A*B	i.	ABC.

3. Which of the following are valid type declarations? If valid, explain why.

a. CHARACTER*5 SUM,B*10   c. REAL Z, INTEGER SUM

b. CHARACTER X*25, Z*300   d. REAL 3.1, 2.6

Answers to Selected Questions

1. a. invalid because of $ sign
   b. invalid because of comma
   c. valid, real
   d. valid, integer
   e. valid, real
   f. invalid because of alphabetic character
   g. invalid because of two decimal points
   h. valid, character
   i. valid, character

3. b. Invalid; maximum character length is 127.
   d. Invalid; REAL must specify a list of variables, not constants.

2.4.7 Integer and Real Arithmetic

The primary distinction between integer and real data is that real data contains a fractional part while integer data does not. Thus when arithmetic is performed using two integer constants and/or variables, *no decimal part is retained*—everything to the right of the implied decimal point is truncated. For example, the integer 7 divided by the integer 4 yields the integer 1, and *not* 1.75!—*the result is truncated, not rounded off*. With two real constants, the fractional part is retained.

EXAMPLES

Expression	Value	
3/4	0	3 and 4 are integers; no fractional part is retained.
8/3	2	8 and 3 are integers; no fractional part is retained.
3./4.	.75	3. and 4. are real; fractional result is computed.
8./3.	2.66666...	Number would be rounded off.
1/2 + 1/2	0	1/2 = 0, since the numerator and denominator are integers!
1./2. + 1./2.	1.	1., 2., and the result are real.

2.4.8 Expressions

An expression can be a constant, a variable, or any combination of constants and/or variables linked by the following arithmetic operators:

+	Addition
−	Subtraction
*	Multiplication
/	Division
**	Exponentiation

Parentheses can be included to denote the order of computations. No two arithmetic operators may be side by side.

Expressions involving real and integer constants/variables are called mixed-mode expressions. For example, both 13*SUM and 1 + 3.2 are mixed-mode expressions. **In mixed-mode operations, the computer converts the integer values to real values before the arithmetic operations are carried out.** Many instructors and professional programmers frown on the use of mixed-mode expressions, since their use can lead to misunderstandings and errors, as shown in the next section.

EXAMPLES

Algebraic Expressions	FORTRAN Expressions
a	A
14	14
$\frac{a}{b} \cdot c$	(A/B*C)
$a \cdot b - 30$	A*B−30.0
$-c$	−C
$(ab)^2$	(A*B)**2
$(-c + b)d$	(−C+B)*D

a^b	A**B
$\sqrt{a}$	A**.5
$\sqrt[4]{(a-b)^3}$	((A-B)**3)**.25
PMT $\dfrac{(1+i \cdot c)^n}{i \cdot c} - 1$	PMT*(1.+I*C)**N/(I*C)-1. (I is REAL)
$a\left(x + \dfrac{b}{2a}\right)^2 + \dfrac{4ac - b^2}{4a^2}$	A*(X+B/(2.*A))**2+(4.*A*C-B*B)/(4.*A**2)
$\dfrac{-2v(x^2 + y^2)}{(u^2 + v^2)^2}$	-2.*V*(X*X+Y*Y)/(U*U+V*V)**2
$\sqrt{\dfrac{2\mu(E + V_o)}{h^2}}$	(2.*MU*(E+VO)/(H*H))**.5
$F\left(\dfrac{\lambda - 1}{\rho} - \dfrac{l(l+1)}{\rho^2}\right)$	F*((LAM-1./RO-L*(L+1./(RO*RO)) (L is REAL)

The following are examples of invalid expressions:

3(A + SUM)	Operator missing after the 3.
A-(B + C * (D-1.)	Unpaired parentheses; should be A − (B + C*(D − 1)).
X * -3.	Two operators side by side; should be X*(− 3).

2.4.9 Evaluation of Expressions

Operations within an expression are performed according to the following rules of precedence:

Operation	Symbol	Precedence
grouping	( )	high precedence
exponentiation	**	
multiplication/division	* /	↓
addition/subtraction	+ −	low precedence

EXAMPLES   Integer arithmetic is assumed in the computations of the following expressions:

1. 3 + 2 * 3 = 3 + 6 = 9
2. 9/4 * 2 = 2 * 2 = 4 (Integer division)
3. (3 + 6)/3 * 6 = 9/3 * 6 = 3 * 6 = 18
4. 3 + 3 * 2 ** 2 = 3 + 3 * 4 = 3 + 12 = 15
5. 3 ** 2 ** 3 = 3 ** (2 ** 3) = 3 ** 8 = 6561

Consecutive exponentiations are evaluated from right to left.

6.	
3 ** 2 + (2 * 2** 3 / 4 + 1) − 2 / 3	Grouping then exponentiation
3 ** 2 + (2 * 8/ 4 + 1) − 2 / 3	Multiplication (left to right)
3 ** 2 + (16 / 4 + 1) − 2 / 3	Division
3 ** 2 + (4 + 1) − 2 / 3	Add (because of parentheses)
3 ** 2 + 5 − 2 / 3	Exponentiation
9 + 5 − 2 / 3	Division
9 + 5 − 0	Addition
14 − 0	Subtraction

Great care must be exercised when evaluating mixed-mode expressions. For example, 5/10 * 2. = 0., while 5/10. * 2 = 1. In the first expression we evaluate 5/10 first; since both numbers are integers, the result is integer 0. The integer 0 is then multiplied by real 2, giving us a *real* 0. In the second expression 5/10. yields .5, since one of the operands is real! 0.5 is then multiplied by integer 2 giving us real 1. The subtleties of this example once again underscore the danger of mixed-mode expressions. To avoid such situations, try and minimize the use of **mixed-mode expressions**.

1. Write FORTRAN expressions for each of the following:

   a. $\dfrac{N(1+N)}{-2}$ **d.** $X^3 - .73X + C$ **g.** $\sqrt{\dfrac{N(SUM) - SUM^2}{N(N-1)}}$

   b. $-Y \cdot X$ **e.** $\dfrac{9}{T} - \dfrac{1}{(T-1)}$ **h.** $\sqrt[6]{(-T)^5}$

   c. $V \cdot T - \dfrac{G \cdot T^2}{2}$ **f.** $\dfrac{(X+Y)(A-B)}{(C+T)^2}$

2. Evaluate the following FORTRAN expressions.

   a. 4. + 3/2   **b.** 4 + 3/2.   **c.** 4.*3/2   **d.** 4.*(3/2)

3. Evaluate the following expressions for A = 3., B = 2. and C = −2.

   a. A + B/C   **c.** 10. − C**B   **e.** (A + B)/B*C

   b. 3.*A**1/B   **d.** 4.*A/B − 3.**(C**B − 1.)   **f.** A − C/B + 3

4. Repeat exercise 3 using integer values for all variables and contants.

Answers

1. **a.** (N*(1+N))/(-2)   **f.** (X+Y)*(A-B)/(C+T)**2.

   b. -Y*X   **g.** ((N*SUM-SUM**2)/(N*(N-1)))**.5

   c. V*T-(G*T**2)/2.   **h.** (-T**5)**(1./6.) or (-T)**(5./6.)

   d. X**3-.73*X+C   Note that (−T)**(5/6) would not be

   e. 9./T-1./(T-1.)   correct, since 5/6 = 0 with integer
                            arithmetic.

2. **a.** 5.   **b.** 5.5   **c.** 6.0   **d.** 4.

3. **a.** 2.   **b.** 4.5   **c.** 6.   **d.** −21.

   e. −5.   **f.** 7.

4. **a.** 2   **b.** 4   **c.** 6   **d.** −21   **e.** −4   **f.** 7

2.4.11 The Replacement Statement

A replacement statement specifies an expression to be evaluated and the location (variable) into which the computed value is to be placed. The general form of the replacement statement is:

$$\boxed{\textit{variable} = \textit{expression}}$$

The value of the expression is first computed, then the result is placed (stored) in the *variable* on the left-hand side of the statement. The equals sign in a replacement statement must be understood to be a replacement sign rather than a mathematical equality. Accordingly, the statement X = X + 1.0 is completely legal: it means add 1.0 to whatever value is in memory cell X and store the result back into X.

Numeric Replacement Statements

First, the expression on the right-hand side of the equal sign is evaluated. If the expression consists of integer operands, then the value of the expression is integer; if the expression is mixed mode or real, the value of the expression is real. The value of the expression is then stored in memory as a real or integer value, depending on the type of the variable on the left-hand side of the equal sign, since that variable determines the type of the value to be stored in memory. Four cases are possible:

1. real variable   = real value   The real value is stored as a real value in the designated variable.

2. real variable   = integer value   The integer value is converted to real and stored in the designated variable.

3. integer variable = real value   All fractional digits are truncated from the real value, and the resulting integer is stored in the designated variable.

4. integer variable = integer value   The integer value is stored in the designated variable.

EXAMPLES

`IX = 3.2`	The value stored in IX will be the integer 3, since IX is integer. When a real value is converted to integer, any fractional part is truncated.
`X = 1`	The value of X will be 1., not 1, since X is real.
`J = 3./2`	The value of the expression is 1.5, but the value stored in J will be 1, since J is an integer variable.
`KX = 4/3+6.8`	4/3 is 1, since both numbers are integers. 1 + 6.8 = 7.8, since one of the operands is real. The value stored, however, is 7, since KX is integer.

Character Replacement Statements

If the receiving field is smaller than the sending field, truncation of excess characters occurs on the right. If the receiving field is larger than the sending field, the receiving field is padded to the right with blanks.

EXAMPLES

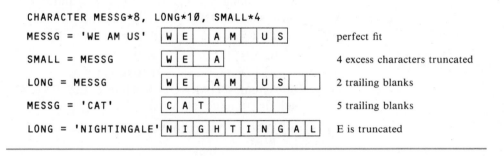

```
CHARACTER MESSG*8, LONG*10, SMALL*4
```

`MESSG = 'WE AM US'`	`W E   A M   U S`	perfect fit
`SMALL = MESSG`	`W E   A`	4 excess characters truncated
`LONG = MESSG`	`W E   A M   U S   `	2 trailing blanks
`MESSG = 'CAT'`	`C A T      `	5 trailing blanks
`LONG = 'NIGHTINGALE'`	`N I G H T I N G A L`	E is truncated

EXAMPLES

The following replacement statements are invalid

`'DOG' = ANIMAL`	Entry on left of equal sign must be a variable.
`3.16 = X`	A variable (memory location), not a constant, must be on the left-hand side of the equals sign; how can one store the value of X into 3.16?
`X+Y = 1.`	An expression cannot be on the left-hand side of the equals sign; how could one store a 1 in the sum of two memory locations?
`HRS*RATE+BONUS`	There is no variable specified into which the result is to be stored.
`MESS = 'BONUS'`	Invalid, if MESS is not decalred as character type.

2.4.12 Do It Now

1. State whether the following are constants, variables, expressions, or statements.

a. '1'	**d.** X = X + X	**g.** 1 − 1
b. '2 + 3'	**e.** Y = Y	**h.** − .3
c. X + 1.	**f.** 1 + 2 + 3.4	**i.** P = −H + R

2. State whether the following are constants, variables, expressions, or statements; if any are invalid, state the reason. Assume Z is character type.

a. 3 = 2 + 1   e. X + Y = X + Y   i. A = (X + Y) / K

b. PAY = HOURS + RATE   f. A = A   j. 'A' = 'A'

c. 6X   g. B + 3 / 2 / −4   k. 3. + SAM.

d. '3 = 4'   h. Z = 'HELLO'

3. For each of the following, assume that A = 2., B = 3. and L = −2; what value will be stored in the variable on the left of the equal sign after execution of each of the following replacement statements?

a. X = A/B   c. QQ = L/3   e. Y = A**L

b. IX = A/B   d. JJ = L/3.   f. IY = A** 1/2 + 1/2

4. State whether each of the following FORTRAN statements is valid; if invalid, explain why.

a. X = 17.5 − B   f. F = E/G + H

b. Q = 3.5 R   g. X**2 = 25.

c. Y + Z = X   h. Z = A + B/C

d. 57 = I   i. R = A/(1. − B/(1. − C/(1. − D/(1. − E))))

e. W = (A + B/C

5. Assuming A = 1.5, B = 3.0, I = 2, and J = 4, evaluate the following replacement statements:

a. X = A − B   d. Y = B**(A − 1.Ø)   g. N = I/3 + J/3

b. K = J/I   e. M = B*A   h. NN = (I + J)/3

c. L = I/J   f. W = I/J   i. Q = A**I

6. Assume CHARACTER RIGHT, LEFT * 6. Determine the value of LEFT resulting from the following code:

```
LEFT  = 'CALCULUS'
RIGHT = LEFT
LEFT  = RIGHT
```

Answers to Selected Questions

2. a. Invalid statement; a variable should be on the left-hand side of the equal sign.

b. Valid statement.

c. Invalid expression or variable name.

d. Valid character variable

k. Invalid expression; period in SAM. is invalid.

3. a. A/B = 2./3. = .6666...; value of X is .6666...7

b. A/B = .6666...; value of IX is integer part of .6666..., which is 0 (without a decimal point).

c. L/3 = −2/3 = 0 (integer arithmetic); value of QQ is 0.0 (it must have decimal point).

d. L/3. = −2/3. = −2./3. = −.6666...; value of JJ is integer part of −.6666... which is 0 (without a decimal point).

e. A**L = 2.**(−2) = 1./4. = .25; value of Y is .25.

f. IY = 1 since (A** 1/2 = (A ** 1)/2 = 2./2 = 1.)

4. **a.** valid   **b.** invalid; missing operator   **c.** invalid; reversed
   d. invalid; reversed   **e.** invalid; missing parenthesis   **f.** valid
   g. invalid; left side   **h.** valid   **i.** valid
   is not a variable.

5. **a.** −1.5   **b.** 2   **c.** 0   **d.** 1.732...   **e.** 4   **f.** 0.0   **g.** 1   **h.** 2   **i.** 2.25

2.4.13 The PARAMETER Statement

The PARAMETER statement allows us to give a name and a value to a constant. The general form of the PARAMETER statement is

PARAMETER (*name1* = *expression1*, *name2* = *expression2*, ...)

where   *name1, name2* ... are valid variable names
         expression1, expression2, ... are usually constants or expressions consisting
             of PARAMETER names defined earlier in a PARAMETER statement.

A new value cannot be assigned to a PARAMETER name through a replacement statement or any other FORTRAN statement, thus the value associated to a PARAMETER name can never be inadvertently changed during the execution of a program.

PARAMETER statements must precede executable statements and follow any specification statements that affects PARAMETER names statement. Thus

```
PARAMETER (SUM=0)
INTEGER SUM
```
is invalid (SUM is implicitly real), but

```
INTEGER SUM
PARAMETER (SUM=0)
```
is valid.

The value of a PARAMETER variable is assigned during the compilation process in contrast to the value given to a variable by a replacement statement during execution of a program.

EXAMPLE

```
INTEGER SUM
REAL PI, FICART, THIRD, PIDIV2, RADIUS, BASE
CHARACTER DATE*8
PARAMETER (PI = 3.1415926, PIDIV2 = PI/2.0, THIRD = 1.0/3.0)
PARAMETER (DATE = '01/02/86', SUM=0, FICART = 0.0715)
   :
AREA = PI * RADIUS**2
VOLUME = THIRD * PI*RADIUS**2*BASE
   :
FICA = GROSS * FICART
WRITE(6,*)DATE
```

One advantage of the PARAMETER statement is that it makes the program easier to read and understand, and in the process, the code becomes more self-documenting. In the preceding example the word PI is used in the formulas instead of the lengthy constant 3.1415926, making the formulas more understandable and easier to write, especially if there are many occurrences of PI throughout the program.

Notice how the PARAMETER statement makes it easy to update the FICA rate. The value of FICART needs to be changed only in the PARAMETER statement, not every time FICART occurs in the program.

Also note how PI is used in the second PARAMETER expression to calculate the value of PIDIV2.

In the case of the FICA rate, it is easier to update its value in the PARAMETER statement than to change its value everywhere in the program where it is used.

Note how PI is used within the second PARAMETER expression.

The value given to a PARAMETER variable occurs during compilation time whereas the value given to a variable through the replacement statement, occurs during the execution of the program.

2.4.14 Order of FORTRAN Statements

We can identify eleven major types of statements in FORTRAN 77. A few have already been discussed in this chapter and many more will be introduced in each of the remaining chapters. Certain restrictions govern the order in which these statements can appear in a FORTRAN program.

Broadly speaking there are executable statements and nonexecutable statements. Executable statements are those statements that cause an action to take place during execution of the program, i.e., after the program has been compiled. Nonexecutable statements are those statements that are used by the compiler to translate the FORTRAN code into object code. These statements specify, describe or classify the various elements of the FORTRAN source code.

In this chapter we have encountered

- Comment statements
- Specification statements: REAL, INTEGER and CHARACTER
- PARAMETER statement
- Executable statements: replacement statement; output statement (WRITE, PRINT*,); OPEN statement; STOP
- END statement

The order in which these statements appear in a program is as follows:

Comment statements	PARAMETER and specification statements
	Executable statements
END statement	

TOP
DOWN

For example a typical program might start with the following statements:

```
REAL COUNT, NORTH
INTEGER SUM, MEAN, N
CHARACTER*10 LIST
PARAMETER (NORTH=362.6, SUM=120)
WRITE ...
```

2.4.15 Functions

You are probably familiar with many mathematical functions such as the square root, exponential, and trigonometric functions. These functions are available to the FORTRAN programmer, along with several other special functions; a few of these are shown in Figure 2.7. (A complete discussion of functions is presented in chapter 8.)

A function operates on one or more values (called arguments) to produce a single resulting value called the functional value. The arguments of a function must be enclosed in parentheses following the name of the function.

A function is used simply by referring to it in an expression in place of a variable or a constant. Thus $4.0 + SQRT(25.0)$ is equal to $4.0 + 5.0 = 9.0$ and $10 + MIN0(3, -4, 7, 10) = 10 - 4$, since -4 is the value returned by the function MIN0.

In the following table of functions, R, R1, and R2 refer to real constants, real variables, or real functions, and I, I1, and I2 refer to integer constants, integer variables, or integer functions.

Function Name	Definition	Examples	
ABS(R) IABS(I)	Absolute value function $\|r\| = \begin{matrix} r \text{ if } r \geq 0 \\ -r \text{ if } r < 0 \end{matrix}$	ABS(1.7) IABS($-$18)	= 1.7 = 18
SQRT(R)	Square root function $\sqrt{r}$ where $r > 0$	SQRT(17.2)	= 4.14...
SIGN(R1,R2) ISIGN(I1,I2)	The value of SIGN(R1,R2) is equal to the absolute value of R1 times the sign of R2.	SIGN(3.0, $-$2.0) = $-$3.0 ISIGN(3,2) = 3	
FLOAT(I) REAL	The value of FLOAT or REAL is equal to the real value of its argument.	FLOAT(3) = 3.	
INT(R)	The value of INT is the integer part of its argument (the digits to the right of the decimal point are dropped).	INT(3.9) INT($-$3.9)	= 3 = $-$3
	To round off R use: INT(R + 0.5) if R $\geq$ 0 or INT(R $-$ 0.5) if R $<$ 0 or simply use INT(R + SIGN(0.5,R)) regardless of sign of R.		
MOD(I1,I2) AMOD(R1,R2)	Remainder function: remainder of 17/5 is 2. In general, remainder = R1 $-$ INT(R1/R2)*R2	MOD(6,4) AMOD(6.,5.) AMOD(4.123, 1.000) MOD($-$5,3) AMOD($-$7.5,2.0)	= 2 = 1. = 0.123 = $-$2 = $-$1.5
MIN0(I1,I2,...) AMIN1(R1,R2,...) MAX0(I1,I2,...) AMAX1(R1,R2,...)	smallest of arguments smallest of arguments largest of arguments largest of arguments	MIN0(2, $-$1,4) AMIN1(3.,9.,6.) MAX0(3,4,IABS($-$6)) AMAX1(3.,4.,SQRT(16.))	= $-$1 = 3. = 6 = 4.
ALOG(R) ALOG10(R)	Natural log: $\log_e(r)$ Common log: $\log_{10}(r)$	ALOG(2.718...) ALOG10(100.0)	= 1. = 2.0
SIN(R) COS(R)	Trigonometric sine: r must be in radians Trigonometric cosine: r must be in radians To evaluate the sine or cosine of an angle d in degrees divide d by 57.3, e.g., $\sin(180°) = \sin(180/57.3) \simeq 0$.	SIN(1.0) COS(3.1)	= 0.8414 = $-$0.99913..
EXP(R)	Exponential function e^r	EXP(1.) = 2.718 EXP($-$1.) = 0.367...	

FIGURE 2.7
COMMON FORTRAN FUNCTIONS

As illustrated in Figure 2.7, the name of the function implicitly determines the type (real or integer) of the functional value; thus SQRT (which starts with S) returns a real value, while IABS (which starts with I) returns an integer value. Note that each function requires a specific type argument, for example, the integer function INT requires a real argument, while the absolute value function IABS requires an integer argument; thus SQRT(10) is an invalid function reference, since 10 is *not* a real value. Also notice that some functions require more than one argument. For example:

```
J = SQRT(16.)
X = (SQRT(16.) + SQRT(25.))/2.
Z = SQRT(SQRT(16.0))
Y = SQRT(X**2 + 1./Z)
X = 2.0*SQRT(X)
```

Since J is an integer, 4. is stored as 4 in J
Value stored in X is 4.5
Argument itself is a function. Z = 2.0
Argument is an expression. Y = $\sqrt{X^2 + 1/Z}$
If X is 9.0, then X becomes 6.0

1. Write FORTRAN statements for each of the following:

   a. $a = \sin^2 x - \cos^2 x$ **d.** Find the largest of A, B, C, D, and E.

   b. $z = e^x - e^{-x}$ **e.** Find the smallest of I, J, K, and 3.

   c. $x = \sqrt{|p - q|}$

2. How could INT be used to round to the nearest hundred? To the nearest thousandth?

3. What will be the value of each of the following if A $=$ 100., B $=$ -2.4, C $=$ 81., D $=$ 0.?

   a. SQRT(C)   **e.** SIGN(B,A)   **h.** ABS(B) + ABS(C)

   b. SQRT(SQRT(C))   **f.** AMIN1(A,B,C,D)   **i.** ALOG10(A)

   c. INT(B)   **g.** AMAX1(A,B,4.*B,C,D)   **j.** SIN(D) + COS(D)

   d. SIGN(A,B)

4. Use the MOD function to determine

   a. whether an integer is even or odd

   b. whether a number is evenly divisible by 7.

1. **a.** `A = SIN(X)**2 - COS(X)**2`

   d. `ALARG = AMAX1(A,B,C,D,E)`

2. To round the value in A to the nearest hundred:

   `A = 100. * INT((A + 50.)/100.)`

3. **a.** 9.   **b.** 3.   **c.** -2 **d.** $-100.$ **e.** 2.4

2.5 LIST-DIRECTED OUTPUT

Output can be produced by either

1. The WRITE statement in conjunction with the FORMAT statement, or

2. The list-directed PRINT/WRITE instructions (no FORMATS are needed).

When the list-directed instructions are used, the system, not the user, decides where the output items are to be placed on the output line(s). (To those familiar with BASIC, the FORTRAN PRINT or WRITE(6,*) instruction is similar to the BASIC PRINT instruction.)

The WRITE/FORMAT instruction is a format-controlled output instruction. The user must provide a FORMAT statement containing various edit codes that specify where each output item is to be printed on the output line. The WRITE statement specifies the list of items to be printed. (To those familiar with BASIC, the WRITE statement is conceptually similar to the PRINT USING.) Formatted output is discussed in chapter 5.

The PRINT or WRITE(6,*) statement is easier and more convenient to use than the WRITE/FORMAT instruction. However, it is important to understand and become familiar with format-controlled output, since formatted output reflects industry procedures. Format-controlled output allows you to produce attractively designed, professional-looking results or reports.

The general form of the list-directed statements is

PRINT*,*list* WRITE(*device-number,**)*list*

Some systems may not support the PRINT* statement.

- In most installations the device number is 6, which refers to the printer. If an asterisk is used for the device number, the system's default output device is used; on microcomputers this is the screen or the keyboard terminal.

- If an OPEN statement is necessary to open your printer file, then the device-number specified in the WRITE statement must be the same as the number specified in the OPEN statement.

- *list* is a string of items that can be constants, variables, functions, or arithmetic expressions. These items should be separated by commas.

When the list of values is written on the output line, each item is separated from the others by spaces. If all the values do not fit on one line, as many lines as needed are used to print the entire list. The number of items per line and the width of each output item vary from one system to the next. Five items per line is common.

Decimal points and fractional values are printed for real numbers.

Exponential notation with the character E is generally used to represent real numbers whose values fall in a certain range. For small numbers this range might be -0.1 to 0.1 and for large numbers outside the $\pm 10^{10}$ range. The system represents these numbers in a format such as

$\pm d.dddddd \, E \pm ddd$, which represents the value $\pm \, d.dddddd \, 10^{\pm ddd}$

where d is a digit (0–9) and E can be read as "times 10 to the power."

EXAMPLES

$$0.900000 \, E - 003 = 0.9 \times 10^{-3} = 0.0009$$
$$1.230000 \, E + 010 = 1.23 \times 10^{10} = 12300000000$$

Figure 2.8 shows a number of examples of format-free WRITE statements. Analyze the output and the various notations for integer, real, and character values. Note the following:

- Lines 23 and 24 produce two blank lines.

- Line 25 writes 0. and $-.00456$ in exponential notation, while all real output items from line 19 use decimal notation.

- Line 25 evaluates expressions and functions. Note that 3/4 evaluates to 0 (integer division).

- Line 26 produces two character strings that are fused together. To avoid this "gluing" effect, change the size of STRING to 16 instead of 15.

2.6 ERRORS AND THE EDITING PROCESS: BUGS

The reader will quickly realize how easily one can make errors on a computer. Errors, commonly called *bugs*, come in four varieties: typographical, syntax, logical, and system errors.

2.6.1 Typographical Errors

Everyone mistypes characters at some time or another. These errors are usually interpreted by the computer as syntax errors. Such errors are self-evident and can be minimized by concentration. A common error is to type the letter *O* instead of the digit zero (0), or the lowercase letter *l* or the upper case I for the digit 1.

```
1:          CHARACTER STRING*15
2:          PARAMETER(PI=3.14159, COEFF=PI/180, GRAVTY=32.16)
3: *
4:          VELOCT = 400.00
5:          DEGREE = 45.00
6:          TIME   = 12.00
7:          RADIAN = DEGREE * COEFF
8:          XVLSTY = VELOCT * COS(RADIAN)
9:          YVLSTY = VELOCT * SIN(RADIAN)
10:         DISTNS = XVLSTY * TIME
11:         HEIGHT = YVLSTY*TIME - (1./2.*GRAVTY)*TIME**2
12: *
13:         WRITE(6,*) 'INITIAL VELOCITY=', VELOCT
14:         WRITE(6,*) 'DEPARTURE ANGLES IN DEGREES=', DEGREE
15:         WRITE(6,*) 'FLIGHT DURATION=', TIME
16:         WRITE(6,*)
17:         WRITE(6,*) 'AT THE END OF', TIME,
18:        1           ' SECONDS, THE MISSILE WILL HAVE COVERED', DISTNS,
19:        2           ' FEET AND ITS ALTITUDE WILL BE', HEIGHT,
20:        3           ' FEET, ASSUMING FLAT TERRAIN AND NO AIR RESISTANCE'
21: *
22:         STRING = 'NOW IS THE TIME'
23:         WRITE(6,*)
24:         WRITE(6,*)
25:         WRITE(6,*) 0., -0.00456, 3/4, 3.0/4.0*2, COS(3.141), SQRT(7.0)
26:         WRITE(6,*) STRING, 'TO STUDY'
27:         STOP
28:         END
```

Output

```
INITIAL VELOCITY=         400.0000000
DEPARTURE ANGLES IN DEGREES=          45.0000000
FLIGHT DURATION=          12.0000000

AT THE END OF          12.0000000 SECONDS, THE MISSILE WILL HAVE COVERED
       3394.1570000 FEET AND ITS ALTITUDE WILL BE       1204.4760000 FEET, ASSUMI
NG FLAT TERRAIN AND NO AIR RESISTANCE.

              0.      -.00456                  3/4          3./4.*2.    COS(3.141)
              |          |                      |              |            |
0.000000E+000 -4.560000E-003                  0       1.5000000 -9.999999E-001
              2.6457510  ◄─────────── SQRT(7.0)
NOW IS THE TIMETO STUDY
              └─ Note fusion of the two strings (line 26)
```

FIGURE 2.8
EXAMPLES OF LIST-DIRECTED OUTPUT

2.6.2 Syntax Errors   Syntax errors reflect the programmer's inability to observe the "grammatical" rules of the FORTRAN language. Syntax errors include misspelled key words, forgotten statement numbers, faulty punctuation, mismatched parentheses, incorrect word order, and so forth. The compiler will identify the line number(s) where the error(s) occurred during the compilation process.

EXAMPLES

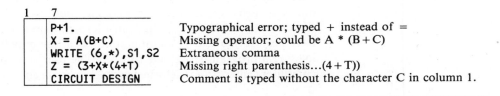

`P+1.`	Typographical error; typed + instead of =
`X = A(B+C)`	Missing operator; could be A * (B + C)
`WRITE (6,*),S1,S2`	Extraneous comma
`Z = (3+X*(4+T)`	Missing right parenthesis...(4 + T))
`CIRCUIT DESIGN`	Comment is typed without the character C in column 1.

Depending on the gravity of the syntax errors, most systems will abort the job at the conclusion of the compilation (why execute a set of unsound instructions?).

2.6.3 Logical Errors   Logical errors are the traditional enemies of beginning and professional programmers alike. Logical errors are present in a program whenever the program does not solve the intended problem, i.e., when the results produced by the computer are incorrect. Such incorrect results may occur because of one silly but critical typographical error or because of incorrect reasoning or an incorrect sequence of instructions. Between these two extremes lie hundreds of other possible sources of errors.

Logical errors are the hardest ones to find in a program because the computer generally prints no error message during the execution of the program, i.e., as far as FORTRAN is concerned, the instructions are all syntactically sound and therefore the results must be correct.

Logical errors are often very well camouflaged and can look perfectly innocent to the programmer as well as to the computer. For example, the instruction AVRGE = SUM/COUNT is a perfectly valid instruction, syntactically speaking, yet it could be a time bomb during the execution of the program if the value of COUNT is 0. If COUNT = 0, the computer will give out an execution error message, since it (like any human being) cannot divide a number by 0. Somehow COUNT should not be 0, and the programmer must play detective in order to find out why the value of COUNT is 0 when that instruction is executed.

Logical errors can also be the result of careless mistakes. For example, you might want to print the result stored in memory location R, but instead you write the instruction WRITE(6,*)S; this instruction yields an incorrect answer, yet as far as FORTRAN is concerned, it is perfectly valid, since WRITE(6,*)S is syntactically correct. The instruction PAY = HOURS + RATE for computing a pay, given a number of hours and a rate, is perfectly valid to the computer, but it is a logical error as far as you are concerned, since the formula is incorrect!

Always remember that the compiler merely translates FORTRAN statements into machine instructions; it does not execute the machine instructions and hence cannot determine whether the instructions make sense or not.

Thus, it is important that the programmer not put blind faith in whatever the computer prints out. The fact that the computer prints out numbers does not necessarily mean that those numbers are correct! The programmer should always check and analyze computer-produced results most carefully.

2.6.4 System Errors

System errors are caused by the components of the computer system itself, such as the telephone lines, the printers, the tapes, or the diskettes. For example, a printer may not be turned on when the CPU needs it, thus generating a special error message. A diskette may be "bad" (especially in microcomputer systems): a user diskette may not have been formatted, or an input/output failure may have occurred when saving or loading a program from tape or disk. The user should contact the lab manager or computer center personnel when system errors occur.

2.6.5 Do It Now

Mrs. X has purchased $12,500 worth of A&L stock, which yields a 13.5% return. Mrs. X pays 27 % of her income to the government. The program below attempts to compute and print the following:

    a. the yearly income from the stock,

    b. the total accumulated principal after one year,

    c. the federal tax to be paid on the stock's earnings and

    d. Mrs. X's net holdings (after federal income tax).

Identify syntax and logical errors in the following program:

```
1:        STOCK = 12,500
2:        INCOME = STOCK * 13.5      Compute income.
3:        WRITE(6,*)INCOME
4: *
5:        INT + STOCK = TOTAL        Compute total principal.
6:        WRITE(6,*)TOTAL
7:        FEDTAX = TOTAL * .27       Compute federal tax on stock income.
8:        HOLDIN = 1.135 * 12500 - .135 * .27 * 12500
9: *      END
```

Answers

Syntax errors:

Line 1   Invalid comma; should be 12500
Line 5   Invalid statement; should be TOTAL = INT + STOCK
Line 9   No END statement (* is column 1)

Logical errors:

Line 2   The percentage should be expressed as .135
Line 2   INCOME is truncated.
Line 7   Federal tax on income should be INCOME * .27 and not TOTAL * .27

Mrs. X's holdings and federal tax are not printed.
There is no STOP instruction.

2.7 YOU MIGHT WANT TO KNOW

1. What happens if I insert extra unnecessary sets of parentheses in an expression?

Answer: Extra sets of parentheses have no effect on the evaluation of an expression. For example:

((40.0 * RATE) + (HOURS − 40.0) * (RATE * 1.5)) is equivalent to
40.0 * RATE + (HOURS − 40.0) * RATE * 1.5

The important point is that parentheses must occur in matched pairs. For each left parenthesis, there must be a right parenthesis. Too many parentheses may slow down the compilation process, however.

2. How does the computer represent repeating decimal numbers (rational numbers)? For example, how can the computer represent exactly 1./3. in decimal form?

Answer: It can't; only the first few digits are retained. For instance, on many systems 1./3. = .3333333 and 8./9. = .8888889

3. I am confused about the difference between STOP and END. Can you help?

Answer: The END statement is processed at compilation time to inform the compiler that there are no more FORTRAN statements to be translated (no FORTRAN code follows; the physical end of the FORTRAN program has been reached—not the physical end of the complete job, control statements and all, but just the FORTRAN source statements). The END statement is not translated into a machine-language instruction. If the END statement is not the last of the FORTRAN statements, the remaining FORTRAN statements will not be read (processed) by the compiler. The world's shortest FORTRAN program is just an END statement all by itself!

The STOP statement on the other hand, is translated into a machine-language instruction and is therefore executed by the CPU during execution time to inform the system that all machine instructions (corresponding to the program) have been carried out, all results (if any) have been printed out, and that as far as this job is concerned there is nothing else to do; i.e., the STOP causes execution to terminate and represents the logical end of the program as opposed to the physical end designated by the END statement. The STOP statement causes control to be returned to the operating system, which will process other programs (if any). As we will see in chapter 3, the STOP statement can be placed anywhere in the program (before the END).

4. What is a bug?

Answer: A "bug" in the computer science jargon simply refers to an error or a mistake of some kind. To "debug" a program means to get rid of the bugs or errors in it.

5. Can an exponent be negative?

Answer: Yes. For example, 3.**(− 2) is evaluated as a $\frac{1.}{3.^2}$ = $\frac{1.}{9.}$

6. In everyday life we don't differentiate between integer and real (floating point) numbers when performing arithmetic operations. Why do we in FORTRAN?

Answer: Actually, we do allow for a difference in everyday computations as well as in FORTRAN. Sometimes we have to figure the position of the decimal point when multiplying or dividing two real numbers. Obviously, operations involving decimal points are more time-consuming than those without a decimal point. On a typical computer, real number operations may be ten times slower than integer number operations.

In a scientific environment, too, it may be necessary to work with very large numbers requiring the use of exponents and decimal points. It would be impractical to write 10^{70} as an integer; hence, an alternative arithmetic is required (real arithmetic). The exponential notation for real numbers is discussed in chapter 5.

7. Is it possible to use nested parentheses to reduce the number of operations required to evaluate an expression?

Answer: Yes. Consider, for example, the evaluation of $2x^3 + 3x^2 - 6x + 1$. A straightforward way to code this expression is:

```
2.*X**3 + 3.*X**2 - 6.*X + 1.
```

Evaluation of this expression will require

2 exponentiations	2 additions
3 multiplications	1 subtraction.

This expression can, however, be simplified by factoring as follows:

$$2x^3 + 3x^2 - 6x + 1 = (2x^2 + 3x - 6)x + 1$$
$$= ((2x + 3)x - 6)x + 1$$

It can then be coded as

```
((2.*X + 3.)*X - 6.)*X + 1.
```

Evaluation of this expression will require

3 multiplications
2 additions
1 subtraction.

2.8 PROBLEM EXAMPLES

2.8.1 An Automatic Change Problem

Problem Specification. Someone purchases an item in a store but does not have the exact change and pays an amount that exceeds the bill. Write a program to calculate the change in dollar bills, quarters, dimes, nickels, and pennies.

Solution. The program to solve this problem is shown in Figure 2.9. Line 10 computes the amount of change in cents. This amount is then divided by 100 to give the number of dollar bills (line 12). Note that the integer division at line 12 truncates all digits to the right of the decimal point. The amount left can then be computed at either line 17 or line 18 (an option that uses the MOD function to compute the remainder). Similar steps are taken at lines 16, 20, and 24 to compute quarters, dimes, and nickels. Note how the number of pennies is computed at line 25.

2.8.2 Test Your Computer—How Good Is It With Numbers?

Finite and Infinite Sums

Consider the following three sums, SUM6, SUM7, and SUM8

$$\text{SUM6} = 9/10 + 9/10^2 + 9/10^3 + 9/10^4 + 9/10^5 + 9/10^6$$
$$\text{SUM7} = 9/10 + 9/10^2 + 9/10^3 + 9/10^4 + 9/10^5 + 9/10^6 + 9/10^7$$
$$\text{SUM8} = 9/10 + 9/10^2 + 9/10^3 + 9/10^4 + 9/10^5 + 9/10^6 + 9/10^7 + 9/10^8$$

```
 1: ******COMPUTERIZED CHANGE SYSTEM
 2: ******GIVEN A BILL AND A PAYMENT COMPUTE THE CHANGE
 3:        REAL BILL, PAYMNT
 4:        INTEGER DOLLAR,HFDLR,QUATER,DIME,NICKEL,CENT
 5:        INTEGER CHANGE, LEFT
 6: *
 7:        OPEN(6,FILE='PRN')
 8:        BILL   =  5.03
 9:        PAYMNT = 10.00
10:        CHANGE = (PAYMNT - BILL) * 100.00
11: ******COMPUTE NUMBER OF DOLLARS
12:        DOLLAR = CHANGE/100
13:        LEFT   = CHANGE - DOLLAR * 100
14: *      LEFT   = MOD(CHANGE, 100)
15: ******COMPUTE NUMBER OF QUARTERS
16:        QUATER = LEFT/25
17:        LEFT   = LEFT - QUATER * 25
18: *      LEFT   = MOD(LEFT,25)
19: ******COMPUTE NUMBER OF DIMES
20:        DIME   = LEFT/10
21:        LEFT   = LEFT - DIME * 10
22: *      LEFT   = MOD(LEFT,10)
23: ******COMPUTE NUMBER OF NICKELS AND PENNIES
24:        NICKEL = LEFT/5
25:        CENT   = LEFT - NICKEL * 5
26:        WRITE(6,*) 'NUMBER OF DOLLARS =', DOLLAR
27:        WRITE(6,*) 'NUMBER OF QUARTERS=', QUATER
28:        WRITE(6,*) 'NUMBER OF DIMES   =', DIME
29:        WRITE(6,*) 'NUMBER OF NICKELS =', NICKEL
30:        WRITE(6,*) 'NUMBER OF PENNIES =', CENT
31:        STOP
32:        END
```

Output

```
NUMBER OF DOLLARS =     4
NUMBER OF QUARTERS=     3
NUMBER OF DIMES   =     2
NUMBER OF NICKELS =     0
NUMBER OF PENNIES =     2
```

FIGURE 2.9
CHANGE CALCULATION

As more terms are added to these sequences, do the successive sums get closer and closer to a particular value, or do the sums grow larger than any arbitrary value by simply adding more and more terms? Does the infinite sum SUMINF, (shown below) get closer and closer to a particular value (converge) or does the value of the infinite sum itself become infinite (diverge)?

$$\text{SUMINF} = 9/10 + 9/10^2 + 9/10^3 + ... + 9/10^{100} + ... 9/10^{1000} + ...$$

In mathematics a sequence of numbers like this one is called a geometric progression; each new term of the sequence is equal to the preceding term multiplied by the number 1/10 (the ratio between two successive terms is constant and equal to 1/10).

The formula for computing the sum of *n* terms of a geometric progression is:

$$\text{Sum of } n \text{ terms} = \frac{\text{first term of sequence} * (1 - \text{ratio}^n)}{1 - \text{ratio}}$$

The formula to compute the sum of the infinite progression is:

$$\text{Sum of infinite terms} = \frac{\text{first term}}{1 - \text{ratio}}$$

Let us write a program to compute the three finite sums SUM6, SUM7, and SUM8, the infinite sum SUMINF and the difference between the infinite sum and each of the finite sums. We will assume that our computer gives 7 significant digits on output. The program is shown in Figure 2.10.

Note that the infinite sum SUMINF is equal to 1. The reader should expect this result, since the infinite sum is actually

$$SUMINF = .9 + .09 + .009 + .0009 + .00009 + \ldots = .99999\ldots = 1 \text{ at infinity!}$$

Note also that the value computed for SUM8 is 1. In fact, as far as the computer is concerned, all finite sums after the first eight terms are included are equal to 1, due to the computer's inability to work with more than seven significant digits.

2.8.3 Test Your Understanding of the Programming Problems

Consider the FORTRAN code in Figure 2.9.

1. What would be the effect of declaring CHANGE as REAL?
2. What would be the effect of typing LEFT as REAL?
3. Could you use the AMOD function instead of the MOD function?

```
 1: ******ERRORS INDUCED BY ARITHMETIC OPERATIONS ON SMALL NUMBERS
 2: ******SUMINF          : SUM OF INFINITE NUMBER OF TERMS
 3: ******SUM6, SUM7, SUM8: 6TH, 7TH, AND 8TH FINITE SUMS
 4: ******DIF6, DIF7, DIF8: DIFFERENCES BETWEEN FINITE & INFINITE SUMS
 5:       REAL  SUM6, SUM7, SUM8, DIF6, DIF7, DIF8, SUMINF
 6: *
 7:       OPEN(6,FILE='PRN')
 8:       SUM6 = .9*(1. - 0.1**6)/0.9
 9:       SUM7 = .9*(1. - 0.1**7)/0.9
10:       SUM8 = .9*(1. - 0.1**8)/0.9
11: ******COMPUTE SUM OF INFINITE TERMS
12:       SUMINF = 0.9/(1.0 - 0.1)
13: ******COMPUTE DIFFERENCES BETWEEN FINITE & INFINITE SUMS
14:       DIF6 = SUMINF - SUM6
15:       DIF7 = SUMINF - SUM7
16:       DIF8 = SUMINF - SUM8
17:       WRITE(6,*) 'INFINITE SUM = ', SUMINF
18:       WRITE(6,*) 'SUM6 = ', SUM6, '   INFINITE SUM - SUM6 = ', DIF6
19:       WRITE(6,*) 'SUM7 = ', SUM7, '   INFINITE SUM - SUM7 = ', DIF7
20:       WRITE(6,*) 'SUM8 = ', SUM8,  ' INFINITE SUM - SUM8 = ', DIF8
21:       STOP
22:       END
```

```
INFINITE SUM =            1.0000000
SUM6 =  9.999990E-001    INFINITE SUM - SUM6 =   1.013279E-006
SUM7 =  9.999999E-001    INFINITE SUM - SUM7 =   1.192093E-007
SUM8 =            1.0000000 INFINITE SUM - SUM8 =        .0000000
```

FIGURE 2.10
FINITE AND INFINITE SUMS

4. Rewrite the code to include half-dollars.

Consider the FORTRAN code in Figure 2.10.

1. Run the program. Are the results identical? If they are not, why?

2. If SUM8 is not 1, determine the first finite sum that is 1. From this observation, infer the number of significant digits that your computer works with.

2.9 EXERCISES

2.9.1 Test Yourself

1. What is the difference between an expression and a statement? Between a constant and a variable? Between integer and real data?

2. Define the terms *source statement, job control instructions, execution time,* and *compile time.*

3. Characterize each of the following as either an integer, a real, or a character constant; or an integer, a real, or a character variable. If some are invalid, explain why.

a. F	**b.** I123	**c.** FORTRAN	**d.** X1.3
e. -1234	**f.** 3ABC	**g.** 'XRAY'S'	**h.** .000000006
i. $+72$	**j.** 4(Y)	**k.** A1B2C.	**l.** 234-567-999
m. $-1,314.6$	**n.** IRAY	**o.** 'COUNT'	**p.** KOUNT
q. $3+4$	**r.** I2+1	**s.** $300.50	**t.** '3<4'

4. Translate the following algebraic expressions into FORTRAN:

a. $x(y + z)$

b. $\frac{a}{b} \cdot c$

c. $\frac{a}{b^5}$

d. $ax^2 + bx + c$

e. $\frac{a}{bs}$

f. $y^{1/3}$

g. πr^2

h. $\frac{a}{x+y} - \frac{.5}{xz}$

i. $2(xy^{-1})$

j. $-x^2$

k. $a^{x+y} + 3.5$

l. $y + a^x$

m. $\frac{y-y_0}{y_1-y_0} \cdot \frac{x-x_0}{x_1-x_0}$

n. $z - 1 + \cfrac{1}{2 + \cfrac{3}{1-x}}$

o. $\frac{-b + \sqrt{b^2 - 4ac}}{2a}$

p. u^{2n}

q. $\sqrt{\dfrac{4(x_1^2 + x_2^2 + x_3^2) - (x_1 + x_2 + x_3)^2}{3(3 - 1)}}$

5. Write the following statements in FORTRAN.

a. $L = A^2 + B^2 - 2AB \cos(C)$ Length of one side of a triangle.

b. $A = P(1 + I/J)^{J \cdot T}$ Compound interest.

c. $A = P(1 + R)^N$ Simple interest.

d. $1/R = 1/R1 + 1/R2 + 1/R3$ Compute R: Total resistance.

e. $Q = .92A(T_1 - T_0)/H$ Heat flow.

f. $E = 1 + X + X^2/2! + X^3/3!$ Approximation of e^x.

g. $Y = Be^{-AX} \cos(\sqrt{B^2 - A^2X - T})$

6. Fill in the blanks with the appropriate words:

    a. The _____ instruction denotes the logical end of a FORTRAN program.

    b. Variables not starting with the letters _____ are real variables.

    c. _____ can be used to refer to or identify a particular FORTRAN instruction.

    d. The _____ instruction denotes the physical end of the FORTRAN program.

    e. Integers and real numbers are examples of _____.

    f. An alternative to format-controlled output is _____ output.

    g. _____ are used to refer symbolically to memory locations.

    h. 3*X + 1 is an example of an _____.

    i. In a FORTRAN statement, positions 73–80 are used for _____.

    j. *Variable = expression* is the general form of a FORTRAN _____.

    k. _____ instructions are generally used in addition to the FORTRAN program to make up a complete job.

    l. The output code generated by the FORTRAN compiler is called _____, while the input to the compiler is called _____.

    m. Two FORTRAN statements with identical statement numbers would result in a _____ time error, while computing the square root of a negative number would result in an _____ time error.

    n. Dividing one integer by another integer will result in _____.

    o. _____ are used to enclose character strings.

7. Identify the order of the operations by placing an appropriate number above each arithmetic operator in the expression, for example:

$$\overset{5}{} \overset{3}{} \overset{6}{} \overset{7}{} \overset{1}{} \overset{4}{} \overset{2}{}$$
$$A + 1 / 3 + B - (3 + 4) / Z ** 2$$

    a. 3 * 4 − (B − C)

    b. 1 / 8 + 5 ** 2 / 4

    c. (−3 + X) * (B + C) + 3 / X + (C − 1)

    d. X / A * 1 − B + (3 − Y)

8. Which of the following are identical to A*(B+C)/D?

    a. (B+C)* A/D   **b.** (A*(B+C))/D   **c.** (B+C)/D*A   **d.** (A/D)*(B+C)

9. What values will be stored in X and Y as a result of the following?

    a. X = 9.   **b.** X = 9.   **c.** X = 9.   **d.** X = 3.
       Y = 4.   Y = 3.   Y = 1Ø.   Y = 8.
       Y = Y−X   X = Y   T = X   Y = .3
                 Y = X   X = Y
                       Y = T

10. Write a FORTRAN replacement to perform the following:

    a. Double what is in C and print out result with the prefix $.

    b. Replace X by half of its square root.

    c. Add X^3 to whatever was in X.

    d. Store the characters SAM in a memory location.

    e. Interchange the values contained in memory locations S and T.

    f. Convert Fahrenheit temperature to Celsius $(C = 5/9(F - 32))$.

11. Are the following statements true or false?

    a. Statement numbers must be sequentially numbered.

    b. Integer variables that have not been typed must start with one of the letters I, J, K, L, M, or N.

    c. The statement END denotes the logical end of the program.

    d. Statement numbers cannot exceed 99999.

    e. Syntax errors are detected at execution time.

    f. The FORTRAN formula $C = 5/9 (F - 32)$ will convert Fahrenheit degrees to Celsius.

    g. The STOP is used by the compiler to terminate the translation process.

    h. SAM. is a valid, real variable name.

    i. Statement numbers must start in column 1.

    j. WRITE(6,*) FLOAT (REAL (3.0)) is a valid statement.

    k. X = X + 1. is a valid FORTRAN expression.

    l. WRITE(*,*) is an invalid output statement.

    m. 4./4/5 evaluates to the same as 4./(4/5).

    n. 2*J = 3 is a valid replacement statement.

    o. The maximum number of characters for a FORTRAN variable name depends on the particular system.

    p. Depending on the integer values I and J and the real variable C, $I*J*C \neq I*C*J$.

    q. K = - (K) is a valid statement.

    r. The argument of the FLOAT function must be real.

    s. The argument of the SIN function must be specified in radians.

    t. All character variables must be declared in a CHARACTER statement.

    u. CHARACTER A, CHARACTER*1 A, CHARACTER A*1 are identical.

12. For A = 3., B = -2., I = 6, and J = 0, evaluate each of the following expressions.

a. A**2 + B	**b.** I + 2/3	**c.** A**B
d. A*3. + B*4.	**e.** A/B	**f.** A/B* 3. + A
g. A/B/2.	**h.** A/B + 2.	**i.** J/I
j. I/J	**k.** A**I	**l.** (A + I)/B
m. A**2**3	**n.** B**B	**o.** J**B

13. What value will be stored in X or IX by each of the following statements, if A = 3.2, B = -2., I = 6, and J = 0?

a. X = I	**b.** IX = A	**c.** X = (I + 3)/2
d. IX = - A + B	**e.** X = I**B	**f.** X = J*I/.1
g. X = B**J	**h.** IX = J*A	

14. As a result of the following program code, indicate what value will be placed in memory locations S, J, and K.

```
I = 4.
A = 1
B = 2
S = (3/I)*3
J = (3./9)*3
K = (A + 2./B)/2
```

15. Show that if I and J are integer variables and C is real, it is possible to have the following situation:

$$\frac{I}{J}\cdot C \neq \frac{I\,C}{J}$$

2.9.2 Programming Exercises

1. Determine the formula for computing the approximate difference between two dates expressed in the form M1, D1, Y1 and M2, D2, Y2 (M = month, D = day, Y = year). Assume there are 365.25 days per year and 30.4 days per month. Then compute the number of years that you have slept since you were born, assuming you sleep eight hours per day.

2. A bullet is fired perpendicular to the ground, with an initial velocity of $v = 100$ m/s. Write the code to determine its height in feet after 14.672 seconds. Use the formula

$$\text{distance} = v_0 t - \frac{1}{2} g t^2$$

where t is the time and g is the force of gravity (9.81 meters/s²). Given the same initial velocity, determine how long it will take the bullet to hit the ground.

3. Mr. X is a widower with three children aged 12, 16, and 19. His monthly salary is $1,023.36. His monthly contribution to a retirement plan is 4.5% of his first nine month's salary. For each child under 18, he receives $119.25 in child support from social security. His monthly social security deduction is 7.15% of his monthly income, and his federal income tax is 13.6% of his yearly gross (deducted on a monthly basis). Monthly payments for life insurance equal 9.6% of his monthly salary after social security and federal tax deductions. Write a program to compute Mr. X's monthly spendable income after taxes, deductions, and supplemental support income.

4. With an interest rate I of 6% and a principal P of $1,956.45 deposited for an 11-year period in a savings account, write a program to compute a total principal T, given the formula:

$$T = P(1 + I)^N \quad \text{where } N \text{ is the number of years.}$$

5. Suppose the interest of exercise 4 is compounded daily for 11 years. Write a program to compute

a. The total principal given by the formula:

$$T = P\left(1 + \frac{I}{J}\right)^{J \cdot N}$$

where J is the number of times the interest is compounded per year.

b. Compute and print the difference between the total amounts when the principal is compounded once and when it is compounded 365 times a year for 11 years. Also print the corresponding interests earned during that period of time.

c. What would the principal be after 11 years and 7 months? (*Hint:* Express *N* as total months divided by 12.)

6. Write a program to evaluate each of the formulas for the indicated values (use $\pi = 3.1416$) and print the answers with appropriate literal headings.

a. Simple interest $i = prt$ for $r = 4\%$ $t = 3$ $p = 100$

b. Volume of a cube $v = c^3$ for $c = 3.167219$

c. Area of a circle $A = \pi r^2$ for $r = 6.2$

d. Volume of a cone $v = \frac{1}{3} \pi r^2 b$ for $r = 9.1$ $b = 4.932747$

[Expected answers: $i = 12.0$, $v = 31.77$, $A = 120.76$ $v = 427.76$]

7. Write a program to compute and print the area and the perimeter of (a) and (b) and the volume of the sphere in (c).

a. 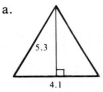   b.   c.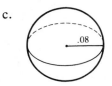

8. Write a program to approximate the Julian date (introduced by Julius Caesar in 46 B.C.) equivalent to the calendar date given in the form: month, day. The Julian date is the day of the year. January 1 has Julian date 1, February 2 has Julian date 33, December 31, has Julian date 365, and so forth. A formula for approximating the Julian date is (month − 1) * 30 + day. Determine the Julian dates for November 7, May 25, and March 21.

9. The truth-in-lending law requires that money-lending institutions disclose the annual interest rate charged on loans. The approximate rate is given by the formula:

$$R = \frac{(2 * N) * F}{A (S + 1)}$$ where   *N* is the number of payments per year
$F = $ the finance charge in dollars
A is the loan amount
$S = $ the total number of scheduled payments.

Write a program to determine the annual percentage rate for a loan of $5,000 for 36 months at 162.50 dollars per month. (Finance charge is the total amount paid minus the amount of the loan, i.e., 36 * 162.5 − 5000 = 850).

10. **a.** Miss T. drove 1050 miles in 17½ hours and spent $86.75 for gas. Her car averages 14.5 miles per gallon. Write a program to compute her average speed, number of gallons used, and the average cost per gallon. The output should be as follows:

```
MILES =            1050
HOURS DRIVEN =     17.5
GAS COST =         86.75
AVERAGE SPEED =    _____
NO. GALLONS =      _____
COST/GALLON =      _____
```

b. Miss T. estimates that she spent 12% of the traveling time on miscellaneous stops. How does this change her average speed?

11. Write a program to produce the following report on the cost c of operating electrical devices:

Cost Analysis

Watts	Hours	Cost/KW	Cost
65	6	.087	--
100	6	.087	--

The formula for computing the cost is

$$C = \frac{W \cdot T \cdot K}{1000} \qquad \text{where} \qquad \begin{aligned} W &= \text{number of watts,} \\ T &= \text{time in hours, and} \\ K &= \text{cost in cents per kilowatt hours.} \end{aligned}$$

12. Write a program to determine the date for any Easter Sunday, computed as follows (let N be the year for which Easter Sunday is to be computed):

Let NA be the remainder of the integer division of N by 19
(for instance, if N = 1914, then NA = 14).
Let NB be the remainder of the integer division of N by 4.
Let NC be the remainder of the integer division of N by 7.
Let ND be the remainder of the integer division of (19·NA + 24) by 30.
Let NE be the remainder of the integer division of (2·NB + 4·NC + 6·ND + 5) by 7.

The date for Easter Sunday is then March (22 + ND + NE). Note that this can give a date in April.

13. For four resistors R_1, R_2, R_3, and R_4 in parallel, the overall resistance R is given by:

$$\frac{1}{R} = \frac{1}{R_1} + \frac{1}{R_2} + \frac{1}{R_3} + \frac{1}{R_4}$$

If R_1, R_2, R_3, and R_4 are respectively 1.5, 3, 4.5, and 6 ohms, write a program to compute R and print the results as follows:

```
R1 = 1.5   R2 = 3.0   R3 = 4.5   R4 = 6.0
THE OVERALL RESISTANCE R = XX.X
```

14. Write a program to determine whether $x = 1.3$ is a root of the equation

$$\frac{17}{3}x^{17} + 4x^8 - .76x^2 - 686 = 0$$

15. Write a program to compute the infinite sum (whenever possible) of each of the following geometric progressions (see section 2.8.2 for formulas):

a. $1 + 2 + 4 + 8 + 16 + \ldots$ **c.** $4 + 2 + 1 + 1/2 + 1/4 + \ldots$

b. $3 - 9 + 27 - 81 + \ldots$ **d.** $9/10 + 9/100 + 9/1000 + \ldots$

16. Mr. Grand wants to purchase a $42,356 Jaguar. He can manage a down payment of $7,800. The trade-in allowance for his old Volvo is $2,945. Current dealer interest rates are an annual 9.6% for 2½ years. What will be Mr. Grand's monthly payment for the next 2½ years? The formula to compute the monthly payment is:

$$R = iP \left[\frac{(1 + i)^m}{(1 + i)^m - 1} \right]$$

where i = interest rate per month
P = principal (purchase price − down payment − trade-in-allowance)
m = the number of monthly payments.

17. Write a program to produce a magic square. In a magic square, the sum of each row, column, and diagonal is equal. For example, the following is a magic square in which the sum is 3:

−2	2	3
6	1	−4
−1	0	4

The secret of the magic square is this: for any values of x, y, and z, a magic square can be formed from:

$x-z$	$x+z-y$	$x+y$
$x+y+z$	x	$x-y-z$
$x-y$	$x+y-z$	$x+z$

In the above example, $x=1$, $y=2$, $z=3$. Choose three numbers and print the corresponding magic square.

18. The Sullivans would like to take a summer trip abroad in a year and a half. They estimate that their expenses will be just over $3,500. They save regularly at a credit union where 6.5% interest is paid on deposits. What should the Sullivans' minimum monthly deposit be to afford the vacation abroad? What would their deposits have to be if they made four equal deposits per year? The formula to calculate the regular deposit R is:

$$R = P \left(\frac{i/n}{(1+i/n)^{n \cdot y} - 1} \right)$$

where P = amount to be saved (future value)
i = interest rate
n = deposits/year
y = number of years

19. Mary and John Soule would very much like to buy the Pitts' house. The Pitts are asking $76,000 conventional with $7,000 down or $84,000 for VA with nothing down. In either case, a 30-year mortgage is sought. Financing charges are 9.5% for VA and 10% for conventional. (Equal monthly payments will be made.) The Soules have another option: Mary's father is willing to give them $9,000 for a down payment, on the condition that they assume with him a 10.5% interest mortgage for the next 22 years and 8 months on the remainder of the conventional price, with equal payments four times a year. In terms of today's dollar value, what is the Soule's best financial arrangement? Identify in each case the total costs involved as well as the interest paid. The formula to compute the regular payments R (monthly, quarterly, etc.) is:

$$R = \frac{iP/n}{1 - \left(\dfrac{i}{n} + 1\right)^{-ny}}$$

where P = principal
          i = interest rate
          n = number of payments/year
          y = number of years. (If the number of years is given in years and months, convert it to months and divide by 12.)

2.9.3 Selected Answers to Test Yourself

1. An expression is a part of a statement; an expression should always be on the right-hand side of the = sign. The value of a constant does not change; the value of a variable can change. Integer data cannot have decimal points; real data always has decimal points.

2. A *source statement* is a statement written in a high-level language such as FORTRAN. *Job control instructions* are required for communication with the computer's operating system to compile and execute a program. *Execution time* is the time during which the computer is executing the translated program. *Compile time* is the time during which the computer is translating a program into machine language.

3.   **a.** real variable
     b. integer variable
     d. invalid variable, contains special character
     f. invalid variable, numeric first character
     g. invalid character constant, missing apostrophe
     i. integer constant
     j. invalid variable, numeric first character and special characters
     l. invalid constant, imbedded −
     m. invalid constant, comma
     o. character constant
     p. integer variable
     q. invalid constant, imbedded +
     s. invalid constant, $ must not be used
     t. valid character constant

4.   **b.** A/B*C
     c. A/B**5
     e. A/(B*S)
     f. Y**(1./3.)

h. $A/(X + Y) - .5/(X*Z)$

i. $2.*(X*Y**(-1))$

j. $-X**2$

l. $Y + A**X$

m. $(Y - Y\emptyset)/(Y1 - Y\emptyset)*(X - X\emptyset)/(X1 - X\emptyset)$

n. $Z - 1. + (1./(2. + 3. /(1. - X)))$

o. $(-B + (B*B - 4.*A*C)**.5)/(2.*A)$

p. $U**(2.*N)$, not $U**2.*N$

q. $((4.*(X1*X1+X2*X2+X3*X3)-(X1+X2+X3)**2)/(3.*(3.-1.)))**.5$

5. a. $A*A + B*B - 2.*A*B*COS(C)$

    b. $P*(1. + AI/J)**(J*T)$

    d. $(1./R1 + 1./R2 + 1./R3)**(-1)$

    e. $.92*A*(T1 - T0)/H$

    g. $B*EXP(-A*X)*COS(SQRT(B*B-A**2*X -T))$

6. a. STOP   **i.** sequencing/identification

    b. I through N   **j.** statement

    c. statement number   **k.** job control

    d. END   **l.** object code, source code

    e. numeric constants   **m.** compilation, execution

    f. list-directed   **n.** truncation of fractional part

    g. Variables   **o.** single quotation marks

    h. mixed mode expression

7.   ②   ③   ①

    a. $3 * 4 - (B - C)$

         ②   ④   ①   ③

    b. $1 / 8 + 5 ** 2 / 4$

           ①   ④   ②   ⑥   ⑤   ⑦   ③

    c. $(- 3 + X) * (B + C) + 3 / X + (C - 1)$

         ②   ③   ④   ⑤   ①

    d. $X / A * 1 - B + (3 - Y)$

8. All are identical

9. b. $X = 3.,\ Y = 3.$

    c. $X = 10.,\ Y = 9.$

    d. $X = 3.,\ Y = .3$

10. b. $X = X**.5/2.$

     c. $X = X + X**3.$

11.			
a. F	**h.** F	**n.** F	**s.** T
c. F	**i.** F	**o.** F	**u.** T
e. F	**j.** T	**p.** F	
f. F	**k.** F	**q.** T	
g. F	**m.** F	**r.** F	

12. **a.** 7.

    b. 6

    c. .111111

    d. 1.

    e. -1.5

    f. -1.5

    g. $-.75$

    h. .5

    i. 0

    j. error.

    k. 729.

    l. -4.5

    m. 6561.

    n. Error, base is negative

    o. undefined.

13. **b.** 3

    c. 4.

    d. -5

    e. .0277778

    g. 1.

    h. 0

14. S = 0.   J = 0 (or 1 on some systems)   K = 1

15. **a.** 3/4*4. = 0. but (3*4.)/4 = 3.

3   READ, Decision Structures, WHILE DO

3.1 PROGRAMMING EXAMPLE

Problem Specification. Each record of an input file contains a student's name and two test scores. Write a program to assign a "fail" grade to students whose average is below 70 and a "pass" grade to those students with a score of 70 or above. The program should also compute the class average.

A program to solve this problem is shown in Figure 3.1. The left-hand column gives the pseudo code, while the column on the right displays the FORTRAN code.

Two new structures are introduced in the pseudo code and in the FORTRAN code:

1. The WHILE DO/ENDWHILE structure, which allows a task to be repeated until a particular condition is met.

2. The IF/THEN/ELSE structure, which allows the computer to carry out one task if a particular condition is met and another task if the condition is not met.

Your FORTRAN compiler may not support the WHILE DO instruction. If it does not, use the instructions typed in red at lines 27, 38, and 39, which will simulate the WHILE DO.

Figure 3.1 also illustrates the READ statement (lines 25 and 37). All microcomputing systems require that an input file be OPENed (line 18) before it can be read by a FORTRAN program. In this case ROSTER.DAT is the name of the catalogued input file that is opened at line 18. Input files are usually created through text editors and catalogued on disk.

Two new programming techniques are illustrated in this program: the counting mechanism at line 30 and the accumulation process (computing a running sum of all scores) at line 28.

3.2 INPUT CONSIDERATIONS

So far we have defined variables (given them a value) by using assignment statements. For example, in the program in Figure 2.8 (computation of the distance covered by a projectile) we assigned fixed values to the velocity, the angle of attack, and the time duration. The resulting program is too specific; experimenting with different velocity

```
1: ******GRADE ROSTER UTILITY FUNCTION
2: ******PROGRAM ASSIGNS A FAIL GRADE FOR SCORES LESS THAN 70
3: ******AND A PASS GRADE OTHERWISE
4: ******PROGRAM COMPUTES THE CLASS AVERAGE SCORE
5: *     COUNTR: COUNTS TOTAL NUMBER OF STUDENTS
6: *     STDAVG: COMPUTES EACH STUDENTS' AVERAGE
7: *     CLSAVG: COMPUTES THE CLASS SCORE AVERAGE
8: *     GRADE : CONTAINS EITHER 'PASS' OR 'FAIL'
9: *     PASLVL: LOWEST PASSING SCORE LEVEL (70)
10: *    EOFREC: SIMULATED END-OF-FILE RECORD FOR INPUT FILE
11: *    SUMTST: ACCUMULATES ALL CLASS SCORES
12:      CHARACTER NAME*10, GRADE*4, PASS*4, FAIL*4, EOFREC*3
13:      REAL    STDAVG,CLSAVG,SUMTST
14:      INTEGER TEST1, TEST2, COUNTR, PASLVL
15:      PARAMETER(PASS='PASS', FAIL='FAIL')
16:      PARAMETER(PASLVL=70,   EOFREC='XXX')
17: *
18:      OPEN(5,FILE='ROSTER.DAT')
19:      OPEN(6,FILE='PRN')
20:      WRITE(6,*)'NAME       ', '           TEST1',
21:     1          '      TEST2', '    GRADE'
22:      WRITE(6,*)
23:      COUNTR = 0
24:      SUMTST = 0.0
25:      READ(5,*)NAME, TEST1, TEST2
26: *
27: 10    IF(NAME .NE. EOFREC)THEN
28:         SUMTST = SUMTST + TEST1 + TEST2
29:         STDAVG = (TEST1 + TEST2)/2.0
30:         COUNTR = COUNTR + 2
31:         IF (STDAVG .GE. PASLVL)THEN
32:            GRADE = PASS
33:         ELSE
34:            GRADE = FAIL
35:         ENDIF
36:         WRITE(6,*)NAME, TEST1, TEST2, '      ', GRADE
37:         READ(5,*) NAME, TEST1, TEST2
38:         GO TO 10
39:      ENDIF
40: *
41:      CLSAVG = SUMTST/COUNTR
42:      WRITE(6,*)
43:      WRITE(6,*)'CLASS AVERAGE =', CLSAVG
44:      STOP
45:      END
```

Pseudo code (left column):

```
* The following pseudo code assigns a
* grade of FAIL or PASS to students
* based on their test average; if the student
* average is below 70, the student receives a
* FAIL grade; otherwise the student gets a PASS.
* The code also computes the class average.
  initialize counters and accumulators

  read the first record

  WHILE end of file not encountered DO
     accumulate test scores
     compute student average
     increment counter
     IF student average ≥ pass level
        give student pass score
     ELSE
        give student fail score
     ENDIF
     write name, test scores, and grade
     read next record
  ENDWHILE

compute class average
write class average
```

Annotations on code:
- Line 27: WHILE (NAME .NE. EOFREC) DO
- Line 39: ENDWHILE

Data File

```
'ABRAMS M'   , 090, 085
'BALLY L'    , 045, 054
'CARICOE L'  , 100, 058
'WALGREEN D' , 077, 065
'XXX'        , 000, 000
```

Output

NAME	TEST1	TEST2	GRADE
ABRAMS M	90	85	PASS
BALLY L	45	54	FAIL
CARICOE L	100	58	PASS
WALGREEN D	77	65	PASS
CLASS AVERAGE =	71.7500000		

FIGURE 3.1
A GRADE ROSTER UTILITY PROGRAM

values, for example, requires recompiling the entire program for each new velocity value. Such a practice is not only time-consuming and inefficient—it also causes the program to lack generality, which is an essential trait of good program design.

Another way to assign a value to a variable is to use the READ statement, which will be discussed in more detail in section 3.3. The READ statement allows the program to accept data by READing data records during the execution of the program.

3.2.1 Data Records and Placement of Data Records in the Complete FORTRAN Job

The way in which FORTRAN processes an input file varies considerably from one computing installation to another. There are essentially two different types of job configurations for the complete FORTRAN job.

Case 1: Mini/Main Frames. Compile—Load and Go

In many systems, the data records that are to be read by the source program are actually entered along with the FORTRAN program, in one package and at the same time. Job control instructions, which are *not* part of the FORTRAN language, separate the FORTRAN source program from the data records. Figure 3.2 illustrates a typical FORTRAN job with this configuration. Note the three types of components that make up the complete job:

1. the job control instructions, which tell the operating system what to do
2. the FORTRAN source program to solve the user's problem
3. the data records that are to be processed by the FORTRAN program

Usually the entire job is entered through a text editor on a terminal. Each line of the job, whether a job control instruction, a source program instruction, or a data line, is typically numbered on the terminal. Note, once again, that with this arrangement the data records are part of the complete job, i.e., if you need to edit the data records, you must bring the complete job—the job control instructions, the FORTRAN program itself, and the data records—back onto the terminal.

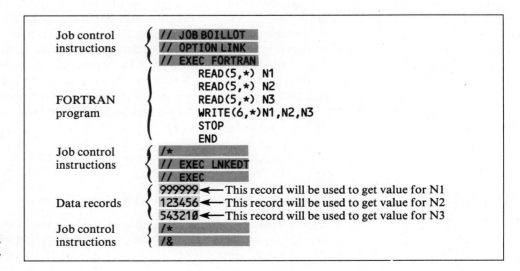

FIGURE 3.2
SAMPLE JOB WITH DATA RECORDS

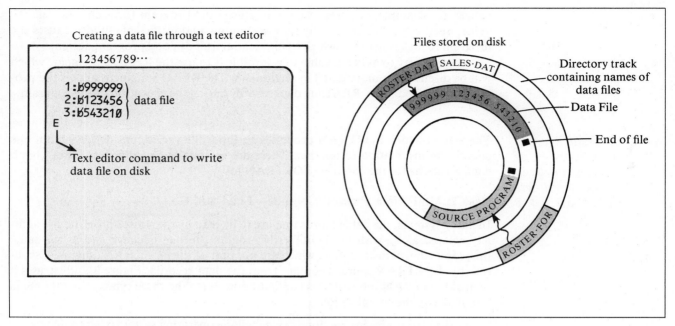

FIGURE 3.3
*INPUT FILE DISPLAYED ON SCREEN AND STORED ON DISK
(MICROCOMPUTERS)*

Case 2: Microcomputers

Through a text editor, the user creates two separate files, the FORTRAN source program and the data file (see Figure 3.3), which are catalogued under different names, for example, ROSTER.FOR for the source program and ROSTER.DAT for the data file. To link the program to the data file, the user must first open the data file with the OPEN instruction. For example, OPEN (5,FILE = 'ROSTER.DAT') tells FORTRAN that whenever a READ(5,*) instruction is encountered in the program, the READ operation is to be carried out on the data records found in file ROSTER.DAT. Thus, the OPEN statement directs the READ operation to the appropriate input file. The numeric label 5 in the OPEN statement is associated with the data file ROSTER.DAT so that a READ (5,*) operation will always be carried out on the input file ROSTER.DAT.

On microcomputers, input files do not have to be closed. (An in-depth discussion of files is found in chapter 9).

*3.2.2 My System
is Different*

Preparing a Simple Program with Input Functions

Use the area on the following page to identify the sequence of steps and commands required on your system to create and run a program that will read an input record and print the input record read.

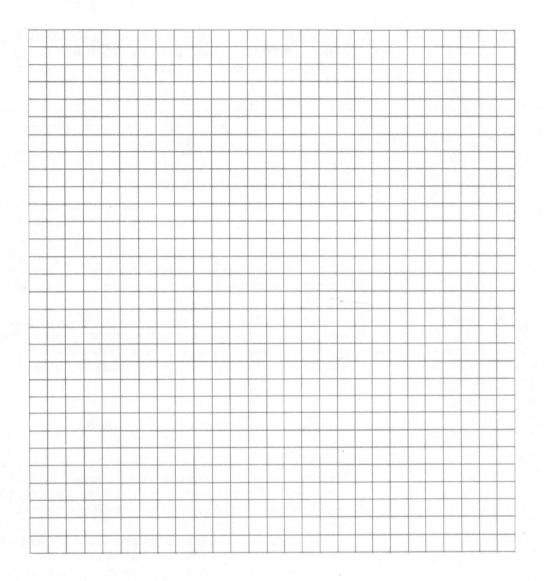

3.3 LIST-DIRECTED INPUT

In many commercial installations, input data is already preformatted, i.e., specific fields are reserved for the various input items. In such situations, only format-controlled input can be used, since the record layout is predefined. Format-controlled input is discussed in chapter 5.

A format-free input is available to the user who is not concerned about the layout of input records. The user simply lists (types) the input items one after the other on data records (data lines), separating each item in the input list by a comma or one or more spaces.

3.3.1 General Forms of   Many systems support the two forms of the READ statement shown in Figure 3.4.
the READ Statement   Some FORTRAN systems, however, will support only one of these forms. Check
                             with your lab manager/instructor to determine the proper form.

Form 1: READ*,*list*
Form 2: READ(*device-number,* *[,END = *statement-number-1*][,ERR = *statement-number-2*]) *list*

---

list is a list of variables separated from one another by commas or spaces

- *device-number* can be an asterisk (*) to indicate the system input device (keyboard/screen) or an integer number (1 through 256) for disk or tape files. Throughout this text, 5 will be used to refer to the input device.

- The END = option allows the user to tell the system what action(s) to take if the end of file is encountered during a READ operation. The system automatically transfers control to *statement-number-1* if the END option is used; if the END option is not used, the program terminates execution with an "end of file" error message.

- The ERR = option allows the user to tell the system what action(s) to take in the event of a READ error, for example, if the data file cannot be located or there is a data type incompatibility during a READ operation (a numeric value contains a letter instead of a digit or a character data item is not enclosed within quotation marks, and so forth). When such an error is detected, the system transfers control to *statement-number-2*.

FIGURE 3.4
GENERAL FORM OF THE READ STATEMENTS

The READ statement reads the input items (which can be real, integer, or character constants) and places them in memory locations corresponding to the variables in the READ list. There must be agreement in type between each variable and the corresponding input item. Data items that are character type must be enclosed in apostrophes.

The system will read as many data records as are needed to satisfy the READ list, but each READ statement processes a new data record.

The END = and the ERR = options are referred to as *interrupts*. The system actually interrupts the FORTRAN program to let it know that something is wrong. For example, if an end-of-file marker is encountered on the input file during a READ operation when the END = option is present, the system simply interrupts the FORTRAN program to determine what action to take at the statement specified by the END = option. (Note that the system automatically writes an end-of-file marker on the data file when the data file is stored on disk.)

In all microcomputing systems where the format-2 READ statement is used, the device number must also be specified in an OPEN statement. A typical form of the OPEN statement is

---

OPEN (*device-number,* FILE = *file-name*)

---

where   *device-number* is an integer constant, typically in the range 1–256;
          file-name is the catalogued name of a data file that is to be read.

The OPEN statement makes a data file available to the FORTRAN program. It tells the system the name of the particular data file that is to be read and the device on which that file resides. To establish a link between the READ statement and its target data file, the device number in the OPEN statement must match the device number in the READ statement.

```
OPEN(5,FILE='MISSILE')
OPEN(2,FILE='TARGET')
    :
READ(5,*)        records are read from the 'MISSILE' data file
READ(2,*)        records are read from the 'TARGET' data file
```

Notice that the OPEN statement must physically precede the READ statement in the program itself. A file is generally only opened once, unless it is closed and then re-opened (file processing is discussed in chapter 9).

On microcomputer systems the disk drive identification can be specified within the file name. Thus OPEN(5,FILE = 'B:MISSILE.DAT') on an IBM PC specifies a data file called MISSILE.DAT that is located on disk drive B. If the drive is not specified, the current default drive is assumed. Device number 5 must be specified in the READ statements that are to read records from file MISSILE.DAT, i.e., READ(5,*) will link the READ operation to records on file MISSILE.DAT.

3.3.2 Examples of List-Directed READ Statements

EXAMPLE 1

Assume the following type declarations:

```
CHARACTER NAME*8
REAL SUM
INTEGER COUNT
```

Memory Storage

a.

```
READ*, NAME,COUNT,SUM
```

One data record

```
'DOE' ,312, 120.07
```

NAME = | D | O | E | | | | | |

SUM = 120.07   COUNT = 312

b.

```
READ*, COUNT,SUM,NAME
```

The system reads as many records as are needed to satisfy the READ list.

Three data records

```
      312
120.07
     'DOE'
```

NAME = | D | O | E | | | | | |

SUM = 120.07   COUNT = 312

c.

NAME = | D | O | E | | | | | |

SUM = 120.07   COUNT = 312

```
READ*, SUM,COUNT,NAME
```

Two data records

```
120.07  312
'DOE'
```

Note the blank spaces separating the data items.

EXAMPLE 2   Assume the following type declarations:

```
CHARACTER FIRM1*5, FIRM2*5
REAL SALES
INTEGER NO
```

a. ```
READ(5,*) FIRM1
READ(5,*) SALES
READ(5,*) NO
```

`'IBM'  10.5  6`

`'GTE'  4.6  17`

`'AT&T', 6.4,  18`

FIRM1 = | I | B | M |   |   |

Invalid READ; real variable SALES would be associated with the character input item 'GTE' on the second record. Recall that each READ starts a *new* record. In this case the items 10.5 and 6 are not read, since only one item is read from the first record!

b. ```
READ(5,*)FIRM1
READ(5,*)SALES
READ(5,*)NO
```

`'IBM'  10.5  6`

`4.6    3.6    2`

`2      4.8    5`

FIRM1 = | I | B | M | | |

SALES = 4.6
NO   = 2

─── Note truncation of K

c. ```
READ(5,*)FIRM1,SALES
READ(5,*)FIRM2,NO
```

`'AMTRAK',  22.5`
`'GE'`
■ End-of-file record

FIRM1 = | A | M | T | R | A |     SALES = 22.5

READ error; no input item is provided for NO in the last record (FIRM2 = 'GE'), so the system reads the next record, which is the end-of-file record.
The program halts execution.

**EXAMPLE 3**    The repetition factor * can be used in the data record as follows:

```
INTEGER A,B,C
REALX,Y,Z,T
READ*,A,B,C,X,Y,Z,T
```

`3*0,  2*1.3,  2*111.0`

Result
A = B = C = 0
X = Y = 1.3
Z = T = 111.0

The asterisk * does not mean multiply; it indicates repetition of the input field.
```

3.3.3 Do It Now

1. Given the following coding segment, identify the value of each of the variables read.

```
CHARACTER NAME*4,LE*2
REAL A,B,C
INTEGER I,J,K
READ*, A,B,C,I
READ*, J
READ*, K,NAME,LE
```

```
2.3  4.1  2.0
```

```
2  3
```

```
5  'ELLA'
```

```
6
```

```
'UNITED',''''
```

2. Indicate actions taken as a result of the following code:

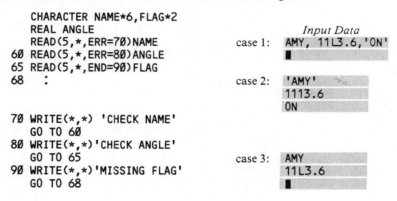

```
        CHARACTER NAME*6,FLAG*2
        REAL ANGLE                        Input Data
        READ(5,*,ERR=70)NAME      case 1:  AMY, 11L3.6,'ON'
   60   READ(5,*,ERR=80)ANGLE              ▮
   65   READ(5,*,END=90)FLAG
   68     :                       case 2:  'AMY'
                                           1113.6
                                           ON
   70   WRITE(*,*) 'CHECK NAME'
        GO TO 60
   80   WRITE(*,*)'CHECK ANGLE'
        GO TO 65                   case 3:  AMY
   90   WRITE(*,*)'MISSING FLAG'            11L3.6
        GO TO 68                            ▮
```

Answers

1. A = 2.3   J = 5
     B = 4.1   K = 6
     C = 2.0   NAME = | U | N | I | T |
     I = 2   LE = | | ' | |

2. Case 1: AMY is not enclosed in single quotation marks (READ error); control is passed to line 70 where an error message is printed. Control is transferred to line 60 which reads the next record (end of file) and the program terminates with an end-of-file error message.

Case 2: NAME = | A | M | Y | | | | , ANGLE = 1113.6, and the system interrupts the FORTRAN program at line 65 since the data read for FLAG is not enclosed in single quotation marks. Since no "ERR = " clause is specified for that READ statement, the program is terminated.

Case 3: The messages CHECK NAME, CHECK ANGLE, and MISSING FLAG are printed and the program resumes at line 68.

3.4 DECISION STRUCTURES

The decision structure allows the program to carry out one task if a particular condition is met and another task if the condition is not met.

3.4.1 Conditions The reader can think of a condition as a statement that is either true or false, for example, the condition "temperature less than 32" is either true or false. Technically speaking, a FORTRAN condition is a logical expression that in its simplest form consists of two arithmetic expressions (or two character operands) linked to one another by one of the relational operators shown in Figure 3.5.

FORTRAN Relational Operators	Mathematical Symbols	Meaning
.EQ.	=	Equal to
.NE.	≠	Not equal to
.LT.	<	Less than
.GT.	>	Greater than
.LE.	≤	Less than or equal to
.GE.	≥	Greater than or equal to

A FORTRAN condition must be enclosed in parentheses, as in the following examples:

```
(HOURS .GT. 40.0)          (SQRT(X**2+Y**2) .GE. Z)
(CITY .EQ. 'PARIS')        ((X+Y)/2.0 .NE. AVG*0.10)
((X-Y)**2 .LT. -Z)         (X .GT. .0001)
```

The computer can compare two numeric operands or two character operands, but it *cannot* compare a numeric operand with a character operand. Numbers (numeric operands) are compared algebraically, based on their signs and magnitudes, for example:

$1 < 23456$ or $-345.76 < -12.01$

Character data are compared character by character from left to right according to the collating sequence shown below. If the two character operands to be compared are of unequal length, the shorter operand is filled with blanks to the right until it is as long as the other operand. In FORTRAN the following collating sequence is always used:

blank < A < B < C < ... < Y < Z   and   0 < 1 < 2 < ... < 8 < 9

Depending on the code used to represent characters internally (EBCDIC or ASCII), the digits may all be "less" than the letters of the alphabet (ASCII code) or "larger" than the letters of the alphabet (EBCDIC code).

EXAMPLES OF
CHARACTER
COMPARISONS

`D E A N`	<	`D E E M`	DEAN less than DEEM since A < E.
`D A D`	>	`C`	DAD is greater than C since D > C.
`D A D`	=	`D A D  `	One trailing blank is provided for the first operand. Both operands are equal.
`N E W   Y O R K`	>	`N E W  `	Four additional blanks are provided to the second operand. The first operand is greater than the second since Y > blank.
`T H E `	>	` T H E`	The first operand is greater than the second since T > blank.
`A 3 B`	?	`3 B 4`	Depends on the internal code used to represent characters.
`3 0`	>	`2 9 3`	Since 3 is greater than 2.

Compound Conditions

Sometimes it may be useful to combine (conjunct) simple conditions. For example, we might want to know whether "temperature is greater than 90 and humidity is less the 78" or "age is less than 18 or age is greater than 65." Such combinations of simple conditions are called *compound conditions*. A compound condition consists of two or more simple conditions linked to one another by one of the two *logical operators* .AND. and .OR., or it may consist of a condition preceded by the logical operator .NOT. The following table illustrates the meaning of the three logical operators:

condition 1 **and** *condition 2*	The resulting compound condition is true if both conditions 1 and 2 are true; otherwise, the compound condition is false
condition 1 **or** *condition 2*	The resulting compound condition is true if one or the other or both conditions are true; otherwise, the condition is false
not *condition*	The resulting compound condition is true if *condition* is false; otherwise, the compound condition is false

The logical operators have the lowest priority in the rules of precedence governing operations, as shown in the following table of precedence:

Operations	Precedence
Grouping via parentheses	Highest
(Arithmetic operations)	.
**	.
*, /	.
+, −	.
(Conditions)	.
.LT.,.GT.,.EQ.,.NE.,.LE.,.GE.	.
(Logical operators)	.
.NOT.	.
.AND.	.
.OR.	Lowest

Parentheses can be used to denote the order in which the compound conditions are to be evaluated. Consider, for example, the two following conditions, which have entirely different meanings depending on where the parentheses are placed:

   1. `(WEIGHT .LT. 140.0 .OR. AGE .LT. 30.0 .AND. EARNIN .GT. 100000.00)`

   2. `((WEIGHT .LT. 140.0 .OR. AGE .LT. 30.0) .AND. EARNIN .GT. 100000.00)`

In the first case, the condition is true if WEIGHT < 140, regardless of age and earnings, whereas in the second case the additional condition EARNIN > 100000 would have to be satisfied before the condition is true.

If no parentheses are present, the rules of precedence govern the order of operations.

EXAMPLE   Assume X = 30., Y = 40., and A = 10.

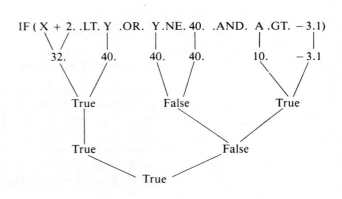

Arithmetic expressions are evaluated first.

Relations are evaluated next.

Logical operations are evaluated last according to the precedence rule.

Caution

The logical operators .AND. and .OR. cannot be side by side in a compound expression. For example,

   `((AGE .GT. 7.) .AND. .OR. .LT. 14.)`   is invalid.

However, the .NOT. operator can be conjuncted to the .AND. or to the .OR., as in

   `((A .GT. B) .AND. (.NOT. (B .LT. C)))`

Relational operators may *not* appear side by side with logical operators. For example

   `(AGE .GE. 25. .AND. .LT. 30.)`   is invalid.

Instead, this condition should be expressed as:

   `(AGE .GE. 25. .AND. AGE .LT. 30.)`

3.8.2 Do It Now

1. A marriage proposal letter will be written when the following compound condition is true.

```
(HAIR .EQ. 'BLACK' .AND. HEIGHT .GT. 5.8 .OR. EARNIN .GT. 100000.)
```

Under how many simple conditions will the letter be written? Specify the various conditions.

2. Assume X = 30.; Y = 40.; A = 1.; B = 4.
Is the following condition true or false?

```
(.NOT.(X + Y .LT. 100. .OR. A .EQ. 1.).AND. B .GT. 3.)
```

3. Which of the following are valid? If invalid, explain why.

   a. `((X+Y)**2 .LT. -1. .AND. Y .GT. Z)`

   b. `(X-Y .EQ. 0. .OR. Z .AND. X .EQ. 0.)`

   c. `(-3. .LT. Z .OR. 1. .EQ. X)`

   d. `(X .NOT. .GT. .4)`

   e. `(.NOT. (Y .NE. -1.))`

Answers

1. A marriage proposal letter will be written under either of the following conditions:

   a. If earnings > $100,000

   b. If hair is black and person is over 5.8 ft. tall.

   c. If both conditions a and b are satisfied.

2. False

3. **a.** Valid.

   b. Invalid; Z .AND. X (.AND. does not join two conditions).

   c. Valid.

   d. Invalid; X .NOT. .GT. (juxtaposition .NOT. .GT. is invalid).

   e. Valid.

3.4.2 The IF THEN ELSE Structure

FORTRAN offers two forms of the decision structure:

1. the simple IF structure, which is a particular case of

2. the general IF THEN ELSE structure.

The general form of the IF THEN ELSE structure is shown in Figure 3.6.

Notice how the indentation of the statements within the IF/ELSE and ELSE/ENDIF statements clearly delineates what actions are to be taken if the condition is true and what actions are to be taken if the condition is false. Indentation is not required, but it is desirable. A common practice is to set off the inner statements two, or three or four positions to the right of the IF, ELSE, and ENDIF key words; these three key words should be aligned themselves.

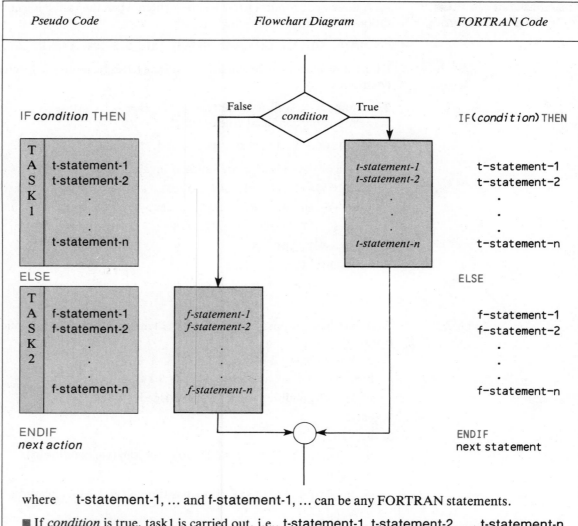

Pseudo Code	Flowchart Diagram	FORTRAN Code

IF *condition* THEN

```
T
A   t-statement-1
S   t-statement-2
K        .
1        .
         .
    t-statement-n
```

ELSE

```
T
A   f-statement-1
S   f-statement-2
K        .
2        .
    f-statement-n
```

ENDIF
next action

False   *condition*   True

t-statement-1
t-statement-2
.
.
.
t-statement-n

f-statement-1
f-statement-2
.
.
.
f-statement-n

IF(*condition*)THEN

```
    t-statement-1
    t-statement-2
         .
         .
         .
    t-statement-n
```

ELSE

```
    f-statement-1
    f-statement-2
         .
         .
    f-statement-n
```

ENDIF
next statement

where   t-statement-1, ... and f-statement-1, ... can be any FORTRAN statements.

- If *condition* is true, task1 is carried out, i.e., t-statement-1, t-statement-2, ..., t-statement-n (all statements up to the ELSE word) are executed; control is then passed to the statement following the ENDIF statement.

- If *condition* is false, task2 is carried out, i.e., f-statement-1, ..., f-statement-n (all statements between the words ELSE and ENDIF) are executed; control is then passed to the statement following the ENDIF statement.

FIGURE 3.6
THE IF THEN ELSE STRUCTURE

EXAMPLE   Pay Computation with Overtime Hours

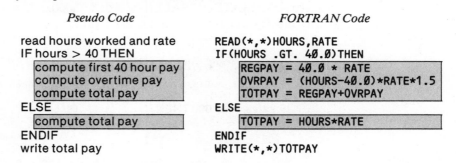

Pseudo Code	*FORTRAN Code*
read hours worked and rate	READ(*,*)HOURS,RATE
IF hours > 40 THEN	IF(HOURS .GT. 40.0)THEN
compute first 40 hour pay	REGPAY = 40.0 * RATE
compute overtime pay	OVRPAY = (HOURS−40.0)*RATE*1.5
compute total pay	TOTPAY = REGPAY+OVRPAY
ELSE	ELSE
compute total pay	TOTPAY = HOURS*RATE
ENDIF	ENDIF
write total pay	WRITE(*,*)TOTPAY

Sometimes an alternative action is not required if a condition is false. In that case the ELSE key word is omitted, leading to the simpler structure shown in Figure 3.7.

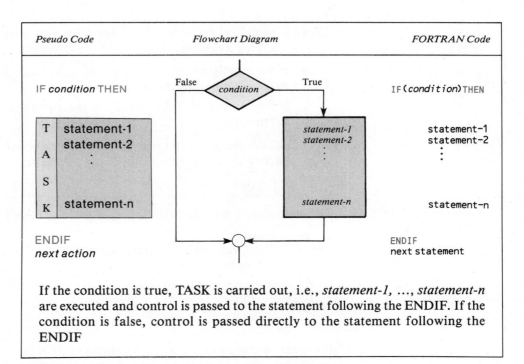

If the condition is true, TASK is carried out, i.e., *statement-1, ..., statement-n* are executed and control is passed to the statement following the ENDIF. If the condition is false, control is passed directly to the statement following the ENDIF

FIGURE 3.7
THE SIMPLE IF/ENDIF STRUCTURE

EXAMPLE   Write the code to read SALES, HOURS, and RATE and compute the resulting pay (HOURS*RATE). If SALES exceeds $10,000, add a bonus equal to 10% of SALES to the pay and print the bonus. Print out the total pay in both cases.

Pseudo Code	*FORTRAN Code*
read sales, hours, and rate	READ(5,*)SALES,HRS,RATE
set bonus to 0	BONUS = 0.
IF sales > 10,000 THEN	IF (SALES .GT. 10000.) THEN
bonus = 10% of sales	BONUS = .1 * SALES
write bonus	WRITE(6,*)BONUS
ENDIF	ENDIF
pay = hours * rate + bonus	PAY = HRS * RATE + BONUS
write pay	WRITE(6,*)PAY

The simple IF structure can be further simplified if the task to be carried out consists of just *one* instruction. The general form of the IF statement (referred to as the *logical* IF) is then:

IF (*condition*) *statement*

where   *statement* can be any type of executable statement other than an IF or a loop type statement.

- If the condition is true, *statement* is carried out, then control is passed to the statement following the IF statement.
- If the condition is false, control is passed to the statement following the IF statement.

Note that only *one* statement may be specified on the same line as the IF statement. Also note the absence of the words THEN and ENDIF.

EXAMPLE   The following code reads an integer number N and determines whether N is even.

```
READ(5,*)N
IF(N - (N/2)*2 .EQ. 0) PRINT*,N,'IS EVEN'
next statement
```

3.4.3 Multilevel IF Structures (Nested IFs)

We often need to include a decision structure within another decision structure. This usually occurs when more than two alternative actions are associated with the value of a single data item. There are always at least three possible approaches to this type of problem:

1. The nested IF ELSE   IF ELSE ... structure
2. The nested IF IF IF ... ELSE ELSE ELSE structure
3. The separate IF ELSE   IF ELSE ... structure

Consider the following problem, where a salesman's commission is based on a graduated sales volume:

Sales	Commission (percentage of sales)
Under $500	2%
$500 and under $5000	5%
$5000 and over	8%

Method 1: The IF ELSE IF ELSE Approach

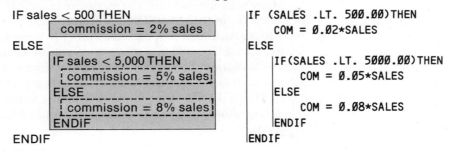

```
IF sales < 500 THEN
    commission = 2% sales
ELSE
    IF sales < 5,000 THEN
        commission = 5% sales
    ELSE
        commission = 8% sales
    ENDIF
ENDIF
```

```
IF (SALES .LT. 500.00) THEN
    COM = 0.02*SALES
ELSE
    IF(SALES .LT. 5000.00) THEN
        COM = 0.05*SALES
    ELSE
        COM = 0.08*SALES
    ENDIF
ENDIF
```

Method 2: The IF IF .. ELSE ELSE Approach

Instead of asking whether SALES is less than 500, we could also solve the problem by asking if SALES is greater than or equal to 500, and if it is, is it greater than or equal to 5,000; we would proceed as follows:

```
IF sales ≥ 500 THEN
    IF sales ≥ 5,000 THEN
        commission = 8% sales
    ELSE
        commission = 5% sales
    ENDIF
ELSE
    commission = 2% sales
ENDIF
```

```
IF(SALES .GE. 500.00) THEN
    IF(SALES .GE. 5000.00) THEN
        COM = 0.08*SALES
    ELSE
        COM = 0.05*SALES
    ENDIF
ELSE
    COM = 0.02*SALES
ENDIF
```

Method 3: The Separate IF ELSE Approach

This approach uses two separate simple IF structures to test for SALES:

```
commission = 2% sales

IF sales ≥ 500 and sales < 5,000 THEN
    commission = 5% sales
ENDIF

IF sales ≥ 5,000 THEN
    commission = 8% sales
ENDIF
```

```
COM = 0.02 * SALES

  IF(SALES .GE. 500.00
1     .AND. SALES .LT. 5000.00)
2       COM = 0.05*SALES

IF(SALES.GE.5000.00) COM=0.08*SALES
```

The selection of one approach over another depends on the level of efficiency and the level of readability desired. Sometimes the first approach may parallel more closely the formulation of the various conditions stated in the problem, i.e., it may provide a more direct translation of the phrasing of the problem. Other times, the second approach might be more suitable.

In terms of efficiency, structured design, style, and elegance, the first and second approaches tower over the third approach. Indeed, if SALES is less than 500, only one IF statement is executed, whereas three IF statements are executed in the third method. However, in terms of readability and comprehension, the third method, lacking any ELSE statements, is extremely direct, affirmative, and to the point. Deep-nested IF/ELSE statements can be very difficult to read and understand, and trying to unravel the conditions under which an innermost ELSE is carried out can be a harrowing experience!

Many program development managers in industry simply do not tolerate the use of nested IFs in their shops, and parenthetically, many also condemn the use of the NOT logical operator, as it creates a barrier to immediate comprehension. Simplicity, clarity, readability, and ease of comprehension are key issues in program development. This author stays above the fracas by simply alerting the reader to the varying schools of thought (and heated differences of opinion) among professionals!

IF THEN [ELSE] structures may be nested within one another as long as they are wholly contained within an IF ELSE segment, an ELSE ENDIF segment, or a simple IF structure.

EXAMPLE 1   Consider the following example, where a simple IF is nested within a full IF.

Hourly employees at the local pulp plant get a $50 Christmas bonus. Salaried employees get a $100 bonus and an extra $20 if they have been with the company more than 10 years. Write the code to compute an employee's pay, given a position code (1 = hourly, 2 = salaried), a pay amount, and a number of years.

```
IF code = 1 THEN              IF(CODE .EQ. 1) THEN
    add $50 to pay                PAY = PAY + 50.00
ELSE                          ELSE
    add $100 to pay               PAY = PAY + 100.00
    IF years > 10 THEN            IF(YEARS .GT. 10.0) THEN
        add $20 to pay                PAY = PAY + 20.00
    ENDIF                         ENDIF
ENDIF                         ENDIF
```

EXAMPLE 2   Note the alignment of the various IF [ELSE] ENDIF statements

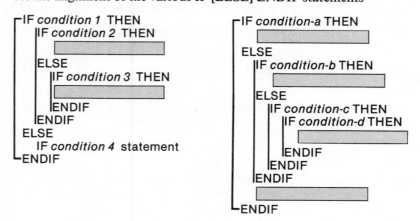

3.4.4 The ELSE IF THEN Structure

The ELSE IF THEN structure is a more compact notation for a series of IF THEN ELSE structures. In the following diagram the numbered blocks 1, 2, 3, and 4 represent tasks.

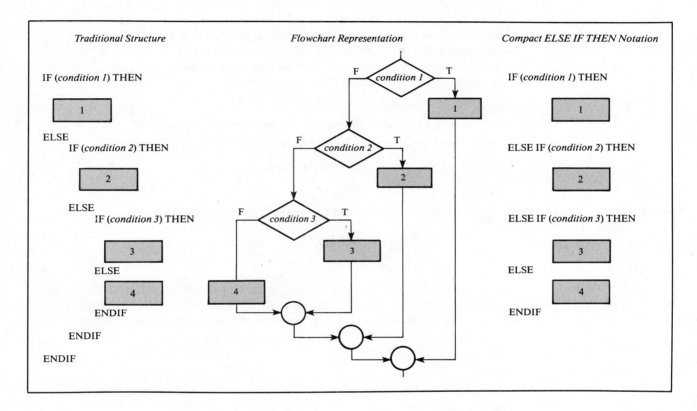

| Traditional Structure | Flowchart Representation | Compact ELSE IF THEN Notation |

Note that in the ELSE IF THEN structure only *one* ENDIF is used and the FORTRAN keywords are not indented. Also note that if block 1 is executed, control is then passed to the ENDIF statement, as it is after execution of blocks 2, 3, and 4.

EXAMPLE

Write the code to read a numerical marital status code (1 = married, 2 = divorced, 3 = single, 4 = widowed) and print the corresponding English word. If the code is neither 1, 2, 3, or 4, print an error message.

```
READ*, MS                    read marital status code
IF(MS.EQ.1) THEN
    PRINT*,'MARRIED'
ELSE IF(MS.EQ.2) THEN
    PRINT*,'DIVORCED'
ELSE IF(MS.EQ.3) THEN
    PRINT*,'SINGLE'
ELSE IF(MS.EQ.4) THEN
    PRINT*,'WIDOWED'
ELSE
    PRINT*, MS, 'IS AN INVALID CODE'
ENDIF
```

3.4.5 Other
Conditional Statements

There are FORTRAN statements other than the logical IF and the IF THEN [ELSE] structures that allow the programmer to transfer to specific statement numbers in a program depending on the outcome of a particular condition. These statements, however, do not form a structure (they have no header or terminal statements), and thus they do not lend themselves very well to a structured design, since they cannot delineate tasks clearly. Use of these statements often leads to entangled designs. For that reason, the three conditional statements listed below are described in appendix A. The reader should be aware of their existence, however, since older FORTRAN programs may still use them. These statements are:

1. The IF (*condition*) GO TO S_1
2. The arithmetic IF statement: IF (*expression*) S_1, S_2, S_3
3. The computed GO TO statement: GO TO (S_1, S_2, ..., S_n), *variable*

where S_1, S_2, ... are statement numbers.

3.4.6 Do It Now

1. A special code K is used for student classifications as follows:

Value of K	Verbal Description
1	Freshman
2	Sophomore

A program is needed that will read a numeric value for K and print the verbal description corresponding to the value of K. If K is not 1 or 2, it should print an error message. Which of the following pseudo code segments will solve the problem?

a.
```
IF K = 1 THEN
    print freshman
ENDIF
IF K = 2 THEN
    print sophomore
ELSE
    print error
ENDIF
```

b.
```
IF K = 1 THEN
    print freshman
ELSE
    IF K = 2 THEN
        print sophomore
    ELSE
        print error
    ENDIF
ENDIF
```

c.
```
IF K = 1 THEN
    print freshman
    IF K = 2 THEN
        print sophomore
    ELSE
        print error
    ENDIF
ENDIF
```

d.
```
IF K = 1 THEN
    print freshman
ENDIF
IF K = 2 THEN
    print sophomore
ELSE
    IF K < 1 or K > 2 THEN
        print error
    ENDIF
ENDIF
```

2. In the commission problem of section 3.4.3, could the solution have been expressed using the following coding segments?

a.
```
COM = 0.05*SALES
IF(SALES .LT. 500.00)COM=0.02*SALES
IF(SALES .GE. 5000.00)COM=0.08*SALES
```

```
b.  COM = 0.05*SALES
    IF(SALES .LT. 500.00)THEN
        COM = 0.02*SALES
        IF(SALES .GE. 5000.00)THEN
            COM = 0.08*SALES
        ENDIF
    ENDIF
```

3. Under what conditions will line 5 be executed?

```
1  IF sales < 500 THEN
2      IF sales < 5,000 THEN
3          commission = 5% of sales
4      ELSE
5          commission = 1% of sales
6      ENDIF
7  ENDIF
```

4. **a.** Are the following two coding segments equivalent?

```
IF(K.EQ.1)THEN              IF(K.EQ.1)THEN
    A = 1.                      A = 1.
ELSE                       ENDIF
    IF(K.EQ.2)THEN         IF(K.EQ.2)THEN
        B = 1.                  B = 1.
    ELSE                   ENDIF
        IF(K.EQ.3)THEN     IF(K.EQ.3)THEN
            C = 1.              C = 1.
        ELSE               ELSE
            D = 1.              D = 1.
        ENDIF              ENDIF
    ENDIF
ENDIF
```

b. Are the following coding segments equivalent (1) if K is neither 1 nor 2, and (2) for all values of K?

```
IF(K.NE.2)THEN             IF(K.NE.1)THEN
    B = 1.                      A = 1.
    IF(K.NE.1)THEN         IF(K.NE.2)THEN
        A = 1.                  B = 1.
    ENDIF                  ENDIF
ENDIF                      ENDIF
```

5. Write the pseudo code to read a value for N and determine whether N lies in the closed interval [−3,2] (including the endpoints).

6. Write the pseudo code to read the X,Y coordinates of point A and determine whether this point lies in the circle centered at the origin with radius 1.67.

7. Write the code to read values for a, b, and c and compute the roots of $ax^2 + bx + c = 0$.

Print NO REAL ROOTS if the discriminant ($b^2 - 4ac$) is negative.
Print SINGLE ROOT = if the discriminant is equal to 0.
Print ROOT1 = _____ ROOT2 = _____ if the discriminant is positive.

8. Write the pseudo code to read three values for X, Y, and Z and print the largest value. If the largest occurs more than once, print a message to that effect.

Selected Answers

   2. **a.** yes **b.** no; 0.08*SALES will never be computed

   3. Never. The condition at line 2 will always be true!

   4. **a.** Not equivalent; see what happens if K = 1, for example.

      b. Case 1, equivalent.
         Case 2, not equivalent.

   5. read N
     IF N $\geq$ − 3 and N $\leq$ 2 THEN
        print 'in interval'
     ELSE
        print 'outside interval'
     ENDIF

   8. Set K to 0
     IF N1 > N2 THEN
        Large = N1
     ELSE
        IF N1 = N2 set K = 1
        Large = N2
     ENDIF
     IF Large > N3 THEN
          Print large
          IF K = 1 Print 'more than one'
     ELSE
        IF Large = N3 THEN
          Print large
          Print 'more than one'
        ELSE
          Print N3
        ENDIF
     ENDIF

3.5 THE GO TO STATEMENT

The general form of the unconditional transfer statement GO TO is:

> GO TO *statement number*

When a GO TO statement is encountered, control is transferred to the statement number designated by the GO TO statement.

    The GO TO statement is used primarily in the loop structure to repeat a task:

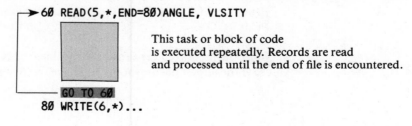

```
60 READ(5,*,END=80)ANGLE, VLSITY



   GO TO 60
80 WRITE(6,*)...
```

This task or block of code
is executed repeatedly. Records are read
and processed until the end of file is encountered.

It is also used in the simulation of the WHILE DO structure.

In a well-structured program, the GO TO statement is not used indiscriminately. It should be used only to create a loop process. Other uses of the GO TO statement generally lead to unstructured designs that are difficult to follow, difficult to understand, and difficult to edit.

3.6 THE LOOP STRUCTURE

As noted in chapter 1, the loop structure is one of the three structures that make it possible to decompose a problem into a task structure. The loop structure can be expressed in pseudo code by using the WHILE DO/ENDWHILE and the DO/CONTINUE LOOP loop structures. Although both of these structures essentially achieve parallel objectives, the WHILE DO structure is more general and more readable than the DO structure; it expresses more naturally and more directly the way in which a task is to be processed repeatedly.

It should be noted, however, that many FORTRAN 77 compilers do not support the corresponding FORTRAN WHILE DO/ENDWHILE statements. That fact should not deter the user from employing the WHILE DO when sketching a program design. In section 3.6.1, the reader will see how simple it is to simulate the WHILE DO/ENDWHILE structure in FORTRAN. The DO/CONTINUE loop structure is discussed in chapter 4.

3.6.1 The WHILE DO/ ENDWHILE Structure

The WHILE DO structure allows a task to be carried out a fixed or a variable number of times—the number of times depends on the outcome of a stated condition. The pseudo code representation of the WHILE DO structure and its corresponding flowchart interpretation are shown in Figure 3.8.

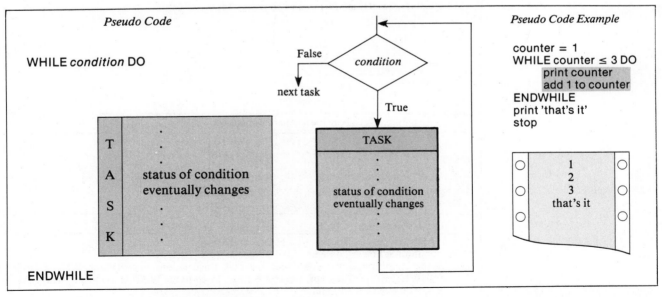

FIGURE 3.8
THE WHILE DO STRUCTURE

If the condition specified in the WHILE DO statement is true, the task (set of instructions between the WHILE and ENDWHILE statements) is carried out; if the condition is false, the task is bypassed and control resumes at the statement following the ENDWHILE. Every time the ENDWHILE statement is encountered, control is passed to the condition specified in the WHILE DO statement to determine whether or not to repeat the task.

If the looping process is ever to end, some instruction(s) within the task must cause a change in the condition—otherwise the task will be repeated forever!

It is very important to understand the following points:

1. The condition tested by the WHILE DO statement is tested first, before the task is carried out. If the condition is already false when the WHILE DO statement is first encountered, the task is *not* carried out and control passes to the statement following the ENDWHILE.

2. Exit from the loop structure is not taken the very moment a variable causes the condition to change from true to false—all remaining instructions in the loop are carried out before exit is taken. Consider the following example:

```
set counter to 0
WHILE counter < 1 DO        Since counter < 1, the specified task is carried out.
    add 1 to counter        At this point the counter is equal to 1 and the condition in
    write counter           the WHILE DO is no longer true. Yet the remaining
ENDWHILE                    instruction(s) in the task are carried out and the value 1
                            is printed.
```

3.6.2 The FORTRAN Implementation of the WHILE DO Structure

The general form of the FORTRAN WHILE DO statement is shown on the left side of Figure 3.9. Many FORTRAN compilers do not support the WHILE DO –this is of little consequence since the WHILE DO can easily be simulated, as shown on the right side of Figure 3.9.

WHILE DO FORTRAN Structure	*Simulated WHILE DO*
WHILE (condition) DO [TASK] ENDWHILE	10 IF (condition) THEN [TASK] GO TO 10 ENDIF
Example: To print the number 1 through 10	
I = 1 WHILE(I .LE. 1Ø)DO WRITE(6,*)I I = I + 1 ENDWHILE	I = 1 10 IF(I .LE. 1Ø)THEN WRITE(6,*)I I = I + 1 GO TO 10 ENDIF
Meaning	

The condition is first evaluated.
■ If the condition is true, the specified task (instructions between the WHILE and ENDWHILE) is carried out. Control is then passed to the WHILE statement, where the condition is evaluated again.
■ If the condition is false, the task is bypassed and control passes to the statement following the ENDWHILE.

FIGURE 3.9
THE WHILE DO AND ITS SIMULATED FORTRAN REPRESENTATION

Recall from chapter 1 that a file is a collection of related records and a record is a collection of related data items. For example, a file might consist of a number of employee records, each consisting of a name, a sex code, an age, and an address entry.

When the user creates a data file and then stores it on disk, the computing system automatically places an end-of-file mark after the last record typed by the user:

Name	Sex	Age	Address
DOE K	1	48	201 NORTH AVE. PENSACOLA FL 32571 ←—1 record
ABRAMS L	2	36	15 CEDAR DR. MILTON FL 32561
.			
.			
GUCCI P	1	28	3248 FAIRPOINT RD. GULF BREEZE FL 32561

File {

■ ◄————————End-of-file market inserted by the text editor/system.

When reading a data file, it is important to avoid reading more records than are present in the file, since such an attempt will result in reading the end-of-file marker. If and when this happens, an end-of-file error message is printed and (if the END option of the READ statement is not used) the program is terminated.

Two programming techniques can be used to process an input file, the automatic end of file and the last record check techniques; the latter is often referred to as the *sentinel* method.

The automatic end-of-file method uses the END= option of the READ statement and is discussed in chapter 4. It is the only method that can be used to process files that do not have sentinel records.

The sentinel technique blends in harmoniously with the WHILE DO structure and does not rely on the END= option of the READ statement. In addition, it is the only method that can be used in an interactive environment where data is read from a terminal.

Both end-of-file methods are widely used, and the reader should be familiar with both approaches. All programs in this chapter will use the sentinel method, while most programs in chapter 4 will use the automatic end-of-file method.

The Sentinel Method

Everyone knows by now that if the program reads the EOF [end-of-file] marker as data, the program will crash, and that steps must be taken to insure that this does not happen. Back in the seventies there was a gothic horror movie titled "The Sentinel." It was about an old priest who lived alone in a decrepit brownstone in a desolate section of the Bronx. Every day he would sit in the window of the tower and watch to see that no one entered the building. But occasionally a visitor would be allowed in, never to be seen again. In truth, this was the gateway to Hades, and it was the old priest's responsibility to guard that an undeserving soul did not suffer the fate which awaited within. And that's exactly the purpose of the sentinel in a data file. It keeps a good program from going to hell.

In the sentinel method we simulate an end-of-file condition by adding to the original data file a last record that is different from any of the records that precede it. The values read from that last record will be so obviously different from the values read from preceding records that the program will know the end of file has been reached. For example, in the above data file, the end of file could be indicated by an unusual name such as 'XXX', or an age value above 200, or a value other than 1 or 2 for the sex code (1 = male, 2 = female). In any event, the simulated end-of-file record must contain as many entries as are present in each of the preceding records. Then, every time a record is read, the program asks, Is the age read greater than 200? If it is, the end of file has been reached; otherwise, more records need to be read and processed.

To see how a sentinel record is used, let us take the above data file and write the code to determine the number of people over 40 years of age. The loop that reads the records will be based on this idea: as long as the age is less than 200, keep reading and processing a new record. A first attempt at the pseudo code solution might be:

```
WHILE age < 200 DO
     read name, sex, age
     count number of people over 40
ENDWHILE
```

input file
```
DOE K, 1, 48  ...
  ⋮
GUCCI, 1, 28  ...
XXX,   0, 200,...
■
```

There are, however, two problems with this code:

(1) the value of age is undefined the first time the WHILE statement is executed, and

(2) the sentinel record is treated as an ordinary record, since an age of 200 is counted as an age over 40!

Obviously the sentinel record should not participate in the count process; otherwise the count of people over 40 will incorrectly include a person 200 years old!

We can avoid these problems by reading the first record by itself before the WHILE DO is carried out and adding another read statement at the foot of the loop:

```
read name, sex, age
WHILE age < 200 DO
     count number
     of people over 40
     read name, sex, age
ENDWHILE
```

READ the first record, which is processed inside the loop. The second record is read by the READ statement at the foot of the loop. If it is the sentinel record, exit out of the loop; otherwise stay in the loop to process the record just read and read the next record.

The first record is read by itself outside the WHILE DO loop, while all other records are read by the READ statement at the foot of the loop (just before ENDWHILE). Because the first READ statement is used to prime values for name, sex, and age so that they are defined the first time through the loop, this method is referred to as the *prime read* method. Its general structure is shown in Figure 3.10.

FIGURE 3.10
*THE PRIME READ
METHOD USING THE
WHILE DO INSTRUCTION*

Steps	*Pseudo Code*
1. Read the first record before the WHILE DO structure.	read *list of variables*
2. Select one of the variables to be read as a sentinel variable and include it in the sentinel condition.	WHILE *sentinel condition not met* DO
3. Place the READ statement just before the ENDWHILE.	process record just read
4. Make sure the data file contains a sentinel value.	read *list of variables* ENDWHILE

EXAMPLE Each record of an input file consists of a student name and a score. Write the pseudo code and the FORTRAN code to print the names of the students whose scores exceed 90.

Let us use a negative score as the sentinel field. We now write the code as follows:

Pseudo Code	Input File		FORTRAN Code
* print student names whose	'ADAMS K'	80	CHARACTER NAME*10
* scores exceed 90	'EXCEL J'	94	INTEGER SCORE,PASS
read name, score	'DONAHUE S'	44	PARAMETER(PASS = 90)
WHILE score ≥ 0 DO	'SIMS K'	91	READ(5,*)NAME,SCORE
IF score > 90 THEN	'LARGO T'	90	10 IF(SCORE .GE. 0)THEN
print name, score	'DITKA S'	60	IF(SCORE .GT. PASS)THEN
ENDIF	'RYAN B'	98	WRITE(6,*)NAME,SCORE
read name, score	'XXXXXX'	−3	ENDIF
ENDWHILE			READ(5,*)NAME,SCORE
			GO TO 10
			ENDIF
			STOP

3.6.4 The Counting Process

Counting is an essential technique in programming. Counting can be used to repeat a procedure a certain number of times (*loop control*), to count the occurrences of specific events, or to generate sequences of numbers for computational uses.

EXAMPLE 1 Number Generation: Odd numbers
Write the pseudo code and the corresponding FORTRAN code to print the numbers 1, 3, 5, ..., 227.

```
                              INTEGER COUNTR
                              COUNTR = 1
set counter to 1          10 IF(COUNTR .LE. 227)THEN
WHILE counter ≤ 227 DO        WRITE(6,*)COUNTR
    print the counter         COUNTR = COUNTR + 2
    add 2 to the counter      GO TO 10
ENDWHILE                      ENDIF
                              STOP
```

Note that when COUNTR becomes 229 in the FORTRAN code, control is passed to the STOP statement and the value 299 is *not* printed. (What would happen if counting (COUNTR = COUNTR + 2) preceded the write instruction?)

EXAMPLE 2

Printing the 7's multiplication table

Write the pseudo code and FORTRAN code to print the 7's multiplication table, as follows:

```
7X  1 =  7
7X  2 = 14
    :
7X 12 = 84
```

In this example, we need to generate a counter that takes on the values 1 through 12. The solution can be written as follows:

```
set counter to 1
WHILE counter ≤ 12 DO
        compute product = 7 × counter
        write 7,counter,product
        add 1 to counter
ENDWHILE
stop
```

```
        INTEGER COUNTR,SEVEN,PRODCT
        PARAMETER (SEVEN = 7)
        COUNTR = 1
10 IF(COUNTR .LE. 12)THEN
        PRODCT = SEVEN*COUNTR
        WRITE(*,*)SEVEN,'*',COUNTR,'=',PRODCT
        COUNTR = COUNTR + 1
        GO TO 10
    ENDIF
    STOP
```

EXAMPLE 3

Each record of an input file contains a name and a sex code (1 = male, 2 = female). Write the code to compute the percentage of females.

Let us use the sex field as a sentinel with value 3. (We could just as well have chosen the name as the sentinel field with value 'XXXX'.)

Pseudo Code

```
* To count all people
total count = 0
* To count all females
fem count = 0
READ name,sex
WHILE sex < 3 DO
        add 1 to total count
        IF sex = 2 THEN
            add 1 to fem count
        ENDIF
        READ name,sex
ENDWHILE
percent = 100*fem count/total count
```

Input File

```
'LONG F'  1
'RUFF P'  2
'SIM L'   1
'SLIM S'  1
'TOE T'   2
'LAST M'  2
'XXXXX'   3
          ↑
    sentinel record
```

FORTRAN Code

```
        INTEGER SEX,TOTAL,FEMALS
        REAL PERCNT
        CHARACTER*4 NAME
        TOTAL  = 0
        FEMALS = 0
        READ(5,*) NAME,SEX
10 IF(SEX .LT. 3) THEN
        TOTAL = TOTAL + 1
        IF(SEX .EQ. 2) THEN
            FEMALS = FEMALS + 1
        ENDIF
        READ(5,*)NAME,SEX
        GO TO 10
    ENDIF
    PERCNT = (100.*FEMALS)/TOTAL
```

3.6.5 The Accumulation Process

We have seen how to count through repeated execution of such statements as $I = I + 1$, where I is initially set to a beginning value. Each time $I = I + 1$ is executed, the value 1 is added to the counter I, which will take on successive values 1, 2, 3, 4, and so on, if I is set initially to zero. Counting can be thought of as "accumulating a count." The main difference between counting and accumulating is that in accumulating, instead

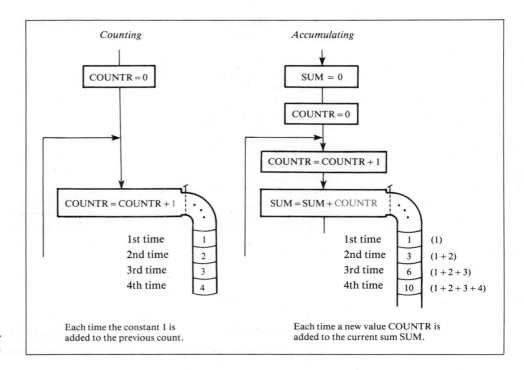

FIGURE 3.11
*COUNTING VERSUS
ACCUMULATING*

of repetitively adding a constant such as 1 to a counter, a variable is added repetitively to an accumulator, which is a special variable used to keep track of running sums (see Figure 3.11). An accumulator can also be used to accumulate a partial product by repetitively multiplying the accumulator by a variable.

EXAMPLE 1   Computing an Average of Scores
    An input file consists of scores arranged in descending numerical order (one score per record). Write the code to read only those scores over 50 and compute and print their average. Stop reading the file as soon as a score 50 or below is encountered. It is possible, of course, that all scores are above 50 or that all scores are 50 or below.

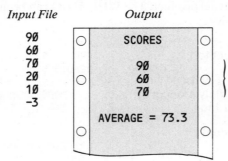

This caption is printed once, outside the loop.
As each score is read, the score is printed. Every time a score is read, it is added to the previous score to form a sum of scores. When these three scores have thus been summed, the sum is divided by 3 to give the average.

    In this problem, we need a counter to count scores and an accumulator to compute the sum of the scores. Note that before entering the loop to read the scores, we need to initialize both the counter and the accumulator to 0 and we need to print the heading SCORES. The pseudo code solution is:

```
print 'scores'        ⎫
set sum scores to 0   ⎬  initialization segment
set counter to 0      
read score            ⎭
WHILE score > 50 DO
      add 1 to counter
      add score to sum scores
      print score
      read score
ENDWHILE
average = sum scores/counter
print average
Stop
```

	SCORE 1st time 60 ↓	SCORE 2d time 90 ↓	SCORE 3d time 70 ↓
	0 + 60	60 + 90	150 + 70

running sums: SUM SCORES

Questions.

1. What happens if all scores are below 50? Change the code appropriately.

2. Change the code to stop reading the input file as soon as the average falls below 80.

EXAMPLE 2   Write the code to read a positive value for N and compute its factorial value (if N is 15, N factorial is the product of the first 15 positive integers starting with 1).

We need:

1. an accumulator *product,* which will be initially 1, then 1 * 2, then 1 * 2 * 3, and so forth, and

2. a counter I to generate the numbers 1, 2, 3, ..., N, which will be used to develop the partial products in *product*

Every time we generate a new value for I, we immediately multiply *product* by I to obtain a new partial product. The WHILE DO can be used to generate the numbers 1, 2, 3, ... as follows:

```
set I to 1                        I = 1
set product to 1                  PROD = 1.
read N                            READ(5,*)N
WHILE I ≤ N DO               10 IF(I .LE. N)THEN
      multiply product by I          PROD = PROD*I
      add 1 to I                     I = I + 1
ENDWHILE                             GO TO 10
write product                     ENDIF
stop                              WRITE(6,*)PROD
                                  STOP
```

PROD will take on the following values: 1, 1*2, 1*2*3, 1*2*3*4,...,1*2*3...*N

EXAMPLE 3 An Approximation to the Sine Function

The general formula for computing an approximation for the sine of x, where x is any angle measured in radians, is:

$$\sin x = \frac{x^1}{1!} - \frac{x^3}{3!} + \frac{x^5}{5!} - \dots - \frac{x^{11}}{11!} + \dots$$

Write the code to read a value for x and compute and print the sine of x using the first terms up to x^{11}. (Recall that 5! (5 factorial) is equal to $1*2*3*4*5$.)

The formula for the sine of x becomes more accurate as more terms of the formula are computed. Let us, for example, compute the sine of $\pi/2$ (which is exactly equal to 1) using the first three terms of the formula. Note that $\pi/2 \approx 1.57080$ radians.

$$\text{sine } (1.57080) = 1.57080 - \frac{(1.57080)^3}{3!} + \frac{(1.57080)^5}{5!}$$

$$= 1.57080 - 0.64597 + 0.07969 = 1.00452$$

This result is fairly accurate, since the real answer is supposed to be 1.

A program to compute the sine of x must do the following:

a. Read x

b. Keep accumulating a product of integers for the denominator in such a way that product is first 1
then $1*2*3$
then $1*2*3*4*5$

c. Accumulate the terms $\dfrac{x}{\text{product}}$, $\dfrac{x^3}{\text{product}}$, $\dfrac{x^5}{\text{product}}$,.... as each new product is computed.

d. Capture $x^1, x^3, x^5, \dots$ through the use of x^{power} where *power* is initially set to 1 and incremented by 2's to obtain successive odd powers of x.

e. Generate the oscillating sequence of terms: $x, -x^3, x^5, -x^7, \dots$.
To do this, we note that $(x)^1, (-x)^3, (x)^5, (-x)^7$ gives rise to $x, -x^3, x^5$ and $-x^7$. Hence we replace x by $-x$ when generating successive terms of the sequence. The resulting FORTRAN code is then:

```
REAL X,PROD,SUM
INTEGER POWER
READ(5,*)X
POWER = 1
PROD = 1.0
SUM = 0.0
WHILE (POWER .LE. 11) DO
    SUM = SUM + (X**POWER)/PROD
    PROD = PROD*(POWER+1)*(POWER+2)
    POWER = POWER+2
    X = -X
ENDWHILE
WRITE(6,*)SUM
STOP
```

Used to compute 1, then $1*2*3$, then $1*2*3*4*5, \dots$
Used to accumulate $x, -x^3/3!, x^5/5!, \dots$
Power is used for the exponent and for PROD.
$\dfrac{x^1}{1}$, $x^1 - \dfrac{x^3}{1\cdot2\cdot3}$, $x^1 - \dfrac{x^3}{1\cdot2\cdot3} + \dfrac{x^5}{1\cdot2\cdot3\cdot4\cdot5}$
Generates $1*2*3$, then $1*2*3*4*5, \dots$

Generate the oscillating sequence $-, +, -, +, \dots$

***3.6.6 Nested
WHILE Statements***

It is often necessary to repeat a loop a certain number of times. This is done by placing a loop within a loop, i.e., making a complete loop part of the body of another loop. In such cases each pass through the outer loop causes the inner loop to run through its complete cycle. The following examples illustrate the mechanism of *nested* loops:

EXAMPLE 1

Multiplication tables

Suppose we were to write the code to print out the multiplication tables from 2 to 12 with blank lines separating each table, as follows:

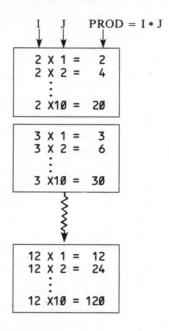

Looking at the tables, we see that we will need two counters: one counter I to take on values 2, 3, ..., 12, and another counter J to cycle through the values 1, 2, 3, ..., 10 for each value of I. The product PROD can easily be computed through the statement PROD = I*J. Every time a multiplication table is completed, we write a blank line. The pseudo code and corresponding FORTRAN code can then be written as follows:

```
set I to 2
WHILE I ≤ 12 DO
    set J to 1
    WHILE J ≤ 10 DO
        compute PROD = I*J
        write I,J,PROD
        add 1 to J
    ENDWHILE
    write blank line
    add 1 to I
ENDWHILE
stop
```

```
      I = 2
10 IF(I .LE. 12)THEN
      J = 1
20    IF(J .LE. 10)THEN
          PROD = I*J
          WRITE(*,*)I,'*',J,'=',PROD
          J = J + 1
          GO TO 20
      ENDIF
      WRITE(*,*)
      I = I + 1
      GO TO 10
   ENDIF
   STOP
```

The process of incrementing the two counters can be visualized as follows:

Outer Loop	Inner Loop
I	J

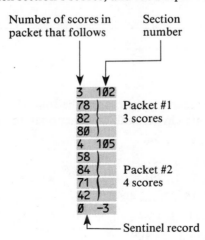

The first time through the outer WHILE loop, I is 2; I remains fixed at 2, and J cycles through the values 1 through 10.

The second time through the outer loop, I is 3; J is reset to 1, then it cycles through all integer values up to 10.

The last time through the outer loop, I is 12. While I remains fixed at 12, J cycles through the values 1 through 10.

EXAMPLE 2   Computing a Percentage of Passing Grades

Problem Specification. An input file consists of several sets of records, each containing grades obtained by different class sections of a particular course (see illustration below). Each set is identified by a header record specifying the number of scores for a particular section and the section number. The sentinel record contains a negative section number.

Write the pseudo code to determine the number and percentage of passing scores for each section (passing scores are those scores above 70). The program should list each section's scores, and the output should be similar to the one shown below:

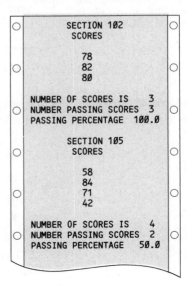

Number of scores in packet that follows

Section number

```
3  102
78 )  Packet #1
82 }  3 scores
80 )
4  105
58 )
84 }  Packet #2
71 }  4 scores
42 )
0  -3
```

Sentinel record

```
         SECTION 102
           SCORES

            78
            82
            80

NUMBER OF SCORES IS    3
NUMBER PASSING SCORES  3
PASSING PERCENTAGE  100.0

         SECTION 105
           SCORES

            58
            84
            71
            42

NUMBER OF SCORES IS    4
NUMBER PASSING SCORES  2
PASSING PERCENTAGE   50.0
```

To understand the problem, we will try to solve it with pencil and paper, using the "dummy" input on previous page. The header record tells us how many scores we need to process, and what the class section number is. The section number is important because we need to print it out. The number of scores tells us how many more scores we need to read before we encounter the next class. For the first class in the example, we need to read three scores: 78, 82, and 80. Since they all exceed 70, the percentage of passing grades is 100 percent and the count of passing scores is 3. Since we have read the three scores, we know that the next record will be a header record and, in our example, we will need to process the four scores of section 105. The logic of the problem is captured in pseudo code in Figure 3.12.

```
*computing a percentage of passing scores
*read first header record
 read no. scores and section number
 WHILE section number > 0 DO
        write section number
*       pass counts passing scores in section and
*       counter counts the number of students in section
        pass = 0
        counter = 1
*       read first score of class
        read score
        WHILE counter ≤ no. scores DO
             write score
             IF score > 70 THEN
                  add 1 to pass
             ENDIF
             add 1 to counter
             read score
        ENDWHILE
*       class data has been read, compute percentage of passing scores
        percentage = pass/counter*100
        write percentage
        read no. scores and section number
 ENDWHILE
 stop
```

FIGURE 3.12
EXAMPLE OF NESTED
WHILE STATEMENTS

3.6.7 Do It Now

1. Write the pseudo code to print the following sequences (the results for part e should be printed in decimal, not fractional, form).

    a. 2, 4, 6, 8, ..., 248

    b. 0, −1, −2, −3, ..., −100

    c. 1, 3, 5, 7, ..., 791

    d. 2, 4, 8, 16, 32, ..., 4096

    e. 1. 1./2. 1./3. 1./4., ..., 1/100.   (1., .5, .3333..., .25,...)

    f. −1, 2, −3, ..., 100

2. Each record of an input file contains a score (1–100). A negative value that is *not* a score identifies the last record of the input file. The following pseudo code is

supposed to print all scores below 50. Why is the logic in the pseudo code incorrect?

```
set score to 0
WHILE score ≥ 0 DO
     read score
     IF score < 50 THEN
          write score
     ENDIF
ENDWHILE
```

3. How many records will be read by the following?

a. I = 9
```
WHILE I ≥ 1 DO
     read record
     subtract 1 from I
ENDWHILE
```

b. I = 1
```
WHILE I ≠ 3 DO
     add 1 to I
     read record
ENDWHILE
```

4. Write the pseudo code to print the **integer** value of X in the range 1 to 10 that satisfies the condition

$$x^2 - x - 6 = 0$$

Exit from the loop as soon as a value for x is found; if there is no such value, print an appropriate message.

5. Write the pseudo code to compute the following expressions.

    a. $5 + 10 + 15 + ... + 675$

    b. $-1 - 2 - 3 - ... - 17$

    c. $1. + 1./2. + 1./3. + ... + 1./100.$

    d. $1 + (1 + 2) + (1 + 2 + 3) + ... + (1 + 2 + 3 + 4 ... + 99 + 100)$

6. Write the pseudo code to read a positive integer value for N and compute and print N factorial (N!). Stop the factorial process if N! > 25,134,798; in such a case, print the value of N.

7. Each record of an input file consists of an age and a sex code (1 = male, 2 = female). The sentinel record contains a negative age. Write the pseudo code to print the percentage of the female population that is over 40.

Answers

1. e. denominator = 1
```
WHILE denominator ≤ 100 DO
     print 1/denominator
     add 1 to denominator
ENDWHILE
```

f. sign = −1
```
counter = 1
WHILE counter ≤ 100
     print sign * counter
     sign = − sign
     add 1 to counter
ENDWHILE
```

4. X = 1
```
WHILE X ≤ 10 and X² − X − 6 ≠ 0 DO
     add 1 to X
ENDWHILE
IF X = 11 THEN
     print 'no roots'
ELSE
     print 'root is', X
ENDIF
```

```
6. read N
   product = 1
   counter = 1
   WHILE counter ≤ N and product ≤ 25,134,798
         product = product * counter
         add 1 to counter
   ENDWHILE
   print product
```

```
7. count = 0
   females over 40 = 0
   read age, code
   WHILE age > 0 DO
         IF code = 2 THEN              (if female)
               IF age > 40 THEN
                   add 1 to females over 40
               ENDIF
               add 1 to count
         ENDIF
         read age, code
   ENDWHILE
   percent = females over 40/count * 100
   print percent
   stop
```

3.7 PUTTING IT TOGETHER: THE PROGRAM DEVELOPMENT PROCESS

3.7.1 Major Programming Activities

Computer programming is a complex, creative task that demands a disciplined, organized approach to problem solving. Students often assume that proficiency in one or more computer languages is all that is required to be a good computer programmer—this is equivalent to assuming that proficiency in English ensures the success of a novelist or proficiency in draftsmanship insures the success of an architect.

The computer programmer must first be able to convert a problem to an *algorithm*, a sequence of well-defined steps that can be carried out by a computer. In some cases, such as computing the area of a rectangular lot, this process is relatively straightforward, since the details of the solution are well understood. In other cases, such as computing the orbit of a spacecraft or predicting weather patterns, the programming process can become quite complex and time-consuming. Even after an algorithm has been developed and converted into a computer language, the programmer must still make sure that the program is correct and will function as desired in all situations. The actual process of writing statements in FORTRAN or some other language often represents only a small portion of the time spent on a programming project.

The program development process involves the following five major activities:

1. Problem Specification
2. Algorithm Design

3. Coding
4. Data validation and testing
5. Documentation

In the following sections we will describe the purpose of each of these activities and techniques of program design.

3.7.2 Problem Specification

A programmer must obviously understand what the problem is before he/she can hope to solve it. The problem specification stage, therefore, requires that the problem originator clearly state the *function* of the program, what *results* it should produce, and any *special considerations* or methods that should be used in arriving at the results. It is then the programmer's responsibility to study the specifications carefully and to seek clarification on any points that are ambiguous or omitted. Even when the problem originator and the programmer are the same person, the success of the programming project depends on a clear understanding of what is to be achieved.

3.7.3 Algorithm Design

Once the programmer understands what is to be accomplished, he/she can proceed with the development of an algorithm. This stage requires two skills: a technique for developing a solution and a mechanism for expressing the solution.

One of the more difficult tasks in programming is developing the logic that controls the order in which instructions are performed. A haphazard approach can result in a situation in which following the order of the instructions is like trying to visually pick out the individual strands in a bowl of spaghetti—the logic of the algorithm is so intertwined that the structure is obscured and difficult to comprehend. Structured programming avoids this problem by restricting the ways in which the control logic can be specified. In the most general sense, structured programming provides an organized and disciplined approach to design, coding, and testing through the use of the three control structures: sequence, selection, and loop.

Top-Down Design

The problem of "not being able to see the forest for the trees" can easily occur in the process of developing algorithms. The computer's limited intuitive abilities (compared to those of a human) require that a great deal of detail be incorporated in any problem solution. A programmer can easily become lost in a maze of details if he/she attempts to fully solve each component of a problem before moving on to the next.

A more productive approach is to first formulate the solution in terms of generalized statements. This first version of the algorithm is typically limited to expressing the general logic of the solution, not the details of any particular computation or any specific action. Once the general algorithm has been developed, it can be refined by adding the details that are necessary to perform the general actions. For a complicated problem, this refinement process may be repeated several times, with each version containing more detail than the last. The process stops when the translation of the algorithm into a programming language is obvious. This approach, referred to as *stepwise refinement*, is part of a design philosophy called *top-down design*. By using top-down design, we can delay becoming involved in details until the problem has been broken into more manageable segments.

EXAMPLE

As an example of top-down design, consider the following problem:

Problem Specification. Lurnalot University in Florida has four student classifications for billing purposes: in-state full-time, out-of-state full-time, in-state part-time, and out-of-state part-time. A student who enrolls for fewer than 12 hours of courses is considered to be a part-time student. The schedule of charges for each classification is summarized in the following table:

Schedule of Charges

	full-time		part-time	
	in-state	out-of-state	in-state	out-of-state
Tuition & Fees	$545	$1,184	$44/hour	$94/hour
Fixed Fee (All students)	$60			
Board	$425			

The university needs a computer program to compute student bills. The input to the program is a file of student records where each record contains a student's (1) name; (2) residence status: the state—Florida or 'FL' implies in-state status; (3) scheduled hours; (4) request for board: 'yes' if requested, 'no' otherwise.

The output should list each student's name and total bill. The input and output have the following form:

Input File

Name	State	Hours	Board
'EDMUND'	'SC',	10	'YES'
'LITTLE'	'SC',	20	'YES'
'ZONE'	'SC',	10	'NO'
'HUGHES'	'SC',	20	'NO'
'DANGER'	'FL',	09	'YES'
'RANT'	'FL',	09	'NO'
'DOE'	'FL',	15	'YES'
'MIGHT'	'FL',	15	'NO'

Output

NAME	STATE	HOURS	BOARD	BILL
EDMUND	SC	10	YES	1425.00
LITTLE	SC	20	YES	1669.00
ZONE	SC	10	NO	1000.00
HUGHES	SC	20	NO	1244.00
DANGER	FL	9	YES	881.00
RANT	FL	9	NO	456.00
DOE	FL	15	YES	1030.00
MIGHT	FL	15	NO	605.00

Task Specifications. We begin by considering the actions that are needed to process one student's bill:

- read the student's record,
- compute the bill,
- write the bill.

These very general actions for a single student must obviously be repeated for each student, so we make our first attempt at an algorithm by including these actions in a loop:

```
* student billing problem.
* version 1—general algorithm
read student record
WHILE the end of the input file is not encountered DO
      compute bill
      write student bill
      read student record
ENDWHILE
stop
```

The statement to "compute bill" is obviously very general, but at this point in the development process we are simply trying to identify the major components of the problem. The next version includes somewhat greater detail on how to compute the bill:

```
* student billing problem
* version 2—add some details on bill computation.
* process individual student bills.
read student record
WHILE the end of the input file is not encountered DO
      initialize bill to fixed fee
      add tuition and fees charge to bill
      if requested, add board charge to bill
      WRITE student bill
      read student record
ENDWHILE
stop
```

These statements are still very general. We still have not considered the details of how to compute the tuition and fees, for example. A further refinement of the algorithm might expand this by distinguishing between full-time and part-time students:

```
* student billing problem
* version 3—additional details on bill computation
* process individual student bills
read student record
WHILE the end of the input file is not encountered DO
      initialize bill to fixed fee
* determine tuition and fee charge
      IF full-time student THEN
            determine full-time tuition and fees charge
      ELSE
            determine part-time tuition and fees charge
      END IF
      add tuition and fees charge to bill
      if requested, add board charge to bill
      write student bill
      read student record
ENDWHILE
stop
```

In this version we continue to delay consideration of the difference between in-state and out-of-state student charges. Incorporating too many details in one refinement step will only obscure the general logic of the algorithm that we are trying to develop.

The final refinement of this algorithm is given in Figure 3.13. Note the addition of the details on how to compute in-state versus out-of-state tuition and fees. The stepwise refinement process is illustrated in Figure 3.14.

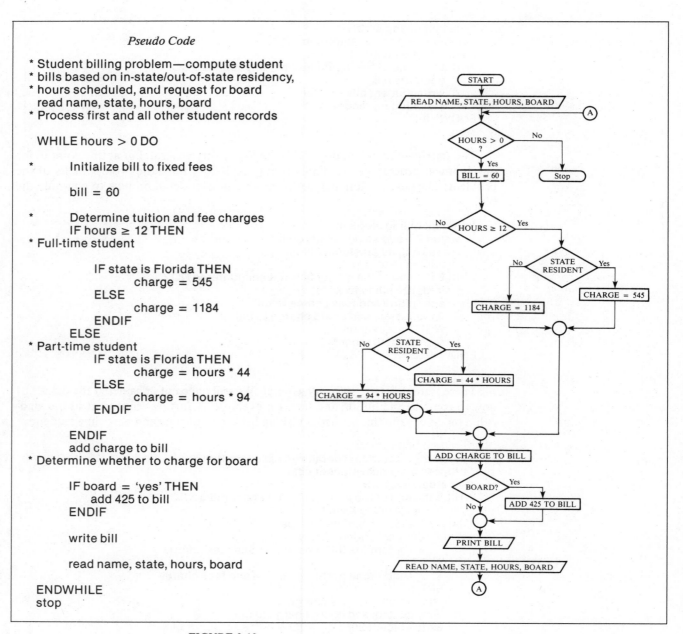

Pseudo Code

* Student billing problem—compute student
* bills based on in-state/out-of-state residency,
* hours scheduled, and request for board
  read name, state, hours, board
* Process first and all other student records

  WHILE hours > 0 DO

*   Initialize bill to fixed fees

          bill = 60

*   Determine tuition and fee charges
          IF hours ≥ 12 THEN
* Full-time student

              IF state is Florida THEN
                      charge = 545
              ELSE
                      charge = 1184
              ENDIF
          ELSE
* Part-time student
              IF state is Florida THEN
                      charge = hours * 44
              ELSE
                      charge = hours * 94
              ENDIF

          ENDIF
          add charge to bill
* Determine whether to charge for board

          IF board = 'yes' THEN
              add 425 to bill
          ENDIF

          write bill

          read name, state, hours, board

  ENDWHILE
  stop

FIGURE 3.13
***PSEUDO CODE AND FLOWCHART FOR STUDENT
BILLING PROBLEM***

3.7.4 Testing the Design

This is probably the most crucial phase in the program development process. Many beginning (and some not-so-beginning) programmers put blind trust in whatever output is produced by their programs, arguing that since no errors showed up during execution, and since captions and numeric values were printed, the results must be correct! Obviously, the results should be checked: this means testing *all* program paths with a barrage of input data. The best way to test your program is to manufacture hypothetical data that will force the program to use each and every path that can be taken during execution of the program (see Figure 3.15). In a parallel context, if you

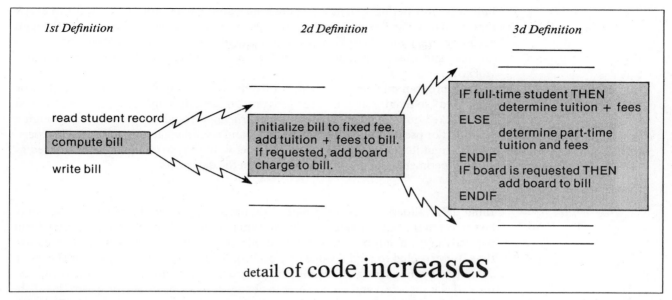

FIGURE 3.14
THE STEPWISE REFINEMENT PROCESS

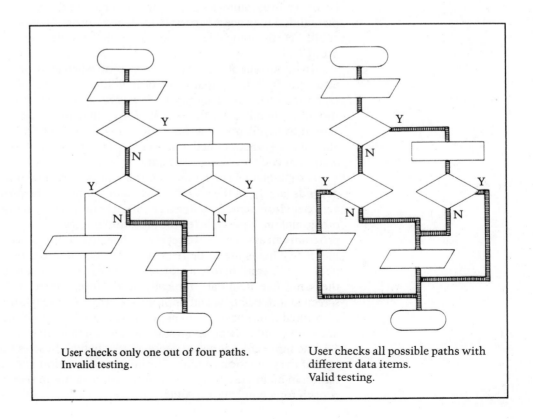

FIGURE 3.15
VALID VERSUS INVALID TESTING

built a lawn-watering system with numerous cutoff valves, you would want to check that no particular line or pipe was obstructed, i.e., that water would flow through each and every line. Checking just one particular circuit or one component of the pipeline and observing that it worked would not imply that the other lines also worked!

In a programming environment, different types of input values may need to be "invented" so that the action of the program on these dummy values can be observed and checked out. This process is known as *tracing* through a program (or through a flowchart or pseudo code). You must follow and record what happens to each experimental input item as it travels through the network of instructions; thus you need as many experimental items as there are paths in the design.

3.7.5 Input Data Validation

Input data validation is another part of design testing. Even though a program may be perfect in the sense that it contains no syntax or logical errors, it may not perform perfectly in the hands of others. For example, what would a program do at execution time if it expected to read a value of 1 or 2 for a particular variable X, but the value submitted by the user was 3? Ideally, the program should inform the user that the value read was incorrect and ask the user to change it to a 1 or 2! The program therefore cannot assume that the value for X will always be a 1 or 2; in fact, when dealing with humans, the value read could be a 1, a 2, or any other character on the keyboard! Hence, to avoid input mistakes the program should test X for the value 1, and then, if X is not 1, test for the value 2. If X is not 2, then someone goofed and an appropriate action should be taken by the computer.

Testing every input item for every imaginable (or unimaginable) value can soon become a programmer's nightmare, and adding the extra code to take care of the input validation process can swell a "skinny" program into the obese league in no time at all! Yet, theoretically, a program should be written in such a way that it is "bullet-proof"!

An important objective to keep in mind when incorporating input data validation into a program is to separate error handling from the logic that treats "clean" data. Upon input, the data should be *immediately* inspected for validity. If it is valid, it should be handled by the routine (task) that processes "clean" data; otherwise it should be handled by another routine that processes "tainted" data. Thus functionality of code is maintained: one section of code takes care of invalid data, and another section of code processes valid data.

The manner in which input data validation is carried out in a FORTRAN program depends largely on the way in which data is input to the program. In an online/interactive environment, data items are often read from the terminal (screen) one after another, making it possible for the program to screen "tainted" items one at a time. The program can ask the user to retype such an item until it is correctly entered. For example, if five items are to be read successively, the program should make sure all five items are "clean" before it starts processing them. In a noninteractive environment, the same five items are typically read from one record. These items should be screened immediately, and appropriate error messages for each type of error should be printed if one or more items are invalid. Only when it is determined that *all* entries are valid should the program start processing these items.

The input environment (interactive or batch) dictates the organization and structure of the validation routine. The program in section 3.8.1 illustrates input data validation in an interactive system, while the program in section 3.8.2 illustrates the approach for a batch file (disk file).

3.8 PROBLEM SOLVING

*3.8.1 Input Validation:
An On-Line Screen-
Driven Billing Program*

Problem Specification. Acme Rental's charges for the use of its rental cars are based on type of car, insurance purchased, mileage, and number of days used. The company rents three types of cars:

Type	Daily Rental	Mileage Charge
1	$40.00	.06
2	$45.00	.08
3	$50.00	.12

The company offers two insurance plans and selects the plan charging the lesser amount:

Plan	Cost
1	$6 per day of use
2	5% of the total combined daily rental and mileage charges, $10 minimum

Write an on-line program to compute a customer's invoice. The desk clerk should enter the data requested by the program through screen prompts: the type of car, the number of miles driven, and the number of days the vehicle was rented. If an invalid entry is typed, the system should inform the clerk about the specific error and allow him/her to retype the entry until it is satisfactory.

When all the data has been entered, the invoice should identify on the screen the type of car, the number of miles driven, the number of days the vehicle was rented, and the amount due. The insurance amount calculated by the computer is the lesser amount of the two insurance plans. A typical session might be:

```
DO YOU WANT TO CONTINUE? (Y=1; N=2)
1
ENTER CAR TYPE (1, 2, OR 3)
6
INVALID CAR TYPE; RETYPE
2
ENTER NUMBER OF DAYS
1O
DAYS MUST BE NUMERIC;  RETYPE
LØ
DAYS MUST BE NUMERIC;  RETYPE
1
ENTER NUMBER OF MILES
1OO
MILES MUST BE NUMERIC; RETYPE
1ØØ

TYPE CAR                 2
MILES DRIVEN           1ØØ
DAYS RENTED              1
INSURANCE PLAN COST        6.ØØØØØØØ
AMOUNT DUE                59.ØØØØØØØ

DO YOU WANT TO CONTINUE? (Y=1; N=2)
```

A program to solve this problem is shown in Figure 3.16.

Program Analysis. The program starts with the input validation task (lines 17–26). First the numeric car type is checked. If a nonnumeric entry is read, an execution-time error occurs and under normal circumstances the program would be terminated (the variable TYPE in the READ list (line 17) expects numeric data). However, with the ERR = option in the READ statement (lines 17 and 20), the system automatically transfers control to a designated program statement when an error is detected during the READ operation. When an invalid car code is typed in the example, control is passed to statement 70, where the user is asked to reenter the car code. The READ statement is then carried out again until there is no READ error. Note that the ERR = option is activated for *any* type of execution-time READ error—in this interactive environment it is safe to assume that the only execution READ error that can occur is a type conflict between the variable and its entered value. If the car code is not 1, 2, or 3, the user is asked to retype the code until it is valid (lines 20–21, a WHILE DO structure).

After the car code has been validated, the days and miles entries are similarly screened for numeric values by the READ statements at lines 24 and 26, both of which have ERR = options.

The program itself is broken down into four tasks:

1. The error validation task (lines 16–26 and 60–65)
2. The daily charge computation (lines 27–34)
3. The insurance plan computation (lines 35–43)
4. The output task—printing the results on the screen (lines 45–53)

Note that the daily rental rates, the mileage rates, and the insurance figures could have been specified as constants in the various formulas (lines 29, 31, 33, 36, and 38). However, if the rental company decided to change its rates, then all constants in the program would have to be located and updated. (Would all of them be found?) One way to avoid this potential problem is to group all constants in the PARAMETER statement—an even more efficient method would be to read the values from a data file to avoid recompiling the program when rates are changed.

Questions

1. Would it be possible to place the READ error routine (lines 58–63) right below line 26?

2. Check your FORTRAN reference manual to determine how to clear the screen after each customer's bill has been displayed on the screen.

3. Change the appropriate instructions in the program so that the customer is never charged more than fifty dollars in the case of insurance plan 2.

```
 1: ** CAR RENTAL PROBLEM
 2: ** WRITE AN ON-LINE INVOICE PROGRAM TO BILL A CUSTOMER FOR RENTAL
 3: ** OF A CAR BASED ON TYPE OF CAR, NUMBER OF MILES DRIVEN, NUMBER
 4: ** OF DAYS USED, AND TWO TYPES OF INSURANCE PLAN.
 5:        REAL INSPER, MINIMN,INSPLN,INSPL1,INSPL2
 6:        REAL RENT1,RENT2,RENT3,CHARG1,CHARG2,CHARG3
 7:        INTEGER TYPE, MILES, DAYS, RESPNS
 8:        PARAMETER(RENT1 =40.00, RENT2 =45.00, RENT3 =50.00)
 9:        PARAMETER(CHARG1=0.06,  CHARG2=0.08,  CHARG3=0.12)
10:        PARAMETER(INSPER=0.05,  MINIMN=10.0,  INSPL2=6.00)
11: **
12:        WRITE(*,*)'DO YOU WANT TO CONTINUE? (Y=1; N=2)
13:        READ(*,*)RESPNS
14: 10     IF(RESPNS .EQ. 1 )THEN
15:            WRITE(*,*)'ENTER CAR TYPE (1, 2, OR 3)'
16: ** ERROR VALIDATION ROUTINE
17: 15         READ(*,*,ERR=70)TYPE
18: 20         IF(TYPE .GT. 3 .OR. TYPE .LT. 1)THEN
19:                WRITE(*,*)'INVALID CAR TYPE; RETYPE'
20:                READ(*,*,ERR=70)TYPE
21:                GO TO 20
22:            ENDIF
23:            WRITE(*,*)'ENTER NUMBER OF DAYS'
24: 30         READ(*,*,ERR=80)DAYS
25:            WRITE(*,*)'ENTER NUMBER OF MILES'
26: 40         READ(*,*,ERR=90)MILES
27: ** COMPUTE DAILY CHARGES (DAILY RENT & MILES)
28:            IF(TYPE .EQ. 1)THEN
29:                CHARGE = RENT1*DAYS + CHARG1*MILES
30:            ELSE IF(TYPE .EQ. 2) THEN
31:                CHARGE = RENT2*DAYS + CHARG2*MILES
32:            ELSE
33:                CHARGE = RENT3*DAYS + CHARG3*MILES
34:            ENDIF
35: ** INSURANCE COST ROUTINE
36:            INSPLN = INSPL2*DAYS
37:            INSPL1 = INSPER*CHARGE
38:            IF(INSPL1 .LE. MINIMN)THEN
39:                INSPL1 = MINIMN
40:            ENDIF
41:            IF(INSPL1 .LT. INSPLN)THEN
42:                INSPLN = INSPL1
43:            ENDIF
44: ** OUTPUT ROUTINE
45:            BILL = INSPLN + CHARGE
46:            WRITE(*,*)
47:            WRITE(*,*)'TYPE CAR        ',        TYPE
48:            WRITE(*,*)'MILES DRIVEN ',           MILES
49:            WRITE(*,*)'DAYS RENTED  ',           DAYS
50:            WRITE(*,*)'INSURANCE PLAN COST', INSPLN
51:            WRITE(*,*)'AMOUNT DUE        ', BILL
52:            WRITE(*,*)
53:            WRITE(*,*)'DO YOU WANT TO CONTINUE? (Y=1; N=2)
54: ** PROCESS NEXT INVOICE
55:            READ(*,*)RESPNS
56:            GO TO 10
57:        ENDIF
58:        STOP
59: ** ERROR ROUTINE IN CASE ENTRY IS NOT CORRECT TYPE
60: 70         WRITE(*,*)'TYPE MUST BE NUMERIC;  RETYPE'
61:            GO TO 15
62: 80         WRITE(*,*)'DAYS MUST BE NUMERIC;  RETYPE'
63:            GO TO 30
64: 90         WRITE(*,*)'MILES MUST BE NUMERIC; RETYPE'
65:            GO TO 40
66:        END
```

Output

```
DO YOU WANT TO CONTINUE? (Y=1; N=2)
1
ENTER CAR TYPE (1, 2, OR 3)
0
INVALID CAR TYPE; RETYPE
0
TYPE MUST BE NUMERIC;  RETYPE
1
ENTER NUMBER OF DAYS
L1
DAYS MUST BE NUMERIC;  RETYPE
5
ENTER NUMBER OF MILES
100
MILES MUST BE NUMERIC; RETYPE
100

TYPE CAR            1
MILES DRIVEN       100
DAYS RENTED          5
INSURANCE PLAN COST     10.3000000
AMOUNT DUE             216.3000000

DO YOU WANT TO CONTINUE? (Y=1; N=2)
1
ENTER CAR TYPE (1, 2, OR 3)
3
ENTER NUMBER OF DAYS
5
ENTER NUMBER OF MILES
5678

TYPE CAR            3
MILES DRIVEN      5678
DAYS RENTED          5
INSURANCE PLAN COST     30.0000000
AMOUNT DUE             961.3600000

DO YOU WANT TO CONTINUE? (YES=1; NO=2)
2
```

FIGURE 3.16
A CAR RENTAL PROBLEM

3.8.2 Input Validation: Processing a Disk Input File

Problem Specification. In section 3.7.3 we discussed top-down design and illustrated the stepwise refinement process with a student billing example. In this section we will add an input validation routine to that example and complete the coding. Recall that each input record consisted of four entries (see Figure 3.17): (1) a name entry (character data enclosed in single quotation marks); (2) a state entry (character data enclosed in single quotation marks); (3) a number of hours or credits (numeric, not to exceed 27); (4) a board entry (character data, either 'YES' or 'NO').

With these four fields in the input records, there are two possible types of input errors:

1. Type mismatch interrupts: character fields are incorrectly typed (missing quotation marks) or character data is read for a numeric variable (for example, lO instead of 1O). If the ERR = option is not specified in the READ statement, errors of this nature will cause the system to terminate execution of the program. Note that when the interrupt occurs, the defective item read from the input record is *not* stored in the designated memory location (variable).

2. The input values read are outside the range of values expected by the program—for example, 'YEA' is an invalid board code and 94 in the credit hours field exceeds the 27 hours limit.

Type mismatches (item 1) are difficult to process when using the unformatted READ statement. Even with the ERR = option, it is practically impossible to read the entire input file and process records that contain type mismatches. Recall that the list-directed READ statement reads one input item at a time, not a logical record (which consists of several input items). Thus if an item read is defective, the READ operation is immediately terminated and the remaining variables (if any) in the READ list are ignored (the data items corresponding to these variables are *not* read). The next READ statement does not start at a new record—it starts at the item to the right of the defective item. The following example illustrates the situation:

```
      CHARACTER NAME*10, STATE*2,BOARD*3
      READ(5,*,ERR=70)NAME,STATE,HOURS,BOARD
60    READ(5,*,ERR=70)NAME,STATE,HOURS,BOARD
      .
      .
70    WRITE(6,*)'MISMATCH TYPE'
      GO TO 60
```

NAME is read and an interrupt occurs because of the missing quotation marks. An error message is printed at line 70, then control is passed to line 60. NAME is read again and its value is now 'SC' (not 'ANTON'), since 'SC' is the item following the last defective item encountered. Another interrupt occurs at STATE since 10 is not character data (missing quotes).

```
LITTLE K, 'SC', 10, 'YES'     logical record
'ANTON P', 'SC', 15, 'NO'     logical record
```

Because of these limitations, we will restrict the way in which invalid data items are to be treated:

1. If an interrupt occurs (READ error), the ERR = option will be used to print a "type conflict" error message, then the program will stop.

2. If a code other than 'YES' or 'NO' is encountered for BOARD, a CHECK BOARD CODE error message is printed. If a value exceeding 27 is read for HOURS, the message CHECK HOURS is printed. If both fields are invalid, then both error messages are printed.

Figure 3.17 illustrates the various types of error messages generated by the program.

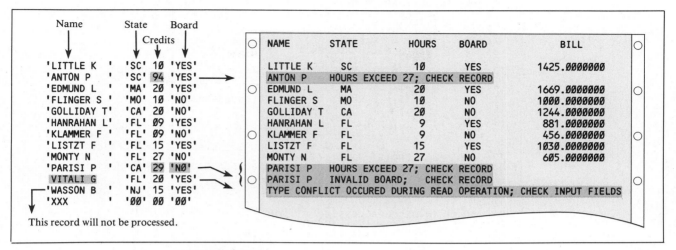

FIGURE 3.17
ERROR MESSAGES

Program Analysis. The FORTRAN code for this problem is shown in Figure 3.18. To ensure a proper program structure, we separate the input validation routine (lines 16–23) from the main logic task that treats valid records. To achieve this separation of functions, we initialize a particular variable (often referred to as a switch) to the value VALID or INVALID, depending on whether the record read is valid or invalid. If the record read is invalid, one or two appropriate error message(s) are printed. We then test the switch to determine whether or not to process the record. Such a variable is called a switch because it is conceptually similar to a railroad switch that is used to select a particular track.

The pseudo code overview of the entire design is:

```
 1:    read 1st record
 2:    WHILE not end of file DO
 3:        set switch to "valid"
 4:        IF record is invalid THEN        input data
 5:            set switch to "invalid"      validation
 6:            print error message(s)
 7:        ENDIF
 8:        IF switch = "valid" THEN
 9:            process valid record          main logic task
10:        ENDIF
11:        read next record
12:    ENDWHILE
```

Questions.

1. Could you rewrite the code without a switch? Discuss the resulting structure and its readability.

2. What would happen if line 3 in the pseudo code were omitted?

```
 1: *****  MATRICULATION FEE PROBLEM
 2: *****  GIVEN A STUDENT ADMISSION FILE COMPUTE STUDENT FEE BASED ON
 3: *****  FULL/PART-TIME & IN/OUT OF STATE STATUS AND BOARD
 4:         CHARACTER NAME*10,BOARD*3,INPUT*7,STATE*2
 5:         INTEGER HOURS
 6:         REAL CHARGE, BILL
 7:         INPUT = 'VALID'               Assume first record is valid.
 8:         OPEN(5,FILE='ROSTER')
 9:         OPEN(6,FILE='PRN')
10:         WRITE(6,*) 'NAME        ',' STATE','            HOURS',
11:     1        '        BOARD',';            BILL'
12:         WRITE(6,*)
13:         READ(5,*,ERR=70) NAME,STATE,HOURS,BOARD
14: 10      IF(NAME .NE. 'XXX') THEN
15: *****  INPUT VALIDATION ROUTINE
16:             IF(HOURS .GT. 27) THEN
17:                 INPUT = 'INVALID'
18:                 WRITE(6,*)NAME,' HOURS EXCEED 27; CHECK RECORD'
19:             ENDIF
20:             IF(BOARD .NE. 'YES' .AND. BOARD .NE. 'NO')THEN
21:                 INPUT = 'INVALID'
22:                 WRITE(6,*)NAME,' INVALID BOARD;   CHECK RECORD'
23:             ENDIF
24:             IF(INPUT .EQ. 'VALID')THEN
25: *****  INVOICE PROCESSING ROUTINE
26:                 BILL = 60.00
27:                 IF(HOURS .GE. 12)THEN
28:                     IF(STATE .EQ. 'FL')THEN
29:                         CHARGE = 545.00
30:                     ELSE
31:                         CHARGE = 1184.00
32:                     ENDIF
33:                 ELSE
34:                     IF(STATE .EQ. 'FL')THEN
35:                         CHARGE = HOURS * 44.00
36:                     ELSE
37:                         CHARGE = HOURS * 94.00
38:                     ENDIF
39:                 ENDIF
40:                 BILL = BILL + CHARGE
41:                 IF(BOARD .EQ. 'YES')THEN
42:                     BILL = BILL + 425.00
43:                 ENDIF
44:                 WRITE(6,*)NAME,'        ',STATE,HOURS,
45:     1               '        ',BOARD,'        ',BILL
46:             ENDIF
47:             INPUT = 'VALID'
48:             READ(5,*,ERR=70)NAME, STATE, HOURS, BOARD
49:             GO TO 10
50:         ENDIF
51:         STOP
52: *****  ERROR ROUTINE IN CASE OF RUN-TIME READ ERROR
53: 70      WRITE(6,*)'TYPE CONFLICT OCCURED DURING READ OPERATION'
54:     1        ,'; CHECK INPUT FIELDS')
55:         STOP
56:         END
```

```
 NAME          STATE          HOURS      BOARD              BILL

 LITTLE K      SC             10         YES          1425.0000000
 ANTON P     HOURS EXCEED 27; CHECK RECORD
 EDMUND L      MA             20         YES          1669.0000000
 FLINGER S     MO             10         NO           1000.0000000
 GOLLIDAY T    CA             20         NO           1244.0000000
 HANRAHAN L    FL              9         YES           881.0000000
 KLAMMER F     FL              9         NO            456.0000000
 LISTZT F      FL             15         YES          1030.0000000
 MONTY N       FL             27         NO            605.0000000
 PARISI P    HOURS EXCEED 27; CHECK RECORD
 PARISI P    INVALID BOARD;   CHECK RECORD
 TYPE CONFLICT OCCURED DURING READ OPERATION; CHECK INPUT FIELDS
```

FIGURE 3.18
STUDENT BILLING PROBLEM

3.8.3 Rocket Trajectory

Problem Specification. In the technical reference manual accompanying the instructions of your store-bought minirocket, you are given its flight characteristics (trajectory function):

$$y = 15 + 1.75t^2 - 0.0046t^4$$

where y is the altitude (in feet) of the rocket at time t (in seconds). The rocket is fired perpendicularly from a 15-foot platform (giving the constant 15 in the function).

You are to write a program to conduct a simulated flight including the following computational tasks:

1. Print the height (altitude) of the rocket at one-second intervals on its way up and on its way down. Include in your output the first negative altitude (rocket impact).

2. At some point in its trajectory, during a one-second time frame, the rocket will switch from ascent to descent. Print the rocket's altitude and the corresponding elapsed time at the beginning and at the end of that one-second time frame. In Figure 3.19, the descent begins between the 14th and 15th seconds (altitude is 181.2 and 175.8 feet, respectively). Make sure these results are printed *after* the altitude table in part (1) is printed.

3. Determine the number of full seconds that elapse before the altitude becomes negative; then, starting at the last computed positive altitude, print the altitude readings at 0.1-second intervals until impact time. In Figure 3.19, this "slow animation" starts at 19 seconds (altitude 47.27 ft) and ends at 19.8 seconds (altitude −5.9 ft).

Problem Analysis. The FORTRAN code to solve this problem is shown in Figure 3.20.

Task (1) can be simply expressed in pseudo code as follows:

```
set seconds to 0
set altitude to 0
WHILE altitude ≥ 0 DO
        add 1 to seconds
        compute altitude using function
        print altitude and seconds
ENDWHILE
```

Since task (2) requires that we print the approximate maximum altitude *after* the altitude and time tables have been printed, we cannot discard a computed altitude (NEWALT) until we find out whether the altitude computed one second later is greater than NEWALT. Therefore we temporarily preserve NEWALT into OLDALT before we compute a new NEWALT (one second later). This process is continued until NEWALT is less than the previous altitude OLDALT, indicating that the rocket has started its descent. At this juncture we save the value of OLDALT (the highest altitude, attained after t whole seconds) into MAXALT, and we save the lower altitude after $t + 1$ seconds (NEWALT) in DESCNT (lines 25–27); now we can print these values after the entire altitude table has been printed (lines 36 and 38).

Notice that as long as the rocket is climbing, lines 25–28 are *not* carried out. Then, as soon as the rocket starts its descent, lines 25–28 are carried out one time, after which they are never carried out again. The variable MISSLE identifies the flight status of the rocket (ascent or descent) and determines whether lines 25–28 are carried

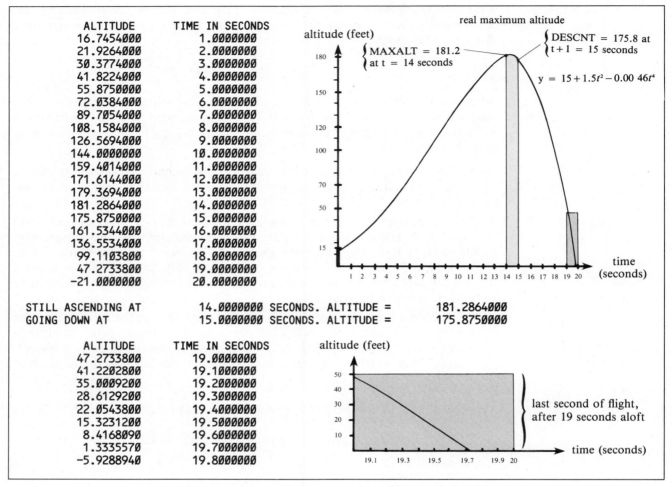

FIGURE 3.19
ROCKET FLIGHT CHARACTERISTICS

out (line 20). Initially MISSLE is set to the value "GOING UP"; it is then set to the value "GOING DOWN" at line 28 when the NEWALT is less than OLDALT. MISSLE acts as a switch—initially it is on, then it is turned off at a particular time; in the meantime, it is constantly monitored to determine what action to take.

When the rocket hits the ground after t full seconds (first time NEWALT is negative) we start task 3 at altitude OLDALT and time $t - 1$ seconds (line 43). The partial last second of flight is retraced at lines 43–49, where the time is incremented in tenths of a second and the corresponding times and altitudes are printed.

Questions and Problems.

1. What would happen if line 28 were omitted?

2. Does the graph in Figure 3.19 give you an idea of the horizontal distance covered? What is the horizontal distance covered theoretically (assume no wind)?

3. Tell how you would change the program so that negative altitudes are not printed in the two altitude tables.

```
 1: * MISSILE TRAJECTORY PROBLEM
 2: * GIVEN A TRAJECTORY FUNCTION CARRY OUT THE FOLLOWING STEPS
 3: * (1) PRINT TABLE OF VERTICAL DISTANCES COVERED PER SECOND
 4: * (2) DETERMINE MAXIMUM ALTITUDE ATTAINED (HEIGHT AND TIME)
 5: * (3) DETERMINE MOMENT OF IMPACT TO NEAREST 1/10 SECOND
 6: *
 7:         CHARACTER MISSLE*8
 8:         REAL SECNDS, OLDALT, NEWALT, MAXALT, DESCNT, TIME
 9: * MISSLE IS USED IN CONJUNCTION WITH APEX COMPUTATION
10:         WRITE(*,*) '          HEIGHT          ','TIME IN SECONDS'
11:         MISSLE = 'GOING UP'
12:         SECNDS = 0.0
13:         NEWALT = 0.00
14: * TASK1: DETERMINE MOMENT OF IMPACT WITH GROUND (ALTITUDE BECOMES < 0)
15: 10      IF(NEWALT .GE. 0.00) THEN
16:             OLDALT = NEWALT
17:             SECNDS = SECNDS + 1
18:             NEWALT = 15.0 + 1.75*SECNDS**2 - 0.0046*SECNDS**4
19: * IF MISSILE IS GOING UP, KEEP TRACK OF ALTITUDE
20:             IF(MISSLE .EQ. 'GOING UP') THEN
21: * SINCE  MISSILE IS CLIMBING KEEP TRACK OF SUCCESSIVE ALTITUDES IN
22: * MAXALT AND CORRESPONDING TIME IN TIME. LAST VALUE IN TIME
23: * WILL BE WHEN MISSILE STARTS DESCENT. TURN MISSLE TO 'GOING DOWN'
24:                 IF(NEWALT .LT. OLDALT) THEN
25:                     MAXALT = OLDALT
26:                     DESCNT = NEWALT
27:                     TIME   = SECNDS
28:                     MISSLE = 'GOING DOWN'
29:                 ENDIF
30:             ENDIF
31:             WRITE(*,*)NEWALT, SECNDS
32:         GO TO 10
33:     ENDIF
34: * TASK2: PRINT LAST ALTITUDE ON WAY UP & 1ST ALTITUDE ON WAY DOWN
35:         WRITE(*,*)
36:         WRITE(*,*)
37:        1'STILL ASCENDING AT ',TIME-1,' SECONDS. ALTITUDE = ',MAXALT
38:         WRITE(*,*)
39:        1'GOING DOWN AT       ',TIME  ,' SECONDS. ALTITUDE = ',DESCNT
40: * TASK3: RE-ENACT LAST PARTIAL SECOND OF FLIGHT TIME
41:         WRITE(*,*)
42:         WRITE(*,*) '          ALTITUDE         ','TIME IN SECONDS'
43:         SECNDS = SECNDS - 1
44:         NEWALT = OLDALT
45: 20      IF(NEWALT .GE. 0.00) THEN
46:             NEWALT = 15.0 + 1.75*SECNDS**2 - 0.0046*SECNDS**4
47:             WRITE(*,*)NEWALT, SECNDS
48:             SECNDS = SECNDS + 0.1
49:         GO TO 20
50:     ENDIF
51:         STOP
52:         END
```

FIGURE 3.20
A ROCKET TRAJECTORY PROBLEM

4. Identify more accurately the maximum altitude attained.

5. Determine the altitude of the missile one full second before its impact. Assume impact occurs when the absolute value of the altitude is less than half a foot.

6. Can you determine a relationship between the height of the platform and the time it takes the rocket to hit the ground? Try to correlate various platform heights with flight time. Then, given a particular platform height, you can predict the flight time of the rocket.

7. Experiment with the exponent of $1.75t^2$, i.e., does $1.75t^4$ instead of $1.75t^2$ cause the rocket to attain twice its maximum altitude? If $1.75t^4$ does not do it, then what exponent causes the rocket to double its altitude (when the platform remains the same)?

8. Display the minirocket firing on your screen by simulating real time frames, i.e., as each real second occurs, display time and altitude on the screen. To simulate a second, execute a dummy instruction 100 or 1000 times, depending on the speed of your computer.

3.8.4 Standard Deviation

Problem Specification. The general formula to compute the standard deviation for n grades $x_1, x_2, x_3, \ldots, x_n$ is

$$\text{standard deviation} = \sqrt{\frac{n(x_1^2 + x_2^2 + x_3^2 + \ldots + x_n^2) - (x_1 + x_2 + x_3 + \ldots + x_n)^2}{n(n-1)}}$$

Write a program to read n grades and compute the average and the standard deviation.

Solution: If you are unsure of the meaning of the standard deviation, consider the following illustration. The following tables show the final scores obtained in two introduction to computers classes taught by two different instructors.

	Class A	Class B	
Average = 50	40	90	Average = 50
	55	20	
	60	80	
	45	10	

At the end of the semester, the two instructors discuss how their classes did that semester. Both recall that their class average was 50, whereupon both express surprise at this coincidence. Little do they realize how different their ranges of scores are. The average does not reflect this. In Class A, all the scores are close together, while in Class B the scores spread out considerably; yet the averages are identical. If the average does not capture the spread of the scores, what mathematical measure does? Answer: the standard deviation.

The standard deviation gives us a feel for the distribution of scores. In Class A the spread between the outermost scores and the average is 10, while in Class B that spread is 40 (90–50 or 10–50). In general, the standard deviation gives an indication of how much, on the average, the scores deviate from the average. A small deviation implies that most of the scores are clustered, while a large deviation implies a large spread among the scores. A deviation of 0 means that all the scores are the same. If the standard deviation is 15 and the score average is 70, this means that the great majority of scores fall in the interval 70 + 15 to 70 − 15 (between 85 and 55).

To understand the mechanics involved, let us compute the standard deviation for class A, where x_1, x_2, x_3, and x_4 are 40, 55, 60, and 45, and $n = 4$.

$$\text{standard deviation} = \sqrt{\frac{\overbrace{4(40^2 + 55^2 + 60^2 + 45^2)}^{\substack{\text{Sum of the squares} \\ \text{of each score}}} - \overbrace{(40 + 55 + 60 + 45)^2}^{\text{Sum of the scores squared}}}{4(3)}} = 9.13$$

Note that the numerator is simply $n*$(sum of all scores^2) $-$ (sum of scores)^2

The program to solve this problem must accumulate two types of sums: the sum of the scores and the sum of the square of each score. Every time a score is read, it is added to the sum of scores ($x_1 + x_2 + x_3 + \ldots$) and it is squared and added to the sum of squares ($x_1^2 + x_2^2 + \ldots$).

This accumulation process continues until the end-of-file is reached, at which time the standard deviation is calculated. The complete program is shown in Figure 3.21.

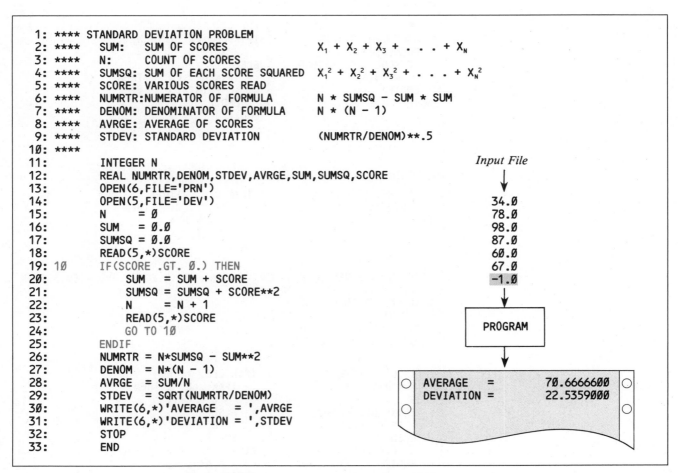

```
 1: **** STANDARD DEVIATION PROBLEM
 2: ****    SUM:   SUM OF SCORES               X₁ + X₂ + X₃ + . . . + Xₙ
 3: ****    N:     COUNT OF SCORES
 4: ****    SUMSQ: SUM OF EACH SCORE SQUARED   X₁² + X₂² + X₃² + . . . + Xₙ²
 5: ****    SCORE: VARIOUS SCORES READ
 6: ****    NUMRTR:NUMERATOR OF FORMULA        N * SUMSQ - SUM * SUM
 7: ****    DENOM: DENOMINATOR OF FORMULA      N * (N - 1)
 8: ****    AVRGE: AVERAGE OF SCORES
 9: ****    STDEV: STANDARD DEVIATION          (NUMRTR/DENOM)**.5
10: ****
11:        INTEGER N
12:        REAL NUMRTR,DENOM,STDEV,AVRGE,SUM,SUMSQ,SCORE
13:        OPEN(6,FILE='PRN')
14:        OPEN(5,FILE='DEV')
15:        N    = 0
16:        SUM  = 0.0
17:        SUMSQ = 0.0
18:        READ(5,*)SCORE
19: 10     IF(SCORE .GT. 0.) THEN
20:            SUM   = SUM + SCORE
21:            SUMSQ = SUMSQ + SCORE**2
22:            N     = N + 1
23:            READ(5,*)SCORE
24:            GO TO 10
25:        ENDIF
26:        NUMRTR = N*SUMSQ - SUM**2
27:        DENOM  = N*(N - 1)
28:        AVRGE  = SUM/N
29:        STDEV  = SQRT(NUMRTR/DENOM)
30:        WRITE(6,*)'AVERAGE   = ',AVRGE
31:        WRITE(6,*)'DEVIATION = ',STDEV
32:        STOP
33:        END
```

Input File

34.0
78.0
98.0
87.0
60.0
67.0
−1.0

PROGRAM

AVERAGE   =   70.6666600
DEVIATION =   22.5359000

FIGURE 3.21
COMPUTING A STANDARD DEVIATION

3.9 EXERCISES

3.9.1 Test Yourself

1. Which of the following pairs of coding segments are equivalent?

a.
```
IF(X .EQ. '1')THEN          IF(X .EQ. '1')THEN
    PRINT*,A                    PRINT*,A
ENDIF                       ELSE
IF(X .EQ. '2')THEN              IF(X .EQ. '2')THEN
    PRINT*,B                        PRINT*,B
ENDIF                           ENDIF
                            ENDIF
```

b.
```
IF(X .GT. 1)THEN            IF(X .GT. 1)THEN
    A = A+1.                    A = A+1.
ELSE                        ENDIF
    IF(X .GT. 2)THEN        IF(X .GT. 2)THEN
        C = C+1.               C = C+1.
    ENDIF                   ENDIF
ENDIF
```

c.
```
IF(KODE .EQ. 1)THEN         IF(KODE .EQ. 1)THEN
    PRINT*,B                    PRINT*,B
    IF(KODE .EQ. 2)THEN     ELSE
        PRINT*,D                IF(KODE .EQ. 2)THEN
    ENDIF                           PRINT*,D
ENDIF                           ENDIF
                            ENDIF
```

In parts (d) through (f), assume K takes on values 1, 2, and 3.

d.
```
IF(K .NE. 1)THEN            IF(K .EQ. 2)THEN
    PRINT*,A                    IF(K .EQ. 3)THEN
ENDIF                              PRINT*,A
                                ENDIF
                            ENDIF
```

e.
```
IF(K .NE. 1)THEN    IF(K .EQ. 1)THEN     IF(K.EQ.2 .OR. K.EQ.3)THEN
    PRINT*,A            PRINT*,B             PRINT*,A
IF(K .NE. 2)THEN    ELSE                 ELSE
    PRINT*,B            PRINT*,A                 PRINT*,B
ENDIF               ENDIF                ENDIF
ENDIF
```

f.
```
IF(K .GT. 1)THEN            IF(K .LE. 1)THEN
    A = A+1.                    IF(K .LE. 2)THEN
ELSE                               C = C+1.
    IF(K .GT. 2)THEN            ELSE
        B = B+1.                    B = B+1.
    ELSE                       ENDIF
        C = C+1.            ELSE
    ENDIF                       A = A+1.
ENDIF                       ENDIF
```

2. Assume that K takes on integer values between 1 and 6 in the following two coding segments. Which variables (A, B, C, D, E, or F) will be printed for each value of K?

a.
```
IF(K .NE. 1)THEN
   IF(K .NE. 4)THEN
      IF(K .GT. 3)THEN
         PRINT*,F
      ELSE
         PRINT*,E
      ENDIF
   ELSE
      PRINT*,D
   ENDIF
ELSE
   IF(K .NE. 2)THEN
      IF(K .GT. 3)THEN
         PRINT*,C
      ELSE
         PRINT*,B
      ENDIF
   ELSE
      PRINT*,A
   ENDIF
ENDIF
```

b.
```
IF(K .GE. 3)THEN
   IF(K .LT. 5)THEN
      PRINT*,A
   ENDIF
ENDIF
IF(K .GT. 3)THEN
   IF(K .EQ. 6)THEN
      PRINT*,B
   ELSE
      IF(K .LE. 6)THEN
         PRINT*,D
      ENDIF
   ENDIF
ELSE
   PRINT*,C
ENDIF
```

3. Are the following statements true or false?

a. Only one STOP statement is allowed per program.

b. Position 1 of an input data record is reserved for comments.

c. A C or an asterisk in position 6 of a FORTRAN statement indicates a continuation from the preceding program line.

d. Data cannot be entered in positions 73–80 of an input record (for a READ operation).

e. Input data records are read at compilation time.

f. A C in position 1 of a FORTRAN statement will cause a compilation error.

g. Running out of input data records will cause a compilation error.

h. The statement 5 GOTO5 is grammatically incorrect.

i. The statement READ(5,*)J,J,J is invalid.

j. The statement GO TO KODE3 is valid.

k. Input data records can immediately follow the READ statement within the FORTRAN program.

4. Omega Triple Pooh sorority girls are very selective about their blind dates. The housemother keeps a record file on members of the local fraternities. Each record contains an age and three numeric entries (1, 2, or 3) describing the following attributes:

Complexion	Build	Trait
fair (1)	tall (1)	meticulous (1)
dark (2)	medium (2)	timid (2)
olive (3)	small (3)	aggressive (3)

All dates must satisfy the following conditions:

a. Tall but not dark, and between the ages of 20 and 30 or

b. medium or small build, but neither meticulous nor with olive complexion, and either under 18 or over 28

c. but under no circumstances small and aggressive and over 75, or timid and tall under 19

Write the code to perform the "blind date" selection for the Pooh women by reading the data file and counting the number of suitable dates.

5. If a year is divisible by 4 it is a leap year, with the following exception: years that are divisible by 100 but not by 400 are not leap years. Thus 1981 is not a leap year, 1984 is a leap year, 2000 is a leap year, but 1900 is not a leap year (not divisible by 400). Write the pseudo code to read a year and determine whether it is a leap year.

6. Write the WHILE DO pseudo code and the WHILE DO equivalent FORTRAN code to generate the following sequences of numbers:

    a. 0, 5, 10, 15, ..., 100

    b. 2, 4, 8, 16, ..., 4096

    c. 1, −2, 3, −4, ..., −100

    d. N, N−1, ..., 3, 2, 1, where N is read from an input record

7. Each record of an input file contains the following data:

Employee number
Employee's yearly base pay
Employment duration in years (1.5 means one year and a half)
Employee classification: 1 = hourly, 2 = salaried
Rating: 1 = satisfactory, 2 = unsatisfactory

The policy for determining employee Christmas bonuses at Santa-Claus Inc. is as follows:

Employees must have been employed with the company at least six months. Employees with a satisfactory rating are paid one week's pay if they are hourly employees or 20% of monthly pay if they are salaried employees. If the rating is unsatisfactory, one day's pay (1/240 of base pay) will be paid to hourly employees and 5% of monthly pay to salaried employees.
Employees with more than 10 years of service and a satisfactory rating receive an additional bonus of $400.

Write the pseudo code to compute the bonus.

8. An input file contains an unknown number of records, each record containing a number between −99 and 99. Write the FORTRAN code to print the numbers read up to and including the first number that changes sign. For example:

Given 3,4,8,4, −3, −2, −1	the program would print	**3,4,8,4,−3**
Given −2,1, −3	the program would print	**−2,1**
Given 1,2,3,4,5,100	the program would print	**1,2,3,4,5**
Given 1,0, −1,2	the program would print	**1,0,−1**

9. Each record of an input file, contains the following fields:

Student name
Age
Sex   (1 = male, 2 = female)
Class   (1 = freshman, 2 = sophomore)

Write a program to list the names of students over 21 years of age and compute the number of male freshmen, the number of female freshmen, the number of male sophomores, and the number of female sophomores.

*3.9.2 Programming
Exercises: General*

1. Final grades in a course are determined by adding scores obtained on three tests, T1, T2, and T3. Students get a PASS grade if the sum of the three scores is above 185 and a FAIL otherwise. Write a program to read three scores and determine the grade. Print the input scores, the average, and the final grade.

2. The FMT Corporation provides home mortgages up to $70,000. The down payment schedule is as follows:

> 3% of the first $30,000
> 10% of the next $22,000
> 20% of the remainder

Enter a mortgage amount and print the down payment required. Reject any application for an amount over $70,000.

3. Each student record consists of a student name and three test scores. The student's average is based on his/her two best scores. Write a program to print the student's name and average on one line and the three test scores on another line (double-space) as follows:

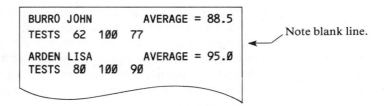

```
BURRO  JOHN          AVERAGE = 88.5
TESTS  62  100  77

ARDEN  LISA          AVERAGE = 95.0
TESTS  80  100  90
```

Note blank line.

4. The formula for computing the simple interest I on a loan of P dollars at an interest rate R for T days is: $I = P * R * T/360$

Write a program to read a dollar amount and an interest rate and produce a table showing the interest to be paid as T varies from 30 days to 4 years in steps of 1 month (30 days). Provide appropriate captions on the output.

5. An input file contains an unknown number of positive and negative numbers varying from $-1,000$ to $+1,000$. Write a program to determine how many positive numbers, how many negative numbers, and how many zeros there are in the input file.

6. a. A file contains ten pairs of grades (one pair per record). Write a program to print out each pair and its corresponding sum.

b. Suppose that the first record in a similar input file contains the number of records that follow, for example:

```
3  ←——————— 3 data records follow
45   60   ⎫
80  100   ⎬ Three data records
36   49   ⎭
```

Modify the program written for part (a) above to process this type of data file.

7. An input file contains 30 grades, one per record. Write a program to compute and print out the number of grades greater than 49 and less than or equal to 63.

8. A data file contains positive and negative numbers varying from -100 to 100. Write a program to compute the sum of the positive numbers and the sum of negative numbers. Print both sums.

9. Mrs. X has just invested $9,000 at 13.5% yearly interest rate (compounded once a year). She has decided to withdraw the accumulated interest as soon as that interest exceeds $11,000.00. Write a program to determine how many years Mrs. X will have to wait before she can withdraw at least $11,000 of accumulated interest. Could you be more specific and identify the number of years and months?

10. The post office charges 22 cents for the first ounce or part thereof for a first class letter and 18 cents for each additional ounce or part thereof. Write a program to accept letter weights in ounces and print the required postage.

11. You own a bookstore that sells both paperback and hardback books. For every book you sell, you have a record with two numbers: the price of the book and either a 0 or a 1 (0 if the book is a paperback, 1 if the book is hardback). Write a program to obtain the following information:

    a. total sales

    b. total number of books sold

    c. average price per book

    d. average price of a paperback book

12. The first record of a store's inventory file contains the current date expressed as YYXXX where YY and XXX represent the year and Julian date. For example, 86245 represents the 245th day of 1986. Each succeeding record contains an item number, the Julian date of the last time an item was sold, the number of items on hand, the cost per item, and the regular selling price. A store plans a sale to try to sell slow-moving items. The purpose of the program is to produce a report showing recommended sale prices as follows:

If an item has not been sold in the last 30 days, discount is 10%.
If an item has not been sold in the last 60 days, discount is 20%.
If an item has not been sold in the last 90 days, discount is 40%.

However, any item that has sold in the last 30 days is not to be placed on sale. If there is only one of an item left in stock, it is not to be placed on sale no matter when the last day of sale occurred. The amount of discount allowed is also subject to the following rule: sale prices cannot be lower than cost.

Write a program to read the input file and produce a report similar to the following one. Continued on next page.

```
CURRENT DATE 86:220

ITEM    LAST SALE    DAYS      NO. IN    COST     REG.     SALE
NO.     DATE         ELAPSED   STOCK              PRICE    PRICE

302     200          20        20        10.00    15.00    15.00
400     189          31        5         6.50     10.00    9.00
101     159          61        15        3.00     5.00     4.00
100     101          119       50        2.00     3.00     2.00
901     100          120       1         12.00    25.00    25.00
999     180          40        2         6.50     7.15     6.50
222     360          225       60        10.00    12.00    10.00
174     100          485       1         30.50    35.50    35.50
```

If your system cannot print seven fields per page width, omit the first two columns. How would you change your program to handle the case where there is an overlap in years, for example, 1987 to 1988?

13. A utility company charges for water consumption as follows:

User Class	Consumption (cubic feet)	Rate/cubic feet
Residential	1st 100	15 cents
	over 100	13 cents
Commercial	1st 100	18 cents
	next 300	15 cents
	over 300	12 cents
Industrial	1st 1,000	14 cents
	over 1,000	10 cents
Institutional		9 cents

Make up an input file and write a program to read the input file and compute and print invoices.

14. Write the code to simulate a gas-pumping machine by displaying a gas-volume window and a cost-volume window. As the gas is being pumped, these two windows should display "rolling" digits, i.e., stationary scrolling of numbers within their windows. Volume is in liters and should be displayed in increments of deciliters (1 deciliter = 1/10 liter). Assume the cost of a liter is 30 cents. A photographic image of the pump taken at each deciliter interval would show the following window contents:

LITERS	COST	
0 0 0 . 0 0	$ 0 0 0 . 0 0	Pump at start.
0 0 0 . 1 1	$ 0 0 0 . 0 3	Pump at first deciliter.
0 0 0 . 2 2	$ 0 0 0 . 0 6	Pump at second deciliter.
.	.	
.	.	
0 4 6 . 1 0	$ 0 1 3 . 8 3	Pump at end of transaction.

Note that only two windows are displayed at any time (liters and cost). Accept a dollar amount and write the code to run the pump until the cost reaches that amount.

15. An input file contains 100 numbers (one number per record). Write a program to read these numbers, and stop whenever the number 4 (by itself) has been read three times. Print the total number of items read. (It is possible that the number 4 may not occur three times.)

16. Computerized checkbook: The first record of an input file contains the balance from the previous month. Each succeeding record contains two entries: a check number and a dollar amount. This dollar amount can be a positive number (deposit) or a negative number (withdrawal). Write a program to produce a checkbook report similar to the following:

Input   *Output*

Current balance

```
     ↓
   3250
   112    -100
   123    -250
   127      50
   128      74
     ↑       ↑
  Check   Amount
  number
```

CHECK NO.	WITHDRAWALS	DEPOSITS	BALANCE
			3250.00
112	100.00		3150.00
123	250.00		2900.00
127		50.00	2950.00
128		74.00	3024.00
		NEW BALANCE	3024.00

17. Each data record in a file contains two items: an age and a code for marital status (1 = single, 2 = married, 3 = divorced, and 4 = widowed). Write a program to compute and print:

  a. The percentage of people over 30 years of age.

  b. The number of people who are either widowed or divorced.

  c. The number of people who are over 50 or less than 30 and who are not married.

Don't forget to print all the input data before printing the results.

18. An IRS agent is checking taxpayers' returns in the $20,000 to $30,000 income bracket (gross earnings). Each record of the returns file contains a social security number, gross earnings, and an amount of tax paid. If taxes paid are below 18.5% of gross earnings, compute the tax due (assume all taxes in that bracket are 18.5% of gross). If the amount due is above $1,400, add a penalty charge of 1.5% of the amount due. Take care of refunds if necessary. Records of gross earnings outside the interval $20,000 to $30,000 are not to be checked. Print appropriate messages with the results.

19. Drs. Smith and Jones both teach principles of management as shown in the teacher/section table shown below. The student file consists of records containing the following information:

Input Record   *Teacher/Section Table*

	Section	Teacher	Time
Student ID	1	Smith	Day
Course Section (1–4)	2	Smith	Night
Grade point average 0.0–4.0	3	Jones	Day
Type code 1 = part-time,	4	Jones	Night
2 = full-time			

Write a program to compute and print:

  a. The percentage of students who are part-time.

  b. The total number of students in Dr. Smith's sections.

  c. A list of the ID numbers of students enrolled in night classes.

  d. The number of day students having a GPA of 2.0 or higher.

  e. The name of the teacher in whose class the highest GPA is found.

20. Employees at Sarah's Style Shop are to receive a year-end bonus. The amount of the bonus depends on the employee's weekly pay, position code, and number of years with the store. Each employee is assigned a bonus based on the following rules:

Position Code	Bonus
1	One week's pay
2	Two weeks' pay; maximum of $700
3	One and a half week's pay

Employees with more than 10 years' experience are to receive $100 in addition to their bonus and employees with less than 2 years' experience are to receive half the bonus derived from the above table.

Write a program to read an employee number, a weekly pay, a position code, and a number of years, then compute and print the employee's bonus.

21. Data for a store shows daily sales for corresponding days of succeeding years. The first value on the record is the amount of sales for a given day in the first year; the second value is the amount of sales for the corresponding day in the second year. Find the number of days in which the second year's daily sales exceeded the first year's daily sales by more than 10% of the first year's sales. The output should be similar to the following:

```
   Sample Data                  Sample Output

   500 550          FIRST YEAR      SECOND YEAR
   400 441             500             550
   300 500             400             441 **
   600 448             300             500 **
                       600             448
1st year   2d year   NUMBER OF SUPERIOR SALES DAYS 2
```

(Note that ** identifies those records for which the second year's daily sales exceeds the first year's daily sales by more than 10%.)

22. Mrs. Spander is spending her money faster than she earns it. She has now decided to keep track of all her expenses. For every purchase or expense, she enters on her home computer the expense description, the amount, and an expense category code (1 = household, 2 = medical, 3 = recreation, 4 = utilities). Then every Sunday night she runs her budget program to obtain an analysis like the one below. Write a program to read the expenses and provide a weekly summary for Mrs. Spander.

```
                        BUDGET ANALYSIS

                 HOUSEHOLD    MEDICAL   RECREATION   UTILITY
                 EXPENSES    EXPENSES    EXPENSES     BILLS

PLANTS             12.33
MOVIES                                    6.50
MORTGAGE          389.75
DENTIST                      154.25
GAS                                                   99.66
VACATION                                1156.56

SUBTOTALS         402.08     154.25     1163.06       99.66

      TOTAL EXPENSES    $1819.05
```

23. The Gull Power Electric Company charges supermarkets and small businesses for electricity according to the following scale:

Kilowatt Consumption	Cost
0–300	$5
301–1000	$5 + 6.113 cents for each kwh over 300 (June thru Oct.)
	$5 + 5.545 cents for each kwh over 300 (other months)
over 1000	Previous rate up to 1000 kwh and 98% of either 5.545 or 6.113 cents for each kwh over 1000, depending on season

Write a program to accept a date (month, day, and year), an account number, a meter number, a current meter reading, and a previous meter reading and produce invoices similar to the following (don't forget the two dotted lines):

```
----------------------------------------------
ACCOUNT NUMBER     METER NUMBER    DATE
    12300              SAE558       04/25/83


METER READING      KW HOURS       AMOUNT
PRESENT PREVIOUS      USED       WINTER RATE
  2335    1998        337          $7.05
----------------------------------------------
```

24. In baseball, a batting average is computed by dividing the total number of hits by the total number of times at bat. The slugging average is computed by dividing the total number of bases by the total number of times at bat—a single is counted as one base, a double as two bases, etc. Write a program that will accept as input the number of singles, doubles, triples, and home runs, and the total number of times at bat for a player. Compute and print the batting average and the slugging average. Use the following test data:

Player	Singles	Doubles	Triples	Home Runs	At Bat
1	5	3	1	2	70
2	3	0	2	1	15
3	10	5	3	0	30

The expected output is:

Player	Batting Average	Slugging Average
1	.157	.314
2	.400	.867
3	.600	.967

25. The present value of an investment P invested at interest rate R for T years with interest compounded N times a year is given by the formula:

$$A = P\left(1 + \frac{R}{N}\right)^{T*N}$$

a. Read P, R, and T and determine the difference between compounding once a year and 365 times a year.

b. Read a principal and an interest rate and, by trial and error, determine the number of years it will take before the original principal is doubled when compounded annually.

26. Salaries at the XYZ Corporation are based on job classification, years of service, education, and merit rating. The base pay for all employees is the same; a percentage of the base pay is added according to the following schedule:

Job Classification	Percentage of Base Pay	Education	Percentage of Base Pay
1	0	1 (high school)	0
2	5	2 (junior college)	10
3	15	3 (college)	25
4	25	4 (graduate degree)	50
5	50	5 (special training)	15

Merit Rating	Percentage of Base Pay	Years of Service	Percentage of Base Pay
0 (poor)	0	0–10 years	5
1 (good)	10	each additional year	4
2 (excellent)	25		

Write a program to accept numerical codes for each of the four variables and calculate the employee's salary as a percentage of a base pay.

27. Write a program to make daily weather reports. Each data record should contain nine integer values giving the following information: current month, day, and year; high temperature for the day, low temperature for the day; year in which the record high for this day was set, record high temperature; year of record low for this day; record low temperature. After reading a data record, print a message of one of the following four types, depending on the data:

a.
```
10/23/84    HIGH TODAY    52
            LOW TODAY     23
```

b.
```
10/24/84    HIGH TODAY    71*
            LOW TODAY     38
*(BEATS RECORD OF 70 SET IN 1906)
```

c.
```
10/25/84    HIGH TODAY    73*
            LOW TODAY    -10**
*(BEATS RECORD OF 68 SET IN 1938)
**(BEATS RECORD OF -8 SET IN 1918)
```

d.
```
10/26/84    HIGH TODAY    22
            LOW TODAY    -18*
*(BEATS RECORD OF -5 SET IN 1900)
```

28. Write a program to perform an analysis of expenses for an automobile trip. Input into the program will be:

    number of days
    estimated mileage for each day
    estimated miles per gallon
    estimated cost of gas per gallon
    estimated cost of room(s) per day
    number of persons
    estimated cost of breakfast/lunch/dinner per person

Assume that no more than four persons can occupy a room; if there are more than four persons, additional rooms will be required. Assume that breakfast on the first day and dinner on the last day are not included in trip expenses. Allow 15% of room plus meals per day per person for incidental expenses. (For example, if two persons are sharing a $40 per night room and total meals per day per person is $15, the estimate for incidental expenses per person per day would be .15 × (40/2 + 15) = 5.25.) Allow 15% of total estimated cost of gas for incidental auto expenses.

Write a report showing all input data and a trip expense budget including:

total automotive costs (gas + incidental)
total cost of meals
total cost of rooms
total cost of incidental expenses
total trip estimated expenses.

3.9.3 Programming Problems: Mathematical and Scientific

1. Consider the polynomial $P(x) = x^2 - 1.596x + .266$, which has a root between 1.3 and 1.4. Use trial and error to find an approximation r to that root such that $|P(r)| < 0.001$. (Recall that a root s of $P(x)$ is such that $P(s) = 0$.)

2. Write a program to read a value for x and compute and print the absolute value of x. Recall that $|x| = x$ if $x > = 0$ and $|x| = -x$ if $x < 0$.

3. Read three values and determine whether they represent the three sides of a right triangle.

4. Write a program to compute the area of a triangle given three sides a, b, and c using the formula:

$$area = \sqrt{s(s-a)(s-b)(s-c)} \quad where \; s = \frac{a+b+c}{2}$$

(*Caution:* Not all possible values of a, b, and c represent a triangle. How could your program detect such values?)
[*Hint:* The sum of any two sides must always be greater than the third.]

5. Read a three-digit number, N, between 100 and 999 and print out each digit as a separate number, i.e., the 100s, and 10s, and the unit's digits.
[*Hint:* divide first by 100, then by 10, using real and integer operations.]

6. Make your family a temperature conversion chart that displays the temperatures in Fahrenheit and centigrade from $-35°F$ to $125°F$. ($F = 9/5*C + 32$).

7. A set of circles have radii of 2, 7, 12, 17, ..., 42, and 47 inches, inclusively. Print out the radius, circumference, and area of each circle.

8. Write a program to perform octal counting up to 27_8, that is, print the numbers 1, 2, ..., 7, 10, 11, ..., 17, 20, 21, ..., 27. Can you generalize your program for counting in octal up to a number N read from a data record?

9. Write a program to read a value for N (N > 0) and

a. Print the positive even integers that are less than or equal to N.

b. Print the first N odd integers starting with 1.

For example, if N = 6, we print 0, 2, 4, 6 for part (a) and 1, 3, 5, 7, 9, 11 for part (b).

10. Read 30 grades already sorted into ascending order and compute the mode. The mode is defined as the score that occurs most frequently. For example, given the grades 10, 15, 15, 17, 17, 17, 20, 21, the mode is 17.

11. Read N grades already sorted into ascending order (N is to be read from the first record) and compute the median. The median is the grade that divides a distribution of scores into two equal parts, for example:

10, 11, 12, 13, 14, 15, 16   The median is 13.

10, 11, 12, 13   The median is $\dfrac{11 + 12}{2} = 11.5$.

12. Write the code to determine whether a particular number K is a prime number. A prime number is a number that is divisible only by itself and 1. One unsophisticated approach would be to divide K by all the numbers starting with 1 up to one less than K. If K is not divisible evenly by any of these numbers, it is prime. Another method, a little more efficient than the first one would be to divide K by all numbers from 2 up to the square root of K.

13. The greatest common factor of two integers is the largest integer that will divide both numbers evenly. For example, the greatest common factor (*gcf*) of 9 and 12 is 3, since 3 is the largest number to divide evenly into both 9 and 12. The *gcf* of 8 and 9 is 1; the *gcf* of 27 and 18 is 9. An interesting algorithm (attributed to the mathematician Euclid) for computing the greatest common factor is shown here in flowchart form. [The remainder of 12 ÷ 9 is 3, while the remainder of 17 ÷ 3 is 2, i.e., 17 ÷ 3 = 5 + 2/17]

Write a program to implement the Euclidean algorithm. Can you explain why it works?

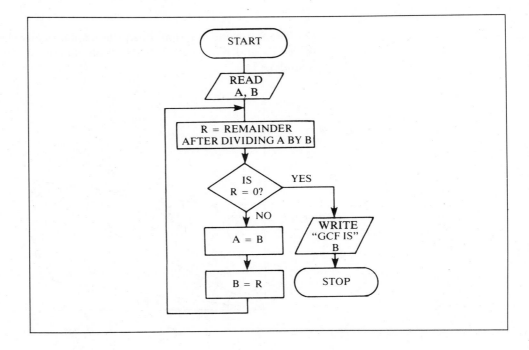

14. The following flowchart calculates the exact date for Easter given any year after 1583. Write a program to compute the Easter date for any given year. In the following formulas, D should be an integer variable.

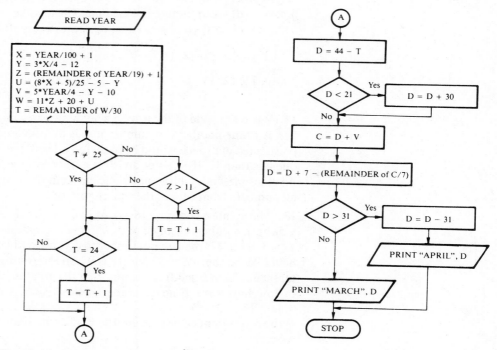

[Remainder of 17/3 is 2; remainder of 16/5 is 1, etc.]

15. The following diagram illustrates geometrically the resultant force F of two forces F1 and F2, given their directions (angles θ_1 and θ_2) and magnitudes (in pounds).

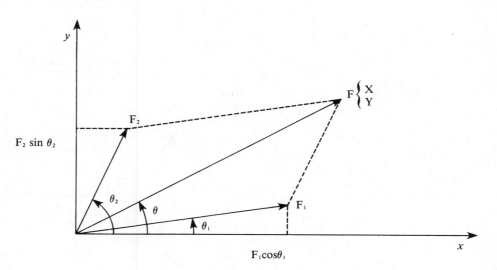

The force F is equal to $\sqrt{X^2 + Y^2}$ where X is the x component of F and Y is the y component of F.

In turn, the X component is equal to the sum of the x components of F1 and F2 and the Y component is equal to the sum of the y components of F1 and F2. Thus

$$X = F_1\cos\theta_1 + F_2\cos\theta_2$$
$$Y = F_1\sin\theta_1 + F_2\sin\theta_2$$

The direction (angle) of the resulting force is given by the formula

$$\theta = \arctan\left(\frac{Y}{X}\right)$$

a. Write a program to read values for F1 and F2 and degree values for θ_1 and θ_2 and compute the force F and its resulting angle.

b. Modify your program so that it increases the angle of F2 (θ_2) in steps of 1 degree and prints the resulting F force. Stop this incremental process when the resulting force is roughly half of the force computed from the original input in part a. Print θ_2.

16. The distance covered by a projectile is essentially a function of the velocity of the projectile and its angle of departure. The following diagram illustrates the trajectory of a projectile fired at angle θ with velocity v.

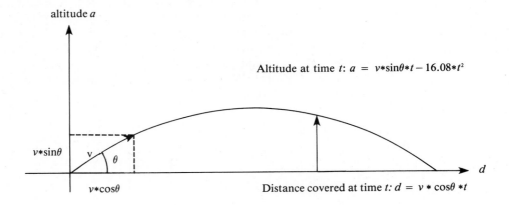

altitude a

Altitude at time t: $a = v*\sin\theta*t - 16.08*t^2$

$v*\sin\theta$

v

θ

$v*\cos\theta$

d

Distance covered at time t: $d = v * \cos\theta * t$

The horizontal distance covered by the projectile is $d = v*\cos\theta*t$, where t is expressed in seconds. Thus if the angle is 90°, the horizontal distance covered is 0 feet—if the angle is 0 degrees, the distance is $v*t$ at time t (just like distance covered by car!).

The vertical distance a (altitude) of the projectile (which is subject to the pull of gravity) is given by $a = v*\sin\theta*t - \frac{1}{2}gt^2$, where $g = 32.16$ feet/s². The altitude is equal to 0 at the time of firing and at the time of impact. Thus the total flight time duration of the projectile can be computed by setting the altitude to 0 and computing the value for t:

If $a = 0$ then $v*\sin\theta*t - 16.08*t^2 = 0$

or $v*\sin\theta - 16.08*t = 0$

or $t = \dfrac{v*\sin\theta}{16.08}$ = total flight time

Write the code to carry out the following:

a. Given $\theta = 45°$ and $v = 300$ feet/s, print a table of altitude and horizontal distance covered by the projectile at 1-second intervals during the flight time. Stop printing the table when the altitude becomes negative. Note that the angles must be expressed in radians (angle in radians $= \theta/180*3.14159$). Also print the exact horizontal distance covered (replace t by $\dfrac{v*\sin\theta}{16.08}$ in the horizontal distance formula).

b. Determine the approximate maximum altitude, i.e., the altitude within a three-foot range of the true maximum altitude, and verify that this altitude is attained at the midpoint in time of the projectile's flight.

c. Determine whether the following hypotheses are true or false:
(1) Given a fixed angle ($\theta = 45°$), doubling the velocity will double the vertical distance covered. If this statement is false, determine the velocity that will double the distance (within 10 feet of twice the original distance).
(2) Given a fixed velocity ($v = 300$ feet/s), doubling the angle will double the projectile's maximum altitude (within 10 feet of twice the original altitude).

d. Determine two sets of values for θ and v so that the horizontal distance covered is 10,400 feet $\pm$ 10 feet.

e. Recalculate part (a) with a head wind (horizontal) of 100 mph.

17. For the derrick shown below, write a program to compute the tension in the cable and the horizontal and vertical components of the reaction at C. Carry out the computation for different boom positions, letting angle A vary from $10°$ to $80°$ in steps of $10°$. Assume that the weight of the boom is 2000 lbs concentrated at its midspan.
[*Check:* When $A = 30°$, T = 4510 lb, reaction at C = 3750 lb horizontal and 7495 lb vertical.]

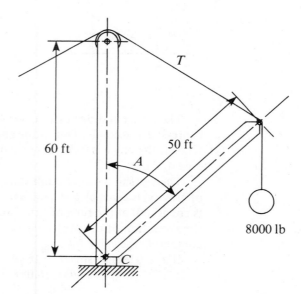

18. A rocket is launched and follows a course given by the equation

$$y = 1.85 \sin\frac{x}{3} + e^{x/2} - 1.35x$$

where x = miles traveled horizontally
        y = miles traveled vertically

An instrument package is released at a height of 4 mi. Write a program to find the horizontal distance from the launch site at which the package is released.
[*Answer:* $x = 4.083$ mi]

19. A solid steel column of circular cross section is needed to support a load of 65,000 lb. The ends of the column are not rigidly fixed but are able to rotate, and the point of application of the load may be as much as 1 in. from the axis of the column. The yield point of the steel is 50,000 lb/in.^{2}, and the desired safety factor is 3. The column is 45 in. long. Write a program to find the required diameter to safely carry the load.

The equation giving the maximum stress in a column of this type is

$$s = \frac{FP}{A}\left(L + \frac{ec}{i^2} \sec \frac{L}{2i} \sqrt{\frac{FP}{AE}}\right)$$

where s = maximum stress = 50,000 lb/in.^{2}
        F = factor of safety = 3
        P = applied load = 65,000 lb
        A = cross-section area (in.)^2 = $\pi d^2/4$ for a circular column
        e = eccentricity of applied load = 1 in.
        c = distance from column axis to extreme edge of cross section = $d/2$ for circular column
        i = radius of gyration = $d/4$ for circular column
        E = modulus of elasticity = 30,000,000 for steel
        L = column length = 45 in.   [*Answer:* Diameter = 15.04 in.]

20. The number e can be defined as the limit of $(1 + 1/n)^n$ as n (integer) gets larger and larger. Write a program to approximate a value for e. Stop when the difference between two successive approximations is less than 0.001. Print out the values for e and n. For example,

$$e_1 = \left(1 + \frac{1}{1}\right)^1 = 2$$

$$e_2 = \left(1 + \frac{1}{2}\right)^2 = 2.25$$

$$e_3 = \left(1 + \frac{1}{3}\right)^3 = 2.37$$

The difference between e_3 and e_2 is still greater than 0.001; hence new values for e must be computed until $e_{n+1} - e_n < 0.001$.

21. The square root of a number A can be computed by successive approximations using the iterative formula $x_{n+1} = \frac{1}{2}(x_n + A/x_n)$, which becomes $X = .5*(X + A/X)$ in FORTRAN. Starting with $x = 1$ as an initial approximation for the square root of A, a new approximation x is computed using the above formula. This new approximation, in turn, can be substituted in the formula to compute a newer approximation x. This process can be continued until the square of the new approximation x is close to A within a prescribed degree of accuracy ϵ ($\epsilon = 0.1, 0.01, 0.001$, etc., depending on the accuracy needed), that is,

$$|x^2 - A| < \epsilon.$$

Write a program to read A and E (ϵ) and compute $\sqrt{A}$. Write an error message if $A \leq 0$. For example, to compute the square root of 24 we start as follows:

$$x_1 = \frac{1}{2}\left(x_0 + \frac{24}{x_0}\right) = \frac{1}{2}\left(1 + \frac{24}{1}\right) = 12.5$$

$$x_2 = \frac{1}{2}\left(x_1 + \frac{24}{x_1}\right) = \frac{1}{2}\left(12.5 + \frac{24}{12.5}\right) = 7.29$$

$$x_3 = \frac{1}{2}\left(x_2 + \frac{24}{x_2}\right) = \ldots$$

22. A certain metal is graded according to the results of three tests that determine whether the metal satisfies the following specifications:

  a. Carbon content is below 0.67.

  b. Rockwell hardness is no less than 50.

  c. Tensile strength is greater than 70,000 psi.

The metal is graded 10 if it passes all three tests, 9 if it passes tests 1 and 2, 8 if it passes test 1, and 7 if it passes none of the tests. Write a program to read a carbon content, a Rockwell constant, and a tensile strength and determine the grade of the metal.

23. Systems of equations can be solved by iterative techniques. For example, to solve the system

$$\begin{cases} 2x + y = 3 \\ x - 3y = 2 \end{cases}$$

we first rearrange the equations to solve for x in terms of y in the first equation and for y in terms of x in the second equation, obtaining

$$\begin{cases} x = (3 - y)/2 \\ y = (x - 2)/3 \end{cases}$$

Starting with an initial approximate solution $x = y = 0$, we refine this approximation by computing a new x and y as follows:

$$\begin{cases} x = (3 - y)/2 = (3 - 0)/2 = 1.5 \\ y = (x - 2)/3 = (1.5 - 2)/3 = -.1666 \end{cases}$$

This procedure is repeated by computing new values for x and y in terms of the values x and y just computed. The process can be terminated by substituting x and y in the original equation and verifying that:

$$\begin{cases} 2x + y \approx 3 & \text{or} & 2x + y - 3 \approx 0 & \text{or} & |2x + y - 3| < \epsilon \\ x - 3y \approx 2 & \text{or} & x - 3y - 2 \approx 0 & \text{or} & |x - 3y - 2| < \epsilon \end{cases}$$

where ϵ is a prescribed degree of accuracy ($\epsilon = 0.01, 0.0001$, etc.)

Write a program to solve the following system of equations using this iterative technique with $\epsilon = 0.01$

$$\begin{cases} 2.56x - .034y = -.56 \\ 3.14x + 1.32y = 50.76 \end{cases}$$

24. Write a program to solve the following system of three equations in three unknowns using the approach in exercise 23. Initially set $x = y = z = 0$ and use $\epsilon = 0.1$.

$$\begin{cases} 3.1x - y + 2z = -.4 \\ x - 10y - 1.3z = 10 \\ -2.1x - 3y + 10z = -103.2 \end{cases}$$

25. Apply Kirchhoff's laws to the circuit shown below and obtain a set of four equations. Solve these equations to obtain the values of the four currents shown.

$$(Answer: i_1 = 52.1 \text{ mA}, i_2 = -60.4 \text{ mA},$$
$$i_3 = -30.4 \text{ mA}, i_4 = 38.8 \text{ mA})$$

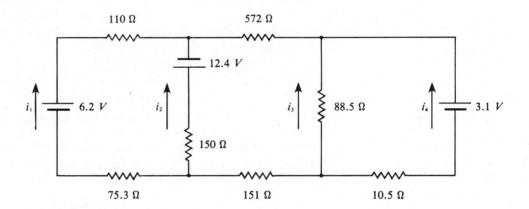

26. Determining the roots of a polynomial, $y = P(x)$, implies finding values, x_i, so that $y = P(x_i) = 0$. One systematic method of determining x is:

Step 1. Determine by visual inspection two values for x, *xpos* and *xneg*, such that $P(xpos) > 0$ and $P(xneg) < 0$. This means that a root of $P(x)$ exists in the interval *xpos, xneg,* since polynomials are continuous functions and the graph of $y = P(x)$ must intersect the x axis somewhere between *xpos* and *xneg:*

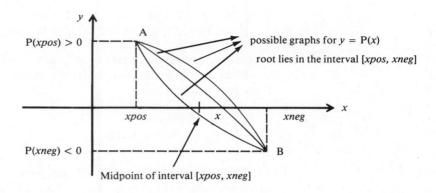

Step 2. For the next approximation x to the root, take the midpoint of the interval *xpos, xneg:*

$$x = \frac{xpos + xneg}{2}$$

Step 3. Determine whether $P(x) > 0$ or $P(x) < 0$. If $P(x) > 0$, then the root must lie between x and *xneg*. If $P(x) < 0$, then the root must lie between x and *xpos*. Then go back to step 2 and recompute a new (refined) approximation, x, making sure to replace *xpos* or *xneg,* depending on the sign of $y = P(x)$, by x.

This algorithm can be terminated when $y = P(x)$ is "sufficiently close" to zero; mathematically speaking, this means $|P(x)| < \epsilon$ where ϵ is a prescribed degree of accuracy.

Using the method described, compute a root of $y = x^3 - 2x^2 + x - 16$ in the interval [3.4]. Start with *xpos* = 4 and *xneg* = 3 and stop when $\epsilon = .1$; i.e., $|P(x)| < .1$.

27. The Fibonacci sequence is formed by assigning the value 1 to the first two terms and then computing each successive term as the sum of the two preceding terms. Thus $a_1 = 1, a_2 = 1, a_3 = a_1 + a_2 = 1 + 1 = 2, a_4 = a_2 + a_3 = 1 + 2 = 3$, and so on. The first ten terms of the Fibonacci sequence are: 1,1,2,3,5,8,13,21,34,55,...

a. Write a program to generate the first 20 terms of the Fibonacci sequence.

b. A number is said to be a Fibonacci number if it occurs as a term of the Fibonacci sequence. Write a program to read a number and determine if it is a Fibonacci number.

28. The golden mean was used by ancient roman architects in the design of structures. A building in which the ratio of the length to the width equalled the golden mean (which is approximately equal to 1.618) was believed to be most pleasing aesthetically. It can be shown that the limit of the ratio of successive terms of the Fibonacci sequence (see exercise 27) is equal to the golden mean. Write a program to compute the terms of the Fibonacci sequence and the ratio of each term to its predecessor. How many terms are required before the difference between successive ratios is less than 0.01? 0.0001? How many terms are required before successive ratios are equal? (The answers to these questions depend on the data representation of your computer; the ratios should become equal in fewer than 100 terms.)

29. The following formula provides an approximation for the nth term in the Fibonacci sequence:

$$0.447264 * (1.61803)^n$$

Write a program to generate the actual terms of the Fibonacci sequence, the approximation, the absolute difference between the actual term and the approximation, and the relative error (difference divided by actual value). What happens to the values of the relative error for successively larger values of n? How "good" is the approximation? Can you improve on the approximation formula?

30. A rent-a-car company has the following system for computing a customer's rental car bill:

Car Type	Rent/Day 150 Miles	Rent/Week 1050 Miles	Extra Mileage	Extra Hours
1	$24.95	$140.00	.18	$3.60
2	$32.95	$184.80	.24	$4.80
3	$44.95	$256.95	.26	$7.00

The daily rate includes an allowance of 150 miles, and the weekly rate includes an allowance of 1050 miles.

The extra mileage column in the above table indicates the additional cost for each mile above the mileage allowance for the different car types.

The extra hours column in the above table specifies the additional hourly charge for each hour that the vehicle is used in excess of one day or in excess of one week.

Passenger collision insurance is optional and costs $3.75 per day.

Destination extra charges: There is no extra charge if the vehicle is returned to the renting station; however, if the receiving station is not the renting station, there is an additional charge of 14 cents per mile for the total number of miles driven (including the mileage allowance).

If a car is rented for fewer than 24 hours, the lesser of the following rates is applied: (1) the number of hours of use times the hourly charge (the extra hours charge in the table), or (2) the daily rental charge.

The final invoice should also include a 4% sales tax.

Write a program to compute a customer's bill, based on the charges described above. For example, the following input parameters are used to generate the sample output shown below:

Input Parameters	Example
Rent code (by the day = 1, by the week = 2)	1
Number of miles driven	1080
Car type	1
Possession of car	
Days	5
Hours	0
Insurance code (1 = yes, 2 = no)	1
Destination extra charge (1 = yes, 2 = no)	1

The output should be similar to:

```
        CAR TYPE        HOURS USED              RENT CODE
           1               120.                      1
MILES DRIVEN              1080.
LESS MILES ALLOWED         750.
CHARGEABLE MILES           330.  a       .18     $ 59.40
NUMBER DAYS                  5.  a     24.95     $124.75

                             SUBTOTAL            $184.15
DESTINATION CHARGES                              $151.20
COLLISION INSURANCE                              $ 18.75

                          TAXABLE CHARGE         $354.10
                          STATE TAX              $ 14.16
                          NET AMOUNT             $368.26
```

3.9.4 Answers to Test Yourself

1. **a.** Identical.

    b. Not identical. For example, suppose X = 3. In case 1, 1 will be added only to A, whereas in case 2, 1 will be added to A and C.

    c. Not identical. D will never be printed in case 1.

    d. Not identical. If K = 2 or 3, then A will be printed in case 1, but A will never be printed in case 2.

    e. The last 2 cases are identical.

    f. Identical.

2. **a.**

K	
1	B
2,3	E
4	D
5,6	F

  b.

K	
1,2	C
3	A,C
4	A,D
5	D
6	B

3. a. F.   **b.** F.   **c.** T.   **d.** F.   **e.** F.   **f.** F.
   g. F.   **h.** F.   **i.** F.   **j.** F.   **k.** F

4. The third test for the "under no condition" should be tested first since the characteristics specified in conditions 1 and 2 could conceivably satisfy condition 3. (Assume all variables are integers.)

```
    IF(.NOT.(HGHT .EQ. 3 .AND. TRAIT .EQ. 3 .AND. AGE .GT. 75
1        .OR.(TRAIT .EQ. 2 .AND. HGHT .EQ. 1 .AND. AGE .LT. 19))) THEN
        IF(HGHT.EQ.1 .AND. COMP.NE.2 .AND. AGE.GE.20 .AND. AGE .LE.30
1                                .OR.
2        HGHT.NE.1 .AND. COMP.NE.3 .AND. TRAIT.NE.1
3                                .AND.
4                (AGE.LT.18 .OR. AGE.GT.28)) KOUNT = KOUNT+1
    ENDIF
```

5. read year
   divide year by 4 and keep remainder r
   IF r = 0 THEN
       divide year by 100 and keep remainder r
       IF r = 0 THEN
           divide year by 400 and keep remainder r
           IF r = 0 THEN
               write leap-year
           ELSE
               write not leap-year
           ENDIF
       ELSE
           write leap-year
       ENDIF
   ELSE
       write not leap year
   ENDIF

6. a.
```
I = 0                      I = 0
WHILE I ≤ 100 DO           5 IF(I .LE. 100)THEN
    print I                    PRINT*, I
    I = I+5                    I = I+5
ENDWHILE                      GO TO 5
                           ENDIF
```

b.
```
I = 2                      I = 2
WHILE I ≤ 4096 DO          5 IF(I .LE. 4096)THEN
    print I                    PRINT*, I
    I = I*2                    I = 2*I
ENDWHILE                      GO TO 5
                           ENDIF
```

c.
```
K = 1                      PARAMETER (K=1, I=1)
I = 1                      5 IF(I .LE. 100)THEN
WHILE I ≤ 100 DO               L = K*I
    print K*I                  PRINT*, L
    K = K-1                    K = -K
    I = I+1                    I = I+1
ENDWHILE                      GO TO 5
                           ENDIF
```

d.
```
  read N
  I = N
  WHILE I ≥ 1 DO
      print I
      I = I − 1
  ENDWHILE
```

```
      READ*, N
      I = N
5   IF(I .GE. 1)THEN
         PRINT*, I
         I = I − 1
         GO TO 5
      ENDIF
```

7.
```
WHILE end-of-file-not-encountered DO
      read emp no, base pay, emp time, class, rating
      IF emp time < .5 THEN
          write 'no bonus'
      ELSE
          IF rating = 1 THEN
              IF class = 1 THEN
                  bonus = base pay/52
              ELSE
                  bonus = .2*base pay/12
              ENDIF
              IF emp time > 10 THEN
                  bonus = bonus + 400
              ENDIF
          ELSE
              IF class = 1 THEN
                  bonus = base pay/240
              ELSE
                  bonus = .05*base pay/12
              ENDIF
          ENDIF
      ENDIF
ENDWHILE
```

8.
```
    READ(5,*)I
    IF(I.LT.-99 OR I.GT.99)STOP
    WRITE(6,*)I
    READ(5,*)K
10  IF(K.GE.-99 .AND. K.LE.99)THEN
        WRITE(6,*)K
        IF(K .NE. 0)THEN
            IF(I*K .LT. 0)STOP
                I=K
        ENDIF
        READ(5,*)K
        GO TO 10
    ENDIF
    STOP
```

```
9.      CHARACTER*8 NAME
        INTEGER FM,FF,SM,SF,AGE,CLASS,SEX
        FM=0
        FF=0
        SM=0
        SF=0
        READ(5,*)NAME,AGE,SEX,CLASS
   10 IF(SEX .LT. 0)THEN
            IF(AGE .GT. 21)WRITE(6,*)NAME
            IF(CLASS .EQ. 1 .AND. SEX .EQ. 1)FM=FM+1
            IF(CLASS .EQ. 1 .AND. SEX .EQ. 2)FF=FF+1
            IF(CLASS .EQ. 2 .AND. SEX .EQ. 1)SM=SM+1
            IF(CLASS .EQ. 2 .AND. SEX .EQ. 2)SF=SF+1
            READ(5,*)NAME,AGE,SEX,CLASS
            GO TO 10
        ENDIF
    5 WRITE(6,*)FM,FF,SM,SF
    8 STOP
        END
```

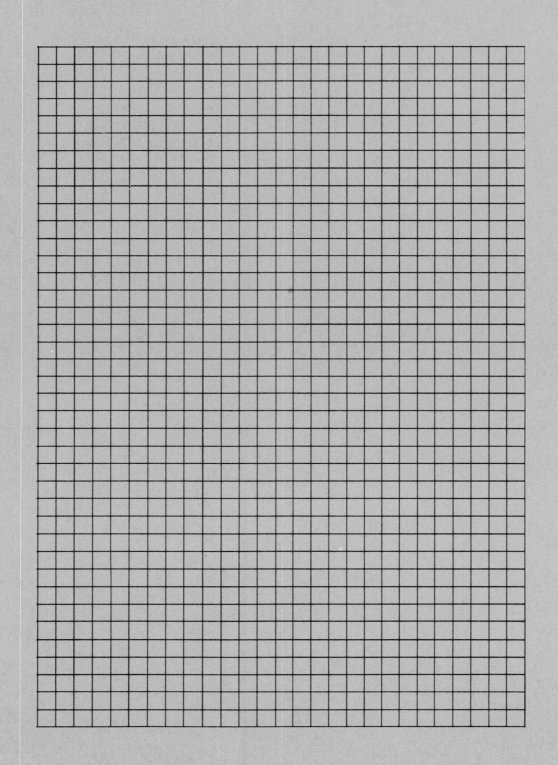

Automatic End of File, DO Structure, Programming Techniques

4.1 PROGRAMMING EXAMPLE

Problem Specification. An input file consists of various class rosters. Each roster starts with a header record identifying the course name and the number of students enrolled in that course (see the sample input file below). Following the header record are the student records (names and scores) for that particular class. Write a program to produce a report similar to the one shown below:

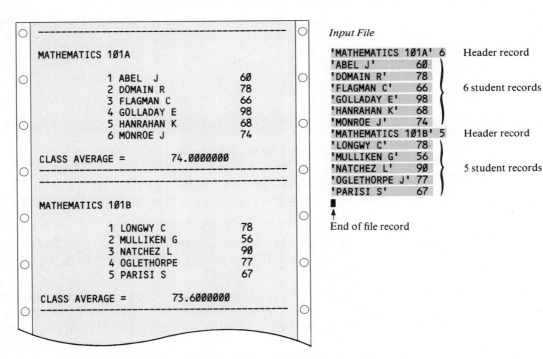

```
-----------------------------------------------

MATHEMATICS 101A

              1 ABEL    J            60
              2 DOMAIN R             78
              3 FLAGMAN C            66
              4 GOLLADAY E           98
              5 HANRAHAN K           68
              6 MONROE J             74

CLASS AVERAGE =        74.0000000
-----------------------------------------------
-----------------------------------------------

MATHEMATICS 101B

              1 LONGWY C             78
              2 MULLIKEN G           56
              3 NATCHEZ L            90
              4 OGLETHORPE           77
              5 PARISI S             67

CLASS AVERAGE =        73.6000000
-----------------------------------------------
```

Input File

```
'MATHEMATICS 101A' 6      Header record
'ABEL J'        60
'DOMAIN R'      78
'FLAGMAN C'     66        6 student records
'GOLLADAY E'    98
'HANRAHAN K'    68
'MONROE J'      74
'MATHEMATICS 101B' 5      Header record
'LONGWY C'      78
'MULLIKEN G'    56
'NATCHEZ L'     90        5 student records
'OGLETHORPE J' 77
'PARISI S'      67
■
↑
End of file record
```

Notice the following features of the output:

■ Dotted lines are printed to act as visual separators between class reports.

■ The header record titles each report.

■ Student records are numbered automatically by the program.

■ The class averages are computed for each class.

The solution to this problem is shown in Figure 4.1. Note the following elements of the FORTRAN language:

1. The DATA statement (line 5) is used to initialize variables to specific values.

2. The END= option in the READ statement (line 7) tells the system what FORTRAN statement to go to in the event of an end-of-file interrupt.

3. The DO and CONTINUE statements (lines 14 and 19) are used for loop control. The statements between the DO and the CONTINUE statements (lines 15–18) are carried out a number of times equal to COUNT, since INDEX goes from 1 to COUNT in increments of 1. The value of COUNT is read from the header record, and thus INDEX takes on values 1, 2, 3, ... up to COUNT. The value of INDEX is printed each time through the loop to provide a numeric label for each student.

Questions.

1. The END= option is missing in the READ statement at line 16. Is this cause for concern? Explain your answer.

2. Add the code to compute the score average of all classes.

4.2 AUTOMATIC END-OF-FILE PROCESSING

The prime READ method used in chapter 3 requires a sentinel record at the very end of the input file and thus leaves itself open to two types of problems:

1. What happens if the sentinel record is inadvertently omitted from the file?

2. What happens if an unknown input file is to be read? Or what happens if our program is to read an input file that is shared by other programs that do not use the prime READ method?

Recall that the last physical record of an input file is an end-of-file mark placed there by the system when the data file is saved onto disk. If this end-of-file mark is read and the END= option is not present in the READ statement, the system terminates execution of the program with an error diagnostic—an unacceptable way to terminate a program. If the END= option is used (automatic end-of-file processing), the system transfers control to the designated statement.

In Figure 4.2, the automatic end-of-file technique is used to process an input file. Note that only one READ statement is used. The pseudo code representation of the automatic end-of-file is somewhat awkward, since statement numbers are not used in pseudo code, but we need to transfer from the READ statement to another statement in the program. Thus we use the conventional but informal expression WHILE not end of file DO, as shown in Figure 4.2.

```
 1: ****COMPUTING CLASS AVERAGES
 2:        CHARACTER LINE*45,NAME*10,HEADER*16
 3:        REAL AVRGE,SUM,COUNT,SCORE
 4:        INTEGER INDEX
 5:        DATA SUM,LINE/0.0, '------------------------------------------'/
 6: ****READ CLASS HEADER RECORDS
 7: 10     READ(5,*,END=90)HEADER,COUNT
 8:        WRITE(6,*)LINE
 9:        WRITE(6,*)
10:        WRITE(6,*)HEADER
11:        WRITE(6,*)
12:        SUM = 0.
13: *
14:        DO 20 INDEX = 1, COUNT
15: ****READ INDIVIDUAL STUDENT NAME & SCORES
16:          READ(5,*)NAME, SCORE
17:          SUM = SUM + SCORE
18:          WRITE(6,*)INDEX, ' ', NAME, SCORE
19: 20     CONTINUE
20: *
21:        AVRGE = SUM/COUNT
22:        WRITE(6,*)
23:        WRITE(6,*)'CLASS AVERAGE =', AVRGE
24:        WRITE(6,*)LINE
25:        GO TO 10
26: 90     STOP
27:        END
```

```
---------------------------------------------

MATHEMATICS 101A


          1 ABEL    J         60
          2 DOMAIN R          78
          3 FLAGMAN C          66
          4 GOLLADAY E         98
          5 HANRAHAN K         68
          6 MONROE J          74

CLASS AVERAGE =       74.0000000
---------------------------------------------
---------------------------------------------

MATHEMATICS 101B


          1 LONGWY C          78
          2 MULLIKEN G         56
          3 NATCHEZ L          90
          4 OGLETHORPE        77
          5 PARISI S          67

CLASS AVERAGE =       73.6000000
---------------------------------------------
```

Input File

'MATHEMATICS 101A'	6	Header record
'ABEL J'	60	
'DOMAIN R'	78	
'FLAGMAN C'	66	6 class records
'GOLLADAY E'	98	
'HANRAHAN K'	68	
'MONROE J'	74	
'MATHEMATICS 101B'	5	Header record
'LONGWY C'	78	
'MULLIKEN G'	56	
'NATCHEZ L'	90	5 class records
'OGLETHORPE J'	77	
'PARISI S'	67	

↑
Physical end of file

FIGURE 4.1
AN EXAMPLE OF A DO LOOP

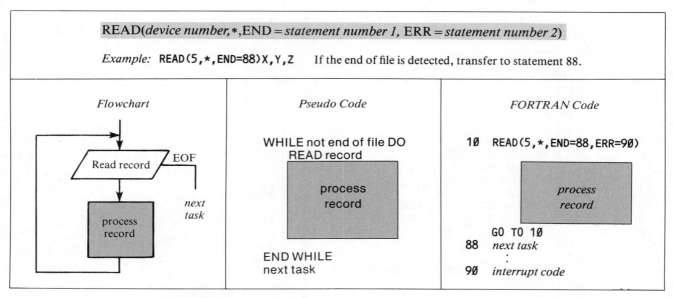

FIGURE 4.2
THE AUTOMATIC END-OF-FILE PROCESS

4.3 DO LOOPS AND THE DATA STATEMENT

4.3.1 The DO/
CONTINUE Loop
Structure

The DO structure represents no new programming concept. In fact, any FORTRAN program can be written without the DO structure. The purpose of the DO is strictly one of convenience to the programmer. It is used primarily for loop control to count the number of times a particular task is to be carried out. Our previous procedure for loop control was to initialize a counter to a certain value, test the counter against a terminal value for loop exit in the WHILE DO statement, and increment the counter within the loop. With the DO structure, these three actions can be specified in just one statement.

The general form of the DO structure and its FORTRAN implementation are:

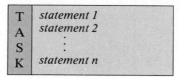

where   *index* is an integer variable that essentially counts the number of times the task will be carried out. Many compilers allow the index to be real.

test is an integer constant or variable against which the index is tested to determine whether or not the task should be repeated. Many compilers allow *test* to be an arithmetic expression (integer or real).

increment is an optional integer constant or integer variable specifying the increment to be added to the index after each execution of the task. If the increment is omitted, its value is assumed to be 1. Many compilers allow increment to be an arithmetic expression (integer or real).

CONTINUE identifies the last statement of the task, thus adding readability, visual clarity, and documentation to the program code. Its statement number corresponds to the statement number specified in the DO statement. All statements between the DO and CONTINUE statements are carried out as many times as dictated by the index.

Caution

1. The increment must not evaluate to 0.

2. The index should not be altered by any statement in the task to be carried out.

(See Appendix A for a discussion of the DO loop in a nonstructured environment.)

Figure 4.3 contains two pseudo code equivalents of a FORTRAN DO structure showing how the index is tested and incremented for positive and negative increments. A more complete discussion of the way in which FORTRAN formally treats the index is found in question 2, section 4.6. In essence, if the increment is positive, the index counts "up"; if the increment is negative, it counts "down." When counting "up," the task is processed once for each value taken on by the index, which takes on values ranging from the initial value up to the last value not greater than *test,* going up in steps of *increment.* The task consists of all statements between the DO statement and

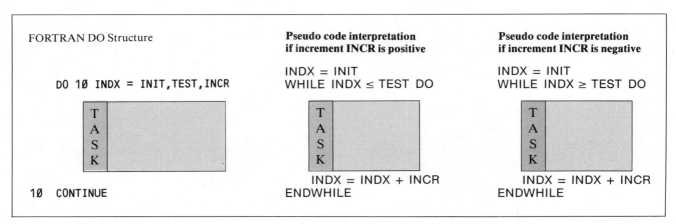

FIGURE 4.3
PSEUDO CODE INTERPRETATION OF THE DO STRUCTURE

the CONTINUE statement. In the following example, the READ and WRITE statements will be carried out 303 times.

EXAMPLE

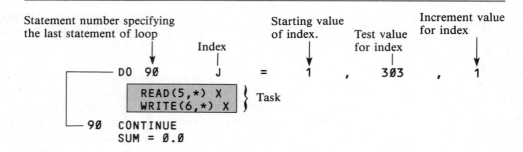

To improve readability, the set of statements corresponding to the task should be indented to the right of the DO and CONTINUE statements.

The following examples illustrate the counting mechanism of the DO statement.

EXAMPLES

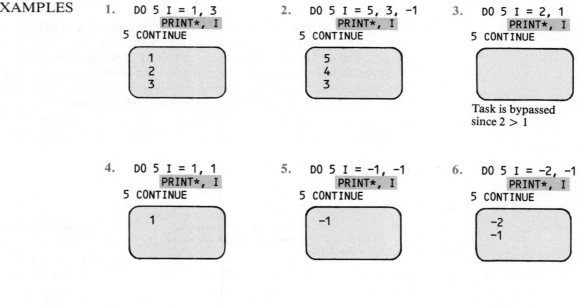

1.
```
DO 5 I = 1, 3
   PRINT*, I
5 CONTINUE
```
```
1
2
3
```

2.
```
DO 5 I = 5, 3, -1
   PRINT*, I
5 CONTINUE
```
```
5
4
3
```

3.
```
DO 5 I = 2, 1
   PRINT*, I
5 CONTINUE
```

Task is bypassed
since 2 > 1

4.
```
DO 5 I = 1, 1
   PRINT*, I
5 CONTINUE
```
```
1
```

5.
```
DO 5 I = -1, -1
   PRINT*, I
5 CONTINUE
```
```
-1
```

6.
```
DO 5 I = -2, -1
   PRINT*, I
5 CONTINUE
```
```
-2
-1
```

7.
```
DO 5 I = -1, -1, -1
   PRINT*, I
5 CONTINUE
```
```
-1
```

8.
```
DO 5 I = -2, -1, -1
   PRINT*, I
5 CONTINUE
```

9.
```
DO 5 X = .5, 1.3, .3
   PRINT*, X
5 CONTINUE
```
```
.5
.8
1.1
```

Sometimes it is convenient to use the index not just as a counting mechanism for loop control but also as a variable (number generator) within the body of the DO loop:

```
DO 15 I = 3,100,2              This code will generate a table of
    ISQRED = I*I               the square root and the squares of
    SQROOT = I**.5             3, 5, 7, ..., 99
    WRITE(6,*)I,ISQRED, SQROOT
15 CONTINUE
```

It is often convenient to express the terminal value of a DO loop as a variable:

```
READ(5,*)N
DO 15 K = 1,N
                    . The task will be repeated N times.
15 CONTINUE
```

The initial, terminal, and increment values can all be expressed as variables:

```
READ(5,*)N,M,INC    Section 4.6 shows how to determine the number of times
DO 15 L=N,M,INC     the task will be executed.

15 CONTINUE
```

It is very important not to change the value of the index while in the DO loop, since this would affect the counting mechanism of the loop:

```
DO 15 J = N1, T1, I1
    J = L + 1  ◄──────── Invalid; the value of the index J is changed.
    K = K * J
15 CONTINUE
```

If the loop goes through its complete cycle, the value of the index during the last pass will be different than the value of the index once exit has been taken from the loop. The difference between them is the increment value (see Figure 4.3). Thus in the following example the final value of INDX at line 6 is 3.

```
DO 5 INDX = 1, 2            1
    PRINT*, INDX ─────────► 2
5 CONTINUE
6 PRINT*, INDX ─────────►   3    ──Value of INDX outside loop
                                   is well defined.
```

The DO loop can be used to process input files containing an unknown number of records, although the sentinel method and the method shown in Figure 4.2 are preferable. Since a test value must be provided for the index of the DO statement, we choose a test value that exceeds the number of records to be read. For example, to process a file having anywhere from 1 to 999 records, we could use the following code:

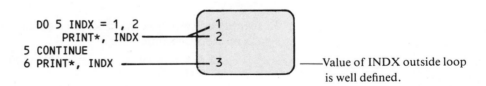

```
DO 5   I = 1, 1000
    READ(5,*, END=88)      The end option of the READ statement will force an
    process record          end-of-file exit from the loop to statement 88. Since it
                            is known that there are a maximum of 999 records.
5 CONTINUE
88 WRITE(6,*)I              I = number of records + 1
```

Note that value of I will be one more than the number of records read, due to the end-of-file record is read. For example, if the file consisted of 64 records, the value of I would be 65.

Decision structures can be part of a DO structure.

EXAMPLE   Each record of a class file (no more than 100 records) contains a score and a sex field (1 = female, 2 = male). Write the FORTRAN code to compute the class score average as well as the score average of all the females.

```
      REAL CLASUM, FEMSUM, CLASAV, FEMAV
      INTEGER STUDNT,SEX,AGE,FEMCT
      DATA FEMSUM,CLASUM,FEMCT/0.,0.,0/
      DO 5  STUDNT = 1, 101              Force an end-of-file transfer.
         READ(5,*,END=88)SCORE,SEX
         IF(SEX .EQ. 1)THEN
            FEMSUM = FEMSUM + SCORE      Accumulate female scores.
            FEMCT  = FEMCT + 1           Count female scores.
         ENDIF
         CLASUM=CLASUM+SCORE
    5 CONTINUE
   88 CLASAV = CLASUM/(STUDNT-1)         Divide by number of records − 1.
      FEMAV  = FEMSUM/FEMCT
```

4.3.2 Do It Now

1. Write the WHILE DO pseudo code to represent the following DO loops:

a.
```
   DO 5 I = 1,3
      PRINT*,I
 5 CONTINUE
```

b.
```
   DO 5 K = 10,5,-2
      PRINT*,K
 5 CONTINUE
```

2. Identify the values taken on by the index in the following examples:

a. `DO 5 X = -2., 2.3, .5`   **b.** `DO 5 I = -3, -4`

c. `DO 5 I = 0, 2`   **d.** `DO 5 I = 3/2, 8/3, 3`

3. Identify any errors in the following coding segments (specify whether they are syntax or execution-time errors):

a.
```
   DO 5 K = -2,N
      PRINT*,K
 5 CONTINUE
```

b.
```
   DO 5 L = 2,3,9
      READ*,J,K,L
      PRINT*,J,K,L
 5 CONTINUE
```

4. What output is produced by the following DO structures?

a.
```
   DO 5 L = 1,4
      PRINT*,L,L**2,L**.5
 5 CONTINUE
```

b.
```
   DO 5 L = 2,21,3
      PRINT*,L
 5 CONTINUE
```

c.
```
   DO 5 T = 3.,1.
      X = T + 1
      PRINT*,X
 5 CONTINUE
```

d.
```
   DO 5 T = 1., -1., -.5
      X = 10. - T
      PRINT*,X
 5 CONTINUE
```

5. Using a DO structure, write the code to generate the following sequences of numbers:

    a. 1, 3, 5, 7, ..., 51

    b. $-10, -9, -8, ..., -1$

    c. $5^2, 6^2, 7^2, ..., 21^2$

    d. 1., .5, .333, ..., 0.010101.. (same as 1., 1./2., 1./3., ..., 1./99.)

6. Using a DO loop, write the code to compute the value of the following expressions:

    a. 1*2*3*4 ... * 16 i.e., 16!

    b. 5 + 10 + 15 + ... + 675

    c. $-1 - 2 - 3 - ... - 17$

    d. 1. + 1./2. + 1./3. ... + 1./100.

    e. 1 + (1 + 2) + (1 + 2 + 3) + ... + (1 + 2 + 3 + 4 ... + 99 + 100)

7. What sum of numbers does the following coding segment compute?

```
   M = 0
   DO 5 K = 1,10
      M = M - (-1)**K * K
 5 CONTINUE
   PRINT*,M
```

8. Using a DO structure, write the FORTRAN code to print all values of x in the range 1 to 10 such that $|x^2 - 3x\sqrt{2} + 4| < 0.1$ [Use increments of .1]. If there are no such values, print an appropriate message.

Answers to Selected Problems

1. a. Set I to 1
    WHILE I ≤ 3 DO
        print*,I
        add 1 to I
    ENDWHILE

    b. Set K to 10
    WHILE K ≥ 5 DO
        print*,K
        add −2 to K
    ENDWHILE

2. a. $-2., -1.5, -1., -.5, 0, .5, 1., 1.5, 2.$

    b. The loop will not be executed since $-3 > -4$

    c. 0, 1, 2

    d. 1

3. a. Statement 16 is undefined (syntax error).

    b. The value of the index L is changed by the READ statement which will cause the loop process to function erratically.

4. a.
```
1    1    1
2    4    1
3    9    1
4   16    2
```

    b. 2, 5, 8, 11, 14, 17, 20

    c. Nothing is printed since the starting value of the index is greater than the terminal value.

    d. 9., 9.5, 10., 10.5, 11.

5. a.
```
   DO 5 I = 1, 51, 2
      PRINT*,I
 5 CONTINUE
```
b.
```
   DO 5 I = -10, -1
      PRINT*,I
 5 CONTINUE
```

c.
```
   DO 5 I = 5, 21
      K = I**2
      PRINT*,K
 5 CONTINUE
```
d.
```
   DO 5 T = 1. 99
      X = 1./T
      PRINT*,X
 5 CONTINUE
```

6. b.
```
   SUM = 0.
   DO 5 I = 5,675,5
      SUM = SUM + I
 5 CONTINUE
   PRINT*,SUM
```
c.
```
   SUM = 0.
   DO 5 I = -1,-17,-1
      SUM = SUM + I
 5 CONTINUE
   PRINT*,SUM
```

d.
```
   SUM = 0.
   DO 5 I = 1,100
      SUM = SUM + 1./I
 5 CONTINUE
   PRINT*,SUM
```
e.
```
   SUM = 0.
   BIGSUM = 0.
   DO 5 I = 1,100
      SUM = SUM + I
      BIGSUM = BIGSUM + SUM
 5 CONTINUE
   PRINT*,BIGSUM
```

7. b. $M = 1 - 2 + 3 - 4 + \ldots + 9 - 10 = -5$

8. Values printed for X are 1.4 and 2.8

```
      INTEGER FLAG
      FLAG = 0
      DO 5 I = 10, 100
         X = FLOAT(I)/10.0
         IF(ABS(X**2 - 3.0*X*SQRT(2.0) + 4.0) .LT. 0.1)THEN
            WRITE(*,*)X
            FLAG = 1
         ENDIF
 5 CONTINUE
      IF(FLAG .EQ. 0)WRITE(*,*)'NO VALUES FOR X'
```

4.3.3 The DO Structure in the Context of Structured Programming

Recall that the basic principles of good structured designs rest on the proper utilization of the three control structures: the sequence, the decision, and the loop structures. The use of these and only these three structures ensures a standardized code in which each structure has only one entry and one exit point. This characteristic lies at the heart of structured programming and makes it possible to move from one task to the next in a very fluid and continuous fashion. Each task is structurally self-contained and independent of the one above or below it. The ENDIF, ENDWHILE and CONTINUE clearly delineate completed tasks while paving the way for new tasks to start.

Historically, the DO structure predates the IF THEN ELSE and the WHILE DO control structures by at least 20 years. Partly for that reason, the DO structure does not have the structural allure of these newer control structures; thus, if used casually, the DO structure can seriously flaw a program design. The DO structure is a good choice for carrying out a task a fixed number of times, but it is not generally recommended if it must contain conditional statements (IF/GO TO or GO TO statements) that transfer control to various statements outside the loop in the following way:

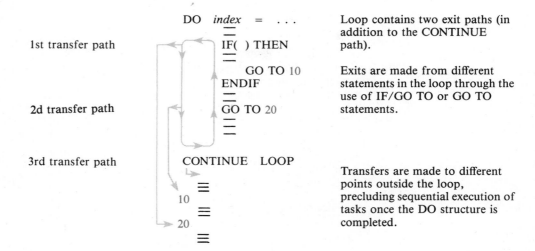

Loop contains two exit paths (in addition to the CONTINUE path).

Exits are made from different statements in the loop through the use of IF/GO TO or GO TO statements.

Transfers are made to different points outside the loop, precluding sequential execution of tasks once the DO structure is completed.

To avoid such multiplicity of paths, the novice programmer is advised to use a WHILE DO structure whenever exit from a loop depends on more than one condition. Using a WHILE DO structure will improve readability and lessen confusion, since *all* conditions can be grouped together in the WHILE DO header statement instead of being scattered throughout a DO structure. In keeping with the principles of good structured design, the WHILE DO structure sports only one exit point.

Remember that if an IF/GO TO or a GO TO statement is used to transfer out of a DO structure, more numeric labels must be created to identify the targets of the GO TO statements. This nurtures a favorable environment for the breeding of spaghetti code—more statement numbers, with an increased chance that some of them will be forgotton in rewrites of the code, not to mention potential disaster if the order of the external statements is changed! One could also argue that the DO loop structure is misleading if a premature exit from it is made, since it does not fulfill its contract of carrying out a task a particular number of times as specified by the DO header statement.

To illustrate the weaknesses of the DO structure, consider the following situation:

One of Man Friday's personnel files contains exactly 100 records; each record contains an employee name, an occupation, and the employee's telephone number. The manager has been asked to obtain the telephone number of the first teacher encountered in the file. If a teacher is found, the program is to print the telephone number and then proceed immediately with task 1; if no teacher is found, an appropriate message is printed and the program is directed to task 2 (search another file, perhaps).

Two solutions are offered; analyze them in terms of readability and structure:

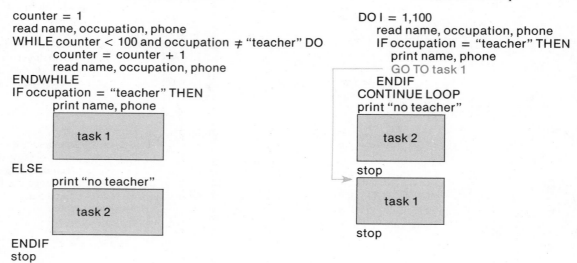

Version 1: WHILE DO

```
counter = 1
read name, occupation, phone
WHILE counter < 100 and occupation ≠ "teacher" DO
        counter = counter + 1
        read name, occupation, phone
ENDWHILE
IF occupation = "teacher" THEN
        print name, phone
```

task 1

```
ELSE
        print "no teacher"
```

task 2

```
ENDIF
stop
```

Version 2: DO Loop

```
DO I = 1,100
        read name, occupation, phone
        IF occupation = "teacher" THEN
                print name, phone
                GO TO task 1
        ENDIF
CONTINUE LOOP
print "no teacher"
```

task 2

stop

task 1

stop

The DO loop version does not have a streamlined design where tasks are carried out sequentially. The code is difficult to read, and the statement *print "no teacher"* must be placed right after the CONTINUE LOOP, since at this juncture, 100 records have been read. If a teacher is found, a GO TO statement must be used to branch out of the loop—this is difficult to do in pseudo code, since line numbers are not allowed (an arrow is used here for the target statement). (Imagine what the pseudo code would look like if more arrows were used with other GO TO statements!) Furthermore, the DO statement is misleading, since the loop **may not** actually be carried out 100 times.

The corresponding WHILE DO statement is very explicit—both conditions are stated at the outset, with no surprise branch later on. In the WHILE DO version, when exit is made out of the loop, the question is asked whether a teacher was found—if the answer is affirmative, task 1 is carried out and if no teacher was found, task 2 is carried out. The logical path in this case is simple and clear!

Once again, in general, it is preferable to use a WHILE DO structure instead of a DO structure whenever a task is not to be carried out a fixed number of times.

4.3.4 Nested DO Structures

Just as WHILE DO and decision structures can be nested within one another, DO structures can also be nested within other DO structures, or for that matter, within WHILE DO or decision structures. The important point to keep in mind is that the nested structure must be wholly contained (header and terminal statement) within the "mother" structure.

Figure 4.4 illustrates different types of imbedded structures.

Once again, control structures must be accessed sequentially. Transfer into a structure should be made only at the header statement of the structure, i.e., the following transfers are invalid:

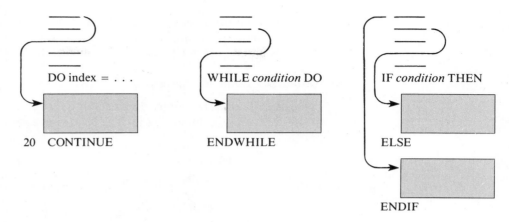

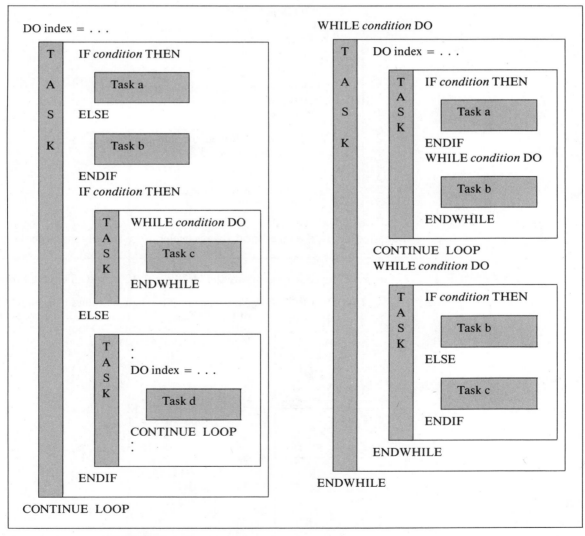

FIGURE 4.4
EXAMPLES OF NESTED STRUCTURES

These diagrams presuppose that IF GO TO or GO TO statements are used. As a general rule, these statements should be used as little as possible—one exception, of course, is the GO TO statement used to simulate the WHILE DO structure.

Nested DO Loop Mechanism

In the case of nested DO loops, each pass through the outer loop causes the inner loop to run through its complete cycle. The following code illustrates the mechanism of nested loops:

Outer loop.
Since I varies from 1 to 3,
the inner loop will be
processed three times.

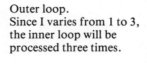

```
DO 20 I = 1,3
   DO 10 J = 1,4
      WRITE(6,*)I,J
10 CONTINUE

20 CONTINUE
```

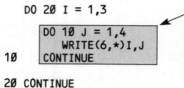

Inner loop.
The inner loop causes the WRITE
statement to be processed four times. Since
the outer loop is processed three times, the
WRITE statement will be processed
altogether 12 times.

This code will produce

I	J	
1	1	First time through the inner loop (outer loop index I = 1).
1	2	
1	3	
1	4	
2	1	Second time through the inner loop (outer loop index I = 2).
2	2	
2	3	
2	4	
3	1	Third time through the inner loop (outer loop index I = 3).
3	2	
3	3	
3	4	

In nested loops, the inner loop always cycles more rapidly than the outer loop.

EXAMPLE 1   Let us write the code to generate the 1's, 2's, ..., 12's multiplication tables.

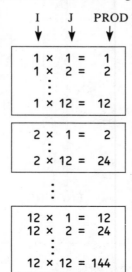

Note that J runs through the values 1 through 12 for each value of I, while I also cycles from 1 to 12 in increments of 1. Therefore we construct an outer DO loop with index I and an inner loop with index J, as follows:

```
INTEGER PROD
DO 10 I = 1, 12
   DO 20 J = 1, 12
      PROD = I*J
      WRITE(6,*)I, 'X', J, '=', PROD
20    CONTINUE
   WRITE(6,*)
10 CONTINUE
```

Note that the WRITE statement after the inner loop prints a blank line between the individual multiplication tables.

EXAMPLE 2   Let us write the code to print a table of monthly mortgage payments like the one below for $60,000, $70,000, and $80,000 homes at interest rates of 11.5, 12.5, and 13.5% over a 30-year period. The formula to compute a monthly mortgage is:

$$\frac{amount*interest\ rate/12}{1-(1/(1+interest\ rate/12))^{years*12}}$$

Looking at the output, we see that we will need two DO loops: an outer loop (line 4) to control the varying mortgage amounts and an inner loop (line 5) to control the varying interest rates. Note how the interest rates are expressed as fractional values (.115, .125, .135) at line 6 for computation purposes and as percentages (11.5, 12.5, 13.5) at line 10 for the printout.

```
1:        INTEGER YRS,AMOUNT,RATE
2:        REAL INTRST,CONST,MONTLY,TOTAL,INTRAT
3:        YRS = 30
4:        DO 10 AMOUNT = 60000,80000,10000
5:           DO 20 RATE = 1150,1350,100
6:              INTRST = RATE/10000.0
7:              CONST  = INTRST/12.0
8:              MONTLY = (AMOUNT*CONST)/(1.0-(1.0/(1.0+CONST))**(YRS*12))
9:              TOTAL  = 12.0*YRS*MONTLY
10:             INTRAT = RATE/100.0
11:             WRITE(*,*)AMOUNT,INTRAT,MONTLY,TOTAL
12: 20       CONTINUE
13:          WRITE(*,*)
14: 10    CONTINUE
15:       STOP
16:       END
```

Mortgage amount	Interest rate	Monthly payment	Total payment
60000	11.5000000	594.1746000	213902.9000000
60000	12.5000000	640.3550000	230527.8000000
60000	13.5000000	687.2473000	247409.0000000
70000	11.5000000	693.2038000	249553.4000000
70000	12.5000000	747.0809000	268949.1000000
70000	13.5000000	801.7886000	288643.9000000
80000	11.5000000	792.2328000	285203.8000000
80000	12.5000000	853.8067000	307370.4000000
80000	13.5000000	916.3298000	329878.7000000

4.3.5 Do It Now

1. How many times will the PRINT statement be executed?

a.
```
   DO 3 I = 2,3
   DO 2 J = 1,4
   DO 1 K = 0,2
      PRINT*,K
1 CONTINUE
2 CONTINUE
3 CONTINUE
```

b.
```
   DO 2 J = 40,60
      DO 1 K = 1,3
         PRINT*,K
1     CONTINUE
2 CONTINUE
```

```
c.   DO 3 I = 2,8,2
         DO 2 J = 1,4
             DO 1 K = 1,4,2
                 PRINT*,K
1            CONTINUE
2        CONTINUE
3 CONTINUE
```

```
d.   DO 5 I = 1,4
         DO 6 J = 2,I
             PRINT*,J
6        CONTINUE
5 CONTINUE
```

2. What output would be produced by each of the following? List all the values taken by I and J during execution of the code.

```
a.       DO 110 I = 2,10,2
             DO 100 J = 1,10
                 WRITE(6,*)I,J
100          CONTINUE
110 CONTINUE
```

```
b.       N = 4
         DO 210 I = 1,N
             DO 200 J = 1,I
                 WRITE(6,*)I,J
200          CONTINUE
210 CONTINUE
```

Answers

1. a. 24; $(2 \times 4 \times 3)$

  b. 63; (21×3)

  c. 32; $(4 \times 4 \times 2)$

  d. 6; $(0, 1, 2, 3)$

2. a.

I	J
2	1
2	2
⋮	⋮
2	10
4	1
4	2
⋮	⋮
4	10
⋮	⋮
10	1
10	2
⋮	⋮
10	10

b.

N	I	J
4	1	1
	2	1
	2	2
	3	1
	3	2
	3	3
	4	1
	4	2
	4	3
	4	4

4.3.6 The DATA Statement

The DATA statement can be used to specify an initial value for a variable. The general form of the DATA statement is:

> DATA *variable list*/*constant list*/[,*variable list*/*constant list*/...]

where   *variable list* is a list of variables separated by commas, and
            constant list is a list of constants separated by commas.
                 PARAMETER constants can be specified in the constant list.

The first variable in the variable list is set to the first value in the constant list, the second variable with the second constant, and so forth. **The number of constants in the constant list must match the number of variables in the variable list, and the type of a variable must match the type of its associated constant.**

The DATA statement should follow such specification statements as the CHARACTER, INTEGER, REAL, and PARAMETER statements. It is recommended (but not necessary) that DATA statements be placed before the first executable statement in the program.

The DATA statement is a nonexecutable statement, i.e., the variables specified by the DATA statement are initialized to their values during the compilation phase. Unlike the variables in a parameter statement, the variables declared in a DATA statement can be reset to different values by replacement statements.

EXAMPLE 1

```
DATA A,J/3.2, 4/
```
The value of A is 3.2 and the value of J is 4 (integer).

Note the agreement in number and type between the variables and constants. J is integer 4 while A is real 3.2.

EXAMPLE 2

The following DATA statements are invalid:

```
INTEGER LL
REAL CODE
DATA A,J,K/3.2,4/        Only two constants for 3 variables!
DATA CODE,LL/0,3.2/      Invalid: type mismatch (missing decimal point after 0).
```

EXAMPLE 3

```
CHARACTER*2,KODE,J,NAME*8
DATA KODE,A,NAME/'MO',3.14,'HILARY'/
```

Memory

KODE: | M | O |

A: 3.14

NAME: | H | I | L | A | R | Y | | |

More than one *variable list/constant list/* can be included in a DATA statement. Repetitions must be separated by a comma as in example 4.

EXAMPLE 4

```
DATA A,B/3.,0./, I,J/1,0/
```

Note the comma.   A is 3.0, B is 0.0, I is 1, and J is 0

Finally, the DATA statement can include repetition factors. Suppose we wanted I, J, and K to be initialized to 0, and A, B, C, and D to be initialized to − 4.1, and NAME1 and NAME2 to 'NAME'. The following statement could be used:

```
CHARACTER*10 NAME1, NAME2
DATA I,J,K/3*0/                    Note the use of the asterisk *
DATA A,B,C,D/4*-4.1/
DATA NAME1,NAME2/2*'NAME'/
```

The asterisks in this context mean repetition, not multiplication.

It is important to remember once again that the DATA statement is a *nonexecutable* statement, that is, the values specified by the DATA statement are initialized during the compilation process. The DATA statement cannot be used during execution to set or reset variables to particular values. The DATA statement can have *no* statement number. Consider the following code:

```
DO 5 K = 1, 3
   DATA R,F/3.0,2.0/
   .
   .
   R = X + 1.0
   .
   .
5 CONTINUE
```

Before the program is executed, the values of R and F are 3.0 and 2.0, respectively. The DATA statement is not carried out at execution time and hence cannot be used to reset variables R and F to 3.0 and 2.0, if R and F have been changed somewhere in the program. Only a replacement or a READ statement can reset R and F to 3. and 2.

4.3.7 Order of FORTRAN statements

New executable FORTRAN statements covered since chapter II are:
Input statement: READ
Decision statements: IF THEN ELSE, If *statement* } chapter III
GO TO statement
WHILE DO
DO/CONTINUE loop; chapter IV
New non-executable statements are:
DATA statement
The current order table of FORTRAN statements is now

Comment statements	PARAMETER and specification statements
	DATA and executable statements
END statement	

4.3.8 Do It Now

1. Consider the following specification statements:

```
INTEGER AA, B2, C, X3
REAL I, J3, L2, B
DATA X3, L2/4, 2.2/
DATA AA, B, B2/4, -6.2, 0/, I, J3/ 2*0.1/
```

What will be the type and initial value of each of the following variables?

a. AA   b. B2

c. C   d. I

e. J3   f. X3

g. L2

2. Given the specification statements

```
REAL A,B,C,D,SEVEN,NBER
INTEGER X,Y,Z
CHARACTER NAME, FIRST
PARAMETER (SEVEN=7.0)
```

identify errors in each of the following DATA statements:

a. DATA/X,Y,Z/1.,2.,3./

b. DATA A,B,C,D/4*0./NAME/'HELLO'/

c. DATA NAME,AB,X,Y/'SEE',2*1., 1,2/

d. DATA X,A,B/3,2.3,'CLOSE'/

e. DATA A,B,D,Y,Z/1.1,2.2,3.,4/, NBER/SEVEN/

Answers

1. a. AA   integer   4   b. B2   integer   0

   c. C   integer   unknown value   d. I   real   0.1

   e. J3   real   0.1   f. X3   integer   4

   g. L2   real   2.2

2. a. First slash is illegal; also, X,Y,Z are integer and the constant list contains real numbers.

   b. Missing comma after second slash. NAME is just one character (HELLO will be truncated to H).

   c. There are four variables but five constants. The character S will be stored in NAME. X is an integer but is assigned the real value 1.

   d. B is not a character constant.

   e. Insufficient number of constants for the variables A, B, D, Y and Z.

4.4 PROGRAMMING TECHNIQUES

Writing a program means decomposing a problem into parts and then selecting appropriate coding techniques for each part. Thus, programming is a finite art: the experienced programmer chooses from his/her pool of coding techniques those techniques best suited for the task, in much the same way that the artist selects the appropriate color from his/her palette. This section describes techniques that are likely to surface in many different problems.

4.4.1 Search for a Maximum/Minimum

It is often necessary to go through a list of values to identify the largest or smallest value in that list. To illustrate such a search technique, consider the following problem:

An input file consists of an unknown number of scores.
Write the code to determine the highest score.

To determine the highest score we must compare each new score with the highest score found so far (let us use the variable name *maximum* for the highest score). In general, if *maximum* is less than the score just read, we replace *maximum* with the new score; otherwise, we keep on reading scores until we find one that is larger than *maximum* (if there is one). When the end of file is encountered, *maximum* is the highest score.

To start the comparison between *maximum* and the other scores, we read the first score in a separate READ statement and call that value *maximum*. (After all, if there were only one score, then *maximum* would be that score.) All other scores are then read by another READ statement.

There are two options:

Option 1: Prime Read Method

```
read score                              INTEGER MXIMUM,SCORE
maximum = score                         READ(5,*)SCORE
WHILE score > 0 DO                      MXIMUM = SCORE
    IF score > maximum THEN        10 IF(SCORE .GT. 0)THEN
        maximum = score                    IF(SCORE .GT. MXIMUM)MXIMUM=SCORE
    ENDIF                                  READ(5,*)SCORE
    read score                             GO TO 10
ENDWHILE                                ENDIF
print maximum                           WRITE(6,*)MXIMUM
```

Option 2: Automatic End of File

```
read maximum                            INTEGER MXIMUM, SCORE
WHILE end of file not encountered DO    READ(5,*,) MXIMUM
    read score                     10 READ(5,*,END=88)SCORE
    IF score > maximum THEN             IF(SCORE .GT. MXIMUM)MXIMUM=SCORE
        maximum = score                 GO TO 10
    ENDIF                          88 WRITE(6,*)
ENDWHILE
print maximum
```

Question. In both options, could we have replaced the first READ statement by the statement MAX = 100? by MAX = 0? by MAX = −10?

4.4.2 Switch or Flag Setting

Sometimes it is necessary to carry out a particular task and then, after that task is completed, determine whether a particular condition prevailed throughout the execution of the task (see example 1 below). In another situation we may need to carry out a subtask within a task one time and then bypass it for the rest of the application (see example 2). Flags or switches are useful in both of these situations.

EXAMPLE 1   An input file consists of temperature readings. Compute the temperature average and determine whether all temperatures read were above 32.

Solution. Either all temperatures will exceed 32 degrees, or they won't (i.e., some will be 32 or less). Let us assume that all will exceed 32 before we even start reading the temperatures. We do this by setting a flag or switch equal to the value "ALL OVER 32". Then we start reading the temperatures. If any temperature read is 32 or less, we change the value of the flag to "NOT ALL OVER 32". When all temperatures have been read, we determine the value of the flag and print the appropriate message.

```
      CHARACTER FLAG*15
      INTEGER COUNT
      REAL SUM,TEMP
      COUNT = 0
      SUM   = 0
      FLAG  = 'ALL OVER 32'
   10 READ(5,*,END=88)TEMP
         SUM   = SUM+TEMP
         COUNT = COUNT+1
         IF(TEMP .LE. 32) FLAG = 'NOT ALL OVER 32'
      GO TO 10
   88 AVRGE = SUM/COUNT
      IF(FLAG .EQ. 'ALL OVER 32')THEN
         WRITE(6,*)'ALL TEMPERATURES EXCEED 32'
      ELSE
         WRITE(6,*)'NOT ALL TEMPERATURES EXCEED 32'
      ENDIF
```

EXAMPLE 2   Given a personnel file, write the code to compute the percentage of employees whose earnings are over $25,000 and print the name of the very first employee with earnings in excess of $100,000.

Solution. Just as in Example 1, we set a flag to a particular value before we start reading the file. In this case, we set the flag to 0 to indicate that we have not yet come across a $100,000 earnings. We then read each record. If a $100,000 earnings is encountered, we print the employee's name and set the flag to 1. Then, when the value of the flag is tested, the code that prints the name of the first person whose earnings exceed $100,000 is bypassed.

```
      CHARACTER NAME*10
      REAL EARNIN, PERCNT
      INTEGER FLAG, COUNT, OVER25
      OVER25 = 0
      COUNT  = 0
      FLAG   = 0                        Set the flag to 0, meaning that so
   10 READ(5,*,END=88)NAME,EARNIN       far we have not encountered a
         COUNT = COUNT + 1              $100,000 earnings!
         IF(FLAG .EQ. 0)THEN
            IF(EARNIN .GT. 100000.)THEN  This code is carried out until an
               WRITE(6,*)NAME            earnings over $100000 is read,
               FLAG = 1                  then the code bypassed.
            ENDIF
         ENDIF
         IF(EARNIN .GT. 25000.)OVER25=OVER25+1
         GO TO 10
   88 PERCNT = (100.0*OVER25)/COUNT
```

EXAMPLE 3

Read an integer number N (no more than eight digits) and print its corresponding digits (excluding leading zeros) one digit per line.

To illustrate the decomposition process on N = 2034, we integer-divide 2034 by 1000 to get a quotient of 2 (the first digit). To obtain the remainder, we multiply the quotient 2 by 1000 (2000) and subtract it from 2034 to get 034. We then integer divide 034 by 100 to get a quotient of 0 (the second digit) and a remainder of 34 ($034 - 0 \times 100$). We then divide 34 by 10 to get 3 (the third digit), and continue the process. The entire process consists of following sequence of operations:

$$
\begin{aligned}
2034/1000 &= 2 \quad \text{and a remainder of 34 (integer division)} \\
34/100 &= 0 \quad \text{and a remainder of 34} \\
34/10 &= 3 \quad \text{and a remainder of 4} \\
4/1 &= 4 \quad \text{and a remainder of 0}
\end{aligned}
$$

Thus to process an eight-digit integer we need to divide by 10^7, 10^6, 10^5, ... 10^0. The code to print each digit is as follows:

```
      INTEGER DIGIT, NUMBER
      READ(*,*)NUMBER
      DO 5 I = 7, 0, -1
          DIGIT  = NUMBER/(10**(I))          Divide first by 10⁷, then by 10⁶, etc.
          WRITE(*,*)DIGIT                     Print the digit
          NUMBER = NUMBER - DIGIT*(10**(I))   Compute the remainder and go on to
    5 CONTINUE                                the next digit.
```

Note that this code prints leading zeros as well as nonzero digits. Thus the WRITE statement must be bypassed until the first nonzero digit is encountered, after which all digits are to be printed. A flag (see line 7) is used to prevent the WRITE instruction from being carried out. When the first nonzero digit is encountered, the flag is changed (line 9) to allow the WRITE operation. The complete code is:

```
 1:       CHARACTER ZERO*8
 2:       INTEGER DIGIT,NUMBER
 3:       ZERO = 'LEADING'              Assume the number has leading zeros.
 4:       READ(*,*)NUMBER
 5:       DO 5 I = 7,0,-1
 6:           DIGIT = NUMBER/(10**(I))
 7:           IF(DIGIT .NE. 0 .OR.      If digit is nonzero or if it is an embedded
 8:    1      ZERO .EQ. 'EMBEDDED')THEN zero, print it.
 9:               WRITE(*,*)DIGIT
10:               ZERO = 'EMBEDDED'     From now on print embedded 0's.
11:           ENDIF
12:           NUMBER = NUMBER - DIGIT*(10**(I))
13: 5        CONTINUE
14:       END
```

4.4.3 Sequence Check

A programmer often needs to process lists of names or item numbers that are supposed to be arranged in a particular order (ascending or descending). It is conceivable, though, that some of these items might be out of order. Thus, when processing the list, it may be necessary to perform a *sequence check* and flag (identify) those elements that are out of sequence. Consider the following problem:

An input file contains a list of scores supposedly arranged in ascending order. Write the code to verify that the list is indeed in ascending order. Print all scores, and place an asterisk by those that are out of sequence.

In a list arranged in ascending order, a number is not in sequence if it is smaller than the preceding in-sequence number. To get a preliminary feel for this problem, let us look at a few lists of numbers:

a. 1, 3, 21, 46   All scores are in sequence.

b. 8, 1, 2, 3, 4, 5   All the scores after the first are out of sequence since they are all less than 8! Note that the first score determines the starting point of the sequence, since the computer can only read one number at a time.

c. 15, 18, 13, 21   Out of sequence, since 13 is less than 18.

d. 15, 18, 12, 15, 60   Out of sequence, since 12 < 18 (18 is last number in sequence).
                             Out of sequence, since 15 < 18.

Note that, in example (d), the score 15 is out of sequence even though it *is* in sequence compared to 12. Since 12 is out of sequence, it should *not* be used in determining whether the next score is in sequence.

To determine whether the scores are in ascending order, we check whether the score just read (let's call it NEW) is larger than the previous score (called OLD). This process is repeated for every new score read. If NEW is greater than OLD, then the two scores are in sequence; otherwise NEW is out of sequence. To understand what happens next, consider a specific example:

$$\text{OLD} \quad \text{NEW}$$
$$\downarrow \quad \downarrow$$
$$...15, \ 18, \ 20,...$$

In this case, NEW is greater than OLD, so 15 and 18 are in sequence. What we want to do now is read the next score 20 (which becomes the new NEW!) and ask whether that NEW score is greater than the one we were calling NEW in the previous comparison (18). However, if we read the next score (20) into NEW, we will destroy the value 18! Hence, before we read NEW (20), we need to save 18 into OLD! Then, on the next go-round, we will be comparing NEW with OLD or 20 with 18.

$$\text{OLD} \quad \text{NEW}$$
$$\downarrow \quad \downarrow$$
$$...15, \ 18, \ 20,...$$

If we did *not* set OLD to NEW before reading the next score, the value of OLD would *never* change, and thus we would always compare a new score with the same OLD score (in this case 15)!

What happens now if NEW is less than OLD? For example,

$$\text{OLD} \quad \text{NEW}$$
$$\downarrow \quad \downarrow$$
$$...15, \ 12, \ 14,...$$

In this case, NEW is less than OLD, so 12 is out of sequence! Before we read the next NEW score (14), we do *not* save 12 into OLD. (If we did, then on the next go-round,

NEW (14) would be greater than OLD (12), implying that 14 is in sequence. This is clearly not the case, since any new score read must be greater than the last in-sequence score (15).) Thus when a score is out of order, we leave OLD unchanged.

    To begin the comparison between NEW and OLD, we read the first score independently of all others and assign that value to OLD. We then use a different READ statement to read all remaining NEW scores. The entire process is shown in pseudo code and in FORTRAN in Figure 4.5.

```
* SEQUENCE CHECK                      * SEQUENCE CHECK PROBLEM
* Read first score and call it old score    INTEGER NEW, OLD
  read old score                       READ(5,*)OLD
  write old score                      WRITE(6,*)OLD
  WHILE not end of file DO          10 READ(5,*,END=88)NEW
      read new score                    IF(NEW .GT. OLD)THEN
      IF new score > old score THEN         OLD=NEW
          set old score = new score         WRITE(6,*)NEW
          write new score               ELSE
      ELSE                                  WRITE(6,*)NEW,'**'
          write new score and asterisk  ENDIF
      ENDIF                             GO TO 10
  ENDWHILE                          88 STOP
  stop                                 END
```

FIGURE 4.5
A SEQUENCE CHECK

4.5 PROGRAMMING EXAMPLES

4.5.1 Critical Speed of a Rotating Shaft

Problem Specification. A gear and a pulley are mounted on a rotating shaft 100 inches long and 2.5 inches in diameter, as shown in Figure 4.6. The gear (85 lbs.) can slide into three fixed grooves on the shaft so that it can mesh with other gears in the machine; the gear's three positions are 20, 30, and 40 inches to the right of the left bearing. The pulley itself (130 lbs.) slides into three variable positions on the shaft, 60, 70, and 80 inches to the right of the left bearing, so that it can be belted to a particular mating pulley. Let us write a program to compute the lowest critical speed for each of the nine gear-pulley combinations.

Analysis. The critical speed is the speed of rotation at which the rotating shaft becomes unstable and pronounced vibrations are encountered. That speed is expressed in revolutions per minute and is given by the formula

$$\text{Critical speed} = \frac{60}{2\pi}\sqrt{\frac{g(W_g*D_g + W_p*D_p)}{W_g*D_g^2 + W_p*D_p^2}}$$

where g is the gravitational constant (386 inches/s²)
          W_g is the weight of the gear
          W_p is the weight of the pulley
          D_g and D_p are the static deflection of the gear and pulley

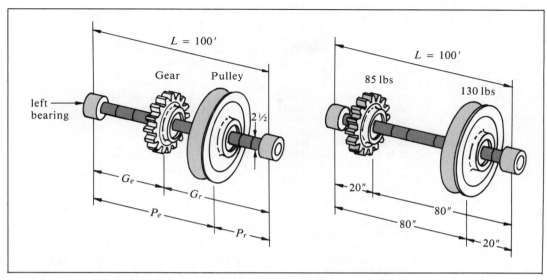

FIGURE 4.6
GEAR AND PULLEY ON A SHAFT

The weight of the pulley and gear causes the shaft to sag. The "sag distance" caused by a single load on a shaft that is not rotating is called the static deflection. In our case, the sag directly under the gear is also affected by the weight of the pulley to its right, and vice versa. The formulas for the gear and pulley deflections are:

$$D_g = \frac{2W_g G_l^2 G_r^2 + W_p G_l P_r (L^2 - P_r^2 - G_l^2)}{6EIL}$$

$$D_p = \frac{2W_p P_l^2 P_r^2 + W_g G_l P_r (L^2 - P_r^2 - G_l^2)}{6EIL}$$

where I is the moment of inertia of a circular shaft $I = \dfrac{\pi \cdot d^4}{64}$ (d = shaft diameter)

E is the metal stress coefficient of the shaft, $E = 30,000,000$.

G_l, G_r, P_l, P_r are the distances from the gear to the left and right bearings and from the pulley to the left and right bearings (see Figure 4.6).

The program to solve this problem is shown in Figure 4.7. Two DO loops are used at lines 27 and 29 to control the various gear and pulley positions. The variable CONST is used at line 32 to simplify the coding of D_g and D_p since the expression it represents is common to both D_g and D_p. In a general situation, the variables specified at lines 19–23 would be either accepted from input (interactive environment) or read from a data file.

```
 1: **** FINDING CRITICAL SPEED OF ROTATING SHAFT
 2: **** DATA DICTIONARY
 3: **** GRWGHT: WEIGHT OF GEAR
 4: **** PUWGHT: WEIGHT OF PULLEY
 5: **** DGEAR : STATIC DEFLECTION OF GEAR
 6: **** DPULLY: STATIC DEFLECTION OF PULLEY
 7: **** GLEFT : DISTANCE BETWEEN LEFT BEARING AND GEAR
 8: **** GRIGHT: DISTANCE FROM GEAR TO RIGHT BEARING
 9: **** PLEFT : DISTANCE FROM LEFT BEARING TO PULLEY
10: **** PRIGHT: DISTANCE BETWEEN PULLEY AND RIGHT BEARING
11: **** CONST : EXPRESSION COMMON TO FORMULA FOR DGEAR AND DPULLY
12: **** INERTA: MOMENT OF INERTIA OF CIRCULAR SHAFT
13: **** LENGTH: LENGTH OF SHAFT
14: **** STRESS:
15:        INTEGER GLEFT, PLEFT
16:        REAL SPEED,LENGTH,STRESS,DIAMTR,GRWGHT,GRIGHT,PRIGHT
17:        REAL PUWGHT,DENOM,CONST,DGEAR,DPULLY
18:        PARAMETER(PI=3.1415926,GRAVTY=386.0)
19:        GRWGHT =  85.0
20:        PUWGHT = 130.0
21:        LENGTH = 100.0
22:        DIAMTR = 2.5
23:        STRESS = 30000000
24:        WRITE(6,*)
25:      1'   GEAR LOCATION','  PULLEY LOCATION','      CRITICAL SPEED'
26:        WRITE(6,*)
27:        DO 10 GLEFT = 20,40,10
28:           GRIGHT = 100.0 - GLEFT
29:           DO 20 PLEFT = 60,80,10
30:              PRIGHT = 100.0 - PLEFT
31:              DENOM  = 6.0*PI*STRESS*LENGTH*DIAMTR**4/64.0
32:              CONST =  GLEFT*PRIGHT*(LENGTH**2 - PRIGHT**2 - GLEFT**2)
33: ****         COMPUTE DEFLECTION FOR GEAR
34:              DGEAR = (2.0*GRWGHT*GLEFT**2*GRIGHT**2+PUWGHT*CONST)/DENOM
35: ****         COMPUTE DEFLECTION FOR PULLEY
36:              DPULLY =(2.0*PUWGHT*PLEFT**2*PRIGHT**2+GRWGHT*CONST)/DENOM
37: ****         COMPUTE CRITICAL SPEED FOR SHAFT
38:              SPEED = 30.0/PI*SQRT(
39:      1         GRAVTY*(GRWGHT*DGEAR + DGEAR + PUWGHT*DPULLY)/
40:      2         (GRWGHT*DGEAR**2 + PUWGHT*DPULLY**2))
41:              WRITE(6,*)GLEFT,PLEFT, '           ',SPEED
42: 20        CONTINUE
43:           WRITE(6,*)
44: 10     CONTINUE
45:        STOP
46:        END
```

GEAR LOCATION	PULLEY LOCATION	CRITICAL SPEED
20	60	818.8417000
20	70	920.0061000
20	80	1131.0870000
30	60	754.9944000
30	70	835.3614000
30	80	986.4850000
40	60	711.4746000
40	70	778.9390000
40	80	900.4072000

FIGURE 4.7
CRITICAL SPEED OF A ROTATING SHAFT

4.5.2 Reports   The observation that computer-produced reports should be easy to read, easy to understand, and attractively designed appears so evident that one might feel this subject warrants no further comment. Yet the physical appearance of a report is of dramatic importance. People in all walks of life make daily decisions based on computer-produced reports—detailed reports, summarized reports, and so forth.

A "good" report is self-explanatory, accurate (obviously), self-contained, and organized in a way that allows the reader to capture the essence of the report as well as the detail. These characteristics should be reflected in a design that is neat, clear, and pleasant to the eye. It is impossible to list all the ingredients that comprise an ideal report; a partial list, however, follows:

1. Major or documentary headings: Identification of the purpose of the report. Date of the report or transaction. Identification of the company, agency, or other producer or subject of the report.

2. Subheadings: Titles or labels should be provided for each column of information listed. (In some cases, underlining improves the appearance of the report).

3. Summary or intermediate results should be printed whenever necessary to provide subtotals for a group of entries that are similar in nature; for instance, sales subtotals for a given salesperson in a sales report, or item subtotals in an inventory.

4. Overall or grand totals reflecting sums of subtotals. A descriptive explanation should precede numerical results.

Consider the following problem:

Problem Specification.   Whenever a meal is sold at Charlie's Eatery, the cost of the order and a corresponding meal code (B = breakfast, L = lunch, D = dinner) are recorded on a terminal. At the end of the day, Charlie would like to obtain the following information:

- the day's total sales
- the average breakfast cost
- the lowest dinner cost

Write a program to read an input file where each record consists of a meal cost (no meal cost should exceed $100.00) and a meal code and produce a report similar to the one shown below. Note the three different types of error messages, depending on whether the meal cost exceeds $100, the meal code is not B, L, or D, or both the meal cost and meal code entries are invalid.

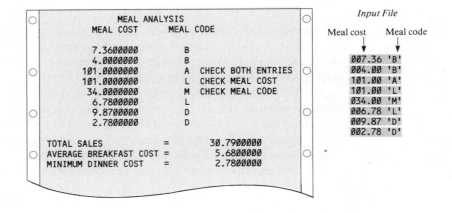

Solution. To compute the daily total sales, the program simply accumulates the various meal costs as they are read. To compute the average breakfast cost, the number of breakfasts must be counted and the breakfast costs accumulated. To find the minimum dinner cost, we can arbitrarily initialize the minimum cost to an unrealistic figure, say $1000, so that when that "minimum" is compared to the first dinner cost, that dinner cost will obviously be less than $1000 and will become the new minimum.

This program requires three techniques: (1) counting (breakfasts), (2) accumulating (total sales and breakfast sales), and (3) finding a minimum value (minimum dinner cost). The entire logic of the problem can be captured in pseudo code as shown below and in FORTRAN code as shown in Figure 4.8. Note the input validation routine at lines 30–40.

Pseudo Code
```
* Charlie's Eatery
  Initialize total sales, breakfast count, breakfast sales to 0
  Initialize minimum dinner cost to $1000.00
  WHILE end of file not encountered DO
        read meal cost, meal code
*       If input record is valid, process it
              IF meal cost < 100 and meal code is valid (B, L, or D) THEN
                    add meal cost to total sales
                    write meal cost and meal code
                    IF meal code = D and meal cost < minimum dinner cost
                        set minimum dinner cost to meal cost
                    ENDIF
                    IF meal code = B THEN
                        add 1 to breakfast count
                        add meal cost to breakfast sales
                    ENDIF
              ELSE
*       If input record contains invalid entries print appropriate error messages
                    IF meal cost > 100 and meal code is not B, L, or D THEN
                        write error message (both entries invalid)
                    ELSE IF meal code not B, L, or D THEN
                        write error message (invalid meal code)
                    ELSE IF meal cost > 100 THEN
                        write error message (invalid meal cost)
                    ENDIF
              ENDIF
  ENDWHILE
  average breakfast cost = breakfast sales/breakfast count
  write total sales, average breakfast cost, minimum dinner cost
  stop
```

4.5.3 Control Breaks

In the preceding section, we discussed the physical aspects of reports, and in chapters 3 and 4 we discussed coding techniques to produce such summary statistics as counts, averages, and grand totals. In real-life applications, more refined summaries are generally needed. For example, in a supermarket an item file might be arranged into categories of goods such as perishables, dairy products, and meats; the manager may need an inventory report by category showing market and cost figures. In a school, a personnel file might be arranged by department number; an administrator may wish to obtain a list and a count of teachers within each department. In a similar situation, a department head may wish to obtain a report at the start of a semester displaying a list of courses broken down into course sections with the name of the teacher for each

```
 1: ***** CHARLIE'S EATERY PROBLEM
 2: ***** TOTCOS: ACCUMULATES ALL MEAL COSTS
 3: ***** TOTBKC: ACCUMULATES ALL BREAKFAST COSTS
 4: ***** BKCNT : COUNTS ALL BREAKFASTS
 5: ***** MINDIN: MINIMUM DINNER COST
 6: ***** MEALC : MEAL COST
 7: ***** MEALKD: MEAL CODE (B=BREAKFAST, L=LUNCH, D=DINNER)
 8: ***** AVGBKF: AVERAGE BREAKFAST COST
 9:         CHARACTER MEALKD*1
10:         REAL TOTCOS,TOTBKC,MINDIN,MEALC,AVGBKF,BKCNT
11:         DATA TOTCOS,TOTBKC,BKCNT,MINDIN/0.,0.,0,1000.0/
12:         WRITE(*,*)'              MEAL ANALYSIS'
13:         WRITE(*,*)'          MEAL COST      MEAL CODE'
14:         WRITE(*,*)
15: 10      READ(5,*,END=88)MEALC,MEALKD
16:         IF(MEALC .LE. 100.00 .AND.
17:      1  (MEALKD.EQ.'B' .OR. MEALKD.EQ.'L' .OR. MEALKD.EQ.'D'))THEN
18: ********** IF NO ERRORS ARE PRESENT IN THE INPUT RECORD
19:            TOTCOS = TOTCOS + MEALC
20:            WRITE(*,*)MEALC,'          ',MEALKD
21:            IF(MEALKD .EQ. 'D' .AND. MEALC .LT. MINDIN)THEN
22:               MINDIN = MEALC
23:            ENDIF
24:            IF(MEALKD .EQ. 'B')THEN
25:               BKCNT = BKCNT + 1
26:               TOTBKC = TOTBKC + MEALC
27:            ENDIF
28:         ELSE
29: ********** IF ERRORS ARE PRESENT IN THE INPUT RECORD
30:            IF(MEALC .GT. 100.00 .AND.
31:      1     MEALKD.NE.'B' .AND. MEALKD.NE.'L' .AND. MEALKD.NE.'D')THEN
32:               WRITE(*,*)MEALC,'          ',MEALKD,'   CHECK BOTH ENTRIES'
33:            ELSEIF
34:      1        (MEALKD.NE.'B' .AND. MEALKD.NE.'L' .AND. MEALKD.NE.'D')THEN
35:               WRITE(*,*)MEALC,'          ',MEALKD,'   CHECK MEAL CODE'
36:            ELSEIF
37:      1        (MEALC .GT. 100.)THEN
38:               WRITE(*,*)MEALC,'          ',MEALKD,'   CHECK MEAL COST'
39:            ENDIF
40:         ENDIF
41:         GO TO 10
42: 88      AVGBKF = TOTBKC/BKCNT
43:         WRITE(*,*)
44:         WRITE(*,*)'TOTAL SALES            =', TOTCOS
45:         WRITE(*,*)'AVERAGE BREAKFAST COST =', AVGBKF
46:         WRITE(*,*)'MINIMUM DINNER COST    =', MINDIN
47:         STOP
48:         END
```

```
          MEAL ANALYSIS
      MEAL COST        MEAL CODE

      7.3600000        B
      4.0000000        B
    101.0000000        A    CHECK BOTH ENTRIES
    101.0000000        L    CHECK MEAL COST
     34.0000000        M    CHECK MEAL CODE
      6.7800000        L
      9.8700000        D
      2.7800000        D

 TOTAL SALES            =      30.7900000
 AVERAGE BREAKFAST COST =       5.6800000
 MINIMUM DINNER COST    =       2.7800000
```

Input File

Meal   Meal
cost   code

007.36 'B'
004.00 'B'
101.00 'A'
101.00 'L'
034.00 'M'
006.78 'L'
009.87 'D'
002.78 'D'

FIGURE 4.8
CHARLIE'S RESTAURANT

section and the total enrollment for each course. Or a publishing company may need a financial sales report broken down by author publications.

The common theme in all of these examples is that input data is frequently arranged into groups of items. These groups must be processed and summarized into a final output product that also preserves group characteristics. Processing this type of data structure requires that we know when a group starts and ends so that we can count the number of group entries, accumulate related entry fields within each group, and so forth. To illustrate such a process, consider the following input file, where each record consists of a salesperson number, a date of sales, an item code and a sales amount. Let us assume that all records for a given salesperson occur in a group; records are not necessarily sorted in sequence by salesperson number.

	Salesperson number	Date of sale	Item code	Sales amount
Records for salesperson 1002	1002	010787	'A1'	22256
	1002	011087	'B3'	07895
	1002	012387	'X2'	09500
Records for salesperson 2103	2103	010887	'BB'	00995
	2103	010987	'B3'	01905
Records for salesperson 3250	3250	011587	'A1'	33378
	3250	011887	'X3'	06795
	3250	012587	'S2'	56000

Given this type of data, a report could be produced to show total sales as well as summary sales for each salesperson. Such a summary report is shown in Figure 4.9. Totals for each salesperson are called *intermediate* or *minor* totals.

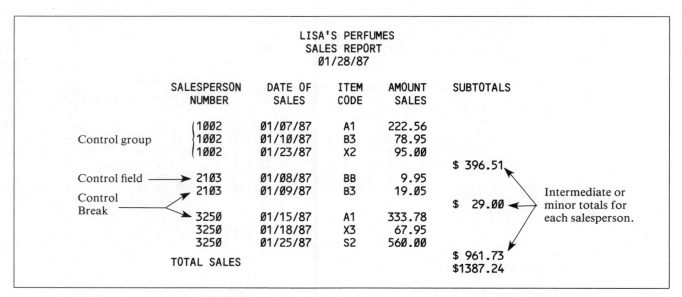

FIGURE 4.9
A SAMPLE CONTROL BREAK REPORT

Notice that in this example the input file is intentionally organized into groups by salesperson number to produce a summary report arranged in a similar fashion. In this application the salesperson number plays a leading role—it determines the grouping of the data on the output report. All other fields play secondary roles. Had management wanted a report summarized by item code or by date, then the item code or date would become the lead or control field, requiring the input file to be arranged by item code or date.

Depending on the type of summary report needed, one particular input field must be designated as a lead field to control the layout of the output report. This, of course, requires that the input data be arranged in appropriate groups. Later on we will see how we can sort an input file by key (control) fields to allow us to produce various types of summary reports based on particular control fields.

Processing an input file organized into control groups requires that we recognize breaks between successive control groups. For that reason, this type of problem is referred to as a *control break problem*. To illustrate the control break programming technique, let us consider a very simple case dealing with a salesperson summary report.

Problem Specification. Each record of an input file contains a salesperson number and a sales amount. Write a program to read an input file like the one shown below and produce a summary sales report similar to the following one:

	Output			Input File
SALESPERSON	SALES	TOTALS		salesperson number ↓ sales ↓
111	100.00			111 100.0
111	50.00			111 050.0
		150.00		222 300.0
222	300.00			333 150.0
		300.00		333 200.0
333	150.00			
333	200.00			
		350.00		
TOTAL SALES		800.00		

Discussion. Let us assign the following names to the various items that are to be processed:

- **salesperson:** refers to the salesperson number read from each record
- **sales:** sales value read from each record
- **total sales:** accumulates all sales
- **subtotal:** accumulates each salesperson's total sales
- **previous salesperson:** Given any two consecutive salesperson groups in the input file, previous salesperson refers to the first salesperson number in the first group.

The basic idea in producing this type of report is to keep accumulating a minor total until a change occurs in the salesperson number. If the record read pertains to the same salesperson as the current group, the sales amount read is added to the current salesperson total (minor total). If the record read pertains to a new salesperson, a *control break* has been found. At this point the minor total for the previous salesperson is printed, the accumulator for the new minor total is reset to 0, and the new salesperson number is stored in previous salesperson.

The decision as to whether the salesperson just read belongs to the current group or to a new group is made by comparing previous salesperson with salesperson. If they are the same, the record read belongs to the current group. Otherwise, a different salesperson number has been read and a control break has occurred.

To start the comparison process between *previous salesperson* and *salesperson,* the first salesperson number is assigned to *previous salesperson.*

The logic of the program is described in pseudo code as follows:

```
* control break logic
      write headings
      read previous salesperson number and sales
      set subtotal and total to sales
      write salesperson number and sales
      WHILE not end of file DO
            read salesperson number and sales
            IF previous salesperson is different from salesperson THEN
*                 Control break occurs
                  write subtotal
*                 Prepare for subtotal of salesperson just read
                  reset subtotal to 0
*                 To compare the next salesperson with the current salesperson
                  reset previous salesperson number to salesperson number
            ENDIF
            add sales to total and to subtotal
            write salesperson number and sales
      ENDWHILE
      write subtotal and total
```

One way to really understand the control break logic is to trace through the pseudo code using a dummy input file and record the various values taken on by all data items. Such a tabulation process is carried out in Figure 4.10; the reader can walk through the code and see what is happening at each step. Take the time to analyze this visual walk-through to see that the logic indeed works! The actual FORTRAN code is shown in Figure 4.11.

Test Your Understanding of the Program

1. Change the pseudo code of the control break problem so that total sales is the result of accumulating the various subtotals.

2. Does the flowchart shown in Figure 4.12 also solve the control break problem? How would you write the pseudo code for this flowchart? What changes would you make to make it a "structured" flowchart?

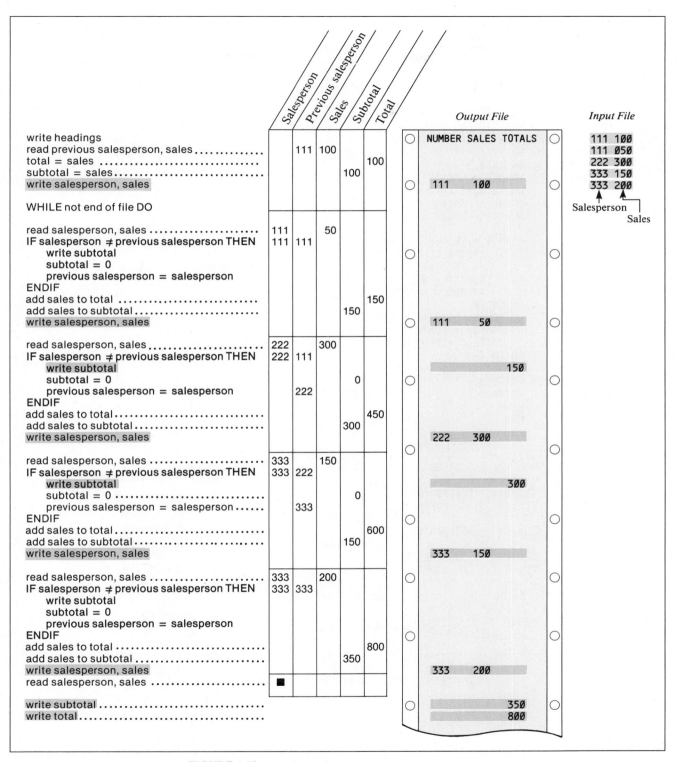

FIGURE 4.10
CONTROL BREAK TABULATION

```
 1: * CONTROL BREAK PROBLEM
 2: *   PRVIUS: PREVIOUS SALESPERSON NUMBER
 3: *   SALSPR: CURRENT SALESPERSON NUMBER
 4: *   TOTAL:  TOTAL SALES FOR ALL SALESPERSONS
 5: *   SUBTOT: TOTAL SALES FOR EACH SALESPERSON
 6: *
 7:       INTEGER PRVIUS,SALSPR
 8:       REAL TOTAL, SALES, SUBTOT
 9:       OPEN(5,FILE='BRKDATA')
10:       WRITE(6,*)'     SALESPERSON     SALES        TOTALS'
11:       WRITE(6,*)
12:       READ(5,*,END=88) PRVIUS,SALES
13:       WRITE(6,*) PRVIUS,SALES
14:       TOTAL  = SALES
15:       SUBTOT = SALES
16: *
17:     7 READ(5,*,END=88)SALSPR, SALES
18:        IF(SALSPR.NE.PRVIUS) THEN
19:           WRITE(6,*)'                            ',SUBTOT
20:           SUBTOT = 0
21:           PRVIUS = SALSPR
22:        ENDIF
23:        TOTAL  = TOTAL + SALES
24:        SUBTOT = SUBTOT + SALES
25:        WRITE(6,*)PRVIUS, SALES
26:        GO TO 7
27: *
28:    88 WRITE(6,*)'                       ',SUBTOT
29:       WRITE(6,*)'     TOTAL SALES      ',TOTAL
30:       STOP
31:       END
```

Output

SALESPERSON	SALES	TOTALS
111	100.0000000	
111	50.0000000	
		150.0000000
222	300.0000000	
		300.0000000
333	150.0000000	
333	200.0000000	
		350.0000000
TOTAL SALES		800.0000000

Input File

Salesman Number → ← Sales

```
100 150.50
100 150.60
200 034.70
300 456.70
400 654.20
400 567.80
```

FIGURE 4.11
A CONTROL BREAK PROBLEM

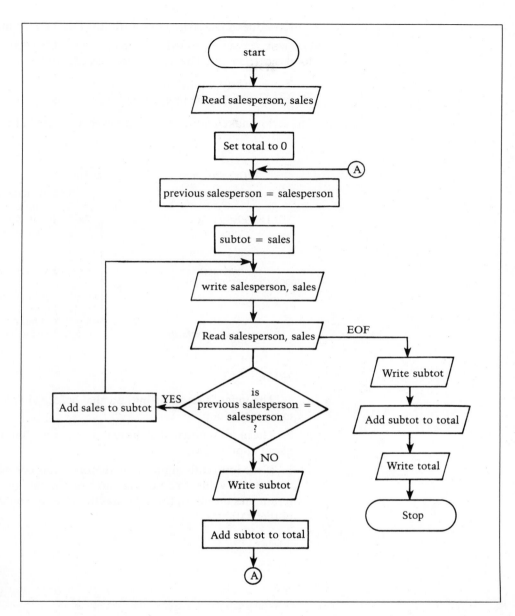

FIGURE 4.12
UNSTRUCTURED
CONTROL BREAK
FLOWCHART

4.6 YOU MIGHT WANT TO KNOW

1. To what depth or level can loops be nested?

Answer: It depends on the compiler. It is safe to assume up to 16 nested loops.

2. If a DATA statement can be replaced by a replacement statement, why use the DATA statement?

Answer: The primary reason is programmer convenience. One DATA statement can initialize a great many variables that otherwise would require many replacement statements.

3. How does a DO structure control the number of times the loop is carried out?

Answer: A counter called the trip counter (TC) calculates the number of times a loop is carried out. The trip counter uses the following formula:

$$TC = \max(0, \text{int}((e_2 - e_1 + e_3) / e_3))$$
where e_1, e_2, e_3 are integer/real expressions.

The actions taken during the loop's execution are as follows:

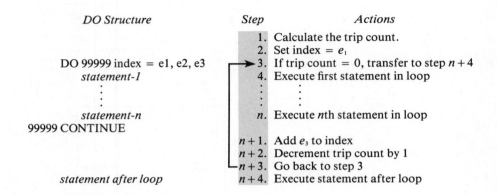

DO Structure	Step	Actions
	1.	Calculate the trip count.
	2.	Set index $= e_1$
DO 99999 index = e1, e2, e3	3.	If trip count $= 0$, transfer to step $n + 4$
statement-1	4.	Execute first statement in loop
$\vdots$	$\vdots$	$\vdots$
statement-n	*n.*	Execute *n*th statement in loop
99999 CONTINUE		
	$n + 1.$	Add e_3 to index
	$n + 2.$	Decrement trip count by 1
	$n + 3.$	Go back to step 3
statement after loop	$n + 4.$	Execute statement after loop

NOTE:

1. The index is set to its initial value before any decision is made whether to execute the loop.

2. The index is updated at the end of each pass but before any decision is made about another pass.

3. If the loop ends abnormally (before it has completed its full cycle), the index has the value it had on the most recent pass through the loop. If the loop terminates normally, the index has the value it would have had on the next (hypothetical) pass.

4.7 ASSIGNMENTS

4.7.1 Test Yourself

1. Using DO loops, write the code to print the following sequences of numbers:

    a. 1,3,5,7, ..., 99

    b. $-1, 1, -1, 1, \ldots$ (25 terms)

    c. 1./1.,   1./1./2.,   1./1./2./3.,   ... 1./2./3./4./ ... /X   (X is read)

    d. N, N − 2, N − 4, ..., 0   where N is an even positive number

    e. 1./9., 1./99., 1./999., ... 1./9999999.

    f. .25, .50, .75, ..., 2.00

2. Write the code to accumulate the following values (use DO loops):

   a. $1^2 + 2^2 + 3^2 + ... + 10^2$

   b. $2 + 4 + 8 + 16 + ... + 1024$

   c. $1 - 2 + 3 - 4 + ... - 1000$

   d. $1 + (1*2) + (1*2*3) + (1*2*3*4) + ... + (1*2*3*...*50)$

   e. $1. + 1./3. + 1./5. + ... + 1./77.$

3. Which of the following are valid DO loops? If a loop is invalid, explain why.

```
a.     DO 10 I = 1,5          b.     DO 6 I = 1,10
         :                             J = I*I + 1
       10 CONTINUE                   6 CONTINUE

c.     DO 30 K = 1,10         d.     DO 15 I = I,6
         DO 40 K = 1,40                :
           :                         15 CONTINUE
       40   CONTINUE
       30 CONTINUE

e.     DO 50 I - 1 = 2,6      f.     DO 60 I = 1,5
         :                             DO 70 J = 1,10,-1
       50 CONTINUE                       :
                                     60   CONTINUE
                                     70 CONTINUE

g.     DO 20 L = 8,1
         DO 30 K = 1,3
           L = L + 1
       30   CONTINUE
       20 CONTINUE
```

4. Write a program to print out the following board (exactly).

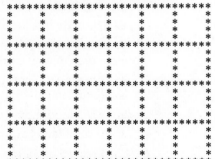

5. How many times will statement 3 be processed?

```
a.     DO 22 I = 1,3          b.     DO 32 I = 2,20
         DO 21 J = 1,4                 DO 33 J = 3,17,5
           DO 20 K = 1,10                 :
        3    X = 1.                    3    X = 1.
       20 CONTINUE                    33   CONTINUE
       21 CONTINUE                    32 CONTINUE
       22 CONTINUE
```

```
c.    DO 18 IØ = 2,8,2              d.    DO 1Ø K = 1,6,2
      DO 15 IM = IØ,2,1                   DO 5 I = 1,K
      DO 1Ø II = 1,4,2                        SUM = SUM + I
 3      X = 1                        5 CONTINUE
1Ø CONTINUE                         1Ø CONTINUE
15 CONTINUE
18 CONTINUE
```

6. Will the following coding segments compute the average of ten grades?

```
a.    SUM = Ø.                      b.    INTEGER SUM
      DO 1Ø I = 1,10                      SUM = Ø.
          READ(5,*)GRADE                  DO 15 I = 1,1Ø
          SUM = SUM + GRADE                   READ(5,*)GRADE
   1Ø CONTINUE                              SUM = SUM + GRADE
      AVERAG = SUM/I                        AVE = SUM/I
                                    15 CONTINUE
                                       WRITE(6,*)AVE
```

7. What will the final value of J be?

```
      J = Ø
      DO 4 I = 1,1Ø
          J = J + .1
    4 CONTINUE
```

8. Which of the following statements are true? If false, explain why.

a. DO 10 IX2 = N, N + 1 is a valid statement.

b. The index of a DO loop can be a real variable.

c. If the initial value of the index of a DO loop is not specified, it is assumed to be 1.

d. A comment statement in the range of a DO loop will be listed at least once and probably more than once, depending on the number of times the body of the loop is executed.

e. The body of a loop will always be processed at least once.

f. A nonexecutable statement in the body of a DO loop can be processed more than once at execution time.

g. When a DO loop has completed its full cycle, the value of its index becomes undefined.

h. A DO loop should always be entered at the DO statement.

i. Accumulating and counting are synonymous terms.

9. Each record of an input file contains the name of a city and its record high temperature for the year. Cities have been sorted in order of ascending temperature. Write the pseudo code to print the name of the first city with a temperature of 100 degrees or above. Flush out all remaining input records, if any (i.e., read remaining records, but do not process them).

10. Each record of an input file contains a dollar amount. Write the pseudo code to print the message 'YES' if *all* the dollar amounts in the file are greater than 10000; otherwise print 'NO'.

11. Each record of an input file consists of an age field and a sex code (1 = male, 2 = female). Write the FORTRAN code to print the age and sex (write "male" or "female") of the youngest person.

12. Refer to example 3 of section 4.4.2 (decomposition of a number into digits) and write the pseudo code to determine whether the number N (a seven digit number) contains the digit 0. Exit from the loop structure as soon as a 0 is found and print a message if the digit 0 is not found.

13. Determine if the digit 0 appears twice in the number N described in exercise 12 above.

4.7.2 Programming Exercises: General

1. Mr. Sly convinced his employers to pay him for 30 days as follows: The first day he gets paid 1 cent, the second day 2 cents, the third day 4 cents, the fourth day 8 cents, and so forth. Each day's pay is twice the previous day's pay. Print a table showing Mr. Sly's earnings during the last 10 days. (Make sure the earnings are displayed in dollar figures.)

2. In a physical education class, students get either a pass or a fail for the course. If the average of the student's three test scores is below 70, the student fails the course. The student's three test scores are recorded as follows:

```
Name    test1  test2  test3
  ↓       ↓      ↓      ↓
DOE K     50     60     70  ⎫
ARMS L    40     80     90  ⎬   Input File
  ⋮                          ⎪
EVANS L   20     45     75  ⎭
```

Write a program to produce the following output using a DO loop to read the input file.

```
STUDENT   TEST1   TEST2   TEST3   AVERAGE   FINAL GRADE

DOE K      50      60      70      60.0       FAIL
ARMS L     40      80      90      70.0       PASS
            .       .       .       .          .
            .       .       .       .          .
            .       .       .       .          .
EVANS M    20      45      75      46.6       FAIL

THE PERCENTAGE OF STUDENTS WHO FAILED IS XXX.X
```

3. Each record of an input file contains a name and a corresponding earnings. Write the code to print the names of the persons with highest and lowest earnings.

a. Assume no two earnings amounts are the same.

b. Assume that equal earnings amounts can exist; print a message if maximum earning is not unique.

4. An input file consists of an unknown number of packets of records, where each packet contains a header record that tells how many records follow in the packet. Each record except the header record contains an ID number and a sex code (1 = male, 2 = female). Write the code to print the ID numbers of all females and the percentage of males in each packet. The input and output have the following forms:

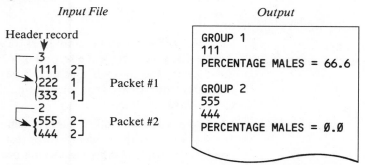

Input File   *Output*

```
GROUP 1
111
PERCENTAGE MALES = 66.6

GROUP 2
555
444
PERCENTAGE MALES = 0.0
```

5. Each record of an input file contains a name and a final test score. The names are supposed to be in descending order. Write a program to print the names that are not in sequence. If all names are in order, print the message "NAMES ARE IN ORDER".

6. An input file contains numbers supposedly arranged in numerical ascending order. Read *all* records and then print the appropriate message: "IN ORDER" or "OUT OF ORDER".

7. A wholesaler accepts a $5,000 promissory note from a retailer at 10% in lieu of cash payment for delivered goods. Write a program to compute the maturity value of the note for a 30-, 60-, and 90-day short-term loan. (The formula for the maturity value if $S = P(1 + I \cdot N)$, where S is maturity value, P is principal, I is interest rate, and N is the number of years, or, if less than 1 year, the number of days/360.)

8. The simple discount is the amount deducted from the maturity value S (see problem 7) of an obligation sold before its date of maturity. The formula is $SD = S \cdot D \cdot N$, where SD = simple discount, S = maturity value, D = discount rate, and N = term of loan, that is, time remaining before maturity.

A wholesaler receives a $10,500 promissory note for goods sold to a retailer. The note matures in N months and bears an I% interest rate. One month later the wholesaler sells the note to a bank at a 9% discount rate. Write a program to compute:

    a. The maturity value of the note for N = 30, 60, and 90 days with interest rate of I = 4%, 5%, and 6% (that is, N = 30 for I = 4%, 5%, and 6%; N = 60 for I = 4%, 5%, and 6%, and so forth).

    b. The proceeds received by the wholesaler as a result of selling the note to the bank for N = 30, 60, and 90 days with interest rate of 4%, 5%, and 6%, respectively.

9. Ms. Small is thinking of borrowing $5,000 for N months at a 12% simple discount rate to purchase a new automobile. Write a program to compute the proceeds of this loan for the following values of N: 6 months, 1 year, 2 years, and 3 years. The proceeds (P) is the sum remaining after the discount is deducted; it is given by the formula: $P = S(1 - SD \cdot N)$ (see problem 8).

10. Each record of a data file contains the following information: a name, a sex code (1 = M, 2 = F), and an amount of earnings. Write a program to print the earnings and the names of females earning between $10,000 and $20,000; also print the lowest earnings and indicate on the output whether it was earned by a male or a female. For example, either of the following outputs could be produced: (notice the MALE and FEMALE captions and not the numeric code).

```
JOMAN              $14300.00
ALLON              $13500.00
LOWEST EARNING = $ 6,736.55 (FEMALE)
```

```
GANDY              $11000.50
LOWEST EARNING = $ 5244.00 (MALE)
```

11. Write a program to compute the weight of a person on the following planets, based on the data:

Planet	Percentage of Earth Weight
Moon	16
Jupiter	264
Venus	85
Mars	38

Create a table with weights ranging from 50 to 250 pounds in steps of 50 pounds. The same program should generate both of the following outputs.

a.

```
EARTH  MOON  JUPITER  VENUS  MARS

  50    xxx    xxx     xxx    xxx
 100     .      .       .      .
  .
  .
  .
 250    xxx    xxx     xxx    xxx
```

b.

```
PLANET  EARTH  WEIGHT

  1       50     xxx
         100     xxx
          .       .
          .       .
          .       .
         250     xxx

  2       50     xxx
         100     xxx
          .       .
          .       .
          .       .
         250     xxx

  4       50     xxx
         100     xxx
          .       .
          .       .
          .       .
         250     xxx
```

In part (b), planet 1 is the moon, planet 2 is Jupiter, etc.
[*Hint:* read planet numbers]

12. An input file consists of several packets of records, each containing grades obtained by different classes. Each packet is identified by a header record specifying the course title and the section number. One student grade (0–100) is typed per record. A sentinel record identifies the end of a packet. Write a complete program to determine the percentage of passing grades for each section (passing grades are grades over 60). List the grades, starting at the top of a new numbered page for each new section. The pages for each section should be numbered 1, 2, 3,. . . . Provide appropriate headers.

To simplify testing your program, assume each output page will contain only four student grades; i.e., assume a page is no more than 10 lines including the various headers. The input and output have the following forms (draw hyphenated lines to indicate end of page):

Input File   *Output*

Course title   Section number
       ↓   ↓
```
ALGEBRA      102  ⎫
90                ⎪
80                ⎬  Packet 1
73                ⎪
 .                ⎪
 .                ⎪
-4                ⎭
ECONOMICS 103  ⎫
22                ⎪
32                ⎬  Packet 2
10                ⎪
-4 ←— Last record of packet
```

```
                                      PAGE 1
   ALGEBRA     SECTION 102

                 GRADES
                   90
                   80
                   73
                   60
   ------------------------------------
                                      PAGE 2
   ALGEBRA     SECTION 102

                 GRADES
                   20
                   37

      PASSING PERCENTAGE = 50.0%
   ------------------------------------
                                      PAGE 1
   ECONOMICS SECTION 103

                 GRADES
                   22
                   32
                   10

      PASSING PERCENTAGE = 0.0%
```

13. The Meals on Wheels Company operates a fleet of vans that deliver cold foods at various local plants and construction sites. The management is thinking of purchasing a specially built $18,000 van equipped to deliver hot foods. This new addition to the fleet is expected to generate after-tax earnings $E_1, E_2, \ldots, E_6$ (as displayed in the following table) over the next six years, at which time the van's resale value will be zero. Projected repair and maintenance $C_0, C_1, C_2, \ldots, C_6$ over the six years are also shown in the table.

Projected Earnings		*Projected Costs*	
		C_0	$18,000 (purchase cost of the van)
E_1	$2,500	C_1	610
E_2	2,500	C_2	745
E_3	3,000	C_3	820
E_4	4,500	C_4	900
E_5	6,000	C_5	950
E_6	6,000	C_6	1,000

a. Write a program to determine whether or not the company should acquire the van. The decision depends on the benefit/cost ratio (BCR) (grossly speaking, earnings/expenditures) given by the formula:

$$BCR = \frac{E_1(1 + i)^6 + E_2(1 + i)^5 + \ldots + E_6(1 + i)^1}{C_0 + C_1(1 + i)^6 + C_2(1 + i)^5 + \ldots + C_6(1 + i)^1}$$

where i is the rate of investment of earnings by the company (use 11% for this problem). If the BCR < 1, then the company should not acquire the van. Use the accumulation process to compute the BCR. The first data record contains E_1 and C_1, the second data record contains E_2 and C_2, and so forth.

b. When shown the projected maintenance costs for the next six years, the repair and maintenance shop foreman argues that these cost figures are unrealistic and proposes instead the following costs for the first through sixth years: 1,000, 1,500, 2,000, 2,000, 2,100, 2,400. Using these figures, determine whether the company should purchase the van.

c. Having found out that the BCR is less than 1 with the projected maintenance costs shown in part (b), the management wants to recompute the BCR with the same figures as in part (b) but setting the resale value of the van at $1,000.00 (the sale of the van represents earnings). Use your program to recompute the BCR.

14. Write a program to produce the following comparative mortgage tables for principals varying from $50,000 to $100,000 in steps of $10,000, interest rates varying from 9.50% to 12.50% in increments of 0.25% and durations of 20, 25, and 30 years.

MORTGAGE PAYMENT PLAN
JOHN DOE

PRINCIPAL	INTEREST RATE	DURATION	MONTHLY-PAYMENT
50000	9.50	20	xxxx.xx
		25	xxxx.xx
		30	xxxx.xx
	9.75	20	xxxx.xx
		25	xxxx.xx
		30	xxxx.xx
	⋮		
	12.50	20	xxxx.xx
		25	xxxx.xx
		30	xxxx.xx
60000	9.50	20	xxxx.xx
		25	xxxx.xx
		30	xxxx.xx
	⋮		
	12.50	20	xxxx.xx
		25	xxxx.xx
		30	xxxx.xx
⋮			
100000	9.50	20	xxxx.xx
		25	xxxx.xx
		30	xxxx.xx
	⋮	⋮	⋮

The formula to compute the monthly payment is:

$$M = \frac{P \cdot I/12}{1 - \left(\dfrac{1}{1 + I/12}\right)^{T \cdot 12}}$$

where

P is the principal
I is the interest rate
T is the mortgage duration in years

Note the blank lines after every third monthly payment.

15. A data file consists of records, each containing the following information concerning items produced at the XYZ manufacturing plant: a department number, an item number, a quantity, and a cost per item. Assume the file has been sorted into order by ascending department number. Write a program to produce a summary report as follows:

DEPARTMENT	ITEM	QUANTITY	COST/ITEM	VALUE	TOTALS
15	1389	4	3.20	12.80	
15	3821	2	7.00	14.00	
					26.80
16	0122	8	2.50	20.00	
					20.00
19	1244	100	.03	3.00	
19	1245	20	4.00	80.00	
19	2469	4	16.00	64.00	
					147.00
				GRAND TOTAL	193.80

Could you alter the program to write each subtotal on the same line as the last entry in each subgroup?

16. Write a program to simulate a bank's handling of a savings account. Each record input into the program contains a transaction amount, a check number, a transaction date (an integer number between 1 and 31), and a transaction code. The records for a particular month should be in ascending date order. The meanings of the transaction code are as follows:

Code	Meaning
1	Balance forward (first record in input file)
2	Deposit
3	Withdrawal
4	End of transactions (the transaction amount is ignored, and the transaction date is used for the final balance)

a. Print a report showing all transactions and the balance after each transaction. The final balance should be clearly labeled. Your report should be similar to the following:

DAY	CHECK NO.	WITHDRAWALS	DEPOSITS	BALANCE
1				3250.00
4	112	100.00		3150.00
6	123	250.00		2900.00
19	127		50.00	2950.00
25	128		74.00	3024.00
31			NEW BALANCE	3024.00

b. Modify part (a) to compute interest and credit it to the account. Assume that interest is based on the average daily balance for the number of days from the beginning of the statement (the date on the balance forward transaction) up to and including the end of the statement (the date of the end of transactions). The interest should be credited to the account on the date of the end of transactions. The average daily balance is computed by adding the daily balances and dividing by the number of days. In the example above, the average daily balance would be

$$\frac{3 \times 3250 + 2 \times 3150 + 13 \times 2900 + 6 \times 2950 + 6 \times 3024 + 3024}{31} = 2987.67$$

since the account had a balance of $3,250 for 3 days, $3150 for 2 days, $2,900 for 13 days, . . ., and a balance of $3024 on the date ending the period. If the interest rate is 4.75%, the account should then be credited with a monthly interest of $11.82.

17. An input file consists of packets of sales transaction records; the first record in any packet identifies a parts number, a parts quantity, and a reorder level. Succeeding records in the packet represent sales transactions (number of parts sold) for the given part. Write a program to produce a sales summary similar to the report shown below and identify any part that needs to be reordered (reorder if the quantity on hand is less than or equal to the reorder level).

Report — STOCK LEVEL ANALYSIS

PARTS NO	SOLD	ON HAND	
111	100		
	30		
		470	
222	50		
		10	REORDER
333	10		
	40		
	20		
	30		
		0	REORDER

Input File — quantity on hand / part number / reorder level

```
111 600 400   } header record
100             number parts
030               sold
222 060 010
050
333 100 030
010
040
020
030
```

18. A large supermarket is organized into departments such as meats, perishables, and dairy products. The supermarket's management would like to follow the monthly sales trends in the various departments. They have instructed their data processing staff to produce monthly reports that will identify departments showing unusually sluggish or unusually active sales: If the current month's sales are more than 15% greater than the average of the previously recorded monthly sales for that department, an appropriate message such as HIGH should be printed. If the current month's sales are less than 90% of the average of the previously recorded monthly sales, then a different message such as LOW should be printed.

All departments have sales records for at least the last three months, and some have records going back beyond three months. The input file consists of records that are arranged in sequence by department number. Within each department, the monthly sales are arranged in ascending date order. Write a program to produce a report similar to the following one (the most recent month is *not* reflected in the average):

Output   *Input*

NO.	DATE	SALES	AVERAGES	ALERT
11	02/01	15000.40		
	03/01	14000.55		
	04/01	14500.20		
	05/01	13800.48	14500.38	
22	01/01	23400.64		
	02/01	30500.88		
	03/01	32600.46		
	04/01	29400.00		
	05/01	25000.00	28975.56	LOW
33	02/01	40000.80		
	03/01	45876.20		
	04/01	44784.88		
	05/01	51080.40	43553.96	HIGH

Dept. Date Amount
No.

11	02	01	15000.40	} Last three months'
11	03	01	14000.55	sales records
11	04	01	14500.20	for dept. 11.
11	05	01	13800.48	← Current monthly
22	01	01	23400.64	sales for dept. 11.
22	02	01	30500.88
22	03	01	32600.46
22	04	01	29400.00
22	05	01	25000.00
33	02	01	40000.80
33	03	01	45876.20
33	04	01	44784.88
33	05	01	51080.40	← Current monthly sales for dept. 33

19. XSTAR is a small company supplying major auto parts companies with a single item. The total fixed costs to run the company amount to $40,000 per year. The company has had a steady dollar breakeven point value (BEP) for the last three years, and the president of the company would like to keep the BEP at about the same level ($117,647) for the coming year. The president believes that the selling price per item could range anywhere from $1.10 to $1.30, but that the variable cost per item should not fall below $.75 nor exceed $.83. To help the president consider the options, write a program displaying different combinations of selling prices ($1.10 to $1.30 in increments of one cent) and corresponding variable costs, all yielding a constant BEP of $117,647; that is, generate a table with headings as follows:

SELLING COSTS	VARIABLE COST/UNIT	BREAKEVEN POINT	DECISION
1.10	73	117647	TOO LOW
1.11		117647	.
.	.	.	.
.	.	.	.
.	.	.	.
1.30	86	117647	TOO HIGH

If the variable cost per unit falls outside the interval of $.75–$.83, state in the decision column that the variable cost is either too low or too high. The formula to compute the BEP is given by:

$$BEP = \frac{\text{total fixed costs}}{1 - \dfrac{\text{variable cost/unit}}{\text{selling price/unit}}}$$

20. The Kiddie Up Company manufactures toys for adults. The company expects fixed costs for the next year to be around $180,000. With the demand for adult toys increasing, the company is looking for sales of $900,000 in the year to come. The variable costs are expected to run at about 74% of sales.

a. Write a program to determine the breakeven point (BEP) (the dollar amount of sales that must be made to incur neither a profit nor a loss), and compute the expected profit. The formula to compute the BEP is

$$BEP = \frac{\text{total fixed costs}}{1 - \dfrac{\text{variable costs}}{\text{sales}}}$$

b. The Kiddie Up Company management is arguing that with the current rate of inflation, variable costs will run higher for the next year—probably anywhere from 75 to 83% of sales. With sales still projected at $900,000, the management directs its data processing staff to generate the following report to determine the breakeven point and the profits and losses for varying variable costs (step of 1%). Sales and fixed costs remain constant.

```
                        KIDDIE UP COMPANY
                     1987 OPERATIONS FORECAST

     PROJECTED SALES: 900000
     FIXED COSTS:     180000

     VARIABLE      VARIABLE COST    BREAK EVEN    PROFIT    DEFICIT
     COSTS         PERCENTAGE         POINT

     675000             75           720000      180000      ***
       .                 .              .           .         .
       .                 .              .           .         .
       .                 .              .           .         .
     747000             83          1058823        ***      158823
```

Write a program to complete this report. Place three stars (★★★) in the profit column if there is no profit. Do the same for deficit.

c. The company employees have just won a new contract. As a result, variable costs are expected to reach 81 or 82% of next year's projected $900,000 sales. A recent internal study carried out by the company on the various aspects of the manufacturing operations disclosed production inefficiencies. Corrective measures could significantly lower fixed costs. Project a range of fixed costs to show a company profit of anywhere from 50 to 100,000 dollars, given that variable costs are expected to reach 81 or 82% of sales next year.

4.7.3 Programming Problems: Scientific/ Mathematical

1. Write programs to accumulate and print the following:

a. $1 + 3 + 5 + 7 + \ldots + 225$ Is accumulation necessary in this problem?

b. $1^1 + 2^2 + 3^3 + 4^4 + \ldots + N^N$,   where N is read from a data record.

c. $2*4*6*8* \ldots *N$ where N is read from a data record.

d. the values for x, y, and z, where $z = x^2 + y^2$, y takes on values 1, 2, and 3, and x takes on values 2, 4, 6, and 8 (use all possible combinations of x and y).

2. Write a program to read a value for N and compute the sum of the squares of the first N even integers. For example, if N = 4, the sum is $2^2 + 4^2 + 6^2 + 8^2$.

3. Write a program to compute:
$$1 + (1+2) + (1+2+3) + (1+2+3+4) + \ldots + (1+2+3+4+\ldots+11).$$

4. Write a program to read a value for N and compute:
$$1*N + 2*N + 3*N + \ldots + 40*N.$$
For example, if N = 3, compute $1\cdot3 + 2\cdot3 + 3\cdot3 + \ldots + 40\cdot3$.

5. Using a DO loop, write a program to determine whether a number N read from a record is prime. A prime number is any number that can be divided only by itself and by 1.

6. Write a program to compute the following sequences of sums:

$S_1 = 1$
$S_2 = 1 + \frac{1}{2}$
$S_3 = 1 + \frac{1}{2} + \frac{1}{3}$
$S_4 = 1 + \frac{1}{2} + \frac{1}{3} + \frac{1}{4}$
.
.
.

How many different sums would you have to compute before a sum exceeds 3.5?

7. Read a positive integer value for N and write the code to:

a. Print the positive even integers that are less than or equal to N; the sequence printed should be in descending order.

b. Print the sum of the first N odd positive integers, starting with 1. For example, if N is 4, then the sum to be printed is $1 + 3 + 5 + 7 = 16$.

8. Write a program to approximate the value of $\pi/4$ using the formula:
$$\frac{\pi}{4} = 1 - \frac{1}{3} + \frac{1}{5} - \frac{1}{7} + \frac{1}{9} - \ldots$$

First approximation is $\pi/4 = 1$
Second approximation is $\pi/4 = 1 - 1/3$
Third approximation is $\pi/4 = 1 - 1/3 + 1/5$
.
.
.

Stop when the difference between two successive approximations is less than 0.01.

9. Write the code to print the following sequence of numbers and stop when the sum of the terms exceeds 1000.

1, 1, 2, 3, 5, 8, 13, ...

[*Hint*: Each term is equal to the sum of the two preceding terms.]

10. The number *e* can be approximated by the formula
$$e_4 = 1 + \frac{1}{1}\left(1 + \frac{1}{2}\left(1 + \frac{1}{3}\left(1 + \frac{1}{4}\right)\right)\right)$$

However, a better approximation would be
$$e_{100} = 1 + \frac{1}{1}\left(1 + \frac{1}{2}\left(1 + \frac{1}{3}\left(1 + \frac{1}{4}\left(1 + \frac{1}{5}\left(1 + \frac{1}{6}\left(\ldots + \frac{1}{99}\left(1 + \frac{1}{100}\right)\right)\right)\right)\right)\right)\ldots\right)$$

Write a program to compute e_{100}.

11. It can be shown that the irrational number $e = 2.71828...$ can be approximated by taking as many terms as desired in the relation

$$e = 1 + 1/1! + 1/2! + 1/3! + 1/4! + ...$$

Write the pseudo code to approximate the value of e using this method. Stop when two successive approximations differ by less than 0.001.

For example: first approximation is 1
second approximation is $1 + 1/1! = 2$
third approximation is $1 + 1/1! + 1/2! = 2.5$
fourth approximation is $1 + 1/1! + 1/2! + 1.3! = 2.666$

12. Write a program to convert binary numbers to decimal. One method that can be used is shown in the following example, where 1011_2 is converted to decimal form:

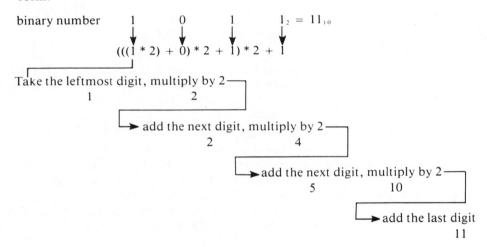

This method assumes that we can decompose a binary number into separate digits. One method of decomposition was shown in example 3 section 4.4.2; the same technique can be used to decompose the binary number 1011_2 into successive digits.

13. Assume each of the variables I, J, K, and L contains a one digit long integer number. Write the code to fuse these 4 digits into the variable M, for example, if $I = 2$, $J = 8$, $K = 3$, and $L = 6$, then $M = (I)(J)(K)(L) = 2836$; M is now a numeric variable equal to 2836.
[*Hint:* This uses the same method as the first part of Problem 12, except that you will multiply by 10, not by 2.]

14. Most periodic functions can be expressed as the sum of an infinite number of sinusoidal waves of different frequencies (a Fourier series). For a square wave of unit amplitude, the ordinate y for any value of x is given as

$$y = \frac{4}{\pi} (\sin x + \frac{1}{3} \sin 3x + \frac{1}{5} \sin 5x + \cdots)$$

Show that this series generates a square wave by computing y for values of x ranging from 0 to 2π in steps of $\pi/10$. Compute each y using the first 50 terms of the Fourier series.

15. A square wave with an amplitude of 1 V and a frequency of 60 Hz is applied to the terminals of a pure inductance of 10 mH. Compute the amplitude of the resulting current wave at 20 intervals over a single cycle of the square wave. Use the first 10 terms of the Fourier expansion for the square wave given in problem 14, replacing x by ωt, where ω is the frequency in radians per second and t is elapsed time.

[*Hint:* At each instant of time, compute the current due to each of the components of the square wave (up to 10) and sum them to get the total current at that instant. Remember that the reactance of the circuit will be different at each frequency.]

[*Check:* the current is 0.301 A at 5 ms]

16. Write a program that will print the inductive reactance, the capacitive reactance, the total impedance, phase angle, and resonant frequency of any circuit having a capacitance of C microfarads, an inductance of L millihenrys, and a resistance of R ohms and subjected to an alternating voltage at a frequency of f hertz. Test the program for $R = 15$, $L = 4.61$, $C = 12.4$, and $f = 450$.
[*Answer:* $X_C = -28.52\ \Omega$,
$X_L = 13.03\ \Omega$, $X = -15.49\ \Omega$, $Z = 21.56\ \Omega$, $\phi = -45.92°$, $f = 665.67$ Hz]

17. Write a program that will compute the total impedance and phase angle for any *RLC* circuit for source frequencies from 0 to 1000 Hz in steps of 50 Hz. Run your program with the circuit values given in problem 16, and plot the resulting points.
[*Check:* At 500 Hz, $X = 18.71$ $\phi = -36.72°$]

18. A circuit in a certain electronic device contains five capacitors and six inductors that can be independently selected, as shown in the diagram. An alternating voltage is applied to the circuit, and it is desired to choose a source frequency that will not cause resonance in the circuit. Write a program that will compute the resonant frequency in hertz for the 30 possible capacitor-inductor combinations.
[*Check:* $F = 438$ Hz when $C = 22\ \mu$F and $h = 6$ mH]

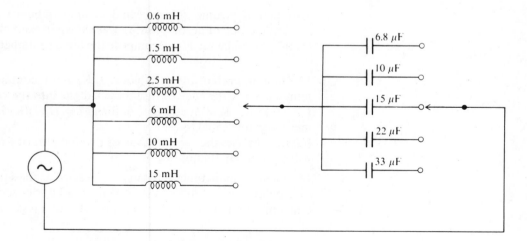

19. *Straight line fitting:* Imagine that you are running an experiment for a physics or a biology project, and you obtain six points with coordinates x and y that you graph carefully as shown. The points seem to fit a straight line, and you would like to find the equation of the line that best fits these points. The equation could then be used to find corresponding y values for points on the x-axis—these points could be between x_1 and x_6 or they could be outside the experimental range.

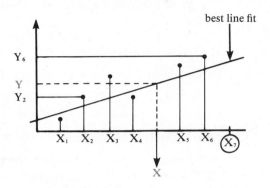

The least squares method can be used to find the equation of the straight line that best fits the experimental points. In this example, we will fit six experimental points (x_1,y_1), (x_2,y_2),...,(x_6,y_6) to the straight line:

$$y = m * x + b$$

where m (the slope) and b (the y intersect) are given by the following formulas:

$$m = \frac{N*SUM_{xy} - SUM_x * SUM_y}{N*SUM_{x^2} - (SUM_x)^2}$$

$$b = \frac{SUM_{x^2}*SUM_y - SUM_x * SUM_{xy}}{N*SUM_{x^2} - (SUM_x)^2}$$

where   N is the total number of points, six in this case
SUM_{xy} is the sum of the $x*y$ product for each point:
   $x_1*y_1 + x_2*y_2 + ... + x_6*y_6$
SUM_y is the sum of the y's, i.e., $y_1 + y_2 + ... + y_6$
SUM_x is the sum of the x's, i.e., $x_1 + x_2 + ... + x_6$
SUM_{x^2} is the sum of all the x's squared, i.e., $x_1^2 + x_2^2 + ... + x_6^2$

Notice that the two denominators are the same.

Write a program to compute m and b for the following two sets of experimental data:

Experiment 1 (6 points)	x	5	29.7	48.4	73	98	8.2				
	y	6.883	-51.13	-94.02	-150	-208.6	0.03				

Experiment 2 (10 points)	x	0.43	0.28	0.39	0.62	0.36	0.7	0.67	0.62	0.23	0.59
	y	0.0047	0.0027	0.0036	0.0065	0.0035	0.007	0.0064	0.0056	0.0021	0.0064

Then compute the difference between each experimental y value and the corresponding y value obtained from the least squares straight line.

Identify the experimental point that seems to be the least accurate in terms of its relationship with the least squares straight line and the other experimental points.

20. The steady-state heat flow through a wall made up of several layers in contact is given by the equation

$$q = \frac{\Delta t}{L_a/k_aA_a + L_b/k_bA_b + L_c/k_cA_c + \cdots + L_n/k_nA_n}$$

where q = total heat flow, Btu/h
  Δt = temperature difference across entire wall, °F
  L = thickness of single layer, ft
  k = thermal conductivity of layer, Btu/ft²h °F/ft
  A = cross-section area, ft²

and the temperature drop across each layer is

$$t = q\,\frac{L}{kA} = qR$$

where R is called the thermal resistance of that layer.

Write a program that will compute the total heat flow through a wall of any number of layers, given the total temperature drop across the wall, and L, k, and A for each layer. Also compute the temperature at the interfaces between layers.

Run your program for a four-layer wall, where one side of the wall is at 80°F and the other side is at 0°F, A (for all layers) is 100 ft², and the conductivities and thicknesses are (starting with the warmer side):

Layer	1	2	3	4
k	0.632	0.068	1.39	0.337
L (ft)	0.578	1.06	0.358	0.783

[*Answer:* q = 419.2 Btu/h, t_1 = 76.17°F, t_2 = 10.82°F, t_3 = 9.74°F]

21. A study was conducted to determine whether using different computer communication modes could affect a student's attitude toward programming. In a computer-related course, 13 students used the batch-processing mode to solve problems on the computer, while 12 other students used the conversational (interactive) mode to solve the same problems. The following entries reflect the average score obtained by each student for the 20 questions of the Attitude Test Toward Programming (ATTP) given at the end of the semester:

Mode of Communication

Batch-Processing	Conversational
2.75	4.15
2.95	3.70
3.00	3.55
3.10	4.45
4.50	4.20
4.75	3.95
2.50	3.80
3.35	4.00
4.00	3.00
3.05	3.65
2.00	4.00
3.35	4.35
4.10	

Students using the conversational approach had a higher average score than students using the batch-processing approach. Write a program to determine if this difference is significant. The difference is significant if $t > 2.069$, where t is given by the following formula:

$$t = \frac{\overline{X}_c - \overline{X}_b}{\sqrt{\dfrac{(N_c - 1)S_c^2 + (N_b - 1)S_b^2}{(N_c + N_b - 2)} \cdot \dfrac{N_c + N_b}{N_c \cdot N_b}}}$$

where $\overline{X}_c$ and $\overline{X}_b$ are the averages of the conversational and batch scores, respectively;

S_c and S_b are the standard deviations for conversational and batch modes respectively (see section 3.8.4 for the programming example of a standard deviation);

N_c and N_b are the number of scores for conversational and batch processing, respectively. [*Expected answer = 2.202*]

22. Legendre Polynomials are defined by the following equations:

$$P_0 = 1$$
$$P_1 = x \text{ where } -1 \le x \le 1$$
$$P_i = \left(\frac{2i - 1}{i}\right)xP_{i-1} - \left(\frac{i - 1}{i}\right)P_{i-2} \text{ for } i = 2, 3,...$$

Write a program to produce a table of Legendre polynomials P_0, P_1, ..., P_{10} for equally spaced values of x such as -1.0, $-.95$, $-.90$,...,$.95$, 1.00.

23. The natural logarithm (base e) of x can be approximated using the series

$$\ln(x) = \left(\frac{x - 1}{x}\right) + \frac{1}{2}\left(\frac{x - 1}{x}\right)^2 + \frac{1}{3}\left(\frac{x - 1}{x}\right)^3 + ...$$

Write a program to approximate the value of $\ln(x)$, with the approximation correct to 3 decimal places. Use the function LOG(X) to compare your results.

24. Write a program to find a five-digit number $d_1d_2d_3d_4d_5$ that when multiplied by a digit k between 2 and 9 will give a result of $d_5d_4d_3d_2d_1$, i.e.,

$$\begin{array}{r} d_1\ d_2\ d_3\ d_4\ d_5 \\ \times\ k \\ \hline d_5\ d_4\ d_3\ d_2\ d_1 \end{array}$$

25. Write a program to compute the area under a curve, $y = f(x)$:

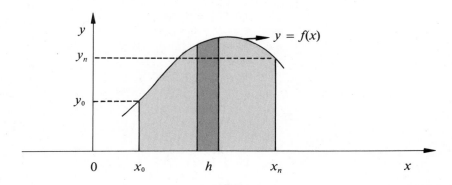

continued on next page

The darkened area under a curve, $y = f(x)$, can be approximated by breaking the interval (x_0, x_n) into n equal intervals of size

$$h = \frac{x_n - x_0}{n}$$

and computing the sum of the areas of the n trapezoids with base h. The smaller the interval h, the closer the approximation is to the exact area. The formula to compute the sum of the areas of the n trapezoids is:

$$A = \frac{h}{2}(y_0 + 2y_1 + 2y_2 + \dots + 2y_{n-1} + y_n)$$

where $y_0, y_1, y_2, \dots, y_n$ are the values of the function at the points $x_0, x_1, x_2, \dots, x_n$. Your program should approximate the area under the curve $y = e^{-x^2/2}$ for x between 1 and 2 for three different values of h, .1, .01, .001. (This is equivalent to obtaining an approximation for the integral $\int_1^2 e^{-x^2/2}$.) The value computed should be approximately 0.34.

26. A *perfect* number is a number that is the sum of all its divisors except itself. Six is the first perfect number; the only numbers that divide 6 evenly are 1, 2, 3, 6, and $6 = 1 + 2 + 3$. An *abundant* number is one that is less than the sum of its divisors (e.g., $12 < 1 + 2 + 3 + 4 + 6$); a *deficient* number is greater than the sum of its divisors (e.g., $9 > 1 + 3$). Write a program to generate a table of the first N integers (N is read from a record) and classify each as perfect, abundant, or deficient.

4.7.4 Selected Answers to Test Yourself

1. a.
```
DO 5 I = 1,99,2
   PRINT*,I
5 CONTINUE
```
b.
```
DO 5 I = 1,25
   PRINT*,(-1)**I
5 CONTINUE
```
c.
```
P = 1.
READ*,X
DO 5 I = 1,X
   P = P/I
   PRINT*,P
5 CONTINUE
```
d.
```
DO 5 I = N,0,-2
   PRINT*,I
5 CONTINUE
```
e.
```
DO 5 I = 1,7
   PRINT*,1./(10**I - 1.)
5 CONTINUE
```
f.
```
DO 5 I = 25,200,25
   P = I/100.
   PRINT*,P
5 CONTINUE
```

2. a.
```
S = 0.
DO 5 I = 1,10
   S = S + I*I
5 CONTINUE
```
b.
```
S = 0.
DO 5 I = 1,10
   S = S + 2.**I
5 CONTINUE
```
c.
```
S = 0.
DO 5 I = 1,1000
   S = S - (-1)**I*I
5 CONTINUE
```
d.
```
P = 1.
S = 0.
DO 5 I = 1,50
   P = P*I
   S = S + P
5 CONTINUE
```
e.
```
S = 0.
DO 5 I = 1,77,2
   S = S + 1./I
5 CONTINUE
```

3. **a.** valid   **b.** valid   **c.** valid   **d.** invalid; inconsist use of the index   **e.** invalid index   **f.** invalid; straddling CONTINUE statements   **g.** invalid; index L is redefined

5. **a.** 120   **b.** 57   **c.** 2   **d.** 9

6. **a.** No; the final value of I will be 11.

   b. No; the average could be 0 because of the integer division!

7. J = 0 since J is implicitly an integer

8. **a.** T   **b.** T.   **c.** F; initial value must always be specified.   **d.** F; the comment will be listed once at compilation time.   **e.** F; if the index is greater than starting value, the loop will be bypassed (if the increment is positive).   **f.** F; nonexecutable statements are processed at compilation time, not execution time.   **g.** F.   **h.** T.   **i.** F.

9.
```
* Flag is a variable name used to record whether or not
* an action has taken place during execution of some code
set flag to 0
WHILE not end of file DO
      read city name, temperature
      IF flag = 0 THEN
            IF temperature ≥ 100 THEN
                  write city name
                  set flag to 1
            ENDIF
      ENDIF
ENDWHILE
```

10. Alternative 1

```
over 10000 = 0
total = 0
WHILE not end of file DO
      read dollar amount
      IF dollar amount > 10000 THEN
            add 1 to over 10000
      ENDIF
      add 1 to total
ENDWHILE
IF over 10000 = total THEN
      write 'yes'
ELSE
      write 'no'
ENDIF
stop
```

Alternative 2

```
WHILE not end of file DO
      read dollar amount
      IF dollar amount ≤ 10000 THEN
            write 'no'
            stop
      ENDIF
ENDWHILE
write 'yes'
stop
```

11.
```
* INITIALIZE THE VARIABLE CONTAINING THE MINIMUM AGE TO 1000!
        CHARACTER DESCR*6
        INTEGER AGE, MINAGE, SEXCOD, SEX
        MINAGE = 1000
     10 READ(5,*,END = 88) AGE,SEXCOD
          IF(MINAGE .GE. AGE)THEN
* STORE THE PERSON'S SEX CODE IN SEX; IF SEXCOD = 1 THEN SEX = 1 ETC.
            SEX = SEXCOD
            MINAGE = AGE
        ENDIF
        GO TO 10
* WHEN THE END OF FILE IS ENCOUNTERED SEX WILL REFLECT SEX OF YOUNGEST PERSON
     88 IF(SEX .EQ. 1) THEN
        DESCR = 'MALE'
      ELSE
        DESCR = 'FEMALE'
      ENDIF
      WRITE(6,*)MINAGE, DESCR
      STOP
      END
```

12.
```
read number
K = 7
digit = 7
WHILE K ≥ 0 and digit ≠ 0 DO
        digit = number /10ᴷ
         number = number − digit * 10ᵏ
         K = K − 1
ENDWHILE
IF digit = 0 THEN
        print 'digit 0 exists
ELSE
        print ' digit 0 is not present'
ENDIF
```

5 Formatted Input/Output and Random Numbers

5.1 PROGRAMMING EXAMPLE

Problem Specification. Assume you are taking out a $1,000 loan at a yearly interest rate of 12% and you intend to repay that loan at $200 (including the interest payment) per month until the loan is fully repaid. You would like to have an amortization schedule like the following one:

```
                    AMORTIZATION TABLE
          PRINCIPAL  $1000.00   INTEREST  12.00%
               REGULAR PAYMENT $ 200.00

    NO.   INTEREST   AMORTIZED   BALANCE   INTEREST TO DATE
     1     10.00      190.00     810.00        10.00
     2      8.10      191.90     618.10        18.10
     3      6.18      193.82     424.28        24.28
     4      4.24      195.76     228.52        28.52
     5      2.29      197.71      30.81        30.81
     6      0.31       30.81       0.00        31.12

    LAST PAYMENT = $ 31.12
```

Write a program to read a loan principal, an interest rate, and a monthly repayment amount and generate an amortization table similar to the one above.

Solution. If no interest were charged, it would take 5 months to repay a $1,000 loan at $200 per month. When interest is charged, the $200 monthly payment must repay the capital and pay the interest on the outstanding balance of the loan. The part of the monthly payment that goes to repay the capital is called the *amortized* amount. The interest taken from the monthly payment is the interest on the unpaid balance; this amount represents the cost of borrowing money.

In this problem, a 12% yearly interest rate means a 1% monthly interest rate, i.e.,

the interest for month 1 is	$1,000 *	0.01 =	$ 10.00
the payment to capital is	$ 200 −	10.00 =	$190.00
the remaining balance is	$1,000 −	190.00 =	$810.00
the interest for month 2 is	$ 810 *	0.01 =	$ 8.10
the payment to capital is	$ 200 −	8.10 =	$191.90
the remaining balance is	$ 810 −	191.90 =	$618.10

This process continues until the remaining balance is less than or equal to $200 (in this example, $30.81). Since that amount will be paid at the end of the last month, an interest of 1% is computed on that amount (31 cents), so that the last payment is $30.81 + .31 = $31.12. At that point the remaining balance is set to 0, and the accumulated interest is $31.12.

The program to solve this problem is shown in Figure 5.1. Note how the layout of the output is determined by the various formatted WRITE statements. Each WRITE statement requires a FORMAT statement. In Figure 5.1 all the FORMAT statements are grouped into one area after the STOP instruction in order not to interfere visually with the logic of the program. Also notice how one FORMAT statement at lines 39–44 captures the entire set of headers and column captions.

Vertical movement of the printer form is controlled by *carriage control codes* enclosed in quotation marks, as shown in the red shaded area at lines 40–44. Each slash indicates the end of a line, and the carriage control code specifies the vertical paper action to be taken by the printer before it starts printing. The carriage control code blank (' ') tells the printer to advance to the next line before printing, the carriage control code 0 (' Ø ') tells it to skip one line (double space), and the carriage control code + (' + ') tells it to stay on the same line, i.e. write on the line that was just printed (this feature is used to underline or to double strike). Carriage control codes will be discussed in more detail in section 5.2.10.

The program also uses a formatted READ statement at line 15 to capture the data on the input record shown in Figure 5.1. Note that no commas or blank spaces separate the three data items on the input record.

5.2 FORMAT-CONTROLLED INPUT AND OUTPUT

Both the READ and the WRITE statement can be used in conjunction with the FORMAT statement to define precisely the layouts of the input and output records. The programmer can, thus, write the various output fields at predetermined positions on the output record (e.g., a printed line), and similarly, the READ statement can read data from specified positions of an input record.

5.2.1 Input and Output Statements

The WRITE Statement

The general form of the WRITE statement is:

> WRITE (*device number, format statement number*) [*output list*]

where   *device number* is an integer constant or an asterisk representing the output device to be used (printer, tape, screen, disk, and so forth). A typical assignment is:

Device Number	Physical Device
*	system output device (screen on microcomputers)
2 or 6	printer
3, 4, 8 or greater	other devices (tapes, disks, etc.).

```
 1: *  AMORTIZATION PROBLEM
 2: *  BALNCE: BALANCE
 3: *  RATE : INTEREST RATE
 4: *  MONPAY: MONTHLY FIXED PAYMENT
 5: *  PAYMNT: COUNTS THE PAYMENTS
 6: *  ACCINT: ACCUMULATED INTEREST
 7: *  AMORT : MONTHLY AMORTIZED AMOUNT
 8: *  INTBAL: INTEREST ON CURRENT BALANCE
 9: *  LASPAY: LAST PAYMENT
10: *
11:       REAL BALNCE,RATE,MONPAY,ACCINT,AMORT,INTBAL,LASPAY
12:       INTEGER PAYMNT
13:       OPEN(5,FILE='INPUT.DAT')
14:       OPEN(6,FILE='PRN')
15:       READ(5,7) BALNCE, RATE, MONPAY
16:       WRITE(6,1)BALNCE, RATE, MONPAY
17:       RATE   = RATE/100./12.          Convert to monthly decimal interest.
18:    PAYMNT = 0                         Counts the number of payments.
19:       ACCINT = 0.00                   Accumulates the monthly interest payments.
20:    10 IF(BALNCE .GE. MONPAY) THEN     Exit from the loop when balance < monthly payment.
21:       PAYMNT = PAYMNT + 1
22:       INTBAL = RATE * BALNCE          Computes interest on current balance.
23:       ACCINT = ACCINT + INTBAL        Accumulate the monthly interests.
24:       AMORT  = MONPAY - INTBAL        Amortized amount = monthly payment − interest
25:       BALNCE = BALNCE - AMORT         New balance = old balance − amortized amount
26:       WRITE(6,5)PAYMNT,INTBAL,AMORT,BALNCE,ACCINT
27:       GO TO 10
28:       ENDIF
29:    20 PAYMNT = PAYMNT + 1             Count the last payment.
30:       INTBAL = BALNCE * RATE          Compute interest on last payment.
31:       ACCINT = ACCINT + INTBAL        Add last interest to accumulated interest.
32:       AMORT  = BALNCE                 Amortized amount equals last balance.
33:       BALNCE = 0.00                   Set balance to 0; loan has been repaid.
34:       WRITE(6,5)PAYMNT,INTBAL,AMORT,BALNCE,ACCINT
35:       LASPAY = AMORT + INTBAL         Add the last month's interest to amortized amount.
36:       WRITE(6,6) LASPAY               Print the last payment.
37:       STOP
38: *
39:     1 FORMAT ('                     AMORTIZATION TABLE'
40:       A/ ' ',''                PRINCIPAL  $',F7.2,4X,'INTEREST    ',F5.2,'%'
41:       B/ ' ','                  REGULAR PAYMENT $',F6.2
42:       C/ '0','  NO.   INTEREST   AMORTIZED    BALANCE   INTEREST TO DATE'
43:       D/ '+',     __   _____   _____   _____   _____'
44:       E/ '  ')
45:     5 FORMAT(' ', 1X, I1, 6X, F5.2, 6X, F6.2, 6X, F6.2, 8X, F5.2)
46:     6 FORMAT('0', 'LAST PAYMENT= $', F6.2)
47:     7 FORMAT(F7.2, F2.0, F6.2)
48:       END
```

```
                    AMORTIZATION TABLE
              PRINCIPAL  $1000.00   INTEREST    12.00%
                   REGULAR PAYMENT $200.00

   NO.    INTEREST    AMORTIZED    BALANCE    INTEREST TO DATE

    1       10.00       190.00      810.00         10.00
    2        8.10       191.90      618.10         18.10
    3        6.18       193.82      424.28         24.28
    4        4.24       195.76      228.52         28.52
    5        2.29       197.71       30.81         30.81
    6         .31        30.81         .00         31.12

   LAST PAYMENT= $ 31.12
```

Input File

```
1000.0012200.00
```
balance   monthly payment
interest rate

FIGURE 5.1
AN AMORTIZATION SCHEDULE

Throughout this text, 6 will be used for the printer and the asterisk for the terminal.

format statement number is an integer number (1 through 99999) identifying the FORMAT statement that describes the position of the output item(s) on the output device.

output list is a list of variable names separated by commas; the values of these variables are to be written on the output device according to the specified format. PARAMETER names cannot be part of the output list. In most FORTRAN 77 versions, the output list can include alphanumeric literals (characters enclosed in quotation marks) and numeric expressions not starting with a left parenthesis (a + sign must precede a left parenthesis).

EXAMPLES

The first WRITE statement can be interpreted as follows: Write the contents of memory locations PAY, HRS, and RATE onto device number 6 (generally a printer) according to the layout description given by the FORMAT labeled 10. The second WRITE statement will print the label 'PAY = ', followed by the result of the evaluation of HRS*RATE.

Printer output lines typically contain 80 or 132 characters (print positions). Many printers used with microcomputers can only handle 8½ inch paper forms, resulting in 80 characters per line with 10 CPI (characters per inch). Many such printers can also print characters in compressed form (17.3 CPI), which allows approximately 132 characters per line, but these characters, of course, are harder to read.

The READ Statement

The general form of the READ statement is:

READ (*device number, format statement number* [,END = sn_1][,ERR = sn_2])*input list*

---

where   *device number* is an integer constant or an asterisk representing the input device to be used. A typical assignment is:

Device Number	Physical Device
*	system input device
1 or 5	disk file
3, 4, 8 or greater	other assigned devices

Throughout this text, the asterisk will refer to the keyboard/screen and device 5 will refer to disk input files.

format statement number is a user-selected format statement number describing the layout of the data on the input record (1 through 99999).

input list specifies the names of the values to be read from the input medium; each data item on the input record will be stored in the corresponding named memory location specified in the variable list. Commas are used to separate the variables.

The END = option allows the user to tell the system what action(s) to take in the event the end of file is encountered during a READ operation. The system automatically transfers control to sn_1 (a particular statement number) if the END option is used; if the END option is not used, the program terminates execution with an "end of file" error message.

The ERR = option allows the user to tell the system what action(s) to take in the event of a READ error, for example, if the data file cannot be located or there is a data type incompatibility (a numeric value contains a letter instead of a digit, and so forth) during a READ operation. When such an error is detected, the system transfers control to sn_2 (a particular statement number).

EXAMPLE

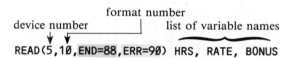

This READ statement can be interpreted as follows: Read three numbers from one or more records (device number 5 may be any input device, depending on the system) and store these three numbers in memory location HRS, RATE, and BONUS, respectively. If an end-of-file record is encountered during the READ operation, control is transferred to statement 88; if an input error occurs (device not ready, invalid data type, and so forth), control is transferred to statement 90.

5.2.2 The FORMAT Statement

The FORMAT statement is a nonexecutable statement that is used in conjunction with the READ and WRITE statements to specify the way in which input/output records are to be arranged.

OUTPUT

The FORMAT statement allows the user to design the layout of the output line by specifying:

- the exact positioning of each result on the output line
- the number of digits to the right of the decimal point
- the number of print positions allocated for each result to be printed.

Each WRITE statement must specify a FORMAT statement number, and each FORMAT statement must have a statement number. The WRITE operation is carried out according to the directions specified in the FORMAT statement. In essence, the WRITE statement specifies the variables that are to be printed and the FORMAT statement directs the way in which the corresponding values are to appear on the output line.

FORMAT statements can be placed anywhere in a program (before the END statement). Some programmers prefer to place all their formats at the end or beginning of their programs, while others like to have them immediately follow their associated WRITE statements. Recall that the link between the WRITE and the FORMAT statement is the format statement number specified in parentheses in the WRITE statement.

The image of the line to be printed is formed in memory before it is actually printed. After all the output values have been placed in their proper positions in the image, the image is printed as one output record (output line) on the printer. However, the first character of the image in memory is *never* printed: it is the carriage control code, which determines what vertical paper action is to be taken before the output line is printed (see sections 5.1 and 5.2.10).

EXAMPLE

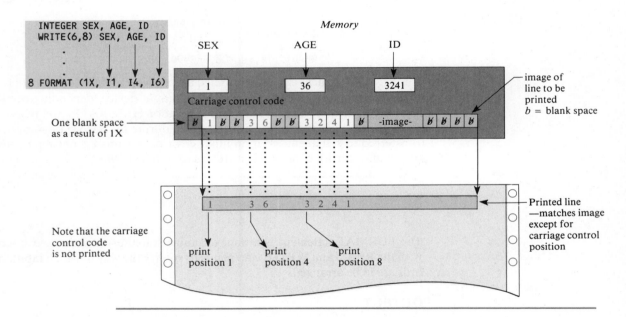

This output operation can be interpreted as follows: Write three numbers (three variables are named) on output device 6 according to the data layout described by the FORMAT statement labeled 8. The image line is created by the FORMAT as follows: A blank space is introduced in the first position as a result of 1X, the value of SEX is placed as an integer value (specified by the I format code) in the next image position (I1), the AGE value is placed in the next four positions (I4), and the ID value is placed in the next six positions (I6). **Note that these values are *right-justified* in the output field** (the right-most digit is placed in the right-most position of the field) and that leading blanks are provided to complete the field width. When the image line is completed in memory, the printer looks at the carriage control code to determine what action to take (space to the next line in this case), then the image line (minus the carriage control code) is printed on the output device. The first character on the output line is a 1, not a blank space.

INPUT

The FORMAT statement is used in conjunction with the READ statement to provide the following information:

- the number of items per record
- the starting position of each data item
- the number of positions used by each data item (item width)
- the type—integer, real, character, . . .—of each data item

The FORMAT statement tells the computer precisely how the READ operation is to be performed, that is, how to process the various data items on the input record. Each READ statement must specify a FORMAT statement number; each FORMAT statement must have a statement number so that it can be referenced. The READ operation is carried out according to the directions described in the FORMAT statement.

Like the FORMAT statements specifying output layouts, FORMAT statements for READ operations can be placed anywhere in the program (before the END statement)—at the beginning or end of the program or immediately following the associated READ statements.

EXAMPLE

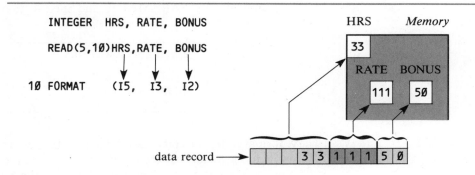

```
INTEGER  HRS, RATE, BONUS

READ(5,10)HRS,RATE, BONUS

10 FORMAT   (I5,  I3,  I2)
```

This input operation can be interpreted as follows: Read three numbers (three variables are named) from a record (device number 5) according to the data layout described by the FORMAT labeled 10. FORMAT 10 can be interpreted as follows: The first number (HRS) will be an integer number (specified by the I format code) found in the first five positions (1–5). The next number (RATE) will be an integer number found in the next three positions (6–8), and the last number (BONUS) will be an integer found in the next two positions (9–10).

General Form of FORMAT statements

The general form of the FORMAT statement is

$$\text{statement number FORMAT } (fd_1, fd_2, \ldots, fd_n)$$

where   *statement number* is the format label referred to in a READ or WRITE statement. $fd_1, fd_2, \ldots, fd_n$ are format codes.

There are two types of format codes:

1. Data format codes identify the type of the item to be read or written, for example, I for Integers, F for real numbers (Floating point), and A for character (Alphanumeric) data.

2. Edit codes control the placement of the various data items in the input/output record. The edit codes are:

- X for spacing
- T for specifying the beginning column position for a data field
- Single quote (') for H to specify literal data (for output records only)
- Slash symbol (/) to indicate transmission of current record to/from input/output device

All format codes must be separated from one another by commas, with the exception of the slash code (/) where the comma is optional.

Order of FORTRAN Statements

With the FORMAT statements the order table of FORTRAN elements becomes

Comment and FORMAT statements	PARAMETER and Specification statements
	Executable statements
END statement	

5.2.3 The X Format Code

The X format code is an edit code used to specify spaces on an input or output record. On output it is generally used to provide margins or to separate output fields by a certain number of blank spaces. The general form of the X format code is:

$$nX$$

where   *n* is an integer specifying the number of spaces (blanks) desired.

EXAMPLE 1

```
    K = 14
    WRITE(6,11)K              image line
 11 FORMAT(3X,I2)
```

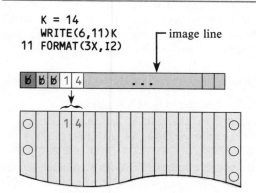

Before printing K, leave two blank spaces (the first space is the carriage control code); then print an integer using two positions (I2).

Note that the X format code does not have a corresponding item in the variable list of the WRITE statement.

EXAMPLE 2

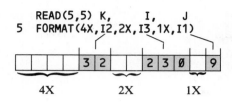

Skip the first four positions. Starting in position 5 read a two-digit integer (32) into K, then skip two positions and read a three-digit integer 230 into I. Finally, skip one position and read 9 into J.

5.2.4 The I Format Code

The I format code is reserved exclusively for integer input/output.

OUTPUT

The general form of the I format code for output is

$$nIw$$

where   I specifies that an integer is to be written.

         w specifies the width of the output field, i.e., the number of print positions reserved for the integer value on the output line.

         n is a duplication factor specifying consecutive occurrences of the I format code.

All values printed are right-justified (the right-most digit is placed on the right-most print position of the output field) with blank spaces inserted to the left in place of leading zeros. Since a negative sign occupies a print position, an extra position for the sign should be included in the field width w if the number is negative.

EXAMPLE 1

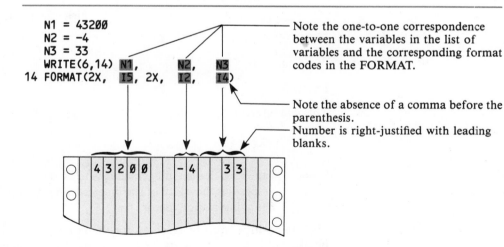

The first variable in the variable list (N1) is associated with the first format code (I5), the second variable (N2) is associated with the second numeric format code (I2), and N3 is associated with the format code I4. Note that N3 has two leading blank spaces.

EXAMPLE 2

```
      K = 35
      J = -5
      WRITE(6,12)K
   12 FORMAT(2X,I3)
      L = -K*J
      WRITE(6,11)L,J
   11 FORMAT(6X,2(I3,1X))
```

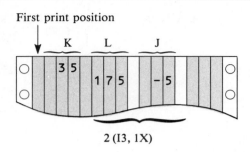

Note that a separate output line is printed for each WRITE statement. The first WRITE statement prints one number on one line, whereas the second WRITE statement prints two entries on a new line. Also note that the duplication field 2(I3,1X) is equivalent to I3,1X,I3,1X.

Care must be exercised to provide a sufficient number of print positions for all the digits including the negative sign, if required. If not enough spaces are allocated, an error message will be printed. The exact form of the message will differ among systems. In the following example a set of asterisks indicates insufficient field width.

EXAMPLE 3

```
      K = 1234
      J = -14
      WRITE(6,15)K,     J,     J


   15 FORMAT (3X,I3,1X,I2,2X,I4)
```

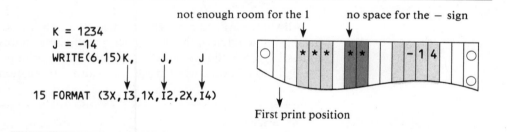

INPUT

The general form of the I format code for input is

$$nIw$$

where   I specifies that an integer value is to be read.
         w specifies the width of the integer field (number of positions).
         n is a duplication factor.

One position must be reserved for the minus sign if the integer is negative. Any blanks within the integer data field, whether leading, imbedded, or trailing, are interpreted as zeros; hence the integer number must be right-justified within the field. Integer data can consist only of the digits 0 through 9 and the + and - sign; any other character entered in an I field will result in an execution-time READ error, which can be detected by the ERR = option in the READ statement.

EXAMPLE

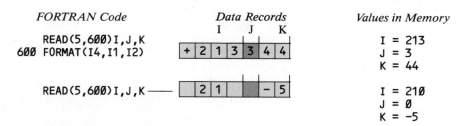

FORTRAN Code	Data Records	Values in Memory

FORTRAN Code:
```
      READ(5,600)I,J,K
600  FORMAT(I4,I1,I2)
```
Data Records (I J K): `+ 2 1 3 3 4 4`

Values in Memory:
I = 213
J = 3
K = 44

FORTRAN Code:
```
      READ(5,600)I,J,K
```
Data Records: `2 1    - 5`

Values in Memory:
I = 210
J = 0
K = −5

In this example the READ list specifies three numbers to be read. Since the FORMAT has three data format codes, the three numbers are to be read from one record. Note that the leading and trailing blanks are read as zeros in the second record. Also note that the plus sign for I in the first data record is not really needed to identify a positive number. Reading starts at the first position of the record unless otherwise specified by T or X edit format codes. Each new field immediately follows the preceding field on the data record, as long as there are no other intervening control format codes in the FORMAT.

5.2.5 The F Format Code

OUTPUT

Real data is described by the F (Floating point) format code, which has the general form

$$nFw.d$$

where   F specifies that a real number is to be printed out.

w specifies the total number of print positions for the number field. It should include sufficient positions for the sign if needed, the digits to the left of the decimal point, the decimal point, and however many digits are needed to the right of the decimal point.

n is the duplication count.

d specifies the number of digits that are to be printed to the right of the decimal point.

The decimal point is *always* printed. It occupies one print position in the output field and hence must be included in the total number of print positions (w) allocated for the real value. One print position must also be allowed for the negative sign if the number is negative.

The F format code can be used *only* for real variables. The reader may wonder why it is necessary to worry about the number of digits to the right of the decimal point on the output. Internally, the computer carries out computations to many decimal places; for example, the result of 10.12*5.24 is stored internally as 53.0288, although the programmer may only be interested in the first two decimal positions (e.g., for dollars and cents). Hence it is always the programmer's responsibility to specify the number of digits wanted for the fractional part of the result. The F format rounds the printed values. Thus if the internal value 14.636 is to be printed with two digits to the right of the decimal point, then 14.64 will be printed; if that same value is to be printed with no digits to the right of the decimal point, 15. will be printed, since 14.6 rounds off to 15.

EXAMPLE 1

```
        A = 63.426
        B = -4.2
        WRITE(6,15) A ,          A,              A,        B,       B
15 FORMAT(1X, F6.3,      F9.5,      1X,    F6.1,    F6.1,    F4.0)
```

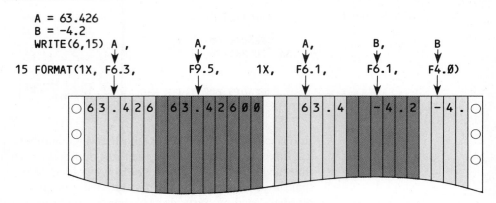

Note that if the number of digits to be printed is less than the width of the field reserved for it, the number is right-justified in the field, with blanks inserted to the left instead of leading zeros.

EXAMPLE 2

```
        A = 12.6534
        B = 13.7
        WRITE(6,16)  A,         A ,      A ,      B
16 FORMAT(2X,   F9.3,      F6.1,    F5.0,    F7.3)
```

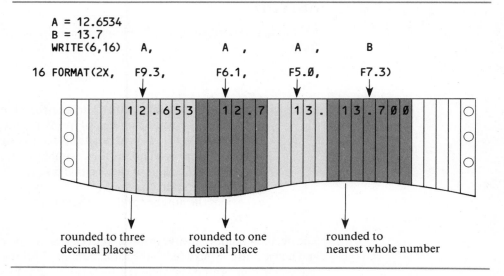

rounded to three   rounded to one   rounded to
decimal places   decimal place   nearest whole number

Note that the value 13.700 is printed for the variable B, since the format specifies three fractional positions.

It is important to understand the way in which digits are printed on output, given the format F$w.d$. The computer first tries to print the d fractional digits, then the decimal point, and finally the remaining digits (the whole part of the number). If there is insufficient space at any time, an execution-time format error occurs.

For example, suppose we wanted to print 56.78 and we specified F4.2. The computer would print the 8, then the 7, then the decimal point, then the 6; at this point the total field width (4) is filled, and a format error occurs (since there is no position left for the 5). Consider another example:

EXAMPLE 3

```
A = -123.456
B = 2509.01
C = 12.
WRITE(6,12) A ,     A ,     B,     C
```

12 FORMAT(1X, F7.3, 1X,F5.1, 1X,F6.2, 1X,F5.4)

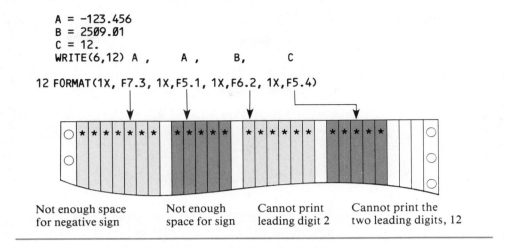

Not enough space for negative sign | Not enough space for sign | Cannot print leading digit 2 | Cannot print the two leading digits, 12

To provide a field (w) sufficiently large to represent a real number, the following rule should be observed:

$$\text{minimum width field } w = d + 1 + (1) + wh$$

Field width — Number of digits to the right of decimal point — Decimal point — Sign, if needed — Number of digits in the whole portion of the number (digits to left of decimal point).

Caution. Real variables that are to be printed must be described by F format codes, similarly, integer variables that are to be printed must be described by I format codes. The following code segment is invalid:

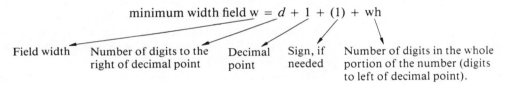

```
      REAL A,B,C
      INTEGER I,J,K
      WRITE(6,100) A , B , C
100   FORMAT (1X, I2, I4, I3)   Should be, for example, FORMAT (1X, F6.2, F4.0, F6.1)
      WRITE(6,200) I, J, K
200   FORMAT (1X,  3F5.1)        should be, for example, FORMAT (1X, 3I5)
```

INPUT

The general form of the F format code is

$$\boxed{n\text{F}w.d}$$

where   F specifies that a real number is to be read.

w specifies the field width (number of positions on input record).

d tells the system where to place the decimal point in the number read into memory, in case no decimal point is present in the number field.

n is the duplication count.

If no decimal point is present in the input field on the data record, w columns (positions) are read, and the number is stored in memory with the decimal point assumed to be d positions to the left of the right-most digit specified in the input field.

EXAMPLE 1

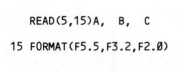

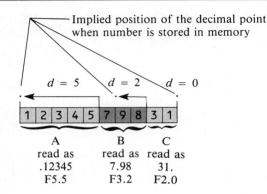

```
        READ(5,15)A,  B,  C

   15 FORMAT(F5.5,F3.2,F2.0)
```

In this example three real numbers are to be read. The first one is located in the first five positions. Since no decimal point is entered in these five positions, the decimal point is assumed to be five positions to the left of the right-most digit ($d = 5$); hence A = .12345, that is, A has five digits to the right of the decimal point. For B, the decimal point is implied to be two positions to the left of the right-most digit, hence B = 7.98. For C, the implied position of the decimal point is at the right-most position of the field ($d = 0$).

If a decimal point is present in the number field, the number and the decimal point are read, as is, into memory, and the implied position of the decimal point given by d in the FORMAT is disregarded. The presence of a decimal point on the data record overrides the specified position d.

However, d must always be specified in the format even though it will not be used when the decimal point is present in the input field.

In all cases d must be such that $d \leq w$. Blanks within the field are treated as zeros. Both the sign and the decimal point (if any) count as separate positions in the input field.

EXAMPLE 2

```
        READ(5,1)X,   Y,   Z

    1 FORMAT (F5.5, 2F3.0)
```

In this example decimal points have been entered in each field, hence the values for X, Y, and Z are those entered in the three fields. The explicit position of the decimal point overrides the implicit position given by d.

In the following example the position of the decimal point is identified explicitly for the variables Y and W and implicitly for the variables X and Z.

EXAMPLE 3

```
READ(5,15)X,  Y,  Z,    W
15 FORMAT(F1.1,F2.0,F3.2,F4.3)
```

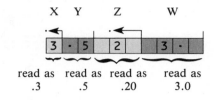

EXAMPLE 4

In this example, a READ error will occur at execution time as a result of the invalid character (−) in the X input field; the second decimal point in the Y field is invalid, as is the character A in the Z field. The program will terminate execution at the very first error with an error message (unless the ERR = option is specified).

```
READ(5,8)X,  Y,  Z

8 FORMAT(F4.2,F5.1,F2.0)
```

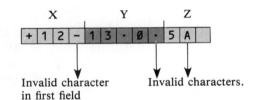

It is permissible to combine both real and integer variables in a READ list. The programmer must then make sure that each variable name in the READ list is properly described by a format code of the corresponding type. If a real variable name is read, its corresponding format code should be F; if an integer variable name is read, its corresponding format code should be I.

EXAMPLE 5

```
READ(5,15) A ,  K ,  B ,  J
15 FORMAT(   F4.2,  I2,  F4.0,  I2)
```

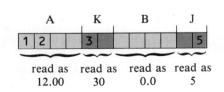

Note the type correspondence between each variable name and its format code.

1. Which of the following output instructions are invalid? Explain why. (Assume 6 represents the output device.)

a.
```
   WRITE(6,10),A,B,C
10 FORMAT(1X,F1.0,F2.0,F3.0)
```

b.
```
   WRITE(6,5)I,J
 5 FORMAT(I1,I4)
```

c.
```
   WRITE(6,16)A,I,J
16 FORMAT(3X,F4.5,I2,I1)
```

d.
```
   WRITE(6,7)A,K,C
 7 FORMAT(F5.2,I3,F4.)
```

e.
```
   WRITE(6,12.)X,Y
12 FORMAT(2X,F3.1,F3.1)
```

f.
```
   WRITE(6,15)I,X,K
15 FORMAT(1X,I2,I3,I1)
```

g.
```
   WRITE(5,9)KL,M1
 9 FORMAT(3X,I3,I3)
```

2. Show the printed output field (print positions) for A, given the following format specifications:

a. A = 743.25   FORMAT(1X,F10.3)

b. A = −643.281   FORMAT(1X,F7.2)

c. A = −4768.6   FORMAT(1X,F6.0)

d. A = 328.74   FORMAT(1X,F5.2)

e. A = .37   FORMAT(1X,F5.2)

3. Which of the following coding segments are valid? If invalid, explain why.

a.
```
   READ (5,10),A,B,C
10 FORMAT(F1.0,F2.0,F3.0)
```

b.
```
   READ(5,5) I,J
 5 FORMAT(I1,I4)
```

c.
```
   READ(5,6)A,I,J
 6 FORMAT(F4.5,I2,I1)
```

d.
```
   READ(5,7)A,B,C
 7 FORMAT(F5.2,I3,F4)
```

e.
```
   READ(5,8)X,J,Y
 8 FORMAT(F3.1,F2.1,I4)
```

f.
```
   READ(5,5)X,I
 5 FORMAT(1X,F5.1 I2)
```

4. Given the following READ statement and data record, what values would be read for I,J,K for the following formats?

```
READ (5,5)I,J,K
```

┌──────── position 1 of input record

| 1 | 3 | | 5 | . | 2 | | | | − | 4 | 6 | 7 | . | 1 | 9 | |

a. 5 FORMAT(I1,I1,I1)

b. 5 FORMAT(2X,1X,I1,1X,I2,I5)

c. 5 FORMAT(I3,I1,1X,I1)

d. 5 FORMAT(I4,I3,I5)

e. 5 FORMAT(7X,I1,I4,I1)

f. 5 FORMAT(2(1X,I1),5X,I3)

5. The following set of numbers is to be recorded as a data file consisting of four records with three entries per record:

Field 1	Field 2	Field 3
−.5	2000.00	.0
100.0	100000.00	.8
47.8	99000.88	.09
3.6	1001.02	.06

Each record of the data file is to be read by the statement
READ(5,6)FLD1,FLD2,FLD3 where 6 is the one and only FORMAT statement
used to read all four records.

a. Show exactly how you would type the four records and specify the FORMAT
used to read these four records. In this part of the problem, enter the decimal
point in each number field of the input record.

b. Repeat part (a) but do not enter the decimal point in the number fields.
What will the FORMAT statement be in this case?

6. What values would be read for A, I, S as a result of the following READ operations?

```
READ(5,5)A,I,S
```

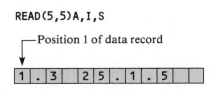

—Position 1 of data record

a. 5 FORMAT(F4.0,I2,3X,F1.1)

b. 5 FORMAT(3X,F4.3,1X,I1,F3.1)

c. 5 FORMAT(2X,F2.1,I3,F3.0)

d. 5 FORMAT(1X,F6.1,I1,F2.2)

e. 5 FORMAT(1X,F1.1,I2,F2.0)

7. Simulate the output produced by the following program segments, indicating
all print positions and blanks.

```
a.    READ(5,10)A,J,X,Z
   10 FORMAT(1X,F3.2,1X,I3,F4.2,F3.0)
      WRITE(5,11)X,A,J,Z
   11 FORMAT(2X,F4.1,2X,F3.1,1X,I3,F2.0)
```

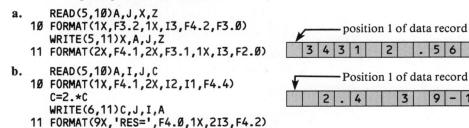

```
b.    READ(5,10)A,I,J,C
   10 FORMAT(1X,F4.1,2X,I2,I1,F4.4)
      C=2.*C
      WRITE(6,11)C,J,I,A
   11 FORMAT(9X,'RES=',F4.0,1X,2I3,F4.2)
```

Answers

1. a. There should be no comma after (6,10); also, the field for A is too small, it
should be at least two positions long.

b. Value of variable I will be used as a carriage control character.

c. F4.5 is an invalid FORMAT code since 5 > 4.

d. F4. is invalid; there must be a digit after the decimal point.

e. No decimal point is used after the format statement number.

f. The variable X must be described with a real format code.

g. Unit 6, not unit 5, represents the output device.

2. a. | | | | | 7 | 4 | 3 | . | 2 | 5 | 0 |

b. | − | 6 | 4 | 3 | . | 2 | 8 |

c. | − | 4 | 7 | 6 | 9 | . |

d. | * | * | * | * | * |

e. | | | | . | 3 | 7 |

3. a. Invalid; comma after (3,10).

b. Valid.

c. Invalid; F4.5.

d. Invalid; integer format for real variable B, and F4 is invalid.

e. Invalid; real format for integer variable J and integer format for real variable Y.

f. Invalid; a comma is needed to separate fields.

4. a. 1, 3, 0

b. 5, 20, -46

c. 130, 5, 2

d. 1305, invalid data, -46

e. 0, -46, 7

f. 3,5, -46

5. a.

```
       - 5 0 0 2 0 0 0 0 0 0 0 0
 1 0 0 0 1 0 0 0 0 0 0 0 0 8 0
 0 4 7 8 0 9 9 0 0 0 8 8 0 9
 0 0 3 6 0 0 1 0 0 1 0 2 0 6
```

```
READ(5,6)FLD1,FLD2,FLD3
6 FORMAT(F4.1, F8.2, F2.2)
```

b.

```
 - . 5 0 0 0 2 0 0 0 . 0 0 . 0 0
 1 0 0 . 0 1 0 0 0 0 0 . 0 0 . 8 0
 4 7 . 8 0 9 9 0 0 0 . 8 8 0 . 0 9
 3 . 6 0 0 1 0 0 1 . 0 2 0 0 . 0 6
```

```
READ(5,6)FLD1,FLD2,FLD3
6 FORMAT(F5.0, F9.0, F3.0)
```

6. a. 1.3, 25, .5

b. 25, invalid data, 50.0

c. 3.0, Invalid data, 1.5

d. Invalid data, 1, .5

e. 0., 30, 25.

7. a. A = 3.43, J = 20, X = .56, Z = 21.

```
       .6    3.4    20**
```

b. A = 2.4, I = 30, J = 9, C = -1.3

```
          RES=  -3.    9  302.40
```

5.2.7 The A Format Code

OUTPUT

The A format code is used to print character data. A stands for *alphanumeric* (letters of the alphabet and other characters). The general format of the A format code is

$$nA[w]$$

where w specifies the width of the output field. If w is omitted, the size of the output field is determined by the size of the variable declared in the CHARACTER statement.

   n is the duplication count.

Variables that are to be printed using the A format *must* be declared in a CHARACTER specification statement.

If the output field w is less than the size v of the variable declared in the CHARACTER statement (i.e., if the text is larger than the output field size), then only the left-most characters of the character variable are printed. If the output field w is longer than the number of characters v of the character variable, the text is right-justified in the field with $w - v$ leading blanks. Analyze the following two examples carefully.

EXAMPLE 1

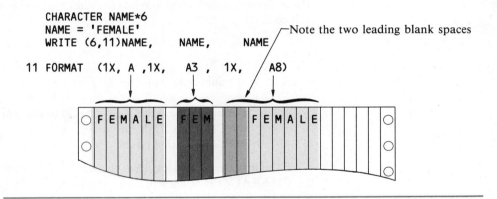

```
CHARACTER NAME*6
NAME = 'FEMALE'
WRITE (6,11)NAME,    NAME,    NAME

11 FORMAT  (1X, A ,1X,  A3 ,  1X,    A8)
```

Note the two leading blank spaces

EXAMPLE 2

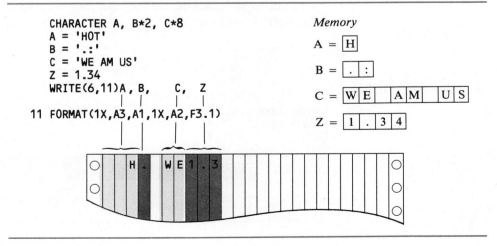

```
CHARACTER A, B*2, C*8
A = 'HOT'
B = '.:'
C = 'WE AM US'
Z = 1.34
WRITE(6,11)A, B,    C,  Z

11 FORMAT(1X,A3,A1,1X,A2,F3.1)
```

Memory

A = ⬚H⬚

B = ⬚.⬚:⬚

C = ⬚WE⬚ ⬚AM⬚ ⬚US⬚

Z = ⬚1⬚.⬚3⬚4⬚

Most FORTRAN versions allow a literal in the output list of the WRITE statement, in which case a corresponding A format code must be specified in the FORMAT.

EXAMPLE

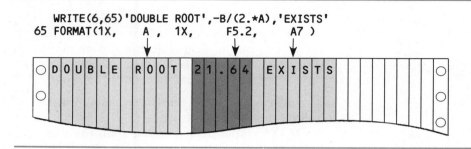

```
      WRITE(6,65)'DOUBLE ROOT',-B/(2.*A),'EXISTS'
   65 FORMAT(1X,   A ,  1X,      F5.2,      A7 )
```

INPUT

The A format code is used to read character type data. The general form of the A format code is:

$$nA[w]$$

where   A specifies that character data is to be read.

      w specifies the width of the input field on the input record. If w is omitted, the size of the input field is equal to the length of the variable specified in the CHARACTER statement.

      n is the duplication count.

If the input field w is less than the size v of the character variable (as declared in the CHARACTER statement), the w characters are read from the input field and stored left-justified in memory with blanks to the right to complete the memory width of the variable. If the input field w is larger than the size v of the character variable, the right-most v characters of the input field are read and stored in memory. Analyze Examples 1 and 2 carefully.

EXAMPLE 1

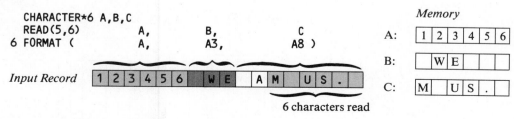

```
      CHARACTER*6 A,B,C
      READ(5,6)        A,      B,          C
   6 FORMAT (         A,      A3,         A8 )
```

EXAMPLE 2

```
        CHARACTER   ME*4,SEX,NAME*8,LOAN*4

        READ(5,10) NAME,SEX,     ME,      LOAN
     10 FORMAT(      A8,     A1,2X,   A3,      A6 )
```

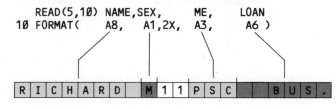

Memory

NAME = | R | I | C | H | A | R | D | |

SEX = | M |

ME   = | P | S | C | |

LOAN = | B | U | S | . |

EXAMPLE 3   Given the following record, the code to read the name, address, account number, and social security number would be:

01 02 03	04 05 06 07 08 09 10 11	12	13 14 15 16 17 18 19 20 21 22 23 24 25	26	27 28 29 30 31 32 33	34	35 36 37 38 39 40 41 42 43
	Name		Address		Acct. Number		Social Security #

```
        CHARACTER NAME*8, ADRESS*13, ACCT*7, SSNO*9
        READ(5,100)NAME,ADRESS,ACCT,SSNO
    100 FORMAT(3X,A,1X,A,1X,A,1X,A)
```

The duplication count can also be used as follows:

EXAMPLE 4
```
        CHARACTER*6, NAME1, NAME2, NAME3
        READ(5,6)NAME1, NAME2, NAME3
      6 FORMAT(3(A7,1X))
```

Value Stored in Memory

NAME1 | S | U | S | A | N |
NAME2 | S | T | E | R | I | X |
NAME3 | S | O | N | I | A |

Data Record

| | | S | U | S | A | N | | A | S | T | E | R | I | X | | S | O | N | I | A | | |

5.2.8 The T Format Code

The T format code is a format control code used to specify the beginning position of a data field on an input or output record. Check your technical reference manual to determine if this feature is available on your system. The general form of the T format code is

$$\boxed{\text{T}n}$$

where   *n* specifies the first column position of an input/output field that is to be printed or read.

The T format code can be used to provide margins and act as a tab feature of sorts; it is also extremely convenient when numerous variables must be read from pre-designed input records or written on forms such as business forms, checks, reports, and so forth. Consider the following examples:

EXAMPLE 1

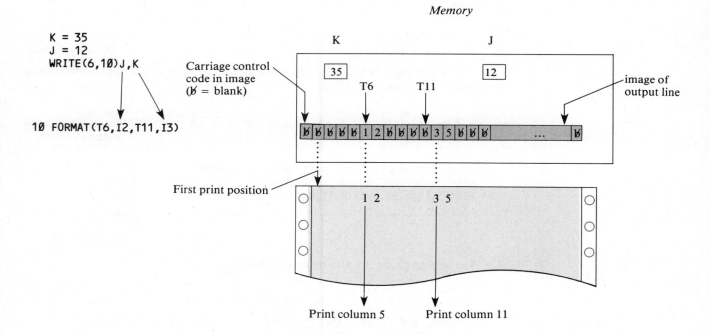

```
K = 35
J = 12
WRITE(6,10)J,K

10 FORMAT(T6,I2,T11,I3)
```

The format code T6 specifies that the output field for J is to start in print position 5 (see the image line above), and T11 specifies that the output field for K is to start in print position 10. The T format code arbitrarily allows the programmer to skip to any desired position on the line. Note that using 5X in the FORMAT instead of T6 would have started J at the same print position.

EXAMPLE 2   To print the various captions and numeric entries of the form shown below, the following code could be used.

```
     WRITE(6,100)
100  FORMAT(T2,'DEPARTMENT',T15,'ITEM',T22,'QUANTITY',T33,'COST/ITEM' ...
        .
        .
     WRITE(6,200)DEPT,ITEM,QTY,COST,VALUE,TOTALS
200  FORMAT(T6,I2,T15,I4,T24,I3,T35,F5.2,T45,F5.2,T53,F6.2)
        .
        .
     WRITE(6,300)GRAND
300  FORMAT(T39,'GRAND TOTAL', 2X,F6.2)
```

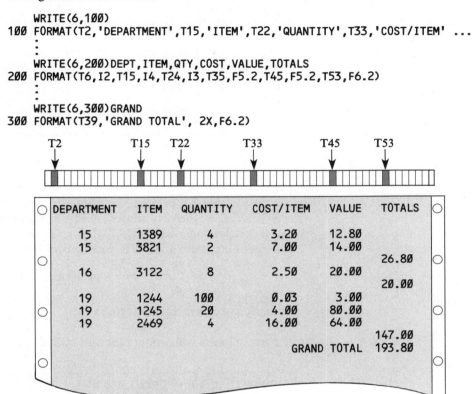

5.2.9 The Format Code for Literal Data (Output only)

Literal data can be specified in a FORMAT in either of two ways:

- using apostrophes (') around a string of characters
- using nH (H is the Hollerith editing code), where n is the number of characters appearing after the H, for example

  3HYES is equivalent to 'YES'
  13HHOW ARE YOU? is equivalent to the literal 'HOW ARE YOU?'
  5HEQUATION will be truncated and appear at execution time as EQUAT

This form of literal specification is rarely used now; it is shown here because it appears in older FORTRAN programs.

The general forms of the literal format codes are:

'literal field'   or n('literal field')   or nH

A single FORMAT statement can describe any number of literals, as in

```
    K = 35
    J = 3
    WRITE(6,11)J,K
 11 FORMAT(2X,'NO-BOYS=',I2,2X,'NO-GIRLS=',I3)
```

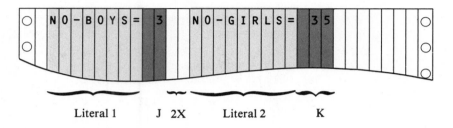

Before the variable J is printed, the printer is asked to start in print position 2 and write NO-BOYS = ; then J is printed. Before K is printed, the printer is asked to space two print positions and write NO-GIRLS = . Then the value for K is printed.

It is possible to have a WRITE statement without any variable list as in

Note, *no* input list

```
    WRITE(6,11)
 11 FORMAT(2X,'XYZ CORPORATION')
```

These statements will produce the output line

Such WRITE statements are generally used to produce headings or page titles.

Finally, the duplication count can be used with literal data as follows:

```
    WRITE(6,7)
  7 FORMAT(1X,80('*'))
```

This will produce a string of 80 asterisks on the output line.

5.2.10 Carriage Control Characters

The first character of every image line sent to the printer is used as a code to determine the vertical spacing on the paper. This code is *never* printed. It is just a signal to the printer to tell it to single-space, double-space, skip to the top of a new page, and so forth. The list in Figure 5.2 summarizes permissible codes and the meaning associated with each.

Code (character)	Meaning
1	Skip to the top of a new page
0	Double-space.
+	Do not space, i.e., stay on the same line. This code is often used for underlining and double striking.
blank	Single-space.
other characters	May have special printer control effects at particular installations.

FIGURE 5.2
*CARRIAGE CONTROL
CHARACTERS*

The vertical movement of the output form (page) is decided upon at the very beginning of the WRITE instruction when the printer interprets the carriage control code. Before the printer writes anything, it checks the carriage control code to see whether to first space a line, double-space, skip to the top of a new page, and so forth. *Then* it writes the output line. The vertical spacing of the form is *not* performed at the end of the WRITE operation.

It is good practice to always start a FORMAT with an explicit carriage control code. The single character literal or an X code at the start of the format enhances clarity and documentation. The following example illustrates the consequences of forgetting the carriage control code.

EXAMPLE 1

```
    AV = 62.0
    WRITE(6,10)AV
10 FORMAT(F4.1,'(AVERAGE)')
```

This would result in the following output

Last printed line.
The 6 of 62.0 is interpreted as a carriage
control character since it is in the
first position of the image line. The
digit 6 might be interpreted as space one
line, or it might mean to skip six pages!

Image of output line in memory

Unpredictable spacing by printer because
carriage control code = 6.

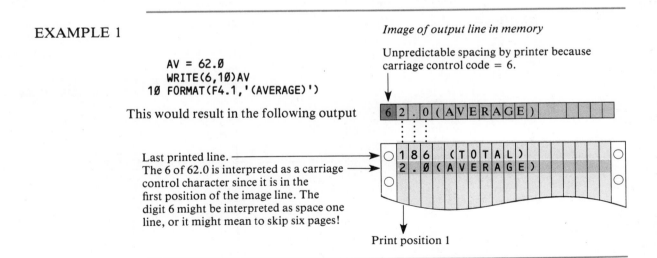

Print position 1

The following examples further illustrate the use of carriage control codes:

EXAMPLE 2

```
      INTEGER PCOUNT
      PCOUNT = 423
      WRITE(6,50)
   50 FORMAT('0','PARTICLE COUNT=',I3)
```

This code segment would yield
the following output:

After completing preceding WRITE,
the printer is still on this line.
As a result of the carriage control
code 0, the paper moves up two lines,
leaving one blank line between the last
line printed and the current line.

Image of output line in memory

Carriage control code of 0
means advance 2 lines before printing.

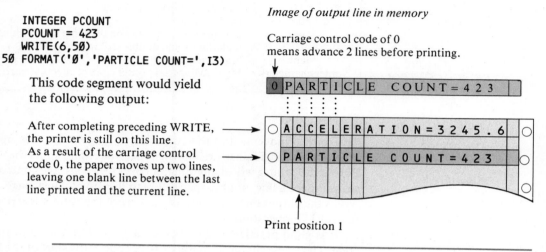

Print position 1

EXAMPLE 3

```
      :
      J = 623
      WRITE(6,15)J
   15 FORMAT('1',I7)
```

This code segment would yield
the following output:

Last printed line

The output is printed at top of
new page.

Image line

carriage control code of 1 means skip to top of next page

```
1          6 2 3
```

DEVIATION IS 17.3

remainder of page

6 2 3

EXAMPLE 4

```
WRITE(6,15)PAY
IF (PAY .GT. 1000.) THEN
      BONUS = .1 * PAY
      WRITE(6,20) BONUS
ENDIF
15 FORMAT(1X,'PAY=',F7.2)
20 FORMAT('+',12X,'BONUS=',F6.2)
```

carriage control + means do not advance to next line.

Last line printed ──────────────────────▶

At the conclusion of WRITE(6,15), the literal message is printed and the printer stays put. The next WRITE statement tells the printer not to advance the form (+) but to print BONUS on the very same line.

If PAY > 1000 a bonus is printed on the same line as the pay, otherwise no bonus is computed or printed.

5.2.11 Do It Now

1. Show the output produced by the following sets of statements, assuming that

A = −123.45
B = 67.2
L = 123
C = −.06

a.
```
    WRITE(6,11)A,L,C
 11 FORMAT(2X,F6.1,2X,I4,1X,F6.3)
```

b.
```
    WRITE(6,12)B,A,C
 12 FORMAT(1X,F3.1,1X,F4.0,1X,F3.1)
```

c.
```
    WRITE(6,13)L,B,C
 13 FORMAT(1X,I2,3X,F6.0,1X,F3.0)
```

d.
```
    WRITE(6,14)A
 14 FORMAT(T3,'A IS',F8.3)
```

e.
```
    CHARACTER GREET*3, PRNN*4
    GREET = 'HELLO'
    PRNN  = 'HE'
    WRITE(6,10)GREET,PRNN,GREET,GREET,PRNN
 10 FORMAT(1X,A5,'F4.1',A1, 1X,A,1X,A2,A3)
```

2. The data record below is to be read by each of the following READ statements. What value will be stored in each variable? (Assume CHARACTER V*4).

Data Record

a.
```
    READ(5,7)I,A,B
  7 FORMAT(1X,I2,F3.0,F3.1)
```

b.
```
    READ(5,8)X,Y,Z,V
  8 FORMAT(F4.2,F2.2,3X,F3.0,A5)
```

    c.   READ(5,9)J1,J2,J3,V   **d.**   READ(5,10)QR,ST,V
          9 FORMAT(4X,I2,I3,I2,T16,A)   10 FORMAT(T2,F3.0,T5,F2.2,5X,A2)

    e.   READ(5,6)V,K
          6 FORMAT(A5,3X,I5)

3. Display the output produced by the following coding segment:

```
      K = 123
      L = -24
      WRITE(6,16)K,L
   16 FORMAT ( I3, 2X,I3)
```

Answers   **1. a.** | | |-|1|2|3|.|5| | | | |1|2|3| |-|0|.|0|6|0| |

                  └— Note round off

    b. |*|*|*| |*|*|*|*| |-|.|1| | | | | | | | | |

    First two fields are too small

    c. |*|*| | | | | | |6|7|.| |-|0|.| | | | | |

    Field too small

    d. | |A| |I|S|-|1|2|3|.|4|5|0| | | | | | |

    e. | | |H|E|L|F|4|.|1|H| |H|E|L| |H|E|H|E| |

             A5   A1   A   A2   A3
        GREET   PRNN GREET GREET PRNN

2. a. I = 23,   A = .45, B = .6

    b. X = -23., Y = .45, Z = 3., V = 'OOPS'

    c. J1 = 45,   J2 = 6,   J3 = 0, V = 'PSbb'

    d. QR = 23., ST = .45, V = '3L'

    e. V = '23.4'; read error, invalid character L.

3.

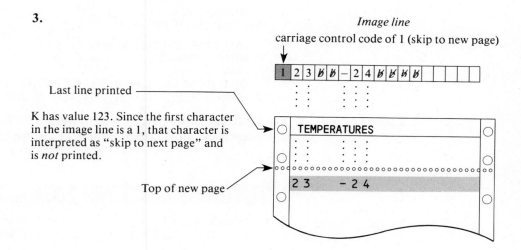

Image line
carriage control code of 1 (skip to new page)

Last line printed

K has value 123. Since the first character in the image line is a 1, that character is interpreted as "skip to next page" and is *not* printed.

Top of new page

TEMPERATURES

23   -24

*5.2.12 The Slash (/)
and Backslash (\)
Format Codes*

So far our FORMAT statements have described one physical input or output record. The close parenthesis in the FORMAT statement indicates the physical end of the record; thus, in an output operation, for example, **the image line will be printed whenever the last close parenthesis in the format is encountered.**

We can use the slash control format code / to describe more than one input or output record with one FORMAT statement. The / format code can be interpreted to mean "end of physical record"; it is used to separate lists of format codes describing different physical records. A comma is optional between the / and other format codes.

For a READ operation, the / implies reading a new record. For a WRITE operation, the / causes whatever is presently in the image line to be printed. Thus many lines can be printed in the course of one WRITE operation (one or more slashes in the FORMAT).

EXAMPLE 1

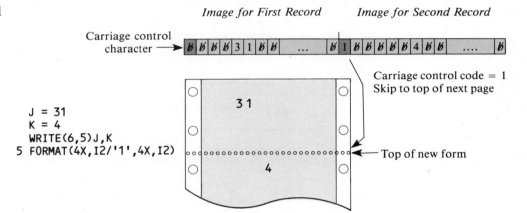

```
J = 31
K = 4
  WRITE(6,5)J,K
5 FORMAT(4X,I2/'1',4X,I2)
```

The slash causes the current image line containing the number 31 to be printed on the next line since the carriage control code for this record is a blank (4X). The next image line is then prepared and printed when format control encounters the rightmost close parenthesis. That image line is printed at the top of a new page since the carriage control code for that record is a 1.

If the format had been FORMAT(4X,I2/1X,I2), J would be printed on one line, then since the carriage control code starting the second record would be blank (1X), the printer would advance to the next line and print K.

EXAMPLE 2

The '+' carriage control code can be used for underlining and double strike (boldface), since the printer stays on the same line. To underline a heading, use the following code (if the underline character is available on your keyboard/printer):

```
  WRITE(6,5)
5 FORMAT(2X,'JULY REPORT'/'+',1X,4('_'),1X,6('_'))
```

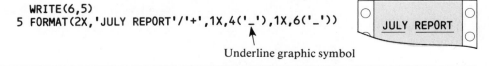

Underline graphic symbol

EXAMPLE 3

```
READ(5,7)A,B,I,J,X
7 FORMAT(F4.1/F4.0,I3/I2,F5.0)
```

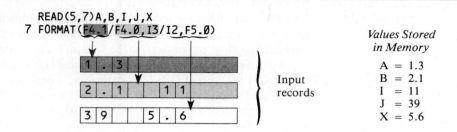

Input records

Values Stored in Memory

A = 1.3
B = 2.1
I = 11
J = 39
X = 5.6

The READ list specifies that five variables are to be read from three records. The value for A is taken from the first data record. The / means "end of this record; select a new record and continue processing at the beginning of the new record." Hence the values for B and I come from the second record, while those for J and X are taken from the third data record.

EXAMPLE 4

position of printer before processing record 1

```
I = 5
J = 6
K = 7
A = 3.43
WRITE(6,1)I,J,K,A

1 FORMAT(1X,I4/ ' ',2X,I4/'0',3X,I3/'1',1X,F3.1)
```

record 1   record 2   record 3   record 4

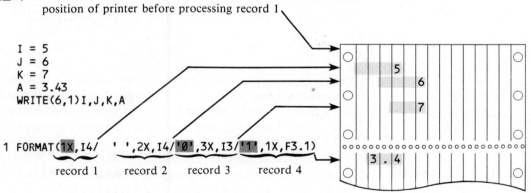

Four variables are to be written on four separate records. The carriage control for the first record is blank (1X), so the printer spaces one line and writes the value for I. The second output record is then processed and the "blank" carriage control character causes the printer to space one line and then print the value for J. Record 3 is then processed—the printer double-spaces and prints the value for K. Finally, the fourth record is processed and the value of A is written at the top of a new page.

EXAMPLE 5 As a result of the following READ statement the values for A and B will be 3. and 4.

First record; the number 3. is read.

End of first record; go to the next record.

End of second record. Data was read from the second record but nothing was transmitted to memory since there were no format codes for that record.

```
      READ(5,5)A,B
 5       FORMAT(F4.0//F4.0)
```

Beginning of third record; the number 4. is read.

| 3 | . | |

| 2 | . | | ← The value 2 is not stored in memory, since the format does not specify a format code for that record.

| 4 | . | |

Three records are read in this example. Any data contained on record 2 is read, but no data on it is transmitted to memory, since the record has no accompanying data format code.

EXAMPLE 6

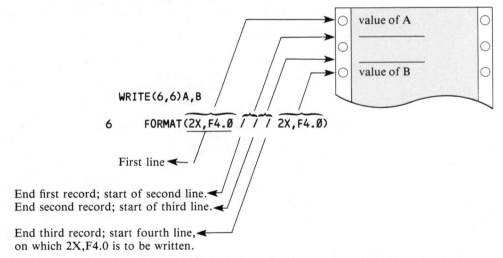

```
      WRITE(6,6)A,B
 6       FORMAT(2X,F4.0 / / / 2X,F4.0)
```

First line ←

End first record; start of second line. ←
End second record; start of third line. ←

End third record; start fourth line, ←
on which 2X,F4.0 is to be written.

In this example, line 1 contains the value of A, and the fourth record (line 4) contains B.

EXAMPLE 7

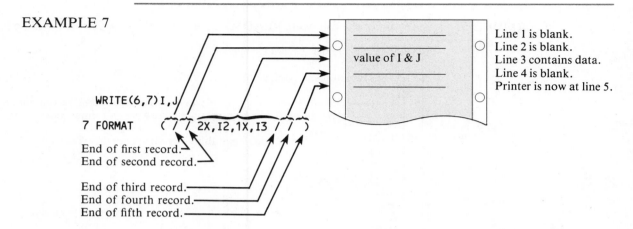

```
      WRITE(6,7)I,J
    7 FORMAT  ( / / 2X,I2,1X,I3 / / )
```

End of first record.
End of second record.

End of third record.
End of fourth record.
End of fifth record.

Line 1 is blank.
Line 2 is blank.
Line 3 contains data.
Line 4 is blank.
Printer is now at line 5.

value of I & J

If the next WRITE statement has a + carriage control character, data will be printed on the fifth line; if it has a (blank) carriage control, line 5 would be blank and printing would start on the following line.

Finally, the slash can be extremely useful for creating headings or distributing data items over more than one record with just one WRITE statement.

EXAMPLE 8

```
      WRITE(6,15)REV ,EXP ,ANC
   15 FORMAT('1'/T50,'PACIFIC COMPANY'/T50,'INCOME STATEMENT'/T53,
     *'JUNE1987'//T45,'REVENUES',T64,F7.2/
     *T45,'EXPENSES',T64,F7.2/T45,'NET INCOME',T64,F7.2)
```

This code will produce the following output:

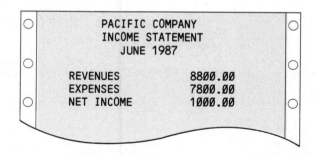

```
        PACIFIC COMPANY
        INCOME STATEMENT
           JUNE 1987

   REVENUES        8800.00
   EXPENSES        7800.00
   NET INCOME      1000.00
```

The Backslash (\ ) (Nonstandard)

In many microcomputer FORTRAN systems, the backslash can be used to carry out input/output functions that are not possible using the traditional carriage control codes.

Whenever the end of the format is reached or a slash is encountered in the format, the current image line is transmitted to the terminal/screen (output operation) or processing of the current input record is terminated (input operation). However, if the last format code is a backslash, the transmission or termination of processing of the record is delayed and input/output statements that follow continue to read from or write into the same record. This feature is often used to reply to a screen prompt on the same line as the prompt itself (example 9) or to reread a particular record using alternative formats (example 10).

EXAMPLE 9

```
1:    WRITE(*,5)'ENTER DEGREES'
2:    READ(*,6)DEGREE
3: 5  FORMAT(1X,A\)
4: 6  FORMAT(1X,I3)
```

EXAMPLE 10

```
1:    READ(5,6)CODE
2:    IF(CODE .EQ. 1)THEN
3:        READ(5,7)FORCE1
4:    ELSE
5:        READ(5,8)FORCE2
6:    ENDIF
7: 6  FORMAT(I2\)
8: 7  FORMAT(F6.2)
9: 8  FORMAT(F10.4)
```

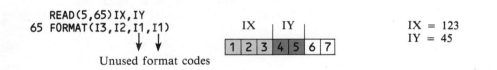

The record read at line 3 or at line 5 is the same record read at line 1. If no backslash had been present at line 7, two records would have been read. The backslash allows us to reread a record in many different ways.

5.2.13 Relationship between the List of Variables and List of Format Codes

If there are more data format codes in a FORMAT statement than there are variables listed in the corresponding READ/WRITE statement, the unused data format codes are ignored.

EXAMPLE 1

```
   READ(5,65)IX,IY
65 FORMAT(I3,I2,I1,I1)
```

Unused format codes

IX = 123
IY = 45

Only two numbers are to be read, and they are described by the first two data format codes, I3 and I2. The remaining format codes (I1 and I1) are not processed, since only two numbers are to be read.

If, on the other hand, there are more variables in the list of variables than there are data format codes, the sequence of format codes is reused starting at the right-most open parenthesis in the FORMAT. A new record is read/written every time format control en.ounters the right-most close parenthesis (last parenthesis in FORMAT).

EXAMPLE 2

		Input File	*Memory*
`READ(5,15)I,J,K`		39	I = 39
`15 FORMAT(I2)`		33	J = 33
		44	K = 44

Format control encounters the right-most close parenthesis after reading I. Therefore the second record is read with format control restarting at the right-most open parenthesis (there is only one in this case); the value 33 is read into J. A third record is read since format control again encounters the right-most close parenthesis. Format control restarts at the right-most open parenthesis, and the value 44 is read into K.

EXAMPLE 3

	Action
`READ(5,5)I,J,K` `5 FORMAT(I3,I2)`	I and J are read from the first record. Format control restarts at the right-most open parenthesis and K is read from the second record using the I3 format.

Input File   *Memory*

1 2 3 4 5   I = 123; J = 45

6 7 8 9 0   K = 678

EXAMPLE 4

```
       READ(5,5)N1,N2,N3,N4,N5,N6,N7,N8
       5 FORMAT(I1,(I2,1X,I3),I4)
              |     |     |    |
              N1    N2    N3   N4
                    N5    N6   N7
                    N8
```

Records

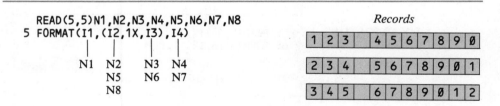

N1, N2, N3, and N4 are read from the first record. N1 = 1, N2 = 23, N3 = 456, N4 = 7890. Format control restarts a new record at I2 and reads N5 = 23, N6 = 56, and N7 = 7890. Format control reads the third record and captures N8 with format I2 (N8 = 34). Remember that format control restarts at the rightmost open parenthesis.

5.2.14 Do It Now

1. Complete the FORMAT of the following FORTRAN code to produce the output shown (minus the dots).

```
    INTEGER QN,QB
    DATA QN,QB/58,64/
    TN = QN*CN
    TB = QB*CB
    SUBTOT = TN + TB
    TAX    = .04*SUBTOT
    GTOT   = SUBTOT + TAX
    WRITE(*,11)QN,CN,TN,QB
  1,CB,TB,SUBTOT,TAX
    STOP
 11 FORMAT
```

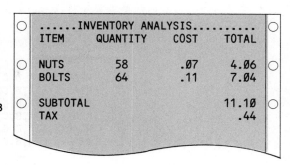

```
......INVENTORY ANALYSIS..........
ITEM      QUANTITY    COST    TOTAL

NUTS         58        .07     4.06
BOLTS        64        .11     7.04

SUBTOTAL                      11.10
TAX                             .44
```

2. Consider the following input file:

```
-324     First record
0064       :
+123       :
0000     Fourth record
```

What will be the value of each variable after the following statements are executed?

    a.   `READ(5,11) A, I2, B`
        `11 FORMAT(F4.0/I4//F4.0)`

    b.   `READ(5,12) X, Y, Z`
        `12 FORMAT(/2F2.0//F2.0)`

3. Suppose $I = 4$ and $A = -3.2$. What output will be produced by each of the following?

    a.   `WRITE(6,13) I, A`
        `13 FORMAT(3X,I3//2X,F4.1)`

    b.   `WRITE(6,14) A, I`
        `14 FORMAT(//'0',F4.1,I3)`

4. In example 9 in section 5.2.12 (backslash), could the same objective have been accomplished by using the + carriage control code in format 6 instead of the backslash in format 5?

5. Identify the number of records (input records or output lines) processed by each of the following pairs of statements. If the statements are invalid, explain why.

    a.   `READ(5,6)A,K,C`
        `6 FORMAT(F5.1)`

    b.   `WRITE(6,6)I,J,I,I,J`
        `6 FORMAT(2I3)`

    c.   `WRITE(6,6)I,A,J,B,K,C`
        `6 FORMAT(1X,I4,F4.1)`

    d.   `WRITE(6,6)I,J`
        `6 FORMAT(1X,I3,I4,'RESULT',I2)`

    e.   `WRITE(6,6)I,A,J,B,K,C`
        `6 FORMAT(1X,I3,F4.1,I2)`

6. Fill in the two boxes for each of the following pairs of READ/FORMAT statements

READ Statement	FORMAT Statement	Number of Records Read	Number of Items Read from Last Record
READ(5,6)A,B,C,D,E,F	FORMAT(7F5.1)		
READ(5,6)A,B,C,D,E,F	FORMAT(6F5.1)		
READ(5,6)A,B,C,D,E,F	FORMAT(5F5.1)		
READ(5,6)A,B,C,D,E,F	FORMAT(4F5.1)		
READ(5,6)A,B,C,D,E,F	FORMAT(3F5.1)		
READ(5,6)A,B,C,D,E,F	FORMAT(2F5.1)		
READ(5,6)A,B,C,D,E,F	FORMAT(F5.1)		

7. Given the following READ statement and corresponding input records, determine the values of N1 through N9.

```
READ(5,6)N1,N2,N3,N4,N5,N6,N7,N8,N9
6 FORMAT(I1,(I2,I1),I3,(1X,2I2))
```
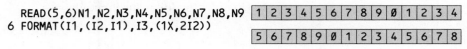

Answers

1.
```
   11 FORMAT('1', '        INVENTORY ANALYSIS'/
    1          ' ', 'ITEM      QUANTITY     COST     TOTAL'/
    2          '0', 'NUTS' ,8X,  I2,  7X, F4.2,3X,F5.2 /
    3          ' ', 'BOLTS',7X,  I2,  7X, F4.2,3X,F5.2 /
    4          '0', 'SUBTOTAL',20X,            F5.2 /
    5          ' ', 'TAX',25X,                 F5.2 /)
```

2. a. A = −324.
      I2 = 64
      B = 0.

   b. X = 0.
      Y = 64.
      Z = 0.

3. a.   **b.**

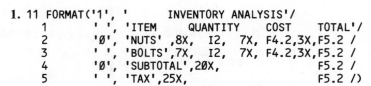
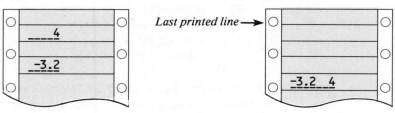

Last printed line →

4. No, the new line created by the + carriage control code would erase the previous screen line.

5. a. Invalid; K should be read under an I format code.

   b. 3

   c. 3

   d. 1 (the literal "RESULT" may or may not be printed, depending on the system used).

   e. Invalid; variable B needs an F format not an I format (I3 is reused).

6. box 1: 1, 1, 2, 2, 2, 3, and 6   box 2: 6, 6, 1, 2, 3, 2 and 1.

7. N1 = 1, N2 = 23, N3 = 4, N4 = 567, N5 = 90, N6 = 12, N7 = 67, N8 = 89, and N9 encounters the end-of-file mark on the next record.

5.3 NUMBER REPRESENTATION

5.3.1 Real Constants in Exponential Form and the E Format Code

A real constant in a FORTRAN program can be represented in two forms: a *basic* form and an *exponential* form. Examples of basic real constants are:

X = −999.9901
Y = 1.00000000000099
Z = 0.00000123

The maximum number of significant digits (see question 7 section 5.6) varies from one computer to the next. If more than the allowed number of significant digits are used, the system will generally represent the constant in double precision mode (see section 5.3.3).

The exponential form for a real constant has the general form:

basic real constant $\mathrm{E} \pm$ *integer exponent*

where   E represents "times 10 to the power." The number of digits allowed in the basic real constant and in the integer exponent varies on different systems.

on microcomputers the exponent range is typically 10^{-38} to 10^{38} while on main frames the range might be 10^{-78} to 10^{75}.

EXAMPLE 1

FORTRAN Exponential Constants	*Value*		
6.2E+4	6.2×10^{4}	=	62000.
−4.32E14	-4.32×10^{14}	=	−432000000000000.
0.034E−2	0.034×10^{-2}	=	.00034
−1.2E−7	-1.2×10^{-7}	=	−.00000012

Exponential form is typically used in place of the basic form for real constants with large or small magnitudes. The exponential form can be used in lieu of the basic form in any arithmetic expression.

EXAMPLE 2

FORTRAN Exponential Form	*Basic Form*
X = −.Ø1E3*Y	X = −1Ø.*Y
Y = 16.2E−4*Z + W	Y = .ØØ162*Z + W
Z = 4.2E+2Ø**2 − Z*.5E−21	Impractical to write in exponential form.

The E Format Code

Input of Exponential Numbers. Numbers in exponential form can be read from data records using the E or the F format code.

The general form of the E format code is:

$$\boxed{n\text{E}w.d}$$

where w represents the number of positions reserved for the data field;

d tells the system where to place the decimal point in the basic real constant in case no decimal point is entered in the input data field.

n is the duplication count.

If there is no decimal point entered in the basic real constant, the decimal point is assumed d positions to the left of the character E in the field. This adjusted value is then raised to the specified integer exponent. If the decimal point is entered as part of the basic real constant, d is ignored and the basic real constant is raised to the specified integer power; d nevertheless must be included in the E format description.

The exponent, if any, must be an integer and must be right-justified in the input field.

EXAMPLE 3

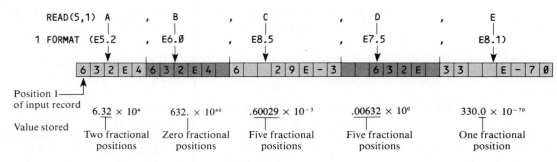

Note that blanks are treated as zeros.

EXAMPLE 4

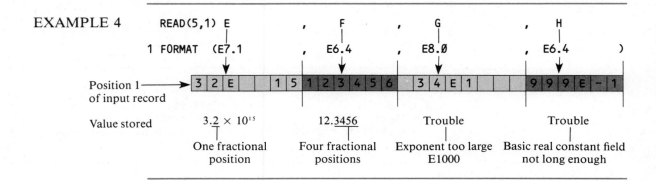

EXAMPLE 5

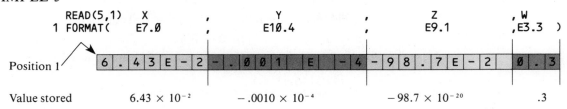

To avoid errors, the programmer should always try to right-justify numbers in their input fields. The exponent portion *must* be right-justified.

Output of Exponential Numbers. An exponential number printed by E*w.d* will generally have the following standardized output form:

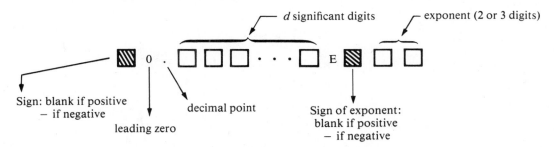

Hence the minimum print positions required to print a negative number with one significant digit are $-0.\,\mathrm{E}-\square\square\square$, so *w* must be greater than or equal to 8 or 9 to print the sign, the leading zero, the decimal point, one significant digit, the E, the sign of the exponent, and the two or three digits for the exponent. (If *w* is not large enough, some systems will not print the leading zero.) Consider the following examples:

Value of Data Item in Memory	Output Format Code	Printed Value	Comments
632000.	E10.3	b̷0.632Eb̷06	Leading blank.
632000.	E8.3	.632Eb̷06	No room for leading zero.
632999.	E9.3	0.633Eb̷06	Round off.
−.83247	E12.5	−0.83247Eb̷00	
−.83247	E13.4	b̷b̷−0.8325Eb̷00	Leading blanks and round off.
−.000004269	E10.3	−0.427E−05	Round off.
−.000004269	E10.1	b̷b̷−0.4E−05	Leading blanks.
−98.5678	E8.1	−0.1Eb̷03	Round off.
−98.5678	E8.0	b̷−0.Eb̷03	No significant digits.
3.256	E8.4	********	Missing at least one space.
123.4567	E15.9	b̷.123456799Eb̷03	The digits 99 are not significant if the system has seven significant digits. The extra digits are randomly generated by the computer and are meaningless.

5.3.2 Do It Now

1. Write each of the following in exponential form.
   a. 13201.47   b. -0.000327

2. Write each of the following as a basic real constant.
   a. 0.332E-4 b. 0.034E4

3. If X $= -6324.705$, what output would be produced by

   ```
   WRITE(6,11)X,X
   11 FORMAT(1X,E14.7,E14.3)
   ```

4. Suppose a data record containing the characters below is read as follows:

   ```
   READ(5,12)Q,R
   12 FORMAT(E8.2,E5.2)
   ```
   | − | | 3 | 2 | E | + | 4 | 1 | . | 3 | 2 | 4 |

   What will be the values of Q and R?

5. What output will be produced by the following fields and output fields:
   a. 3.162   E10.2
   b. $-0.12345678E04$ E9.4
   c. $-0.12345678E4$ E11.4
   d. 392.1E-23 E10.2

Answers

1. a. .1320147E5   b. $-0.327E-3$
2. a. 0.0000332   b. 340.
3.

   | − | 0 | . | 6 | 3 | 2 | 4 | 7 | 0 | 5 | E | | 0 | 4 | | | | | − | 0 | . | 6 | 3 | 2 | E | | 0 | 4 |

4. Q $= -3200.$
   R $= 1.324$
5. a. ᵇᵇ0.32Eᵇ01   b. Insufficient field width
   c. $-0.1235E$ᵇ04   d. ᵇᵇ0.39E-20

5.3.3 Double Precision Numbers and the D Format Code

Some applications require a greater number of significant digits than can be maintained using real type data. Many computers offer an extended version of real (floating-point) data representation called *double precision;* double precision allows the retention of more significant digits. The DOUBLE PRECISION specification statement is used to declare those variables for which more significant digits are required. Double precision numbers generally have twice the number of significant digits of REAL numbers; they occupy more memory space, of course, and double precision arithmetic is slower than single precision (REAL) arithmetic.

The general form of the DOUBLE PRECISION statement is

> DOUBLE PRECISION *list of variables*

Each variable in the *list of variables* is assigned double precision mode. DOUBLE PRECISION affects *only real numbers, not integer numbers.* Integers cannot be declared as DOUBLE PRECISION integers. This does not mean that a variable name starting with I through N cannot be declared in a DOUBLE PRECISION list—it can, but it will represent a double precision real number.

EXAMPLES

```
DOUBLE PRECISION X,I
X = 123456789012345.            Both X and I are double precision.
I = .123456789012345D40         Exponential form using D instead of E.
                                (D represents "times 10 to the power."
```

DOUBLE PRECISION is a nonexecutable specification statement subject to the same restrictions as other specification statements.

Double precision constants can be represented in a basic form similar to the basic real constants. For example, on IBM systems the constant 63217869.2, which contains more than seven significant digits, is a double precision constant in basic form.

There is also an exponential form for double precision constants; it is analogous to the exponential form for real constants except that the character D is used in place of E.

EXAMPLE

$6.2D + 4$ has value 62000.
$- .0326798432156D - 4$ has value $- .00000326798432156$

Double precision constants and variables can be mixed with real and integer constants and variables in any arithmetic expression. When any double precision operand and a non-double-precision operand are involved in an arithmetic operation, the non-double-precision operand is converted to double precision. The operation is then carried out using double precision arithmetic, and the final result of the expression is a double precision number.

EXAMPLE

```
DOUBLE PRECISION T,X     First C**K is performed in real mode.
X = I*J/C**K + T         Then I*J is performed in integer mode.
                         Then (I*J)/(C**K) is performed in real mode.
                         Then (I*J)/(C**K) + T is performed in double precision.
                         Finally, the double precision result is stored in the double
                         precision variable X.
```

If a replacement statement places a double precision value into a real variable, significant digits may be lost. Consider the following example, which assumes that a real variable can hold at most seven significant digits:

```
DOUBLE PRECISION X,Y                Results
REAL A,B
X = 1.23456789D3          X will contain 1234.56789
A = 1.23456789D3          A will contain 1234.568 (rounded off)
Y = 999999999.D0          Y will contain 999999999.
B = 999999999.D0          B will contain 1000000000 (rounded off)
I = 1.29456789D1          I will contain 12 (truncation).
J = 999999999             J will contain 999999999 or fewer digits, or compilation
                          error (integer overflow) may occur.
```

The D format code can be used for input/output of double precision data. The general form of the D format code is D*w.d*. The D format code is used in exactly the same as the E format code (section 5.3.1).

The F format code can also be used for double precision input and output, as in the following example:

```
      DOUBLE PRECISION X,Y
      READ(5,1)X,Y
      WRITE(6,2)X,Y
    1 FORMAT(D8.0,D10.4)
    2 FORMAT(2X,F9.0,3X,D18.5)
```

The F format code does not use an exponent, hence the width of the F field must be large enough to accommodate many trailing zeros!

5.3.4 Do It Now

1. Determine the word length and other details of double precision data representation for the computer you are using.

2. What output would be produced by each of the following:

   a.
   ```
         DOUBLE PRECISION X,Y
         X = 123.456789
         Y = 1.6D-4
         WRITE(6,14)X,Y
      14 FORMAT(1X,D14.7,D8.1)
   ```

   b.
   ```
         DOUBLE PRECISION QR,ST
         QR = 1.2D0 + (-.12E1)
         ST = .123456789D+4
         UV = ST
         WRITE(6,15)QR,ST,UV
      15 FORMAT(1X,F4.0,D17.9,E16.9)
   ```

Answers

2. a. `|  |0|.|1|2|3|4|5|6|8|D|+|0|3|  |0|.|2|D|-|0|3|  |  |  |  |  |`

   b. `|  |  |0|.|  |  |0|.|1|2|3|4|5|6|7|8|9|D|+|0|4|  |0|.|1|2|3|4|5|6|8|0|0|E|+|0|4|  |`

5.4 RANDOM NUMBERS

5.4.1 An Overview

Random numbers are introduced here because some of the exercises in this chapter and the following ones will require the use of random numbers to simulate certain real-life events. Such exercises can be interesting and fun, since in many instances the outcome cannot be predicted (unless you have a knowledge of statistics). Random numbers are often used in programs that simulate probabilistic events. For example, consider the throwing of a die. The outcome of this event can be 1, 2, 3, 4, 5, or 6; each outcome is equally likely to occur. A program can use random numbers in the range 1 to 6 to simulate the outcome of a single throw of a die.

There is no standard method for generating random numbers in a FORTRAN program. However, most computer installations have random number routines stored in their libraries and these routines can be accessed by the user. Typically there is a built-in function (it might be called RANDOM, RANF, or RAND) that returns a random number in some range. For example, Y = RAND(1) will cause the computer to store in Y a random number between 0. and 1. Every time this statement is executed, a new random value will be stored in Y.

EXAMPLE

```
   Y1 = RAND(1)
   Y2 = RAND(1)
   Y3 = RAND(1)
   WRITE(6,3)Y1,Y2,Y3
 3 FORMAT(1X,F10.6)
```

Output

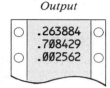

```
.263884
.708429
.002562
```

You must determine the specifics of random number generation for your installation before attempting any programming exercises using random number generation. If you have no random number generator routine, you can append to your FORTRAN program the random number program shown in Figure 5.3.

The random number function can be very useful in the simulation of random events or in games where the computer is one of the players. Many times, though, the fractional numbers (between 0 and 1) generated by RAND are not too convenient in that particular form. Suppose, for example, that we wished to pick integer random numbers between 1 and 6 to simulate the throw of a die. How can we go from a fractional number in the interval [0,1] to an integer in the interval [1,6]? The following sequence of transformations illustrates how this can be accomplished.

	Value of RAND Case 1	Value of RAND Case 2	Value of RAND Case 3
T1 = RAND(1)	.263884	.708429	.002562
T2 = RAND(1)*6.	1.583304	4.250574	.015372
T3 = RAND(1)*6.+1.	2.583304	5.250574	1.015372
I = RAND(1)*6.+1.	2	5	1

Hence the formula I = RAND(1)*6. + 1. can be used to transform the set of random fractional numbers between 0 and 1 into the set of integers 1, 2, 3, 4, 5, and 6!

In general, to generate real or integer random numbers between LOW and HIGH, the following formulas can be used:

Real values between LOW and HIGH: X = RAND(1)*(HIGH − LOW) + LOW
Integer values between LOW and HIGH: I = RAND(1)*(HIGH − LOW + 1) + LOW

5.4.2 An Example

To determine the probable outcome of a particular event, a program can be written to simulate that event a great number of times and to count the various outcomes. The more the event is simulated, the more accurate the projection of the frequency of the different outcomes. For example, to determine the probability of tossing a 5 with a die, we would simulate tosses and count the number of times a 5 comes up. One thousand tosses would probably result in an answer close to 167 (1/6 of the tosses).

The program shown in Figure 5.3 simulates the tossing of a die 100, 1000, and 10,000 times. It counts the occurrences of each outcome (1, 2, 3, 4, 5, and 6) and prints the proportion of each that occurred. The estimate of the probability of each possible occurrence is the number of occurrences divided by the number of repetitions. The expected value for the probability is .167. The output of the program in Figure 5.3 shows that as the number of repetitions increases, the estimate for the probability of each outcome comes closer to the expected value.

5.4.3 Do It Now

1. Using RAND(1) to generate random integer numbers between 0. and 1.

   a. Write the formula to pick random integer values between 5 and 30.

   b. Write the formula to pick random integer values 1, 11, 21, 31, ..., 101.

   c. Write the formula to pick random integer values between −10 and +10.

2. Write a program for the following game between the computer and a player. The computer picks a random number between 1 and 10 and a player must guess the number picked by the computer. The dialogue between computer and player should be similar to

```
MY NAME IS ZEN. WHAT'S YOUR NAME?
? AMY
AMY I'M GOING TO CHOOSE A NUMBER BETWEEN 1 AND 10. PLEASE GUESS IT
ENTER GUESS
? 7
NO, TRY AGAIN
? 2
NO, TRY AGAIN
? 9
TERRIFIC AMY! WOULD YOU LIKE TO PLAY ANOTHER GAME?
? YES
ENTER GUESS
? 3
NO, TRY AGAIN
? 6
TERRIFIC AMY! WOULD YOU LIKE TO PLAY ANOTHER GAME?
? NO
THANK YOU AMY FOR PLAYING WITH ME
```

3. Write the code to drill a student on the multiplication tables 1 through 12. The student should be allowed three tries, after which the program should print the correct result and present a new multiplication problem.

Answers to Selected Problems

1. **a.** K = RAND(1)∗26 + 5

   b. K = INT(RAND(1)∗11 + 1)∗10 − 9

   c. K = RAND(1)∗21 − 10

```
 1: **** COMPUTING FREQUENCIES
 2: **** RAND: NAME OF FUNCTION WHICH RETURNS RANDOM NUMBERS BETWEEN Ø & 1
 3: **** NUMBR: AN INTEGER BETWEEN 1 AND 6
 4: ****
 5:      INTEGER TIMES, INDX, NUMBR, INDX1
 6:      REAL N1,N2,N3,N4,N5,N6
 7:      TIMES = 1Ø
 8:      DO 1Ø INDX = 1, 3
 9:          TIMES = 1Ø*TIMES
1Ø:          N1 = Ø.Ø
11:          N2 = Ø.Ø
12:          N3 = Ø.Ø
13:          N4 = Ø.Ø
14:          N5 = Ø.Ø
15:          N6 = Ø.Ø
16:          DO 2Ø INDX1 = 1, TIMES
17:              NUMBR = RAND(1)*6.Ø + 1.Ø
18:              IF(NUMBR .EQ. 1) THEN
19:                  N1 = N1 + 1.
2Ø:              ELSEIF (NUMBR .EQ. 2) THEN
21:                  N2 = N2 + 1.
22:              ELSEIF (NUMBR .EQ. 3) THEN
23:                  N3 = N3 + 1.
24:              ELSEIF (NUMBR .EQ. 4) THEN
25:                  N4 = N4 + 1.
26:              ELSEIF (NUMBR .EQ. 5) THEN
27:                  N5 = N5 + 1.
28:              ELSE
29:                  N6 = N6 + 1.
3Ø:              ENDIF
31: 2Ø       CONTINUE
32:          WRITE(*,3Ø)TIMES,N1/TIMES,N2/TIMES,N3/TIMES
33:      1          ,N4/TIMES,N5/TIMES,N6/TIMES
34: 3Ø       FORMAT(1X, 'REPETITIONS=',I5,3X,
35:      1          ' N1',' N2',' N3',' N4',' N5',' N6'
36:      2          /1X, '              ',8X, 6(F5.4,1X) /'Ø')
37: 1Ø   CONTINUE
38:      STOP
39:      END
4Ø: **** TYPE THE FOLLOWING CODE IF YOU NEED A FUNCTION WHICH RETURNS
41: **** REAL RANDOM NUMBERS BETWEEN Ø AND 1. THE ABOVE PROGRAM MADE
42: **** USE OF THE FOLLOWING CODE
43:      FUNCTION RAND(K)
44:      INTEGER IM, IB, IA
45:      DATA IM, IB, IA/ 24211, 32767, 19727/
46:      IA = MOD(IM*IA, IB)
47:      RAND = FLOAT(IA)/FLOAT(IB)
48:      RETURN
49:      END
```

REPETITIONS= 100	N1	N2	N3	N4	N5	N6
	.1900	.1700	.1600	.1600	.1500	.1700
REPETITIONS= 1000	N1	N2	N3	N4	N5	N6
	.1620	.1700	.1660	.1680	.1660	.1680
REPETITIONS=10000	N1	N2	N3	N4	N5	N6
	.1669	.1663	.1668	.1666	.1669	.1665

FIGURE 5.3
PROBABILITY OF OCCURRENCE

5.5 PROGRAMMING EXAMPLES

5.5.1 The Monte Carlo Method

Random numbers can be used to solve some mathematical problems for which other methods of solution are known. This method is called the Monte Carlo method. An elementary example of such a problem is the task of estimating the value of π. The value of π is known to be approximately 3.14159, but it is an irrational number (i.e., its decimal representation does not repeat or terminate).

Consider a circle with area equal to π as shown below:

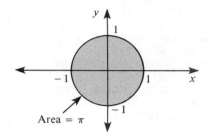

The equation for the circle is $x^2 + y^2 = 1$. Its radius is equal to 1 and therefore its area is π:

$$\text{area} = \pi r^2 = \pi 1^2 = \pi$$

Since the area of the whole circle is π, the area of that portion of the circle in the first quadrant is $\pi/4$:

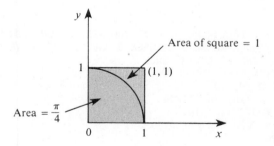

If we choose points with coordinates (x, y) in the first quadrant, some points will lie in the circle and some will lie outside the circle.

A point with coordinates x, y lies in (or on) the circle if

$$x^2 + y^2 \leq 1$$

A method to estimate the value of $\pi/4$ (and thereby the value of π) is to choose a large number of points at random in the square shown above and count the number of points that lie inside the circle. The count of inside points divided by the total count times the area of the square is an estimate of the area of a quarter of the circle ($\pi/4$). Let us write a program to estimate the value of π using this method.

Suppose, for example, that 10,000 points are chosen and 7800 of them lie inside or on the quarter circle. Then .78 (7800/10000) is the proportion of points that lie inside or on the quarter circle. Therefore .78 × 4 = 3.12 is the estimate for the area of the whole circle (π).

The procedure required to carry out this task is shown in pseudo code as follows:

```
initialize counter to zero
DO 10,000 times
    choose a point that lies in the square in first quadrant
    IF the point is in the circle THEN
        add 1 to counter
    ENDIF
CONTINUE LOOP
estimate = (counter/10,000)*4
print estimate
stop
```

The points in the square all have x and y coordinates in the range 0 to 1. We can, therefore, use the output of the RAND function directly as the values of x and y.

A solution for this problem is shown in Figure 5.4.

```
 1: **** MONTE CARLO METHOD FOR COMPUTING PI
 2: **** RAND: NAME OF FUNCTION RETURNING RANDOM NUMBERS BETWEEN Ø & 1
 3: **** COUNT: COUNTS NUMBER OF POINTS INSIDE CIRCLE
 4: **** X & Y: COORDINATES OF RANDOM POINTS IN 1ST QUADRANT
 5:       INTEGER COUNT,INDX
 6:       REAL X,Y,PI
 7:       COUNT = Ø
 8:       DO 1Ø INDX = 1, 1ØØØØ
 9:          X = RAND(1)
1Ø:          Y = RAND(1)
11:          IF(X**2 + Y**2 .LE. 1.Ø) COUNT = COUNT + 1
12: 1Ø    CONTINUE
13: **** COMPUTE ESTIMATE FOR PI
14:       PI = (COUNT/1ØØØØ.)*4.Ø
15:       WRITE(*,5)PI
16:  5    FORMAT(1X,'ESTIMATE FOR PI = ', F6.4)
17:       STOP
18:       END
19: **** TYPE THE FOLLOWING CODE IF YOU NEED A FUNCTION WHICH RETURNS
2Ø: **** REAL RANDOM NUMBERS BETWEEN Ø AND 1. THE ABOVE PROGRAM MADE
21: **** USE OF THE FOLLOWING CODE
22:       FUNCTION RAND(K)
23:       INTEGER IM, IB, IA
24:       DATA IM, IB, IA/ 24211, 32767, 19727/
25:       IA = MOD(IM*IA, IB)
26:       RAND = FLOAT(IA)/FLOAT(IB)
27:       RETURN
28:       END
```

```
ESTIMATE FOR PI = 3.146Ø
```

FIGURE 5.4
A COMPUTATION FOR π

5.5.2 A Random Walk

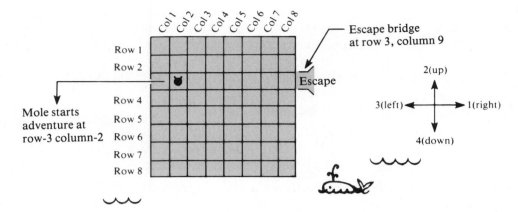

The above diagram represents an island surrounded by water. The island can be thought of as a square grid divided into 8 rows and 8 columns. One bridge leads off the island at row 3 and column 9. Let us place an imaginary mole at the black square (row = 3, column = 2). The mole moves one square at a time in one of 4 directions: right, up, left, or down. A random number between 1 and 4 is used to move the mole one grid point at a time in any of the four directions. Let us arbitrarily associate a move to the right with the number 1, a move up with the number 2, and so forth. The mole keeps moving from one square to the next as directed by the random number until the mole either falls into the water or gets to the bridge and escapes.

Write a program to determine the mole's chances of escape. Express its chances in percentage form, for example, 1.8%.

In this problem, the sequence of moves resulting in either an escape or an accident (falling in the water) is called an "adventure." Adventures can last anywhere from two moves (shortest distance to water) to hundreds of moves (see diagram below).

One Short, Sad Adventure   *One Long, Happy Adventure*

2 moves: drown   23 moves: escape

Obviously, 10 or even 50 such adventures may not be enough to determine the mole's chances of escape. The mole may never escape in its first 50 adventures. For the results to be meaningful, let us give the mole the opportunity to have 500 distinct adventures, i.e., let us restart the mole at the starting block 500 times and count the number of times it escapes and the number of times it falls into the water.

The key questions in this problem are: How do we move the mole around? And how do we know when the mole falls in the water or escapes?

Initially we position the mole at row 3 and column 2 by writing R = 3 and C = 2. (We will use the variables R and C to keep track of the row and column positions of the mole.) We then generate a random number K between 1 and 4 (K = RAND(1)*4 + 1, for example) to tell us the direction of the next move (1 = right, 2 = up, 3 = left, 4 = down).

If K has value 2, we move the mole up one square, i.e., we go from row 3 to row 2. Hence we need to subtract 1 from the current value of R (R = R − 1).

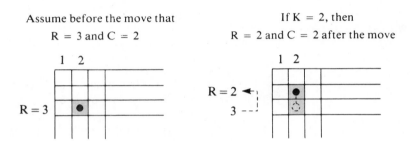

Assume before the move that R = 3 and C = 2

If K = 2, then R = 2 and C = 2 after the move

Note that when moving in an upward direction, the column C does not change.

In general, if the mole is at position (R,C) and the random number is 2 (move up), we set R = R − 1.

If K has value 3, and we are initially at R = 3 and C = 2, we need to move the mole from column 2 to column 1 (C = C − 1).

If K has value 4, we need to add 1 to R (R = R + 1).

If K has value 1, we need to add 1 to C (C = C + 1).

After we move the mole to its new position, we must check to see whether the mole is in the water (R = 0, R = 9, C = 0, C = 9), or whether it has escaped (R = 3, C = 9). It is fairly evident that when the mole is moving upward, it can have an accident only at row 0 (when moving up, the mole cannot hit the water to the left or to the right or backwards!). Hence, if the row is not 0, the mole is still on the island and we need to pick another random number for the next move. If, on the other hand, the mole moves left (K = 3), we need to check whether column C is 0; obviously we do not need to check for R = 0, C = 9, or R = 9 when moving in a leftward direction.

When moving down, we should check if R = 9 (accident) and when moving to the right we should check if C = 9. If C = 9, the mole can escape if the row R is 3. Hence, when moving right, we should check for C = 9 and R = 3. If both these conditions are satisfied, we increment the escape counter by 1. If C = 9 but R = 3, the mole has had an accident. If C does not equal 9, then the mole is still on the island, and we go to the random number generator for the next move.

An adventure ends when the mole either hits the water or escapes. Before we start a new adventure by repositioning the mole at its starting block (R = 3 and C = 2), we must determine whether we have gone through 500 adventures. If we have completed 500 adventures, we compute the percentage of escapes by computing E * 100/500 or E/5 (E is the number of escapes). Note that the number of escapes plus the number of accidents should equal 500.

```
Initialize escape counter to 0.
DO 1,000 adventures
     Place mole at starting point (row = 3, column = 2)
     WHILE mole is in island DO
             Pick up random direction
             Adjust row/column accordingly
     ENDWHILE
     IF mole escapes THEN
          add 1 to escape counter
     ENDIF
CONTINUE LOOP
percentage = escape counter/10
write percentage
stop
```

FIGURE 5.5
*PSEUDO CODE FOR
RANDOM WALK*

The logic of the problem is captured in pseudo code form in Figure 5.5, and the FORTRAN code is shown in Figure 5.6.

Question. How does one decide whether 100, 500, or 1000 adventures are reasonable figures for this type of problem?

Answer. One could start with 100 adventures and then try 500 adventures. If the result for the 500 adventures is approximately five times that for 100 adventures, the experiment could be run with 100 adventures. On the other hand, if the ratio between the two results is not close to 5:1, we could go to 2500 adventures and see if the result correlates with 500 adventures. This process should be repeated until a constant relation is found.

5.6 YOU MIGHT WANT TO KNOW

1. How can I print a blank line?

Answer: Omit the output list in the WRITE statement, for example:

```
   WRITE(6,3)
 3 FORMAT(1X)  or  FORMAT( )
```

2. What if my printer can accommodate up to 80 characters, but my FORMAT specifies more than 80 characters? What will happen to the extra characters?

Answer: Some systems might truncate the line to 80 characters, others will stop execution of the program with an execution-time format error, and some will wrap around to the next line.

3. How many WRITE statements can reference a FORMAT statement?

Answer: As many as desired. One FORMAT can be shared by many WRITE statements (or READ statements).

4. How can I read or write complex numbers?

Answer: See appendix D.

```
 1: **** MOLE MAZE
 2: **** ROW   : KEEPS TRACK OF ROW POSITION
 3: **** COLUMN: KEEPS TRACK OF COLUMN POSITION
 4: **** ESCAPE: COUNTS THE NUMBER OF ESCAPES
 5: **** PERCNT: COMPUTES PERCENTAGE OF ESCAPES
 6: **** TRIP  : COUNTS THE NUMBER OF ADVENTURES
 7: **** K     : RANDOM DIRECTION FOR MOLE
 8:        INTEGER ROW,COL,TRIP,K
 9:        REAL PERCNT,ESCAPE
10:        ESCAPE = 0.
11: **** START 1,000 ADVENTURES
12:        DO 5000 TRIP = 1,1000
13: ****       PLACE MOLE AT POSITION ROW=3 & COLUMN=2 TO START ADVENTURE
14:            ROW = 3
15:            COL = 2
16: ****       STAY IN THE MAZE UNTIL MOLE EITHER DROWNS OR ESCAPES
17: 10         IF(ROW.GT.0 .AND. ROW.LT.9 .AND. COL.GT.0 .AND. COL.LT.9)THEN
18: ****           PICK UP A RANDOM DIRECTION
19:                K = RAND(1)*4.0 + 1.0
20:                IF(K .EQ. 1) THEN
21:                    COL = COL + 1
22:                ELSEIF(K .EQ. 2)THEN
23:                    ROW = ROW - 1
24:                ELSEIF(K .EQ. 3)THEN
25:                    COL = COL - 1
26:                ELSEIF(K .EQ. 4)THEN
27:                    ROW = ROW + 1
28:                ENDIF
29:                GO TO 10
30:            ENDIF
31:            IF(ROW.EQ.3 .AND. COL.EQ.9)ESCAPE = ESCAPE + 1
32: 5000 CONTINUE.
33:        PERCNT = ESCAPE/10.
34:        WRITE(*,20)PERCNT
35:        STOP
36: 20     FORMAT(1X,'PERCENTAGE OF ESCAPES IS', F5.2)
37:        END
38: **** THE FOLLOWING CODE IS THE RANDOM NUMBER GENERATOR FUNCTION
39:        FUNCTION RAND(K)
40:        INTEGER IM,IB,IA
41:        DATA IM,IB,IA/24211,32767,19727/
42:        IA = MOD(IM*IA, IB)
43:        RAND = FLOAT(IA)/FLOAT(IB)
44:        RETURN
45:        END
```

FIGURE 5.6
MOLE MAZE PROGRAM

5. I am performing some arithmetic computations on some data, and I do not know how many digits I should reserve for my output field (I,F) in the FORMAT.

Answer: Most of the time you can estimate an upper limit for the magnitude and the number of fractional digits. Otherwise, make your field as large as possible— I20 or F20.6, for example. The result will be right-justified anyway, with blanks on the left. If you are working with very large magnitudes, use the E format discussed in section 5.3.

6. What happens if I write the following code?

```
   READ(5,6)I,J,K
 6 FORMAT(I3,T2,I3,T1,I1)
```

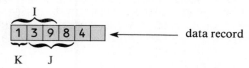

Answer: In many systems the T feature permits restarting a READ operation at different positions in a record. In this case, I = 139, J = 398, K = 1

7. What are "significant digits"?

Answer: Generally speaking, significant digits are those digits used to represent any number. Leading zeros (before or after the decimal point) are not significant. For example:

    1001.56   has six significant digits
    0012.4   has three significant digits
    .000315   has three significant digits ($.000315 = .315 \times 10^{-3}$)
    120000.   has two significant digits ($120000 = .12 \times 10^{6}$)

Computers represent numbers and carry out operations using a fixed number of significant digits, *n*, which depends on the computer's hardware. Any number or any result of an operation must then be expressed as accurately as possible with those *n* digits.

Since computers cannot, in general, represent nonterminating decimal numbers exactly, those numbers are rounded off or truncated, depending on the computer. Rounding off a number to *n* significant digits amounts to finding the closest approximation to that number with *n* or fewer nonzero digits; all digits to the right of the *n*th significant digit are discarded. If the first discarded digit is 5 or greater, 1 is added to the *n*th digit; otherwise, the *n*th digit is unchanged.

EXAMPLE

The following numbers are rounded off to seven significant digits (as on IBM systems):

    41.239824   rounded to 41.23982 $= .4123982 \times 10^{2}$
    .0011145678   rounded to .001114568 $= .1114568 \times 10^{-2}$
    315.00075   rounded to 315.0008 $= .3150008 \times 10^{3}$
    1000001499999.98 rounded to 1000001000000.00 $= .1000001 \times 10^{13}$

In the last example, note the loss of precision in the final number representation (499,999.98!).

---

8. Does "significance" of digits imply accuracy of result? That is, if the computed result of an operation is carried out to seven significant digits, does this mean that the computer result represents the first seven digits of the true answer?

Answer: No. Significance and accuracy of results are not synonymous. Consider the following example: Two carpenters must saw a board in seven equal parts. They use a computer for their calculations and it carries out operations to seven significant digits. Both carpenters measure the boards independently of one another and both feel very satisfied with the accuracy of their measurement of the board—40.01 and 39.89 inches, respectively. A computer is used to perform the division by 7 and the printout yields an answer of 5.715714 (40.01/7) and 5.698541 (39.89/7) for one-seventh of the board. The very presence of seven digits on the computer printout form might so overwhelm the carpenters that each might think that all seven of his/her digits must be correct. Yet the two results have only one digit in common! How many of these digits are then truly meaningful? One? Two? Accuracy depends on the exactness of the measurements, not on the seven significant digits; a very precise measurement (one with many digits) can be terribly inaccurate if there is something wrong with the instrument. Many programmers have blind faith in computer printouts; yet much of a computer's input data in real life deals with approximate measurements of weights, distances, temperatures, forces, and so forth. The number of significant digits will not affect the precision of results to any great extent. Hence results should always be interpreted with the greatest of care even if 15 digits are used to express a result and even if DOUBLE PRECISION is used.

If it is known that the input data are 100% accurate, then of course the number of significant digits used in carrying out operations can affect the accuracy of the results. The reader might be interested in the subject of error analysis, which treats the effects of significant digits or rounding off on numerical operations.

9. It is true that most decimal numbers don't have an exact internal representation on the computer?

Answer: Yes. In fact 99.999 ...% of the numbers that we use in everyday life are not represented exactly on a computer; this is not surprising when we realize that the set of real numbers on a computer is finite. Numbers with small magnitudes have the best chance of being the most accurately represented on a computer. There are literally thousands and thousands more computer real numbers in the interval {0,1} than there are, say, in the interval between 100,000 and 100,001; and the interval or gap between any two successive computer real numbers widens dramatically as the numbers grow in magnitude. For example, on IBM systems the real number following 3,000,000,000 is 3,000,001,000, not 3,000,000,001 (using single precision).

It should be noted, however, that all *integers* are represented exactly in memory up to the number of significant digits allowed by the computer system. Integers are represented exactly in memory because the integer conversion to binary is exact. In the case of floating-point number conversion, the fractional part generally does not convert to binary exactly; for example, $0.1_{10} = 0.00011001100 ..._2$, which must be truncated or rounded off.

10. I need more significant digits than DOUBLE PRECISION can give me on the system that I use. What can I do?

Answer: You will have to write your own code. See exercises 10, 11 and 12, section 6.7.3, for some thoughts on this matter.

5.7 ASSIGNMENTS

5.7.1 Test Yourself

1. Are the following statements true or false?

   a. FORMATS must be placed before the STOP statement.

   b. A READ and a WRITE statement may share the same FORMAT.

   c. WRITE(6,6) is an invalid WRITE statement.

   d. In describing the output format F*w.d* for a real number, the value *d* should always be less than or equal to *w*.

   e. The output field F3.1 allows one fractional digit and three digits to the left of the decimal point.

   f. The F format code automatically rounds off numbers on output.

   g. A format for an input operation should always follow the corresponding READ instruction.

   h. Formats are not required to have statement numbers.

   i. Formats are nonexecutable statements.

   j. The statement READ(5,5)J,J,J is invalid.

   k. In a READ operation, FORMAT (T2, . . .) and FORMAT (2X, . . .) will cause reading to start at the same record position.

   l. The statements
```
READ(5,6)X,I,Y
      6 FORMAT(F5.1/I3/F5.1)
```
   will read three records.

   m. The statements
```
READ(5,7)I,X,K
      7 FORMAT(I1,F1.1,I2,F2.2,F3.3)
```
   will read five records.

   n. The statements
```
READ(5,6)I,J
      6 FORMAT(I2/'+',I3)
```
   will read the same record twice.

   o. The first character of an input record is interpreted as a carriage control code.

2. What output will be produced by each of the following program segments?

   a.
```
      X = 3.2
      Y = X*.16
      WRITE(6,10)X,Y
   10 FORMAT(3X,F4.0,T10,F9.2,
      1'ALL')
```

   b.
```
      I = +1632
      J = -4
      K = I/J
      WRITE(6,11)I,J,K
   11 FORMAT(T8,I4,3X,I1,'+',I5)
```

   c.
```
      XXX = 4.3257
      YYY = -.0007
      ZZZ = XXX+YYY
      WRITE(6,12)XXX,YYY,ZZZ
   12 FORMAT(T2,F7.3,F7.3,F7.3)
```

   d.
```
      ABC = 19.2
      IJ3 = 4
      WRITE(6,13)ABC,IJ3
   13 FORMAT(2X,I4,3X,F6.0)
```

   e.
```
      I = .8
      J = .6
      Z = I+J
      WRITE(6,11)Z
   11 FORMAT(1X,F2.0,'I2,F4.1')
```

   f.
```
      I = 11
      WRITE(6,12)I
   12 FORMAT(I2)
      WRITE(6,13)
   13 FORMAT('1','1','ALL')
```

3. How many records will be processed by the following READ instructions using the various accompanying FORMATs?

5 FORMAT(3F5.1)

a. READ(5,5)A,B,C with FORMATs 5 FORMAT(F5.1,F5.1)

5 FORMAT(4F5.1)

b. READ(5,6)I,J,K,L,M,N 6 FORMAT(I1,I2,I2)

with FORMATs 6 FORMAT(I1,I2,I3,I4)

7 FORMAT(F5.1,I3,F4.1)

c. READ(5,7)A,I,D with FORMATs 7 FORMAT(F5.1/I2)

7 FORMAT(F5.1)

4. Determine the number of records processed (read) by the READ statement and the number of lines generated by the WRITE statement, given the various formats:

READ(5,5)I,J   WRITE(6,6)I,K

a. 5 FORMAT(I4/I3)   **f.** 6 FORMAT(/1X,I2///1X,I3)

b. 5 FORMAT(/I4,I3)   **g.** 6 FORMAT('0',I2/1X,I3/1X)

c. 5 FORMAT(/I4,I3/1X)   **h.** 6 FORMAT(//T2,I2/1X,I3)

d. 5 FORMAT(//I4,I3/1X)   **i.** 6 FORMAT(//1X,I2/1X/I4///1X)

e. 5 FORMAT(//I4//I3//1X)   **j.** 6 FORMAT(/'0',I2/'0',I3)

5. Write a program to print out the following board using two DO loops.

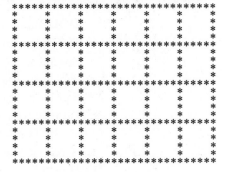

6. What advantage is there in using double precision mode variables and constants? What is the price that you pay for double precision mode, however?

7. What restrictions are there on the placement of specification statements in FORTRAN programs?

8. Express each of the following exponential constants in basic form:

a. 3.2E − 4   **e.** 432.4D2

b. .0034E10   **f.** − 163.94872D − 10

c. − 132.4E6   **g.** 1632543.11D − 8

d. − 132.4E − 6   **h.** .0000324D15

9. What value will be stored for each of the following data items as a result of a READ operation? The result should be expressed as $0.ddddddd \times 10^{exp}$, where d and exp are the significant digits and the decimal exponent, respectively.

Input Data	READ FORMAT Code	Value Stored
a. 632E4	E5.2	
b. -.623E14	E8.2	
c. 1234E-2	E7.0	
d. -1234E-5	E8.2	
e. 69.52D4	D7.2	
f. 000003241	E9.3	
g. -00002561E4	E11.4	
h. 333.447E-50	E11.0	

10. What output will be produced for each of the following?

Value in Memory	Output FORMAT Code	Output Results
a. .0032456	E8.2	
b. - 98.9437	E17.1	
c. .0032456	E11.4	
d. 31245.E - 31	E15.2	
e. - 12340000.	E13.4	
f. - 12340000.	D16.7	
g. - .0000006972	E8.1	
h. + 212.E + 26	E7.1	
i. 212.E26	E6.1	
j. 123.4567891	E17.10	
k. 123.4567891	D16.8	

11. Are the following statements true or false?

a. DOUBLE PRECISION IXNAY creates a more precise integer.

b. DATA statements must be the first statements in a FORTRAN program.

c. Specification statements are nonexecutable statements.

d. The A format code can be used to read any data that can be read by an I,F,E or D format code.

e. Double precision numbers provide twice as many significant digits as ordinary real constants.

f. A real constant has the same internal representation as an exponential real constant.

g. Double precision numbers also exist for integers.

h. The statement DOUBLE PRECISION I,J,K is valid.

i. The REAL statement may be used to define a double precision constant.

j. The statement X = 12345678901134.56 causes X to become a double precision variable.

k. Integers are always fixed in length in terms of memory representation. For instance, the constants 1 and 1234567 use the same number of bits.

l. Double precision always provides a greater number of significant digits and a greater range for the exponent.

m. The F, E, and D format codes can be used to read real numbers in nonexponential form.

*5.7.2 Programming
Exercises*

1. Each record of a data file contains 60 characters of text. Write the FORTRAN code to print the text with a left margin of 10 characters.

2. You work for a federal prison and are asked to provide certain information about the prisoners. Each prisoner's record consists of a name, a sentence length in months, the month entered prison, the year entered prison, and the age of prisoner when incarcerated. Write a program to indicate release time information about each prisoner: age, year, and month at release time. The input and output might be similar to:

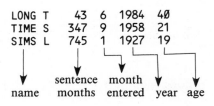

LONG T	43	6	1984	40
TIME S	347	9	1958	21
SIMS L	745	1	1927	19

name sentence months month entered year age

| | SENTENCE | ENTERED PRISON | | RELEASED PRISON | |
	MONTHS	AGE	YR	MONTH	AGE	YR	MONTH
LONG T	43	40	1984	6	44	1988	1
TIME S	347	21	1958	9	50	1987	8
SIMS L	745	19	1927	1	81	1989	2

3. A loan is taken out at a particular interest rate and is repaid at a fixed monthly amount. The monthly transactions can be summarized in an amortization table like those shown below:

```
                    AMORTIZATION TABLE
        PRINCIPAL  $1000.00  INTEREST 12.00  DURATION 3 MONTHS
                    REGULAR PAYMENT   $300.00

        NO.   INTEREST    AMORTIZED    BALANCE   INTEREST TO DATE
         1     10.00       290.00      710.00         10.00
         2      7.10       292.90      417.10         17.10
         3      4.17       417.10        0.00         21.27

        LAST PAYMENT = $421.27
```

```
                    AMORTIZATION TABLE
        PRINCIPAL   750.00  INTEREST 12.00  DURATION 3 MONTHS
                    REGULAR PAYMENT   $300.00

        NO.   INTEREST    AMORTIZED    BALANCE   INTEREST TO DATE
         1      7.50       292.50      457.50          7.50
         2      4.57       295.43      162.07         12.07
         3      1.62       162.07        0.00         13.69

        LAST PAYMENT = $163.69
```

Write a program similar to the program in Figure 5.1 to read a loan amount, a monthly payment, an interest rate, and the term of the loan (such as 5 months, or 1 year and 3 months) and produce a repayment schedule similar to those shown. Note that in such a case the last payment may very well exceed the regular monthly payment.

4. In a physical education class, students get either a pass or a fail for the course. If the average of the student's three test scores is below 70, the student fails the course. The student's three test scores are recorded on records, as follows:

```
          Test1   Test2   Test3

   CANN    50      60      70
   TODD    40      80      90      } Input File
     .
   LOT     20      45      75
```

Write a program to produce the following output:

```
STUDENT    TEST1    TEST2    TEST3    AVERAGE    FINAL GRADE

  CANN      50       60       70        60         FAIL
  TODD      40       80       90        70         PASS
   .         .        .        .         .           .
   .         .        .        .         .           .
   .         .        .        .         .           .
  LOT       20       45       75        46         FAIL

THE PERCENTAGE OF STUDENTS WHO FAILED IS XXX.X
HIGHEST AVERAGE WAS OBTAINED BY TODD
(HIGHEST AVERAGE WAS ALSO OBTAINED BY OTHER STUDENTS)
```

Print this message if appropriate.

5. Each record of an input file consists of the following six items:

Item	Description/code
1. Marital status	(1 = single, 2 = married, 3 = divorced, 4 = widowed)
2. Sex	(1 = female, 2 = male)
3. Age	(1 = over 30, 2 = under 30)
4. Contentment	(1 = happy, 2 = unhappy)
5. Family name	
6. First name	

For example, an input record might appear as

Marital status   Sex   Age   Contentment

2   2   1   2   OAKS ZAN

Write a program using only *one* WRITE statement to transcribe this data into sentences with the following structure:

first name family name IS { OVER 30 / UNDER 30 } . { SHE / HE } IS { SINGLE / MARRIED / DIVORCED / WIDOWED } AND { HAPPY / UNHAPPY } .

For example, given the above input record, the program should produce the following sentence:

ZAN OAKS IS OVER 3Ø. HE IS MARRIED AND UNHAPPY.

6. Write a program to read a principal, an interest rate, and a mortgage duration and produce an amortization schedule similar to the one shown below (see Figure 5.1). Note that in the example shown below the entire report consists of 8 pages, of which only the first and last are shown. Be sure to number each page and print the last payment.

First page (1)

```
          AMORTIZATION TABLE        PAGE 1
PRINCIPAL $40000.00  INTEREST 7.75  DURATION 25 YEARS
          REGULAR PAYMENT  $302.10
```

NO.	INTEREST	AMORTIZED AMOUNT	BALANCE	INTEREST TO DATE
1	258.33	43.77	39956.20	258.33
2	258.05	44.05	39912.20	516.38
3	257.77	44.33	39867.90	774.15
4	257.48	44.62	39823.20	1031.63
5	257.19	44.91	39778.30	1288.82
6	256.90	45.20	39733.10	1545.72
7	256.61	45.49	39687.60	1802.33
8	256.32	45.78	39641.90	2058.65
9	256.02	46.08	39595.80	2314.67
10	255.72	46.38	39549.40	2570.39
11	255.42	46.68	39502.70	2825.81
12	255.12	46.98	39455.70	3080.93

YR. 1 3080.93 544.27

NO.	INTEREST	AMORTIZED AMOUNT	BALANCE	INTEREST TO DATE
1	254.82	47.28	39408.50	3335.75
2	254.51	47.59	39360.90	3590.26
3	254.21	47.89	39313.00	3844.47
4	253.90	48.20	39264.80	4098.37
5	253.58	48.52	39216.30	4351.95
6	253.27	48.83	39167.40	4605.22
7	252.96	49.14	39118.30	4858.18
8	252.64	49.46	39068.80	5110.82
9	252.32	49.78	39019.00	5363.14
10	252.00	50.10	38968.90	5615.14
11	251.67	50.43	38918.50	5866.81
12	251.35	50.75	38867.80	6118.16

YR. 2 3037.23 587.97

NO.	INTEREST	AMORTIZED AMOUNT	BALANCE	INTEREST TO DATE
1	251.02	51.08	38816.70	6369.18
2	250.69	51.41	38765.30	6619.87
3	250.36	51.74	38713.50	6870.23
4	250.02	52.08	38661.50	7120.25
5	249.69	52.41	38609.00	7369.94
6	249.35	52.75	38556.30	7619.29
7	249.01	53.09	38503.20	7868.30
8	248.67	53.43	38449.80	8116.97
9	248.32	53.78	38396.00	8365.29
10	247.97	54.13	38341.90	8613.26
11	247.62	54.48	38287.40	8860.88
12	247.27	54.83	38232.60	9108.15

YR. 3 2989.99 635.21

Last page (8)

```
          AMORTIZATION TABLE        PAGE 8
PRINCIPAL $40000.00  INTEREST 7.75  DURATION 25 YEARS
          REGULAR PAYMENT  $302.10
```

NO.	INTEREST	AMORTIZED AMOUNT	BALANCE	INTEREST TO DATE
1	62.64	239.46	9459.37	49515.90
2	61.09	241.01	9218.36	49577.00
3	59.54	242.56	8975.80	49636.60
4	57.97	244.13	8731.67	49694.50
5	56.39	245.71	8485.96	49750.90
6	54.81	247.29	8238.67	49805.70
7	53.21	248.89	7989.78	49858.90
8	51.60	250.50	7739.28	49910.50
9	49.98	252.12	7487.16	49960.50
10	48.35	253.75	7233.41	50008.90
11	46.72	255.38	6978.03	50055.60
12	45.07	257.03	6721.00	50100.70

YR. 23 647.37 2977.83

NO.	INTEREST	AMORTIZED AMOUNT	BALANCE	INTEREST TO DATE
1	43.41	258.69	6462.31	50144.10
2	41.74	260.36	6201.95	50185.80
3	40.05	262.05	5939.89	50225.90
4	38.36	263.74	5676.16	50264.20
5	36.66	265.44	5410.72	50300.90
6	34.94	267.16	5143.55	50335.80
7	33.22	268.88	4874.68	50369.00
8	31.48	270.62	4604.05	50400.50
9	29.73	272.37	4331.68	50430.30
10	27.98	274.12	4057.56	50458.20
11	26.21	275.89	3781.67	50484.40
12	24.42	277.68	3503.99	50508.90

YR. 24 408.20 3217.00

NO.	INTEREST	AMORTIZED AMOUNT	BALANCE	INTEREST TO DATE
1	22.63	279.47	3224.52	50531.50
2	20.83	281.27	2943.25	50552.30
3	19.01	283.09	2660.16	50571.30
4	17.18	284.92	2375.24	50588.50
5	15.34	286.76	2088.48	50603.90
6	13.49	288.61	1799.87	50617.30
7	11.62	290.48	1509.39	50629.00
8	9.75	292.35	1217.04	50638.70
9	7.86	294.24	922.80	50646.60
10	5.96	296.14	626.66	50652.50
11	4.05	298.05	328.61	50656.60
12	2.12	328.61	0.00	50658.70

LAST PAYMENT = $330.73

YR. 25 149.84 3503.99

7. A large clothing store keeps track of its inventory by department (1 = men's wear, 2 = ladies' wear, 3 = girl's wear, and 4 = boys' wear). The store's inventory file consists of four packets of data, each packet representing a particular department. A typical input file is shown below; each record consists of a department number, an item description, an item quantity, a cost figure, and a market figure (cost to the customer).

	Item	Cost to Store	
Dept. No.	Quantity		Cost to Customer

```
1SUITS   0300100092
1COATS   0200060065
1SHIRTS  1000012013
1DRESSES0400060065
2COATS   0185184200
2SHOES   0600040030
3JEANS   0200040035
3SHOES   0200030034
4JEANS   0300042043
```

a. Write a program to process the input file to compute the store's inventory at lower cost (the lesser of cost or market value for each whole department). The output should be similar to the following:

```
                    PAN AMERICAN APPAREL COMPANY
                         INVENTORY EVALUATION
                              05/06/86

                           UNIT COST              EXTENDED
              QUANTITY    COST    MARKET       COST        MARKET      LOWER COST

MENS DEPT
  SUITS        300       100.00   92.00       30000.00    27600.00
  COATS        200        60.00   65.00       12000.00    13000.00
  SHIRTS      1000        12.00   13.00       12000.00    13000.00
  TOTAL                                   $  54000.00  $ 53600.00   $  53600.00
LADIES DEPT
  DRESSES      400        60.00   65.00       24000.00    26000.00
  COATS        185       184.00  200.00       34040.00    37000.00
  SHOES        600        40.00   30.00       24000.00    18000.00
  TOTAL                                   $  82040.00  $ 81000.00   $  81000.00
GIRLS DEPT
  JEANS        200        40.00   35.00        8000.00     7000.00
  SHOES        200        30.00   34.00        6000.00     6800.00
  TOTAL                                   $  14000.00  $ 13800.00   $  13800.00
BOYS DEPT
  JEANS        300        42.00   43.00       12600.00    12900.00
  TOTAL                                   $  12600.00  $ 12900.00   $  12600.00

INVENTORY AT LOWER COST                                              $161000.00
```

The program should compute the subtotals for each of the four departments as well as the grand total.

b. Compute the lower cost inventory line by line instead of for the whole department. For example, for the men's department the lower cost inventory is 27,600 + 12,000 + 12,000 = 51,600.00

8. A resistor network using standard EIA resistors consists of three meshes, as shown in the schematic diagram below. One thousand volts D.C. is impressed across the input. The values of the various resistors are shown in the schematic diagram. Assume the wattage rating of the resistors is adequate. Write a program to calculate the total current, in amperes, supplied by the 1000-volt supply to the network.

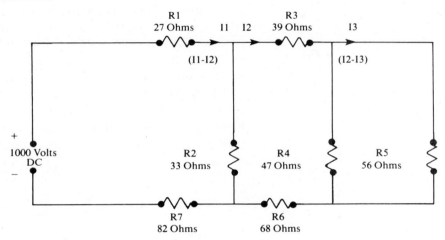

Use Cramers rule to solve for I1, I2, and I3 using

$$aI1 + dI2 + gI3 = j$$
$$bI1 + eI2 + hI3 = k$$
$$cI1 + fI2 + iI3 = l$$

$$I1 = \frac{\begin{vmatrix} j & d & g \\ k & e & h \\ l & f & i \end{vmatrix}}{\begin{vmatrix} a & d & g \\ b & e & h \\ c & f & i \end{vmatrix}} \quad I2 = \frac{\begin{vmatrix} a & j & g \\ b & k & h \\ e & l & i \end{vmatrix}}{\begin{vmatrix} a & d & g \\ b & e & h \\ c & f & i \end{vmatrix}} \quad I3 = \frac{\begin{vmatrix} a & d & g \\ b & e & h \\ c & f & i \end{vmatrix}}{\begin{vmatrix} a & d & g \\ b & e & h \\ c & f & i \end{vmatrix}}$$

where the determinant $\begin{vmatrix} a & d & g \\ b & e & h \\ c & f & i \end{vmatrix} = a(e \cdot i - f \cdot h) - d(b \cdot i - c \cdot h) + g(b \cdot f - c \cdot e)$

5.7.3 Exercises Involving Random Numbers

1. Write a program to generate 100 random real numbers and 100 random integers in the range 0–10. Determine the average of the numbers. What would you expect the results to be?

2. Write a program to determine the least number of random integer numbers between 1 and 100 that must be generated so that the average of these numbers lies in the interval 47 to 53.

3. Marc and Laura each toss a six-sided die. Write a program to simulate the toss of a die and find the probability that they will toss the same number.

4. Sue Ellen and Anabelle each toss a pair of six-sided dice. Write a program to find the chance that both will toss a 2 (i.e., each tosses two 1's)? a 3? a 4? a 12? Simulate the toss of a die.

5. Charlie tosses a pair of six-sided dice. What number (sum of the face values of both dice) is most likely to be thrown (a 2 is a combination of 1 and 1; a 7 is a combination of 4 and 3, 5 and 2, or 6 and 1, and so forth). Simulate the toss of a die.

6. A dog is lost at node 0 in a tunnel (see diagram). It can move one node at one time in either direction right or left with equal probability (1 = right, 2 = left). When the dog hits node L_2, however, a force of nature always propels him directly to node L_4. The dog escapes from the tunnel when he either hits L_5 or R_4. Write a program to determine:

   a. Whether the dog has a better chance to exit from the right or the left: in fact, what are the odds that he will exit from R_4? from L_5? Restart the dog at node 0 a thousand times and count the number of times he escapes through R_4 or L_5.

   b. How long, on the average, the dog stays in the tunnel (each node takes one minute to cover).

   c. Do the same problem as in part a, but let node L_2 propel the dog to L_4 only when traveling in a left direction. If node L_2 is reached when traveling to the right, the node L_2 has no effect.

NODE 0

7. John Jones has $200,000 to invest in speculative gold stock. The gold mines are of such a nature that they either go broke, leaving stock worthless, or strike gold and make the stockholders wealthy. Mr. Jones's goal is to retire with $2,000,000. He plans to invest in blocks of $100,000. He estimates that the probability of losing each $100,000 investment is 75%, while the probability of making $1,000,000 from the same investment is 25%. In the latter case, he will sell the stock and make further $100,000 investments of the same nature.

   a. What is the probability of Mr. Jones's retiring with $2,000,000? [*Hint:* Simulate the 75%/25% lose/win probability by generating random numbers in the range 1 to 4. Arbitrarily choose one number to represent a win. The probability of getting any value in this range is 1/4 = 25%.] Simulate 100 such investment sequences and count the wins (makes $2,000,000) and losses (goes broke); from these figures, determine the probability of Mr. Jones's successful retirement.

   b. Determine whether, in the course of the 100 investment trials, Mr. Jones ever won $1,000,000 only to lose it, i.e., does he ever win $1,000,000 but fail to retire with $2,000,000?

   c. Instead of a return of $1,000,000 for a $100,000 investment, suppose that the return was only $500,000. How would this change Mr. Jones's chances of success? Experiment with returns varying from $300,000 to $3,000,000 in steps of $100,000 and see how the odds for successful retirement change.

8. You are now at the famous Monte Carlo casino and you have $1,000 to burn. You are not a sophisticated roulette player, so you decide to place bets on the even or odd. The roulette ball lands on any of 37 numbers (0–36). The number 0 is the house's lucky number, and the croupier rakes in everything on the board (i.e., you lose your bet). Correct bets on even or odd squares double your input bet. A correct bet on any of the numbers 1 through 36 gives you 20 times the original amount you bet. Write a program to continuously accept bets (from input device) and print your remaining balance. The game should go on till you have either run out of cash or doubled your initial investment. Play 10 such games and keep track of how many you win and how many you lose. What are your chances of doubling your initial investment?

Suppose now you always bet $10 at a time; what are your chances to win more than $3,000? Would your chance of making $3,000 increase if your betting amount was fixed at $100 instead of $10?

9. A submarine has been trapped in an enemy bay with only one escape channel leading out of the bay. The bay is surrounded by mines as shown below. All navigating equipment is malfunctioning, and the blind submarine is now moving randomly in any of the four cardinal directions one square at a time. If the sub hits any of the mines, it is instantly destroyed. The sub escapes when it reaches row 2 column 5.

a. Write a program to determine the sub's chances of escape from its present position (row 4, column 2).

b. Compute the submarine's chances of escape for each of the squares in the above grid.

c. Allow the submarine to restart at row 4, column 2 10,000 times. In those 10,000 attempts, determine the least number of steps the submarine took to escape. Do you think the answer will be 5?

d. Assume there is another moving blind submarine in row 3, column 4. What are the chances of the submarines' colliding with each other? Take into account the fact that both submarines can escape!

e. Change the program to allow the submarine to travel in any diagonal direction also. Do you expect the sub's chances of escape are improved with the sub's increased versatility?

10. Refer to the mole problem of Section 5.5.2.

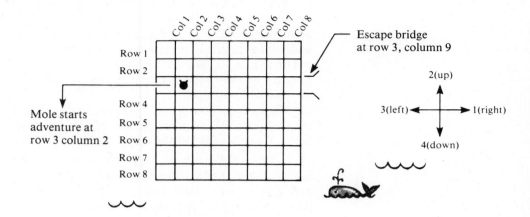

Escape bridge
at row 3, column 9

Mole starts
adventure at
row 3 column 2

a. Compute the average number of moves the mole takes before it either has an accident or escapes. Use 500 adventures.

b. In the course of the 1000 adventures, record the maximum and minimum number of steps taken by the mole before it escapes.

c. The above island (maze) has now been transformed into a closed arena from which no mole can escape. One mole is placed in row 1, column 1 and another mole in row 6, column 6. Moles move about the arena as described in part a above. Upon hitting a wall, the mole bounces back to the position it occupied prior to hitting the wall. Both moles move at the same time. Write a computer program to determine, on the average, how many mole moves are made before a mole collision occurs.

11. Write a program using the Monte Carlo method to estimate the area under the curve $y = x^2$ in the interval 0 to 2.

[*Hint:* Consider the graph of the function shown below:

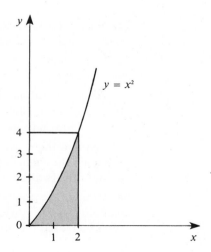

The area of the rectangle that contains the region to be approximated is $4 \times 2 = 8$. Generate points at random in this rectangle: y coordinate in range 0 to 4, x coordinate in range 0 to 2. Count the number of points below or on the curve, i.e., points for which $y \le x^2$. The desired estimate is the number of points that lie below the curve divided by the total number of points and multiplied by the area of the rectangle. The expected value is 2.66.

12. Write a program using the Monte Carlo method to estimate the area under the curve $y = 2x^2 - x + 3$ in the interval 2 to 4. [*Hint:* Graph the function first.]

5.7.4 Answers to Test Yourself

1. **a.** F; FORMATs must be placed before the END statement.
   b. T
   c. F
   d. F; d should be less than w.
   e. F; there will be only two digits to the left of the decimal point.
   f. T
   g. F
   h. F
   i. T
   j. F
   k. F; T2 starts in position 2 while 2X causes the field to start in position 3.
   l. T
   m. F; one record will be read.
   n. F; carriage control applies only to output.
   o. F; position 1 can be used for input.

2. **a.** `        3.              .5 1 A L L`
   b. `              1 6 3 2      * +   - 4 0 8`
   c. `    4 . 3 2 6   - 0 . 0 0 1     4 . 3 2 5`
   d. ABC and IJ3 should be defined respectively by F and I format codes.
   e. `0 . I 2 , F 4 . 1`

   Some systems will not write text after list is satisfied.

   f. `1`   top of new page

   `1 A L L`   top of new page

3. **a.** 1,2,1.   **b.** 2,2.   **c.** 1,3, error (I is integer, but is described by F type).

4. **a.** 2.   **b.** 2.   **c.** 3.   **d.** 4.   **e.** 7.   **f.** 5.   **g.** 4.
   h. 4.   **i.** 8.   **j.** 5.

6. Double precision mode allows more significant digits to be computed but takes more time to compute and more space to store each value.

7. Specification statements must precede executable statements.

8.
  a. 0.00032
  b. 34000000
  c. − 132400000
  d. − .0001324
  e. 43240
  f. − .000000016394872
  g. 0.0163254311
  h. 32400000000

9.
  a. 0.6320000×10^5
  b. $-0.6230000 \times 10^{14}$
  c. 0.1234000×10^2
  d. $-0.1234000 \times 10^{-3}$
  e. 0.6952000×10^6
  f. 0.3241000×10^1
  g. -0.2561000×10^4
  h. $0.3334470 \times 10^{-47}$

10.
  a. `0.32E-02`
  b. `        -0.1E 03`
  c. `0.3246E-02`
  d. `      0.31E-26`
  e. `  -0.1234E 08`
  f. `  -0.1234000D 08`
  g. `-0.7E-06`
  h. `0.2E 29`
  i. `.2E 29`
  j. `0.1234567891E 03`
  k. `  0.12345679D 03`

11.
  a. F.   DOUBLE PRECISION is only for real numbers
  b. F.
  c. T.
  d. T.   No arithmetic can be carried out on those numbers.
  e. F.   Depends on the system
  f. T.
  g. F.
  h. T.
  i. F.
  j. F.   Only if X is a DOUBLE PRECISION variable
  k. T.
  l. F.   Range is not necessarily greater
  m. T.

One Dimensional Arrays

6.1 ONE-DIMENSIONAL TABLES

6.1.1 Background and Justification

Some problems can be solved only with the use of tables; consider the following examples.

EXAMPLE 1

Suppose an input file consists of five records, where each record contains a score. We want to print the difference between each score and the average score. Computing the average of the scores poses no problem: each time a score is read, it can be accumulated into a variable SUM through a statement such as SUM = SUM + SCORE. But a problem arises when the average has been computed and it is time to determine the difference between each score and the average: the scores that have been read are no longer in memory, since each score was stored successively in the same data item (SCORE).

Determining the difference between each score and the average requires the computer to remember (store) the scores as they are read so that after the average is computed, the computer can remember (retrieve) each score one at a time and compute the difference between it and the average. The computer can remember these scores only if it stores them in different memory locations, i.e., if each score is provided with a separate name, as is done in Figure 6.1. But the code in Figure 6.1 is laborious and impractical because each score is individually processed. What would happen if the input file consisted of 100 scores or, even worse, an unknown number of scores?

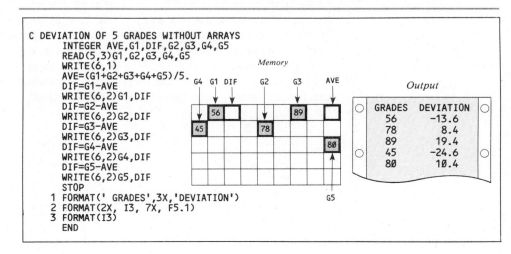

```
C DEVIATION OF 5 GRADES WITHOUT ARRAYS
      INTEGER AVE,G1,DIF,G2,G3,G4,G5
      READ(5,3)G1,G2,G3,G4,G5
      WRITE(6,1)
      AVE=(G1+G2+G3+G4+G5)/5.
      DIF=G1-AVE
      WRITE(6,2)G1,DIF
      DIF=G2-AVE
      WRITE(6,2)G2,DIF
      DIF=G3-AVE
      WRITE(6,2)G3,DIF
      DIF=G4-AVE
      WRITE(6,2)G4,DIF
      DIF=G5-AVE
      WRITE(6,2)G5,DIF
      STOP
   1 FORMAT(' GRADES',3X,'DEVIATION')
   2 FORMAT(2X, I3, 7X, F5.1)
   3 FORMAT(I3)
      END
```

Memory

Output

GRADES	DEVIATION
56	-13.6
78	8.4
89	19.4
45	-24.6
80	10.4

FIGURE 6.1
AVERAGE AND DEVIATION WITHOUT AN ARRAY

Obviously, all the scores have to be stored in memory if we want to be able to refer to them at any given time in our program. The score storage structure in Figure 6.1 certainly does that, but it does not allow us to refer to a score by its position in the list of scores, i.e., it cannot easily answer the following types of questions:

- How far down the list is the score whose value is 98? Is it the 9th, 10th, or 20th score?
- Which is the largest score? Is it the 2d, the 3d, the 4th, . . . ?
- What is the value of the 11th score?
- How can we read a value for INDEX (a number between 1 and the number of scores) and then print all scores from INDEX to the end of the list (in other words, if INDEX is 7, then print the 7th, 8th, 9th, . . . score; or if INDEX is 11, start printing with the 11th score)?

The data structure in Figure 6.1 does *not* provide us with such capability.

What we need is an indexing data structure (a high-sounding name for a list or a table) that enables us to refer to an element in a table by its position. In FORTRAN a table is called an *array*. Thus, if score is the name of the entire list of scores, then score(3) would refer to the 3d score in that list (the number 3 enclosed in parentheses is called a *subscript*). Similarly, if INDEX has value 4, then score (INDEX) would refer to score(4) or the 4th score of the list. With this subscripting capability, we can index an array and access successive array entries simply by manipulating the subscript (adding 1 to the subscript to get the next array entry). Thus, a problem such as "given an array of 100 scores, determine how many exceed the value 90" can be restated as "determine the number of times score (INDEX) is greater than 90 for values of INDEX ranging from 1 to 100 in increments of 1."

Similarly, the scores can be read into the score array by means of the statement READ (5,6) SCORE (INDEX), where INDEX (in this example) varies from 1 and 100. Thus the first time the read instruction is carried out, INDEX is 1 and we read the first score into memory location score (1); INDEX is then 2 and we read the next score into score(2), and so forth.

Score(1) is called a *subscripted variable*. Subscripted variables can be processed in exactly the same way as ordinary variables. For example, given the variable X and score(2), we can write score(2) = 48 just as we can write X = 48. The main difference between the two is that we know what item in memory precedes score (2) (i.e., score(1)) and what item follows it (i.e., score(3)), whereas we do *not* know what item comes in memory before or after such grades as G1, G2, G3 (see Figure 6–1). This indexing structure makes it possible to process an array of items. So far we have been able to process only one item of information at a time. **Now, with arrays, we can process lists of items—a very powerful capability indeed!**

EXAMPLE 2   Here is another problem that would be difficult to solve without tables: Given the tax table in Figure 6.2, write a program to compute the amount of tax owed on an adjusted gross income read from an input record.

The problem is, how can the computer compute the tax if it doesn't have the tax tables in its memory? This type of problem obviously requires a data structure different from any we have encountered so far. One approach might be to create an income array INCOME, a tax array TAX, and a percent-over array PERCENT as shown in Figure 6.3 and store these arrays in memory. Then, for example, we could compute the tax due on an adjusted income of $9,800 by successively comparing $9,800 with the first, second, third, . . . entries of table INCOME until an entry is found that is larger than 9800; in this case, it would be the fourth entry of array INCOME or INCOME(5). The tax due on $9,800 would then be:

DUE = $502.60 + 14% over $7,910

DUE = 4th entry of **TAX** + 4th entry of **PERCENT** * (9800 − 4th entry of **INCOME**)

DUE = **TAX(4)** + **PERCENT(4)** * (9800 − **INCOME(4))**

The last statement is actually the correct FORTRAN expression to compute the tax due (see problem 18 in section 6.7.2).

ADJUSTED INCOME	BUT NOT OVER—	TAX	OF THE AMOUNT OVER—
$ 0	$ 3,540	$ 0.00 + 0%	$ 0
3,540	5,720	0.00 + 11%	3,540
5,720	7,910	239.80 + 12%	5,720
7,910	12,390	502.60 + 14%	7,910
12,390	16,650	1,129.80 + 16%	12,390
16,650	21,020	1,811.40 + 18%	16,650
21,020	25,600	2,598.00 + 22%	21,020
25,600	31,120	3,605.60 + 25%	25,600
31,120	36,630	4,985.60 + 28%	31,120
36,630	47,670	6,528.40 + 33%	36,630
47,670	62,450	10,171.60 + 38%	47,670
62,450	89,090	15,788.00 + 42%	62,450
89,090	113,860	26,976.80 + 45%	89,090
113,860	169,020	38,123.30 + 49%	113,860
169,020	.....	65,151.70 + 50%	169,020

FIGURE 6.2
A TAX TABLE

ADJUSTED INCOME	BUT NOT OVER—	TAX	OF THE AMOUNT OVER—
$ 0	$ 3,540	$ 0.00 + 0%	$ 0
3,540	5,720	0.00 + 11%	3,540
5,720	7,910	239.80 + 12%	5,720
7,910	12,390	502.60 + 14%	7,910
12,390	16,650	1,129.80 + 16%	12,390
16,650	21,020	1,811.40 + 18%	16,650
21,020	25,600	2,598.00 + 22%	21,020
25,600	31,120	3,605.60 + 25%	25,600

INCOME	TAX	PERCENT
$ 0	$ 0.00	. 0
3,540	0.00	.11
5,720	239.80	.12
7,910	502.60	.14
12,390	1,129.80	.16
16,650	1,811.40	.18
21,020	2,598.00	.22
25,600	3,605.60	.25
31,120	4,985.60	.28
36,630	6,528.40	.33
47,670	10,171.60	.38
62,450	15,788.00	.42
89,090	26,976.80	.45
113,860	38,123.30	.49
169,020	65,151.70	.50

INCOME(4)

$9,800 (gross)

FIGURE 6.3
STRUCTURING A TAX TABLE

6.1.2 Definition of an Array

In FORTRAN and in most nonbusiness programming languages, tables are called *arrays*.

In terms of structure, an array is an area of memory that has been divided into a number of equal contiguous parts. For example, the following diagram represents an array:

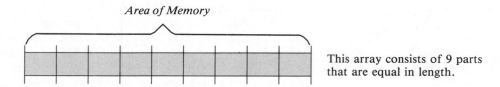

Area of Memory

This array consists of 9 parts that are equal in length.

In terms of syntax, this area of memory is given a name that identifies the entire family or collection of equal parts called *elements*. Each element bears the name of the array, followed by a subscript enclosed in parentheses. The name of the array and the number of elements must be declared in a type statement (INTEGER, REAL, and so forth).

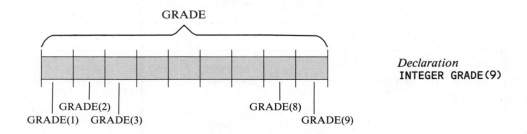

GRADE

Declaration
INTEGER GRADE(9)

GRADE(2)   GRADE(8)
GRADE(1)   GRADE(3)   GRADE(9)

In terms of data, an array is a collection of data values with identical characteristics whose use in a program warrants their being organized under one common name as multiple occurrences of related values. For example:

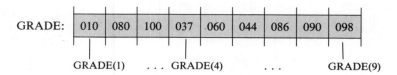

GRADE: | 010 | 080 | 100 | 037 | 060 | 044 | 086 | 090 | 098 |

GRADE(1)   . . . GRADE(4)   . . .   GRADE(9)

All nine related values are captured under one name to facilitate processing.

The problem of Figure 6.1 can be solved with or without arrays. Each method uses the same number of memory locations (see Figure 6.4). If we call the array "GRADE," a block of five sequential memory locations GRADE(1), GRADE(2), ..., GRADE(5) is reserved for the five grades; five memory locations are also used for the individual by labeled grades G1, G2, G3, . . . in Figure 6.1. What makes the array concept different and powerful is that the elements of the array can be indexed with a subscript, thereby greatly simplifying the task of manipulating array elements for processing and for input/output operations.

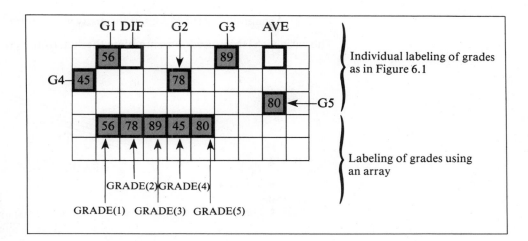

FIGURE 6.4
INDIVIDUALLY LABELED GRADES VERSUS AN ARRAY OF GRADES

The grade problem in our example can be broken into the following three tasks:

1. reading the grades from the input file into the array GRADE,

2. accumulating the grades in the array and computing the average,

3. printing the grades and the deviations (grade − average).

Some of these tasks could be consolidated, but we will illustrate these three tasks independently to illustrate the use of arrays in different situations.

Task 1. Reading the five grades into the array GRADE

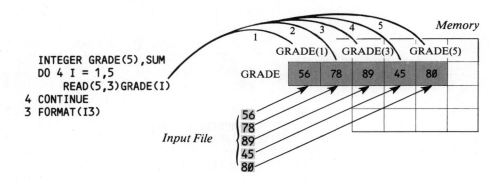

```
        INTEGER GRADE(5),SUM
        DO 4 I = 1,5
            READ(5,3)GRADE(I)
      4 CONTINUE
      3 FORMAT(I3)
```

Note that the statement READ GRADE(I) is processed five times as I takes on values 1 to 5. I is both the array subscript and the index of the DO loop. Initially I is 1, so the first time the READ statement is executed, GRADE(I) will refer to GRADE(1) and the value read from the input file will be stored in GRADE(1); the second time, I is 2, GRADE(I) will identify GRADE(2), and a new grade will be stored in GRADE(2). Eventually, I will be 5, GRADE(I) will refer to GRADE(5), and the last grade will be read into GRADE(5), completing the task of reading the grades into the array.

Task 2. Accumulating the grades in the array and computing the average

The variable SUM is used to accumulate the sum of the grades:

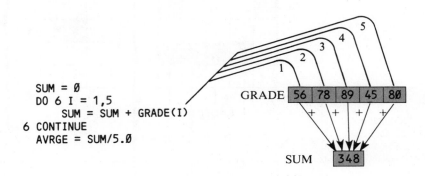

```
SUM = 0
DO 6 I = 1,5
     SUM = SUM + GRADE(I)
6 CONTINUE
  AVRGE = SUM/5.0
```

The 1st time (I = 1) through the loop, SUM =   0 + GRADE(I) =   0 + GRADE(1) =   0 + 56 = 56
The 2d time (I = 2) through the loop, SUM =   56 + GRADE(I) =   56 + GRADE(2) =   56 + 78 = 134
The 3d time (I = 3) through the loop, SUM = 134 + GRADE(I) = 134 + GRADE(3) = 134 + 89 = 223
The 4th time (I = 4) through the loop, SUM = 223 + GRADE(I) = 223 + GRADE(4) = 223 + 45 = 268
The 5th time (I = 5) through the loop, SUM = 268 + GRADE(I) = 268 + GRADE(5) = 268 + 80 = 348

Note that the grades are *not* read from the array by means of the READ statement—they are simply retrieved or accessed from memory by their own names, such as GRADE(1). (READ is used only to read data from an input file.)

Task 3. Printing the elements of array GRADE and the deviations from the average

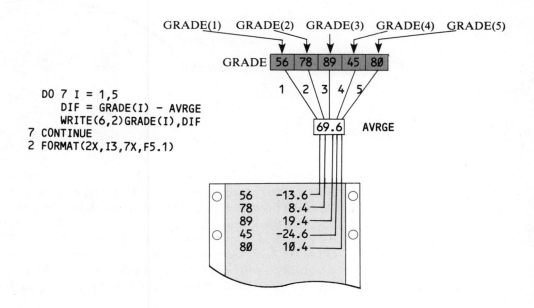

```
DO 7 I = 1,5
     DIF = GRADE(I) - AVRGE
     WRITE(6,2)GRADE(I),DIF
7 CONTINUE
2 FORMAT(2X,I3,7X,F5.1)
```

```
* GRADE DEVIATION PROBLEM USING ARRAYS
*   GRADE:   ARRAY TO HOLD GRADES
*   SUM:     ACCUMULATES SUM OF GRADES
*   I:       SUBSCRIPT FOR ARRAY GRADE
*   AVRGE    GRADE AVERAGE
*   DIF:     DIFFERENCE BETWEEN GRADE AND AVERAGE
*       INTEGER GRADE(5),I,SUM
        REAL AVRGE
        WRITE(6,1)
        DO 5 I = 1, 5
            READ(5,3)GRADE(I)
    5   CONTINUE
        SUM = 0
        DO 6 I = 1,5
            SUM = SUM + GRADE(I)
    6   CONTINUE
        AVRGE = SUM / 5.0
        DO 7 I = 1, 5
            DIF = GRADE(I) - AVRGE
            WRITE(6,2)GRADE(I),DIF
    7   CONTINUE
        STOP
    1   FORMAT(' GRADES',3X,' DEVIATION')
    2   FORMAT(2X, I3, 7X, F5.1)
    3   FORMAT(I3)
        END
```

Reserve 5 memory locations for array GRADE.

Read all grades into array.
When I = 1, GRADE(I) is GRADE(1) and 56 is read into GRADE(1).
Do the same thing for I = 2, 3, 4, and 5.
Initialize sum of grades to 0.

Add all grades one at a time to SUM.

Compute the average of the grades.

Compute the difference between each grade and average.
Print the grade and corresponding difference.

Output

GRADES	DEVIATION
56	-13.6
78	8.4
89	19.4
45	-24.6
80	10.4

Input File

```
056
078
089
045
080
```

FIGURE 6.5
COMPUTING A DEVIATION OF GRADES

The first time through the loop, I = 1, and GRADE(1) and DIF = GRADE(1) − AVRGE are printed. By varying the subscript from 1 to 5, all the elements of the array and their differences from the average are printed.

The entire program is shown in Figure 6.5.

6.1.3 Do It Now

1. Could the grades be read into the array and accumulated at the same time?

2. How could the program of Figure 6.5 handle 97 grades?

3. Think of a problem that you could not solve easily without arrays.

Answers   **1.** Yes. Use the following code:

```
INTEGER GRADE(97),SUM
SUM = 0
DO 5 I = 1,5
    READ(5,3) GRADE(I)
    SUM = SUM + GRADE(I)
5 CONTINUE
```

2. Change the three DO statements to DO n I = 1, 97

3. Sorting a list of names.

6.2 FORTRAN STATEMENTS

6.2.1 Array Declarator Statements

The following specification statements can be used to declare arrays:

DIMENSION REAL INTEGER DOUBLE PRECISION CHARACTER	*array name*$_1$ (*ul*) [,*array name*$_2$(*ul*) ...] format-1
	array name$_1$ ([*ll*:]*ul*) [,*array name*$_2$ ([*ll*:]*ul*) ...] format-2

where   *array name*$_1$, *array name*$_2$, ... are names of the various arrays (any valid variable names)

format-1 and format-2 are used to declare the size (dimension) of the individual array(s). Some FORTRAN systems will permit only format-1 (check your technical manual). Format-1 is the most commonly used format, but format-2 can also be used advantageously, depending on the nature of the problem to be solved.

In format-1, *ul* is an unsigned integer constant representing the maximum number of memory locations reserved for each array. Array subscripts can then vary from 1 to the upper limit *ul*. See Figure 6.6.

In format-2, *ll* and *ul* (*ll* < *ul*) are signed integer constants representing the lower and upper limit integer values that the subscript can take. If both *ll* and *ul* are used, they must be separated by a colon (:). In format-2, both *ll* and *ul* can be negative, or *ll* can be negative and *ul* positive, or both *ll* and *ul* can be positive.

Note that the subscript values must stay within the closed interval [*ll*:*ul*] in the case of format-2 and within [1, *ul*] in format-1. If the subscript takes on a value outside the declared interval, an execution-time error will occur with an "invalid index" error message. Note once again that *ll* and *ul* are both integer constants that can be expressed as either numeric constants or PARAMETER constants but *not* as variables.

Declaration	Subscript range	Memory representation		Total number of elements

1. INTEGER SCORES(100) — Subscript range: $\{1,2,3,\dots,100\}$

Memory representation (positions 1, 2, 3, 4, 46, 100): 50 | 60 | 84 | 36 | ⋯ | 76 | | | | | — SCORES(46) — Total: 100

2. INTEGER CLASS(9:12) — Subscript range: $\{9,10,11,12\}$

Memory representation (positions 9, 10, 11, 12): 904 | 800 | 780 | 726 ← CLASS(12) — Total: 4

3. REAL TEMP(-10:10) — Subscript range: $\{-10,-9,\dots,0,1,\dots,10\}$

Memory representation (positions −10, −9, 0, 9, 10): 3.2 | 3.01 | ⋯ | 1.9 | ⋯ | 1.2 | 1.1 — TEMP(9) — Total: 21

4. REAL GRADES(0:9) — Subscript range: $\{0,1,2,\dots 9\}$

Memory representation (positions 0, 1, 2, 9): 30. | 20. | 60. | ⋯ | 44. — Total: 10

5. CHARACTER*10 NAME(36) — Subscript range: $\{1,2,3,\dots,36\}$

Memory representation (positions 1, 2, 36): TIM | SUE | ⋯ | ANTONY — Total: 36

6. DIMENSION Y(-100:-50) — Subscript range: $\{-100,-99,\dots,0,\dots,-50\}$

Memory representation (positions −100, −99, −98, −50): −3.2 | −1.6 | 0.1 | 1.2 | ⋯ | 13.6 — Y(−50) — Total: 51

FIGURE 6.6
EXAMPLES OF ARRAY DECLARATIONS

Any array used in a program must first be declared in a type or DIMENSION statement; any number of arrays can be declared in one type or DIMENSION statement, for example, the statements

```
INTEGER STUDNT
PARAMETER (STUDNT=63,NMBER=20)
DIMENSION X(6),K(3)
INTEGER TABLE(STUDNT),VECTOR(NMBER),TAB
```

declare X as a real array and K, TABLE, and VECTOR as integer arrays.

If the DIMENSION statement is used to declare arrays, then the name of the array determines the array type (integer if the array name starts with I through N, real otherwise).

In general it is a good idea to use a PARAMETER statement to declare the size of an array. If you do not use a PARAMETER statement and you decide to change the size of a particular array in your program, you will need to retype all numeric references to the array size limits in the program. If the size is declared as a parameter constant, only the PARAMETER size field needs to be edited. This makes the program more general and easier to read.

Examples of array declarations are shown in Figure 6.6. In example 2, the elements of the array CLASS could be used to represent the total number of students in grades 9 through 12. Thus, CLASS(9) would reflect the total number of freshmen, CLASS(10) the number of sophomores, etcetera. The notation CLASS(9) is more meaningful than CLASS(1) since the subscript 9 refers to the ninth grade (freshman class). In example 3, the array TEMP might be used to record the time it takes to freeze a body of water at various temperatures (− 10 degrees up to 10 degrees in increments of 1 degree). Thus, TEMP(-10) = 3.2 might mean that it takes 3.2 minutes to freeze tap water in a -10 degree environment. TEMP(-9) = 3.4 might mean that it takes 3.4 minutes at -9 degrees, etcetera. Note again the direct relationship between subscript value and corresponding array element, which gives a better identification of the array element.

Recall that type specification statements should precede executable statements and DATA statements. A typical FORTRAN program might start as follows:

```
INTEGER SIZE
PARAMETER (NUMBER=3Ø, SIZE=2Ø)
INTEGER GRADE(NUMBER),SUM(SIZE)     All 30 elements of GRADE are integer values.
REAL A(336),K(32),T,L               Two arrays and two variables.
DOUBLE PRECISION B(5),LT(6)          Both B and LT are double precision (real) arrays.
CHARACTER*1Ø NAME(5Ø),PIT(7)        Each element of these two arrays contains 10 characters.
CHARACTER STAR(6)*8,TAB(15)*3       Elements of STAR and TAB are 8 and 3 characters long.
DATA T,L/2*Ø./
READ(5,6)...
```

The following array declaration statements are invalid:

DIMENSION A(3.)	Invalid limit; the limit must be an integer constant.
DIMENSION A(N)	N is not an integer constant (unless N is a PARAMETER constant).

These examples stress again that the size of an array must be declared with an *integer* value in a type or DIMENSION statement. **The size of an array may *not* be declared as a variable.** The maximum value that can be specified as an array size depends on the size of the particular computer's memory.

Character arrays are conceptually similar to numeric arrays. For example, if TEXT is an array declared as CHARACTER*5 TEXT(6) then TEXT(1), TEXT(2), ..., TEXT(6) are the six elements that make up array TEXT. Each array element consists of five characters, for example, array TEXT might have the following configuration:

TEXT(1)	TEXT(2)	TEXT(3)	TEXT(4)	TEXT(5)	TEXT(6)
P A R I S	R O M E	M I L A N O S L O		B O N N	T U N I S

Note that declaring an array does *not* initialize the array elements to any particular values; it simply reserves memory locations.

6.2.2 Subscripts

Subscripts must be used to refer to array elements. A subscript can be an integer constant, an integer variable, or an integer expression (some compilers also allow real expressions for subscripts). For example, if INDX is a variable containing the value 4, then GRADES(INDX) refers to the 4th element of GRADES, since INDX contains 4.

As far as we are concerned, GRADES(INDX) is simply GRADES(4), which in turn might contain the value 64. If the value of INDX changes and becomes 5, then GRADES(INDX) refers to GRADES(5), whose value might be equal to 89.

It is important to differentiate between the subscript value and the corresponding array element value. The value of A(3) generally has nothing to do with the number 3; for instance, A(3) might equal 8.9. Also, the same subscript can be used to refer to two different array elements, for example, A(I) and L(I).

Suppose arrays A and L and variables I and R have the following values:

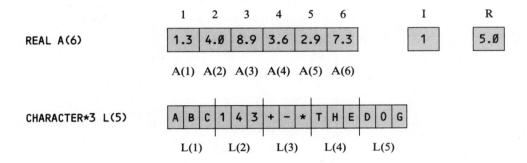

The following examples illustrate the use and meaning of the subscripts (assuming the subscript expression can be real).

Subscript Form	Example	Meaning
constant	A(4)	The value in the fourth location of A is 3.6.
constant	A(3.7)	When the subscript is real, it is truncated to just the whole number portion. This refers to the third element of array A, or 8.9.
variable	A(I)	The subscript is evaluated first. Since $I = 1$, this refers to the first element of A, which is 1.3.
variable	A(R)	Since R is 5., the value of A(R) would be 2.9, since A(R) is equivalent to A(5).
expression	A(24./R-2.3)	The arithmetic expression is evaluated first to $4.8 - 2.3 = 2.5$, which is then truncated to 2. A(2) is the second element in array A, or 4.
library function	A(SQRT(4.))	Since the square root of 4. is 2., this also refers to the second element in array A.
subscripted variable	A(A(4))	Since the fourth element in array A is 3.6, this example becomes A(3.6), which is A(3) or 8.9.
constant	L(3)	Third element of array $(+ - *)$.
expression	L(2*I)	$2*I = 2$, so this refers to the second element, i.e., characters 1, 4 and 3.
expression	2.*A(2*I-1)/A(2)	$A(2*I - 1) = 1.3$. Therefore the entire expression is equal to $2.*1.3/4. = 0.65$

CAUTION

1. When you have dimensioned an array to a particular size such as REAL X(33), you must make sure that any subscripts used with array X do not exceed 33. This is easier said than done! If you use X(I) anywhere in a replacement statement or in an input or output statement, the value of I *must* be less than or equal to 33 and greater than or equal to 1. If I is not in the interval 1 through 33, some systems will give an execution-time error message such as "invalid index"; other systems may process A(I) with unpredictable results (see question 7 section 6.6). After all, what would you do if you had a list of 10 names and someone asked you, "What is the name of the 15th person on your list?"!

    Consider the following example:

    ```
    DIMENSION A(100),B(10)
    I = 101
    Y = A(I)           Invalid use of A(I), since I = 101, which exceeds 100.
    B(11) = 3.         Invalid; maximum subscript for B is 10.
    DO 10 I = 1,11     On the last pass of the DO loop, I will be eleven,
          B(I) = 0.    causing an invalid reference to B(11).
    10 CONTINUE
    ```

2. In a replacement statement, you *must* use subscripts to refer to an array element. Using the name of an array without subscripts is illegal in a replacement statement:

    ```
    REAL WEEK(52)    ⟵ invalid              ⟵ valid
    DAY = WEEK/7.0               DAY = WEEK(3) /7.0
    WEEK = 7.0                   WEEK(2) = 7.0
    ```

3. When declaring an array in a type specification statement, make sure you specify the size of the array with an integer constant. If a program written for some particular application requires that array X be large enough to contain 10 elements one day and 100 elements another day, *don't* write the following:

    ```
    REAL X(N)
    READ*, N         (Decide on the size depending on the application)
    ```

    This method will *not* work. Use the statement REAL X(100) and don't fret about the fact that you may not be using all array cells.

6.2.3 Do It Now

1. Write type statement(s) to create an array Q containing 10 real elements and an array R containing 25 character elements, each 3 characters long.

2. Suppose arrays X and T are as follows:

```
        DIMENSION X(7)                        CHARACTER*4 T(3)

| -3.0 | 2.3 | 0.0 | 3.0 | -2.0 | 6.0 | 10.0 |   T: | H | E |   | I | S |   | T | 0 | 0 |   | M | E |

X(1) X(2) X(3) X(4) X(5) X(6) X(7)            T(1)        T(2)        T(3)
```

and suppose I = 3 and J = 2. Evaluate each of the following expressions:

a. X(3)

b. X(1 + 4)

c. X(1) + X(4)

d. X(I)

e. X(I − J)

f. X(I) − X(J)

g. X(X(4))

h. (X(7) − 3) / X(4)

i. X(X(I/J)**.5 + 1) / 2.0

j. X(2*I + 1) − X(J/I)

k. T(2)

l. X(J)**2

m. X(J**2)

3. Which of the following are legal array declarations for arrays A and B?

a. INTEGER B(3)

b. CHARACTER A(100),B(N)

c. REALA(1)

d. INTEGER(2*100)

e. CHARACTER A(3)*2,B(4)*5

f. CHARACTER*2A(3),B(2)*3

g. DIMENSION A(0:0)

h. DIMENSION B(-3)

i. REAL SQRT(17)

j. REAL WRITE (6:5)

k. REAL READ(5:6)

Answers

1. REAL Q(10)
   CHARACTER*3 R(25)

2. a. 0.

   b. −2.

   c. −3. + 3. = 0.

   d. 0.

   e. −3.

   f. 0 − 2.3 = −2.3

   g. X(3) = 0.

   h. 2.333333

   i. Invalid; square root of negative number.

   j. X(0) is undefined.

   k. SØTO

   l. 5.29

   m. 3.0

3. a. Valid.

   b. Invalid. Variable N is not allowed.

   c. Valid.

   d. Invalid. Expression is not allowed.

   e. Valid.

   f. Valid.

   g. Valid.

   h. Invalid. If only one limit is used, it must be positive.

   i. Valid. There are no reserved words in FORTRAN.

   j. Invalid. Lower limit must be less than upper limit.

   k. Valid.

6.3 ARRAY MANIPULATION

When working with arrays, it is often necessary to initialize arrays to certain values, create duplicate arrays, interchange elements within arrays, merge two or more arrays into one, search or accumulate array entries, or sort arrays. This section illustrates some of the commonly used array manipulation techniques so that the reader can become more familiar with the array index mechanism. In the following examples, it is assumed that values have already been stored in the various arrays.

6.3.1 Array Initialization and Duplication

The following code sets all elements of array A to zeros, sets each element of array B to the variable X, sets $C(1) = 1$, $C(2) = 2$, ..., $C(N) = 10$, and creates a copy of array D in array S.

```
PARAMETER (N=10)
REAL A(N),B(N),C(N),S(N),D(N)
READ*,X
DO 5 I = 1,N                As I varies from 1 to 10,
      A(I) = 0.             A(1), A(2), ..., A(10) are set to 0., one at a time,
      B(I) = X             B(1), B(2), ... are set to the value X,
      C(I) = FLOAT(I)      C(1) = 1., C(2) = 2., ..., C(10) = 10.,
      S(I) = D(I)          S(1) = D(1), S(2) = D(2), ..., S(10) = D(10)
5 CONTINUE
```

Sometimes it may be necessary to set an array C equal to the sum of two other arrays A and B in such a way that $C(1) = A(1) + B(1)$, $C(2) = A(2) + B(2)$, ..., $C(100) = A(100) + B(100)$. The following code could be used:

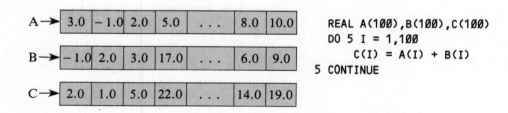

```
REAL A(100),B(100),C(100)
DO 5 I = 1,100
      C(I) = A(I) + B(I)
5 CONTINUE
```

Suppose we want to initialize two arrays A and B, as follows:

$A(1) = B(10) = 1.$ The code on the right   REAL A(10),B(10)
$A(2) = B(9) = 2.$ could be used: DO 5 I = 1,10
$A(3) = B(8) = 3.$ A(I)   = REAL(I)
                                                              B(11-I) = REAL(I)
$A(10) = B(1) = 10.$ 5 CONTINUE

Note that $11 - I$ generates the numbers 10, 9, 8..., 1 as I ranges from 1 to 10. If I ranged from 1 to N, the subscript $N + 1 - I$ would generate the numbers $N, N - 1, N - 2, ..., 3, 2, 1$.

6.3.2 Reversing Arrays

Suppose A is an array of size N, where N has been defined previously, and we want to reverse the array, i.e., interchange A(1) with A(N), A(2) with A(N−1), A(3) with A(N−2), and so forth. The following code could be used (assuming A has already been loaded):

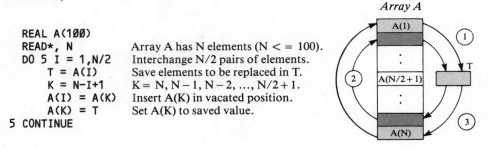

Array A

```
REAL A(100)
READ*, N            Array A has N elements (N < = 100).
DO 5 I = 1,N/2      Interchange N/2 pairs of elements.
    T = A(I)        Save elements to be replaced in T.
    K = N-I+1       K = N, N−1, N−2, ..., N/2+1.
    A(I) = A(K)     Insert A(K) in vacated position.
    A(K) = T        Set A(K) to saved value.
5 CONTINUE
```

Since each interchange step involves a pair of elements (A_1, A_N), (A_2, A_{N-1}), ..., the interchange process needs to be repeated only N/2 times. If N is odd, the middle element remains the same. T is a temporary location needed to save A(1) before we move A(N) into A(1). If we simply wrote A(1) = A(N), the value of A(1) would be lost.

6.3.3 Accumulation of Array Elements

To compute the product of the elements of the array A = | 10 | 20 | 30 | 40 | 50 |, the following code could be used:

```
PARAMETER (N=5)
INTEGER P,A(N)
P = 1               P is initially set to 1 before the loop is entered.
DO 5 K = 1,N        The first time through the loop, P = P*A(1) = 1*10 = 10
    P = P*A(K)      The second time through the loop, P = P*A(2) = 10*20 = 200
5 CONTINUE
                    :
```

To compute the sum of two arrays A and B such that S = A(1) + B(1) + A(2) + B(2) + ... + A(50) + B(50) we could use:

```
PARAMETER (N=50)
REAL A(N),B(N)
S = 0.0
DO 5 K = 1,N
    S = S + A(K) + B(K)
5 CONTINUE
```

EXAMPLE

Assume arrays X and Y contain 10 x and y coordinates of a vector V. Let us compute the dot product $x_1 y_1 + x_2 y_2 + ... + x_{10} y_{10}$. The following code could be used:

```
PARAMETER (N=10)
REAL X(N),Y(N),DOTPRD
DOTPRD = 0.0                         Set dot product to 0, outside loop.
DO 5 I = 1,N
    DOTPRD = DOTPRD + X(I)*Y(I)      Accumulate the xᵢyᵢ.
5 CONTINUE
```

6.3.4 Array Merge

Suppose A, B and C are arrays of size 10 and we want the array C to contain the data $A_1, B_1, A_2, B_2, ..., A_{10}, B_{10}$ arranged in that order. Any of the following codes could be used:

1.
```
    K = 1
    DO 10 I = 1,10
        C(K) = A(I)
        K    = K + 1
        C(K) = B(I)
        K    = K + 1
10 CONTINUE
```

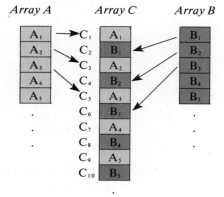

2.
```
    K = 1
    DO 10 I = 1,20,2
        C(I)   = A(K)
        C(I+1) = B(K)
        K      = K + 1
10 CONTINUE
```

3.
```
    DO 10 I = 1,10
        C(2*I-1) = A(I)
        C(2*I)   = B(I)
10 CONTINUE
```

$2*I - 1$ generates the odd entries of C
$2*I$ generates the even entries of C

6.3.5 Array Searches

EXAMPLE 1

Assume array A already contains N grades and we want to determine the number of grades over 53. The following code can be used:

```
    K = 0
    DO 10 I = 1,N
        IF(A(I) .GT. 53.)K = K+1
10 CONTINUE
```

If $A(I) > 53$ increment counter K by 1. Otherwise compare next grade with 53.

EXAMPLE 2

Assume array SCORES contains 100 scores that are supposed to be in ascending order. Write the pseudo code to perform a sequence check and write an error message if the scores are out of sequence. If the scores are in sequence, write an appropriate message. Stop as soon as the first out-of-sequence score is detected.

```
k = 2
WHILE k ≤ 100 and scores(k – 1) ≤ score(k) DO
        k = k + 1
ENDWHILE
IF k > 100 THEN
        Print 'numbers are in sequence'
ELSE
        Print 'numbers not in sequence'
ENDIF
STOP
```

Process the scores until one is found to be out of sequence or the end of the array has been reached. If the index k = 101, then all scores are in sequence. Otherwise they are not in sequence.

EXAMPLE 3   Assume an array G contains 10 scores and we want to determine the highest score. One way to do this is to use a variable MAX to contain the current highest score and keep comparing MAX with the next score. If the next score is larger than MAX, then MAX is set to that score; otherwise MAX is compared to the score that follows. Initially, MAX is set to the first score.

```
INTEGER G(10),MAX
MAX = G(1)                        Set MAX initially to the first score.
DO 50 I = 2,10                    Start comparing MAX with the second entry.
    IF(MAX .LT. G(I))MAX=G(I)     If the largest score (MAX) so far is less than
50 CONTINUE                        the new score G(I), replace MAX by new score
PRINT*,'LARGEST VALUE', MAX       G(I). Otherwise, look at the next score.
```

This code does not, however, indicate the position of the largest element of the array G, i.e., it does not show whether the largest number was found at the 5th or 7th position, for example. That could be done with the following code, where POS is used to indicate the position of largest number.

```
INTEGER POS,G(10)
MAX = G(1)
POS = 1                        Assume largest element is in position 1
DO 50 I = 2,10                 (subject to later change).
    IF(MAX .LT. G(I))THEN
        MAX = G(I)             Every time a new larger number is found, store it in
        POS = I                MAX and keep track of its array position in POS.
    ENDIF
50 CONTINUE
PRINT*, 'LARGEST NUMBER IS',MAX,'AT POSITION',POS
```

6.3.6 Do It Now

1. What will be the content of each element of the array Y after the following code is executed:

```
INTEGER Y(10)
Y(1) = 1
Y(2) = 1
DO 5 I = 3,10
    Y(I) = Y(I-1) + Y(I-2)
5   CONTINUE
```

2. Write the code to fill successive elements of an array with the values 5, 7, 9, 11, ..., 225. Do not use a READ statement to read the values 5, 7, 9 ..., 275.

3. Assume array X has 50 elements. Write the code to compute the sum of the squares of the elements of X.

4. Array C with N elements is supposed to be in ascending order. Write the code to perform a sequence check and print all numbers that are out of sequence.

5. Array C contains 17 elements. Print the element in C closest to 5.37 and identify its position, i.e., was that element the first? second? fourteenth?

6. Given an array G containing 5 scores, would the following code print the position of the highest score and the highest score itself?

```
K = 1
DO 5 I = 2,5
    IF(G(K) .LT. G(I)) K = I
5 CONTINUE
PRINT*,'POSITION HIGHEST SCORE IS',K,'HIGHEST SCORE IS',G(K)
```

Answers

1.

1	1	2	3	5	8	13	21	34	55
Y_1	Y_2	Y_3	Y_4	Y_5	Y_6	Y_7	Y_8	Y_9	Y_{10}

2.
```
INTEGER A(111)            INTEGER A(111)
K = 1                     DO 5 I = 1,111
DO 5 I = 5,225,2    or        A(I) = 2*I + 3
    A(K) = I              5 CONTINUE
    K = K + 1
5 CONTINUE
```

3.
```
S = Ø.
DO 5 I = 1,5Ø
    S = S + X(I)**2
5 CONTINUE
```

4.
```
T = C(1)
DO 5 I = 2,N
    IF(T .LT. C(I)) THEN
        T = C(I)
    ELSE
        PRINT*,C(I)
    ENDIF
5 CONTINUE
```

5.
```
K = 1
X = ABS(C(1)-5.37)
DO 5 I = 2,17
    D = ABS(C(I)-5.37)
    IF(D .LT. X)THEN
        X = D
        K = I
    ENDIF
5 CONTINUE
PRINT*,'POSITION IS',K,'NUMBER IS',C(K)
```

6. Yes; K will identify the position of the highest score, while G(K) will be the highest score.

6.4 INPUT AND OUTPUT OF ARRAYS

There are essentially two methods for loading (reading) and writing out arrays. The first method uses the *explicit* form of the DO loop, and the second method uses an implied form of the DO loop that is equivalent to listing all array entries individually in the READ/WRITE list. The second method is called the *implied DO list*; it can do everything that the explicit form of the DO loop does and much more, as will be seen in the following sections, where the two methods are discussed in more detail.

6.4.1 Explicit Use of the DO Loop

A straightforward approach for reading five grades from five data records (one grade per record) into an array GRADE is to use five READ statements, each specifying one of the five memory locations into which the grades are to be stored:

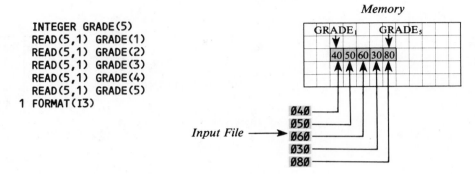

```
      INTEGER GRADE(5)
      READ(5,1) GRADE(1)
      READ(5,1) GRADE(2)
      READ(5,1) GRADE(3)
      READ(5,1) GRADE(4)
      READ(5,1) GRADE(5)
    1 FORMAT(I3)
```

This method is clearly tedious. A preferable approach is to read GRADE(I) as I varies from 1 to 5, i.e., the READ statement is part of a DO loop where the array subscript is also used as the index of the DO loop. For example, to read five data items from five records (one data item per record), the following code can be used:

EXAMPLE 1

```
      INTEGER GRADE(5)
      DO 10 I = 1,5
         READ(5,1) GRADE(I)
   10 CONTINUE
    1 FORMAT(I3)
```

The first time through the loop, I is 1 and GRADE(1) is read from the data record. The second time through the loop, I is 2 and the data item on the second record is stored into GRADE(2). Finally, I is 5 and the fifth data item (from the fifth record) is read into GRADE(5). Because there is only one variable in the READ list, the corresponding format should specify only one data format code.

To read two numbers per record into two different arrays HR and RATE, the following code can be used:

EXAMPLE 2

```
      REAL RATE(10)
      INTEGER HR(10)
      DO 10 I = 1,10
         READ(5,5)HR(I),RATE(I)
   10 CONTINUE
    5 FORMAT(I3,3X,F4.0)
```

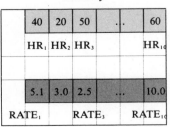

Input Data

040ᵇᵇᵇ05·1
020ᵇᵇᵇ03·0
050ᵇᵇᵇ02·5
          ⋮
060ᵇᵇᵇ10·0

EXAMPLE 3   Assume that each element of array SALES contains a daily sales amount and that you want to print the daily sales with each corresponding day. The following code could be used:

```
REAL SALES(7)
WRITE(6,12)
DO 10 I = 1,7
    WRITE(6,11)I,SALES(I)
10 CONTINUE
11 FORMAT(1X,I2,5X,F6.2)
12 FORMAT(' DAY',4X,'SALES')
```

Output

DAY	SALES
1	101.00
2	200.00
3	50.50
4	35.50
5	100.00
6	300.00
7	50.00

Note that I represents the day and SALES(I) represents the sales for the corresponding day, i.e., SALES(I) is the sales for the Ith day.

EXAMPLE 4   If two numbers per record are to be read into an array A of size 6, the following code can be used:

```
REAL A(6)
DO 10 I = 1,5,2
    READ(5,5)A(I),A(I+1)
10 CONTINUE
5 FORMAT(2F5.1)
```

Input File

```
0003000040
00060-0020
0009100060
```

Memory

3.0	4.0	6.0	−2.0	9.1	6.0
A_1	A_2	A_3	A_4	A_5	A_6

If six numbers were to be read per record, the READ list in the DO loop would have to specify $A(I), A(I+1), A(I+2), A(I+3), A(I+4), A(I+5)$ and the index increment would have to be 6, making the DO loop method unwieldy. In this case the DO list is advantageous.

6.4.2 Implied DO List   The implied DO list is essentially a shorthand notation for listing subscripted variables in a READ/WRITE list. Instead of writing

```
READ(5,5)A(1),A(2),A(3),A(4),A(5),A(6)
```

we can use a more compact and convenient notation:

```
READ(5,5) (A(I),I=1,6,1)   note the required parentheses
WRITE(6,7)I
```

This statement is interpreted as follows: Read the numbers A(I) as I ranges from 1 to 6 in steps of 1. The incremental step can be omitted, resulting in an automatic increment of 1. Six values will then be read from one or more records, as determined by the number of data format codes in the format. Once again, the implied DO list specifies the total number of values to be read into memory or written out, and the format specifies how many of these values will be read per record (or written per line).

As with the DO loop, the index of the DO list is defined at the conclusion of the READ operation if the DO list goes through its complete cycle; in the above example the value printed for I would be 7 (see page 174). The value of the index is also preserved if transfer is made out of the DO list through the "END = " option of the READ statement. Consider the following examples:

EXAMPLE 1

```
REAL A(5)                    REAL B(5)
READ(5,10)(A(I),I=1,5)       WRITE(6,10)(B(I),I=1,5)
10 FORMAT (F5.0)             10 FORMAT(2X,2F6.0)
```

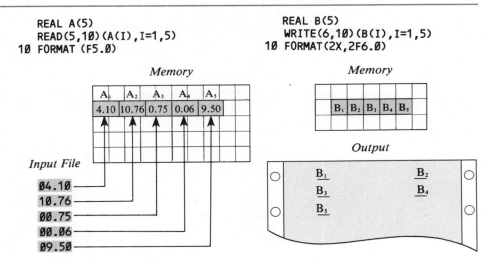

In both cases five elements are to be read or written. The format specifies the number of entries per record. For the READ operation there is one item per record, hence five records will be read. For the WRITE operation there are two items (2F6.0) per line; hence three lines will be printed, with only one item printed on the last line.

EXAMPLE 2

```
READ(5,10)(A(I),I=1,13)       WRITE(6,20)(A(I),I=1,13)
10 FORMAT(3F5.0)              20 FORMAT(1X,7F6.0)
```

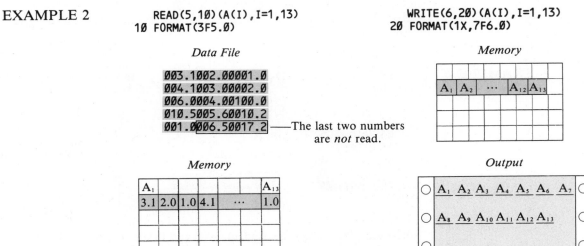

In both cases 13 elements are processed. For the READ operation there are three items per record (3F5.0); hence, five records will be read, reading only the first entry on the fifth record. For the WRITE operation, 7 items are printed per line (7F6.0); hence, two lines will be printed, with only six fields printed on the second line.

EXAMPLE 3   Printing the index of the DO list

```
        WRITE(6,12)
        READ (5,5)(SALES(I),I=1,7)

        WRITE(6,11)(I,SALES(I),I=1,7)
    5 FORMAT(F5.2)
   11 FORMAT(1X,I2,4X,F6.2)
   12 FORMAT(' DAY',4X,'SALES')
```

— 14 entries in all are written (same as 1, $SALES_1$, 2, $SALES_2$, …, 6, $SALES_6$, 7, $SALES_7$)

— 2 entries per line

Input File	Memory	Output
10100	SALES	DAY SALES
20000	101.0	1 101.00
05050	200.0	2 200.00
03550	50.5	3 50.50
10000	:	4 35.50
30000	:	5 100.00
05000	50.0	6 300.00
		7 50.00

Seven sales are read into array SALES. The list of variables in the WRITE statement specifies 14 items to be printed: 1,SALES(1), 2,SALES(2), …, 7,SALES(7). The output format indicates that only two entries are to be printed per line. If FORMAT 11 had been (7(I3,6X,F6.2)), then the 14 values would have been printed on the same line.

EXAMPLE 4

```
    READ(5,10)(A(I),B(I),I=1,5)              WRITE(6,10)(A(I),B(I),I=1,5)
 10 FORMAT(2F5.0)                         10 FORMAT(3F6.0)
```

Input File	Memory	Output
012.4001.5	A_1 A_2 A_5	A_1 B_1 A_2
001.3003.0	12.4 1.3 3.0 34.5 10.6	B_2 A_3 B_3
003.0010.4		A_4 B_4 A_5
034.5010.6	1.5 3.0 10.4 10.6 90.8	B_5
010.6109.8	B_1 B_2 B_5	

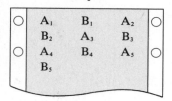

Both examples process the elements A(I) and B(I) as I varies from 1 to 5. The implied DO list is equivalent to the list of variables A(1),B(1),A(2),B(2),A(3),…,A(5),B(5).

The READ statement reads pairs of A and B elements, hence five data records are needed. In the WRITE operation, three numbers are written per line (3F6.0).

EXAMPLE 5

```
WRITE(6,4)(A(I),I=1,5),(B(I),I=1,4)        WRITE(6,6)(A(I),I=1,5),(B(I),I=1,4)
4 FORMAT(1X,3F4.0)                         6 FORMAT(1X,6F4.0/1X,3F4.0)
```

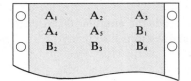

In both examples, nine values are to be printed. Format 4 specifies three entries per line, hence three lines with three entries will be printed. Format 6 specifies six values on the first line and three values on the second line.

EXAMPLE 6

```
CHARACTER*3 TEXT(15)                       WRITE(6,4)(TEXT(K),K=1,15)
READ(5,6)(TEXT(I),I=1,15)                  4 FORMAT(1X,3A4,A1)
6 FORMAT(2A3,A1,1X,A4)
```

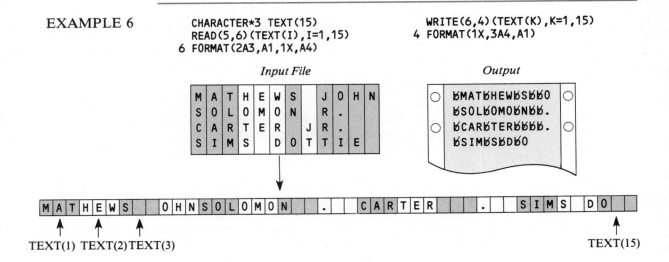

Recall that on input if w of Aw is greater than the length l of the variable to be read (l is defined in the CHARACTER statement), then the right-most l characters of the input data field are read into the variable; likewise on output, if w is greater then l, then the l characters are right-justified in the output field with $w - l$ leading blanks.

EXAMPLE 7   Suppose the correct answers to a multiple choice test (maximum of 25 questions) are recorded on an input record with the first entry on the record indicating the number of test questions that follow, for example

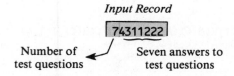

Input Record

74311222

Number of   Seven answers to
test questions   test questions

The following code first reads the number of test questions (7) into N and then reads the N answers to the test questions into array TEST. The TEST array is then printed out on one line.

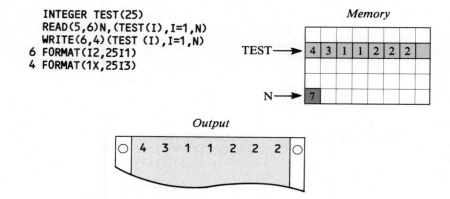

```
      INTEGER TEST(25)
      READ(5,6)N,(TEST(I),I=1,N)
      WRITE(6,4)(TEST (I),I=1,N)
    6 FORMAT(I2,25I1)
    4 FORMAT(1X,25I3)
```

Memory

TEST → | 4 | 3 | 1 | 1 | 2 | 2 | 2 |

N → | 7 |

Output

| 4 | 3 | 1 | 1 | 2 | 2 | 2 |

Note that formats 6 and 4 specify 25I1 and 25I3. Since N will always be less than or equal to 25, only N entries will be printed per line.

EXAMPLE 8   Suppose that for a particular report the following heading is required at the top of a new page:

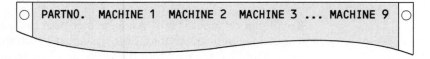

PARTNO.   MACHINE 1   MACHINE 2   MACHINE 3 ... MACHINE 9

The literal "MACHINE" is repeated nine times, and the numbers 1,2,3,...,8,9 can be generated by the implied DO list, as follows:

```
      WRITE(6,1)(I,I=1,9)   Write I as I varies from 1 to 9.
    1 FORMAT('1',9X,'PARTNO.',2X,9('MACHINE',I1,2X))
```

EXAMPLE 9   It is often desirable to produce graphic output from a computer program. A scientific problem might require the graph of a function; a business problem might require a bar graph. Consider, for example, the following problem. Data regarding company sales for a week have been tabulated as shown:

Day	Sales
1	3
2	7
3	10
4	6
5	8
6	2
7	0

To visualize the sales trend, we can represent each day's sales with an equivalent number of * symbols. The output on the right might be suitable.

DAY	SALES
1	***
2	*******
3	**********
4	******
5	********
6	**
7	

The program to solve this problem is shown in Figure 6.7 (we assume SALES does not exceed 20). The variable STAR is initialized to the character *; every time a day's sales (SALES) is read, a number of stars (*) equal to SALES is printed by the implied DO list in statement 15.

```
C BAR GRAPH EXAMPLE
C    SALES:   DAILY SALES VOLUME
C    DAY:     TO COUNT THE DAYS
C    STAR:    GRAPHIC SYMBOL FOR PLOTTING
         INTEGER SALES,DAY
         CHARACTER STAR
         DATA STAR/'*'/
         WRITE(6,1)                              Skip to next page to print titles.
         DO 20 DAY = 1,7
             READ(5,2) SALES                     Read sales for the day.
             IF(SALES.EQ.0) THEN                 If sales are 0, print only the day.
                 WRITE(6,3)DAY
             ELSE
15               WRITE(6,3)DAY,(STAR,J=1,SALES)  Print the day and number of stars
             ENDIF                               corresponding to the sales for that day.
20       CONTINUE
         STOP
   1     FORMAT(1X,'DAY',T8,'SALES')
   3     FORMAT(T3,I1,T8,20A1)                   Assume maximum of 20 sale entries.
   2     FORMAT(I2)
         END
```

FIGURE 6.7
*EXAMPLE OF A
BAR GRAPH*

In conclusion, the implied DO list is a convenient method for loading or writing out arrays. The implied DO list cannot be used if the data items are to be analyzed as they are read into memory or written out. For example, if one wishes to read an array and stop the reading process when a particular item is encountered in the input file, an explicit DO loop must be used, since the implied DO list does not allow testing while reading; similarly, an explicit DO loop must be used for writing arrays if the array elements are to be analyzed as they are written out.

*6.4.3 Format Reuse
and the Slash*

In general, if n variables are specified in a READ/WRITE list, the system scans for n corresponding data format codes (I,F,A,E,D) in the FORMAT statement. If there are m data format codes in the FORMAT and m is less than n (fewer format codes than variables), some of the format codes will be reused. After the first m variables have been processed, reading or writing will start at the beginning of a new record and scanning for data format codes will resume at the right-most *open* (left) parenthesis in the format in order to complete processing the $n - m$ variables left in the READ/WRITE list.

EXAMPLE 1

```
      DATA I,J,K,L,M,N/1,2,3,10,11,12/
      WRITE(6,5) I,J,K,L,M,N
    5 FORMAT(1X,I1,I2,(1X,I2,I2))
```

right-most
open parenthesis ──────── carriage control code for 2d record

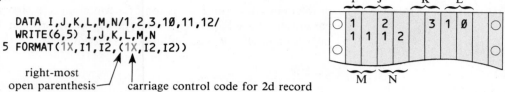

Variables I,J,K, and L will be printed on the first line; at this point format control encounters the very last parenthesis in the format, signaling the end of the record (the end of the line, in this case); format control then resumes scanning at the right-most open parenthesis and prints M and N on the second line since the carriage control for the new record is blank (1X).

EXAMPLE 2

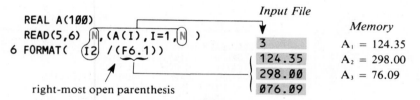

```
      REAL A(100)
      READ(5,6) N,(A(I),I=1,N )
    6 FORMAT( I2 /(F6.1))
```

right-most open parenthesis

Input File

3
124.35
298.00
076.09

Memory

$A_1 = 124.35$
$A_2 = 298.00$
$A_3 = 76.09$

In this example, N is first read, and then N is used as the terminal value in the implied DO list to control the number of variables to be read. All values for the array A will be read under the format F6.1, since after encountering the right-most parenthesis, format scanning resumes at the right-most *open* parenthesis, forcing a new record. If we had used (I2/F6.1) instead, then A(2) would be read with format code I2, which would be invalid.

EXAMPLE 3

```
      WRITE(6,10)(K(I),I=1,20)
   10 FORMAT(1X,I1/1X,2(I1,1X,I1),2(1X,I1,I1))
```
──────── Rightmost open parenthesis

Output Listing

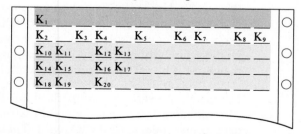

After the right-most parenthesis has been encountered the first time, FORMAT control will resume scanning at 2(1X,I1,I1), which is equivalent to 1X,I1,I1,1X,I1,I1. From then on, all the variables in the WRITE list will be processed according to this format, beginning a new line each time. Note that scanning does *not* resume at

(1X,I1,I1) but at 2(1X,I1,I1), i.e., the duplication factor 2 is included. Also note the importance of 1X in 2(1X,I1,I1)—it serves as carriage control. If the 1X had been omitted, then part of K_{10}, K_{14}, and K_{18} would *not* be printed.

EXAMPLE 4

```
WRITE(6,12)P,(A(I),B(I),I=1,3),(C(I),I=1,3)
12 FORMAT(1X,F5.1/T10,(1X,2F3.0))
```

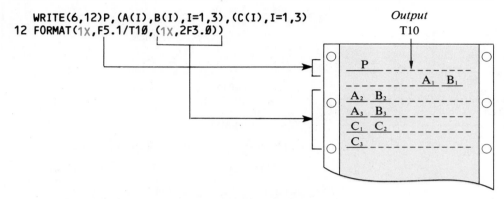

Output
T10

P	
	A_1 B_1
A_2 B_2	
A_3 B_3	
C_1 C_2	
C_3	

Note that after P, A_1, and B_1 are written, all remaining variables are written under the same format (1X,2F3.0). If we had used (1X,F5.1/(T10,2F3.0)), then A_2, B_2, A_3, B_3, C_1, C_2, and C_3 would be aligned under A_1 and B_1.

EXAMPLE 5

```
WRITE(6,5)A,B,C,D,E,F,G,H,S,T,V,W,X
5 FORMAT(F5.0/2(3X,F3.0),2(1X,F3.0),F3.0)
```

Once the right-most parenthesis has been encountered, a new line is started and format control starts at the right-most open parenthesis, i.e., 2(1X,F3.0),F3.0). All remaining variables in the WRITE list are written according to this partial format code.

Output

A				
B	C	D	E	F
G	H	S		
T	V	W		
X				

6.4.4 Do It Now

1. Given the data file shown below, what values will be stored in arrays X and Y as a result of executing the following instructions? (Repeat each part of the problem with all the FORMATS shown for that part.) Assume REAL X(5), Y(5).

a.
```
   READ(5,6)(X(I),I=1,5)
1  FORMAT(F2.0)
2  FORMAT(5F2.0)
```

b.
```
   READ(5,6)(X(I),Y(I),I=1,5)
1  FORMAT(2F2.0)
2  FORMAT(3F2.0)
3  FORMAT(10F1.0)
```

Data File

0	2	0	3	0	0	0	0	1	2
0	4	–	6	0	0	0	0	2	2
0	5	0	7	0	0	0	0	0	0
–	2	–	1	0	0	0	0	1	4
0	0	0	0	0	0	0	0	0	0

```
c.    READ(5,6)(X(I),I=1,5,2),(Y(I),I=2,5,2),X(2)
   1  FORMAT(2F2.0)
   2  FORMAT(3F2.0)

d.    READ(5,6)N,(X(I),Y(I),I=1,N)
   1  FORMAT(I2,6F2.0)
   2  FORMAT(/I2,4F2.0/6F1.0)
   3  FORMAT(I2,3F2.0)

e.    I = 0
  10  READ(5,14)A,B
      IF(A .NE. 0.) THEN
           I = I+1
           X(I) = A
           Y(I) = B
      ENDIF
      GO TO 10
  30  ...
  14  FORMAT(2F2.0)
```

Data File

0	2	0	3	0	0	0	0	1	2
0	4	-	6	0	0	0	0	2	2
0	5	0	7	0	0	0	0	0	0
-	2	-	1	0	0	0	0	1	4
0	0	0	0	0	0	0	0	0	0

2. Determine the number of lines printed by

```
WRITE(6,4)(X(I),I=1,3),Z,(Y(I),I=1,4)
```

using the following FORMATS

a. FORMAT(1X,F5.0)   d. FORMAT(1X,/1X,F4.0)

b. FORMAT(1X,9F5.0)   e. FORMAT(1X,6F4.0/1X,F4.0)

c. FORMAT(1X,3F5.0)

3. What will be printed by the following WRITE statements? Give the value of the variable, if known, or the variable name if the value is unknown.

a. WRITE(6,4)(A(I),I,I=1,2)

b. WRITE(6,5)(B(I),I,C(I),I=1,3)

c. WRITE(6,6)(K,A(I),B(I),I=1,5,2)

4. Assume CHARACTER*3 A(4) and the data file shown below.

S	O	M	E		P	E	O	P	L	E	
S	E		T	H	I	N	G	S	E		A
S		T	H	E	Y		A	R	E		A
N	D	S	A	Y		W	H	Y			

Display the contents of array A resulting from the following input statements:

```
READ(5,6)(A(I),I=1,4)
```

a. FORMAT(3A3)   c. FORMAT(1X,A3)   e. FORMAT(A6)

b. FORMAT(A1)   d. FORMAT(2A2)   f. FORMAT(2A5)

5. An input file consists of 100 records, where each record contains a student name, a 3-digit ID, a final score in management, and a final score in algebra.

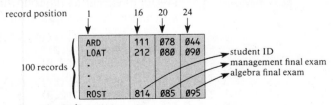

Write the code to load all the algebra scores into array A and all the names into array NAME using (a) the DO loop and (b) the DO list.

Answers   **1.**

a. 1   X

2.	4.	5.	−2.	0.

    2   X

2.	3.	0.	0.	12.

b. 1   X

2.	4.	5.	−2.	0.

Y

3.	−6.	7.	−1.	0.

    2   X

2.	0.	−6.	5.	0.

Y

3.	4.	0.	7.	−2.

    3   X

0.	0.	0.	0.	1.

Y

2.	3.	0.	0.	2.

c. 1   X

2.	7.	3.	?	4.

Y

?	−6.	?	5.	?

    2   X

2.	0.	3.	?	0.

Y

?	4.	?	−6.	?

d. 1   X

3.	0.	?	?	?

Y

0.	12.	?	?	?

N

2

    2   X

−6.	0.	0.	0.	?

Y

0.	22.	5.	7.	?

N

4

    3   Invalid format I2 for Y(2)

e.   X

2.	4.	5.	−2.	?

Y

3.	−6.	7.	−1.	?

    2. a. 8   **b.** 1   **c.** 3   **d.** 16   **e.** 3

    3. a. A(1), 1, A(2), 2

       b. B(1), 1, C(1), B(2), 2, C(2), B(3), 3, C(3)

       c. K, A(1), B(1), K, A(3), B(3), K, A(5), B(5)

    4. A_1 A_2 A_3 A_4

a.	S	O	M	E		P	E	O	P	S	E	E
b.	S			S			S			N		
c.	O	M	E	E	E			T	H	D		S
d.	S	O		M	E		S	E		E		
e.	E		P		T	H	H	E	Y	S	A	Y
f.	M	E		O	P	L	E		T	N	G	S

5. a.
```
      CHARACTER*15 NAME(100)
      INTEGER A(100)
      DO 5 I = 1,100
          READ(5,6)NAME(I),A(I)
    5 CONTINUE
    6 FORMAT(A15,8X,I3)
```

b.
```
      CHARACTER*15 NAME(100),X
      INTEGER A(100)
      READ(5,6)(NAME(I),X,A(I),I=1,100)
    6 FORMAT(A15,A8,I3)
```
Note that X, is a dummy variable.

6.4.5 End-of-File Conditions

More often than not, an input file consists of an unknown number of records. If the input data is to be read into arrays, how do we know how many entries to reserve for our arrays? The type or DIMENSION statements require an integer constant for the size of the array—we cannot specify a variable size for the array (such as REAL X(N) where N varies from one application to the next). One way to take care of the problem is to estimate a maximum size. Individual problems frequently specify the maximum number of records to be processed, so use that maximum! Remember, not all reserved array entries have to be used.

In the next paragraphs we will illustrate two methods for dealing with an unknown number of input records. Let us consider the following problem:

Each record of an input file contains a student's name and two test scores. Write the code to:

1. store the students' names and corresponding test averages into arrays NAME and AVRGE, and

2. print the number of records processed (assuming no more than 100 records).

Prime Read Method

Using the test scores as sentinel values, the following pseudo and FORTRAN codes could be used:

Pseudo Code

```
indx = 0
read lname, test1, test2
WHILE test1 > 0 DO
        indx = indx + 1
        name(indx) = lname
        avrge(indx) = (test1 + test2)/2
        read lname, test1, test2
ENDWHILE
print 'no. records is', indx
```

```
      INTEGER SIZE
      PARAMETER (SIZE=100)
      REAL AVRGE (SIZE),TEST1, TEST2
      CHARACTER*10 NAME(SIZE)
      INDX = 0
      READ(5,1)LNAME,TEST1,TEST2
   10 IF(TEST1 .GT. 0.0)THEN
         INDX        = INDX + 1
         NAME(INDX)  = LNAME
         AVRGE(INDX) = (TEST1+TEST2)/2.
         READ(5,1)LNAME,TEST1,TEST2
         GOTO 10
      ENDIF
      WRITE(6,2)INDX
    1 FORMAT(A10,2F3.0)
    2 FORMAT(...
```

Note that the final value of INDX reflects the total count of records read (not including the sentinel record).

Automatic End-of-File Methods

Automatic End-of-File Method Without the DO List.
Two options are presented:

Option 1

```
      CHARACTER*10 NAME(101)
      REAL AVRGE(100),TEST1, TEST2
      I = 1
    7 READ(5,9,END=8)NAME(I),TEST1,TEST2
         AVRGE(I) = (TEST1+TEST2)/2.
         I = I + 1
         GO TO 7
    8 I = I - 1
      WRITE(6,5)I
```

Option 2

```
      CHARACTER*10 NAME(100),LNAME
      REAL AVRGE(100),TEST1, TEST2
      I = 0
    7 READ(5,9,END=8)LNAME,TEST1,TEST2
         I = I + 1
         NAME(I) = LNAME
         AVRGE(I) = (TEST1+TEST2)/2.
         GO TO 7
    8 WRITE(6,5)I
```

In option 1 the names are directly read into array NAME; however, the terminal value of the index I is one more than the number of grades read, since I counts the end-of-file record. Hence 1 must be subtracted from I. In option 2 the index I reflects the exact number of grades read; however, the name is read into LNAME first, before the name is stored into the array.

Note that in this type of problem, the DO list can not be used efficiently in the READ statement, since each record is to be processed as it is read (compute test average). A READ statement similar to the one in exercise 5b, section 6.4.4 could be used, however.

Automatic End of File With the DO List. Temperature readings have been recorded 50 per record. Write the code to read an input file consisting of no more than 10 such (full) records, compute and print the average temperature, and then print the temperature readings one entry per line.

```
      REAL TEMP(500),AVE,SUM
      READ(5,6,END=88) (TEMP(I),I=1,500)    Read at most 500 entries.
   88 N = I-1                                Subtract 1 for the end-of-file record.
      SUM = 0.
      DO 5 I = 1,N                           There are N temperature readings.
          SUM = SUM+TEMP(I)
    5 CONTINUE
      AVE = SUM/N
      WRITE(6,4) AVE, (TEMP(I),I=1,N)        Write the temperature readings
    4 FORMAT(1X,F5.1)                        one per line.
    6 FORMAT(50F4.1)
```

If there are exactly 10 records, the value of I at statement 88 will be 501, since the loop has gone through its entire cycle. If, on the other hand, fewer than 10 records are read, then the final value of I will cause TEMP(I) to read the end-of-file record. Thus, in either case, the value 1 needs to be subtracted from I (statement 88) to reflect the number of temperature readings.

6.4.6 Nested DO Lists

Implied DO lists can be nested, and in such a case each DO list must have a different index. Consider the following example:

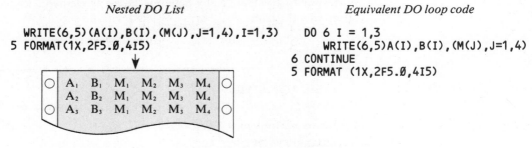

Nested DO List

```
WRITE(6,5)(A(I),B(I),(M(J),J=1,4),I=1,3)
5 FORMAT(1X,2F5.0,4I5)
```

Equivalent DO loop code

```
DO 6 I = 1,3
    WRITE(6,5)A(I),B(I),(M(J),J=1,4)
6 CONTINUE
5 FORMAT (1X,2F5.0,4I5)
```

In the following statement,

Inner loop   Outer loop

```
WRITE(6,5)(A(I),B(I),(M(J),J=1,3),I=1,2)
```

the list of variables is equivalent to $A_1,B_1,M_1,M_2,M_3,A_2,B_2,M_1,M_2,M_3$. The outer loop subscript changes more slowly than the inner loop subscript; the inner loop subscript runs through its complete range of values for each value of the outer subscript. Thus:

I is first 1 and J runs through 1,2,3
I is then 2 and J runs through 1,2,3

6.4.7 Common Misunderstandings

One of the most confusing aspects of input/output of arrays is the relationship between the list of variables specified by the READ/WRITE statement and the corresponding FORMAT. Consider the following example (which is frequently misinterpreted)—how many data records will be read by the following code?

```
DO 5 I = 1,9
    READ(5,6)A(I)
5 CONTINUE
6 FORMAT(3F5.3)
```

The reader might think that this code will read A(I) as I goes from 1 to 9 and that three records will be read altogether since three numbers are specified in the FORMAT. That is not the case.

Initially I is 1, and the first time through the loop the READ statement becomes READ(5,6)A(1). This statement says "read just one element, A(1)"; the format says "the maximum number of entries that can be read from a record is three," but that's just a maximum—in this case the program will only read one element since only one variable is specified. Hence, one record will be read for each pass of the DO loop, so altogether nine records will be read.

Contrast the preceding code with the following one:

```
    READ(5,6)(A(I),I=1,9)
6 FORMAT(3F5.3)
```

In this case the READ statement says "read nine elements altogether." The FORMAT says "three elements per record." Hence, to satisfy the READ list, three records will have to be read altogether.

6.4.8 Initialization of Arrays Thru the DATA Statement

We have already used the DATA statement to establish initial values for nonsubscripted variables. It can also be used to initialize arrays. Recall that the DATA statement should be placed after the various type statements. The DATA statement initializes an array either by explicitly listing the named array elements and their corresponding values, or by defining the array elements through the DO list, or by specifying the name of the array by itself with no subscripts.

EXAMPLE 1

```
   REAL A(5),B(100)
a. DATA A(1),A(2),A(3),A(4),A(5) /1.,2.1,-3.,4.,5.6/
b. DATA (A(I),I=1,5)/1.,2.1,-3.,4.,5.6/
c. DATA A/1.,2.1,-3.,4.,5.6/    (see section 6.4.9)
d. DATA (B(I),I=1,10),(B(I),I=90,100)/10*1.0,11*2.0/
```

Explicit form.
DO list.
Array name by itself.

In case (c), where the name of the array is used without subscripts, the constant list must contain as many values as there are array elements (as specified in the array declarator type statement). For example a compilation error will occur if four values are specified in the DATA list for an array A whose size is 5. In case (d), B_{11} through B_{89} are not initialized to any values.

Note that the asterisk (*) in the constant list (see example (d)) means duplication of a constant, *not* multiplication.

EXAMPLE 2

To initialize 100 elements of arrays A and B to zeros and blanks values respectively, we write:

```
INTEGER A(200)
CHARACTER*3 B(100)
DATA (A(I),I=1,100)/100*0 /, B/100*' ' /
```

A(101),A(102),...,A(200) remain undefined.

6.4.9 Processing Arrays without Subscripts

A reference to an array name without subscripts is valid only in input/output statements and in the DATA statement. Thus, if A is an array, we cannot write A = 0 and hope that all elements of A will be set to 0.

Array Name with Input/Output Statements

If an array name is used by itself without subscripts in a READ or WRITE operation, *all* the elements of the array (as many as are declared in the type or DIMENSION statement) are either read or written.

EXAMPLE

```
REAL X(10)
READ(5,6)X
```
is equivalent to
```
REAL X(10)
READ(5,6)(X(I),I=1,10)
```

Care must be exercised when using names of arrays without subscripts in an input/output operation. Consider the following code:

```
REAL HRS(3),RATE(3)              40.bb05.50
READ(5,3)HRS,RATE                20.bb03.00  ◄──── Input File
3 FORMAT(F3.0,2X,F5.2)           50.bb02.50
```

This code would load arrays HRS and RATE as follows:

HRS	RATE		HRS	RATE
40.0	3.0		40.0	5.5
5.5	50.0	*not*	20.0	3.0
20.0	2.5		50.0	2.5

The statement READ(5,3)HRS,RATE reads the list of variables:

HRS(1),HRS(2),HRS(3),RATE(1),RATE(2),RATE(3)

Array Name with the DATA Statement

An array name without subscripts or DO list can be specified in a DATA statement—the size of the constant list must equal the size of the array as declared in the type statement.

EXAMPLE

```
REAL A(50)
DATA A/25*0.0,25*1.0/    valid, since size of A is 50
DATA A/49*0.0/           invalid, since only 49 constants are specified
```

6.4.10 Do It Now

1. Specify the list (or values) of the variables generated by the following nested DO lists:

    a. `WRITE(6,4)(I,I=1,10),(I,I=10,-1,-1)`

    b. `WRITE(6,5)(A(I),B(I),I,I=1,K)`

    c. `WRITE(6,5)(A(I),(B(J),I,J=1,2),A(I+1),I=1,2)`

    d. `WRITE(6,5)(A(I),(B(J),C(J),J=1,2),I=1,2)`

2. Write the code to produce the following outputs:

    a.
```
10 10 10 10 10 10 10 10 10 10
   9  9  9  9  9  9  9  9  9
   8  8  8  8  8  8  8  8
   :
   2  2
   1

   1
```

    b.
```
1
2  2
3  3  3
4  4  4  4
:
10 10 10 10 10 10 10 10 10 10
```

3. How many records will be read by the following?

    a.
```
    DO 5 I = 1,9
        READ(5,6)A(I),B(I)
  5 CONTINUE
  6 FORMAT(F5.1)
```

    b.
```
    DO 5 I = 1,3
        READ(5,6)(A(J),J=1,4)
  5 CONTINUE
  6 FORMAT(3F4.0)
```

4. How many lines will be printed when the WRITE statement is used with each of the different formats?

```
WRITE(6,4)(I,A(I),I=1,5)
```

    a. `FORMAT(1X,F4.1)`

    b. `FORMAT(1X,I1,F4.1)`

    c. `FORMAT(1X,2(I1,F4.1))`

    d. `FORMAT(1X,I1,F4.1,I1)`

5. An input file consists of an unknown number of scores ranging from 1 to 100. Write the code to determine the number of scores below the average. Assume there is at least one score.

Answers
1. **a.** 1,2,3,4,5,6,7,8,9,10,10,9,8,7,6,5,4,3,2,1,0, − 1

b. $A_1 B_1 1 A_2 B_2 2 ... A_K B_K K$

c. $A_1 B_1 1 B_2 1 A_2 A_2 B_1 2 B_2 2 A_3$

d. $A_1 B_1 C_1 B_2 C_2 A_2 B_1 C_1 B_2 C_2$

2. **a.**
```
    DO 5 I = 10,1,-1
        WRITE(6,6)(I,K=1,I)
    5 CONTINUE
    6 FORMAT(1X,10I3)
```
b.
```
    DO 5 I = 1,10
        WRITE(6,6)(I,K=1,I)
    5 CONTINUE
    6 FORMAT(1X,10I3)
```

3. **a.** 18   **b.** 6 (2 records per READ statement)

4. **a.** Invalid; the variable I needs an I type format.

b. 5

c. 3; the last line will print 5 and A(5).

d. Invalid. A(2) is read with I1 format.

5.
```
    INTEGER SCORE(100),BELOW
    REAL SUM,AVE
    SUM = 0.0                      Accumulates the scores.
    I = 1                          Index for the array SCORE.
    BELOW = 0                      Counts the number of scores below the average.
  4 READ(5,6,END=88)SCORE(I)       Read a score.
        SUM = SUM+SCORE(I)         Add it to the sum.
        I = I+1                    Count it.
        GO TO 4                    Go back and read more records.
 88 AVE = SUM/(I-1)                I − 1 because of the end-of-file record.
    DO 5 K = 1,I-1                 Process I − 1 scores.
        IF(SCORE(K).LT.AVE)BELOW = BELOW+1
  5 CONTINUE
    WRITE(6,3)BELOW
```

6.5 PROGRAMMING EXAMPLES

6.5.1 Table Look-Up

Table look-up is a fast and efficient method to directly access data in a table without searching the table elements, something like looking up your taxes in the tax table (fast and painful!).

Problem/Specification. United Package Service operates under a cost delivery system based on article weight and destination zone. The rate table per pound is as follows:

Zone Code	Cost Per Pound	Meaning
1	$ .55	The cost to ship 1 pound to zone 1 is $ .55
2	$ .80	The cost to ship 1 pound to zone 2 is $ .80
3	$1.03	The cost to ship 1 pound to zone 3 is $1.03
4	$1.30	.
5	$1.75	.
6	$2.01	.

Let us write a program that will read an input file where each record contains two entries: a destination zone and a shipment weight. The program will print the destination zone, the weight, and the corresponding shipping cost.

To understand the problem, let us look at the following example. Suppose we wanted to send a two-pound parcel to zone 6. We would look up the zone 6 and identify the corresponding cost per pound entry, which is $2.01. Since the parcel weighs two pounds, the total cost would be $2 * 2.01 = 4.02$. An attractive output design might be:

```
ZONE    WEIGHT    COST

  6       2.0     4.02
  2       3.5     2.80
```

A convenient way to look up the cost associated with a particular zone is to create an array RATE such that RATE(1) = $.55, RATE(2) = $.80, ..., RATE(6) = $2.01. In this way, if the zone is 6, for example, we can immediately look up the sixth entry of RATE ($2.01). In general, the cost associated with zone ZONE is simply RATE (ZONE). Hence if we read a zone ZONE and a weight WGHT, the corresponding shipment cost is simply WGHT * RATE (ZONE).

The program in Figure 6.8 reads a zone ZONE and a weight WGHT, and prints ZONE, WGHT, and the resulting cost RATE(ZONE)*WGHT.

6.5.2 Inventory Update Program

Problem/Specification. An input file consists of two sets of records:

1. The first set of records is the master file, which reflects an item inventory at the start of the business day. Each master file record contains a part number and a corresponding item stock quantity. The end of the master file is identified by a record containing negative entries. Let us assume that the master file contains no more than 100 records.

2. The second set of records, which follows the master file, reflects the transactions for the various items during that day. Transaction records have the same format as the master file records: they contain the item number and the corresponding total number of items sold that day. Note that a particular item number may occur in more than one transaction record.

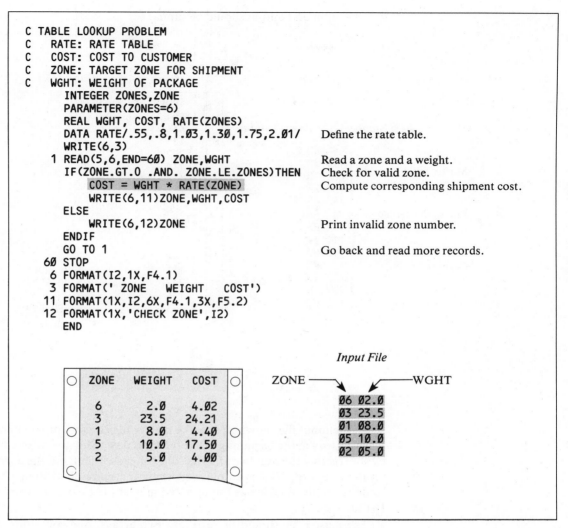

```
C TABLE LOOKUP PROBLEM
C   RATE: RATE TABLE
C   COST: COST TO CUSTOMER
C   ZONE: TARGET ZONE FOR SHIPMENT
C   WGHT: WEIGHT OF PACKAGE
      INTEGER ZONES,ZONE
      PARAMETER(ZONES=6)
      REAL WGHT, COST, RATE(ZONES)
      DATA RATE/.55,.8,1.03,1.30,1.75,2.01/      Define the rate table.
      WRITE(6,3)
    1 READ(5,6,END=60) ZONE,WGHT                  Read a zone and a weight.
      IF(ZONE.GT.0 .AND. ZONE.LE.ZONES)THEN       Check for valid zone.
          COST = WGHT * RATE(ZONE)                Compute corresponding shipment cost.
          WRITE(6,11)ZONE,WGHT,COST
      ELSE
          WRITE(6,12)ZONE                         Print invalid zone number.
      ENDIF
      GO TO 1                                     Go back and read more records.
   60 STOP
    6 FORMAT(I2,1X,F4.1)
    3 FORMAT(' ZONE   WEIGHT   COST')
   11 FORMAT(1X,I2,6X,F4.1,3X,F5.2)
   12 FORMAT(1X,'CHECK ZONE',I2)
      END
```

ZONE	WEIGHT	COST
6	2.0	4.02
3	23.5	24.21
1	8.0	4.40
5	10.0	17.50
2	5.0	4.00

Input File

ZONE ⟶   ↙ ⟵WGHT

```
06 02.0
03 23.5
01 08.0
05 10.0
02 05.0
```

FIGURE 6.8
A TABLE LOOK-UP PROBLEM

Write a program to update the master file against the transaction file to produce a new master file at the end of the day.

1. A reorder notice should accompany any item number for which fewer than 10 items remain in stock.

2. A list of invalid item numbers, if any, should be printed before the final master file is printed. Invalid items are incorrectly recorded items in the transaction file for which there are no corresponding items in the master file.

The input and output should be similar to:

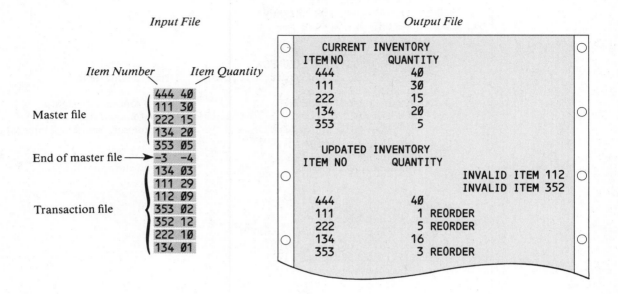

Input File		Output File

In the input file shown above, the master file consists of five items that represent the inventory at the beginning of the business day. Sales are reflected in the master file by subtracting the number of units sold for each item from the corresponding master item quantity. For example, originally there are 20 of item 134; 4 of these are sold during the day, hence the updated master file quantity for item 134 should be 16 (20 − 4).

The master file should be read into two arrays, one containing the master item numbers (in this case there are five) and the other containing the corresponding item quantities.

We then read the transaction file one record at a time; every time an item is read (sold), the master file is updated to reflect the current number of items on the shelf. The master table must be searched to identify which master file item number is to be updated. In the first transaction for item 134, we look for an entry equal to 134 in the master item table; in this case it is the 4th entry of the table. We then subtract the item quantity (3) from the 4th element of the master file quantity table.

If there is an incorrect item number in the transaction file, then there is no matching item in the master item table. If the entire master array is searched and no matching entry is found, the incorrect item number is printed. When all transaction records have been read, the updating process is complete and the master file is printed, two entries at a time. If the quantity entry is less than 10, a reorder message is printed.

The logic to solve this problem is shown in pseudo code in Figure 6.9 and in FORTRAN in Figure 6.10.

Test Your Understanding of the Program

1. Give at least two good reasons why transaction records are not stored in an array. Project coding consequences if array was used.

2. Change the code so that the master file and transaction files are read from two separate input files.

3. In the FORTRAN program of Figure 6.10, show what happens at line 27 if K = 100 and no match is found. How would you correct the problem without changing the size of the array INVEN? [*Hint:* set a flag if a match exists in order to exit from the loop.]

4. Make the necessary changes to the code so that the list of invalid items physically follows the updated inventory. In the present case this list precedes the updated inventory.

write captions
set count to 0
read item, quantity
WHILE item > 0 DO
    write item, quantity
    count = count + 1
    inven (count) = item
    quan (count) = quantity
    read item, quantity
ENDWHILE
	Read, load and print master file

write captions
WHILE end of file not encountered DO
    read item, quantity
    set index to 1
    WHILE index ≤ count and item ≠ inven (index) DO
        index = index + 1
    ENDWHILE
    IF index = count + 1 THEN
        write 'invalid item', item
    ELSE
        quan (index) = quan (index) − quantity
    ENDIF
ENDWHILE
	Process transaction records
	
	Search master file for a matching transaction item.
	
	If there is no match, write error message
	
	else update item quantity.

DO index = 1 to count
    IF quan (index) < 10 THEN
        write inven (index), quan (index), 'reorder'
    ELSE
        write inven (index), quan (index)
    ENDIF
CONTINUE LOOP
	Analyze updated master file
	
	Print reorder message for items whose stock level is less than 10.

FIGURE 6.9
AN INVENTORY UPDATE PROGRAM

```
1: C INVENTORY UPDATE PROGRAM
2: C    INVEN: ARRAY TO STORE ITEM NUMBERS
3: C    QUAN:  ARRAY TO STORE ITEM QUANTITIES
4: C    ITEM:  ITEM NUMBER READ
5: C    QTY:   ITEM QUANTITY READ
6: C    COUNT: COUNTS ITEMS IN MASTER FILE
7: C    K:        INDEX USED TO COUNT ITEMS
8:          INTEGER INVEN(100), QUAN(100)
9:          INTEGER ITEM, QTY, K, COUNT
10:         OPEN (6,FILE='PRN')                  open the printer file
11:         OPEN (5,FILE='INVENDAT')             open the input data file
12:         WRITE(6,20)
13:         WRITE(6,30)
14:         COUNT = 0
15: 1       READ(5,40) ITEM,QTY
16:         IF(ITEM .GT. 0) THEN
17:             WRITE(6,3) ITEM,QTY
18:             COUNT        = COUNT + 1
19:             INVEN(COUNT) = ITEM
20:             QUAN(COUNT)  = QTY
21:             GO TO 1
22:         ENDIF
23:         WRITE(6,15)
24:         WRITE(6,30)
25: 5       READ(5,40,END=8) ITEM,QTY
26:         K = 1
27: 6       IF(K.LE.COUNT .AND. ITEM.NE.INVEN(K))THEN    Search master array for a
28:             K = K + 1                                matching item number.
29:             GO TO 6
30:         ENDIF
31:         IF(K .GT. COUNT)THEN                  If K > count, the entire array was searched and no match
32:             WRITE(6,60) ITEM                  was found in the master file.
33:         ELSE
34:             QUAN(K) = QUAN(K) - QTY           If K ≤ count, a match was found before the end of the
35:         ENDIF                                 master was reached.
36:         GO TO 5
37: 8       DO 20 K = 1, COUNT
38:             IF(QUAN(K) .LT. 10) THEN
39:                 WRITE(6,70)INVEN(K),QUAN(K)
40:             ELSE
41:                 WRITE(6,50)INVEN(K),QUAN(K)
42:             ENDIF
43: 10      CONTINUE
44:         STOP
45: 15      FORMAT('0   UPDATED INVENTORY')
46: 20      FORMAT('     CURRENT INVENTORY')
47: 30      FORMAT(' ITEM NO       QUANTITY')
48: 40      FORMAT(I3,1X,I2)
49: 50      FORMAT(3X,I3,12X,I2)
50: 60      FORMAT(26X,'INVALID ITEM',I4)
51: 70      FORMAT(3X,I3,12X,I2,' REORDER')
52:         END
```

FIGURE 6.10
AN INVENTORY UPDATE PROGRAM

6.5.3 A Frequency
Distribution

Problem/Specification. Each record of an input file contains integer temperatures between −50° and 50°. Write a program to determine the number of times each temperature occurs. The input and output will have the following form:

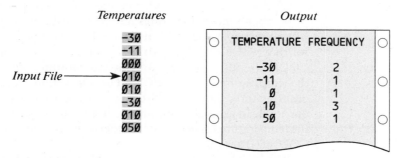

Temperatures

Input File ⟶

```
-30
-11
000
010
010
-30
010
050
```

Output

O	TEMPERATURE	FREQUENCY	O
O	−30	2	O
O	−11	1	O
	0	1	
O	10	3	O
	50	1	

Given a list of temperatures in the range −50° to 50°, we must determine how many times temperature −50° appears, how many times −49° appears, and so forth. It is possible that many of these temperatures will not appear at all in the input list.

Since we do not know what temperatures will occur, we need 101 different counters to count all possible temperature occurrences. Also, since it would be quite impractical to have 101 differently labeled variable names to count the occurrence of each temperature, we will use 101 array elements as counters. We need to choose which of the array elements will count which temperature. We decide on the following scheme:

COUNT(−50)   will count the occurrence of temperature −50°
COUNT(−49)   will count the occurrence of temperature −49°
          .
          .
          .
COUNT(0)   will count the occurence of temperature 0°
          .
          .
          .
COUNT(50)   will count the occurrence of temperature 50°, and in general
COUNT(TEMP) will count how many times the temperature TEMP appears in the input list.

Thus, every time we read a TEMP, we will use that TEMP as the subscript of COUNT to designate which counter to increment, i.e., we add 1 to COUNT(TEMP):

COUNT(TEMP) = COUNT(TEMP) + 1

After all temperatures have been read, the array of counters will appear as follows:

Input Temperatures   *Set of 101 Counters*

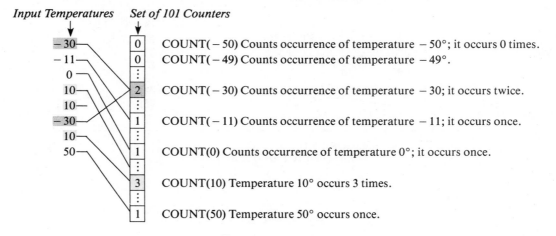

	COUNT(−50) Counts occurrence of temperature −50°; it occurs 0 times.
	COUNT(−49) Counts occurrence of temperature −49°.
	COUNT(−30) Counts occurrence of temperature −30; it occurs twice.
	COUNT(−11) Counts occurrence of temperature −11; it occurs once.
	COUNT(0) Counts occurrence of temperature 0°; it occurs once.
	COUNT(10) Temperature 10° occurs 3 times.
	COUNT(50) Temperature 50° occurs once.

Every time we read a temperature TEMP we add 1 to the appropriate counter through the statement COUNT(TEMP) = COUNT(TEMP) + 1, i.e., if TEMP = −30, then COUNT(−30) = COUNT(−30) + 1, meaning that the count of temperature −30° is equal to the old count of temperature −30° plus 1. Obviously, COUNT(−30) and all other counters should also be initialized to 0's.

When all the temperatures have been read, we must print all those temperatures whose frequency counts are nonzero. Thus we must go through the array of counters, starting with COUNT(−50) and asking the question: Is COUNT(−50) = 0? If COUNT(−50) = 0, there were no temperatures equal to −50°, so we do not print the temperature −50°. If COUNT(−50) = 3, this means that the temperature −50° occurred three times in the list, so we write the temperature and its corresponding frequency 3. In general, if the answer to the question "Is COUNT(I) = 0?" is yes, then the temperature I is *not* printed; otherwise, the temperature I and the frequency count COUNT(I) are printed.

The FORTRAN code for this problem is shown in Figure 6.11.

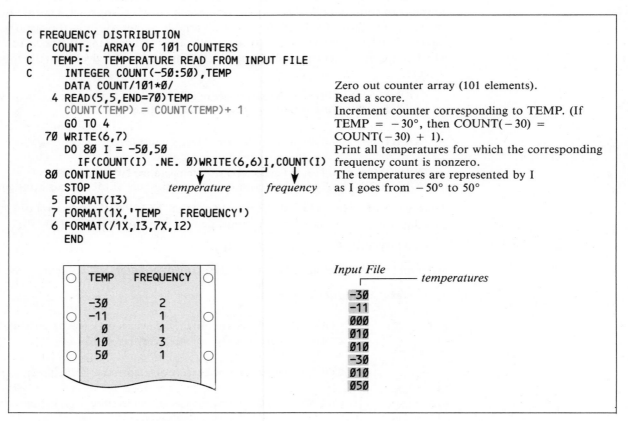

FIGURE 6.11
A FREQUENCY DISTRIBUTION

Test Your Understanding of the Program

1. Suppose your compiler did not allow for lower and upper subscripts in the declaration of the COUNT array in Figure 6.11. What would you do?

2. Modify the program of Figure 6.11 to produce a sorted list of temperatures, i.e., if temperature 44 occurs 3 times, print 44, 44, 44. Temperatures should be written one per line.

3. Modify the program to process an input file consisting of *one* input record containing all scores. The first entry in the record specifies the number of scores in the record, for example

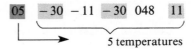

5 temperatures

6.5.4 Array Input/Output

To be admitted to the Mensa club, candidates must score a minimum of 74 points on a particular intelligence test. Each candidate's name and test score are recorded on records as shown in Figure 6.12. Write a program to read an input file (no more than 50 records) to produce the report shown in Figure 6.12, which consists of:

1. Two separate paragraph listings of names of successful and unsuccessful candidates. Each line should contain four names.

2. Two consecutive vertical lists of names and scores of successful and unsuccessful candidates (one name and corresponding score per line).
If there are no successful candidates, the caption "SUCCESSFUL CANDIDATES" should not be printed; follow the same rule for unsuccessful candidates.

A program to solve this problem is shown in Figure 6.12. Since the names of the candidates must be printed by group (success/failure), two arrays are needed to store the names of successful candidates and unsuccessful candidates.

A name and a score are read from a record (line 17). If the score is less than 74, the name is stored in the array FNAME and its corresponding score in array FAIL. The index F is used to place each name and score in successive array locations. Arrays PNAME, PASS, and index P are used similarly to record the passing candidates' data. When the end of file is reached, P contains the number of passing candidates while F contains the number of failing candidates.

The implied DO list WRITE(6,2)(PNAME(I),I = 1,P) at line 30 specifies the list of all passing candidates, while FORMAT 2 tells the computer to print first a heading, then four names per line under the heading. Similarly, the names of passing candidates and their scores are specified by the statement WRITE(6,4)(PNAME(I), PASS(I),I = 1,P) (line 35). FORMAT 4 specifies that one name and one score are to be printed per line. Note the position of the literals PASSING and FAILING in FORMAT 4 (line 42), and note the use of the parentheses in (12X,A8,1X,I3)) to force format control to restart at the right-most open parenthesis in the format to print all remaining names and scores. Note also, that if P = 0 (no passing candidates) or F = 0 (no failing candidates), the corresponding captions will not be printed (lines 35 and 37).

```
 1: C INPUT OUTPUT OF ARRAYS
 2: C    PNAME: TABLE OF NAMES OF PASSING CANDIDATES
 3: C    FNAME: TABLE OF NAMES OF FAILING CANDIDATES
 4: C    PASS:  ARRAY CONTAINING PASSING SCORES
 5: C    FAIL:  ARRAY CONTAINING FAILING SCORES
 6: C    P:     VARIABLE USED TO INDEX "PASSING" ARRAY
 7: C           ALSO COUNTS NUMBER OF PASSING CANDIDATES
 8: C    F:     VARIABLE USED TO INDEX "FAILING" ARRAY
 9: C    NAME:  CANDIDATE'S NAME READ FROM INPUT RECORD
10: C    SCORE: CANDIDATE'S SCORE READ FROM INPUT RECORD
11: C    MESSG: CHARACTER VARIABLE TO HOLD CAPTIONS FOR OUTPUT PURPOSES
12: C
13:        CHARACTER*8 PNAME(50),FNAME(50),NAME
14:        CHARACTER*23 MESSG
15:        INTEGER PASS(50),FAIL(50),SCORE,P,F
16:        DATA P,F/0,0/,MESSG/'SUCCESSFUL CANDIDATES'/
17:     10 READ(5,1,END=88)NAME,SCORE
18:            IF(SCORE .LE. 74) THEN
19: C          CANDIDATE FAILS; RECORD NAME & SCORE IN "FAIL" ARRAYS
20:                F = F + 1                              Counts failing candidates
21:                FNAME(F) = NAME
22:                FAIL(F)  = SCORE
23:            ELSE
24: C          CANDIDATE PASSES; RECORD NAME & SCORE IN "PASS" ARRAYS
25:                P = P + 1                              Counts passing candidates
26:                PNAME(P) = NAME
27:                PASS(P)  = SCORE
28:            ENDIF
29:            GO TO 10
30:     88 WRITE(6,2) MESSG, (PNAME(I),I=1,P)             This statement is bypassed if P = 0.
31:        MESSG = 'UNSUCCESSFUL CANDIDATES'
32:        WRITE(6,2) MESSG, (FNAME(I),I=1,F)             This statement is bypassed if F = 0.
33:        WRITE(6,3)
34:        MESSG = 'PASSING'
35:        WRITE(6,4) MESSG, (PNAME(I),PASS(I),I=1,P)     Bypassed if P = 0.
36:        MESSG = 'FAILING'
37:        WRITE(6,4) MESSG, (FNAME(I),FAIL(I),I=1,F)     Bypassed if F = 0.
38:        STOP
39:      1 FORMAT(A8,I3)
40:      2 FORMAT('0',A23//(1X,4A9))
41:      3 FORMAT('0',11X,'NAMES    SCORES')
42:      4 FORMAT('0  ',A9,A8,1X,I3/(12X,A8,1X,I3))
43:        END
```

SUCCESSFUL CANDIDATES

ADAMS	PENSKE	MICHAEL	SALAAM
JONES	CLARK	WILLS	MOUTON
HENGSIU			

UNSUCCESSFUL CANDIDATES

LOUD	LAZY	MILLS	ANTONE
MONISH	GAMBINO	BOILLOT	DERNIER

	NAMES	SCORES
PASSING	ADAMS	74
	PENSKE	81
	MICHAEL	90
	SALAAM	100
	JONES	76
	CLARK	79
	WILLS	94
	MOUTON	86
	HENGSIU	96
FAILING	LOUD	56
	LAZY	48
	MILLS	44
	ANTONE	46
	MONISH	46
	GAMBINO	35
	BOILLOT	48
	DERNIER	10

Input File

Name	Score
ADAMS	074
PENSKE	081
LOUD	056
MICHAEL	090
LAZY	048
MILLS	044
ANTONE	046
MONISH	046
SALAAM	100
GAMBINO	035
BOILLOT	048
JONES	076
CLARK	079
WILLS	094
DERNIER	010
MOUTON	086
HENGSIU	096

FIGURE 6.12
INPUT OUTPUT OF ARRAYS

6.5.5 Sorting Two methods for sorting, the bubble sort and the mini/max sort, are discussed in this section. Both methods are easy to understand, and they will give the reader some insight into the sorting process. In the "real world" of sorting, however, these two methods may not be suited to sort very large arrays; other very excellent sorts such as the Shell-Metzner sort are available (see exercise 39 in section 6.7.2).

The Bubble Sort

Let us illustrate the bubble sort with an example.

Assume the following list of numbers is to be sorted in *ascending* sequence:

| 4 | 5 | 3 | 2 |

The bubble sort begins by comparing the first and second numbers and interchanging the first number with the second number if the first number is greater than the second number. Then we move on to the second and third numbers and perform an interchange if the second is greater than the third (this time we interchange 5 and 3). Then we move on to the third and fourth numbers (5 and 2) and perform an interchange if necessary (in this case we interchange 2 and 5). In this way we ensure that the largest number is continuously moved to the right. At the end of this first pass through the list, the order is:

| 4 | 3 | 2 | 5 |

We now repeat the procedure on a second pass:
Compare the first pair 4, 3 and interchange to obtain 3, 4.

Compare the second pair 4, 2 and interchange to obtain 2, 4.

Compare the third pair 4, 5; no interchange.

Actually, we did not need to process the third pair, since we already know that the largest number is in the last position. At the end of the second pass, the second largest number is in the second-to-last position and the order is:

| 3 | 2 | 4 | 5 |

We now carry out the same procedure for the third time.

Compare the first pair 3, 2 and interchange to obtain 2, 3.

Compare the second pair 3, 4; no interchange.

Compare the third pair 4, 5; no interchange.

Actually, we only needed to compare the first pair of numbers, since we know the last two numbers are already in order.
Thus at the end of the third pass the numbers are sorted.

first pair | 4 | 5 | 3 | 2 |

second pair | 4 | 5 | 3 | 2 |
                 | 4 | 3 | 5 | 2 |

third pair | 4 | 3 | 5 | 2 |
                 | 4 | 3 | 2 | 5 |

The largest number is now in the right-most position

first pair | 4 | 3 | 2 | 5 |
                 | 3 | 4 | 2 | 5 |

second pair | 3 | 4 | 2 | 5 |
                 | 3 | 2 | 4 | 5 |

third pair | 3 | 2 | 4 | 5 |

The second-largest number is now in the next-to-last position.

first pair | 3 | 2 | 4 | 5 |
                 | 2 | 3 | 4 | 5 |

second pair | 2 | 3 | 4 | 5 |

third pair | 2 | 3 | 4 | 5 |

                 | 2 | 3 | 4 | 5 |

In general, if an array contains N numbers, we will need $N-1$ passes to sort the array, although in some cases fewer than $N-1$ passes may be needed. For example, an array with 10 elements may be in order after only four passes. Once the numbers are in order, no further interchange of numbers will occur on subsequent passes. The code determines when the numbers are in order by setting a flag to the value 0 prior to executing a particular pass. If, any interchange of entries occurs during that pass, the flag is then set to 1. Thus, if the flag has value 0 at the conclusion of a pass, the entries are in order.

In our example, notice that the largest number is pushed into position 4 at the end of pass 1. Thus in pass 2 the interchange process stops at the third entry of the array, since the largest number is already in place as a result of pass 1. At the conclusion of pass 2, the second-largest number in the array is now in position 3. Thus each pass analyzes a shrinking number of elements (one element less than the previous pass).

The pseudo code and FORTRAN code to sort an array into ascending order are shown in Figures 6.13 and 6.14, respectively.

```
*Bubble Sort Algorithm
 read numbers into array
 size = number of elements read
 set flag to 1
 pass = 1
 WHILE pass ≤ size − 1 and flag = 1 DO
     flag = 0
     DO index = 1, size − pass
         IF array (index) > array (index + 1) THEN
             temporary = array (index)
             array (index) = array (index + 1)
             array (index + 1) = temporary
             flag = 1
         ENDIF
     CONTINUE LOOP
     pass = pass + 1
 ENDWHILE
 write sorted array elements
```

FIGURE 6.13
BUBBLE SORT
PSEUDO CODE

6.5.6 The Mini/Max Sort

Another method that can be used to sort a table of numbers into ascending (or descending) order is to determine the location (position) of the smallest element in the table and then interchange that element with the first element of the table. Thus at the end of the first search pass, the smallest element is in the first position. The table is then searched for the next smallest element, with the search starting at position 2 of the table; the smallest element found in the second pass is then swapped with the number in position 2 of the table. At the end of the second search pass, the first two elements of the table are in ascending sequence order. The search for the next smallest number starts in position 3, and the same search-and-interchange process is repeated

```
1: * BUBBLE SORT PROGRAM. ASCENDING ORDER SORT
2: * ARRAY: ARRAY OF NUMBERS TO BE SORTED
3: * SIZE:   NUMBER OF ELEMENTS TO BE SORTED
4: * PASS:   COUNTS NUMBER OF PASSES
5: * FLAG:   TERMINATES SORT IF NUMBERS ARE IN ORDER (FLAG = "NO INTERCHANGE")
6: * TEMPRY: USED TO INTERCHANGE A PAIR OF NUMBERS
7: * N:      MAXIMUM NUMBER OF ELEMENTS IN ARRAY
8:          PARAMETER(N=10)
9:          INTEGER ARRAY(N),SIZE,PASS,TEMPRY,INDX,I
10:         CHARACTER FLAG*15
11:         OPEN(5,FILE='SORTDAT')
12:         READ(5,3,END=88)(ARRAY(I),I=1,N)
13: 88      SIZE = I - 1
14:         WRITE(6,1)(ARRAY(I),I=1,SIZE)
15:         FLAG = 'INTERCHANGED'
16:         PASS = 1
17: 5       IF(PASS .LE. SIZE-1 .AND.
18:     A           FLAG .EQ. 'INTERCHANGED')THEN
19:            FLAG = 'NO INTERCHANGE'
20:            DO 10 INDX = 1, SIZE - PASS
21:               IF(ARRAY(INDX) .GT. ARRAY(INDX+1))THEN
22:                  FLAG        = 'INTERCHANGED'
23:                  TEMPRY      = ARRAY(INDX)
24:                  ARRAY(INDX) = ARRAY(INDX+1)
25:                  ARRAY(INDX+1) = TEMPRY
26:               ENDIF
27: 10         CONTINUE
28:            PASS = PASS + 1
29:            GO TO 5
30:         ENDIF
31:         WRITE(6,2)(ARRAY(I),I=1,SIZE)
32:         STOP
33: 1       FORMAT(1X,'UNSORTED NUMBERS:',10I4)
34: 2       FORMAT(1X,'SORTED NUMBERS  :',10I4)
35: 3       FORMAT(I3)
36:         END
```

Outer loop: controls the number of passes.
Note the exit from the loop if numbers are in sequence.
Assume no interchange in the next pass.
The first pass shifts the largest number into the rightmost position of the array (ARRAY (SIZE)).
The second pass shifts the second-largest number into the next-to-last position of the array, i.e., into ARRAY(SIZE − 1).
SIZE − PASS represents the size of the ever-shrinking array as it gets smaller with each pass.
If FLAG = 'INTERCHANGED', the numbers are still not in sequence.
If an interchange occurs during a particular pass, set the flag to "interchanged".

```
UNSORTED NUMBERS:  42  -3  45  34  56 -34  10  10  78
SORTED NUMBERS  : -34  -3  10  10  34  42  45  56  78
```

FIGURE 6.14
A BUBBLE SORT

until the last two (right-most) table elements are processed. Using this sorting procedure, a table of N elements will require N − 1 passes for the search-and-interchange procedure. During the first pass, N elements will be compared, while in the last pass only two elements will be compared. Let's see how this sort process works, using the same example we used with the bubble sort:

Array — location of smallest element is 4.

	Array	

Begin first pass | `4 5 3 2` | Find location of smallest value and switch places with first value (ARRAY(1)). | Search for smallest value starts at position 1.
End first pass | `2 5 3 4` | |

Begin second pass | `2 5 3 4` | Find location of smallest value and switch places with first value of remaining array, i.e., ARRAY(2). | Search for smallest value starts at position 2.
End second pass | `2 3 5 4` | |

Begin third pass | `2 3 5 4` | Find location of smallest value and switch places with first value of remaining array (ARRAY(3)). | Search for smallest value starts at position 3.
End third pass | `2 3 4 5` | |

To understand the complete sort program, let's start by writing the code for the first pass, which determines the position of the smallest element of the table and performs the interchange of the smallest number with the number in the first position of the table. Assume ARRAY contains a number of elements equal to SIZE.

In the following code, K keeps track of the position of the current smallest number as the code analyses each successive element of ARRAY. Referring to the example above, in the first pass, K is initially 1 and eventually takes on the value 4, since the smallest number (2) is in position 4.

```
      INTEGER SIZE
      SMALL  = ARRAY(1)
      K      = 1
      DO 6 J = 2, SIZE
         IF (SMALL .GT. ARRAY(J))THEN
             SMALL = ARRAY(J)
             K     = J
         ENDIF
6     CONTINUE
      TEMPRY    = ARRAY(K)
      ARRAY(K)  = ARRAY(1)
      ARRAY(1)  = TEMPRY
```

Assume the smallest value is ARRAY(1) before the search starts. Assume the position K of smallest value is 1, subject to later change. Start comparing SMALL with the remaining values. If SMALL ≤ ARRAY(J), then SMALL is still the smallest and its position K does not change. If SMALL > ARRAY(J), then the new smallest value is at location J, so we set K equal to J and we reset SMALL to ARRAY(J) to keep track of current smallest value.

After the loop is completed, we switch the smallest value with the value in the first position.

To generalize from this code segment to the complete sort program, K must start with the value 1 for the first pass, then the value 2 for the second pass, and so forth, up to SIZE − 1 for the last pass (the number of passes is one less than the number of elements). The interchange process will require that we move ARRAY(2) to TEMPRY on the second pass, ARRAY(3) to TEMPRY on the third pass, and so forth. Hence an additional (outer) loop is required to control K and to position the succeeding smallest values into locations ARRAY(1), ARRAY(2), ARRAY(3), . . ., ARRAY(SIZE). The complete code is shown in Figure 6.15.

6.5.7 Graph Plotting General Considerations

Let us write a program to graph the function $y = f(x) = x^2/5 + 1$ in the first quadrant, for values of x ranging from 1 to 7 in steps of 1. Before we write the program, let us get a general idea about how to proceed by looking at the function $y = x^2/5 + 1$. Graphing the function means plotting various points that belong to the curve and then joining these points together. We pick various values of x such as 1, 2, 3, ..., 7,

```
C MINI/MAX ASCENDING ORDER SORT PROGRAM
C    SMALL:   TEMPORARY LOCATION TO HOLD SMALLEST SCORE
C    K:       TEMPORARY LOCATION TO IDENTIFY POSITION OF SMALLEST SCORE IN ARRAY
C    ARRAY:   ARRAY OF VALUES TO BE SORTED
C    N:       NUMBER OF VALUES IN ARRAY
C    PASSES:  NUMBER OF PASSES (N - 1)
C    TEMPRY:  TEMPORARY LOCATION FOR INTERCHANGE PROCEDURE
C
         INTEGER ARRAY(26),N,PASSES,TEMPRY,SMALL,K
         READ(5,3,END=88)(ARRAY(I),I=1,26)
88       N = I - 1
         WRITE(6,1) (ARRAY(I),I=1,N)
         PASSES = N - 1
         DO 5 L = 1, PASSES
            SMALL = ARRAY(L)
            K = L
            DO 6 J = L+1, N
               IF(SMALL .GT. ARRAY(J))THEN
                  SMALL = ARRAY(J)
                  K     = J
               ENDIF
6           CONTINUE
            TEMPRY   = ARRAY(K)
            ARRAY(K) = ARRAY(L)
            ARRAY(L) = TEMPRY
5        CONTINUE
         WRITE(6,2) (ARRAY(I),I=1,N)
         STOP
1        FORMAT(' UNSORTED VALUES:',25I4)
2        FORMAT(' SORTED VALUES  :',25I4)
3        FORMAT(I3)
         END
```

N keeps track of the number of scores.

Number of passes.
L controls the number of passes. Before starting a pass, assume SMALL = ARRAY(L) is the smallest value and that its location in the array is K = L.
Find the real smallest value SMALL and its location K in the array.
SMALL is smallest number so far.
Current position of smallest number is K.

At end of loop, smallest number is ARRAY(K).
Interchange the smallest value found during the first pass with the first element, then the smallest value found during the second pass with the second element, and so forth.

```
UNSORTED VALUES:   12   45  100    3   98   67   76
SORTED VALUES  :    3   12   45   67   76   98  100
```

FIGURE 6.15
THE MINI/MAX SORT

then we determine the corresponding values for y and plot the corresponding points $P_1, P_2, ..., P_7$ as follows:

x	$y = f(x)$
1	1.2
2	1.8
3	2.8
4	4.2
5	6
6	8.2
7	10.8

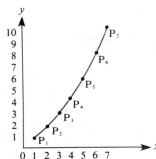

It is a little more difficult to print the graph of this function using the computer, because the printer paper moves up in increments of one line. Thus it is difficult to print P_1 first and then print P_2 above P_1 since succeeding lines are printed down on the printed form. One could argue "why not print P_7, then P_6, and so on down to P_1 to keep the points coming down the printer page using incremental values of y equal to 10, 9, 8, ..., 1"; to do that we could compute the corresponding values of x using the formula $x = \sqrt{5y - 5}$ instead of $y = x^2/5 + 1$. This method, of course, would work in this particular case, but what if you had to graph the function $y = x^4 - 16x^3 + 2x^2 - 1$? How would you compute x in terms of y?

We will solve this problem by using the vertical axis as the x axis so that each new printer line corresponds to a unit increment of x; the horizontal axis will be the y axis. For each value of x, we will print a graphic symbol y units away from the x axis. With the axes switched this way, the graph of the function will appear as:

x	y	y **rounded**
1	1.2	1
2	1.8	2
3	2.8	3
4	4.2	4
5	6.	6
6	8.2	8
7	10.8	11

Physical Positioning of y *on paper*   y axis

* is 1 position away from x axis

* is 2 positions away from x axis

line array containing graphic symbol * at position y, while all remaining positions are blanks.

x axis

From this diagram, the graphing of a function $y = F(x)$ becomes more evident. We use an array to print one horizontal line at a time. The line array is initially set to blanks. For a given value of x, the corresponding value of the function y is computed, and a graphic symbol such as * is inserted at position y in the line array. The array (line) is then printed, and the process is repeated for the different values of x. Thus any graph can be visualized as follows on your printer:

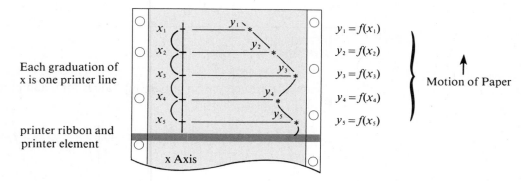

Each graduation of x is one printer line

printer ribbon and printer element

x Axis

$$y_1 = f(x_1)$$
$$y_2 = f(x_2)$$
$$y_3 = f(x_3)$$
$$y_4 = f(x_4)$$
$$y_5 = f(x_5)$$

Motion of Paper

The code to graph the function $y = \dfrac{x^2}{5} + 1$ is shown in Figure 6.16 for values of x ranging from 1 to 10 in increments of 1 (line). The value .5 is added to y to round off the position value of y in the LINE array.

Other functions might require additional code. Care must be exercised if y is negative. In this case, an appropriate constant equal to the largest negative y value plus 1

```
C PLOTTING Y = X**2/5 + 1 FOR X = 1 TO 10
C    LINE: ARRAY CONTAINING BLANKS EXCEPT FOR GRAPHIC SYMBOL *
C          THE LINE ARRAY SIMULATES THE LINE TO BE PRINTED
C    X:    RANGES IN VALUE FROM 1 TO 10 IN INCREMENTS OF 1 LINE
C    Y:    DISTANCE BETWEEN A POINT ON THE CURVE AND THE X AXIS
C       PARAMETER (N=21)
        CHARACTER LINE(N)
        INTEGER X
        REAL Y
        DATA LINE/N*' '/          Initialize array line to blanks.
        WRITE(6,2)
        DO 5 X = 1, 10
          Y = X**2/5.0 + 1.0    Compute the value of the function.
          LINE(Y + .5) = '*'    Insert the asterisk in its proper place in the line.
          WRITE(6,1)X,Y,LINE    and write out the line array.
          LINE(Y + .5) = ' '    Blank out the asterisk to prepare for the next line.
    5   CONTINUE
        STOP
    1   FORMAT(1X,I2,3X,F4.1/'+',13X,NA1)
    2   FORMAT(' X      Y')
        END
```

Output

X	Y
1	1.2
2	1.8
3	2.8
4	4.2
5	6.0
6	8.2
7	10.8
8	13.8
9	17.2
10	21.0

$y = \frac{x^2}{5} + 1$

FIGURE 6.16
PLOTTING THE FUNCTION $Y = X^2/5 + 1$

should be added to all the values of y so that the resulting subscript of the line array is greater than or equal to 1. If your system supports negative subscripts, then such steps are unnecessary.

If the changes in the magnitude of y are fractional, y should be scaled (multiplied by a constant) appropriately; for example, if for $x = 2$ the value of y is 1.3 and if for $x = 3$ the value for y is 1.4, you might wish to multiply y by 10 to obtain 13 and 14; then the graphic symbol on the first line will be one position to the left of the graphic symbol on the second line. Otherwise the graph might be represented by a vertical straight line, since LINE(1.3) = LINE(1.4) = LINE(1).

6.5.8 Polynomial and Sine Curves

Let us plot two functions side by side: $y = x^2 + x - 6$ in the interval $(-4, 3.6)$ and $y = \sin x$ in the interval 0 to 7.2. For $y = x^2 + x - 6$, our approach is as follows:

1. Fill an array PLINE with blanks.

2. Compute a value YPOLY $= x^2 + x - 6$ for $x = -4$, insert the symbol * in position YPOLY of the array (PLINE(YPOLY) = '*') and print the array PLINE.

3. Repeat steps 1 and 2 for values $x = -3.6, -3.2, ..., 3.6$ (the incremental value is arbitrarily set to 0.4 and represents succeeding lines on the printed form).

There is one minor problem: For some values of x, YPOLY is negative (see Figure 6.17); YPOLY cannot be negative (unless your system supports negative subscripts), since it is used as a subscript of PLINE to indicate the position of the symbol * on the output line. This problem can be solved by adding to $x^2 + x - 6$ a constant C that will neutralize the largest negative value of $x^2 + x - 6$ in the given interval and ensure that YPOLY ≥ 1. Adding such a constant does not change the shape of the graph but shifts the x axis to the right by C. In this example, a constant C $= 7.25$ could be used, since the largest negative value for YPOLY is -6.25 (when $x = -.5$).

With YPOLY $= x^2 + x - 6 + 7.25$, the smallest and largest value for YPOLY in the interval are YPOLY $= 1$ ($x = -.5$) and YPOLY $= 18$ ($x = 3.6$). Hence the array PLINE must be dimensioned to a size of at least 18.

```
C PLOTTING A POLYNOMIAL AND A SINE FUNCTION
C   XPOLY: X VALUE FOR THE POLYNOMIAL
C   XSINE: X VALUE FOR THE SINE
C   YPOLY: VALUE OF THE POLYNOMIAL FUNCTION
C   YSINE: VALUE OF THE SINE FUNCTION
C   PLINE: IMAGE OF THE LINE TO BE PRINTED FOR POLYNOMIAL
C   SLINE: IMAGE OF THE LINE TO BE PRINTED FOR THE SINE
C
        CHARACTER PLINE(28), SLINE(28)
        REAL XPOLY, XSINE, YPOLY, YSINE
        DATA PLINE,SLINE/56*' '/                    Initialize both line arrays to blanks.
        WRITE(6,9)
        XPOLY = -4.0
        XSINE = 0.0
     18 IF(XPOLY .LE. 4.0) THEN
            YPOLY = XPOLY**2 + XPOLY - 6.
            YSINE = SIN(XSINE)
            PLINE(YPOLY + 7.25)  = '*'
            SLINE(8*(YSINE + 2)) = '*'
            WRITE(6,11)XPOLY,YPOLY,PLINE,XSINE,YSINE,SLINE
            XPOLY = XPOLY + .4
            XSINE = XSINE + .4
            PLINE(YPOLY + 7.25)  = ' '            Erase the graphic symbol.
            SLINE(8*(YSINE + 2)) = ' '            Erase the graphic symbol.
            GO TO 18
        ENDIF
        STOP
      9 FORMAT(3X,'X',4X,'Y'/'+',34X,'X',4X,'Y')      Print captions.
     11 FORMAT(2F5.1,2X,28A1/'+',31X,2F5.1,28A1)      Print both graphs on same line.
        END
```

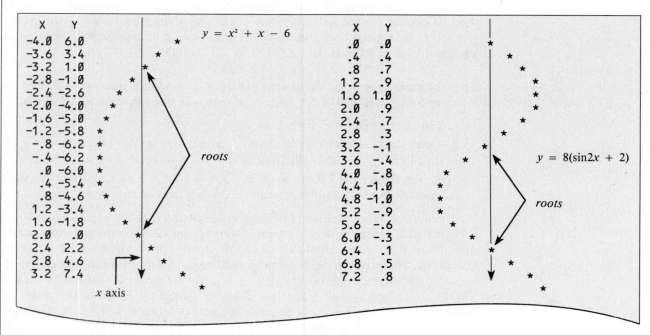

FIGURE 6.17
PLOTTING TWO FUNCTIONS

In the case of the sine function, a constant of 2 is added to YSINE = SIN(X) to ensure that YSINE ≥ 1, since SIN(X) = −1 for some values of *x*.

Plotting YSINE = SIN(X) + 2 is somewhat meaningless, since most of the values taken by YSINE will be in the interval 1 to 2. To magnify or stretch the graph over a wider area of print columns, we can multiply SIN(X) + 2 by a factor (let us use 8 in this case) that will spread out YSINE from a minimum of 1*8 when SIN(X) = −1 to a maximum of 3*8 = 24 when SIN(X) = 1. An array of a size of at least 24 must be reserved for the array to print the sine function. Multiplying the function by 8 does not plot the original function exactly, but it gives a fairly good idea of the shape of the curve while preserving the roots (see Figure 6.17).

6.5.9 Format Reuse: A Class Schedule

Consider, for example, the following problem, which requires the reuse of the format: Each pair of records of an input file contains a student's class schedule for the week. The first record contains the student's Monday schedule (identical to Wednesday's and Friday's), and the second record contains the student's Tuesday schedule (same as Thursday's). Write a program to produce weekly class schedules comparable to the following:

TIME	M	T	W	TH	F
8	DP101		DP101		DP101
9		FH100		FH100	
10	MS312		MS312		MS312
11		BY101		BY101	
12	EH202		EH202		EH202
13					
14					
	TOTAL CLASS MEETINGS 13				

Each data record is divided into seven fields reflecting the times when classes may meet:

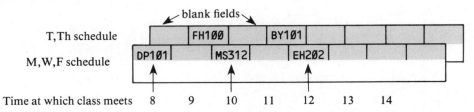

A program to solve this problem is shown in Figure 6.18. If the final caption "TO-TAL CLASS MEETINGS =" were to be omitted from the report, the following, much simpler format could be used instead of format 2.

```
      FORMAT('Ø','TIME',3X,'M',6X,'T',6X,'W',5X,'TH',6X,'F'
   1        //(1X,I3,5(2X,A5)))
```

Each line following the header line is printed according to this format, starting at the right-most open parenthesis.

```
C CLASS SCHEDULE
C   MWF:   CONTAINS MONDAY WEDNESDAY FRIDAY SCHEDULE
C   TTH:   CONTAINS TUESDAY THURSDAY SCHEDULE
C   MEET:  COUNTS THE NUMBER OF CLASS MEETINGS
      CHARACTER*5 MWF(7), TTH(7)
    5 READ(5,1,END=8)MWF, TTH
      MEET = 0
      DO 10 J = 1, 7
         IF(MWF(J) .NE. ' ') MEET=MEET+3
         IF(TTH(J) .NE. ' ') MEET=MEET+2
   10 CONTINUE
      WRITE(6,2)(J, (MWF(J-7),TTH(J-7),L=1,2),MWF(J-7),J=8,14),MEET
      GO TO 5
    8 STOP
C
    1 FORMAT(7(A5,1X))
    2 FORMAT('0','TIME',3X,'M',6X,'T',6X,'W',5X,'TH',6X,'F'/'0',
     *        7(I3,5(2X,A5)/)/6X,'TOTAL CLASS MEETINGS = ',I2)
C
      END
```

Read M,W,F schedule first and then the T, Th schedule

3 meetings for any class on M W and F

2 meetings for any class on T and Th

J prints the time at which courses are offered.

Seven lines, each containing a time (I3) and 5 course titles 5(2X,A5).
Note the use of the slash to cause 7 lines to be printed.

```
TIME    M       T       W       TH      F

   8    DP101           DP101           DP101
   9            FH100           FH100
  10    MS312           MMS312          MS312
  11            BY101           BY101
  12    EH202           EH202           EH202
  13
  14

        TOTAL CLASS MEETINGS = 13
TIME    M       T       W       TH      F

   8    HS202           HS202           HS202
   9    FH100           FH100           FH100
  10    GE321           GE321           GE321
  11            BY101           BY101
  12            EH202           EH202
  13            G2322           G2322
  14

        TOTAL CLASS MEETINGS = 15
TIME    M       T       W       TH      F

   8            HS202           HS202
   9
  10
  11
  12    CS100           CS100           CS100
  13    MS201           MS201           MS201
  14    PE101           PE101           PE101

        TOTAL CLASS MEETINGS = 11
```

Input File

Time at Which Class Meets

8	9	10	11	12	13	14

record #1
DP101   MS312   EH202
FH100   BY101

record #2
HS202 FH100 GE321
BY101 EH202 G2322

record #3
CS100 MS201 PE101
HS202

TTh at 8   MWF at 12   MWF at 14

MWF at 13

FIGURE 6.18
CLASS SCHEDULE

6.6 YOU MIGHT WANT TO KNOW

1. Is there any limit to the size of an array?

Answer: Yes, the maximum size for an array is a function of the memory size of the system in use.

2. Does a DIMENSION or a type statement initialize array elements to any specific values?

Answer: No, it is the programmer's responsibility to initialize arrays.

3. What differentiates a FORTRAN function from a subscripted variable? For instance, when I write $Y = SIN(X)$, is $SIN(X)$ a subscripted variable?

Answer: Unless you dimension an array called SIN in your program, SIN(X) is not a subscripted variable name but a function name.

4. Can I use an implied DO list in an arithmetic statement to process an array? For example, can I write:

```
(A(I),I=1,10) = 0.   or
SUM = (TAB1(I) + TAB2(I),I=1,10)
```

Answer: No, implied DO lists are valid only in input/output and DATA statements.

5. What happens if I use a subscripted variable name in my program and I forget to declare it as an array?

Answer: No compilation error will occur, since the compiler will think that it is a function. An error will occur later on, since no such function has been defined.

6. Can the same index be used more than once in an implied DO lists, for example,

```
READ(5,5)((A(I),I=1,5),SAM,I=1,9)
```

Answer: No, the inner implied DO list A(I),I = 1,5 will change the value of I used to control the outer implied DO list (I = 1,9). Note, however, that the following is permissible:

```
READ(5,6)(A(I),I=1,4),(B(I),I=1,6),I
```

In this case I is used to control three independent entities.

7. My friend was running a FORTRAN program with a statement $X = A(J)$, in which J exceeded the limit expressed in the REAL statement that declared A as an array. Although the program gave erroneous results, no error message was printed. Why?

Answer: The programmer uses the REAL statement to inform the compiler of the maximum number of memory locations for the array. If the user inadvertently at execution time refers to an array element A(J) in which J exceeds the size declared in the REAL statement, some systems may fail to inform the user that the array dimension has been exceeded and may actually process A(J) as that element J positions away from the first element of A. This response can destroy data or machine instructions representing FORTRAN instructions, depending on the value of J and depending on whether A(J) is on the left or the right of the equals sign in a replacement statement. With many versions of FORTRAN, however, if the index goes outside its specified range during execution, an error message is printed and execution of the program terminates at that point.

6.7 EXERCISES

6.7.1 Test Yourself

1. In terms of memory arrangement, what is the difference between a three-element array and any three variable names?

2. State whether the following statements are true or false:

   a. The REAL statement is an executable statement.

   b. An implied DO list is an executable statement.

   c. A FORMAT is an executable statement.

   d. END is a nonexecutable statement.

   e. The DATA statement is an executable statement.

   f. If A is an array, then READ(5,1)A will cause reading of just A(1).

   g. Subscripted variables can be used in any FORTRAN statement in the same way that nonsubscripted variables are used.

   h. The INTEGER and REAL statements can be placed anywhere in the program.

   i. If K = 3 and L = 3, then G(K) = G(L).

   j. If X(I) = X(J), then I = J.

   k. The value printed for I is 7 after WRITE(6,5)(B(I),I = 1,6),I

   l. If K is the location (position) of the largest value in array X, then X(K) is the largest value.

   m. Given CHARACTER A(20), the instruction READ(5,1) A(1) will store in A(1) a maximum of 20 characters.

   n. X(A(31)) is a valid subscripted variable.

   o. X(7) = 'BOY' is a valid replacement statement.

3. Assume G is an array consisting of five entries,

$$\text{REAL G(5)} \longrightarrow \boxed{1.4 \mid 3. \mid -4. \mid 1. \mid 3.}$$

Are the following statements valid or invalid? If valid, specify the resulting values; if invalid, explain why.

```
a. L = G(1)              d. K = -2
b. L = 2                    K = G(K**2-1)+K**2
   L = G(G(L))
                         e. L = 2
c. K = 1                    G(2*L) = 'HELLO'
   G(K) = G(K)+1
                         f. G(3) = (G(2)-3.)/G(G(4)-1.)
```

4. A and B are integer arrays of size 5; both are initially set to zeros. Use the code in parts a, b, c, and d to read the indicated data files and identify the contents of A and B.

Case 1 refers to 10 input records, while case 2 refers to just 1 record.

Case 1. Input File   Case 2. Input File

```
                    Ø1ØØØ1ØØ
                    Ø2ØØØ2ØØ
                    Ø3ØØØ3ØØ
                    Ø4ØØØØØØ
        10 records  Ø5ØØØØØØ    Ø1Ø2Ø3Ø4Ø5Ø6Ø7Ø8Ø9101112
                    Ø6ØØØØØØ
                    Ø7ØØØØØØ
                    Ø8ØØ-2ØØ           ↓
                    Ø9ØØØØØØ        1 record
                    1ØØØØØØØ
```

```
a.      DO 5 I = 1,3
            READ(5, )A(I),A(I+1),B(I)    Case 1:   FORMAT(3I2); FORMAT(I2)
        5 CONTINUE                       Case 2:   FORMAT(12I2)

b.      READ(5, )(A(I),B(I),I=1,5)       Case 1:   FORMAT(I2); FORMAT(3I2)
                                         Case 2:   FORMAT(12I2)

c.      READ(5, )(A,(B(J),J = 1,5,2)     Case 1:   FORMAT(I2)
                                         Case 2:   FORMAT(12I3)

d.      DO 5 I = 1,3
            READ(5,2)A(I)                Case 1:   FORMAT(4I2)
            READ(5,2)(B(J),J=1,5)        Case 2:   FORMAT(12I2)
        5 CONTINUE
```

5. Determine the number of records processed by the following codes:

```
a.      DO 1Ø I = 1,5              c.      DO 1Ø K = 1,6,2
            READ(5,6)A(I)                      READ(5,7)(A(I),I = 1,K)
        1Ø CONTINUE                       1Ø CONTINUE
        6 FORMAT(3F5.Ø)                   7 FORMAT(3F5.Ø)

b.      DO 1Ø J = 1,9             d.      REAL A(4),J
            READ(5,6)A(J),B(J)               DO 5 I = 1,4
        1Ø CONTINUE                              WRITE(6,6)J,A
        6 FORMAT(F5.3)                    5 CONTINUE
                                          6 FORMAT(1X,2F4.1)
```

6. Convert the following implied DO lists to the explicit DO loop form:

```
a.      READ(5,5)(A(I),I = 1,6)
        5 FORMAT(2F5.Ø)

b.      READ(5,6)(A(I),K(I),I = 2,9,2)
        6 FORMAT(2(F5.1,I2))
```

7. Specify the exact output (print positions, etc.) for the following WRITE operations, given the following arrays A and B and the constant K:

array A | 1.5 | – 3.2 | 3. | 4.8 | .34 | K | 3 | array B | – 1. | 2. | 3. |

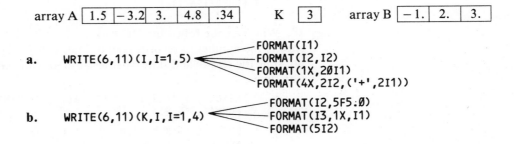

```
a.      WRITE(6,11)(I,I=1,5)  ——— FORMAT(I1)
                              ——— FORMAT(I2,I2)
                              ——— FORMAT(1X,2ØI1)
                              ——— FORMAT(4X,2I2,('+',2I1))

b.      WRITE(6,11)(K,I,I=1,4) ——— FORMAT(I2,5F5.Ø)
                               ——— FORMAT(I3,1X,I1)
                               ——— FORMAT(5I2)
```

c.   `WRITE(6,11)(J,(A(I),I=1,5),J=1,2)` ⟵   `FORMAT(I2,5F4.0)`
                                        `FORMAT(I1/5F4.0,I2/5F4.0)`
                                        `FORMAT(I2/(5F4.0))`

d.   `WRITE(6,11)((A(I),I=1,2),(B(I),I=1,2),L=1,2)` ⟵   `FORMAT(2F4.0,3F3.1)`
                                        `FORMAT(1X,F4.1)`
                                        `FORMAT(12F3.0)`

8. Write possible formats for the following input/output statements.

    a. `READ(5,5)(A(I),I = 1,5),(K(I),I = 1,1000)`

    b. `WRITE(6,5)(A(I),B(I), I,I = 1,500)`

    c. `WRITE(6,5)(A(I),I = 1,3),(JPAY(I),I = 1,1000),COST, K`

9. Given the input data file shown below, specify the contents of arrays X and or Y.

Data File

```
bbb1.3bbb4.2bbb6.8bbb1.9bbb3.3 ⟵ First record
4.1    -2.3    6.0    8.5    4.1
7.8     2.1    0.6    4.9   -2.0          [b = blank space]
18.3    7.1    4.2    8.1    7.3
0.0    10.0   20.0   30.0   40.0 ⟵ Last record
```

a.
```
      INTEGER C
      REAL X(5)
      C = 1
    3 READ(5,1)X(C)
      IF(C.NE.5) THEN
          C = C + 1
          GO TO 3
      ENDIF
    1 FORMAT(F6.1)
```

b.
```
      INTEGER C
      REAL X(3),Y(2)
      READ(5,1)X,Y
    1 FORMAT(5F6.1)
```

c.
```
      INTEGER C
      REAL X(5)
      C = 1
    3 READ(5,1)X(C)
      IF(C.NE.5) THEN
          C = C + 2
          GO TO 3
      ENDIF
    1 FORMAT(F6.1)
```

d.
```
      REAL X(4),Y(3)
      READ(5,1)X
      READ(5,1)Y
    1 FORMAT(4F6.1)
```

e.
```
      REAL X(3),Y(3)
      READ(5,1)(X(I),Y(I),I=1,3)
    1 FORMAT(5F6.1)
```

f.
```
      REAL X(3),Y(3)
      READ(5,1)(X(I),I = 1,3),(Y(I),I=1,3)
    1 FORMAT(4F6.1)
```

g.
```
      INTEGER C
      REAL X(5)
      READ(5,1)X(5)
      READ(5,1)X(1),X(4)
      X(3) = X(1)*5
      X(2) = X(1) + X(5)
    1 FORMAT(F6.1)
```

h.
```
      REAL X(16)
      READ(5,1)(X(I),A,I = 1,4)
    1 FORMAT(3F6.1)
```

10. Which of the following DO lists are invalid? If the implied DO list is valid, specify the number of records read or lines written. If the implied DO list is invalid, state the reason and state whether an error will occur at compilation or execution time.

    a.
```
      READ(5,5)(A(I),I = 1,5),(B(J),J = 1,3)
    5 FORMAT(3F5.2)
```

    b.
```
      WRITE(6,6)(K,A(I),B(I),I,I = 1,5)
    6 FORMAT(I2,2F3.0,I3)
```

```
c.      READ(5,5)(A(J),B(J),J = 1,9)
      5 FORMAT(F5.1)

d.      WRITE(6,8)(A(J),J = 1,N,K-J)
      8 FORMAT(F10.1)

e.      READ(5,7)A,(A(J),J = 1,7),B,KK
      7 FORMAT(4F3.0)

f.      READ(5,8)(A(I),(B(J),J = 1,5),I = 1,5)
      8 FORMAT(F5.1)

g.      WRITE(6,11)(PAY(J),J = 1,3)
     11 FORMAT(2F6.1)

h.      WRITE(6,4)(I,(A(I),I = 1,3),B,K = 1,5)
      4 FORMAT(1X,I1,3F5.0,F3.0)
```

11. Given an array A of size 100, write two codes to generate each of the following outputs; one code should use the implied DO list for the WRITE statement and the other should use the explicit DO loop.

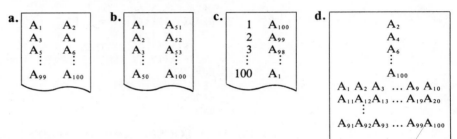

12. Array POS contains 12 numbers. Using only one WRITE statement, write the code to produce exactly the following output:

```
POS LISTING: 1  2  3  4
             5  6  7  8
             9 10 11 12
```

13. Given the following complete programs, infer potential execution-time/logical errors:

```
a.   DIMENSION A(100)          c.   DIMENSION A(100)
     I = 1                          WRITE(6,5)A
     X = 4.                         READ(5,5)(A(I),I = 1,110)
     A(J) = X**2+2.*X+I          5  FORMAT(10F5.0)
     STOP                           STOP
     END                            END

b.   DIMENSION A(100)          d.   DIMENSION A(6)
     I = 1                          DO 10 I = 1,5
     X = 4                             READ(5,7)A(I),A(I + 1)
     A(I) = X**A(J)              7     FORMAT(2F5.0)
     STOP                        10 CONTINUE
     END                            STOP
                                    END
```

14. Specify the list of variables that are read or written by the following instructions; for example the list might be: N, L, M_1, M_2,... . Indicate the position of each of the variables on the input or output record. (Repeat part b for each of the FORMATs given.)

a.
```
    INTEGER M(20)
    WRITE(6,5)(N,L,(M(J),J = 1,4),K,K=1,2)
  5 FORMAT(1X,3I3/(1X,4I2))
```

b.
```
    REAL T(10)
    READ(5,6)A,B,(T(I),I = 1,5)
  6 FORMAT(3F5.1)
  6 FORMAT(3F5.1/F5.1)
  6 FORMAT(F5.1/(2F5.1))
```

c.
```
    WRITE(6,4)(A(I),I = 1,7)
  4 FORMAT(1X,2F4.0/1X,2(F3.1,1X)/2(1X,F3.0))
```

15. Find at least five syntax errors in the following code:

```
    REALA(10),B(20),X
    DIMENSION A(10),C(3)
    DATA C/4,5,6/
 20 READ(5,1)(A(I),I = 1,10)
    DO 3 I = 1,10
       IF(A(I).GE.X) THEN X = A(I)
       IF(A(I).LT ISMALL) ISMALL = A(I)
  3 CONTINUE
    IF(X = 0)X=0.001
    STOP
    END
```

16. Array SOCSEC contains 100 different social security numbers. Write the code to determine whether the number in T matches any number in array SOCSEC. The code should print either MATCH or NO MATCH.

17. An input record contains an unknown number of numbers (at least 51 but no more than 100). Write the code to read the first 20 numbers into array A, the next 30 into array B, and the remainder into array C.

18. Arrays A and B contain integers between 1 and 100. Array A has 10 elements, and array B has 16. Write the code to print the numbers that are common to both arrays and the number of equal elements.

For example given arrays A and B shown below the output would be as follows:

Arrays

A: | 3 | 5 | 3 | 7 | 9 |

B: | 5 | 3 | 7 | 3 | 8 |

Output

```
            3
            5
            7
NUMBER OF EQUAL ITEMS = 3
```

19. First load an array A with 20 integers between 1 and 20. Then write the code to perform a frequency distribution on the numbers in array A. The output should list the numbers in ascending order and their corresponding frequency, as follows:

```
NUMBERS    1  3  4  5  10  12  13  14  15  17  18  19
FREQUENCY  1  4  2  1   1   1   2   2   1   2   2   1
```

20. Write the code to determine whether an array that has 10 numbers (not necessarily integers) has any two equal entries.

21. Array A consists of 11 entries; the first 10 entries contain numbers arranged in ascending sequence. Read a number X and insert it in its proper position in array A. For example, if X = 23 and array A is

| 10 | 20 | 30 | 40 | 50 | 60 | 70 | 80 | 90 | 95 | |

The edited array is:

| 10 | 20 | 23 | 30 | 40 | 50 | 60 | 70 | 80 | 90 | 95 |

22. Write the code to produce the following multiplication tables

```
1 X  1 =  1    2 X  1 =  2    3 X  1 =  3  . . .    10 X  1 =  10
1 X  2 =  2    2 X  2 =  4    3 X  2 =  6           10 X  2 =  20
1 X  3 =  3    2 X  3 =  6    3 X  3 =  9           10 X  3 =  30
       :              :              :                     :
1 X 12 = 12    2 X 12 = 24    3 X 12 = 36           10 X 12 = 120
```

6.7.2 Programming Problems: General/Business

1. Assume array A with 50 elements has already been loaded. Write the code to compute the sum of the squares of the elements of array A.

2. A and B are tables of size 100 and 50, respectively. Write the code to store the numbers 1, 2, 3, ..., 100 in table A and to store the first 50 positive odd integers starting with 101 in table B. Do not read data from input records.

3. A data file is composed of two packets of scores. The first packet contains final scores obtained by an algebra class, while the second packet contains scores obtained by an accounting class. The packets are separated by a negative number. Read the class scores into two arrays and print the number of scores in each packet. The input file (one entry per record) has the following form:

$$10, 80, 64, ..., 86, 44, 28, -3, 43, 74, ..., 86, 94, 21, -7$$

Algebra scores   Accounting scores
At most 100 scores   At most 50 scores

4. An input file consists of an unknown number of scores ranging from 1 to 100. Write a program to determine the number of scores below the average. Print the scores and the count of scores below the average.

5. Each record of an input file (maximum 15 records) consists of an account number and an amount deposited. Write the code to:

  a. Print the account numbers of all the accounts in which $50,000 or more has been deposited.

  b. Then print the numbers of all the accounts in which amounts between $10,000 and $50,000 have been deposited.

6. For each student in a class, there is one record with his/her name and 10 test scores. The student's average is based on his/her nine best scores. Write a program to produce an output similar to the following:

```
              GRADE REPORT
NAME: WOODRUFF    AVERAGE = 60.0
TESTS:  10   20   30  40  50  60  70  80  90  100

NAME: ZIEGLER     AVERAGE = 58.9
TESTS:  100  50   60  40  35  65  80  20  30  70
```

7. Write the code to produce the following tables:

```
a. 1 2 3 4 5 6 7 8 9 10      b. 1 2 3 4 5 6 7 8 9 10
   1 2 3 4 5 6 7 8 9            2 3 4 5 6 7 8 9 10
   1 2 3 4 5 6 7 8                3 4 5 6 7 8 9 10
   1 2 3 4 5 6 7                    4 5 6 7 8 9 10
   1 2 3 4 5 6                        5 6 7 8 9 10
   1 2 3 4 5                            6 7 8 9 10
   1 2 3 4                                7 8 9 10
   1 2 3                                    8 9 10
   1 2                                        9 10
   1                                            10

c. 10                        d.                    1
   10 9                                          2 1
   10 9 8                                      3 2 1
   10 9 8 7                                  4 3 2 1
   10 9 8 7 6                              5 4 3 2 1
   10 9 8 7 6 5                          6 5 4 3 2 1
   10 9 8 7 6 5 4                      7 6 5 4 3 2 1
   10 9 8 7 6 5 4 3                  8 7 6 5 4 3 2 1
   10 9 8 7 6 5 4 3 2              9 8 7 6 5 4 3 2 1
   10 9 8 7 6 5 4 3 2 1        10 9 8 7 6 5 4 3 2 1
```

8. The following diagram shows Pascal's triangle for N = 6:

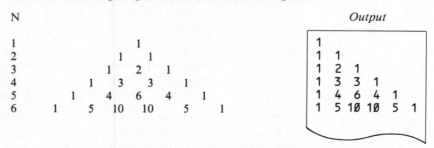

Find the rule for generating successive rows of Pascal's triangle and use it in a program that will accept a value of N and print the appropriate triangle.

9. Write a program to calculate the exact Julian date equivalent to the date specified in the form: month, day, year. The Julian date is the day of the year: January 1 has Julian date 1, February 2 has Julian date 33, December 31 has Julian date 365, and so forth. Use a table showing the number of days that have occurred since the beginning of the year for each month, i.e.

Month	Days
1	0
2	31
3	59
4	90
:	:

How would you change your program to account for leap years, in which February has one more day. [*Hint:* See exercise 8 page 55 and ex.5 page 116.]

10. Write a program to convert dates in the form month-number, day, year to the form month-name, day, 19year. For example, the input 11 18 84 should produce the output NOVEMBER 18, 1984.

11. Write a program that will input a value for N and draw the following axis graduated in units of 5:

```
If N = 31   ----5----Ø----5----Ø----5----Ø-
If N =  7   ----5--
If N =  3   ---
```

12. Use exercise 11 to draw a graduated axis for the bar graph problem on page 285. The last graduation symbol should reflect the maximum sales for the week, as shown in the following example:

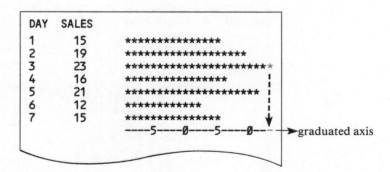

13. The correct answers (1,2,3, or 4) to a multiple choice test of 10 questions are recorded on the first record of an input file. Succeeding records contain the name of a student and the student's 10 answers. Write the code to compute each student's final score (each correct answer is worth 10 points). The input and output have the following form:

Input File

```
1123142433
JONES   1123142433
HILL    1123111324
CLAM    4123142432
```

Output

NAME	SCORES	GRADE
JONES	1 1 2 3 1 4 2 4 3 3	100
HILL	1 1 2 3 1 1 1 3 2 4	50
CLAM	4 1 2 3 1 4 2 4 3 2	80

14. At the beginning and at the end of each month, members of the U-WATCH-UR-WEIGHT club are weighed in. Each member's name and initial and terminal weights are typed on a record. Write a program to read such records and print out each member's name, initial and final weight, and weight loss. Also print the average weight loss for the group and the number of members whose weight loss was greater than the average weight loss. For example:

```
    GREEN    200   180   20   *
    FARAH    130   120   10
    TODINI   161   154    7

AVERAGE WEIGHT LOSS IS 12.3 POUNDS
1 MEMBER WITH WEIGHT LOSS OVER 12.3 POUNDS
```

Note that a * is printed beside the name of each member whose weight loss is above the average.

15. An encyclopedia company has hired part-time salespeople. The name of each salesperson and the number of encyclopedia sets he/she has sold are recorded on separate data records (one record per salesperson). Each salesperson is paid $90.00 for each set sold, as well as $15.00 extra for each set (or fraction) sold over the average number of sets sold by all the salespeople. For example, if the average number of sets sold is 5.8 and a salesperson has sold 8 sets, the difference is 2.2, which counts as 3 sets over the average (the fractional part counts as an entire set). Write a program to print the name, the number of sets sold, and the amount earned by each employee. Don't forget to print the average number of sets sold.

16. Klinkon Headquarters has received personnel secrets for the spaceship Renderprize from two of its spies:

The First Spy Reports

Number	Name
455-30-1980	Kiik
465-29-9136	Skolly
408-32-6166	Spark
432-98-2316	Thekov
492-38-7213	Uhula
433-27-8107	McJoy
446-66-2366	Lusu

The Second Spy Reports

Number	Title
465-29-9136	Engineer
432-98-2316	Navigator
446-66-2366	Navigator
433-27-8107	Doctor
455-30-1980	Captain
408-32-6166	First Officer
492-38-7213	Communications

As a Klinkon programmer, your job is to program the computer to match up crew member names with their titles. (Star Fleet Command has evidence that when Klinkon programmers make syntax errors, they mysteriously disappear!) Write the code to produce a list of numbers and the corresponding names and titles, i.e.

```
455-30-1980   KIIK     CAPTAIN
465-29-9136   SKOLLY   ENGINEER
    :           :          :
    :           :          :
```

17. A table contains 27 numbers that can be either positive or negative. Write a program to print the positive numbers and the negative numbers 4 per line as follows:

```
-14   -12   -34   -56
 -2    -6   -45   -67
        .
        .
        .
-34   -23

 12    56    9Ø    21
 56    89     6     4
        .
        .
        .
 78
```

If there are no positive numbers, just print the negative ones (and vice versa).

18. Using the schedule shown below, write a program to read an adjusted gross income and compute and print the amount of tax owed.

Over—	But Not Over—	Amount	Of the Amount Over—
$0	$2,390	—0—	
2,390	3,540	$0.00 + 11%	$2,390
3,540	4,580	126.50 + 12%	3,540
4,580	6,760	251.30 + 14%	4,580
6,760	8,850	556.50 + 15%	6,760
8,850	11,240	870.00 + 16%	8,850
11,240	13,430	1,252.40 + 18%	11,240
13,430	15,610	1,646.60 + 20%	13,430
15,610	18,940	2,082.60 + 23%	15,610
18,940	24,460	2,848.50 + 26%	18,940
24,460	29,970	4,283.70 + 30%	24,460
29,970	35,490	5,936.70 + 34%	29,970
35,490	43,190	7,813.50 + 38%	35,490
43,190	57,550	10,739.50 + 42%	43,190
57,550	85,130	16,770.70 + 48%	57,550
85,130	-----	30,009.10 + 50%	85,130

19. The following integers have been recorded on a record:

36, 27, 43, 18, 5, 6, 9, 33, 45, 34, 22, 42

Read these numbers into an array and write a program to accomplish the following:

a. Compute the average (mean) of these 12 numbers, rounded to the nearest whole number.

b. Compute the difference between each of these 12 numbers and the mean (subtract the mean from each number), and store each of these deviations in an array.

c. Determine which of the 12 numbers in the array deviates the most from the mean (i.e., which deviation has the largest absolute value) and print that number (not its deviation). Continued on next page.

The output should be as follows:

```
ARRAY    DEVIATION
 36          9
 27          Ø
 43         16
 :           :
 :           :
 42         15

MEAN ROUNDED IS 27
NUMBER DEVIATING MOST FROM MEAN IS 5
```

20. Professor X records her final grades as follows: The first data item N (N < 20) in the record identifies the number of grades for her entire class. N is followed by N grades entered on the same record. Write a program to produce a grade frequency report. A sample input and output are shown below:

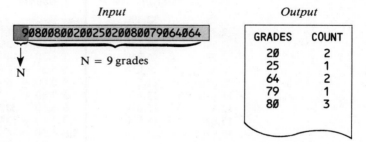

Input

9080080020025020080079064064

N

N = 9 grades

Output

GRADES	COUNT
2Ø	2
25	1
64	2
79	1
8Ø	3

21. A very simple method to encode a message is to replace each letter of the message with another according to some scheme such as

letter   A B C D E ... Y Z
substitute Z Y X W V ... B A

Write a program to encode a message using this method.

22. Each record of an input file contains a variable number of zon zero scores reflecting the number of students in a particular class. Each record consists of no more than 10 entries, and a zero identifies the end of the scores if fewer than 10 scores are typed on a record. For example:

010020030000000000000000000000   record consists of 3 scores
010020030040050060070080090100   record consists of 10 scores

Write a program to compute the average of each record, as well as the overall average. Print the scores of each record using one line per record and then print all the scores read, 10 per line. Also print the count of scores that are below the average of all scores read. Assume there are no more than 100 scores in the input file. The output should be similar to the following:

```
CLASS 1    10 20 60                          AVERAGE = 30.00
CLASS 2    10 10 10 20 20 20 30 30 30 20      AVERAGE = 20.00
OVERALL    10 20 60 10 10 10 20 20 20 30
           30 30 20                          AVERAGE = 22.30
NUMBER OF SCORES BELOW OVERALL AGERAGE = 9
```

23. **a.** Without reading any data records (initialize the three following arrays to the constants specified below), create and print the following inventory file for an auto parts dealer:

Part Number	Quantity	Cost/Part
115	50	90
120	60	91
125	70	92
130	80	93
135	90	94
.	.	.
160	140	99

For example, there are 50 of item 115 at a cost of 90 cents each.

b. During the day, sales transactions are recorded on records as follows:

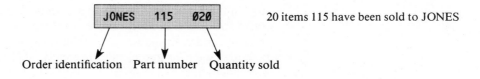

20 items 115 have been sold to JONES

Order identification   Part number   Quantity sold

A part number may occur more than once in the transaction file.

Write a program to read the transaction records and update the corresponding item stock levels. If an order exceeds the available stock quantity, sell all existing stock items (if any) and print the number of items still owed to the customer. (See sample output on next page.)

When the entire transaction file has been read, print an updated inventory consisting of a part number, a current stock level, a delivered quantity, a cost, and a reorder quantity column. Each entry in the reorder column should be equal to the total number of items sold that day (including items not delivered but already paid for). Thus, in the example below, 105 of item 135 were sold, but 15 were undelivered. Since the original stock level was 90, 105 items must be reordered.

The cost of any item for which no sales were made is to be discounted by 10%, rounded to the nearest penny and flagged as such on the output.

Incorrect part numbers read in the transaction file must be listed after the updated inventory report. A record number should identify the invalid number. (See next page for sample input and output.)

The input and output files have the form:

Output

```
NAME        ITEM NO     ON ORDER

SIMS         135            5
SOUL         135           10
CROSS        120            3


PART        STOCK       DELIVERED              REORDER
NUMBER      LEVEL       QUANTITY      COST     QUANTITY

115          40            10        90.00       10
120           0            60        91.00       63
125          70             0        83.00               DISCOUNT
130           5            75        93.00        5
135           0            90        94.00      105
 .            .             .          .          .
 .            .             .          .          .
 .            .             .          .          .
160           .             .          .          .

CHECK RECORD 2: NO EXISTING PART 117
CHECK RECORD 9: NO EXISTING PART 126
```

Transaction File

Part number	Quantity
DOE	115	5
LONG	126	20
LIU	120	60
JONES	115	5
WONG	130	75
SIMS	135	95
SOUL	135	10
CROSS	120	3
DIM	117	5

24. On NBC's *Today* show weather report, temperatures from various cities in the United States are listed by geographical area. Temperature readings are collected from various weather-measuring stations and typed on records in no special sequence order. Each record contains the name of the city, the corresponding temperature, and a geographical code area (1 = East Coast, 2 = Midwest, 3 = South, 4 = Pacific).

a. Write a program segment to produce a list of cities and their temperatures by geographical area in the order the cities are encountered in the input file. The output should identify each geographical area by name, as shown below:

Input

```
BOSTON    45   1
FRESNO    66   4
NEW YORK  51   1
MOBILE    73   3
MADISON   -5   2
CHICAGO   57   2
MIAMI     88   3
```

Output

```
EAST COAST
                     BOSTON    45
                     NEW YORK  51
MIDWEST
                     MADISON   -5
                     CHICAGO   57
SOUTH
                     MOBILE    73
                     MIAMI     88
PACIFIC
                     FRESNO    66
          :
HIGHEST TEMP:    MIAMI    88
```

b. Write another program segment to list cities in ascending temperature order (four cities per printed line) as follows:

```
MADISON -5  BOSTON   45  NEW YORK  51  CHICAGO  57
FRESNO  66  MOBILE   73  MIAMI     88
```

25. Write a program to determine the day of the week for any date in the twentieth century. Use the following algorithm:

Let J be the Julian date (see problem 9 in this section) and Y be the year (last two digits only).

    a. Compute $X = 365.25*Y + J$

    b. If the decimal part of X is zero, subtract one from X.

    c. Compute the remainder after dividing the integer part of X by seven.

    The remainder corresponds to the days of the week as follows:
        0 = Sunday, 1 = Monday, 2 = Tuesday, ...

26. The Meals on Wheels Company operates a fleet of vans used for the delivery of cold foods at various local manufacturing plants and construction sites. The management is thinking of purchasing a specially built $18,000 van equipped to deliver hot foods. This new addition to the fleet is expected to generate after-tax earnings E_1, E_2, ..., E_6 (as displayed below) over the next six years, at which time the van's resale value will be zero. Projected repair and maintenance costs C_0, C_1, C_2, ..., C_6 over the six years are shown below.

Projected Earnings		*Projected Costs*		
E_1	$2,500	C_0	$18,000	(purchase cost of the van)
E_2	2,500	C_1	1,000	
E_3	3,000	C_2	1,500	
E_4	4,500	C_3	2,000	
E_5	6,000	C_4	2,000	
E_6	6,000	C_5	2,100	
		C_6	2,400	

The decision to purchase the van depends on the benefit/cost ratio (BCR) (grossly speaking, earnings/expenditures) given by the formula

$$BCR = \frac{E_1(1+i)^6 + E_2(1+i)^5 + \ldots + E_6(1+i)^1}{C_0 + C_1(1+i)^6 + C_2(1+i)^5 + \ldots + C_6(1+i)^1}$$

where i is the rate of investment of earnings by the company. If BCR > 1, then the company should acquire the van. Write a program to determine how high the investment rate (i) would have to be raised to permit the purchase of the vehicle. Write a program to compute the BCR for investment rates starting at 6% and increasing by amounts of 0.1%. The output should be as follows: (see next page)

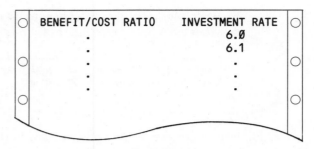

Stop when the BCR is greater than 1 and print the following message:

```
PURCHASE OF VAN REQUIRES INVESTMENT RATE OF XX.XX.
```

27. The department of psychology offers a maximum of ten sections of introduction to psychology. Each section contains no more than 25 students. At the end of the semester, final grades for each section are recorded as follows:

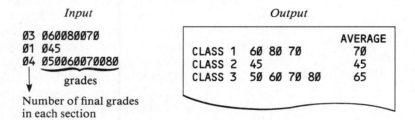

    a. Write a program to produce the output shown above.

    b. Write a program to produce the following output showing the class averages:

```
CLASS 1    CLASS 2    CLASS 3 ... CLASS?
  70         45         65          ?
```

Note that there might be fewer than ten classes.

28. An input file consists of an unknown number of grades in random order. Compute and print the median. The median is the score that divides a distribution of scores into two equal parts. For example,

    10, 30, 87, 12   The median is $(12 + 30)/2 = 21$
                                (Half are above 21, half are below 21.)

    53, 16, 99   The median is 53 (Half are above 53, half below 53.)

  29. Write a program to record in an array P the relative ascending order position of each element of array A. For example, if

array A = | 51 | 20 | 90 | 80 | 100 | then   array P = | 2 | 1 | 4 | 3 | 5 |

The interpretation for array P is:

1 is stored in P(2), to indicate that the second element of A is the smallest (20).
2 is stored in P(1), to indicate that the first element of A is the 2d smallest (51).
.
.
.
5 is stored in P(5), to indicate that the fifth element of A is the largest (100).

The following code would then print the elements of A in ascending numerical sequence

```
WRITE(6,6)(A(P(I)),I=1,5)
```

In what programming situation would this sort algorithm be preferable to the bubble or mini/max sorts?

30. You work for the National Weather Service. They are going to measure changes in wind direction by sending up 3 balloons on each of 5 different days. Each of the 15 balloons is assigned a unique identification number (ID) between 100 and 999 (in no particular order). One balloon is released in the morning, one is released at noon, and one is released in the evening on each of the five days. When the balloons are returned, the ID number (integer), the day each balloon was sent up (1, 2, 3, 4, or 5), and the distance traveled (real number) will be recorded, with one record for each balloon (see the test data at the end of the problem). Write a program to:

a. Read the test data records shown (one at a time) into three arrays.

b. Sort the arrays into ascending order by ID number.

c. Print the sorted arrays with three entries per line (ID, day, and distance).

d. Find the maximum distance traveled for each day (there will be five maximums). Print the ID, day, and maximum distance for each of the five days (print the results for the first day, then the second, third, etc.).

e. Find the average distance traveled by balloons released on the first and fifth days combined, and print this average distance (one result).

Input: 15 records with 3 data items/record: ID, day and distance.

Output: 15 printed lines of sorted ID's and corresponding days and distances (ID, day, distance).

5 printed lines of maximum distances for each day (1 through 5) (ID, day, distance).

1 printed line showing the average distance traveled on the first and fifth days combined (average).

Use the following test data.

Identification	Day	Distance
123	2	143.7
269	3	976.4
120	1	370.2
460	5	980.8
111	1	111.3
986	4	1320.6
629	3	787.0
531	2	429.2
729	2	726.1
833	4	433.1
621	3	962.4
143	4	714.3
972	5	320.1
410	5	820.4
511	1	1240.0

31. At the Kilpatrick Community College, General Mathematics MS101 has always been offered in the traditional teacher/lecture format. This year, for the first time, students may take MS101 using a self-paced approach to instruction through a computer-assisted instructional method (CAI). Because of the novelty of the CAI approach, the mathematics faculty has formulated the following policies concerning grades and tests for those taking MS101 in the CAI mode:

1. Students may take one, two or three tests during the semester.

2. The final score is based on the student's average score, scaled as follows: If the CAI class average AV is less than 80 (the standardized average for the traditional teacher/lecture form), then the difference 80 − AV should be added to each student's average score; otherwise, the difference, AV − 80, is subtracted from each student's average. The input data is formatted as follows:

Input record

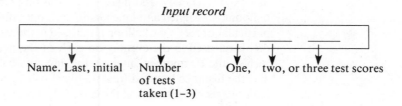

Write a program to produce the following score information. For example, the following input data would produce the output shown:

Input

```
BOILLOT M 1 90.5
HORN L    2 86.0  9.0
GLEASON G 3 60.0 80.0 100.0
```
Name | Number of Tests | Scores

Output

STUDENT NAME	AVERAGE	SCALED AVERAGE
BOILLOT M.	90.5	84.5
HORN L.	87.5	81.5
GLEASON G.	80.0	74.0

AVERAGE 86.0

Can you rewrite the code for this exercise in such a way that each student's scores are printed after the student name but before the average as follow:

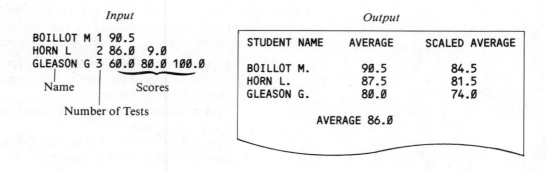

STUDENT NAME	SCORES	AVERAGE	SCALED AVERAGE
BOILLOT M.	90.5	90.5	84.5
HORN L.	86.0 89.0	87.5	81.5
GLEASON G.	60.0 80.0 100.0	8.0	74.0

32. The Triple Star Corporation maintains a file in which each record contains a date (year) and the yearly sales in millions of dollars. These figures lie between 0 and 60 million. Write a program to produce a graph of this data, similar to the following one:

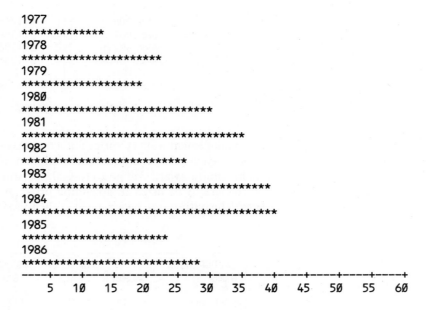

Make sure your program prints the last unit line, i.e., ---- + ---- + ---- and the graduations 0,5,10,15, ... Make your own data file.

33. You are the organizer for the National Swimming Finals. You want to have a program that will seed the swimmers in the correct preliminary heat (race). You have 36 swimmers, each with an identification number and a submitted time. The swimming pool has only six lanes, so only six swimmers can swim at a time. The procedure for seeding is to (1) sort the swimmers according to submitted times, and (2) assign to the first heat the swimmers with the first, seventh, thirteenth, ..., and thirty-first fastest times. (Note that a person whose time is 52.1 is *faster* than someone whose time is 55.8.) The swimmers in the second heat should be those with the second, eighth, fourteenth, ..., and thirty-second fastest times. Swimmers should be assigned to the other four heats in a similar manner.
Write a program to:

a. Read a file in which each record contains an integer ID and a submitted time, and store these data into an integer array and a real array.

b. Sort both arrays in ascending order *by time*.

c. Starting with the first heat, print the heat number (integer), then print the ID number and time of each swimmer in that heat in ascending order by time. Repeat for each heat.

d. Print on a separate line (1) the number of swimmers who swam faster (less time) than the average submitted time and (2) the average submitted time.

34. The BOISUPP company employs a variable number of salespersons. The input file consists of records of sales by each salesperson; the records are already sorted in ascending order by salesperson number but not by date. For example, a typical data file might be:

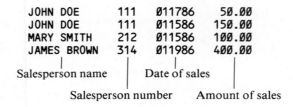

```
JOHN DOE      111    011786    50.00
JOHN DOE      111    011586   150.00
MARY SMITH    212    011586   100.00
JAMES BROWN   314    011986   400.00
```
| |
Salesperson name   Date of sales

Salesperson number   Amount of sales

The management wants to print out a monthly sales report to summarize the total sales for each salesperson and the total amount of all sales. Also, a salesperson-of-the-month award will go to the salesperson with highest sales for the month. Entries are to be listed in ascending order by salesperson number and date of sales. The output is to be arranged in the following form:

```
SALESPERSON              DATE OF   AMOUNT OF   TOTAL SALES/
NAME            NUMBER     SALES       SALES    SALESPERSON

JOHN DOE         111     01 15 86    150.00
                         01 17 86     50.00        200.00

MARY SMITH       212     01 15 86    100.00        100.00

JAMES BROWN      314     01 19 86    400.00        400.00

                                   TOTAL SALES     700.00

**AWARD GOES TO JAMES BROWN**
```

Write a program to read a transaction file and produce a summary report like the one shown. Be sure you include more than one transaction for some of the salespersons and note that in such cases you print the number of the salesperson only once.

35. A radio station has hired you to write a program to help them plan their air time. You are given twenty input records at most, with the following entries on each record:

1st entry: Record identification
2nd entry: Record type (1 = Punk rock, 2 = Acid rock, 3 = Classical)
3rd entry: Playing time (3.6 means 3 minutes and 6/10 of a minute)

Write a program to

a. Read the input file and store the record identification, the record type, and the playing time into three separate tables.

b. Sort the three tables in ascending order by playing time.

c. Print the sorted tables with each record identification, record type, and corresponding playing time on one output line (3 data items/line).

d. Determine total playing time for each type of record and print the results in the form:

```
PUNK ROCK   14.6
ACID ROCK   21.Ø
CLASSICAL    9.2
```

e. Determine the classical record with the playing time closest to 2.4 minutes and print the located record's identification and playing time.

36. Wrap-around sales averaging. The management at Food Stores, Inc., likes to compare their monthly sales with a running average of their sales for the preceding 11 months. Write a program to read sales data for the preceding 11 months (Jan. to Nov. '86) and read "dummy" sales projections for the next 12 months (Dec. '86 through Nov. '87). Then compute the preceding 11-month's running average for Dec. '86 through Nov. '87. The process can be visualized as follows:

Jan.–Nov. 1986											Dec. '86–Nov. '87								11 months running average
J	F	M	A	M	J	J	A	S	O	N	D	J	F	M	A	M ... N		
10	11	12	10	11	14	10	11	12	11	12	13							11.27
	11	12	10	11	14	10	11	12	11	12	13	16						11.54
		12	10	11	14	10	11	12	11	12	13	16	11					12.00
			10	11	14	10	11	12	11	12	13	16	11	13				11.90

For the month of December, for example, management will compare the December volume (13) with the running average of the 11 previous months 11.27 [(10 + 11 + 12 + 10 + 11 + 14 + 10 + 11 + 12 + 11 + 12)/11]

The output should be similar to:

MONTHS	11-MONTH RUNNING AVERAGE	MONTH SALES
DECEMBER	11.27	13
JANUARY	11.54	16
FEBRUARY	12.ØØ	11
MARCH	11.9Ø	13

37. The Language Department at Johns College offers five courses and is now registering students. Each student completes a form with his/her name and one course number. A student can take more than one course, in which case he/she fills out different forms. The list of courses, the maximum enrollment per class, and the room number in which each class meets are as follows:

Course	Size	Room No.
FRE 110	5	204
FRE 120	10	200
GER 100	6	100
SPN 100	10	212
SPN 105	15	220

a. Each record of the input file consists of a student name and a course number. Write a program to read this file and provide the following enrollment information:

Input

```
ADAMS   FRE   110
BEVIS   GER   100
ADAMS   FRE   120
ADAMS   SPN   100
KERR    SPN   105
```

Output

COURSE	ROOM NO	ENROLLMENT	MAX ENROLLMENT
FRE 110	204	5	5
FRE 120	200	6	10
.			
.			
.			
SPN 105	220	4	15

If a course if filled, either identify that course by placing a * next to the maximum enrollment figure or list the students who could not enroll.

b. At the conclusion of the enrollment procedure, the department head would like to be able to inquire directly in this data base to obtain any of the following information:

Information Required	Query Code	Item
A list of student names in any particular course	1	Course number
A list of courses taken by a particular student	2	Student name
An actual class size for a particular room	3	Room number

(Query code 4 stops the inquiry process.)

For example, the following set of queries would produce the output below:

Query Code

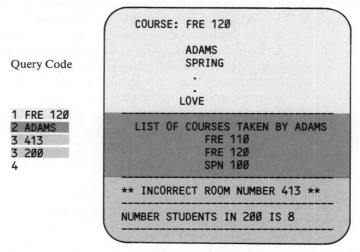

```
1 FRE 120
2 ADAMS
3 413
3 200
4
```

```
          COURSE: FRE 120

              ADAMS
              SPRING
                .
                .
              LOVE
─────────────────────────────────
       LIST OF COURSES TAKEN BY ADAMS
               FRE 110
               FRE 120
               SPN 100

**  INCORRECT ROOM NUMBER 413  **
───────────────────────────────────
NUMBER STUDENTS IN 200 IS 8
───────────────────────────────────
```

Write a program to accept the query information and produce the requested information (perform input validation on all fields). Another option for inquiries (instead of numerical codes) is to have the computer display a menu of inquiries.

38. Systems planning involves estimating development time and projection of costs associated with the completion of a particular task. An example might be planning the construction of a house. A list of tasks and a time schedule might be:

Sequence of Events	Task Description	Time in Days
1	Laying of foundation	15
2	Plumbing installment	12
3	Frame and roof	20
4	Electrical work	7
5	Plastering	4
6	Carpentry	7
7	Landscaping	3

Write a program to produce a bar graph like the following one to represent the duration of each task.

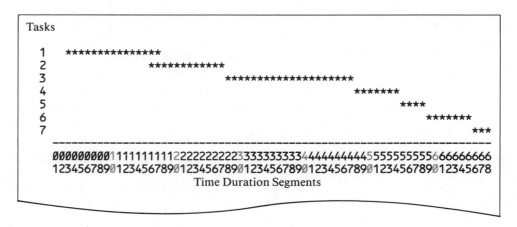

```
Tasks

1    ***************
2                 ************
3                             ********************
4                                                 *******
5                                                        ****
6                                                            *******
7                                                                   ***
     ---------------------------------------------------------------------
     000000000011111111112222222222333333333344444444445555555555666666666
     123456789012345678901234567890123456789012345678901234567890123456789012345678
                         Time Duration Segments
```

39. Two sort methods have been presented in this chapter, the bubble and the mini/max sort. These two sorting techniques are not the most efficient methods, however. One extremely efficient sorting method is the Shell-Metzner sort. In an article entitled "A Comparison of Sorts" in *Creative Computing*, Volume 2, John Grillo compared the three methods and determined that to sort 100,000 numbers would take 7.1 days, 3.8 days, and 15 minutes for the bubble, mini/max, and Shell-Metzner sort, respectively. To sort 10,000,000 numbers would take 93 years, 50 years, and 2.5 days respectively! Write a program to sort N numbers using the following pseudo code:

```
set flag to 1, and position to N
WHILE position > 1 or flag = 1
  flag = 0
  position = (position + 1)/2
  DO I = 1, N - position
    IF X(I) > X(I + position)THEN
       interchange X(I) with X(I + position) and set flag to 1
    ENDIF
    CONTINUE LOOP
ENDWHILE
stop
```

6.7.3 Programming Problems: Scientific/ Mathematical/Use of Random Numbers

1. This exercise requires interactive communications with a terminal. Write a program in which you pick a number between 1 and 10 and the computer tries to guess it randomly, using random numbers between 1 and 10. The computer should not guess the same number twice.

2. A weighted average is computed as

$$f_1 x_1 + f_2 x_2 + f_3 x_3 + \ldots + f_n x_n \text{ where } f_1 + f_2 + f_3 + \ldots + f_n = 1.$$

Write a program to read n values of f and x and compute the weighted average. Write an error message if the sum of the f's is not equal to 1. Test your program with the following:

n	f_1	x_1	f_2	x_2	f_3	x_3	Expected Output
3	.4	3	.5	2	.1	5	2.7
2	.6	4	.6	8			Error message

3. Write a program to read an unknown number of grades and calculate the standard deviation of those grades using the following formula:

$$sd = \sqrt{\frac{(x_1 - \bar{x})^2 + (x_2 - \bar{x})^2 + (x_3 - \bar{x})^2 + \ldots + (x_n - \bar{x})^2}{n(n - 1)}}$$

where n = number of grades;
$\bar{x}$ = average of grades;
$x_1, x_2, x_3, \ldots, x_n$ are the grades.

5. Write a program to generate 1,000 random integer numbers between 1 and 100 and print their frequency. Compare the observed frequency with the expected frequency for randomly selected numbers.

6. You are designing an eight-stringed musical instrument to span the octave starting with middle C. The strings are to be steel (density = 450 lb/ft³), 24 in. long, and are to be one of the following commercially available diameters, in inches:

0.0320, 0.0359, 0.0403, 0.0453, 0.0508

The tension in any string must not exceed 500 lbs or be less than 150 lbs. The eight required frequencies (in hertz) are

261.6, 293.7, 329.6, 349.2, 392.0, 440.0, 493.9, 523.3

The fundamental frequency of a vibrating string is

$$f = \frac{1}{2L} \sqrt{\frac{F}{M}}$$

where L is the string length, F is the tension, and M is the mass per unit length.

Write a program that will choose the thinnest string meeting the above requirements, and compute the tension in the string for each of the eight required frequencies.

(*Check:* At 392 Hz, D = 0.0320 in. and F = 192 lbs)

7. **a.** In the maze game of chapter 5 section 5.5.3 you placed a mole 500 times at row 3, column 4 of the island and counted the number of times the mole escaped. Now, if the mole were clever, it could remember the route it took the first time it found the way out, so that from then on it would never drown! Write a program to do just that; i.e., keep track in an array of the sequence of steps leading to a safe exit and reject any sequence of steps leading to drowning. Sooner or later the mole will find a way out; then that path will be recorded in an array, and from that point on the mole will always escape.

b. Of course, the mole's first path to freedom may not be the shortest way out. Write a program to force the mole to select the shortest escape path out of the first 20 escape routes it finds. From then on the mole should remember that particular path. Print the mole's final exit path using a coordinate system, for example,

(3,4) (3,3) (4,3) ...

↓   ↘

row   column

8. Using the bar graph method discussed in section 6.4.2, produce abstract computer art as follows: Fill an array S of size 60 with random numbers between 1 and 100 and graph the corresponding bar graph for each element of S.

9. Using the bar graph method discussed in section 6.4.2:

a. write the code to graph the function $y = x^2$ and $y = 10 |\sin x|$ to obtain graph similar to the ones shown below. Scale to reasonable page width.

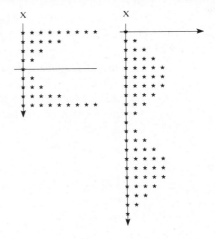

Recall that the vertical axis represents the independent variable (x) and the horizontal axis represents the dependent variable (y). Rotation of the graphs 90° counterclockwise will yield the usual positions of the x and y axes.

b. Repeat part *a* to graph the same functions as follows:

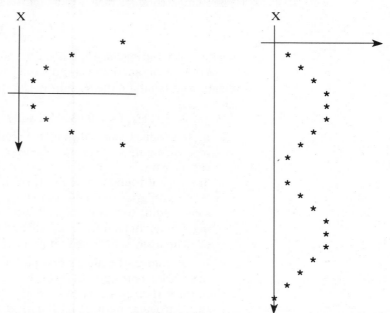

10. Load an array of size 8 with any digits from 1 to 9, then write the code to store these eight digits as a single number in memory location NUMBER.

For example, if A = | 3 | 5 | 2 | then NUMBER = 352.

A(1)   A(2)   A(3)

(*Hint:* NUMBER $= ((0 + A(1)*10) + A(2))*10 + A(3) = (3*10 + 5)*10 + 2 = 352$)

11. Read a three-digit number, N, and store each individual digit of N in three consecutive array locations. For example, if N = 193, then J(3) = 1, J(2) = 9, J(1) = 3.

(*Hint:* Divide N by 100 to get J(3) = 1, then divide N − J(3)*100 (93) by 10 to obtain J(2) = 9, and so on.)

12. Write a program to compute $n! = n(n - 1)*(n - 2)* \ldots *2*1$ for values of n that are so large that the result cannot fit in a single integer memory location. For example, 25! = 15,511,210,043,330,985,984,000,000. One way to solve the problem is to use an array to store the answer (each array element contains a digit), using one array memory location per digit. Thus 12! = 479,001,600 would be stored as follows (see exercise 10):

J(8)   J(6)   J(4)   J(2)
J(9) | J(7) | J(5) | J(3) | J(1)

| 4 | 7 | 9 | 0 | 0 | 1 | 6 | 0 | 0 |

To compute 13!, multiply each memory location by 13 (taking care to move the carries) to obtain:

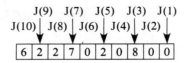

13. Two integer numbers containing a maximum of 18 digits each are contained on two data records. Write a program to compute the sum of these numbers.

14. A data record contains the degree n and the coefficients $a_n, a_{n-1}, \ldots a_1, a_0$ of a polynomial function: $f(x) = a_n x^n + a_{n-1} x^{n-1} + \ldots + a_1 x + a_0$. Write a program to produce a table of values of $f(x)$ for x varying from 0 to 5 in units of .5. Assume the maximum value of n is 10.

15. *Binary Search.* In this chapter we discussed a sequential method of searching for a particular entry in an array. Sequential searches are time-consuming in the sense that searching starts with the first entry and proceeds through successive entries. A shorter search is the binary search, which is essentially a guessing game. The binary search, however, requires that the array already be arranged in a particular order (ascending or descending). The array is split into two sections at the midpoint; then the desired entry is either in the right section or in the left section. If it is in the right section, that section is again split into two subsections, and the desired number is in one of the subsections. This splitting-in-half procedure is carried out until the desired entry has been found. The *binary search* divides the table in half, then in quarters, then in eighths, then in sixteenths, and so on.

A table with 4 entries	(2^2) requires at most 2 comparisons.
A table with anywhere from 5 to 8 entries	(2^3) requires at most 3 comparisons.
A table with anywhere from 9 to 16 entries	(2^4) requires at most 4 comparisons.
A table with anywhere from 17 to 32 entries	(2^5) requires at most 5 comparisons.
.	.
.	.
.	.
A table with up to 1024 entries	(2^{10}) requires at most 10 comparisons.

Hence, to search for a specific value in a table with 1024 entries (2^{10}) requires only 10 comparisons!

When the table is split into sections, the endpoints of a section are identified by two pointers, L (left) and R (right). Initially L = 0 and R = number of entries + 1. To see how the method works and how the pointers are moved, study the following example, where we want to determine whether 51 is in table A, which has 11 elements.

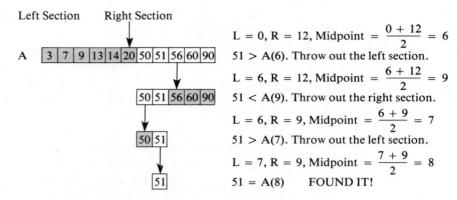

Left Section   Right Section

A

$L = 0$, $R = 12$, Midpoint $= \dfrac{0 + 12}{2} = 6$

$51 > A(6)$. Throw out the left section.

$L = 6$, $R = 12$, Midpoint $= \dfrac{6 + 12}{2} = 9$

$51 < A(9)$. Throw out the right section.

$L = 6$, $R = 9$, Midpoint $= \dfrac{6 + 9}{2} = 7$

$51 > A(7)$. Throw out the left section.

$L = 7$, $R = 9$, Midpoint $= \dfrac{7 + 9}{2} = 8$

$51 = A(8)$ FOUND IT!

Note that the number 51 was found in four moves, compared to the eight moves that would have been required if a sequential search had been performed.

Write a program to perform a binary search on an array containing no more than 50 elements.

6.7.4 Answers to Test Yourself

1. All can hold the same amount of information. The notion of "order" does not exist for locations X1, X2, and X3, i.e., no one can predict what variable follows X2. In contrast, we know that the item physically next to X(2) in memory is X(3).

2. **a.** F.   **b.** T except in DATA statement   **c.** F.   **d.** T.   **e.** F.
   f. F.   **g.** T   **h.** F.   **i.** T.   **j.** F.   **k.** T.
   l. T.   **m.** F.   **n.** T.   **o.**   T if X is character type.

3. **a.** 1   **b.** −4   **c.** 2.4   **d.** 0

   e. Invalid; G is not a character array.   **f.** Invalid; G(0) is invalid.

4. **a.** case 1:   FORMAT(3I2)   A = |1|2|3|0|0| B = |1|2|3|0|0|

      FORMAT (I2)   A = |1|4|7|8|0| B = |3|6|9|0|0|

   case 2:   FORMAT(12I2)   A = |1|2|0|0|0| B = |3|0|0|0|0|
      end of file encountered when trying to read A(2) the 2nd time around

   b. case 1:   FORMAT(I2)   A = |1|3|5|7|9| B = |2|4|6|8|10|

      FORMAT(3I2)   A = |1|1|0|3|3| B = |0|2|2|0|4|

   case 2:   FORMAT(12I2)   A = |1|3|5|7|9| B = |2|4|6|8|10|

   c. case 1:   FORMAT(I2)   A = |1|2|3|4|5| B = |6|0|7|0|8|

   case 2:   Read error format on some systems: too few digits on input record.

   d. case 1:   FORMAT(4I2)   A = |1|4|7|0|0| B = |8|0|-2|0|9|

   case 2:   FORMAT(12I2)   A = |1|0|0|0|0| B = |0|0|0|0|0|
      end of file encountered when trying to read B(1) for first time.

5. a. 5.   **b.** 18.   **c.** 4.   **d.** 12

6. a.
```
DO 1 I = 1,6,2
1 READ(5,5) A(I),A(I + 1)
```

   b.
```
DO 2 I = 2,9,4
2 READ(5,6)A(I),K(I),A(I + 2),K(I + 2)
```

7. a. (1.) Skip to the top of a new page, space down four lines (no printed output).

    (2.) 1   2
          3   4
          5

    (3.) 1   2   3   4   5

    (4.) 5 _ _ _ _ _ 1 _ _ 2 + 3   4
       ↳because of carriage control code +

   b. (1.) Invalid; mixed modes.

    (2.) _ _ 3 _ _ 1
          _ _ 3 _ _ 2
          _ _ 3 _ _ 3
          _ _ 3 _ _ 4

    (3.) 3 _ _ 1 _ _ 3 _ _ 2 _ _ 3
          3 _ _ 3 _ _ 4

   c. (1.) _ _ 2 . _ − 3 . _ _ 3 . _ _ 5 . _ _ 0 . _ _
          2 _ _ 2 . _ − 3 . _ _ 3 . _ _ 5 . _ _ 0 .

    (2.) Starting on a new page, 2nd line
          _ 2 . _ _ − 3 . _ _ 3 . _ _ 5 . _ _ 0 . _ 2
          _ 2 . _ _ − 3 . _ _ 3 . _ _ 5 . _ _ 0 . _ _

    (3.) 1
          _ 2 . _ − 3 . _ _ 3 . _ _ 5 . _ _ 0 .
    J cannot be described by an F format when the format is reused.

   d. (1.) _ 2 . _ _ − 3 . * * * 2 . 0 1 . 5
          _ − 3 . _ _ − 1 . 2 . 0 _ _ _

    (2.) _ 1 . 5
          _ − 3 . 2
          _ − 1 . 0
          _ 2 . 0
          _ 1 . 5
          _ − 3 . 2
          _ − 1 . 0
          _ 2 . 0

    (3.) 2 . − 3 . − 1 . 2 . 2 . − 3 . − 1 . 2 .

8. a. `5 FORMAT(5F1Ø.Ø/(1ØI8))`

   b. `5 FORMAT(1X,2F1Ø.Ø,I5)`

   c. `5 FORMAT(1X,3F1Ø.Ø/1ØØ(1X,1ØI6/),2X,F5.Ø,I3)`

9.

		1	2	3	4	5
a.	X	1.3	4.1	7.8	18.3	0.
b.	X	1.3	4.2	6.8		Y 1.9 3.3
c.	X	1.3		4.1		7.8
d.	X	1.3	4.2	6.8	1.9	Y 4.1 −2.3 6.
e.	X	1.3	6.8	3.3		Y 4.2 1.9 4.1
f.	X	1.3	4.2	6.8		Y 1.9 4.1 −2.3
g.	X	4.1	5.4	20.5	7.8	1.3
h.	X	1.3	6.8	−2.3	7.8	A = 2.1

10. a. Valid; 3 records.

   b. Valid; 5 records.

   c. Valid; 18 records.

   d. Invalid; possible problems with $K - J$ (execution time).

   e. Invalid; integer variable read with real format code (execution-time error).

   f. Valid; 30 records.

   g. Valid; 2 records.

   h. Valid; 5 records.

11.

```
a.    WRITE(6,5)(A(I),I = 1,1ØØ)              DO 1Ø I=1,1ØØ,2
      5 FORMAT(T1Ø,F5.Ø,1X,F5.Ø)            1Ø WRITE(6,5)A(I),A(I+1)

b.    WRITE(6,5)(A(I),A(I+5Ø),I=1,5Ø)         DO 1Ø I=1,5Ø
      5 FORMAT(T1Ø,F5.Ø,1X,F5.Ø)            1Ø WRITE(6,5)A(I),A(I+5Ø)

c.    WRITE(6,5)(I,A(1Ø1-I),I = 1,1ØØ)        DO 1Ø I=1,1ØØ
      5 FORMAT(T1Ø,I3,1X,F5.Ø)              1Ø WRITE(6,5)I,A(1Ø1-I)

d.    WRITE(6,5)(A(I),I = 2,1ØØ,2),(A(I),I = 1,1ØØ)
      5 FORMAT(5Ø(T1Ø,F5.Ø/)/(2X,1ØF5.Ø))
```

12.

```
   WRITE(6,5)(I,I = 1,12)
   5 FORMAT(T5,'POS LISTING:',(T2Ø,4I3))
```

13. a. Value of J is undefined; this could destroy a memory location and blow the program. Run time "invalid index" message possible.

   b. Value of J is undefined, but this cannot blow the program; the results may be meaningless. Run time "invalid index" message possible.

   c. Program may blow since values will be read into A(101), A(102), ..., A(110), which have not been reserved for the array A. Error message possible.

   d. The values initially read for A(2), A(3), A(4), and A(5) will be destroyed by successive values.

14. a.

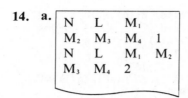

N	L	M_1	
M_2	M_3	M_4	1
N	L	M_1	M_2
M_3	M_4	2	

b.

Format 1

A	B	T_1
T_2	T_3	T_4
T_5		

Format 3

A	
B	T_1
T_2	T_3
T_4	T_5

Format 2

A	B	T_1
T_2		
T_3	T_4	T_5

c.

A_1	A_2
A_3	A_4
A_5	A_6
A_7	

15. The size of array A should not be declared in both the REAL and the DIMENSION statement.

The list of constants in the DATA statement should be real constants.

FORMAT 1 is omitted.

THEN X is a valid variable name!

.LT should be written as .LT.

X = 0 is incorrect in the last IF statement.

16.
```
        CHARACTER*9 SOCSEC(100),T
        READ*,T
        I = 1
      5 IF(I.LE.100 .AND. SOCSEC(I).NE.T)THEN
            I=I+1
            GO TO 5
        ENDIF
        IF(I .EQ. 101)THEN
            PRINT*, 'NO MATCH'
        ELSE
            PRINT*, 'MATCH'
        ENDIF
```

17.
```
        REAL A(20),B(30),C(51)
        READ(5,6,END=88)A,B,C
     88 ----
```

```
18.    INTEGER A(10),B(16),K(100)
       DATA K/100*0/
       READ(5,1)(A(I),I=1,10),B
       DO 5 I = 1,10
           DO 6 J = 1,16
               IF(A(I).EQ.B(J))K(A(I))=1
6      CONTINUE
5 CONTINUE
       L = 0
       DO 7 I = 1,100
           IF(K(I) .NE. 0)THEN
               PRINT*,I
               L = L+1
           ENDIF
7 CONTINUE
       PRINT*,'NUMBER EQUAL ITEMS=',L


19.    INTEGER A(20),K(20),NUMB(20),FREQ(20)
       DATA K/20*0/
       READ(5,1)A
       DO 5 I = 1,20
           K(A(I)) = K(A(I))+1
5 CONTINUE
       L = 0
       DO 6 I = 1,20
           IF(K(I) .NE. 0)THEN
               L = L+1
               NUMB(L) = I
               FREQ(L) = K(I)
           ENDIF
6 CONTINUE
       WRITE(6,8)(NUMB(I),I=1,L)
       WRITE(6,9)(FREQ(I),I=1,L)
8 FORMAT(' NUMBERS  ',20I4)
9 FORMAT(' FREQUENCY',20I4)
       STOP


20.    REAL A(10)
       READ(5,1)A
       DO 5 I = 1,9
           DO 6 J = I+1,10
               IF(A(I).EQ.A(J))GOTO9
6      CONTINUE
5 CONTINUE
       PRINT*,'NO EQUAL ENTRIES'
       STOP
9 PRINT*,'MATCH EXISTS'
       STOP
```

```
21.    REAL A(11)
       READ(5,9)(A(I),I=1,10),R
       I=1
   5   IF(I.LE.10 .AND. A(I).LE.R)THEN
           I=I+1
           GO TO 5
       ENDIF
       IF(I .EQ. 10) THEN
           A(11)=R
       ELSE
           DO 6 J = 11,I+1,-1
               A(J) = A(J-1)
   6       CONTINUE
           A(I) = R
       ENDIF
       STOP


22.    INTEGER K(10)
       DO 5 J = 1,12
           DO 6 I = 1,10
               K(I) = I*J
   6       CONTINUE
           WRITE(6,4)(I,J,K(I),I=1,10)
   5   CONTINUE
   4   FORMAT(10(I3,'X',I3,'=',I3,3X))
```

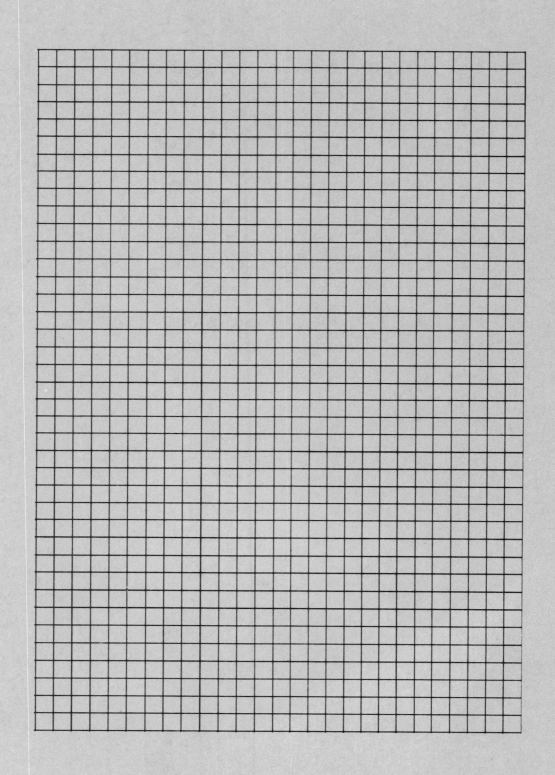

7 Two-Dimensional Arrays

7.1 Two-Dimensional Arrays

7.1.1 Background and Justification

Much of the information that we deal with in our everyday lives is arranged in rows and columns. In a movie house, in an airplane, or in a typical classroom, seats can be identified by their row and column positions. For some of us, looking up our taxes means reading a number at the intersection of an income level row and a number of dependents column. Chessboards and teachers' grade notebooks are also examples of two-dimensional tables or two-dimensional arrays.

The power of a two-dimensional array lies in its "lookup" procedure, which allows us to access any entry in the table directly, without searching through array entries. We access an array entry by specifying its row and column.

EXAMPLE 1

In the sales tax deduction table shown below, the deduction allowed a family with four children and an income of $8,000 to $8,999 is $117.

		Number of Children					
Income Table	1	2	3	4	5	6
$ 0,000.	35.	48.	49.	59.	59.	60.
$ 3,000.	44.	58.	61.	71.	73.	75.
$ 4,000.	51.	68.	72.	82.	85.	88.
$ 5,000.	58.	76.	82.	91.	97.	100.
$ 6,000.	64.	84.	91.	100.	107.	112.
$ 7,000.	70.	92.	100.	109.	117.	123.
$ 8,000. →	76.	99.	108.	117.	127.	133.
$ 9,000.	81.	106.	116.	124.	136.	143.
$10,000.	86.	112.	124.	131.	145.	153.
$11,000.	91.	118.	132.	138.	154.	163.
$12,000.	96.	124.	139.	145.	162.	172.
$13,000.	101.	130.	146.	151.	170.	181.
$14,000.	106.	136.	153.	157.	178.	190.
$15,000.	110.	141.	160.	163.	186.	198.
$16,000.	114.	146.	167.	169.	194.	206.
$17,000.	118.	151.	173.	175.	201.	214.
$18,000.	122.	156.	179.	181.	208.	222.
$19,000.	126.	161.	185.	186.	215.	230.

7th entry (pointing to $8,000 row, 76.)

Once the correct income entry has been located in the INCOME table (position 7 for $8,000), we simply look up the figure at the seventh row and fourth column of the table, i.e., we can use the number of children to identify the proper column directly (with no IF statements). This table is an example of a two-dimensional array consisting of 18 rows and 6 columns; entries in the table can be successively accessed by varying the row and/or column subscript.

EXAMPLE 2　　Consider the following class roster, where each horizontal line consists of a student name and three test scores.

	Test 1	Test 2	Test 3
Adams	78	44	94
Boring	58	66	84
Cattix	49	58	64
Stout	59	68	91

Here the data is physically arranged in rows and columns. The class roster is another example of a two-dimensional array from which it is easy to retrieve information. For example, to determine STOUT's score on the second test, we simply look up the entry found at the intersection of the fourth row and the second column. If we name the score array SCORE, then each array entry can be identified by the name of the array and its row and column. For example:

SCORE (4, 1) = 59 and SCORE (2, 3) = 84

Note that the first subscript always refers to the row, while the second subscript refers to the column.

EXAMPLE 3　　Mr. Spandex does his daily grocery shopping at four stores (he store-hops for bargains) and he records his daily purchases at the various stores as follows:

	Store 1	Store 2	Store 3	Store 4	Explanation
Day 1	10.00	20.00	10.50	40.45	On day 1 he spent $10 at store 1, $20 at store 2, ...
Day 2	0.00	15.00	20.00	35.55	On day 2 he spent $0 at store 1, $15 at store 2, ...
Day 3	10.90	31.65	30.78	12.64	
Day 4	0.00	0.00	9.87	5.50	
Day 5	21.35	32.56	3.75	1.98	On day 5 he spent $21.35 at store 1, $32.56 at store 2, ...

Over the weekend, Mr. Spandex likes to analyze his grocery expenses by asking such questions as:

1. How much did I spend on Monday, on Tuesday, ..., on Friday?

2. How much did I spend for the whole week at store 1, store 2, ..., store 4?

3. On which day did I spend the least? the most?

4. At which store(s) did I spend the least? the most?

5. Which store(s) did I not go to on a particular day?

6. What are my total weekly expenses?

7. What were my expenses for a given day?

8. What was the average amount spent that week at each of the stores?
...and his questions go on and on!

If the weekly data was stored in a two-dimensional array A, Mr. Spandex could find out what he spent on day 3 at store number 4 simply by typing the following instruction: WRITE(*,*) A(3,4).

The use of a two-dimensional array greatly simplifies the coding process, since a particular array element can be captured by specifying a value for days and stores. Similarly, columns or rows of array elements can be processed by fixing one subscript and letting the other vary from 1 to 4 (store) or 1 to 5 (day).

7.1.2 Programming Example

Let us write a program to read any three digits in the interval 0–9 (for example, 0, 1, and 2) and rewrite them in block form as:

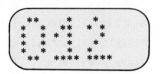

Note that each block digit can be treated as a one-dimensional array consisting of 6 character elements; thus, the digit 1 can be stored in block form in the array CHARACTER*4 ONE(6) as:

ONE(1) = [ ][ ][*][ ]
ONE(2) = [ ][*][*][ ]
ONE(3) = [*][ ][*][ ]
ONE(4) = [ ][ ][*][ ]
   :   :

To write the ONE digit block, we could use the following code:

```
      DO 5 I = 1,6
          WRITE(6,4) ONE(I)
 5    CONTINUE
 4    FORMAT(1X,A4)
```

To write the string of three block digits 3 2 1 would require the code

```
      DO 5 I = 1,6
          WRITE(6,4) THREE(I), TWO(I), ONE(I)
 5    CONTINUE
 4    FORMAT(1X,A4,1X,A4,1X,A4)
```

where THREE and TWO are arrays representing the block digits 3 and 2.

Given a random sequence of digits, how do we specify the list of arrays to be printed, that is, how do we establish a relationship between the single digits in the input and the digit blocks to be printed? For example, if we read the digits 9, 0, and 6, how do we tell the program to WRITE(6,4)NINE(I),ZERO(I),SIX(I) as I varies from 1 to 6?

Using a two-dimensional array provides a simple solution. As shown in Figure 7.1, we create a two-dimensional array BLOCK consisting of six rows and ten columns. The first column of BLOCK, which starts with BLOCK(1,0), represents the block digit 0; the second column, which starts with BLOCK(1,1), represents the block digit 1, and so forth. Thus if we want to write the sequence of block digits corresponding to 9, 0, and 6, we simply print the 9th, 0th, and 6th column elements of BLOCK from the first row down to the sixth row, one row per line. The array BLOCK thus establishes a direct relationship between the three single digits and their corresponding block images. For 9, 0, 6 the list of elements to be printed would be:

List of elements   *Selected columns of BLOCK array*

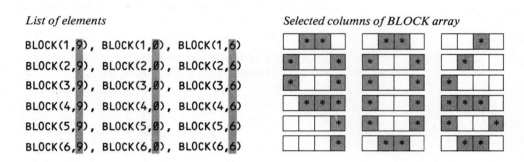

BLOCK(1,9), BLOCK(1,0), BLOCK(1,6)

BLOCK(2,9), BLOCK(2,0), BLOCK(2,6)

BLOCK(3,9), BLOCK(3,0), BLOCK(3,6)

BLOCK(4,9), BLOCK(4,0), BLOCK(4,6)

BLOCK(5,9), BLOCK(5,0), BLOCK(5,6)

BLOCK(6,9), BLOCK(6,0), BLOCK(6,6)

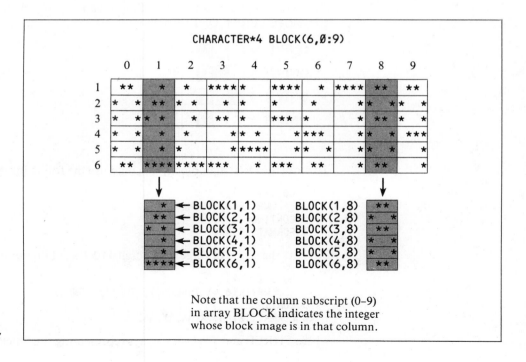

FIGURE 7.1
BLOCK DIGIT DIAGRAMS

```
 1: **BLOCK:   2-DIMENSIONAL ARRAY CONTAINING DIGITS Ø-9 IN BLOCK FORM
 2: **         EACH DIGIT IS A 6 BY 4 DOT MATRIX
 3: **DIGIT:   DIGITS TO BE EXPANDED INTO BLOCK FORM
 4: **N:       NUMBER OF DIGITS TO BE BLOWN UP
 5: **
 6:            CHARACTER*4 BLOCK(6,Ø:9)
 7:            PARAMETER(N=3)
 8:            INTEGER DIGIT(N)
 9:            OPEN(5,FILE='DIGIT.DAT')
10: **         READ THE BLOCK CHARACTERS Ø THRU 9
11: **         INTO THE 2-DIMENSIONAL ARRAY BLOCK
12:            DO 5 I = 1, 6
13:               READ(5,6)(BLOCK(I,J),J=Ø,9)
14: 5          CONTINUE
15: **         READ THE DIGITS TO BE MAGNIFIED
16:            READ(*,7)(DIGIT(I),I=1,N)
17: **         TRANSLATE AND WRITE THE DIGITS JUST READ
18: **         INTO CORRESPONDING BLOCK CHARACTERS
19:            DO 8 I = 1, 6
20:               WRITE(6,10)(BLOCK(I,DIGIT(J)),J=1,N)
21: 8          CONTINUE
22:            STOP
23: 7          FORMAT(3I1)
24: 6          FORMAT(10A4)
25: 10         FORMAT(1X,3(A4,1X))
26:            END
```

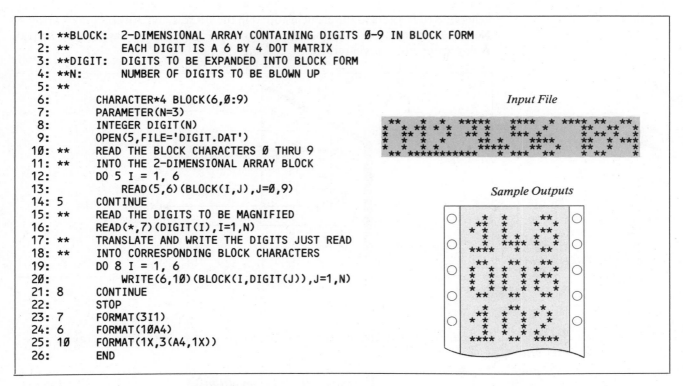

Input File

Sample Outputs

FIGURE 7.2
A DIGIT ENHANCEMENT PROCESS

To simplify matters further, the three digits can be read into a one-dimensional array DIGIT. If the digits 9, 0, and 6 are read, DIGIT(1) = 9, DIGIT(2) = 0, and DIGIT(3) = 6, and the corresponding sequence of block elements to be printed is:

BLOCK(I,DIGIT(1)), BLOCK(I,DIGIT(2)), BLOCK(I,DIGIT(3))   as I varies from 1 to 6

BLOCK(I,9)   BLOCK(I,Ø)   BLOCK(I,6)

The program to solve this problem is shown in Figure 7.2. Note how the block digits are read into array BLOCK at line 13, one row at a time as J varies from 0 through 9.

7.2 FORTRAN STATEMENTS

7.2.1 Two-Dimensional Arrays

In chapter 6 we discussed one-dimensional or linear arrays, where only one subscript is needed to address an element of the array. With two-dimensional tables or arrays, we address a particular array element by specifying the row and the column. Thus, the element in the second row and third column of array A is addressed as A(2,3). In general, A(I,J) refers to the element found in the Ith row and Jth column of array A. Note the comma separating the two subscripts. Figure 7.3 displays a 3 by 3 array. Analyze the subscripts carefully.

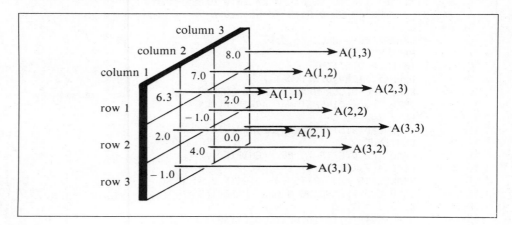

FIGURE 7.3
*A TWO-DIMENSIONAL
ARRAY*

7.2.2 *Array Declaration Statements and Subscripts*

The general form of the declaration statement for a two-dimensional array is:

$$
\begin{Bmatrix} \text{DIMENSION} \\ \text{Type statement} \end{Bmatrix}
\begin{cases}
name_1 \; (ll,ul) \; [,name_2(ll,ul)] \; \ldots & \text{format-1} \\[2ex]
name_1 \; ([ll:]ul,[ll:]ul) \; [,name_2([ll:]ul,[ll:]ul) \ldots]) & \text{format-2}
\end{cases}
$$

where $name_1$, $name_2$ are names of the various arrays;
ll and ul are lower and upper subscript limits as described in section 6.2.1. The first subscript refers to the row subscript, while the second subscript refers to the column subscript.

Examples of two-dimensional array declarations are shown in Figure 7.4.

Subscript expressions for two-dimensional arrays follow the same rules as subscripts for one-dimensional arrays. The following references to a two-dimensional array are valid:

T(3*X,I + 2)   If X = 1.4 and I = −1, then we have T(4,1).
B(10/L,J*2)   If L = 3 and J = 1, then we have B(3,2).
C(SQRT(X),X**2)   If X = 9, then we have C(3,81).
A(− 3:I + 1,2*K:I) If I = 6 and K = 2, we have A(− 3:7,4:6)

In these examples, the subscript expressions are first evaluated and then truncated to their integer values. Note that functions *can* be part of subscript expressions. As in the case of one-dimensional arrays, some FORTRAN versions may restrict subscript expressions to integer expressions.

Declaration	Subscript Range	Memory Representation	Number of Elements
1. INTEGER CLASS(3,2)	row {1, 2, 3} col {1, 2}	CLASS(1,2) ... CLASS(3,1)	6
2. REAL X(-2:1,0:4)	row {-2, -1, 0, 1} col {0, 1, 2, 3, 4}	X(-2,4) ... X(0,0)	20
3. CHARACTER*3 L(2,3)	row {1, 2} col {1, 2, 3}	JOE SUE JIM L(1,2) NIK MAT TIM L(2,3)	6

FIGURE 7.4
EXAMPLES OF ARRAY DECLARATIONS

7.2.3 Do It Now

Consider the following arrays A and B:

A

1.	-2.	.5	3.
3.	0.	0.	-1.
2.	1.	5.	6.
3.	1.	0.	1.

B

10.	5.
0.	6.
-1.	.5

1. Determine the following values:
   a. A(3,4) = ?
   b. A(2,3) + B(1,2) = ?
   c. A(3,2) * A(4,3) = ?
   d. B(2,1) + B(2,2) = ?
   e. 1/(A(4,4)*2) + B(3,1) = ?

2. List the variable names (not the values) for the following:
   a. the diagonal elements of A
   b. the 2d row of B
   c. the 3d column of A

3. If I = 2, J = 4, what values will be printed by the following codes?

a. `PRINT*,A(J,I)`

b. `PRINT*,B(I + 1,2)`

c.
```
   S = Ø.Ø
   DO 5 K = 1,3
      S = S + A(I,K)
 5 CONTINUE
   PRINT*,S
```

d.
```
   DO 5 L = 1,4
      M = 5 - L
      PRINT*,A(M,J)
 5 CONTINUE
```

e.
```
   DO 5 L = 1,2
      PRINT*, B(L,L)
 5 CONTINUE
```

Answers

1. a. 6.   **b.** 5.   **c.** 0.   **d.** 6.   **e.** -0.50

2. a. A(1,1), A(2,2), A(3,3), A(4,4)

   b. B(2,1), B(2,2)

   c. A(1,3), A(2,3), A(3,3), A(4,3)

3. a. 1.   **b.** 0.5   **c.** 3.   **d.** 1., 6., -1., 3.   **e.** 10., 6.

7.2.4 Processing Two-Dimensional Arrays

Two-dimensional arrays can be processed in essentially the same way as one-dimensional arrays, except that an additional subscript must be used. In general, this means that we will need two loops: one to control the rows and one to control the columns. The order of these loops, i.e., which one is the inner one, is generally immaterial, since a table can be processed in row fashion or in column fashion. The following examples illustrate some common procedures.

EXAMPLE 1   Initializing all elements of an array to 0

```
REAL A(1Ø,6), B(1Ø,6)      REAL A(1Ø,6), B(1Ø,6)
DO 6 I = 1,1Ø              DO 6 J = 1,6
   DO 5 J = 1,6               DO 5 I = 1,1Ø
      A(I,J)=Ø.Ø                 A(I,J)=Ø.Ø
      B(I,J)=Ø.Ø                 B(I,J)=Ø.Ø
6    CONTINUE             5    CONTINUE
5 CONTINUE                6 CONTINUE
```

The elements are zeroed out   The elements are zeroed out
in row fashion.   in column fashion.

The DATA statement could also be used to initialize two-dimensional arrays as follows:

```
INTEGER B(-2:4,8)          There are 7 × 8 = 56 elements in array B
REAL A(1Ø,6)
DATA A,B/6Ø*Ø.Ø,56*Ø/
```

EXAMPLE 2   Array Addition

We would like to add the two arrays

A =
1	2	3
2	1	4

and array   B =
−1	2	0
1	3	4

to obtain another array C such that each element of C is equal to the sum of the corresponding elements of A and B, i.e.

C =
1 + (−1)	2 + 2	3 + 0
2 + 1	1 + 3	4 + 4

or   C =
0	4	3
3	4	8

In general, we want $C(I,J) = A(I,J) + B(I,J)$ as I goes from 1 to 2 and as J goes from 1 to 3:

```
      INTEGER A(2,3),B(2,3),C(2,3)
      DO 5 I = 1, 2                              DO 6 J = 1, 3
          DO 6 J = 1, 3          or                  DO 5 I = 1, 2
              C(I,J)=A(I,J)+B(I,J)                        C(I,J)=A(I,J)+B(I,J)
      6     CONTINUE                             5     CONTINUE
      5 CONTINUE                                 6 CONTINUE
```

EXAMPLE 3   Array Search

Suppose we are to identify the row and column position of the largest number in array A. To start the search process, we assume the largest number is at row R = 1 and column C = 1. We then compare A(R,C) with the entries of the array, moving successively along rows from one to the next (we could also move along columns). Whenever we find an entry larger than A(R,C), we reset R and C to the row and column position of the larger number just found:

```
      INTEGER ROW,COL
      REAL A(10,15),MAX
      ROW = 1
      COL = 1
      MAX = A(1,1)
      DO 5 I = 1,10
         DO 6 J = 1,15
            IF(MAX .LT. A(I,J))THEN
                ROW = I
                COL = J
                MAX = A(I,J)
            ENDIF
      6     CONTINUE
      5 CONTINUE
```

Assume the largest number is at row 1 and column 1 (subject to later change, of course).

Determine if MAX is still largest. Since MAX is no longer the largest (A(I,J) is larger), reset ROW and COL to the location of the current largest number (A(I,J)).

EXAMPLE 4 Row Summation and Column Interchange

Given an array A of size 10 by 17, write the code to:

1. Add all the entries of the Nth row of array A, where N is accepted from input.
2. Interchange column 3 with column 17.

The row sum is $SUM = A(N,1) + A(N,2) + A(N,3) + \ldots + A(N,16) + A(N,17)$; the row index is fixed to N, while the column index varies from 1 to 17.

The interchange procedure can be accomplished by successively moving each element of column 3 into a temporary location, TEMP, then moving the corresponding element of column 17 into the vacated column 3 position, and finally moving the saved value in TEMP into the corresponding location of column 17, as shown below. If no temporary location were used, the elements of column 3 would be destroyed by the statement $A(I,3) = A(I,17)$, as I ranges from 1 to 10.

The code to perform the sum and the interchange procedure is:

```
REAL A(10,17)
   :
   :
READ(5,1)N
SUM = 0.0
DO 20 J = 1,17
     SUM = SUM+A(N,J)
20 CONTINUE
   DO 30 I = 1,10
       TEMP = A(I,3)
       A(I,3) = A(I,17)
       A(I,17) = TEMP
30 CONTINUE
 1 FORMAT(I2)
```

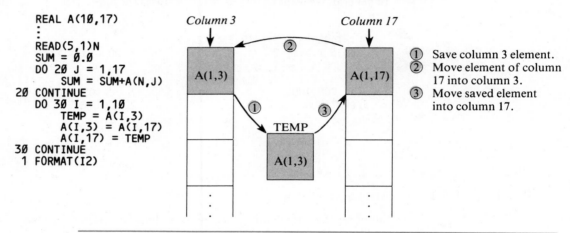

① Save column 3 element.
② Move element of column 17 into column 3.
③ Move saved element into column 17.

EXAMPLE 5 Row Summation for an Entire Array

Given the array A, shown below, we would like to compute the sum of the elements of the first row and store that sum in S(1), compute the sum of the elements of the second row and store it in S(2), and so forth.

A				S		Compute sum of each row
1	4	7		12		$S(1) = 1 + 4 + 7$
2	5	8		15		$S(2) = 2 + 5 + 8$
3	6	9		18		$S(3) = 3 + 6 + 9$

Two methods are shown:

Row Method. The sum of each row can be computed by fixing the row index I of A to 1 and varying the column index from 1 to 3, and repeating the same process for I equal to 2 and 3.

```
      INTEGER S(3),A(3,3)
      DATA S/3*0/              Initialize S(1), S(2) and S(3) to zeroes.
      DO 5 I = 1,3
         DO 6 J = 1,3       I = 1  S(1) = S(1)+A(1,1)+A(1,2)+A(1,3) = 1+4+7 = 12
            S(I)=S(I)+A(I,J) I = 2  S(2) = S(2)+A(2,1)+A(2,2)+A(2,3) = 2+5+8 = 15
    6    CONTINUE            I = 3  S(3) = (S3)+A(3,1)+A(3,2)+A(3,3) = 3+6+9 = 18
    5 CONTINUE
```

Column Method. The same results can be obtained, in a less apparent way, if we interchange the two DO loops as follows:

```
      DATA S/3*0/          J = 1                 J = 2                  J = 3
      DO 6 J = 1,3
         DO 5 I = 1,3    S₁ = A₁₁            S₁ = A₁₁ + A₁₂        S₁ = A₁₁ + A₁₂ + A₁₃
            S(I)=S(I)+A(I,J) S₂ = A₂₁        S₂ = A₂₁ + A₂₂        S₂ = A₂₁ + A₂₂ + A₂₃
    5    CONTINUE        S₃ = A₃₁            S₃ = A₃₁ + A₃₂        S₃ = A₃₁ + A₃₂ + A₃₃
    6 CONTINUE
```

7.2.5 Do It Now

1. What values will be stored in array X after each of the following codes is executed?

a.
```
      INTEGER X(3,4)
      DO 5 I = 1,3
         DO 6 J = 1,4
            X(I,J) = I*J
    6    CONTINUE
    5 CONTINUE
```

b.
```
      INTEGER X(3,4)
      L = 1
      DO 5 I = 1,4
         DO 6 J = 1,3
            X(J,I) = L
            L = L+1
    6    CONTINUE
    5 CONTINUE
```

2. If A is a table of size 10 by 6, write the code to initialize the first column of A with 1's, the second column with 2's, the third column with 3's, ..., and column 6 with 6's.

3. Write the code to load a 10 by 10 array with 100 random numbers between 0 and 1, *then* compute the average of all the entries of the array. What would you expect the answer to be?

4. Write the code to input a value for C and print the largest value in column C of the array A(3,7).

5. Given an array A of size 6 by 6, write the code to compute the sum of the elements of its first diagonal and the sum of the elements of its second diagonal. These diagonals are defined as follows:

1st diagonal   2d diagonal

Answers

1. a.

1	2	3	4
2	4	6	8
3	6	9	12

X:

b.

1	4	7	10
2	5	8	11
3	6	9	12

X:

2.
```
    INTEGER A(10,6)
    DO 5 J = 1,6
        DO 6 I = 1,10
            A(I,J) = J
6       CONTINUE
5   CONTINUE
```

3.
```
    REAL A(10,10)
    DO 5 I = 1,10
        DO 5 J = 1,10
            A(I,J) = RAND(1)
5   CONTINUE
    SUM = 0.
    DO 6 I = 1,10
        DO 4 J = 1,10
            SUM = SUM + A(I,J)
4       CONTINUE
6   CONTINUE
    PRINT*,SUM/100.0
```
The answer should be close to 0.5.

4.
```
    INTEGER A(3,7),C
    READ*,C
    L = A(1,C)
    DO 5 I = 2,3
        IF(L.LT.A(I,C))L=A(I,C)
5   CONTINUE
    PRINT*,L
```

5.
```
    REAL A(6,6)
    D1 = 0.0
    D2 = 0.0
    DO 5 I = 1,6
        D1 = D1 + A(I,I)
        D2 = D2 + A(I,7-I)
5   CONTINUE
    PRINT*,D1, D2
```

7.2.6 Input and Output of Two-Dimensional Arrays

In the example in section 7.1.2 we loaded a two-dimensional array with data arranged in row fashion as follows:

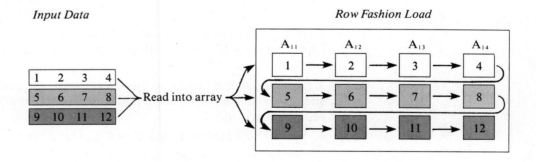

Input Data   *Row Fashion Load*

It is, of course, also possible to load a two-dimensional array in column fashion *if* the data file specifies a sequence of entries that reflect a column arrangement. For example, to load the above array with the same numbers, but in column fashion, we must have the following input file:

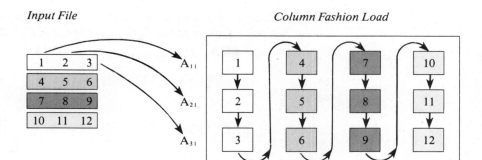

Input File   Column Fashion Load

Various methods of loading an array in row or column fashion are illustrated in Figure 7.5. Study this figure carefully; options 3 and 4 are probably the methods used most frequently. Note that options 4 and 5 do not necessarily require that the input

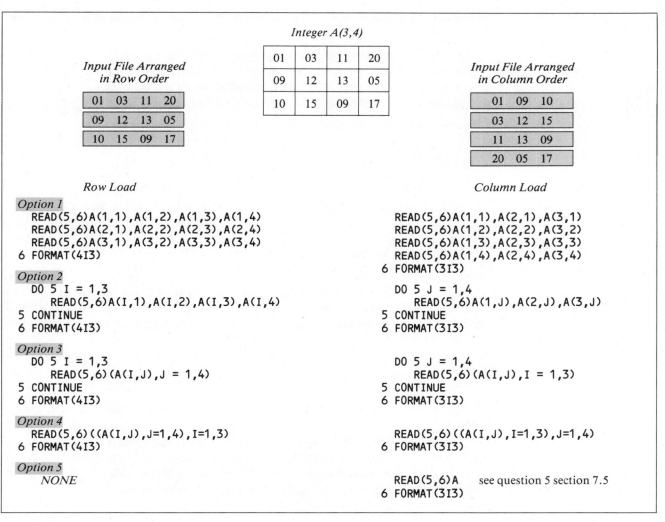

Integer A(3,4)

01	03	11	20
09	12	13	05
10	15	09	17

Input File Arranged
in Row Order

```
01  03  11  20
09  12  13  05
10  15  09  17
```

Input File Arranged
in Column Order

```
01  09  10
03  12  15
11  13  09
20  05  17
```

Row Load

Option 1
```
  READ(5,6)A(1,1),A(1,2),A(1,3),A(1,4)
  READ(5,6)A(2,1),A(2,2),A(2,3),A(2,4)
  READ(5,6)A(3,1),A(3,2),A(3,3),A(3,4)
6 FORMAT(4I3)
```

Option 2
```
  DO 5 I = 1,3
     READ(5,6)A(I,1),A(I,2),A(I,3),A(I,4)
5 CONTINUE
6 FORMAT(4I3)
```

Option 3
```
  DO 5 I = 1,3
     READ(5,6)(A(I,J),J = 1,4)
5 CONTINUE
6 FORMAT(4I3)
```

Option 4
```
  READ(5,6)((A(I,J),J=1,4),I=1,3)
6 FORMAT(4I3)
```

Option 5
```
     NONE
```

Column Load

```
  READ(5,6)A(1,1),A(2,1),A(3,1)
  READ(5,6)A(1,2),A(2,2),A(3,2)
  READ(5,6)A(1,3),A(2,3),A(3,3)
  READ(5,6)A(1,4),A(2,4),A(3,4)
6 FORMAT(3I3)
```

```
  DO 5 J = 1,4
     READ(5,6)A(1,J),A(2,J),A(3,J)
5 CONTINUE
6 FORMAT(3I3)
```

```
  DO 5 J = 1,4
     READ(5,6)(A(I,J),I = 1,3)
5 CONTINUE
6 FORMAT(3I3)
```

```
  READ(5,6)((A(I,J),I=1,3),J=1,4)
6 FORMAT(3I3)
```

```
  READ(5,6)A     see question 5 section 7.5
6 FORMAT(3I3)
```

FIGURE 7.5
VARIOUS METHODS OF LOADING A TWO-DIMENSIONAL ARRAY

data be arranged as shown in Figure 7.5. The input data could also be recorded on just one record in row or column sequence and be read into array A as follows:

Input Record

Row order
(option 4)

```
01 03 11 20 09 12 13 05 10 15 09 17    READ(5,6)((A(I,J),J=1,4),I=1,3)
                                       6 FORMAT(12I3)
```

Column order
(option 4, 5)

```
01 09 10 03 12 15 11 13 09 20 05 17   {READ(5,6)((A(I,J),I=1,3),J=1,4)
                                      {READ(5,6)A
                                      6 FORMAT(12I3)
```

Note the simple method in option 5 for loading an array when the data file is organized in column sequence. READ(5,6)A is equivalent to READ(5,6)((A(I,J), I = 1,3),J = 1,4) if the array A is declared as INTEGER A(3,4).

Consider the following examples of array input/output.

EXAMPLE 1   Assume three arrays A, B, and C are to be read row-wise, according to the data layout shown below:

record #1   A(1,1) A(1,2) A(1,3) B(1,1) B(1,2) B(1,3) B(1,4) C(1)
record #2   A(2,1) A(2,2) A(2,3) B(2,1) B(2,2) B(2,3) B(2,4) C(2)
record #3   A(3,1) A(3,2) A(3,3) B(3,1) B(3,2) B(3,3) B(3,4) C(3)
record #4   A(4,1) A(4,2) A(4,3) B(4,1) B(4,2) B(4,3) B(4,4) C(4)

The implied DO list to load these arrays might be

```
1 FORMAT(8F5.0)
  READ(5,1)((A(I,J),J=1,3),(B(I,K),K=1,4),C(I),I=1,4)
```

This can be interpreted as

When I = 1, read A(1,J) as J = 1 to 3, then B(1,K) as K = 1,4 and C(1)

or

read A(1,1), A(1,2), A(1,3), B(1,1),...,B(1,4), C(1)

then repeat the process for I = 2, 3, and 4.

Altogether, three elements of A, four elements of B, and one element of C will be read from each record as I ranges from 1 to 4. Hence (3 + 4 + 1)·4 = 32 elements will be read. The list of variables contains 32 elements, and the format specifies eight values per record, hence four records will be read.

EXAMPLE 2   In this example, the array B is to be read column-wise and the elements of C are reversed

record #1   A(1,1) A(1,2) A(1,3) B(1,1) B(2,1) B(3,1) B(4,1) C(4)
record #2   A(2,1) A(2,2) A(2,3) B(1,2) B(2,2) B(3,2) B(4,2) C(3)
record #3   A(3,1) A(3,2) A(3,3) B(1,3) B(2,3) B(3,3) B(4,3) C(2)
record #4   A(4,1) A(4,2) A(4,3) B(1,4) B(2,4) B(3,4) B(4,4) C(1)

The following code might be used to read this data:

```
  READ(5,1)((A(I,J),J=1,3),(B(K,I),K=1,4),C(5-I),I=1,4)
1 FORMAT(8F5.0)
```

If the preceding method is too confusing, a combination of a DO loop and an implied DO list can be used as follows:

```
      DO 10 I = 1,4
          READ(5,1) (A(I,J),J=1,3), (B(K,I),K=1,4), C(5-I)
   10 CONTINUE
```

EXAMPLE 3   Two-dimensional arrays are very useful when printing tables of numbers that require some form of column/row identification and headings. Consider example 3 in section 7.1.1, where A is an "expense" array; we would like to print the input data in the following form:

```
DAY 1    10.00    20.00    10.50    40.45
DAY 2     0.00    15.00    20.00    35.55
DAY 3    10.90    31.65    30.78    12.64
DAY 4     0.00     0.00     9.87     5.50
DAY 5    21.35    32.56     3.75     1.98
```

The following code can be used to generate this output:

Day   Store

```
      WRITE(6,1)(I,(A(I,J),J=1,4),I=1,5)
    1 FORMAT(8X,'DAY',I2,5X,4F11.2)
```

The DO list generates $1,A_{11},A_{12},A_{13},A_{14},2,A_{21},A_{22},A_{23},A_{24},3,\ldots,5, A_{51},A_{52},A_{53},A_{54}$ on 5 lines.

We could also generate the more sophisticated output

```
                  SHOPPING ANALYSIS
            STORE 1    STORE 2    STORE 3    STORE 4

DAY 1        10.00      20.00      10.50      40.45
DAY 2         0.00      15.00      20.00      35.55
DAY 3        10.90      31.65      30.78      12.64
DAY 4         0.00       0.00       9.87       5.50
DAY 5        21.35      32.56       3.75       1.98
```

with just one WRITE statement:

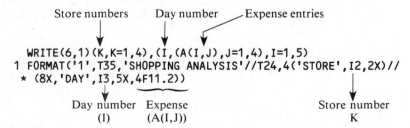

```
      WRITE(6,1)(K,K=1,4),(I,(A(I,J),J=1,4),I=1,5)
    1 FORMAT('1',T35,'SHOPPING ANALYSIS'//T24,4('STORE',I2,2X)//
     * (8X,'DAY',I3,5X,4F11.2))
```

However, the beginning programmer may prefer to use two or three separate WRITE statements.

EXAMPLE 4   Professor X's grade roster file (100 records maximum) contains the following information:

Name	Number test scores (N ≤ 4)	Test scores (max of 4)			
ANTON	3	080	074	068	
BEVIS	1	070			
HUGHES	4	020	030	060	080
TERN	2	074	086		
WATS	3	080	060	020	

Input File

Write the code to read the students' names and number of tests into one-dimensional arrays NAME and NO and the grades into a two-dimensional array GRADES (to be processed later on) producing the following report as the input file is read.

Arrays in Memory

Name

ANTON
BEVIS
HUGHES
TERN
WATS
⋮

No

3
1
4
2
3
⋮

Grades

80	74	68	
70			
20	30	60	80
74	86		
80	60	20	
⋮	⋮	⋮	⋮

Report

NAME	TESTS	TEST 1	TEST 2	TEST 3	TEST 4
ANTON	3	80	74	68	
BEVIS	1	70			
HUGHES	4	20	30	60	80
TERN	2	74	86		
WATS	3	80	60	20	
⋮	⋮	⋮	⋮	⋮	⋮

The following code could be used:

```
      CHARACTER*8  NAME(100)
      INTEGER GRADES(101,4),NO(100),N
      WRITE(6,1)(I,I=1,4)
      DO 5 I = 1,100
         READ(5,8,END=88)NAME(I),N,(GRADES(I,J),J=1,N)
         WRITE(6,2)NAME(I),N,(GRADES(I,J),J=1,N)
         NO(I) = N
    5 CONTINUE
   88 STOP
    1 FORMAT(' NAME',5X,'TESTS',2X,4('TEST',1X,I1,2X))
    2 FORMAT(1X,A8,3X,I1,5X,4(I3,5X))
    8 FORMAT(A8,4X,I1,4X,4(I3,2X))
      END
```

7.2.7 Do It Now

Given the data file shown below, specify the contents of the array INTEGER A(3,4) after carrying out the following input instructions. Assume that array A initially is set to 0's.

Input File
```
01020304  ◄— 1st Record
05060708
09101112
```

1. a.
```
    DO 5 I = 1,3
  5     READ(5,6)(A(I,J),J = 1,3)
  6 FORMAT(4I2)
```

b.
```
    DO 5 I = 1,3
  5     READ(5,6)(A(J,I),J = 1,3)
  6 FORMAT(4I2)
```

c.
```
    READ(5,6)((A(I,I),J=1,4),I=1,3)
  6 FORMAT(4I2)
```

d.
```
    READ(5,6)A
  6 FORMAT(4I2)
```

2. Given the arrays REAL A(3,4) and INTEGER B(3,4), write the necessary WRITE instruction and FORMAT statement to produce each of the following output arrangements. (Use only one WRITE statement for each part.)

    a. First row of A on one line, first row of B on next line, ... (continuing to alternate in this way).

    b. All entries of A in row fashion followed by all entries of B in row fashion, all on one line.

    c. All entries of A in row fashion on one line, followed by all entries of B in row fashion on the next line.

    d. $A_{11} B_{11} A_{12} B_{12} A_{13} B_{13} \ldots A_{34} B_{34}$, all on just one line.

    e. First column of A on first line, second column of A on second line, ..., fourth column of A on fourth line, followed by first column of B on fifth line, second column of B on sixth line, ...

    f. First row of A on line 1, second row of A on line 2, third row of A on line 3, first row of B on line 4, second row of B on line 5, ...

    g. All entries of A in column fashion, one entry per line, followed by all entries of B in column fashion, one entry per line.

3. Write the code to produce the following report for Professor X (see example 4 in section 7.2.6). Read the names and grades in the same arrays as given in the example.

NAME	TESTS	TEST 1	TEST 2	TEST 3	TEST 4	AVERAGE
ANTON	3	80	74	68		74.0
BEVIS	1	70				70.0
HUGHES	4	20	30	60	80	47.5
TERN	2	74	86			80.0
WATS	3	80	60	20		53.3
AVERAGE		64.8	62.5	49.3	80.0	

Input File
```
ANTON   3080074068
BEVIS   1070
HUGHES  4020030060080
TERN    2074086
WATS    3080060020
```

Answers

1. a.
```
 1   2   3  0
 5   6   7  0
 9  10  11  0
```

b.
```
 1   5   9  0
 2   6  10  0
 3   7  11  0
```

c.
```
 4   0   0  0
 0   8   0  0
 0   0  12  0
```

d.
```
 1   4   7  10
 2   5   8  11
 3   6   9  12
```

2. **a.**
```
WRITE(6,6)((A(I,J),J = 1,4),(B(I,J),J = 1,4),I = 1,3)
6 FORMAT(1X,4F6.0/1X, 4I6)
```

b.
```
WRITE(6,6)((A(I,J),J=1,4),I=1,3),((B(I,J),J=1,4),I=1,3)
6 FORMAT(1X,12F6.0,2X,12I3)
```

c. Same WRITE statement as part b, with
```
6 FORMAT(1X,12F6.0/1X,12I3)
```

d.
```
WRITE(6,6)((A(I,J),B(I,J),J = 1,4),I = 1,3)
6 FORMAT(1X,12(F6.0,1X,I3))
```

e.
```
WRITE(6,6)A,B
6 FORMAT(4(1X,3F6.0/),(1X,3I3))
```

f. Same WRITE statement as part b with
```
6 FORMAT(3(1X,4F6.0/),(1X,4I3))
```

g.
```
WRITE(6,6)A,B
6 FORMAT(12(1X,F6.0/),(1X,I3))
```

3.

```
C COLNO(4):  RECORDS NUMBER OF ENTRIES IN EACH COLUMN
C            I.E., COLNO(1) = 5 AND COLNO(4) = 1 IN THIS EXAMPLE
C COLSUM(4): RECORDS THE SUM OF ENTRIES OF EACH COLUMN
C            I.E., COLSUM(1) = 324  AND COLSUM(4) = 80 IN THIS EXAMPLE
C TESTAV(4): COMPUTES THE AVERAGES OF EACH COLUMN
C            I.E., TESTAV(1) = 324/5 =64.8 AND TESTAV(4) = 80/1 = 80
C
      REAL TESTAV(4),AVER,SUM
      CHARACTER*8 NAME(100)
      INTEGER GRADES(101,4),N,COLNO(4),COLSUM(4)
      DATA COLNO,COLSUM/8*0/
      WRITE(6,1)(I,I=1,4)
      DO 5 I = 1,100
         READ(5,8,END=88)NAME(I),N,(GRADES (I,J),J=1,N)
         WRITE(6,2)NAME(I),N,(GRADES(I,J),J=1,N)
         SUM = 0.0
         DO 6 J = 1, N
            SUM = SUM + GRADES(I,J)
            COLSUM(J) = COLSUM(J)+GRADES(I,J)
            COLNO(J)  = COLNO(J) + 1
6        CONTINUE
      AVER = SUM/N
      WRITE(6,3)AVER
5     CONTINUE
88    DO 7 I = 1, 4
         IF(COLNO(I) .EQ. 0)GO TO 12
         L = I
         TESTAV(I)=COLSUM(I)/(REAL(COLNO(I)))
7     CONTINUE
12    WRITE(6,4)(TESTAV(I),I=1,L)
      STOP
1     FORMAT(' ',NAME',5X,'TESTS',2X,4('TEST',1X,I1,2X),2X,'AVERAGE'/)
2     FORMAT(1X,A8,3X,I1,5X,4(I3,5X))
3     FORMAT('+',50X,F5.1)
4     FORMAT('0','AVERAGE',10X,4(F5.1,3X))
8     FORMAT(A8,I1,4I3)
      END
```

Input File

Name	N	Grades
ANTON	3	080074068
BEVIS	1	070
HUGHES	4	020030060080
TERN	2	074086
WATS	3	080060020

Compute sum of each row.
Accumulate four separate column sums.
Count number of entries in each of the four columns.
Compute average of scores for each row.

If a column contains no entries, exit from loop.
Count number of averages to be printed.
Compute average of each column.

Write out the column averages.

7.3 PROGRAMMING EXAMPLES

7.3.1 Programming Example

Recall Mr. Spandex (section 7.1.1), who does his daily grocery shopping at four stores and records his daily purchases in table form:

Day	Store			
	1	2	3	4
1	10.00	20.00	10.50	40.45
2	0.00	15.00	20.00	35.55
3	10.90	31.65	30.78	12.64
4	0.00	0.00	9.87	5.50
5	21.35	32.56	3.75	1.98

Let us write a program to help Mr. Spandex:

1. Load the expense table into a 5 by 4 array called A (5 rows and 4 columns).
2. Print the total expenses for each day.
3. Print the amount he spent on any given day at any given store.

Task 1 Loading the array A

To load the various entries into the array A, we first record the entries in row sequence on five input records, simulating the original data arrangement:

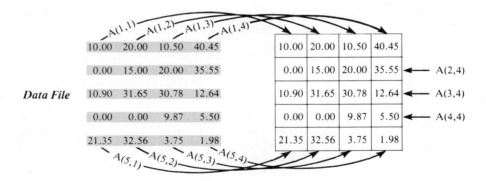

Specifying the proper sequence of the array elements in the READ/WRITE list is a basic task when an input or output operation is to be performed on a two-dimensional array. There are always alternative ways to accomplish this task; some are more compact and efficient than others, but there may be several acceptable solutions (see Figure 7.5).

Task 2   Printing the Total Daily Expenses

To compute the total daily expenses, we must add the elements of a particular row. Since each row can be thought of as a one-dimensional array, we are essentially accumulating the elements of a one-dimensional array. For example, to compute the sum of the first row, we could write

```
SUM = A(1,1)+A(1,2)+A(1,3)+A(1,4)    or      SUM = 0.0
                                             DO 7 STORE = 1,4
                                                 SUM = SUM + A(1,STORE)
            varying column index            7 CONTINUE
```

Since the same process needs to be repeated for each of the remaining rows (row 2 through row 5), we let the row index DAY vary from 1 to 5:

```
      INTEGER DAY,STORE
      DO 6 DAY = 1,5                    Process 5 days (rows).
          SUM = 0.0                     Initialize the accumulator for total expenses to 0.
          DO 7 STORE = 1,4              Each row consists of 4 column entries (stores).
              SUM = SUM + A(DAY,STORE)  Add the 4 column entries of a given row to compute
    7     CONTINUE                      the total expenses for the particular day.
          WRITE(6,2)SUM                 Print each day's total expenses.
    6 CONTINUE
    2 FORMAT (F6.2)
```

Task 3   Interactive Communication between Mr. Spandex and His Computer

To enable Mr. Spandex to determine how much he spent at a particular store on a particular day, we add the following code.

```
      INTEGER DAY,STORE
   11 WRITE(*,3)                           Write message on screen instead of printer.
      READ(*,4)DAY,STORE                   Read from the screen. Mr. Spandex enters day and store.
      IF(DAY .NE. 0) THEN
        WRITE(*,8)A(DAY,STORE),DAY,STORE   Print expense for a given day and store.
        GO TO 11
      ENDIF
    9 STOP
    8 FORMAT(' YOU SPENT',F6.2,' DOLLARS ON DAY',I2,' AT STORE',I2)
    3 FORMAT(' ENTER DAY AND STORE. TO STOP ENTER 00')
    4 FORMAT(2I1)
```

The complete program to solve this three-part problem is shown in Figure 7.6.

```
 1: C GROCERY SHOPPING ANALYSIS
 2: C    A(5,4): ARRAY CONTAINING WEEKLY EXPENSES BY DAY & STORE
 3: C    SUM:    USED TO ACCUMULATE TOTAL DAILY EXPENSES
 4: C    DAY:    IDENTIFIES THE DAY
 5: C    STORE:  IDENTIFIES A PARTICULAR STORE
 6: C
 7:        REAL A(5,4), SUM
 8:        INTEGER DAY, STORE
 9:        DO 5 DAY = 1, 5
10:          READ(5,1)(A(DAY,STORE),STORE=1,4)
11:      5 CONTINUE
12:        DO 6 DAY = 1, 5                    Process 5 days.
13:          SUM = 0.0                        Set the sum of expenses for each day to 0.
14:          DO 7 STORE = 1, 4                Add the expenses at the 4 stores for a given day.
15:            SUM = SUM + A(DAY,STORE)
16:      7     CONTINUE
17:          WRITE(*,2)DAY, SUM
18:      6 CONTINUE
19:     11 WRITE(*,3)                         Write the cue on the screen (terminal).
20:        READ(*,4)DAY, STORE               Enter the day and store on the screen (terminal).
21:        IF(DAY .NE. 0) THEN
22:          WRITE(*,8)A(DAY,STORE),DAY,STORE      Print answers on terminal.
23:          GO TO 11
24:        ENDIF
25:        STOP
26:      8 FORMAT(' ',YOU SPENT',F6.2,' DOLLARS ON DAY',I2,' AT STORE',I2)
27:      3 FORMAT(' ',ENTER DAY AND STORE. TO STOP ENTER 00')
28:      4 FORMAT(2I1)
29:      1 FORMAT(4F5.2)
30:      2 FORMAT(' ','TOTAL DAILY EXPENSES FOR DAY',I2,' IS',F6.2)
31:        END
```

```
TOTAL DAILY EXPENSES FOR DAY 1 IS 80.95
TOTAL DAILY EXPENSES FOR DAY 2 IS 70.55
TOTAL DAILY EXPENSES FOR DAY 3 IS 85.97
TOTAL DAILY EXPENSES FOR DAY 4 IS 15.37
TOTAL DAILY EXPENSES FOR DAY 5 IS 59.64
ENTER DAY AND STORE. TO STOP ENTER 00
32

YOU SPENT 31.65 DOLLARS ON DAY 3 AT STORE 2
ENTER DAY AND STORE. TO STOP ENTER 00
11

YOU SPENT 10.00 DOLLARS ON DAY 1 AT STORE 1
ENTER DAY AND STORE. TO STOP ENTER 00
34

YOU SPENT 12.64 DOLLARS ON DAY 3 AT STORE 4
ENTER DAY AND STORE. TO STOP ENTER 00
00
```

Input File

	A(1,1)	A(1,2)	A(1,3)	A(1,4)
day 1	10.00	20.00	10.50	40.45
day 2	00.00	15.00	20.00	35.55
day 3	10.90	31.65	30.78	12.64
day 4	00.00	00.00	09.87	05.50
day 5	21.35	32.56	03.75	01.98

FIGURE 7.6
A GROCERY SHOPPING ANALYSIS

7.3.2 A Frequency
Distribution

Problem/Specification. Data have been gathered on the smoking habits of students at a university. Each record in the study, consists of a student's class (1 = freshman, 2 = sophomore, 3 = junior, 4 = senior, 5 = graduate) and a code representing the student's smoking habits (1 = don't smoke, 2 = one pack or less a day, 3 = more than one pack a day). Let us write a program to generate a frequency table showing students' smoking habits by class (see diagram below).

This problem essentially deals with counting, i.e., we need to count how many freshmen do not smoke, how many freshmen smoke one pack or less a day, how many freshmen smoke in excess of one pack, and so forth. Altogether we need 15 counters (5 student classifications and 3 habits). One simple way to solve the problem manually is to draw a table with 5 rows and 3 columns and proceeds as follows:

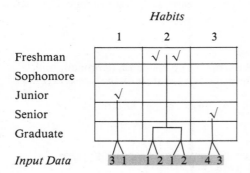

If the first record is 3,1 (3 = junior, 1 = doesn't smoke), we place a check mark in the box at row 3 and column 1. We read the next record (1,2) and check the corresponding box. We repeat the process until we run out of records, then we add up the checks in each box.

This table shows the counts (frequencies) obtained by processing the four data records shown.

To simulate this process in our program, we create a two-dimensional array COUNT with 5 rows and 3 columns, where each entry serves as a counter. Initially, these counters are set to 0; then every time we read a class and a habit code, we add 1 to the corresponding array entry, e.g., if class = 1 and habit = 2, we add 1 to COUNT(class,habit), which is COUNT(1,2) in this case. When all records have been read, COUNT (I,J) will contain the count of class I students with smoking habit J. The input and output will have the following form:

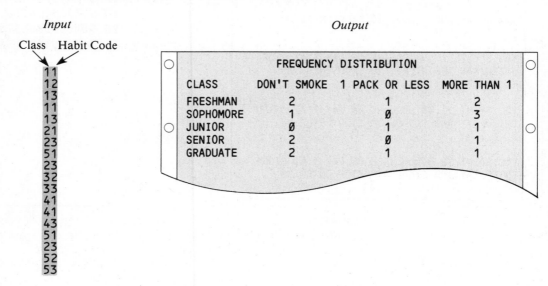

The program to solve this problem is shown in Figure 7.7.

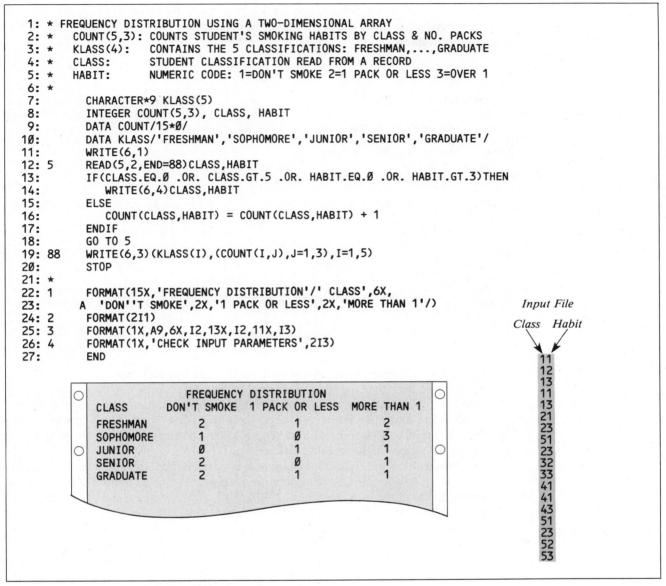

```
 1: * FREQUENCY DISTRIBUTION USING A TWO-DIMENSIONAL ARRAY
 2: *    COUNT(5,3): COUNTS STUDENT'S SMOKING HABITS BY CLASS & NO. PACKS
 3: *    KLASS(4):   CONTAINS THE 5 CLASSIFICATIONS: FRESHMAN,...,GRADUATE
 4: *    CLASS:      STUDENT CLASSIFICATION READ FROM A RECORD
 5: *    HABIT:      NUMERIC CODE: 1=DON'T SMOKE 2=1 PACK OR LESS 3=OVER 1
 6: *
 7:        CHARACTER*9 KLASS(5)
 8:        INTEGER COUNT(5,3), CLASS, HABIT
 9:        DATA COUNT/15*0/
10:        DATA KLASS/'FRESHMAN','SOPHOMORE','JUNIOR','SENIOR','GRADUATE'/
11:        WRITE(6,1)
12: 5      READ(5,2,END=88)CLASS,HABIT
13:        IF(CLASS.EQ.0 .OR. CLASS.GT.5 .OR. HABIT.EQ.0 .OR. HABIT.GT.3)THEN
14:           WRITE(6,4)CLASS,HABIT
15:        ELSE
16:           COUNT(CLASS,HABIT) = COUNT(CLASS,HABIT) + 1
17:        ENDIF
18:        GO TO 5
19: 88     WRITE(6,3)(KLASS(I),(COUNT(I,J),J=1,3),I=1,5)
20:        STOP
21: *
22: 1      FORMAT(15X,'FREQUENCY DISTRIBUTION'/' CLASS',6X,
23:      A  'DON''T SMOKE',2X,'1 PACK OR LESS',2X,'MORE THAN 1'/)
24: 2      FORMAT(2I1)
25: 3      FORMAT(1X,A9,6X,I2,13X,I2,11X,I3)
26: 4      FORMAT(1X,'CHECK INPUT PARAMETERS',2I3)
27:        END
```

```
                 FREQUENCY DISTRIBUTION
  CLASS        DON'T SMOKE   1 PACK OR LESS   MORE THAN 1

  FRESHMAN          2              1               2
  SOPHOMORE         1              0               3
  JUNIOR            0              1               1
  SENIOR            2              0               1
  GRADUATE          2              1               1
```

```
Input File

Class  Habit

  1 1
  1 2
  1 3
  1 1
  1 3
  2 1
  2 3
  5 1
  2 3
  3 2
  3 3
  4 1
  4 1
  4 3
  5 1
  2 3
  5 2
  5 3
```

FIGURE 7.7
A FREQUENCY DISTRIBUTION PROGRAM

7.3.3 An On-line Airline Reservation Problem

You have been asked to write an on-line reservation system for a small commuter airline company. Each plane has 5 rows of seats, with 4 seats per row, and can carry up to 20 passengers. The ticket agent is to ask each passenger's name and his or her row and seat preference; the name and seat request are then entered on a computer terminal as shown on the following page. If the seat requested is available, the system should reserve that seat. If that seat is already taken, the system is to assign the first available seat, starting with row 1, row 2, ..., up to row 5. A message should appear on the screen as soon as the seating capacity has been reached. When all passenger requests have been taken care of, the program should then print the seating arrangement, by passenger name:

```
ENTER ROW THEN SEAT AND NAME
11BOILLOT
ENTER ROW THEN SEAT AND NAME
11ADKINS
ENTER ROW THEN SEAT AND NAME
44FORD
ENTER ROW THEN SEAT AND NAME
44CABERAS
ENTER ROW THEN SEAT AND NAME
00000000

        FINAL SEATING ARRANGEMENT
ROW 1  BOILLOT  ADKINS   CABERAS  _____
ROW 2  _____  _____  _____  _____
ROW 3  _____  _____  _____  _____
ROW 4  _____  _____  _____  FORD
ROW 5  _____  _____  _____  _____
```

System displays the cue on the terminal. The agent enters the passenger's request and name.
11 means row 1 and seat 1.

When the agent enters the special code 00, the system prints the seating arrangement.

Note that ADKINS is assigned 1,2 and that CABERAS is assigned 1,3!

(Note that the program instructs the printer to underline each seat.)

We will represent the plane's seating configuration with a 5 by 4 array SEAT, which will eventually contain all the passenger's names. Initially we set these 20 seats to blanks to indicate nonreserved seats. Thus SEAT(3,4) = ' ' means that seat number 4 in the 3d row is empty. If a passenger wishes to reserve SEAT(3,4), we store the passenger's name in that array location.

If there are fewer than 20 passengers at departure time, the agent enters a special code (R = 0) to terminate the reservation process; the system then prints the seating arrangement of the airplane (lines 27–30). If all seats are taken, the system alerts the agent and prints the final seating arrangement.

The program to solve this problem is shown in Figure 7.8.

7.3.4 A Bar Graph

The daily volume of a major stock exchange is given in millions of shares for the three weeks starting July 8:

JULY 8		JULY 15		JULY 22	
VOLUME	WORKDAY	VOLUME	WORKDAY	VOLUME	WORKDAY
5	1	5	1	3	1
7	2	3	2	2	2
8	3	5	3	1	3
9	4	4	4	2	4
7	5	2	5	4	5

```
1: * AIRPLANE SEATING RESERVATION SYSTEM
2: *    SEAT(5,4): ARRAY DISPLAYING PLANE SEATING ARRANGEMENT
3: *    R:           PASSENGER'S ROW REQUEST
4: *    C:           PASSENGER'S SEAT PREFERENCE (COLUMN)
5: *
6:       CHARACTER*8 SEAT(5,4), NAME
7:       INTEGER R, C
8:       DATA SEAT/20*' '/                    Initialize all seats to blanks.
9:    35 WRITE(*,1)                           System writes cue on terminal
10:       READ(*,2)R,C,NAME                   Accept a passenger seating request.
11:       IF(R .NE. 0) THEN                   If no more passengers, print the seating arrangement.
12:          IF(SEAT(R,C) .EQ. ' ') THEN      If seat is not taken,
13:             SEAT(R,C) = NAME              reserve it.
14:             GO TO 35
15:          ELSE                             Otherwise check for 1st available seat starting at (1,1).
16:             DO 5 I = 1,5
17:                DO 7 J = 1, 4
18:                   IF(SEAT(I,J) .EQ. ' ')THEN    Assign passenger a seat other than
19:                      SEAT(I,J) = NAME           the one requested.
20:                      GO TO 35
21:                   ENDIF
22:  7             CONTINUE
23:  5          CONTINUE
24:             WRITE(*,3)                    If we have gone through both DO loops,
25:          ENDIF                            all the seats must be taken, i.e., plane is full.
26:       ENDIF
27:       WRITE(*,4)
28:       DO 8 I = 1, 5                       Print the plane's seating arrangement.
29:          WRITE(*,6)I, (SEAT(I,J),J=1,4)
30:  8    CONTINUE
31:       STOP
32:  1 FORMAT(' ','ENTER ROW THEN SEAT AND NAME')
33:  2 FORMAT(2I1,A8)
34:  3 FORMAT(' ','PLANE IS FILLED TO CAPACITY'/)
35:  4 FORMAT(15X,'FINAL SEATING ARRANGEMENT'/)
36:  6 FORMAT(' ','ROW ',I1,2X,4(A8,2X)/'+',7X,4(8('_'),2X))     Underline seats.
37:    END
```

FIGURE 7.8
AN ON-LINE RESERVATION SYSTEM

Write a program to produce the bar graph shown below for the 15 work days starting
July 8. The transactions have been recorded on 1 record as follows:

record: 5 7 8 9 7 5 3 5 4 2 3 2 1 2 4

Understanding the Problem

In this problem we will use an array G consisting of at least 9 rows (for the maximum volume during the entire 15-day period) and 15 columns (for the 15 days). Initially, we set the array G to blanks. We then read the transaction for the first day of the first week (5) and insert five asterisks in the first column of G. We then proceed with the next transaction volume (7) and insert seven asterisks in the second column to represent the second day's volume. These steps are repeated up to the 15th day, where we insert asterisks in G(1,15), G(2,15), G(3,15), and G(4,15). The process can be visualized as follows:

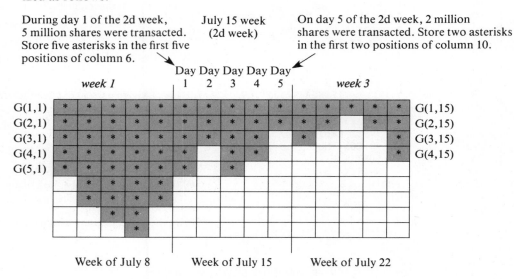

During day 1 of the 2d week, 5 million shares were transacted. Store five asterisks in the first five positions of column 6.

July 15 week (2d week)

On day 5 of the 2d week, 2 million shares were transacted. Store two asterisks in the first two positions of column 10.

In this diagram, the bar graph peaks down rather than up—to flip it up we print row 9 on the first line, row 8 on the second line, and so forth:

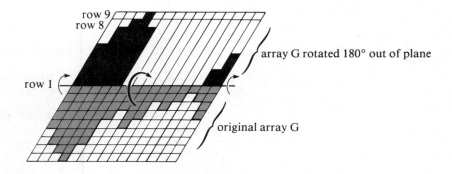

row 9
row 8
row 1
array G rotated 180° out of plane
original array G

The problem can be broken down into the following activities:

1. Initialize array G(9,15) with blank characters.

2. Read the number of transactions for the first day and call it V.
   Store V asterisks in the first column of G.
   Then read the number of transactions for the second day, call it V.
   Store V asterisks in the second column of G.
   Repeat these steps for days 3, 4, ..., 15.

3. Print the array G, starting with row 9, then row 8, ..., and finally row 1.

4. Print the graduations for the day axis, i.e., 1 2 3 4 5 1 2 3 ... .

The FORTRAN code to solve this problem is shown in Figure 7.9. Notice how the horizontal graduations are printed.

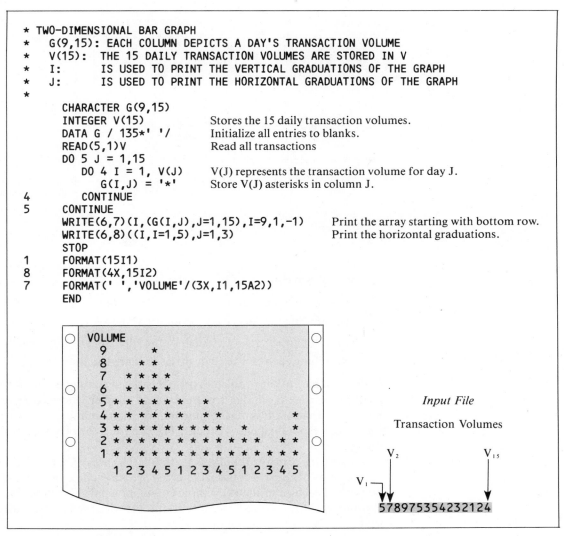

```
*  TWO-DIMENSIONAL BAR GRAPH
*    G(9,15): EACH COLUMN DEPICTS A DAY'S TRANSACTION VOLUME
*    V(15):   THE 15 DAILY TRANSACTION VOLUMES ARE STORED IN V
*    I:       IS USED TO PRINT THE VERTICAL GRADUATIONS OF THE GRAPH
*    J:       IS USED TO PRINT THE HORIZONTAL GRADUATIONS OF THE GRAPH
*
       CHARACTER G(9,15)
       INTEGER V(15)              Stores the 15 daily transaction volumes.
       DATA G / 135*' '/          Initialize all entries to blanks.
       READ(5,1)V                 Read all transactions
       DO 5 J = 1,15
          DO 4 I = 1, V(J)        V(J) represents the transaction volume for day J.
             G(I,J) = '*'         Store V(J) asterisks in column J.
4         CONTINUE
5      CONTINUE
       WRITE(6,7)(I,(G(I,J),J=1,15),I=9,1,-1)   Print the array starting with bottom row.
       WRITE(6,8)((I,I=1,5),J=1,3)              Print the horizontal graduations.
       STOP
1      FORMAT(15I1)
8      FORMAT(4X,15I2)
7      FORMAT(' ','VOLUME'/(3X,I1,15A2))
       END
```

FIGURE 7.9
A TWO-DIMENSIONAL BAR GRAPH

7.3.5 A Warehouse Problem

You own six warehouses across the country; each warehouse stocks five particular items. The stock quantities of each of the five items are recorded in a data file, with one record for each warehouse. Write a program to read the data into a two-dimensional array and produce the output shown on the next page.

Identify on the output any item that has zero stock in three or more warehouses. Also print those warehouses and item numbers where the stock is below 10. When listing those item numbers with stock levels less than 10, note that commas separate each item, i.e., the list should terminate with an item number, not a comma.

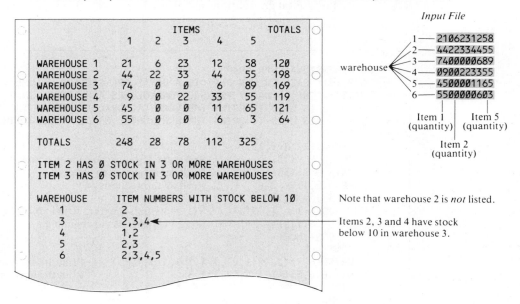

The problem consists of four parts:

1. Computing the sum of each row of the array.
2. Computing the sum of each column of the array.
3. Searching each column to determine whether 3 or more entries are 0.
4. Searching each row to find entries that are less than 10.

The last part of the problem is probably the most interesting. It requires us to look at a row and identify in that row the column number whose corresponding array element is less than 10. It is that column number (item number) that we need to print and not the corresponding entry (stock). The program to solve this problem is shown in Figure 7.10.

Initially the array COLSUM is set to 0's. The array COLSUM is used to compute the five sums of the five columns of array W. As each record is read, we accumulate the sums of each row (line 19) while accumulating partial column totals (line 20). Line 22 prints each row as well as the sum of its entries. When the entire array has been printed, we print the column totals (line 24).

In the third part of the problem, we check each column (line 29) for entries that have value 0. If there are three or more zero entries in a particular column, we print the column number (item number) and the message. K is used as a counter to count each occurrence of a zero entry. If K is less than 3, no message is printed.

In the fourth part of the problem, we analyze each row and record in the array BELOW the item numbers whose stock level is below 10. The variable M counts these items (line 39); when each row has been analyzed we print the M elements of array BELOW. A comma is inserted between each item (line 43). To avoid printing a comma to the right of the last entry, we print BELOW(M) (the last entry) all by itself.

```
 1: C WAREHOUSE PROBLEM
 2: C    W(6,5):    6 WAREHOUSES EACH CONTAINING 5 DIFFERENT ITEMS
 3: C    ROWSUM:    ACCUMULATES SUM OF EACH ROW OF W
 4: C    COLSUM(5): ACCUMULATES SUM OF EACH COLUMN OF W
 5: C    K:         COUNTS NUMBER OF WAREHOUSES WITH Ø STOCK LEVEL FOR A GIVEN ITEM
 6: C    BELOW(5):  IDENTIFIES ITEMS WITH STOCK < 1Ø FOR A GIVEN WAREHOUSE
 7: C    COMMA:     REPRESENTS A COMMA TO SEPARATE ITEM NUMBERS
 8: C    M:         COUNTS NUMBER OF ITEMS WHOSE STOCK LEVEL IS < 1Ø IN EACH ROW
 9:       INTEGER W(6,5), COLSUM(5), ROWSUM, BELOW(5)
10:       CHARACTER COMMA
11:       DATA COMMA / ','/,COLSUM / 5*Ø/
12: C
13:       READ(5,1)((W(I,J),J=1,5),I=1,6)
14:       WRITE(6,2)(I,I=1,5)
15: C
16:       DO 5 I = 1, 6
17:          ROWSUM = Ø
18:          DO 6 J = 1, 5
19:             ROWSUM = ROWSUM + W(I,J)
20:             COLSUM(J) = COLSUM(J) + W(I,J)
21: 6        CONTINUE
22:          WRITE(6,3)I,(W(I,J),J=1,5),ROWSUM
23: 5     CONTINUE
24:       WRITE(6,4)COLSUM
25: C
26:       DO 7 J = 1, 5
27:          K = Ø
28:          DO 8 I = 1, 6
29:             IF(W(I,J) .EQ. Ø)K = K + 1
30: 8        CONTINUE
31:          IF(K .GE. 3) WRITE(6,9)J
32: 7     CONTINUE
33: C
34:       WRITE(6,11)
35:       DO 20 I = 1, 6
36:          M = Ø
37:          DO 30 J = 1, 5
38:             IF(W(I,J) .LT. 1Ø)THEN
39:                M = M + 1
40:                BELOW(M) = J
41:             ENDIF
42: 30       CONTINUE
43: 21       IF(M .GT. Ø) WRITE(6,12)I, (BELOW(L),COMMA,L=1,M-1), BELOW(M)
44: 20    CONTINUE
45:       STOP
46: C
47: 1     FORMAT(5I2)
48: 2     FORMAT(24X,'ITEMS',10X,'TOTALS'/16X,5(I1,4X)/)
49: 3     FORMAT(' ','WAREHOUSE ',I1,3X,5(I2,3X),I3)
50: 4     FORMAT('Ø','TOTALS',7X,5(I3,2X)/)
51: 9     FORMAT(' ','ITEM ',I1,' HAS Ø STOCK IN 3 OR MORE WAREHOUSES')
52: 11    FORMAT('Ø','WAREHOUSE',5X,'ITEM NUMBERS WITH STOCK BELOW 1Ø')
53: 12    FORMAT(5X,I1,10X,5(I1,A1))
54:       END
```

Compute row end column totals. *(lines 16–23)*

Determine any item that has 0 stock in three or more warehouses. *(lines 26–32)*

Print warehouse and item numbers with stock levels less than 10. *(lines 34–44)*

FIGURE 7.10
A WAREHOUSE PROBLEM

7.4 THREE-DIMENSIONAL ARRAYS

7.4.1 Definition and Background Information

A three-dimensional array is a data structure whose elements can be accessed using three subscripts. A three-dimensional table can be visualized as a rectangular parallelepiped sliced into several two-dimensional tables (planes).

Three-dimensional arrays are declared through the DIMENSION or the type statement, just as one- and two-dimensional arrays are declared; three size limits must be declared for a three-dimensional array.

Consider the following two arrays: REAL Q(3,2,4), TABL(3,4,2)

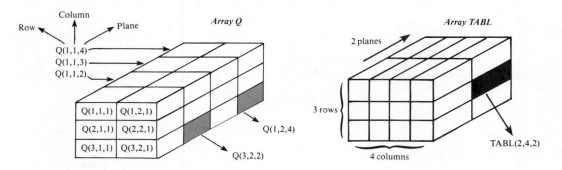

Any element of the three dimensional array Q can be referred to by Q(R,C,D),

where   R indicates the row.
         C indicates the column.
         D indicates the plane, i.e., which of the two-dimensional arrays the element is in.

The rules for subscripts are similar to those for one- and two-dimensional arrays.

Input/output and processing techniques for three-dimensional arrays are similar to the techniques for two-dimensional arrays.

EXAMPLE

A Three-Dimensional Table Problem

Each record of an input file (maximum of 50 records) consists of a student name followed by 8 scores. The first four scores are mathematics test scores, and the last four scores are computer science test scores. Write a program to compute the class average (all tests in both disciplines) and "pass" those students whose averages on both mathematics and computer tests are above the overall class average (place two asterisks by their grades). Sample input and output files are as follows:

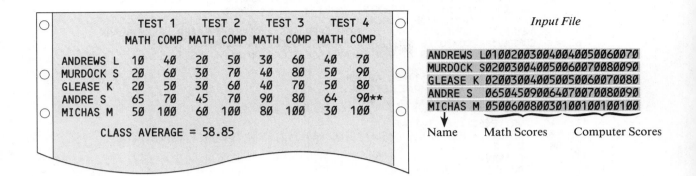

Input File

		TEST 1		TEST 2		TEST 3		TEST 4	
		MATH	COMP	MATH	COMP	MATH	COMP	MATH	COMP
ANDREWS L		10	40	20	50	30	60	40	70
MURDOCK S		20	60	30	70	40	80	50	90
GLEASE K		20	50	30	60	40	70	50	80
ANDRE S		65	70	45	70	90	80	64	90**
MICHAS M		50	100	60	100	80	100	30	100

CLASS AVERAGE = 58.85

```
ANDREWS L010020030040040050060070
MURDOCK S020030040050060070080090
GLEASE K020030040050050060070080
ANDRE S065045090064070070080090
MICHAS M050060080030100100100100
```

Name   Math Scores   Computer Scores

The FORTRAN code to solve this problem is shown in Figure 7.11. (Note how the input data is read into the three-dimensional array SCORES at line 14). The SCORES array can be visualized as a three-dimensional table as follows:

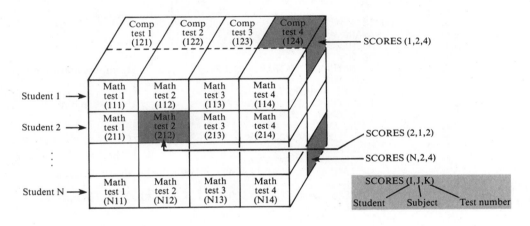

7.5 You Might Want to Know

1. Does FORTRAN allow arrays of more than three dimensions?

Answer: Some versions of FORTRAN allow 31 dimensions for an array (Burroughs 6700/7700), while most others offer 7 dimensions.

2. What will happen to my program if I use an illegal subscript reference? For example, what happens if my array is declared by DIMENSION X(3,5) and I make a reference to X(5,7)?

Answer: The handling of this problem may differ among FORTRAN systems. Many FORTRAN compilers translate an array reference into an address without checking whether the subscripts are in the range allowed by the declarator state-

```
 1: * A 3-DIMENSIONAL ARRAY PROBLEM
 2: *    SCORES(50,2,4): MAXIMUM OF 50 STUDENTS; 2 SUBJECTS, 4 TESTS
 3: *    NAME(50): ARRAY OF STUDENTS' NAMES
 4: *    N:        NUMBER OF STUDENTS
 5: *    AWARD:    CONTAINS '**' IF BOTH AVERAGES > CLASS AVERAGE, ELSE BLANK
 6: *    COMPAV:   COMPUTES STUDENT'S AVERAGE SCORE ON COMPUTER TESTS
 7: *    MATHAV:   COMPUTES STUDENT'S AVERAGE SCORE ON MATH TESTS
 8: *
 9:         CHARACTER NAME(51)*9, AWARD*2
10:         REAL MATHAV, COMPAV, CLASAV
11:         INTEGER SCORES(51,2,4), N
12: *
13:         WRITE(6,1) (I,I=1,4)
14: 10      READ(5,2,END=88) (NAME(I),((SCORES(I,J,K),K=1,4),J=1,2),I=1,51)
15: 88      N = I - 1
16:         CLASAV = 0.0
17:         DO 5 I = 1, N
18:            DO 6 J = 1, 2
19:               DO 7 K = 1, 4
20:                  CLASAV = CLASAV + SCORES(I,J,K)          } Compute class average.
21: 7             CONTINUE
22: 6          CONTINUE
23: 5       CONTINUE
24:         CLASAV = CLASAV/(8*N)
25: *
26:         DO 11 I = 1, N
27:            AWARD = '  '
28:            MATHAV = 0.0
29:            DO 8 K = 1,4
30:               MATHAV = MATHAV + SCORES(I,1,K)             } Compute math average.
31: 8          CONTINUE
32:            MATHAV = MATHAV/4.
33:            IF(MATHAV .GT. CLASAV) THEN                    No award if math average ≤ class average.
34:               COMPAV = 0.0
35:               DO 9 K = 1, 4
36:                  COMPAV =COMPAV + SCORES(I,2,K)           } Compute computer test average.
37: 9             CONTINUE
38:               COMPAV = COMPAV/4.                          } If both test averages > class average,
39:               IF(COMPAV .GT. CLASAV) AWARD='**'           the student is awarded stars (**)
40:            ENDIF
41:            WRITE(6,3)NAME(I),((SCORES(I,J,K),J=1,2),K=1,4),AWARD
42: 11      CONTINUE
43:         WRITE(6,4)CLASAV
44:         STOP
45: *
46: 1       FORMAT(16X,4('TEST ',I1,6X)/14X,4('MATH COMP   ')/)
47: 2       FORMAT(A9,8I3)
48: 3       FORMAT(1X,A9,4(4X,I3,2X,I3),A3)
49: 4       FORMAT('0',14X,'CLASS AVERAGE = ',F6.2)
50:         END
```

	TEST 1		TEST 2		TEST 3		TEST 4	
	MATH	COMP	MATH	COMP	MATH	COMP	MATH	COMP
ANDREWS L	10	40	20	50	30	60	40	70
MURDOCK S	20	60	30	70	40	80	50	90
GLEASE K	20	50	30	60	40	70	50	80
ANDRE S	65	70	45	70	90	80	64	90**
MICHAS M	50	100	60	100	80	100	30	100

CLASS AVERAGE = 58.85

Input File

Scores(1,1,1)   Scores(1,1,2)   Scores (1,2,4)

```
ANDREWS L010020030040040050060070
MURDOCK S020030040050060070080090
GLEASE K 020030040050050060070080
ANDRE S  065045090064070070080090
MICHAS M 050060080030100100100100
```

FIGURE 7.11
A THREE-DIMENSIONAL ARRAY PROBLEM

ment. If the address is invalid (outside the user's program), an execution-time diagnostic will be produced. If the address is valid, the data or instruction contained in that location will be fetched or changed, depending on whether X(5,7) is to the left or to the right of the equal sign in a replacement statement. The effects of such a mistake may be apparent when the desired output is not produced by the program. The cause of the error may be difficult to determine, since the erroneous output will usually provide no clue that can be traced to an invalid array reference. Screening subscripts for valid ranges is strongly recommended.

3. Can I initialize two- or three-dimensional arrays in a DATA statement?

Answer: Yes. For example:

```
REAL X(3,2,4)
DATA(((X(I,J,K),I=1,3),J=1,2),K=1,4)/12*2.,6*1.,6*2.1/
```
or
```
DATA X/12*2., 6*1., 6*2.1/
```

meaning: $X(1,1,1)$ through $X(3,2,2) = 2.$
            $X(1,1,3)$ through $X(3,2,3) = 1.$
            $X(1,1,4)$ through $X(3,2,4) = 2.1$

4. Is there any limit to the size of a multidimensional array?

Answer: Theoretically, no. Practically, yes. Restrictions on array sizes are dictated by the size of the memory of the particular system. For example, on a system with a memory size of 512,000 bytes, the statement INTEGER A(100,50,50) exceeds the memory size since array A occupies 1 million bytes (1 array element = 4 bytes). On larger systems the operating system may take up a large portion of memory; the programmer requiring large arrays should check on memory available.

5. How are three-dimensional arrays stored in memory?

Answer: Internally, multi-dimensional arrays are stored as a linear sequence of elements in column order. For example, an array A with three rows and three columns is stored as follows:

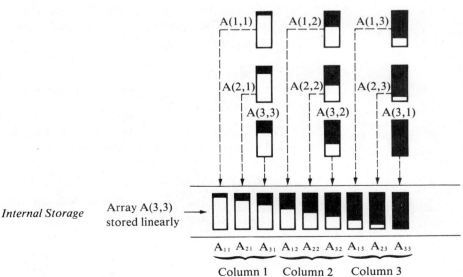

Internal Storage   Array A(3,3) stored linearly

A_{11} A_{21} A_{31} A_{12} A_{22} A_{32} A_{13} A_{23} A_{33}

Column 1   Column 2   Column 3

Although the array A is stored column-wise in memory, A does not have to be read into memory by columns. It can be read row-wise as in:

READ(5,3)(A(I,J),J, = 1,3),I = 1,3)

Three-dimensional arrays are stored linearly in memory. The internal order of storage for the array A(3,5,3) is column-wise across each depth plane.

Order

A(1,1,1)
A(2,1,1)
A(3,1,1)
A(1,2,1)
A(2,2,1)
A(3,2,1)
A(1,3,1)
A(2,3,1)
A(3,3,1)
A(1,4,1)
A(2,4,1)
A(3,4,1)
A(1,5,1)
A(2,5,1)
A(3,5,1)
A(1,1,2)
A(2,1,2)
A(3,1,2)
A(1,2,2)
.
.
.

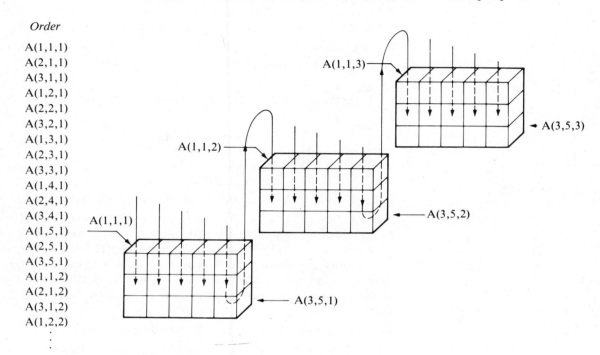

6. Can a multidimensional array be processed without subscripts in a READ/WRITE statement?

Answer: Yes, an array name can be used in a READ or WRITE list without subscripts. The elements will be processed in column order.

Consider the following example:

```
    REAL X(3,4)
    READ(5,3) X ◄————— Note that subscripts are not used.
  3 FORMAT(3F4.Ø)
```

This code will read all 12 elements of X, with three data items per record. The data will be read into the array as follows:

X(1,1) X(2,1) X(3,1) ⎫
X(1,2) X(2,2) X(3,2) ⎪
X(1,3) X(2,3) X(3,3) ⎬ order in which data items will be read from input file.
X(1,4) X(2,4) X(3,4) ⎭

These array considerations apply to output as well. For example, suppose the array IX contains the following data:

IX =

17	9	8	73
4	6	18	14
5	10	21	5

The following WRITE statements are equivalent:

```
INTEGER IX(3,4)                    INTEGER IX(3,4)
    :                                  :
    :                                  :
WRITE(6,10)IX                      WRITE(6,10)((IX(I,J),I=1,3),J=1,4)
10 FORMAT(2X,3I3)                  10 FORMAT(2X,3I4)
```

yielding the output:

Output

```
17    4    5
 9    6   10
 8   18   21
73   14    5
```

7.6 EXERCISES

7.6.1 Test Yourself

1. Which of the following are valid array declarations? Specify errors, if any.

   a. INTEGER A(100,3),IB(3,5)

   b. DIMENSION A3(3),A4(4,4)

   c. CHARACTER ST(50,40),J(3,1,7)*3

   d. DIMENSION Z100

   e. DIMENSION UT(3.,2)

   f. REAL N,X(3,2,N)

   g. INTEGER Z(7,2:3,4,5:6)

   h. DIMENSION (MIKE)10

   i. DIMENSION BIG(3:0,2)

   j. DOUBLE PRECISION I(2,2)

2. List the internal order of storage for arrays A and B specified by:

```
INTEGER A(2,4),B(3,1,4),K(2,2,2)
```

3. Explain in words what arrays TC and TR will contain as a result of the following code:

```
REAL A(5,4),TC(4),TR(5)
DATA TC,TR/9*0./
READ array A from input file
DO 3 J = 1,4
   DO 2 I = 1,5
      TC(J) = TC(J) + A(I,J)
      TR(I) = TR(I) + A(I,J)
2     CONTINUE
3 CONTINUE
```

4. Using implied DO lists, write I/O statements corresponding to the following lists of variables:

    a.   `WRITE(6,10)A(4),A(5),A(6),A(7),...,A(90)`

    b.   `WRITE(6,4) B(1),B(3),B(5),B(7),B(9),...,B(99)`

    c.   `READ(5,2) C(2,1),C(2,2),C(2,3),C(2,4),C(2,5)`

    d.   `READ(5,1) A(1,1),B(1),A(2,1),B(2),A(3,1),B(3)`

    e.   `WRITE(6,5) K,A(1,1),B(1),B(2),B(3),K,A(2,1),B(1),B(2),B(3)`

    f.   `READ(5,3) A(1,1),A(1,2),A(1,3),B(2,1),B(2,2),B(2,3),C(1),`
        `*          C(2),C(3)`

    g.   `WRITE(6,1) A(1,1),B(1,1),C(1,1),I,A(1,2),B(1,2),C(1,2),I,`
        `*          A(1,3),B(1,3),C(1,3),I`

    h. `WRITE` *the values* 1 2 3 4 1 2 3 4 1 2 3 4 (12 values)

5. Generate the corresponding READ/WRITE list of variables for the following implied DO lists, and specify the number of records that would be processed by the accompanying FORMATs.

    a.   `((A(I,J),I = 1,3),J = 1,2)`   `FORMAT(8F3.1)`

    b.   `((A(I,J),I,I = 1,3),J = 1,2)`   `FORMAT(2(F3.1,I2)/F3.1,I2)`

    c.   `((A(I,J),I = 1,3),J,J = 1,3)`   `FORMAT(3F3.1,I1/(3F3.1,I1))`

    d.   `((A(I,J),B(I,J),J=1,2),I=1,3)` `FORMAT(F3.1)`

    e.   `(C(I),(A(I,J),J = 1,3),`
        `*(P(K,I),K = 1,2),I = 1,2)` `FORMAT(6F4.1)`

    f.   `(((A(I,J,K),I=1,2),K=1,3),J=1,2)` `FORMAT(11F3.0)`

6. Assume arrays A, JSUM, and VAR contain the following data:

A(3,4)

1.	2.	3.	4.
5.	6.	7.	8.
9.	10.	11.	12

JSUM(3,4)

10	20	30	40
50	60	70	80
90	100	110	120

VAR

500.

Write the necessary implied DO lists to generate the following output using only these three arrays (no computations are to be performed). Show the format statements, too.

```
a. 1.  2.  3.  4. ... 12. 10 20 30 40 ... 120 500.

b. 1.  2.  3.  4.    10  20  30  40      500.
   5.  6.  7.  8.    50  60  70  80      500.
   9. 10. 11. 12.    90 100 110 120      500.

c. 1.  5.  9.     500.     10 50  90
   2.  6. 10.     500.     20 60 100
   3.  7. 11.     500.     30 70 110

d. 1. 10  2.  20  3.  30  4.  40
   5. 50  6.  60  7.  70  8.  80
   9. 90 10. 100 11. 110 12. 120

e. 1. 10  5.  50 9.  90  2.  20 6.  60 10. 100
   3. 30  7.  70 11. 110 4.  40 8.  80 12. 120
```

For part e, you may want to use a combination of a DO loop and an implied DO list.

7. Write one READ statement with a DO list and an appropriate FORMAT statement to read each of the following input files:

a. A_{11} A_{21} A_{31} A_{41}
  A_{12} A_{22} A_{32} A_{42}
  A_{13} B_{23} A_{33} A_{43}

b. A_{11} A_{12} A_{13}
  A_{14} A_{15} A_{16}
  B_1 B_2 B_3
  B_4 B_5 B_6

c. A_{11} B_{11} A_{21} B_{21}
  A_{31} B_{31} A_{41} B_{41}
  A_{51} B_{51} A_{61} B_{61}

d. A_{11} B_{11} A_{21} B_{12}
  A_{31} B_{13} A_{41} B_{14}
  A_{51} B_{15} A_{61} B_{16}

e. A_{11} A_{12} A_{13} B_{11} B_{12}
  A_{21} A_{22} A_{23} B_{21} B_{22}
  $\vdots$ $\vdots$
  A_{91} A_{92} A_{93} B_{91} B_{92}

f. A_{11} A_{12} ... A_{19}
  A_{21} ... A_{29}
  $\vdots$
  A_{81} ... A_{89}
  B_{11} B_{21} B_{31}
  B_{41} B_{12} B_{22}
  B_{32} B_{42}

8. An array A of size 5×5 is to be read from five records (five entries per record, one record for each row). Write the codes to

a. Read in the array and write it out in row form (one row per line), then print each column on one line, i.e., $A_{11}, A_{21}, ..., A_{51}$ on one line, $A_{12}, A_{22}, ..., A_{52}$ on the second line, and so forth.

b. Calculate the sum of the elements in the third row.

c. Find the largest value in the first column.

d. Create an array B consisting of five elements initialized to zero. Calculate the sum of each column of A, storing the result in the corresponding column position of B.

e. Add the corresponding elements of rows 2 and 3 of the array A, storing the results in row 3; i.e., $A(3,1) = A(3,1) + A(2,1)$, and so forth.

f. Interchange column 3 and column 4.

g. Compute the sum of the entries of the main diagonal ($A_{11}, A_{22}, A_{33}, ..., A_{55}$).

h. Compute the sum of the entries of the secondary diagonal and determine the largest entry of that diagonal. (The secondary diagonal consists of elements $A_{15}, A_{24}, A_{33}, A_{42}, A_{51}$)

i. Print the smallest element of the array A and its position in the array (row, column).

9. List the internal sequence of arrays X(3,2) and Y(2,3,2).

10. Write the READ statement to read in two arrays C and D of size 5×5 given the following input description (5 entries per record):

1,2,3,4,5	1,2,3,6,8	4,5,6,7,8	4,5,6,7,6 ...
Row 1 of C	Row 1 of D	Row 2 of C	Row 2 of D

11. Given array R(4,6,5) write the code to compute the sums of each row of R and store the sums in a two-dimensional array S(4,5) in such a way that:
S(1,1) = sum of row 1, plane 1; S(1,2) = sum of row 1, plane 2; ...; S(2,3) = sum of row 2, plane 3.

12. Assume an array F of size 40 by 17 already contains data. Write the code to store the rows of the array F sequentially into a one-dimensional array G of size 680 (40 × 17), as follows:

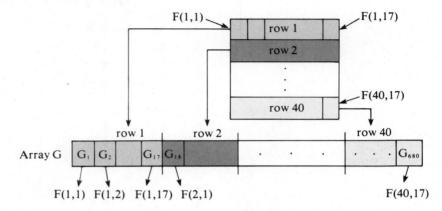

13. Assume the array A(10,3) has been read in; write a program segment to compute the sum of the elements of the array A and print the following output with *one* WRITE statement.

```
                        FINAL
      COLUMN 1    COLUMN 2    COLUMN 3    ...    COLUMN 10
        A₁ ₁        A₂ ₁        A₃ ₁      ...      A₁₀ ₁
        A₁ ₂        A₂ ₂        A₃ ₂      ...      A₁₀ ₂
        A₁ ₃        A₂ ₃        A₃ ₃      ...      A₁₀ ₃
      SUM OF ALL ELEMENTS IS XXX.X
```

14. Mr. Spandex (see section 7.3.1) would like to use the computer to help him further analyze his daily grocery shopping.

		\multicolumn{4}{c}{Store}		
		1	2	3	4
	1	10.00	20.00	10.50	40.45
	2	0.00	15.00	20.00	35.55
Day	3	10.90	31.65	30.78	12.64
	4	0.00	0.00	9.87	5.50
	5	21.35	32.56	3.75	1.98

Write the code to help him answer the following questions:

    a. How much did he spend for the whole week at store 1, store 2, ..., store 4?

    b. On which day did he spend the least? the most?

    c. At which store(s) did he spend the least? the most?

    d. Which store(s) did he not go to on a particular day?

e. What are his total weekly expenses?

f. What is the average daily expense at each store? The output should have the following form:

	STORE 1	STORE 2	STORE 3	STORE 4
DAY 1	10.00	20.00	10.50	40.45
DAY 2	.00	15.00	20.00	35.55
DAY 3	10.90	31.65	30.78	12.64
DAY 4	.00	.00	9.87	5.50
DAY 5	21.35	32.56	3.75	1.98
AVERAGE	8.45	19.84	14.98	19.22

15. In the bar graph of Figure 7.9, replace the graphic symbol * by the darker rectangular symbol ■ to print a more forceful bar graph. Your output should be similar to Graph 2.

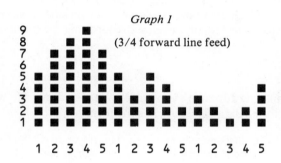

Graph 1

(3/4 forward line feed)

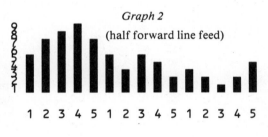

Graph 2

(half forward line feed)

[*Hint:* Use a combination of multistrike characters, for example, M, W, A, *, L, and E, to obtain the symbol ■. You can change the line spacing on a printer attached to a microcomputer by executing the following BASIC instruction: LPRINT CHR\$(27)CHR\$(*n*) where *n* = 36 for normal line spacing (1/6 of an inch) and any value less than 36 for a smaller line spacing.]

16. The result of multiplying two arrays A(5,4) and B(4,3) is another array C of size 5 by 3, defined as follows (matrix multiplication):

$$
\begin{matrix} A \end{matrix}
\begin{pmatrix} A_{11} & A_{12} & A_{13} & A_{14} \\ A_{21} & A_{22} & A_{23} & A_{24} \\ A_{31} & A_{32} & A_{33} & A_{34} \\ A_{41} & A_{42} & A_{43} & A_{44} \\ A_{51} & A_{52} & A_{53} & A_{54} \end{pmatrix}
\times
\begin{pmatrix} B_{11} & B_{12} & B_{13} \\ B_{21} & B_{22} & B_{23} \\ B_{31} & B_{32} & B_{33} \\ B_{41} & B_{42} & B_{43} \end{pmatrix}
=
\begin{pmatrix} C_{11} & C_{12} & C_{13} \\ C_{21} & C_{22} & C_{23} \\ C_{31} & C_{32} & C_{33} \\ C_{41} & C_{42} & C_{43} \\ C_{51} & C_{52} & C_{53} \end{pmatrix}
$$

where

$$C_{11} = A_{11} * B_{11} + A_{12} * B_{21} + A_{13} * B_{31} + A_{14} * B_{41}$$
$$C_{21} = A_{21} * B_{11} + A_{22} * B_{21} + A_{23} * B_{31} + A_{24} * B_{41}$$
$$C_{31} = A_{31} * B_{11} + A_{32} * B_{21} + A_{33} * B_{31} + A_{34} * B_{41}$$
$$C_{41} = A_{41} * B_{11} + A_{42} * B_{21} + A_{43} * B_{31} + A_{44} * B_{41}$$
$$C_{51} = A_{51} * B_{11} + A_{52} * B_{21} + A_{53} * B_{31} + A_{54} * B_{41}$$

$$C_{12} = A_{11} * B_{12} + A_{12} * B_{22} + A_{13} * B_{32} + A_{14} * B_{42}$$
$$C_{22} = A_{21} * B_{12} + A_{22} * B_{22} + A_{23} * B_{32} + A_{24} * B_{42}$$
$$C_{32} = A_{31} * B_{12} + A_{32} * B_{22} + A_{33} * B_{32} + A_{34} * B_{42}$$
$$C_{42} = A_{41} * B_{12} + A_{42} * B_{22} + A_{43} * B_{32} + A_{44} * B_{42}$$
$$C_{52} = A_{51} * B_{12} + A_{52} * B_{22} + A_{53} * B_{32} + A_{54} * B_{42}$$

$$C_{13} = A_{11} * B_{13} + A_{12} * B_{23} + A_{13} * B_{33} + A_{14} * B_{43}$$
$$C_{23} = A_{21} * B_{13} + A_{22} * B_{23} + A_{23} * B_{33} + A_{24} * B_{43}$$
$$C_{33} = A_{31} * B_{13} + A_{32} * B_{23} + A_{33} * B_{33} + A_{34} * B_{43}$$
$$C_{43} = A_{41} * B_{13} + A_{42} * B_{23} + A_{43} * B_{33} + A_{44} * B_{43}$$
$$C_{53} = A_{51} * B_{13} + A_{52} * B_{23} + A_{53} * B_{33} + A_{54} * B_{43}$$

Write a program to read an array A of size 5 by 4 and an array B of size 4 by 3 and compute the product array C of size 5 by 3. For example:

$$
A \begin{pmatrix} 1 & 2 & 3 & 4 \\ 6 & 7 & 8 & 9 \\ 5 & 4 & 3 & 2 \\ 2 & 3 & 4 & 5 \\ 1 & 2 & 3 & 4 \end{pmatrix} \times B \begin{pmatrix} 1 & 2 & 3 \\ 4 & 5 & 6 \\ 7 & 8 & 7 \\ 3 & 4 & 5 \end{pmatrix} = C \begin{pmatrix} 42 & 52 & 56 \\ 117 & 147 & 161 \\ 48 & 62 & 70 \\ 57 & 71 & 77 \\ 42 & 52 & 56 \end{pmatrix}
$$

[*Hint*: Note that any element of C is such that:
C(I,J) = A(I,1)*B(1,J) + A(I,2)*B(2*J) + A(I,3)*B(3,J) + A(I,4)*B(4,J) where I varies from 1 to 5 and J varies from 1 to 3, i.e., C(I,J) is equal to the product of the Ith row of A and the Jth column of B as illustrated above.]

17. A company has two factories; each contains three shops, and each shop has five machines. A study of the repair records of machines (machine down-time expressed in hours) is to be made. The log of repairs is recorded in table A. The technical manager may want to compute the number of hours lost for each machine in shop 1, factory 2, or find out which shops in the two factories exceeded 100 hours in down-time for machine 4, and so forth.

Using a three-dimensional table to identify the various factories, shops, and machines can greatly facilitate the logic of programs to answer these questions. An array to store the data on the repair records can be specified by:

REAL A(3,5,2)

shop　machine　factory

The repair data for each shop has been entered in a file where factory 1 data precedes factory 2 data. The data has the form:

Hours lost on machine 1, shop 1, factory 1　　Hours lost on machine 4, shop 1, factory 1

A(1,1,1)	A(1,2,1)	A(1,3,1)	A(1,4,1)	A(1,5,1)	Shop 1	Factory 1
A(2,1,1)	A(2,2,1)	A(2,3,1)	A(2,4,1)	A(2,5,1)	Shop 2	
A(3,1,1)	A(3,2,1)	A(3,3,1)	A(3,4,1)	A(3,5,1)	Shop 3	
A(1,1,2)	A(1,2,2)	A(1,3,2)	A(1,4,2)	A(1,5,2)	Shop 1	Factory 2
A(2,1,2)	A(2,2,2)	A(2,3,2)	A(2,4,2)	A(2,5,2)	Shop 2	
A(3,1,2)	A(3,2,2)	A(3,3,2)	A(3,4,2)	A(3,5,2)	Shop 3	

Write a program to compute the average time lost on each machine. Sample output and input files are shown below:

```
            FACTORY  1
SHOP 1   1.1   2.2   3.3   4.4   5.5
SHOP 2   1.1   1.2   1.3   1.4   1.5
SHOP 3   0.1   0.2   0.3   0.4   0.5
            FACTORY  2
SHOP 1   3.0   4.0   5.0   6.0   7.0
SHOP 2   4.0   5.0   6.0   7.0   8.0
SHOP 3   1.0   2.0   3.0   4.0   5.0
AVERAGES 1.7   2.4   3.1   3.9   4.6
```

Input File

A(1,2,1)　　A(1,4,1)

A(1,1,1)　A(1,3,1)　A(1,5,1)

```
01.102.203.304.405.5
01.101.201.301.401.5
00.100.200.300.400.5
03.004.005.006.007.0
04.005.006.007.008.0
01.002.003.004.005.0
```

A(3,2,2)　　A(3,4,2)

A(3,1,2)　　A(3,3,2)　　A(3,5,2)

*7.6.2 Programming
        Problems:
    Business/General*

1. An array A has size 4 by 9. Write the code to interchange the first column with the ninth column, the second column with the eighth column, and so forth.

2. Each record in a file consists of six data items, a student name followed by five test scores, for example:

```
DOE 10 20 30 40 50

SLY 10 10 70 60 40
```

Five Test Scores

There are at most 100 records. Read the test data into a two-dimensional table. For example, A(3,I), with I ranging from 1 to 5, represents the third student's test scores. Compute the average score for each student and the average score on each test. The output should have the following format:

NAME	TEST1	TEST2	TEST3	TEST4	TEST5	AVERAGE
DOE	10	20	30	40	50	30.0
SLY	11	10	71	60	40	38.4
AVERAGE/TEST	10.5	15.0	50.5	50.0	45.0	

3. The personnel department of a small insurance company maintains a payroll file for its insurance representatives, who work in different states. Each employee's record contains (among other information) the following data:

Employee Name	Hours Worked	Rate of Pay	State Tax
Anton D.	45	10.00	.05

Write a program to read an unknown number of input records (maximum 100). Load array NAME with the employee names and load a two-dimensional array A with the corresponding three entries from each record. *Then*

a. Compute and print each employee's pay before and after tax.

b. Compute the total payroll for the firm (not including state tax withdrawals).

c. Give a $1,000 bonus to the employee with lowest hourly rate who has worked more hours than any other employee. Such a condition may or may not be satisfied.

Overtime is paid at 1.5 times the regular rate. The output should be similar to

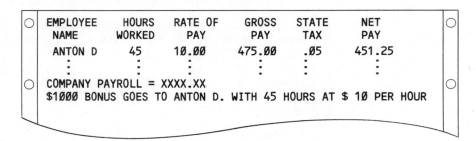

EMPLOYEE NAME	HOURS WORKED	RATE OF PAY	GROSS PAY	STATE TAX	NET PAY
ANTON D	45	10.00	475.00	.05	451.25

COMPANY PAYROLL = XXXX.XX
$1000 BONUS GOES TO ANTON D. WITH 45 HOURS AT $ 10 PER HOUR

4. Write a program to compute itemized sales tax deductions using the following instructions and table:

Your itemized deduction for general sales tax paid can be estimated from these tables. To use the tables:

Alabama

Step 1—Figure your total available income.

Step 2—Count the number of exemptions for you and your family. Do not count exemptions claimed for being 65 or over or blind as part of your family size.

Step 3 A—If your total available income is not over $40,000, find the income line on the table and read across to find the amount of sales tax for your family size.

Step 3 B—If your income is over $40,000, but not over $100,000, find the deduction listed on the income line "$38,001–$40,000" for your family size. For each $5,000 (or part of $5,000) of income over $40,000, increase the deduction by the amount listed on the line "$40,000–$100,000."

Income	Family Size					Over
	1	2	3	4	5	5
$1–$8,000	93	115	122	131	142	160
$8,001–$10,000. . . .	109	132	142	153	165	185
$10,001–$12,000. . .	124	147	161	173	187	208
$12,001–$14,000. . .	138	161	178	191	206	228
$14,001–$16,000. . .	152	174	194	209	225	248
$16,001–$18,000. . .	164	186	210	226	242	266
$18,001–$20,000. . .	176	197	225	242	259	284
$20,001–$22,000. . .	188	208	239	257	275	301
$22,001–$24,000. . .	199	218	253	271	290	317
$24,001–$26,000. . .	210	228	266	285	305	332
$26,001–$28,000. . .	221	238	279	299	320	347
$28,001–$30,000. . .	231	247	291	313	334	362
$30,001–$32,000. . .	241	256	303	326	347	376
$32,001–$34,000. . .	251	265	315	338	360	390
$34,001–$36,000. . .	261	274	327	350	373	403
$36,001–$38,000. . .	271	282	338	362	386	416
$38,001–$40,000. . .	280	290	349	374	399	429
$40,001–$100,000 . .	14	15	17	19	20	21

(See Step 3B)

Step 3 C—If your income is over $100,000, your sales tax deduction is limited to the deduction for income of $100,000. To figure your sales tax deduction, use Step 3 B but don't go over $100,000

5. A data file (maximum of 100 records) contains the following information:

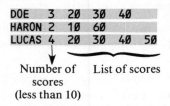

```
DOE    3  20  30  40
HARON  2  10  60
LUCAS  4  20  30  40  50
```

Number of   List of scores
scores
(less than 10)

If the average of all the scores in the input file is less than 80, five points are added to the average of each student; otherwise 5 points are subtracted from the average of each student. Write a program to produce the following output:

NAME	TEST1	TEST2	TEST3	TEST4	...	TEST10	AVERAGE	UPDATED AVERAGE
DOE	20	30	40				30.0	35.0
HARON	10	60					35.0	40.0
LUCAS	20	30	40	50			35.0	40.0
:	:	:	:	:			:	:

6. Dr. X is an information-science teacher. He keeps track of his students' names and their respective grades as follows:

Student	Grade 1	Grade 2	Total
Margulies	91	56	147
Gleason	40	50	90
Horn	50	65	115
Monish	70	70	140
⋮	⋮	⋮	⋮

a. Write a program to read input records and create this two-dimensional table (with three numeric entries) for about ten students.

b. Add the necessary code to allow Dr. X to correct his file in the event grades are recorded incorrectly. Grade changes are read according to the following format:

STUDENT NAME   GRADE 1   GRADE 2

For grades that need not be changed, enter a negative number. For example, HORN − 1 98 means change HORN's second grade to 98 and compute the new total. When all changes have been made, print or display the updated roster.

7. At the end of every semester, Dr. Landrum, head of the business data systems department, likes to check grade reports of the department's freshman class (100 students at most). Each student's final grades in three subject areas are entered on records, one record per student, for example:

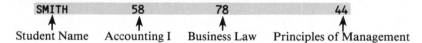

SMITH	58	78	44

Student Name   Accounting I   Business Law   Principles of Management

Enter in an array NAME all student names and enter each student's grades into a corresponding two-dimensional array G. For example, G(3,2) represents the third student's score in Business Law.

Write a program for Dr. Landrum, using the array G to

a. Compute the average score of each student across all disciplines.

b. Compute the freshman average scores for Accounting I, for Business Law, and for Principles of Management.

c. Provide a list of all students whose three final scores are all above the freshman average scores for each of the three subject areas.

d. Award a prize to student(s) with highest scores in Principles of Management. Print the name(s) of the recipient(s).

e. Award a scholarship to any student who obtains the three highest scores in the three subject areas (if there is such a student). Continued on next page.

The output should be similar to the following report:

```
        SEMESTER END REPORT
              BUSINESS
          ACCT. I    LAW      MANAGEMENT    AVERAGE
HORNET       40        50          60         50.0
BOIL         50        90          40         60.0
SMITHEN      20        60          10         30.0

CLASS AVERAGE  36.7     66.7        36.7

STUDENT NAMES WHOSE 3 TESTS EXCEED THE 3 CLASS AVERAGES
                        BOIL
AWARD GOES TO HORNET
SCHOLARSHIP IS AWARDED TO NO ONE
```

8. Read into an array named WORD eight of each of the following: nouns, pronouns, verbs, adverbs, adjectives, and articles (repeated if necessary) and store their corresponding numerical word codes into an integer array called KODE. The word codes are: 1 = pronoun, 2 = verb, 3 = adverb, 4 = adjective, 5 = noun, 6 = article. A typical input file might appear as:

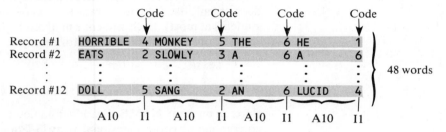

After reading this input file, the two arrays WORD and KODE would appear as follows:

WORD	HORRIBLE	MONKEY	THE	HE	EATS	SLOWLY	...	DOLL	SANG	AN	LUCID

KODE	4	5	6	1	2	3	...	5	2	6	4

KODE(1)   KODE(2)   KODE(48)

a. Write a program to load an array TABLE(8,6) in such a way that column 1 of TABLE contains all the pronouns, column 2 contains all the verbs, and so forth; then write out TABLE to produce the following arrangement:

PRONOUNS	VERBS	ADVERBS	ADJECTIVES	NOUNS	ARTICLES
HE	EATS	SLOWLY	HORRIBLE	MONKEY	THE
⋮	⋮	⋮	⋮	⋮	⋮
	SANG		LUCID	DOLL	AN

b. Using the random-number generator routine to extract entries from the 48-word array (not from the six sorted word arrays), construct two English sentences to fit the following grammatical structure:

Article, noun, verb, adjective. Pronoun, verb, article, adverb, adjective, noun.

For example, the following sentences might be generated:

`THE ANIMAL IS TALL. HE IS A VERY BEAUTIFUL MONKEY.`

Analyze the selected numerical codes to keep rejecting words until they satisfy the desired grammatical structure. [*Hint*: You might want to store the numerical word codes for the sentence in an array where NUM(1) = 6, NUM(2) = 5, NUM(3) = 2, ..., NUM(10) = 5 and compare NUM(I) with KODE(J), where I varies from 1 to 10 and J is a random number between 1 and 48.]

9. Grid analysis is a marketing strategy technique used to examine product-related needs of customers. The following market grid for apartments was developed in Dallas to help builders better understand the needs (grey squares) of customers:

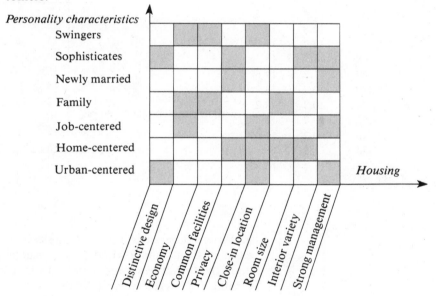

Write a program to read the data shown (using any code you wish) into an array and perform the following functions:

a. Accept one personality characteristic from input and list corresponding housing needs. For instance, given the following response and cue

`ENTER PERSONALITY CHARACTERISTICS? FAMILY`

The computer should print

```
FOR FAMILY CHARACTERISTIC THE NEEDS ARE:
    1 ECONOMY
    2 COMMON FACILITIES
    3 ROOM SIZE
```

b. Accept one housing need from input and list personality characteristics sharing that need. Use the same input/output format as in part (a).

c. Accept one housing need from input and list the personality characteristics that do *not* require that need.

d. Accept a pair of personality characteristics and list all the corresponding needs. For example, newlywed, urban-centered: distinctive design, privacy, close-in location, strong management.

10. The table on the left shows life expectancy, and the table on the right shows how long a savings amount will last if it is invested at a fixed interest rate and a fixed percentage of the amount is withdrawn consistently every year. For example, if one's savings earns 10% interest and one withdraws 10% of the amount every year, the withdrawal process can go on indefinitely; however, if 11% of the amount is withdrawn every year, then the withdrawal process will last only 25 years.

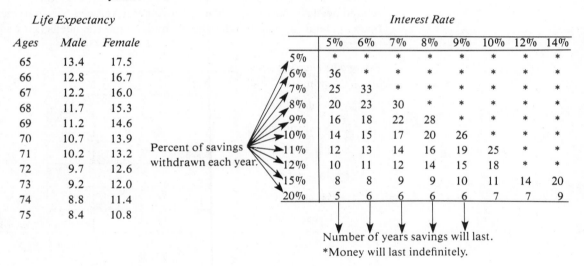

Life Expectancy

Ages	Male	Female
65	13.4	17.5
66	12.8	16.7
67	12.2	16.0
68	11.7	15.3
69	11.2	14.6
70	10.7	13.9
71	10.2	13.2
72	9.7	12.6
73	9.2	12.0
74	8.8	11.4
75	8.4	10.8

Interest Rate

Percent of savings withdrawn each year.

	5%	6%	7%	8%	9%	10%	12%	14%
5%	*	*	*	*	*	*	*	*
6%	36	*	*	*	*	*	*	*
7%	25	33	*	*	*	*	*	*
8%	20	23	30	*	*	*	*	*
9%	16	18	22	28	*	*	*	*
10%	14	15	17	20	26	*	*	*
11%	12	13	14	16	19	25	*	*
12%	10	11	12	14	15	18	*	*
15%	8	8	9	9	10	11	14	20
20%	5	6	6	6	6	7	7	9

Number of years savings will last.
*Money will last indefinitely.

a. Write a program to store both tables in memory, and write the code to read an interest rate and a withdrawal percentage and determine the number of years the withdrawal process can continue. For example, a savings amount earning 8% interest with an 11% withdrawal rate will last for 16 years.

b. Given an individual's age (65 or over), a sex code, a savings amount, and an interest rate, determine the largest possible yearly savings withdrawal that will leave the individual as close to broke as possible (as allowed by the table) at the time of death!

For example, a male, age 75, with $10,000 in savings at 10% interest rate, has a life expectancy of 8.4 years. His maximum percentage of withdrawal is then 15%. Twenty percent would be too high (the withdrawal process could last only 7 years). Hence his maximum yearly withdrawal would be $1500. (This would still leave a little extra for funeral expenses!)

Another example: A male, age 65, with $10,000 savings invested at 7% interest rate, has a life expectancy of 13.4 years. His maximum withdrawal would be 11%, for a yearly withdrawal of $1,100.

11. You are tallying returns from a primary election in which five candidates were running for office: Aiken, Andover, Hilary, Martin, and Watson. Each vote is recorded on one record with two entries per record. The first entry is a number identifying the party of the voter (1 = Democrat, 2 = Republican, 3 = Independent). The second entry identifies the name of the candidate.

    a. Write a program to determine the total number of votes obtained by each candidate. If a candidate obtains six or more votes from any party, print the number of votes from that party and the party. For example:

```
CANDIDATE    TOTAL VOTES      PARTY          NUMBER OF VOTES

AIKEN            4

WATSON                        DEMOCRAT             6
WATSON           21           INDEPENDENT          10

ANDOVER          8

HILARY           14           INDEPENDENT          10

MARTIN                        DEMOCRAT             6
MARTIN                        REPUBLICAN           6
MARTIN           20           INDEPENDENT          8
```

Note for example that Mr. Watson must have gotten five votes from the Republican party; the name of the party is not printed, however, since he did not obtain at least six votes in that party.

    b. List the candidates who obtained votes from each of the three parties. For the example given above, the output might be:

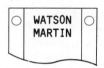

```
WATSON
MARTIN
```

    c. Identify candidates who were elected by one or more Democrats, by one or more Republicans, etcetera. Given the above input, the output could be as follows:

```
BY AT LEAST 1 DEMOCRAT:     AIKEN    ANDOVER MARTIN WATSON
BY AT LEAST 1 REPUBLICAN:   MARTIN   HILARY  WATSON
BY AT LEAST 1 INDEPENDENT:  ANDOVER HILARY  MARTIN WATSON
```

12. A large computer company decided some years ago to study whether there was any relationship between the major of a college student and his or her success in the computer field. Four hundred graduates were selected as follows: 70 in mathematics, 156 in engineering, and 174 in liberal arts. At the end of the company training period, overall scores revealed the following:

	Performance		
	Excellent	Fair	Unsatisfactory
Mathematics	37	23	10
Liberal arts	56	76	42
Engineering	25	64	67

The formula used to determine whether "major" is a significant factor in success is:

$$x = \frac{1}{4} \sum_{j=1}^{3} \sum_{i=1}^{3} (f_{ij} - e_{ij})^2 = \frac{1}{4} [(f_{11} - e_{11})^2 + (f_{12} - e_{12})^2 + (f_{13} - e_{13})^2 + (f_{21} - e_{21})^2 + \ldots + (f_{33} - e_{33})^2]$$

where f_{ij} is $\dfrac{(\text{sum of row } i) \cdot (\text{sum of column } j)}{\text{sum of all entries of performance array}}$

(row and column refer to the above performance array)

For example, $f_{23} = \dfrac{(56 + 76 + 42) \cdot (10 + 42 + 67)}{400}$

e_{ij} is number of students in cell at row i and column j. For example, $e_{23} = 42$.

Write a program to read the given numbers in an array and determine whether there is a relationship between major and future success in the computer field. If $x > 9.488$, the relationship exists; otherwise, it does not.

13. The region shown below is a two-dimensional model of a section of a nuclear reactor. The point marked S is the source of particles that are free to travel one mesh step in any direction with equal probability. Points marked A are centers of absorption; any particle reaching such a point is considered to have been absorbed. Points marked R are reflectors that return a particle to the point from which it came, taking a total of two steps for the process. Points marked E indicate that a particle escapes through the absorbing medium. Blank points are scattering centers from which the particle moves one mesh step in any direction with equal probability. Motion can be in the horizontal or vertical direction only. The source is to be considered a normal mesh point.

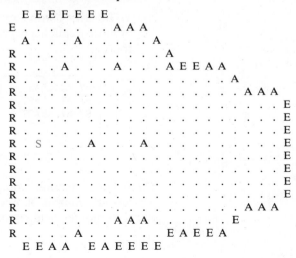

Write a program to start individual particles one at a time from point S and follow them one at a time to their escape or absorption.

    a. Run 500 particles; keep track of each particle in an array that records the number of steps taken and whether the particle was absorbed or escaped. Terminate any particles remaining in the reactor after 500 moves and count them (such particles are neither absorbed nor escaped).

    b. Print out the percentage of particles that escaped and the percentage that were absorbed.

    c. Print out the number of particles that escaped versus the number of steps taken (so many escaped on the fifth step, so many escaped on the sixth step, and so forth). Do the same for the particles that were absorbed.

    d. Print how many particles escaped through the right-most points.

The output should be similar to:

```
PERCENTAGE ESCAPED                 .        XXX.X
PERCENTAGE ABSORBED                         XXX.X
ESCAPES THROUGH RIGHT-MOST POINTS    XX
PARTICLES OVER 500 MOVES             XX

    ABSORBED    ESCAPED    NO. STEPS
       2           0           4
       4           3          10
       0          22          96
       :           :           :
       :           :           :
      24           0         126
       :           :           :
       0           1         500
```

Interpretation: Two particles were absorbed in 4 steps.
                  Four particles were absorbed in 10 steps; three particles escaped in 10 steps (output line 2); and so forth.
The number-of-steps column should be in ascending order.

    Use a random number generator to generate the numbers 1, 2, 3, and 4 and associate these four random numbers with the four directions of motion.

14. An input file contains at most 100 records. Each record contains a student name, the number of tests the student took that semester, and the test scores themselves (see the following sample input). Students may take only the final if they want to, or both the 12 weeks test and the final, or the 6 and 12 weeks tests and the final. The tests are recorded on the input record in the following order:
final, 12 weeks test (test 2), 6 weeks test (test 1).

    Write the code to first read the input data into arrays NAME, GRADES, and N (number of tests), but do *not* do any accumulation or computation during this initial reading phase. After the scores have been read into the two-dimensional table GRADES, process the data. List the names, the scores, and the test averages of all students who took three tests. Provide similar lists of the students who took two tests and those who took one test. Finally, print the class averages for the three tests.

No grades other than the scores read from the input record should be stored in the GRADES table; i.e., unused elements of GRADES should not be initialized to 0's or to any other values.

The input and output have the following form:

Sample Input

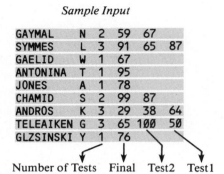

```
GAYMAL     N  2  59   67
SYMMES     L  3  91   65   87
GAELID     W  1  67
ANTONINA   T  1  95
JONES      A  1  78
CHAMID     S  2  99   87
ANDROS     K  3  29   38   64
TELEAIKEN  G  3  65  100   50
GLZSINSKI  Y  1  76
```

Number of Tests   Final   Test2   Test1

Sample Output

NAME		TEST 1	TEST 2	FINAL	AVERAGE
SYMMES	L	87	65	91	81.0
ANDROS	K	64	38	29	43.7
TELEAIKEN	G	50	100	65	71.7
GAYMAL	N		67	59	63.0
CHAMID	S		87	99	93.0
GAELID	W			67	67.0
ANTONINA	T			95	95.0
JONES	A			78	78.0
GLZSINSKI	Y			76	76.0
AVERAGE		67.0	71.4	73.2	

Array GRADES

59	67	
91	65	87
67		
95		
78		
99	87	
29	38	64
65	100	50
76		

Array N

2
3
1
1
1
2
3
3
1

15. *A Digital Data Noise-Elimination Problem.* A common problem in the collection of digital data via telecommunications is the phenomenon of noise—momentary fluctuations in the signal. When the transmitted data represents an image, as in pictures transmitted by satellites and space vehicles, noise results in obviously invalid random black, white, and gray spots when the image is reconverted to visual form. In order to eliminate at least some noise from a picture, it is possible to examine the image in digital form prior to converting it to visual form and replace noise elements by an estimate of the correct signal. Noise elements can be found by examining the difference between each element and the elements surrounding it. Noise elements generally differ drastically from the surrounding elements, for example, a white element surrounded by black elements or a black element surrounding by white. An estimate of the correct signal can be made by replacing the noise element by the average of the surrounding elements.

Write a program to eliminate noise from a digitized image stored in a 30 × 30 array. Each element of the array represents one "spot" in the image and stores a value from 0 to 9. Zero represents white; 9 represents black; the values between 0 and 9 represent shades of gray. An element is assumed to be a noise element if it differs in absolute value by 4 or more from five of its surrounding elements. For example, consider the element A(3,3) in the array below. There are eight elements surrounding A(3,3); the relevant differences are:

$$|7 - 3| = 4$$
$$|6 - 3| = 3$$
$$|9 - 3| = 6$$
$$|9 - 3| = 6$$
$$|2 - 3| = 1$$
$$|8 - 3| = 5$$
$$|8 - 3| = 5$$
$$|1 - 3| = 2$$

Array A →

7	2	1	2	5
6	7	6	9	7
8	9	3	2	2
7	8	8	1	2
5	6	7	1	7

Five of the differences are greater than or equal to 4, hence the element can be classified as a noise element. Noise elements should be replaced by the average of the surrounding elements, in this case

$$A(3,3) = \frac{7 + 6 + 9 + 9 + 2 + 8 + 8 + 1}{8} = 6$$

Assume boundary elements (rows 1 and 30 and columns 1 and 30) are not distorted. How would you change your program to account for possible distorted boundary elements?

16. *A Digital Image Enhancement.* Another problem in the analysis of images in digitized form is that objects are sometimes difficult to recognize because of insufficient contrast between the object and its background. One method that can be used to enhance digital images is to reduce the number of distinct shades of gray from the number represented in the initial signal (ten in the previous problem) to a lesser number such as five (black, white, and three shades of gray), three (black, white, and gray), or even two (black and white). This process is somewhat like increasing the contrast on a black-and-white television set. With increased contrast some detail is lost but the remaining images are more prominent.

Write a program to enhance contrast in the 30 × 30 digitized images described below. Perform three enhancements: translate the image from the original ten different values to five (low contrast), three (medium contrast), and two (high contrast) different values using the following table of transformations:

Original Value	Low Contrast	Medium Contrast	High Contrast
0	0	0	0
1	0	0	0
2	2	0	0
3	2	4	0
4	4	4	0
5	4	4	9
6	6	4	9
7	6	9	9
8	8	9	9
9	8	9	9

For example, given the following 3 × 3 digitized image, we generate 3 "contrast" images:

| Original Image | Low Contrast | Medium Contrast | High Contrast |

Original Image			*Low Contrast*			*Medium Contrast*			*High Contrast*		
7	6	9	6	6	8	9	4	9	9	9	9
9	6	2	8	6	2	9	4	0	9	9	0
8	8	1	8	8	0	9	9	0	9	9	0

The following examples show two images that have been digitized and processed for high and low contrast images. To give the images more tone/contrast, many characters have been multistruck with different characters to give the picture varying tones of gray. Each printer line was made to advance half its usual vertical spacing. For a hint on how to proceed, look at the program at the end of this chapter on page 412.

Original Digital Image   *Low Contrast Image*   *High Contrast Image*

Digitized Image   *Low Contrast Image*   *High Contrast Image*

17. The world is at war, and the only hope to conquer the enemy is to destroy its command post. Army intelligence agents have intercepted a chart (see diagram that follows) of an area in the Mohave desert showing exactly where the enemy command post is located. This chart divides a certain region of the desert into areas of square yards. Each square yard on the chart is identified by two numbers. The first number represents its north-south position on the chart, and the second number represents its east-west position on the chart. The chart shows a total of ten yards running north to south and a total of ten yards running east to west. The top of the chart is north and the bottom is south (rows), while the left side of the chart is west and the right side is east (columns). (For example, area (1,1) on the chart is the area in the upper left corner and (10,10) is the area on the lower right corner; area (3,4) means the third area down and the fourth area to the right.) To fully protect the enemy's command post, explosive land mines are planted in every square yard around the post except for a *single* path so that men and supplies can move in and out. Any person who steps on any portion of the square yard with a mine will be blown up. Using the provided chart, you are to follow the path free from mines and destroy the enemy command post, being careful not to step on any areas with mines.

Initialize a two-dimensional array with 1's for the squares in the gray area and 0's for the path free of mines (light area).

Output:

a. Print out the map of 0's and 1's using an attractive format.

b. Once all the data is read, you are to follow the path that must be taken to safely reach the command post and print out the two integer identification numbers for each area you travel through (including the area where you start and end).

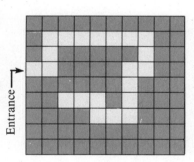

The following assumptions must be made:
  (1) The path starts at (4,1).
  (2) You cannot go back and retrace your steps.
  (3) When the path ends and you can go no further (mines are all around you), you have reached the command post and are not to try to travel any further!
  (4) You can travel only north, south, east, or west (you cannot travel diagonally).
  (5) Once you have found the correct path, you radio the path coordinates to your second-in-command, who is to follow your footsteps directly to the command post, without ever testing for mines. To ensure that he obeys, you order him to replace all 0's of the clear path by 3's and to print the region once he is safe at the command post.

18. The Furnishmatic Warehouse Company is a national distribution center for five types of furniture items: chairs, tables, desks, beds, and sofas. Each item comes in two styles, referred to henceforth as style A and style B. The company keeps track of outgoing shipments as follows: The first five records of the daily transaction file identify the particular furniture items by numeric code and specify the stock on hand for each item at the start of the business day. These five records are not updated during the day. Subsequent records identify transaction shipments as they occur during the day; these records specify the numeric code for the item, the quantity shipped, and the particular style. The following example shows the form of the input file:

Item code	In stock Style A	In stock Style B		Item code
1	2000	1000		1 = Chairs
2	1000	0500		2 = Tables
3	0500	0200	*Header Records*	3 = Desks
4	1000	1000		4 = Beds
5	0500	0200		5 = Sofas
1	100	A		
1	050	B		
2	400	A	*Shipments*	
1	100	B		
5	100	B		

a. Write the program to produce the following end-of-day transaction summary:

	SHIPMENTS		ENDING STOCK LEVEL	
	STYLE A	STYLE B	STYLE A	STYLE B
CHAIRS	100	150	1900	850
TABLES	400	0	600	500
DESKS	0	0	500	200
BEDS	0	0	1000	1000
SOFAS	0	100	500	100

b. This part requires interactive communication with the computing system. Write the code to carry out the inquiries described in the following paragraphs.

The warehouse agent would like to make the inventory processing system more flexible; in addition to entering the regular item transactions shown in part (a), he would like to ask the computer questions. The agent settles on two forms of inquiry. One informs him of the current stock level of all items when he types the query code INVEN on the screen (terminal). The computer's response should appear on the screen as follows:

	STYLE A	STYLE B
CHAIRS	1900	850
TABLES	600	500
DESKS	500	200
BEDS	1000	1000
SOFAS	500	100

The other form of inquiry allows the agent to enter a numeric item code and a style; the computer responds with the number of such items that have already been shipped out. The query and the response should appear on the screen as follows:

```
1   B
CHAIRS    STYLE B    SHIPMENT: 150
```

In order for the agent to enter regular transactions in addition to the two forms of inquiry discussed above, the program must be written in such a way that the terminal constantly polls the agent by leaving the following messages on the terminal when idle:

```
TO ENTER REGULAR TRANSACTIONS:          ENTER 1
TO DISPLAY CURRENT INVENTORY:           ENTER INVEN
TO DETERMINE NUMBER OF ITEMS SHIPPED:   ENTER 2
TO TERMINATE:                           ENTER 3
```

For example, a typical dialogue between agent and terminal might be as follows (the characters in red identify the agent's inquiries):

```
TO ENTER REGULAR TRANSACTIONS          ENTER 1
TO DISPLAY CURRENT INVENTORY           ENTER INVEN
TO DETERMINE NUMBER OF ITEMS SHIPPED   ENTER 2
TO TERMINATE                           ENTER 3
1
ENTER TRANSACTION
1   100   A
TO ENTER REGULAR TRANSACTIONS ENTER 1
TO DISPLAY CURRENT INVENTORY ENTER INVEN
TO DETERMINE NUMBER OF ITEMS SHIPPED ENTER 2
TO TERMINATE ENTER 3
INVEN
              STYLE A      STYLE B
CHAIRS        1900         1000
TABLES        1000         500
DESKS         500          200
BEDS          1000         1000
SOFAS         500          200
TO ENTER REGULAR TRANSACTIONS ENTER 1
TO DISPLAY CURRENT INVENTORY ENTER INVEN
TO DETERMINE NUMBER OF ITEMS SHIPPED ENTER 2
TO TERMINATE ENTER 3
2
ENTER SELECTION
1   B
CHAIRS    STYLE B   SHIPMENT: 80
```

c. The agent still feels that the process in part (b) is awkward. He would rather have the computer display a menu of possible inquiries to which he could give a simple response. For example, a menu to take care of part (b) of this exercise would appear on the screen as:

```
STOCK LEVEL MENU
WHAT TYPE OF ITEM?
1

WHAT STYLE?
B
WHAT DETAIL CODE?
2
```

Write the code to allow this type of interaction.

19. A matrix is a rectangular array of numbers. Addition and multiplication of matrices is illustrated in the following examples (also see exercise 16, section 7.6.1):

Addition

$$\begin{pmatrix} a_{11} & a_{12} & a_{13} \\ a_{21} & a_{22} & a_{23} \end{pmatrix} + \begin{pmatrix} b_{11} & b_{12} & b_{13} \\ b_{21} & b_{22} & b_{23} \end{pmatrix} = \begin{pmatrix} a_{11}+b_{11} & a_{12}+b_{12} & a_{13}+b_{13} \\ a_{21}+b_{21} & a_{22}+b_{22} & a_{23}+b_{23} \end{pmatrix}$$

Multiplication

$$\begin{pmatrix} a_{11} & a_{12} & a_{13} \\ a_{21} & a_{22} & a_{23} \end{pmatrix} \cdot \begin{pmatrix} b_{11} & b_{12} \\ b_{21} & b_{22} \\ b_{31} & b_{32} \end{pmatrix} = \begin{pmatrix} a_{11}\cdot b_{11}+a_{12}\cdot b_{21}+a_{13}\cdot b_{31} & a_{11}\cdot b_{12}+a_{12}\cdot b_{22}+a_{13}\cdot b_{32} \\ a_{21}\cdot b_{11}+a_{22}\cdot b_{21}+a_{23}\cdot b_{31} & a_{21}\cdot b_{12}+a_{22}\cdot b_{22}+a_{23}\cdot b_{32} \end{pmatrix}$$

In general, if A is m by n (m rows and n columns) and B is n by q, then the product matrix C = A·B is of size m by q. The number of columns in A must equal the number of rows in B. Such matrices are said to be *conformable*.

a. Write a program to read two 4 by 3 matrices and compute their sum and difference (to subtract, the corresponding entries are subtracted).

b. Write a program to read a 3 by 3 matrix A and a 3 by 3 matrix B. Compute A·B and (A + B)·(A − B).

c. Write a program to read a value for N and compute A^N where A is a 3 by 3 matrix that has been read in.

$$A^N = \underbrace{A\cdot A\cdot\ldots\cdot A}_{N\text{ matrices}}$$

d. Read in a square matrix A and print out its tranpose A^T (the rows of A^T are equal to the columns of A; row i of A^T = column i of A).

20. The XYZ Company manufactures four products: P1, P2, P3, P4. Each of these products must undergo some type of operation on five different machines:

A, B, C, D, E. The time (in units of hours) required for each of these products on each of the five machines is shown below:

	A	B	C	D	E
P1	0.2	0.2	0.1	0.58	0.15
P2	0.26	0.1	0.13	0.61	0.3
P3	0.5	0.21	0.56	0.45	0.27
P4	0.6	0.17	1.3	0.25	0.31

For example, product P1 requires 0.2 hour on machine A, 0.2 hour on machine B, 0.1 hour on machine C, and so on.

a. The XYZ Company has been requested to fill an order of 356 of product P1, 257 of product P2, 1,058 of product P3, and 756 of product P4. Write a program to determine the total number of hours that *each* machine will be used. [*Hint*: Express the table as a 4 by 5 matrix; express the order as a 1 by 4 matrix, and multiply the two matrices. You do not need to know about matrices to solve this problem, however!]

b. The XYZ Company is renting the five machines A, B, C, D, E from a tooling company. The hourly rental cost for each machine is as follows:

Machines	A	B	C	D	E
Rental cost/hour	$10.00	$5.75	$3.50	$10.00	$5.76

Write a program to compute the total rental expense for all the machines. [*Hint*: Express the rental costs as a 1 by 6 matrix and multiply by the matrix result from part (a). This problem can be solved without matrices.]

21. Write a program to verify that for any conformable matrices X, Y, and Z of your choice the following are true:

a. $(X + Y) \cdot Z = X \cdot Z + Y \cdot Z$

b. $(X \cdot Y) \cdot Z = X \cdot (Y \cdot Z)$

c. $X \cdot X^{-1} = X^{-1} \cdot X = I$

The inverse of a matrix (X^{-1}) is only defined for square matrices. Not all square matrices have inverses, however. A matrix X multiplied by its inverse yields the identity matrix I, which consists of 1's down the main diagonal and 0's elsewhere. For part (c) above use the following matrices

$$X = \begin{pmatrix} 1 & 2 & -3 \\ 4 & -1 & 2 \\ 14 & -1 & 3 \end{pmatrix} \quad \text{and } X^{-1} = \begin{pmatrix} -1 & -3 & 1 \\ 16 & 45 & -14 \\ 10 & 29 & -9 \end{pmatrix}$$

22. Let us refer to A′ (A prime) as the transpose of matrix A (see problem 20d). Write a program to demonstrate that

$$(A')^{-1} = (A^{-1})'$$

Use the X matrices shown in exercise 21.

23. An *n* by *n* matrix A is said to be *symmetric* if and only if A = A′. Write a program to demonstrate that

a. $A \cdot A'$ is symmetric and

b. $A + A'$ is symmetric.

24. A strictly triangular matrix is a square matrix with all entries on and below the main diagonal equal to zero. Write a program to demonstrate that if A is a 4 by 4 strictly triangular matrix, then $A^4 = A \cdot A \cdot A \cdot A$ is the zero matrix (in general, A^n is the zero matrix if A is an n by n strictly triangular matrix).

25. Write a program to verify that $DET(A \cdot B) = DET(A) \cdot DET(B)$, where A and B are square matrices and DET refers to the determinant of the matrix.

26. Write a program to verify that the determinant of a triangular matrix is equal to the product of its diagonal elements; use a square matrix of size 4.

27. An iterative method[1] for computing the inverse of a matrix A is given by

$$A^{-1} = I + B + B^2 + B^3 + B^4 + ...,$$

where $B = I - A$ (I is the identity matrix). Compute the inverse of

$$A = \begin{pmatrix} 1/2 & 1 & 0 \\ 0 & 2/3 & 0 \\ -1/2 & -1 & 2/3 \end{pmatrix}$$

Stop at B^{10} in the expansion for A^{-1}. Check the result by computing $A^{-1}*A$.

28. The trace of a matrix is defined as the sum of its diagonal elements. Let A be a 5 by 5 matrix and B be a 5 by 5 matrix. Write a program to determine that $tr(A \cdot B) = tr(B \cdot A)$ and $tr(A + B) = tr(A) + tr(B)$.

29. A method for computing the inverse of any matrix on a computer is as follows:

$$A^{-1} = -\frac{1}{c_n}(A^{n-1} + c_1 A^{n-2} + c_2 A^{n-3} + ... + c_{n-1}I)$$

where the c's are all constants defined as

$c_1 = -tr(A)$ (See exercise 28 for the definition of the trace.)
$c_2 = -1/2(c_1 tr(A) + tr(A^2))$
$c_3 = -1/3(c_2 tr(A) + c_1 tr(A^2) + tr(A^3))$
$\vdots$
$c_n = -1/n(c_{n-1} tr(A) + c_{n-2} tr(A^2) + ... + c_1 tr(A^{n-1}) + tr(A^n))$

Write a program to compute the inverse of a 5 by 5 matrix A and check that it is indeed the inverse by verifying that $A \cdot A^{-1} = I$, where I is the identity matrix.

For example, the inverse of a 2 by 2 matrix X is $X^{-1} = -\frac{1}{c_2}(X + c_1 I)$ where $c_2 = -1/2(c_1 tr(X) + tr(X^2))$ and $c_1 = -tr(X)$.

---

[1] This method will work only when the eigenvalues of A are less than 1 in absolute value.

30. The following is the daily schedule of a small Pennsylvania airline.

Flight Number	Origin	Stops	Plane Capacity	Departure Time
700	State College	Harrisburg Baltimore Washington	5	7:05 A.M.
701	Washington	Harrisburg State College	5	9:00 A.M.
430	State College	Harrisburg Baltimore Washington	5	4:15 P.M.
431	Washington	Baltimore Harrisburg State College	5	6:15 P.M.

Write a program for maintaining passenger reservations for three days. If a plane is full, assume the passenger will accept the next available flight. After all transactions have been processed, print a listing by flight and stops of the passengers scheduled. The planes are very small; there is a maximum of five passengers per flight. Use a three-dimensional array to store reservations.

The output should have the following form:

```
DATE    FLIGHT                          PASSENGER
2/25    700     STATE COLLEGE TO        B. BALDRIGE
                HARRISBURG              H. DAVIS
                                        .
                HARRISBURG TO           B. BALDRIGE
                BALTIMORE               H. DAVIS
                                        .
                BALTIMORE TO            H. DAVIS   (Baldrige gets off at Baltimore)
                WASHINGTON
        701     WASHINGTON TO           A. CHARLES
                HARRISBURG              .
                                        .
                HARRISBURG TO           (Charles gets off in Harrisburg)
                STATE COLLEGE           .
                                        .
        430     STATE COLLEGE TO        .
                HARRISBURG              .
                        .               .
                        .               .
        431     .                       .
                .                       .
                .                       .
2/26    700     .                       .
        .       .       .               .
        .       .       .               .
```

Use the following list of reservation requests:

Transactions (Requests for Seats)

Name	Date Desires	From	To	Flight Number
B. Baldrige	2/25	State College	Baltimore	700
W. Bartlett	2/26	Harrisburg	State College	431
W. Broderick	2/25	Harrisburg	Washington	430
R. Cheek	2/26	Baltimore	State College	431
E. Cooley	2/27	State College	Washington	700
H. Davis	2/25	State College	Washington	700
S. Dalles	2/26	Harrisburg	State College	431
L. Donald	2/25	Baltimore	Washington	700
F. John	2/26	Baltimore	Harrisburg	431
L. Line	2/26	Washington	State College	431
M. Dohert	2/25	State College	Baltimore	700
W. Howard	2/26	Washington	Harrisburg	431
J. Jacks	2/25	Washington	State College	431
J. Jacks	2/26	State College	Washington	430
G. Holland	2/26	Harrisburg	Washington	700
G. Holland	2/27	Washington	Harrisburg	431
C. Italia	2/26	State College	Washington	700
C. Italia	2/26	Washington	Harrisburg	431
H. Kent	2/25	Baltimore	Harrisburg	431
H. Kent	2/27	Harrisburg	Baltimore	430
C. Murray	2/25	State College	Washington	700
C. Murray	2/26	Washington	State College	431
R. Steel	2/25	State College	Washington	700
R. Steel	2/25	Washington	State College	431
A. Charles	2/25	Washington	Harrisburg	701
A. Charles	2/26	Harrisburg	Washington	430
A. Jabbari	2/25	State College	Washington	700
B. Jolly	2/27	Baltimore	Harrisburg	431
J. Hay	2/26	State College	Harrisburg	430
D. Day	2/27	Washington	State College	431
C. Mead	2/25	State College	Baltimore	700
Z. Mattern	2/26	Washington	Harrisburg	431
D. Davidson	2/25	Harrisburg	State College	431
M. West	2/26	State College	Washington	700
L. Mudd	2/27	Baltimore	Harrisburg	431
R. Frat	2/25	Washington	Harrisburg	701

7.6.3 Answers to Test Yourself

1. **a.** Valid.

   b. Valid.

   c. Valid.

   d. Missing parentheses.

   e. Real number is invalid for size specification.

   f. Variable may not be used to specify array size.

   g. Valid.

   h. Misplaced parentheses.

   i. Lower bound must be less than upper bound.

   j. Valid.

2. A(1,1),A(2,1),A(1,2),A(2,2),A(1,3),A(2,3)A(1,4),A(2,4)
B(1,1,1),B(2,1,1),B(3,1,1),B(1,1,2),B(2,1,2),B(3,1,2),B(1,1,3),B(2,1,3),
B(3,1,3),B(1,1,4),B(2,1,4),B(3,1,4),
K(1,1,1),K(2,1,1),K(1,2,1),K(2,2,1), K(1,1,2),K(2,1,2),K(1,2,2),K(2,2,2)

3. TC will contain the sum of each column of A.
TR will contain the sum of each row of A.

4. **a.** WRITE( )(A(I),I = 4,90)

   b. WRITE( )(B(J),J = 1,99,2)

   c. READ( )(C(2,K),K = 1,5)

   d. READ( )(A(J,1),B(J),J = 1,3)

   e. WRITE( )(K,A(I,1),(B(J),J = 1,3),I = 1,2)

   f. READ( )(A(1,J),J = 1,3),(B(2,J),J = 1,3),(C(J),J = 1,3)

   g. WRITE( )(A(1,J),B(1,J),C(1,J),I,J = 1,3)

   h. WRITE( )((I,I = 1,4), J = 1,3)

5. **a.** A(1,1),A(2,1),A(3,1),A(1,2), A(2,2),A(3,2). 1 record.

   b. A(1,1),I,A(2,1),I,A(3,1),I,A(1,2),I,A(2,2), I,A(3,2),I. 4 records.

   c. A(1,1),A(2,1),A(3,1),J,A(1,2),A(2,2),A(3,2),J,A(1,3),A(2,3),A(3,3),J. 3 records.

   d. A(1,1),B(1,1),A(1,2),B(1,2),A(2,1),B(2,1),A(2,2),B(2,2),A(3,1),B(3,1),A(3,2),B(3,2). 12 records.

   e. C(1),A(1,1),A(1,2),A(1,3),P(1,1),P(2,1),C(2),A(2,1),A(2,2),A(2,3),P(1,2),P(2,2). 2 records.

   f. A(1,1,1),A(2,1,1),A(1,1,2),A(2,1,2),A(1,1,3),A(2,1,3),A(1,2,1),A(2,2,1),A(1,2,2),A(2,2,2),A(1,2,3),
   A(2,2,3). 2 records.

6. **a.** WRITE( )((A(I,J),J = 1,4),I = 1,3),(JSUM(I,J),J=1,4),I=1,3),VAR
   FORMAT (2X,12F4.0,12I4,F5.0)

   b. WRITE( )((A(I,J),J = 1,4),(JSUM(I,J),J = 1,4),VAR,I = 1,3)
   FORMAT(2X,4F4.0,4I4,F5.0)

   c. WRITE( )((A(I,J),I = 1,3),VAR,(JSUM(I,J),I = 1,3),J = 1,3)
   FORMAT(2X,3F4.0,F5.0,3I4)

   d. WRITE( )((A(I,J),JSUM(I,J),J = 1,4),I = 1,3)
   FORMAT(4(F5.0,I5))

   e. WRITE( )((A(I,J),JSUM(I,J),I = 1,3),J = 1,4)
   FORMAT(6(F5.0,I5))

7. **a.** READ( )((A(I,J),I = 1,4),J = 1,3)
   FORMAT(4F5.0)

   b. READ( )(A(1,J),J = 1,6),(B(I),I = 1,6)
   FORMAT(2(3F5.0/),(3F3.0))

   c. READ( )(A(I,1),B(I,1),I = 1,6)
   FORMAT(2(F4.0,1X,F5.0))

   d. READ( )(A(I,1),B(1,I),I = 1,6)
   FORMAT(2(F5.0,F6.0))

   e. READ( )((A(I,J),J = 1,3),(B(I,J),J = 1,2),I = 1,9)
   FORMAT(3F5.0,2F3.0)

   f. READ( )((A(I,J),J = 1,9),I = 1,8),((B(I,J),I = 1,4),J = 1,2)
   FORMAT(8(9F3.0/),(3F4.0))

```
8. a.    DIMENSION A(5,5),B(5)
         READ(5,1)((A(I,J),J=1,5),I=1,5)
       1 FORMAT(5F10.0)
         WRITE(6,2)((A(I,J),J=1,5),I=1,5)
         WRITE(6,2)((A(I,J),I=1,5),J=1,5)
       2 FORMAT(2X,5F10.0)

   b.    SUM = 0.
         DO 3 I = 1,5
            SUM = SUM + A(3,I)
       3 CONTINUE

   c.    ALARG = A(1,1)
         DO 4 I = 2,5
            IF(ALARG.LT.A(I,1))ALARG=A(I,1)
       4  CONTINUE

   d.    DO 5 I = 1,5
            B(I) = 0.
       5 CONTINUE
         DO 6 I = 1,5
         DO 6 J = 1,5
            B(J) = B(J) + A(I,J)
       6 CONTINUE

   e.    DO 7 I = 1,5
            A(3,I) = A(3,I)+A(2,I)
       7 CONTINUE

   f.    DO 8 I = 1,5
              HOLD = A(I,3)
              A(I,3) = A(I,4)
              A(I,4) = HOLD
       8 CONTINUE

   g.    SUM2 = 0.
         DO 9 I = 1,5
            SUM2 = SUM2 + A(I,I)
       9 CONTINUE

   h.    SSUM = 0.
         SLARG = A(1,5)
         DO 16 I = 1,5
            J = 6 - I
            SSUM = SSUM + A(I,J)
            IF(SLARG.LT.A(I,J))SLARG = A(I,J)
      16 CONTINUE

   i.    KROW = 1
         KOLUMN = 1
         ASMAL = A(1,1)
         DO 5 I = 1,5
         DO 5 J = 1,5
            IF(ASMAL.GT.A(I,J))THEN
               ASMAL = A(I,J)
               KROW = I
               KOLUMN = J
            ENDIF
       5 CONTINUE
         PRINT*, ASMAL, KROW, KOLUMN
```

9. $X(1,1)$, $X(2,1)$, $X(3,1)$, $X(1,2)$, $X(2,2)$, $X(3,2)$
   $Y(1,1,1)$, $Y(2,1,1)$, $Y(1,2,1)$, $Y(2,2,1)$, $Y(1,3,1)$, $Y(2,3,1)$
   $Y(1,1,2)$, $Y(2,1,2)$, $Y(1,2,2)$, $Y(2,2,2)$, $Y(1,3,2)$, $Y(2,3,2)$

```
10. READ(5,3)((C(I,J),J=1,5),(D(I,J),J=1,5),I=1,5)

11.   REAL R(4,6,5),S(4,5)
      DATA S/20 * 0./
      DO 5 I = 1,4
         DO 5 J = 1,6
            DO 5 K = 1,5
               S(I,K) = S(I,K) + R(I,J,K)
    5 CONTINUE

12.   REAL F(40,17),G(680)
         :
         :
      K = 1
      DO 10 I = 1,40
      DO 10 J = 1,17
         G(K) = F(I,J)
         K = K + 1
   10 CONTINUE

13.   REAL A(10,3)
      SUM = 0.
      DO 10 I = 1,10
      DO 10 J = 1,3
         SUM = SUM + A(I,J)
   10 CONTINUE
      WRITE(6,5)(J,J = 1,10),((A(I,J),I = 1,10),J = 1,3),SUM
    5 FORMAT(T30,'FINAL'/T5,10('COLUMN',I3,2X)/3(T5,10F6.1/)/T5,
     *'SUM IS',F5.1)

14. C GROCERY SHOPPING ANALYSIS
    C   A(5,4): ARRAY CONTAINING WEEKLY EXPENSES BY DAY & STORE
    C   SUM:    USED TO ACCUMULATE TOTAL DAILY EXPENSES
    C   DAY:    IDENTIFIES THE DAY
    C   STORE:  IDENTIFIES A PARTICULAR STORE
    C
          REAL A(5,4), SUM, COLUMN(4)
          INTEGER DAY, STORE
          DO 5 I = I, 5
             READ(5,1)(A(I,J),J=1,4)
    5     CONTINUE
          DO 4 J = 1,4
             SUM = 0.
             DO 6 I = 1,5
                SUM = SUM + 4(I,J)
    6     CONTINUE
             COLUMN(J) = SUM/5.
    4     CONTINUE
          WRITE(6,7)(I,I=1,4),(I,(A(I,J),J=1,4),I=1,5),COLUMN
          STOP
    7     FORMAT(8X,4('STORE ',I1,3X)//5(' DAY',I1,3X,4(F5.2,5X)/),
     A          ' AVERAGE ',4(F5.2,5X))
    1     FORMAT(4F5.2)
          END
```

Hint for problem 17 (digitized images)

```
            CHARACTER ICON(5),MOD(30,30)
            INTEGER IMAGE(30,30)
            DATA ICON/' ','0','1','X','*'/
            READ(5,15)LIM1,LIM2          LIM1 = number rows; LIM2 = number columns.
            READ(5,25)((IMAGE(K,L),L=1,LIM2),K=1,LIM1)
            WRITE(6,90)
            WRITE(6,30)((IMAGE(K,L),L=1,LIM2),K=1,LIM1)
            N=1
77          IF(N.EQ.2) THEN              digitized image       contrast character
                WRITE(6,60)                     code                 ICON
                KODKEY = 5                        ↓                    ↓
                KODADD = 4              0,1        blank
            ELSE                        2,3        0
                WRITE(6,40)             4,5        multistrike 0 and 1
                KODKEY = 2             6,7        multistrike 0, 1, and X
                KODADD = 1             8,9        multistrike 0, 1, X and *
            ENDIF
            KODMIN = 0              Any contrast characters can be chosen.
            DO 200 K = 1, LIM1
               DO 250 I = 1 ,5
                  DO 300 L = 1, LIM2
                     NUMCOM = (IMAGE(K,L)/KODKEY) + KODADD - KODMIN
                     IF (NUMCOM .LT. 1) NUMCOM = 1
                     IF(N.EQ.2 .AND. IMAGE(K,L).LT.5)NUMCOM = 1
300               MOD(K,L) = ICON(NUMCOM)
                  WRITE(6,10)(MOD(K,M),M=1,LIM2)
250            KODMIN = KODMIN + 1
               KODMIN = 0
200         WRITE(6,20)
            N = N + 1
            IF(N.LT.3) GO TO 77
            STOP
15          FORMAT(2I2)
25          FORMAT(30I1)      number of elements per line (LIM2)
40          FORMAT(/1X,'LOW CONTRAST IMAGE'/1X)
60          FORMAT(/1X,'HIGH CONTRAST IMAGE'/1X)
10          FORMAT('+',30A1)
20          FORMAT(1X)
90          FORMAT(1X,'ORIGINAL DIGITAL IMAGE'/1X)
30          FORMAT(1X,30I1)
            END
```

15.
```
C TWO-DIMENSIONAL BAR GRAPH
C    G(9,5): EACH COLUMN REPRESENTS A DAY'S TRANSACTION VOLUME
C    V(15):  THE 15 DAILY TRANSACTION VOLUMES ARE STORED IN V
C    I:      IS USED TO PRINT THE VERTICAL GRADUATIONS OF THE GRAPH
C    J:      IS USED TO PRINT THE HORIZONTAL GRADUATIONS OF THE GRAPH
C    SYMBOL(6) IS USED FOR MULTISTRIKING GRAPHIC SYMBOLS
      CHARACTER G(9,15), SYMBOL(6)
      INTEGER V(15)
      DATA G /135*' '/
      DATA SYMBOL /'M','W','A','*','L','E'/
      READ(5,1)V
      DO 5 J = 1,15
         DO 4 I = 1, V(J)
            G(I,J) = '*'
4        CONTINUE
5     CONTINUE
      DO 40 I = 9, 1,-1
         DO 60 K = 1,6
            DO 50 J = 1, 15
               IF(G(I,J) .NE. ' ') G(I,J)=SYMBOL(K)
50          CONTINUE
            WRITE(6,10)I,(G(I,J),J=1,15)
60       CONTINUE
         WRITE(6,9)
40    CONTINUE
      WRITE(6,8)((I,I=1,5),J=1,3)
      STOP
1     FORMAT(15I1)
8     FORMAT(4X,15I2)
10    FORMAT('+',2X,I1,15A2)
9     FORMAT(1X)
      END
```

Multistrike these 6 characters to obtain ■.

Same as in Figure 7.9.

Print each line 6 times on top of itself.

Print the graduations 1 2 3 4 5 1 2 3 4 5 . . . .

16.
```
      INTEGER A(5,4), B(4,3), C(5,3),SUM
      READ(5,1)((A(I,J),J=1,4),I=1,5)
      READ(5,2)((B(I,J),J=1,3),I=1,4)
      DO 4 I = 1,5
         DO 5 J = 1, 3
            SUM = 0
            DO 6 K = 1, 4
               SUM = SUM + A(I,K) * B(K,J)
6           CONTINUE
            C(I,J) = SUM
5        CONTINUE
4     CONTINUE
      WRITE(6,3)((A(I,J),J=1,4),I=1,5)
      WRITE(6,7)((B(I,J),J=1,3),I=1,4)
      WRITE(6,8)((C(I,J),J=1,3),I=1,5)
      STOP
1     FORMAT(4I1)
2     FORMAT(3I1)
3     FORMAT(1X,4I3)
7     FORMAT(1X,3I3)
8     FORMAT(1X,3I6)
      END
```

```
17. C PROCESSING A THREE-DIMENSIONAL ARRAY
    C   A(3,5,2):  HOURS LOST FOR 3 SHOPS, 5 MACHINES & 2 FACTORIES
    C   LOSTIM(5): CONTAINS HOURS LOST FOR EACH OF THE 5 MACHINES
    C
          REAL A(3,5,2), LOSTIM(5)
          INTEGER SHOP, MACHIN, FACTRY
          READ(5,1)(((A(I,J,K),J = 1,5), I = 1,3),K = 1,2)
          DO 30 MACHIN = 1, 5
             LOSTIM (MACHIN) = 0.0
             DO 20 FACTRY = 1, 2
                DO 15 SHOP = 1, 3
                   LOSTIM(MACHIN) = LOSTIM(MACHIN) + A(SHOP,MACHIN,FACTRY)
    15          CONTINUE
    20       CONTINUE
             LOSTIM(MACHIN) = LOSTIM(MACHIN)/6.
    30    CONTINUE
          DO 40 FACTRY = 1, 2
             WRITE(6,2)FACTRY,(SHOP,(A(SHOP,MACHIN,FACTRY),MACHIN=1,5),SHOP=1,3)
    40    CONTINUE
          WRITE(6,3)(LOSTIM(MACHIN),MACHIN = 1,5)
          STOP
    C
     1 FORMAT(5F4.1)
     2 FORMAT('0',16X,'FACTORY',I3/ (' SHOP',I2,4X,5F6.1))
     3 FORMAT('0','AVERAGES',1X,5F6.1)
          END
```

Program Modularization
Subroutine and Function
Subprograms

8.1 PROGRAM MODULARIZATION

8.1.1 Case Study 1:
Decomposition of a
Problem into Modules

In the following example we will break down the logic of a program into separate physical entities that we will call *modules*. Each module will perform one generalized task. In FORTRAN these modules are referred to as *subprograms,* implying that they are not complete programs but are one of the parts of the solution to a particular problem.

One characteristic of a module is that it can be executed from any other module, that is, each module has a built-in linkage that allows it to be accessed (called) by any module and that also allows it to return to the calling module when execution of the module is completed. A special module often referred to as the *coordinating module* (or main program in FORTRAN) contains the code that activates (passes control to) the other modules in a predefined order. A program that consists of a coordinating module and its network of modules is said to have *modular structure,* since it is made up of independent modules with clearly defined objectives. A modular system is elegant and powerful because each module or subprogram can be designed, coded, edited, and tested independently of the others.

Decomposing a problem into modules is referred to as *modularization.* A similar principle is used in many manufacturing processes such as modular-home construction, where independent home modules (kitchens, bathrooms, etcetera) are designed at some company headquarters, built and tested at a particular plant(s), and assembled and tested as a whole unit at the construction site.

Problem/Specification. Employees at Sarah's Style Shop are to receive a year-end bonus. The amount of the bonus depends on the employee's weekly pay, position code, and number of years with the store. Each employee is assigned a bonus based on the following rules:

Position Code	Bonus
1	One week's pay
2	Two weeks' pay; maximum of $700
3	One and a half week's pay

Employees with more than 10 years' experience are to receive an additional $100, and employees with fewer than 2 years' experience are to receive half of the bonus determined by their position code.

Write a program to read an input file where each record contains a name, a weekly pay, a position code, and a number of years' experience and compute the employee's final bonus amount.

The input data should be validated to ensure that the position code is valid (1, 2, or 3) and that the weekly pay does not exceed $1,000. In the event of invalid data, appropriate error messages should be printed, along with the sequence number of the invalid record.

A typical input file and output report are shown at the bottom of Figure 8.1.

Program Development. The program to solve this problem must perform the following three tasks:

1. Validating the input data.
2. Determining the bonus amount based on the position code.
3. Modifying the bonus amount, depending on the years of experience.

We will write three separate subprograms to perform these three distinct tasks and we will name them as follows:

- CHECK   This module will validate the weekly pay and the position code and write error messages (if necessary).
- BONUS   This module will compute the bonus amount based on the position code.
- SUPPLEMENT   This module will modify the bonus amount based on years of experience.

Another module called the coordinating module must then be written to coordinate and activate the sequence in which these three modules are to be called (used).

The overall control sequence can be depicted in the following chart, sometimes referred to as a *hierarchy chart:*

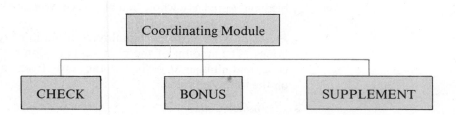

We can then write each module in pseudo code:

Coordinating Module

```
WHILE end of file not encountered DO
      read name, weekly pay, position code, and years
      set error flag to "no errors"
      make position code. weekly pay, and error flag available to CHECK
      and transfer to CHECK module
                                    ◄── upon return from CHECK
      IF error flag = "no errors" THEN
          make the following variables available to BONUS: position code, weekly
          pay, and another variable (amount), which will be used by BONUS to store
          the computed bonus amount; transfer to BONUS module
                                    ◄── upon return from BONUS
          make years and amount available to SUPPLEMENT and transfer to
          SUPPLEMENT module
                                    ◄── upon return from SUPPLEMENT
          write name and amount
      ENDIF
ENDWHILE
```

CHECK | position code, weekly pay, and error flag are made available to module
error flag returns a value to calling program

```
*Keep track of the record count in case record is invalid
 add 1 to record counter
 IF weekly pay > 1000 THEN
     write "invalid pay", record counter
     set error flag to "error"
 ENDIF
 IF position code is not 1, 2 or 3 THEN
     write "invalid code", record counter
     set error flag to "error"
 ENDIF
 return to calling module
```

BONUS | position code and weekly pay are made available to module
amount returns a value to calling module

```
IF position code = 1 THEN
    amount = weekly pay
ELSE
    IF position code = 2 THEN
        amount = 2 * weekly pay
        IF amount > 700 amount = 700
    ELSE
        amount = 1.5 * weekly pay
    ENDIF
ENDIF
return to calling module
```

SUPPLEMENT	years and amount are made available to module amount returns a value to calling module
IF years > 10 amount = amount + 100 IF years < 2 amount = amount/2 return to calling module	

Subprogram CHECK. If subprogram CHECK is to validate the input data, it must be told the name of the items to be validated, that is, CHECK needs to be able to access the contents of memory locations *weekly pay* and *position code.* CHECK must also be able to report to the coordinating program whether either or both items are invalid. Indeed, if one or both are invalid, then the coordinating program must skip subprograms BONUS and SUPPLEMENT. This reporting between CHECK and the coordinating program is accomplished by a flag that is set to the value "no error" in the main program, before control is passed to CHECK. If CHECK detects invalid fields, it then resets the flag to the value "error". Upon return to the main program, the flag is tested to determine whether a bonus is to be computed for the record read.

Altogether, then, CHECK must be able to link with three variables defined outside the CHECK program. These variables or *arguments,* must be passed (made available) from the calling program (in this case, the main program) to the called program (in this case, CHECK). The weekly pay and position code are *input arguments* to the CHECK subprogram, that is, these arguments simply feed information to CHECK— they are not changed by CHECK. The error flag, on the other hand, can be viewed as an *output argument,* since CHECK alters its value before returning to the calling program.

In FORTRAN a subprogram is named in a SUBROUTINE statement. Thus, "SUBROUTINE CHECK" gives the name CHECK to a subprogram. The subprogram's arguments (if any) are specified in the SUBROUTINE statement as follows:

```
SUBROUTINE CHECK (PAY, CODE, FLAG)     three arguments enclosed in parentheses
```

We can now formally state the validation problem: Given PAY, CODE, and FLAG, write a subprogram called CHECK to:

1. Print an error message if PAY exceeds 1000 and/or CODE is neither 1, 2, or 3.

2. Set FLAG to the value "ERROR" if one or both of these conditions are met.

The CALL statement, which is specified in the CALLing or main program, passes control from the calling program to subprogram CHECK:

```
CALL CHECK (PAY, CODE, FLAG)      in the CALLing program
```

It is interesting to note that the argument names specified in the SUBROUTINE statement can be different from the corresponding names specified in the calling sequence. While the names may be different, their values will be the same (as long as they are of matching types). Thus the linkage between programs could have been accomplished just as well by writing:

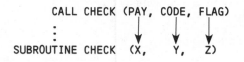

```
          CALL CHECK (PAY, CODE, FLAG)     X refers to same memory location as PAY.
          :                                Y refers to same memory location as CODE.
SUBROUTINE CHECK  (X,    Y,    Z)          Z refers to same memory location as FLAG.
```

In this case X refers to PAY, that is, X is just another name for memory location PAY. X is called a *dummy argument* since it does not actually reserve any memory storage (PAY does). Likewise, Y refers to CODE and Z to FLAG. The task to be carried out by CHECK could then be restated as:

1. Print an error message if X > 1000 and/or Y is neither 1, 2, or 3.

2. Set Z to the value "ERROR" if one or both of these conditions are met.

Lines 25–50 of Figure 8.1 give the complete FORTRAN code for subroutine CHECK.

The three subroutine arguments PAY, CODE, and FLAG at line 25 correspond to the actual arguments PAY, POSKOD, and ERRFLG at line 14 in the main program, where the CALL statement activates the subroutine. Note that the value of ERRFLG is set to the value "NO ERRORS" at line 13, but that value can be changed in the CHECK subprogram if an invalid input item is found (line 45). Remember that ERRFLG and FLAG are one and the same—if we change FLAG, we automatically change ERRFLG, too, i.e., FLAG and ERRFLG point to the same memory address.

The counter I at line 38 counts the number of records read and can therefore be used to identify the sequence number of invalid records. Because I is initialized in a DATA statement (line 37), it is not reset to 0 at line 37 every time CHECK is called. Also note that since I does not appear anywhere else except in subroutine CHECK, its memory storage location is defined in the memory area reserved for the CHECK program (unlike the storage locations of the three arguments).

Once the pay and position code have been validated, control is passed back to the calling program at line 49 by the special statement RETURN.

Note the documentation at lines 26–33. Arguments can be used in any of three ways:

1. Input: the subprogram uses the value(s) of the argument but does not change it (e.g., PAY and CODE at lines 27–29).

2. Input/output: argument value is used as input but is also changed by the subprogram (e.g., an array to be sorted).

3. Output: the value sent by the calling program is not used by the subprogram. The argument is simply used to return a value to the calling program (e.g., FLAG, line 41).

Subprogram BONUS. In this subprogram (lines 52–72) the names of the dummy arguments at line 52 are identical to the actual arguments at line 16, with the exception of AMOUNT and AMT. Still, POSKOD must be typed as an integer at line 59 since POSKOD is typed as an integer in the calling program (line 9)—corresponding arguments must match in type.

Note that AMOUNT is defined in the main program and is therefore assigned a memory location in the main program. Yet the main program does not store a value in AMOUNT—the BONUS subprogram does, at lines 62, 65, 66, and 68. The argument AMT, an output argument, actually refers to memory location AMOUNT, which is defined in the main program.

Subprogram SUPPLM. In this subprogram (lines 74–85) the two arguments are YEARS (input argument) and AMOUNT (input/output argument). Either $100.00 is added to AMOUNT (years > 10), or AMOUNT is divided by 2 (years < 2), or AMOUNT stays the same (years between 2 and 10). Recall that the initial value of AMOUNT is actually calculated in subprogram BONUS, not in the main program.

```
 1: ***** YEAR-END BONUS PROBLEM
 2: ***** NAME:    EMPLOYEE NAME
 3: ***** ERRFLG: FLAG IS SET IF INVALID DATA IS READ
 4: ***** POSKOD: POSITION CODE IN COMPANY (1, 2, OR 3)
 5: ***** PAY:     EMPLOYEE WEEKLY PAY
 6: ***** YEARS:   YEARS OF SENIORITY IN COMPANY
 7: ***** AMOUNT: BONUS AMOUNT
 8:        CHARACTER NAME*10,ERRFLG*10
 9:        INTEGER POSKOD,YEARS
10:        REAL PAY,AMOUNT
11:        WRITE (6,25)
12: 10     READ(5,*,END=88)NAME,PAY,POSKOD,YEARS
13:        ERRFLG = 'NO ERRORS'
14:        CALL CHECK(PAY,POSKOD,ERRFLG)
15:        IF(ERRFLG .EQ. 'NO ERRORS')THEN
16:           CALL BONUS(POSKOD,PAY,AMOUNT)
17:           CALL SUPPLM(YEARS,AMOUNT)
18:          WRITE(6,20)NAME,AMOUNT
19:        ENDIF
20:        GO TO 10
21: 88     STOP
22: 20     FORMAT(1X,A,1X,F7.2)
23: 25     FORMAT(1X,'NAME',8X,'BONUS')
24:        END
25:        SUBROUTINE CHECK(PAY,CODE,FLAG)
26: ***** ARGUMENT DEFINITIONS
27: *****    INPUT ARGUMENTS
28: *****       PAY:  EMPLOYEE WEEKLY PAY
29: *****       CODE: EMPLOYEE POSITION CODE
30: *****    OUTPUT ARGUMENT
31: *****       FLAG: IS SET IF PAY OR CODE ARE INVALID
32: ***** LOCAL VARIABLES
33: *****    I: IDENTIFIES NUMBER OF INVALID RECORD
34:        CHARACTER FLAG*9
35:        INTEGER CODE, I
36:        REAL PAY
37:        DATA I/0/
38:        I = I + 1
39:        IF(PAY .GT. 1000.00)THEN
40:           WRITE(6,10)I
41:           FLAG = 'ERROR'
42:        ENDIF
43:        IF(CODE .EQ. 0 .OR. CODE .GT. 3)THEN
44:           WRITE(6,11)I
45:           FLAG = 'ERROR'
46:        ENDIF
47: 10     FORMAT(3X,'INVALID PAY AMOUNT     AT RECORD',I3)
48: 11     FORMAT(3X,'INVALID POSITION CODE AT RECORD',I3)
49:        RETURN
50:        END
```

Line 13 — Assume the data read contains no errors (valid code and pay).
Line 14 — Send PAY and POSKOD values to the validation routine.
Lines 15–18 — If all input values are valid (no errors found in validation subroutine), go and compute the bonus AMOUNT based on the position code and pay (line 16) and either add 100 to AMOUNT, split AMOUNT in half, or leave AMOUNT unchanged, depending on number of years (line 18).
Line 20 — Go and read the next record (line 20).

Lines 28 — PAY refers to the same memory location as PAY in calling program.
Line 29 — CODE refers to the same memory location as POSKOD in calling program.
Line 31 — FLAG refers to the same memory location as ERRFLG in calling program.
Line 33 — I counts the number of records to identify those records containing invalid data.

Lines 39–41 — Write error message if PAY > 1000 and set flag to indicate invalid input.

Lines 43–45 — Write error message if code is not 1, 2, or 3 and set flag to indicate invalid input.
Note that one input record can give rise to two error messages.

```
51: *
52:         SUBROUTINE BONUS(POSKOD,PAY,AMT)
53: ****  ARGUMENT DEFINITIONS
54: ****     INPUT ARGUMENTS
55: ****        POSKOD: EMPLOYEE POSITION CODE
56: ****        PAY:    EMPLOYEE WEEKLY PAY
57: ****     OUTPUT ARGUMENTS
58: ****        AMT: BONUS AMOUNT
59:         INTEGER POSKOD
60:         REAL PAY,AMT
61:         IF (POSKOD .EQ. 1)THEN
62:           AMT = PAY
63:         ELSE
64:           IF(POSKOD .EQ. 2)THEN
65:             AMT = 2*PAY
66:             IF(AMT .GT. 700.00)AMT = 700.00
67:           ELSE
68:             AMT = 1.5 * PAY
69:           ENDIF
70:         ENDIF
71:         RETURN
72:         END
73: *
74:         SUBROUTINE SUPPLM(YEARS,AMOUNT)
75: ****  ARGUMENT DEFINITIONS
76: ****     INPUT ARGUMENTS
77: ****        YEARS: YEARS WITH THE COMPANY
78: ****     OUTPUT/INPUT ARGUMENTS
79: ****        AMOUNT
80:         INTEGER YEARS
81:         REAL AMOUNT
82:         IF(YEARS .GT. 10)AMOUNT=AMOUNT+100.00
83:         IF(YEARS .LT. 2) AMOUNT=AMOUNT/2.0
84:         RETURN
85:         END
```

POSKOD refers to the same memory location as POSKOD in calling program.
PAY refers to the same memory location as PAY in calling program.
AMT refers to the same memory location as AMOUNT in calling program.

AMT is equal to one week's pay.

AMT is twice the weekly pay but is set to 700 at line 66 if twice the PAY exceeds 700.

AMT is one and a half times the weekly pay.

YEARS refers to the same memory location as YEARS in calling program.
AMOUNT refers to the same memory location as AMOUNT in calling program.

Add 100 to AMOUNT if over 10 years.
Divide AMOUNT by 2 if under 2 years.

Output

```
NAME         BONUS

ARMSTRONG   100.00
DENTON      200.00
BREWTON     700.00
MOULTON     150.00
DEVINE       50.00
LOUDERMILK  200.00
  INVALID PAY AMOUNT      AT RECORD 7
  INVALID POSITION CODE AT RECORD 8
  INVALID PAY AMOUNT      AT RECORD 9
  INVALID POSITION CODE AT RECORD 9
HIGGINS     485.13
```

Input File

```
'ARMSTRONG',  100.00,1,05
'DENTON',     100.00,2,05
'BREWTON',    500.00,2,05
'MOULTON',    100.00,3,05
'DEVINE',     100.00,1,01
'LOUDERMILK',100.00,1,20
'SUZUCKI',   1001.0,1,11
'MAUPASSANT',456.00,4,02
'OMBOKO',    2000.0,5,21
'HIGGINS',    256.75,3,12
```

FIGURE 8.1
A MODULARIZED PROGRAM

8.1.2 Case Study 2: Multiple Use of a Generalized Module

In this example a particular task is to be carried out more than once at various points in a program. Rather than physically inserting the code for the task at the various points where it is needed, we simply write the generalized code once and branch to it (call it) whenever it is needed. This practice not only reduces the bulk of the program (lines of code) but also modularizes the program.

Problem/Specification. Given an unknown dollar amount, write a program to break down the dollar amount into the least number of quarters, dimes, nickels, and pennies.

One approach to this problem is shown in flowchart form in Figure 8.2, where we subtract successively 25, 10, and 5 from the amount to compute the number of quarters, dimes, and nickels. Note that block 1 in the flowchart of Figure 8.2 can be carried out any number of times, block 2 at most twice (there can be no more than two dimes), and block 3 at most once.

Also note that the type and order of operations in each block are identical. The only differences are in the names of the variables and the constants used (25, 10, and 5). Therefore we can write a generalized subroutine to perform any block operation (1, 2, or 3) using one dummy variable name to act as the various counters (quarter, dime, and nickel) and another dummy variable to represent the various amounts to be subtracted (25, 10, and 5). The resulting subroutine code would then be:

```
1:  SUBROUTINE CHANGE (AMOUNT, COIN, VALUE)
2:        AMOUNT = AMOUNT - VALUE
3:        COIN   = COIN + 1
4:  RETURN
5:  END
```

Note that

> if COIN = QUARTER and VALUE = 25, lines 2 and 3 represents block 1;
> if COIN = DIME   and VALUE = 10, lines 2 and 3 represents block 2;
> if COIN = NICKEL   and VALUE = 5, lines 2 and 3 represents block 3.

Figure 8.3 contains the complete program code. Subroutine CHANGE (lines 25–40) is called at lines 8, 12, and 16 for successively different values of AMT, COIN, and VALUE. The two arguments AMT and COIN are used as two-way communication links—two-way in the sense that the calling program sends values to the subroutine through AMT and COIN, and these values are in turn modified by the subroutine and sent back to the calling program. Thus they are both input and output arguments. The third argument VALUE is a one-way communication link transmitting a constant from the main program to the subroutine; thus VALUE is just an input argument. Note that all three subroutine arguments are declared as integers since they are integer values in the calling program.

8.1.3 Function Subprograms

In chapter 2 we discussed the square root function as well as other types of functions. A statement such as Y = SQRT(16.0) causes the computer to transfer to a system subprogram called SQRT. This subprogram computes the square root of the given argument (16.0 in this case) and returns a single value called the functional value (4 in this case). Such subprograms are called function subprograms since, generally speaking, they return only one value.

In this example, where we are given a one-dimensional array consisting of N numeric values, we will write one function subprogram to return the array element with

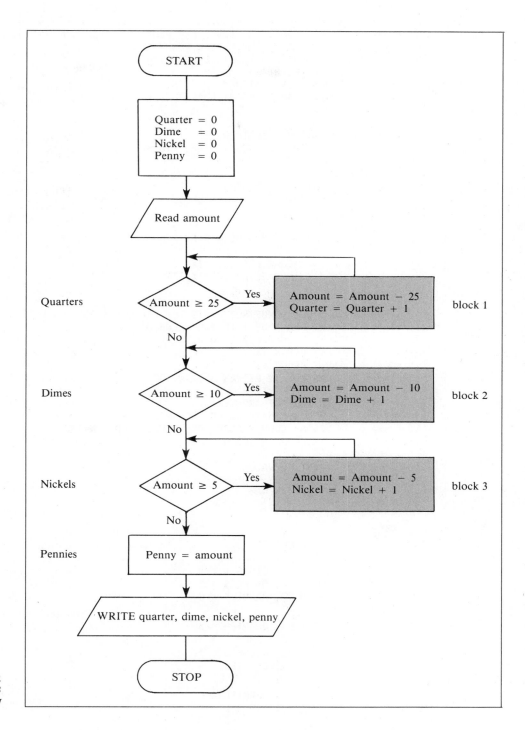

FIGURE 8.2
A CHANGE-MAKING
ALGORITHM

```
 1: *****SUBROUTINE PROBLEM: AUTOMATIC CHANGE PROGRAM
 2: *****GIVEN ANY NUMBER OF PENNIES, FIND THE LEAST NUMBER OF COINS
 3: *****(QUARTERS, DIMES, NICKELS, AND PENNIES) AMOUNTING TO THE PENNY SUM
 4:        INTEGER QUARTR,DIME,NICKEL,PENNY,AMOUNT
 5:        DATA    QUARTR,DIME,NICKEL,PENNY/4*Ø/
 6:        READ(*,*)AMOUNT
 7: 25     IF(AMOUNT .GE. 25)THEN
 8:           CALL CHANGE(AMOUNT,QUARTR,25)
 9:           GO TO 25
1Ø:        ENDIF
11: 1Ø     IF(AMOUNT .GE. 1Ø)THEN
12:           CALL CHANGE(AMOUNT,DIME,  1Ø)
13:           GO TO 1Ø
14:        ENDIF
15:        IF(AMOUNT .GE. 5)THEN
16:           CALL CHANGE(AMOUNT,NICKEL, 5)
17:        ENDIF
18:        PENNY = AMOUNT
19:        WRITE(*,1)QUARTR,DIME,NICKEL,PENNY
2Ø:        STOP
21: 1      FORMAT(1X,'QUARTERS=',I2/1X,'DIMES   =',I2
22:     *         /1X,'NICKELS =',I2/1X,'PENNIES =',I2)
23:        END
24: *
25: ***** SUBROUTINE CHANGE SUBTRACTS THE VALUE CALLED "VALUE"
26: ***** FROM AMT AND ADDS 1 TO THE VALUE OF COIN
27:        SUBROUTINE CHANGE(AMT,COIN,VALUE)
28: *      ARGUMENT DEFINITIONS
29: *         INPUT ARGUMENTS
3Ø: *****        VALUE: IS EITHER 25, 1Ø, OR 5
31:              INTEGER VALUE
32: *****      INPUT/OUTPUT ARGUMENTS
33: *****        AMT:  REMAINING DOLLAR AMOUNT
34: *****        COIN: COUNTS QUARTERS, DIMES, AND PENNIES
35:              INTEGER AMT,COIN
36: *
37:        AMT  = AMT  - VALUE
38:        COIN = COIN + 1
39:        RETURN
4Ø:        END
```

Line 8 annotation:
$$AMOUNT = AMOUNT - 25$$
$$QUARTR = QUARTR + 1$$

Line 12 annotation:
$$AMOUNT = AMOUNT - 10$$
$$DIME = DIME + 1$$

Line 16 annotation:
$$AMOUNT = AMOUNT - 5$$
$$NICKEL = NICKEL + 1$$

Line 27 annotation:
AMT refers to AMOUNT
COIN refers to either QUARTR, DIME, or NICKEL

```
75                          ← input value
QUARTERS= 3
DIMES   = Ø
NICKELS = Ø
PENNIES = Ø

94
QUARTERS= 3
DIMES   = 1
NICKELS = 1
PENNIES = 4

36
QUARTERS= 1
DIMES   = 1
NICKELS = Ø
PENNIES = 1
```

Program is run three times.

FIGURE 8.3
AN AUTOMATIC CHANGE PROGRAM

the smallest absolute value and another function subprogram to compute the absolute value. The complete program is shown in Figure 8.4. We organize our program by dividing it into three modules:

1. The main program (lines 1–14).

2. The function subprogram MINIMN (lines 16–37), which searches for the smallest array value.

3. The function ABSVAL (lines 39–48), which computes the absolute value.

We can draw the following hierarchy chart for this program:

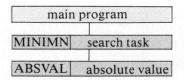

Notice how the function MINIMN is used at lines 12, 30, and 33 and how ABSVAL is used at lines 30, 33, 49, and 50. Notice also how the arguments are used in the function subprograms to carry out the desired computations. Just as in the case of subroutines, corresponding arguments between calling and called functions share the same memory storage. Thus array TABLE at line 20 actually refers to the same memory storage as ARRAY at line 12, LENGTH refers to N at line 12, and X takes on successive values TABLE(1), ..., TABLE(N) at lines 30, 32 and 33.

Finally, note how the functional values are transmitted back to the calling program by the replacement statements MINIMN = *functional value* (lines 30 and 33) and ABSVAL = *functional value* (lines 49 and 50), that is, the value of the function is passed through the name of the function, *not* through an argument.

Since a function returns a particular value to the calling program, the value returned can be integer, real, double precision, logical, complex, or character type. Thus, the function itself should be typed. In Figure 8.4 we have typed MINIMN and ABSVAL as INTEGER at lines 20 and 42, since both functions return integer values. If the function is not typed, then the value returned is either integer or real as defined implicitly by the name of the function. It is always a good practice to type functions, just as we have always typed variables and array names. The function names should be typed both in the function program and in the program that calls them.

At this point, some readers may wonder whether function subprograms could alternatively be written as subroutine subprograms. The answer is yes, as shown in Figure 8.5. The resulting code is a little more unwieldy, since the functional values must be returned through arguments. Recall that FORTRAN was intended for solving scientific problems where functions are routinely used—therefore FORTRAN allows the user to define functions that correspond to the scientific formulation of the problem.

```
 1: ***** FUNCTION SUBPROGRAM PROBLEM
 2: ***** THIS PROGRAM READS N ELEMENTS INTO ARRAY "ARRAY" AND
 3: ***** PRINTS THE SMALLEST ABSOLUTE VALUE OF THE ARRAY'S ELEMENTS
 4: ***** PROGRAM PARAMETERS
 5: *****     N: SIZE OF ARRAY TO BE PROCESSED
 6:           PARAMETER(N=10)
 7: ***** PROGRAM VARIABLES
 8:           INTEGER ARRAY(N)
 9: ***** FUNCTIONS USED
10:           INTEGER MINIMN
11:       READ(5,*)ARRAY
12:       WRITE(6,*)' MINIMUM VALUE=',MINIMN(ARRAY,N)
13:       STOP
14:       END
15: *
16: ******FUNCTION SUBPROGRAM MINIMN
17: ***** GIVEN AN ARRAY "TABLE" OF SIZE "LENGTH", THIS
18: ***** FUNCTION RETURNS THE TABLE ENTRY WITH LOWEST
19: ***** ABSOLUTE VALUE
20:       INTEGER FUNCTION MINIMN(TABLE,LENGTH)
21: ***** ARGUMENT DEFINITIONS
22: *****     INPUT ARGUMENTS
23: *****         TABLE:  NAME OF ARRAY
24: *****         LENGTH: SIZE OF ARRAY
25: *****
26:               INTEGER TABLE(LENGTH),LENGTH
27: ***** FUNCTIONS USED
28:           INTEGER ABSVAL
29: *
30:       MINIMN = ABSVAL(TABLE(1))
31:       DO 10 I = 2, LENGTH
32:          IF(MINIMN .GT. ABSVAL(TABLE(I)))THEN
33:             MINIMN=ABSVAL(TABLE(I))
34:          ENDIF
35: 10    CONTINUE
36:       RETURN
37:       END
38: *
39: ***** FUNCTION SUBPROGRAM ABSVAL
40: ***** THIS FUNCTION RETURNS THE ABSOLUTE VALUE OF
41: ***** ITS ARGUMENT "X"
42:       INTEGER FUNCTION ABSVAL(X)
43: ***** ARGUMENT DEFINITIONS
44: *****     INPUT ARGUMENT
45: *****        X: VALUE FOR WHICH ABSOLUTE VALUE IS
46: *****            SOUGHT
47:            INTEGER X
48: *
49:       ABSVAL = X
50:       IF(X .LT. 0.0)ABSVAL = -X
51:       RETURN
52:       END
```

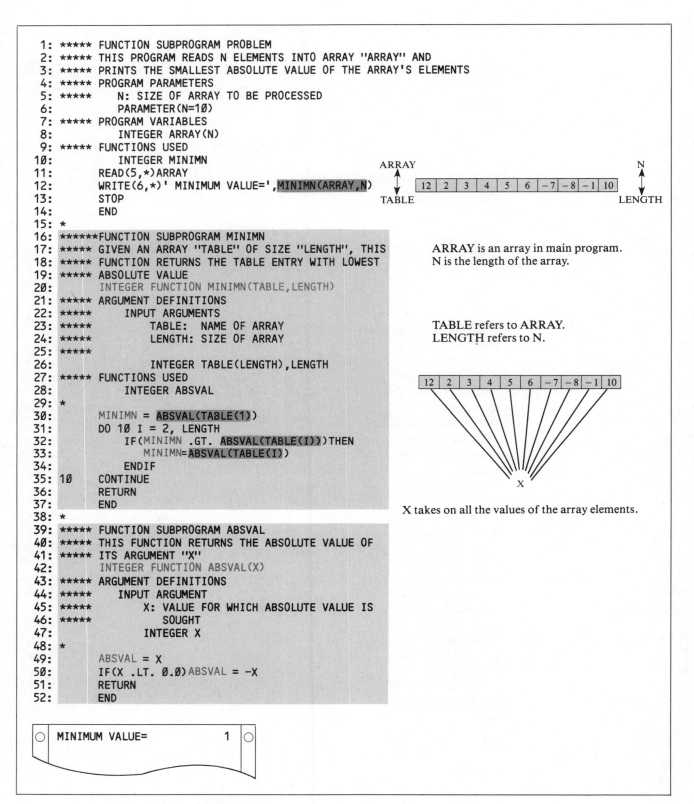

ARRAY is an array in main program.
N is the length of the array.

TABLE refers to ARRAY.
LENGTH refers to N.

X takes on all the values of the array elements.

```
MINIMUM VALUE=        1
```

FIGURE 8.4
A FUNCTION SUBPROGRAM EXAMPLE

```
 1:*******FUNCTION SUBPROGRAM CODED AS A SUBROUTINE
 2:        PARAMETER(N=10)
 3:        INTEGER  ARRAY(10)
 4:        OPEN (5,FILE='DATA')
 5:        READ(5,*)ARRAY
 6:        CALL SEARCH(ARRAY,10,MINIMN)
 7:        WRITE(6,*)' MINIMUM VALUE=',MINIMN
 8:        STOP
 9:        END
10:        SUBROUTINE SEARCH(TABLE,LENGTH,MINIMN)
11:        INTEGER LENGTH,TABLE(LENGTH),ABSVAL
12:        CALL ABS(TABLE(1),ABSVAL)
13:        MINIMN = ABSVAL
14:        DO 10 I = 1, LENGTH
15:            CALL ABS(TABLE(I),ABSVAL)
16:            IF(MINIMN .GT. ABSVAL)MINIMN=ABSVAL
17: 10     CONTINUE
18:        RETURN
19:        END
20:        SUBROUTINE ABS(X,ABSVAL)
21:        INTEGER X,ABSVAL
22:        ABSVAL = X
23:        IF(X .LT. 0.0)ABSVAL = -X
24:        RETURN
25:        END
```

FIGURE 8.5
*FUNCTION CODED
AS SUBROUTINE*

8.2 SUBPROGRAMS

Subprograms are a powerful, convenient, and sometimes necessary programming tool to help you better structure, document, code, test, and debug your programs.

8.2.1 Program Structure: Modularity

As the examples in section 8.1 have shown, one way to improve the structure of a program is to decompose the original problem or task to be solved into independent modules and then execute these modules in a predefined sequence. In the process, you must clearly identify and document each module and show the order in which the modules are to be executed. Such a well-organized approach results in code that is easier to write, follow, test, and debug and is easier for others to read. You will also find that you will use the GOTO statement less frequently. This in itself is very important, since undisciplined use of the GOTO statement often gives rise to the "spaghetti code syndrome." Reading such code makes it very difficult for the reader to remember where in the program one is coming from and where one is going! Breaking a program into modules minimizes the need for GOTO statement and improves the clarity and readability of the resulting code.

Decomposing a problem into smaller modules allows one to focus more easily on a particular part of the problem without worrying about the overall problem. The modules become easier to solve and are much more manageable when each performs a very specific function. Typically, you can code each module independently of the others and even test and debug each module separately. Once all modules are working properly, you can link them together by writing the coordinating module (the main program), which specifies the order in which the modules are to be executed. These principles are illustrated in Figure 8.6. Note that the resulting program consists of five modules: the coordinating module and the four subtask modules A, B, C, and D.

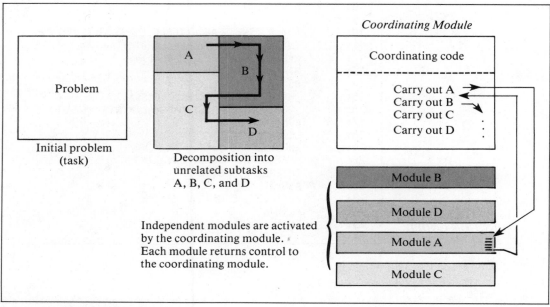

FIGURE 8.6
PROGRAM DECOMPOSITION

In a modular environment, each module can be respecified as a sequence of smaller modules describing what is to be done at increasing levels of detail. The technique of expanding a program plan into several levels of detailed subplans and presenting the program structure as a hierarchy of tasks is sometimes referred to as *top-down* design. A hierarchy chart, sometimes called a structured diagram, is a useful tool for illustrating module relationships and hierarchies. Figure 8.7 shows a hierarchy chart for the problem of Figure 8.6.

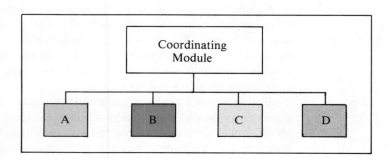

FIGURE 8.7
A HIERARCHY CHART

An interesting analogy to the modularization process is the manufacturing principle of Henry Ford:

Realizing that there were very few people skilled enough to build an entire automobile, as up until that time the only way cars were being built was by hand in small shops by small groups of highly skilled men, Ford proceeded to break down this immense task into its constituent parts: body, interior, chassis and drive-train. Since these jobs were still far too complex for the average worker, he refined each subtask: the drive-train into engine, driveshaft and rear-end, the chassis into springs, frames and axles, and so on. Still too complex! The engine is composed of the block, pistons, crank, cam, valves, head, carburetor, generator, radiator, etc. . . . Finally, when he had broken-down the automobile into small enough parts, Ford was able to hire and train an average man to do one of the tasks necessary to produce a particular part. Once tested, each part was assembled with the rest and became a Model T. And that's how Henry Ford became the man we most associate with the assembly line, and, in the process, one of the wealthiest and most influential men in the world.

By breaking down a problem into independent modules, a lead programmer in charge of a very complex problem can easily assign various team members the responsibility for developing one or more modules. These modules can then be compiled, run and tested independently. (Making one change in one module is a very local intervention that does not require an understanding of all other modules. On the other hand, making one change in a nonmodular program held together by myriads of GOTO statements not only requires an understanding of the whole program but can well result in dramatic repercussions throughout the program if the change is logically or syntactically incorrect. Masses of error messages and needless output are then generated—not to mention the time wasted for each compilation attempt.) When all modules are completed, they can be joined together to form the complete program, which can then be tested.

In summary, modularization helps the programmer write better structured programs that are generally more compact and thus easier to work with and more readable. A subprogram can also reduce the code required for procedures or tasks that are to be performed repeatedly at different places in a program.

Subprograms that are to be used frequently should be compiled, debugged, and stored in a library. Storing a subprogram in a library saves computer time, since the subprogram need not be recompiled each time it is to be used. User-written subprograms can be shared through "share" libraries. Comment statements containing a brief description of the subprogram and its use (calling sequence) should be included in the listing of the subprogram. Documentation is very important in subprograms. Comments should be used to identify input arguments, output arguments, local variables, and names of function subprograms that are called (invoked) in the subprogram itself.

8.2.2 Function Subprograms

The function subprogram is one form of a programmer-defined function. Another form is the arithmetic statement function, which is discussed in Appendix E. A function subprogram can be compiled separately and executed by another program.

Function subprograms are usually written to carry out generalized procedures that are data-independent, for example, determining the largest element of any array, computing the average or the standard deviation of any set of grades, and so forth. Arguments (sometimes called *dummy* arguments because they are used as place holders) are used to illustrate the way in which the task (function) is to be carried out.

Function subprograms can be catalogued in the system or user libraries if they are to be shared by other users or used repeatedly by the programmer. They can also be a physical part of the entire program, i.e., submitted with the main program every time the program is run.

Functions can executed from another program (another main program or other subprograms) by using the name of the function and specifying a list of arguments.

The Function Invocation Statement

The general form of a function invocation statement (function reference) is:

$$\text{function name } (a_1, a_2, a_3, \ldots, a_n)$$

where   *function name* is the name of the function (any valid variable name) and $a_1, a_2, a_3, \ldots, a_n$ are arguments to be passed to the function subprogram. These arguments can be variables, subscripted variable names, array names, constants, expressions, or function names.

The value of the function is returned through the name of the function (acting as a variable). If the function is not typed, the value returned by the function is implicitly typed by the function name (if the name begins with I,J,K,L,M, or N, the function value is integer; otherwise, it is real).

Consider the following examples:

```
X = 3. * SUB(Y)/SAM + 3.6        One argument is passed to the function.
AX = A(T,J,3) + B(X**2,1.5)      The function A has three arguments, while
                                 the function B has two arguments.
IF(TRAP(X,K) - 8.3)THEN          The function TRAP is part of an IF
  .                              statement. It is first evaluated, then its value
  .                              is compared to 8.3.
Z = S1(A, B(1), 3*I + K, J)      S1 has four arguments.
T = SUB2(SIN(X),Y) - SUB2(3.1,0.0)  Arguments can be functions, too.
```

You may wonder how the compiler differentiates between a function and a reference to an array; for example, B(3) could be a reference to a function or to an element of the array B. If the variable B is typed as an array, then B is an array; if B is not typed as an array, the compiler will treat any reference to B as a reference to a function subprogram even if the user has never defined a function B (after the compilation process, an error will occur when the system tries to locate the function B in its libraries and cannot find such a function!).

The FUNCTION Definition Statement

The first statement in every function subprogram must be the FUNCTION statement. The general form of this statement is:

$$[type] \text{ FUNCTION } function\ name\ (p_1, p_2, p_3, \ldots, p_n)$$

where   *function name* is the name of the function, and

$p_1, p_2, p_3, \ldots, p_n$ are dummy arguments used to pass the data to and from the calling program. These arguments can be variable names, expressions, array names, or function names. **Subscripted variables and constants are not permitted as arguments in the function definition** (although they are permitted in the function invocation statement).

type is an optional parameter that specifies the mode of the value returned by the function. Functions can be typed as REAL, INTEGER, CHARACTER, CHARACTER*n, DOUBLE PRECISION, COMPLEX, or LOGICAL. It is a good practice to always type the function both in the subprogram and in the program that calls the function. If *type* is omitted, the function value is implicitly defined by the function name (if the name starts with I,J,K,L,M, or N, the value is integer; otherwise, it is real).

The dummy arguments used in the subprogram are dummy names for the actual arguments listed in the invocation statement. When the function is executed, the dummy arguments take on the values of the "real" arguments specified in the calling program. More precisely, the function processes the real arguments directly through the dummy arguments.

The arguments in the invocation statement should correspond in number, order, and type with the dummy arguments of the FUNCTION statement. The corresponding argument names may be the same or different. The order of the arguments in the invocation statement and in the FUNCTION statement must be the same; that is, there must be a one-to-one correspondence between the two sets of arguments.

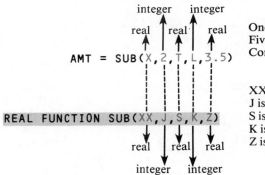

One-to-one correspondence between arguments. Five arguments in both calling and called programs. Corresponding arguments are of same type.

XX is the same as X.
J is the same as 2(J = 2).
S is the same as T.
K is the same as L.
Z is the same as 3.5 (Z = 3.5).

If an argument in a function subprogram is an array name, the array name must be declared in a DIMENSION or type statement in the function subprogram.

Passing Back the Value of the Function

The value of the function that is computed in the function subprogram is passed back to the calling program by setting the function name all by itself equal to the functional value (*name of function = functional value*). For example, if the function AVRGE computes the average of its three arguments X1, X2, and X3, we would write:

name of function ⟶ `AVRGE = (X1+X2+X3)/3.0` ⟵ *functional value*

Once again, *every* function must contain the statement:

name of function = functional value

since this is the *only* way a function can be assigned a value.

The RETURN and END Statements

As in all programs we have written so far, the last statement in a function subprogram must be the END statement.

The RETURN statement, which is optional in FORTRAN 77, returns control to the calling program from the function subprogram. There can be many RETURN statements in a function subprogram.

Position of Subprograms in the Complete Program (JOB)

All user-defined function or subroutine subprograms are separate logical entities and as such are generally compiled independently of one another. On some systems, special system control statements (job control, workflow, and so forth) may be required to separate each program from the others. On other systems, the various subprograms are simply typed one after the other following the END statement of each subprogram, with no special separator statements required between them. Figure 8.8 illustrates the two most common setups. The student should determine the proper control statements required by his/her computer system. In many systems the input data is not part of the job stream but is stored as a separate file on disk.

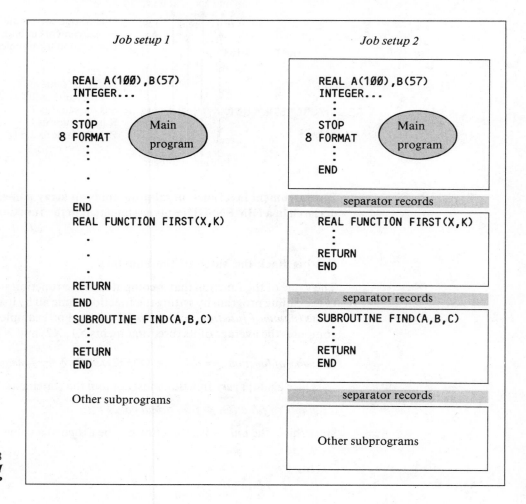

FIGURE 8.8
*SUBPROGRAM
JOB MAKEUP*

EXAMPLES OF
FUNCTION
SUBPROGRAMS

1. Function ALARG returns the larger value of any two arguments.

Calling Program   *Function Subprogram*

```
                              REAL FUNCTION ALARG(A,B)
        :                     REAL A,B
        :                     IF(A .GT. B) THEN
Z = ALARG(X,Y)                    ALARG = A
WRITE(6,3)Z                   ELSE
        :                         ALARG = B
        :                     ENDIF
IF(ALARG(Z,T).LT.3.1)THEN...  RETURN
                              END
```

2.
```
REAL QUIZZ,Y,T                REAL FUNCTION QUIZZ(J,K,L)
        :                     INTEGER J,K,L
        :                     QUIZZ = REAL(J + K + L)/3.0
IF(QUIZZ(30,40,50).GT.T)THEN  RETURN
        :                     END
        :
Y = QUIZZ(J,30,L)
```

Note the REAL specification in both programs. QUIZZ returns a real value.

3.
```
REAL BAKER, A                 REAL FUNCTION BAKER (X,Y,J)
I = 2                         REAL X,Y
A = 7.0                       INTEGER J
Y = BAKER(3.2, 9.8*A, I)          :
        :                         :
        :
```
The arguments of BAKER must be two real values followed by an integer value.

When control is passed to BAKER,
X = 3.2, Y = 9.8*7 = 68.6, and J = 2

4. In this example, the function name participates as a variable in the subprogram. The function SUM computes the sum of the entries of a 10-element real array.

```
INTEGER A(10),B(10)           REAL FUNCTION SUM(Z)
REAL SUM                      INTEGER Z(10)
        :                     SUM = 0.
        :                     DO 10 I = 1,10
X = SUM(A)                        SUM = SUM + REAL(Z(I))
        :                10    CONTINUE
Y = SUM(B)                    RETURN
        :                     END
```

Note the array declaration statement required in the subprogram. SUM (the name of the function) is used as an accumulator.

5. Function LARG returns the largest element in a real array of size 10.

```
REAL A(10),B(10),LARG         REAL FUNCTION LARG(X)
        :                     REAL X(10)
X = LARG(A) + LARG(B)         LARG = X(1)
                              DO 10 I = 2,10
                                  IF(LARG.LT.X(I)) LARG = X(I)
                        10    CONTINUE
                              RETURN
                              END
```

When the RETURN statement is executed, control is passed to the point at which the function was invoked. First LARG(A) is executed, then LARG(B), then the sum of the two largest numbers is stored in X.

6. This example illustrates character arguments.

The function RATE(USAGE) returns $\left\{\begin{array}{l}\text{the value 'LOW'} \quad\text{if USAGE} \leq 300.\\ \text{the value 'MEDIUM' if } 300 < \text{USAGE} \leq 500.\\ \text{the value 'HIGH'} \quad\text{if USAGE} > 500.\end{array}\right.$

```
CHARACTER*6 RATE,POWER          CHARACTER*6 FUNCTION RATE(USAGE)
READ(*,*) USAGE,X               REAL USAGE
POWER = RATE(USAGE)             IF(USAGE .LE. 300.) THEN
   .                                RATE = 'LOW'
   .                            ELSE IF (USAGE .LE. 500.) THEN
POWER = RATE(X)                         RATE = 'MEDIUM'
   .                                ELSE
   .                                    RATE = 'HIGH'
                                ENDIF
                                RETURN
                                END
```

7. The character function HINAME returns the name that is alphabetically last in a list of names stored in array NAME.

```
CHARACTER*15 NAME(50)               CHARACTER*15 FUNCTION HINAME(NOM)
CHARACTER*15 HINAME                 CHARACTER*15 NOM(50)
   .                                HINAME = NOM(1)
   .                                DO 6 I = 2,50
IF(HINAME(NAME).GT.'ZEUS')THEN          IF(HINAME.LT.NOM(I))HINAME=NOM(I)
   .                              6 CONTINUE
   .                                RETURN
                                    END
```

It is often necessary to write function subprograms that will process arrays of varying sizes. In this case an integer variable may be used to specify the size of the array in the DIMENSION or type statement in the function subprogram (but not in the program where memory is actually reserved for the array). A more detailed discussion of variable dimension for multidimensional arrays is presented in example 5 section 8.2.4.

8. In this example, the subprogram processes arrays of varying sizes. The number of rows and the number of columns are passed as the second and third arguments. The function AVER computes the average of the grades stored in arrays CLASS1, CLASS2, and CLASS3. Using the variable dimension in the function subprogram allows the user to write *one* subprogram to find the grade average of *any* size grade array.

Calling Program   *Function Subprogram*

```
REAL CLASS1(10,10)                  REAL FUNCTION AVER(ARAY,NR,NC)
REAL CLASS2(5,5)                    REAL ARAY(NR,NC)
REAL CLASS3(7,17)                   INTEGER NR,NC
REAL AVER, A,B,C,TOT                AVER = 0.
READ(5,6)CLASS1,CLASS2,CLASS3       DO 6 I = 1,NR
A = AVER(CLASS1,10,10)                 DO 5 J = 1,NC
B = AVER(CLASS2,5,5)                        AVER = AVER + ARAY(I,J)
C = AVER(CLASS3,7, 17)            5     CONTINUE
TOT = (A+B+C)/3.0                       AVER = AVER/(NR*NC)
   .                              6 CONTINUE
   .                                RETURN
                                    END
```

variable dimension

Since subprograms are separate programs that are treated independently by the compiler, identical variable names that are totally unrelated can appear in the calling and called programs with no risk of confusion; likewise, duplicate statement numbers in the calling and called programs are permissible, since the programs are compiled separately. For that reason, if the programmer wishes to refer in a function subprogram to a variable that is defined in the calling program, he/she cannot use the same name and hope that it will refer to the variable with the identical name in the calling program. The only way to "communicate" variables between programs is either through the COMMON statement (see Appendix F) or by passing the variable name as an argument in the function-calling sequence. Consider the following example:

9.

Calling Program	*Subprogram*
``` REAL A(10),B(6),SUM READ(*,*)P,Q,A SUM = 0. DO 8 I = 1,6 SUM = SUM + A(I) 8 CONTINUE R = SUM + P T = ADD(P,Q,R) ⋮ ```	``` FUNCTION ADD(X,Y,Z) SUM = X + Y + Z PROD = X*Y*Z 8 IF(SUM.GT.PROD)THEN ⋮ 8 ADD = ... GO TO 8 ENDIF ```

The only variables common to the two programs are P and X, Q and Y, and R and Z. The variable SUM in the main program has *no* relationship to the variable SUM in the subprogram; similarly, statement 8 in the main program will not be confused with statement 8 in the subprogram.

10. The following examples show *invalid* function references or function definition statements:

Calling Program	*Function Subprogram*	*Comments*
`X = AMAX(2.1,3,4.)`	`FUNCTION AMAX(X,Y,Z)`	"3" is integer and "Y" is real.

`INTEGER SMALL`
`   ⋮`
`J = SMALL(3.1,X)`
	`FUNCTION SMALL(T,X)`	Type mismatch—SMALL is an integer function in the calling program and a real function in the function subprogram.

`S = COT(A,B,T(3))`	`FUNCTION COT(X,Y,Z)` `X = COT(T,Z,P)`	Recursion is not permissible, i.e., a function cannot invoke itself.
`REAL Q(100)` `C = DAM(Q(1),Q(2),-4)`	`FUNCTION DAM(T(1),T(2),J)` `REAL T(100)`	Function arguments may not be subscripted variable names.
`MIM = SUB(X,2*J,9.8)`	`FUNCTION SUB(X,J)`	Arguments disagree in number.

`INTEGER CART(10)`
`   ⋮`
`X = TIP(3.9,X,CART)`
	`FUNCTION TIP(X,Y,Z)`
	`   TIP = (X + Y)/2.`
	`     ⋮`
		Z must be declared as an array in the function subprogram.

`READ*, INCOME` `G = TAX(INCOME)`	`FUNCTION TAX(INCOME)` `REAL TAX`	The type statement must precede the word FUNCTION.

`A = PAY(EARN,DEP,3)`
`PRINT*,A`
`C = PAY(10.,A*2+K)`
`   ⋮`
	`FUNCTION PAY (A,B,N)`
	`PAY = A*B+N`
	`RETURN`
	`END`
		PAY must be invoked with three arguments.

1. Determine which of the following calling program/function subprograms pairs are invalid. Give reasons.

	Calling Program	*Function Subprogram*
a.	`X = MAX(2.1,3.1,4)`	`FUNCTION MAX(X,Y,Z)`
b.	`IF(LOW(I,J,K))THEN`	`FUNCTION LOW(K,I,J)`
c.	`REAL MALL` `X = MALL(X,T)`	`FUNCTION MALL(X,T)`
d.	`REAL A(5)` `INTEGER X,S` `Z = A(X,K,3*S)`	`FUNCTION A(I,J,T)`
e.	`T = BAD(1,2.+S,3*I)`	`FUNCTION BAD(I,J,K)`
f.	`M = TUT(SQRT(R),S)`	`FUNCTION TUT(RT,T)`
g.	`S = MAD(3.,2*S,-1)`	`FUNCTION MAD(X,Y,K)`
h.	`P = MAT(ABS(K),2,SIN(T))`	`FUNCTION (X,I,T)`

2. Write a function subprogram to compute the determinant of a 2 by 2 matrix.

[*Note:* Determinant of $A = |A| = \begin{vmatrix} a_{11} & a_{12} \\ a_{21} & a_{22} \end{vmatrix} = a_{11} \cdot a_{22} - a_{21} \cdot a_{12}$]

3. Write a function to calculate the approximate number of days that have elapsed between two dates, M1, D1, Y1 and M2, D2, Y2, where M, D, and Y refer to month, day, and year.
[*Hint*: There are an average of 365.25 days in each year and an average of 30.4 days in each month; express both quantities in days.]

4. Write a function subprogram to compute the cost of postage for a first class letter weighing P ounces. The postage is 22 cents for the first ounce and 17 cents for each additional ounce or part thereof.

5. Write a function subprogram to compute the dot product of two vectors X and Y, each with N coordinates.

6. Write a function for the binomial expression

$$C(n,m) = \frac{n!}{m!(n-m)!}$$

$C(n,m)$ represents the number of ways to choose m objects from n different objects. For example, if six people are on a ship and the lifeboat can hold only two, then

$$C(6,2) = \frac{6!}{2!4!} = \frac{6 \cdot 5 \cdot 4 \cdot 3 \cdot 2 \cdot 1}{(2 \cdot 1) \cdot (4 \cdot 3 \cdot 2 \cdot 1)} = 15$$

$C(6,2) = 15$ represents the number of different combinations of people who could be saved.

Answers

1. a. Invalid; 4 and Z different types.

   b. Valid.

   c. Invalid; the function type must be the same in the calling program and in the function definition.

   d. Invalid reference to a singly dimensioned array A.

e. Invalid; 2 + S and J different types.

f. Valid.

g. Valid.

h. Invalid; function has no name.

2.
```
REAL FUNCTION DET(A)
REAL A(2,2)
DET = A(1,1) * A(2,2) - A(2,1) * A(1,2)
RETURN
END
```

3.
```
REAL FUNCTION MDIF(M1,D1,Y1,M2,D2,Y2)
REAL M1,D1,M2,D2,Y1,Y2,JD1,JD2,MDIF
JD1 = 365.25 * Y1 + REAL(M1-1) * 30.4 + D1
JD2 = 365.25 * Y2 + REAL(M2-1) * 30.4 + D2
MDIF = ABS(JD1 - JD2)
RETURN
END
```

4.
```
REAL FUNCTION POSTGE(P)
REAL P
POSTGE = .22
IF(P .GT. 1.) POSTGE = .22 + .17*REAL(INT(P-.000001))
RETURN
END
```

5.
```
REAL FUNCTION DOT (X,Y,N)
REAL X(N),Y(N)
DOT = 0.0
DO 5 I = 1,N
    DOT = DOT+X(I)*Y(I)
5 CONTINUE
RETURN
END
```

6.
```
INTEGER COMB,FACT
READ(5,1)N,M
COMB=FACT(N)/(FACT(M)*FACT(N-M))
WRITE(6,2)N,M,COMB
STOP
2 FORMAT(' COMBINATIONS OF',I3,'ITEMS' / 1X, 'TAKEN',I3,' AT A TIME IS',I4)
1 FORMAT(2I2)
END
INTEGER FUNCTION FACT(N)
FACT = 1
DO 10 I = 1,N
   FACT = FACT*I
10 CONTINUE
RETURN
END
```

8.2.4 Subroutines

A subroutine is an independently compiled block of code. As the prefix *sub-* implies, a subroutine is not really a complete program; if it were executed by itself, it would not produce meaningful results. Subroutines are usually written to carry out generalized procedures that are data-independent, for example, sorting or merging arrays of any size. Arguments (sometimes called *dummy arguments*) provide the data for the subroutine to use in its procedure. These arguments must be specifically identified by the program that uses the subroutine. The name of the particular array to be sorted and the exact number of grades for which an average is to be computed are examples of arguments that might be passed to a subroutine.

The reader may think there is no conceptual difference between a function subprogram and a subroutine subprogram—that is true! The only difference is that functions return only one result to the calling program, while subroutines can return any number of results.

A subroutine is executed from another program (a main program or another subprogram) through the CALL statement.

The CALL Statement

The general form of the CALL statement is:

> CALL *subroutine name* [$(a_1, a_2, a_3, ..., a_n)$]

where   CALL is a required key word;
        subroutine name is the name of the subroutine (any valid variable name);
        $a_1, a_2, ..., a_n$ are arguments to be passed to the subroutine. These arguments can be variables, subscripted variables, array names, constants, expressions, or function names.

        Arguments are used either to transmit data to the subroutine or to receive data (values, results) from the subroutine. Arguments are optional.

EXAMPLES

```
CALL SUB(X)
CALL NEWPAG
CALL POLL(A,B(1),3*I+K,J)

CALL SUB2(SIN(X),Y)
```

One argument is passed to the subroutine called SUB.
No arguments (print headings only, for example).
Four arguments are passed to the subroutine; $3*I + K$ is evaluated and passed to the 3rd argument of POLL.
The sine of X will be evaluated and the value passed to the first argument of SUB2.

The SUBROUTINE Statement

The SUBROUTINE statement must be the first statement in every subroutine subprogram. The general form of the SUBROUTINE statement is:

> SUBROUTINE *subroutine name* [$(p_1, p_2, p_3, ..., p_n)$]

where   SUBROUTINE is a required key word;
        subroutine name is the name of the subroutine (any valid variable name) which cannot be typed; $p_1, p_2, p_3, ..., p_n$ are dummy arguments used to communicate data to and from the calling program. These arguments can either be variables, array names, or function names but not subscripted variable names or constants.

If an argument is an array name, the array name must be declared in a type or DIMENSION statement within the subroutine. The size of the array should be the same as the size of the corresponding argument (array) in the calling program; variable array dimensions can also be used (see example 5 in this section).

The dummy arguments used in the subroutine refer to the actual names or arguments listed in the invocation statement of the calling program. When the subroutine is executed, the dummy arguments take on the values of the "real" arguments specified in the CALL statement of the calling program. More precisely, the subroutine processes the real arguments through the dummy arguments.

The arguments in the CALL statement should correspond in number, order, and type to the dummy arguments of the SUBROUTINE statement. The names used may be the same or different. The order of the arguments in the CALL statement and in the SUBROUTINE statement must be the same; that is, there must be a one-to-one correspondence between the two sets of arguments.

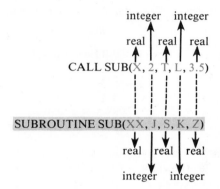

One-to-one correspondence between arguments.
Five arguments in both calling and called programs.
Type between corresponding arguments preserved.

XX is same as X.
J is same as 2 (J = 2).
S is same as T.
K is same as L.
Z is same as 3.5 (Z = 3.5).

The optional RETURN statement returns control to the statement immediately following the CALL statement in the calling program. Many RETURN statements can be included in a subroutine. The END statement should be the last statement in a subroutine subprogram.

All user-defined subroutines are separate physical and logical entities and are compiled independently of one another. The compiler treats each subroutine as a separate program in the job. The various subroutines should be placed immediately after the END statement of the main program; their order is immaterial. Each one should start with the SUBROUTINE statement and terminate with the END statement. The physical positioning of the various subprograms in the complete job is illustrated in Figure 8–8 page 432.

The ordering of the various FORTRAN statements within the FORTRAN program is shown as follows:

Comment statements	FUNCTION and SUBROUTINE statements	
	FORMAT statements	PARAMETER and specification statements
		DATA and executable statements

EXAMPLES

1.

Main Program	Subprogram	Comments
DATA X,Y/3.,4./	SUBROUTINE ADD(A,B,C)	1. C is same as R.
CALL ADD(X,Y,R)	C = A + B	The value of R is 7.
WRITE(6,*)R	RETURN	C = R = 3. + 4.
CALL ADD(X,R,Z)	END	
WRITE(6,*)Z		2. C is same as Z.
		C = Z = 3. + 7.

In the first call to ADD, arguments A, B, and C correspond to X, Y, and R, respectively. In the second call to ADD, arguments A, B, and C correspond to X, R, and Z, respectively. The value printed for R is 7.0 while the value printed for Z is 10.0.

It should be emphasized again that a subroutine can change the value of a variable in the main program. Consider the following example:

2.

Main Program	Subprogram	Comments
	SUBROUTINE TRI(X,C)	
⋮	⋮	
A = 4.0	X = 7.0	The subroutine changes
CALL TRI(A,B)	C = 3.1	the value of A to 7.0
WRITE(6,1)A	RETURN	since X really refers to A.
⋮	END	

A is 4. when the call is made to the subroutine; on return to the main program, the value for A will be 7.; the value for B will be 3.1.

The value of any expression in the CALL statement is calculated before passing values of parameters to the subroutine.

3.

Main Program	Subprogram
⋮	SUBROUTINE SUB4(A,B,C)
X = 3.0	⋮
Y = 2.0	
CALL SUB4(X,X+Y,3.*Y)	

The value of A will be 3.0; the value of B will be 5.0; the value of C will be 6.0.

If an array is to be passed to a subroutine, the name of the array is specified in the CALL statement. The argument array name used in the subroutine must be specified in a type or DIMENSION statement in the subprogram, and its size must equal the size of the corresponding array in the calling program.

4.

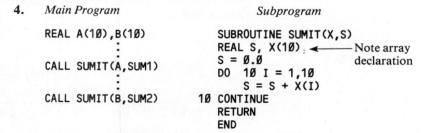

Two calls to subroutine SUMIT are made. As a result, SUM1 and SUM2 will contain the sums of the elements of arrays A and B, respectively.

5. Variable dimensioning of arrays

Arrays that are passed as arguments from one program to another through the CALL sequence must be declared as arrays in the subprogram through appropriate type statements. If the size of the array to be processed in the subprogram is to be the same size as the corresponding array in the main program (or calling program), the size of the subprogram array can be set to the particular size of the array defined in the calling program. Suppose, for example, we wished to add two arrays, A and B, of the same size (adding corresponding elements), and store the resulting entries in a third array, C. The following code could be used.

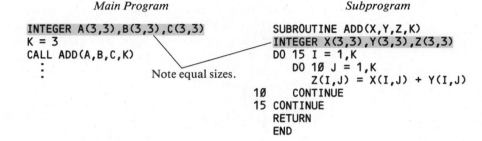

Main Program

```
INTEGER A(3,3),B(3,3),C(3,3)
K = 3
CALL ADD(A,B,C,K)
   .
   .
   .
```

Note equal sizes.

Subprogram

```
SUBROUTINE ADD(X,Y,Z,K)
INTEGER X(3,3),Y(3,3),Z(3,3)
DO 15 I = 1,K
   DO 10 J = 1,K
      Z(I,J) = X(I,J) + Y(I,J)
10    CONTINUE
15 CONTINUE
RETURN
END
```

The only drawback to subroutine ADD is that it is coded to add only arrays of size 3 by 3. The generality of the subroutine is restricted, since it cannot be used to add arrays that are of size 2 by 2, 5 by 5, and so forth. One way to remedy this problem is to use the variable type declaration feature, which allows the user to adjust the size of the array in the subroutine to the size of the corresponding array in the main program (calling program). In this way a subroutine can process arrays of different sizes. For example, the problem of adding corresponding elements of two arrays could be coded as follows:

Main Program

```
INTEGER A(3,3),B(3,3),C(3,3)
INTEGER T(2,3),Q(2,3),R(2,3)
M = 3
N = 3
CALL ADD(A,B,C,M,N)
   .
   .
   .
CALL ADD(T,Q,R,2,3)
```

Subprogram

```
SUBROUTINE ADD(X,Y,Z,M,N)
INTEGER X(M,N),Y(M,N),Z(M,N)
DO 15 I = 1,M
   DO 10 J = 1,N
      Z(I,J) = X(I,J) + Y(I,J)
10    CONTINUE
15 CONTINUE
RETURN
END
```

In the first call to ADD, X, Y, and Z are 3 by 3 arrays, while in the second call arrays X, Y, and Z are 2 by 3.

6. The following are incorrect SUBROUTINE statements:

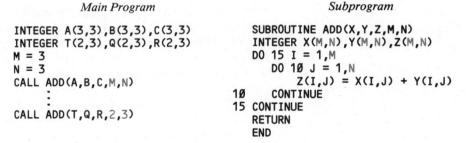

Main Program	Subprogram	Comments
CALL SUM(A,B,C)	SUBROUTINE SUM(A,B)	Invalid. Two subroutine arguments.
CALL PROD(A,3,N)	SUBROUTINE PROD(X,Y,I)	Type mismatch in second argument.
CALL TOT(X,3.1,2)	SUBROUTINE TOT(X,B(1),J)	B(1) not allowed as argument.
CALL SIS(T(3),M)	SUBROUTINE SIS(S,4)	4 is not an argument name.
CALL TW(A + B,C)	SUBROUTINE TW(X + Y,D)	X + Y is an invalid argument.

8.3 FORTRAN-SUPPLIED FUNCTIONS

In chapter 2 we discussed certain FORTRAN-supplied functions such as the square root function and the absolute value function. These functions are examples of *intrinsic* functions. A list of intrinsic functions is shown in Figures 8.9 and 8.10. Each intrinsic function requires a particular type argument, while the value of the intrinsic function is determined by the type of the function name. Thus, the ABS function requires a real argument, and the value returned by the ABS function is real. Many FORTRAN 77 compilers allow intrinsic functions to be used generically, that is, one name covers all intrinsic names for one particular function while the argument is not restricted to any specific type. The value returned by the generic function has the same type as its argument(s). For example, the generic name for the absolute value function is ABS and the argument can be integer, real, complex, or double precision. Thus ABS(X) returns a real value while ABS(N) returns an integer value. In Figures 8.9 and 8.10 the generic functions are identified by the dagger (†) symbol.

The general form of a function reference for a FORTRAN-supplied function is:

> *function name* (*argument expression*[,...])

where   *function name* is the name of the function.

        argument expression (there must be at least one) can be a constant, a variable, another function reference, or an expression containing constants, variables, arithmetic operations, and function references. The argument expression is evaluated to a single value, which is then passed to the function as an argument.

Logically, we can think of the function as being evaluated at the point it is used (where it appears in the statement). Internally, a transfer is made to a set of instructions that calculates the value of the function based on the value of the argument(s). Control is then returned to the point where the function was called. Some functions can have more than one argument, as in the case of the function MIN, which selects the smallest value of its integer arguments:

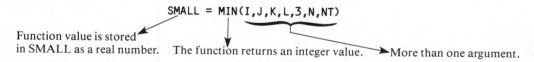

SMALL = MIN(I,J,K,L,3,N,NT)

Function value is stored in SMALL as a real number.   The function returns an integer value.   More than one argument.

The argument of the function must always be enclosed in parentheses. The argument itself may also contain parentheses, as in:

Outer parentheses identify the argument.

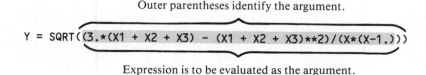

Y = SQRT((3.*(X1 + X2 + X3) − (X1 + X2 + X3)**2)/(X*(X−1.)))

Expression is to be evaluated as the argument.

Arguments: R = real, I = integer, C = complex, D = double precision	† : generic functions

Function	*Form*	*Argument*	*Value*	*Example*

Absolute value
$\|x\| = x$ if $x \geq 0$
$\|x\| = -x$ if $x < 0$
	ABS(R)†
	IABS(I)
	CABS(C)
	DABS(D)
		1 real
		1 integer
		1 complex
		1 double precision
			real
			integer
			real
			double precision
				`ABS(1.7)   = 1.7`
				`ABS(-2)    = 2`
				`ABS(3.,2.) = `$\sqrt{13}$

Square root $\sqrt{x}$	SQRT(R) R ≥ 0 CSQRT(C) DSQRT(D)	1 real 1 complex 1 double precision	real complex double precision	`SQRT(3.) = 1.732...` `SQRT(2)  is invalid.`
Exponential e^x	EXP(R)† CEXP(C) DEXP(D)	1 real 1 complex 1 double precision	real complex double precision	`EXP(1.)  = 2.718...` `EXP(-1.) = 0.367...`
Natural log $\text{Log}_e(x)$	ALOG(R) R > 0 CLOG(C) DLOG(D)	1 real 1 complex 1 double precision	real complex double precision	`LOG(2.718...) = 1.` `ALOG(2)  is invalid.`
Common log $\text{Log}_{10}(x)$	ALOG10(R) R > 0† DLOG10(D)	1 real 1 double precision	real double precision	`LOG10(100.) = 2.` `LOG10(20.)  = 1.301...`

Trigonometric functions: Given the angles, find the value of corresponding trigonometric functions. Sine, cosine, and tangent require arguments in radians; to use degrees, divide by 57.3 (180/π = 57.3), e.g., SIN(π) = SIN(180°/57.3)

Function	*Form*	*Argument*	*Value*	*Example*
Sine	SIN(R)† CSIN(C) DSIN(D)	1 real 1 complex 1 double precision	[−1. to 1.]	`SIN(90./57.3) = 1.` `SIN(1.) = .8414`
Cosine	COS(R)† CCOS(C) DCOS(D)	1 real 1 complex 1 double precision	[−1. to 1.]	`COS(3.1) = -.999...`
Tangent	TAN(R)† DTAN(D)	1 real 1 double precision	−∞. to +∞.	`TAN(1.571) = -4900...`

The arc functions: Given the arc values, find the corresponding angles. The values returned by these functions are expressed in radians: multiply by 57.3 to get degrees. DASIN, DACOS, DATAN and DATAN2 are double precision functions.

Function	*Form*		*Argument*	*Value*	*Example*
Arcsine	ASIN(R)	$-1 < R \leq 1$†	1 real	$[-\pi/2, \pi/2]$	`ASIN(.5) = 0.523...`
Arcosine	ACOS(R)	$-1 < R \leq 1$†	1 real	$[0, \pi]$	`ACOS(.5) = 1.047...`
Arctangent	ATAN(R)	$-\infty < R < +\infty$†	1 real	$[-\pi/2, \pi/2]$	`ATAN(1.) = 0.785...`
Real arc tangent R1/R2	ATAN2(R1,R2)	$-\infty < R1, R2 < \infty$†	2 real	$(-\pi, \pi]$	`ATAN2(5.8,-4.7) = 2.251`

For the hyperbolic functions, the arguments must be in radians.

Function	*Form*	*Argument*	*Value*	*Example*
Hyperbolic sine	SINH(R)† DSINH(D)	1 real	real	`SINH(.2) = 0.201...`
Hyperbolic cosine	COSH(R)† DCOSH(D)	1 real	real	`COSH(.2) = 1.02...`
Hyperbolic tangent	TANH(R)† DTANH(D)	1 real	real	`TANH(2.99) = .994...`

The following three functions can be used to operate on the real and the imaginery parts of a complex number:

Function	*Form*	*Argument*	*Value*	*Example*
Imaginary part	AIMAG(C)	1 complex	real	`AIMAG(7.0,-2.0) = -2`
Real part	REAL(C)†			
Conjugate	CONJG(C)	1 complex	complex	`CONJG(7.0,-2.0) = (7.0,2.0)`
Convert to complex	CMPLX(R1,R2)†	2 real	complex	`COMPLX(3.,4.) = 3+4i`

FIGURE 8.9
FORTRAN-SUPPLIED MATHEMATICAL FUNCTIONS

8.3.1 Mathematical
Functions

Standard built-in mathematical functions are shown in Figure 8.9. Note that there are restrictions on the ranges of values acceptable as arguments; for example, the square root and logarithmic functions cannot have negative arguments. If an invalid argument is detected by a function, an error message will be printed. Certain intrinsic functions also require a particular type argument (real, integer, and so forth); a real argument can be either single or double precision.

EXAMPLES

```
Y = SQRT(A**2 + B**2)
IF(ABS(Y) .LT. 0.01)THEN
```
Evaluate the expression $\sqrt{a^2 + b^2}$.
If the value of y is in the range $-0.01 < y < 0.01$, carry out task.

```
I = COS(X)**2 + C*EXP(-SIN(X))
```
Evaluates to $\cos^2 x + ce^{-\sin x}$. The result is truncated since it is stored in I.

```
Q = LOG(R)
```
The natural logarithm (base e) is computed. If r is negative, an error message will be printed, since logarithms of negative numbers are not defined.

8.3.2 Special Functions

Certain other functions shown in Figure 8.10 are also intrinsic functions.

The type conversion functions INT, IDINT and REAL are used to change the type of an argument. (Type conversion, of course, can also be accomplished with a replacement statement in which the type of the expression on the right is different from that of the variable on the left.) The type conversion functions allow this operation to be performed within an arithmetic expression.

EXAMPLE 1

The INTeger function converts to integer type, truncating any fractional part. If A = 3. and B = 2. then INT(A/B) + INT(A/4.) = 1 + 0 = 1

Some functions such as the transfer of sign (SIGN) and positive difference (DIM) functions require two arguments. SIGN (x,y) is equal to the absolute value of x times the sign of y while the value of DIM (x,y) is $x - y$ if that difference is positive, zero otherwise.

EXAMPLE 2

Function Reference	Value	Function Reference	Value
SIGN(3, −2)	−3	DIM(3, −2)	5
SIGN(3,2)	3	DIM(3., 2.5)	0.5
SIGN(−3., −2.)	−3.	DIM(−3, −2)	0
SIGN(−3,2)	3	DIM(−3.,2.)	0.

Some other functions may have any number of arguments; the functions that return the largest or smallest argument of a sequence of arguments require at least two arguments, all of the same type.

Arguments: R = Real, I = Integer, C = Complex, D = Double precision	† generic functions				
Function	*Purpose*	*Form*	*Argument*	*Value*	*Example*
Type conversion	Conversion to integer truncates fractional part	INT(R)† IDINT(D) AINT(R)†	1 real 1 double 1 real	integer integer real	INT(3.6)=3 INT(-2.5)=-2 INT(-3.79)=-3 AINT(3.6)=3.0
	Conversion to real Conversion to real Conversion to single precision Conversion to double precision	REAL(I)† FLOAT(I) SNGL(D) DBLE(R)	1 integer 1 integer 1 double 1 real	real real real double	FLOAT(3)=3.0
Nearest whole number	Rounds to nearest real number	ANINT(R)† DNINT(R)	1 real 1 double	real double	ANINT(-3.7)=-4.
Nearest integer	Rounds to nearest integer	NINT(R)† IDNINT(R)	1 real 1 double	integer integer	NINT(3.7)=4
Positive difference	Whichever of the following two values is larger: R1 − R2 or 0	DIM(R1,R2)† IDIM(I1,I2)	2 real 2 integer	real integer	DIM(3.2,1.0)=2.2 IDIM(1,3)=0
Remainder	Remainder $= x_1 - \text{INT}\left(\frac{x_1}{x_2}\right)*x_2$ (remainder of $\frac{17}{5} = 2$)	AMOD(R1,R2) MOD(I1,I2)† DMOD(D1,D2)	2 real 2 integer 2 double	real integer double	MOD(6,4)=2 AMOD(6.,5.)=1. MOD(-5,3)=-2 AMOD(-7.5,2.)=-1.5 AMOD(4.123,1.)=.123
Transfer of sign	x_1, x_2 = arguments of sign function $\lvert x_1 \rvert$ if $x_2 \geq 0$ $-\lvert x_1 \rvert$ if $x_2 < 0$	SIGN(R1,R2)† ISIGN(I1,I2) DSIGN(D1,D2)	2 real 2 integer 2 double	real integer double	ISIGN(2,-3)=-2 ISIGN(-2,-3)=-2 SIGN(-4.,2.)=4.0
Choose largest value	Largest of $(x_1, x_2, \ldots, x_n)$	MAX(...)† AMAX1(R1,R2,...) MAX0(I1,I2,...) DMAX1(D1,D2,...) MAX1(R1,R2,...) AMAX0(I1,I2,...)	≥ 2 generic ≥ 2 real ≥ 2 integer ≥ 2 double ≥ 2 real ≥ 2 integer	real integer double integer real	AMAX1(-1.,-2.,-3.)=-1. MAX0(-2,7,3)=7 MAX1(2.3,0,4.)=4 AMAX0(2,1,3)=3.0
Choose smallest value	Least of $(x_1, x_2, \ldots, x_n)$	MIN(...)† AMIN1(R1,R2,...) MIN0(I1,I2,...) DMIN1(D1,D2,...) MIN1(R1,R2,...) AMIN0(I1,I2,...)	≥ 2 generic ≥ 2 real ≥ 2 integer ≥ 2 double ≥ 2 real ≥ 2 integer	real integer double integer real	AMIN1(8.,3.1,0.3)=0.3 MIN0(3,2,0,-1)=-1 MIN1(3.1,2.0,1.0)=1 AMIN0(1,2,8)=1.0

FIGURE 8.10
OTHER FORTRAN-SUPPLIED FUNCTIONS

EXAMPLE 3   Suppose J = 3 and K = −2

Generic Function Reference	*Intrinsic Function Reference*	*Value*
MIN (3,9,7, − 1,4)	MIN0 (3,9,7, − 1,4)	− 1
MAX (3.,9.,7., − 1.,4.)	AMAX1 (3.,9.,7., − 1.,4.)	9.
MIN (J, K, J∗K, J + K)	MIN0 (J, K, J∗K, J + K)	− 6
MAX (J,K,J∗K,J + K,14)	MAX0 (J,K,J∗K,J + K,14)	14

1. Write FORTRAN statements for each of the following:

   a. $\sin x + \cos x$

   b. $\sin^2 x + \cos^2 x$

   c. $\tan x^{-1}$

   d. $\ln(x+y)$

   e. $|a+b|$

   f. $\sqrt{a+b}$

   g. $(\tan x)^{-1}$

   h. $\dfrac{1}{\sin x^2 + \cos x^2}$

   i. $e^x + e^{-x}$

   j. $\sqrt{\sin^2 x + \cos^2 x}$

   k. $|a-b|\,|x-y|$

2. What is the value of each of the following if A $= -3.$ and B $= 4.$?

   a. SQRT(A + B)

   b. ABS(A + B)

   c. LOG(EXP(B))

   d. LOG10(A + B)

   e. LOG(A)

3. An observer on shore sights a ship one mile away, moving along a line perpendicular to the line of sight. One hour later the observer sights the ship and finds an angle of 25° between the two sightings. Write a program to calculate how far the ship has traveled.

4. Write a single FORTRAN statement for each of the following:

   a. Place the largest value of a one-dimensional array A of length 5 into variable X.

   b. Compute the remainder after dividing X by Y.

   c. Compute the square root of integer variable I.

5. What will be the value of each of the following expressions if A $= -3.$ and B $= 4.$?

   a. INT (A)

   b. SIGN (A,B)

   c. DIM (A,B)

   d. MAX (A, 2.*A, B)

   e. MIN (A, 2.*A, B)

   f. MOD (B,A)

6. What will be the values of the following expressions?

   a. INT(0.5)

   b. INT(1.9)

   c. INT(-1.5)

   d. INT(1-2.9)

   e. REAL(-5)

   f. NINT(-1.1)

   g. NINT(-0.75)

   h. AINT(0.7)

   i. AINT(-1.5)

   j. ANINT(0.6)

   k. ANINT(-2.5)

   l. MOD(17,13)

   m. MOD(2.14,1.)

   n. MAX(ABS(-1.3),2.,ABS(2.1))

   o. MIN(-1,-3,NINT(-2.5))

7. The date for any Easter Sunday in any year can be computed as follows (let Y be the year):

   Let A be the remainder of the division of Y by 19.
   Let B be the remainder of the division of Y by 4.
   Let C be the remainder of the division of Y by 7.
   Let D be the remainder of the division of (19A + 24) by 30.
   Let E be the remainder of the division of (2B + 4C + 6D + 5) by 7.

   The date for Easter Sunday is March (22 + D + E), which may give a date in April. Write the code to read a year and determine its Easter date.

8. A prime number is a number that is evenly divisible only by 1 and by itself. Write the code to print all prime numbers between 5 and 10,000. To determine whether a number N is prime, it suffices to check whether N is divisible by any integer up to $\sqrt{N}$. For example, to determine whether 43 is prime, one needs only to check if 43 is divisible by 2, 3, 4, 5, and 6.

Answers

1. **a.** SIN(X) + COS(X)

   b. SIN(X)**2 + COS(X)**2

   c. TAN(X**(−1)) or TAN(1./X)

   d. LOG(X + Y)

   e. ABS (A + B)

   f. SQRT(A + B)

   g. 1./(TAN(X)) or TAN(X)**(−1)

   h. 1./(SIN(X**2) + COS(X**2))

   i. EXP(X) + EXP(−X)

   j. SQRT(SIN(X)**2 + COS(X)**2)

   k. ABS(A − B)*ABS(X − Y)

2. **a.** 1.   **b.** 1.   **c.** 4.   **d.** 0.

   e. Error. Argument must be > 0.

3.

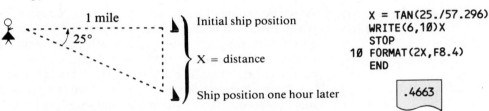

```
X = TAN(25./57.296)
    WRITE(6,10)X
    STOP
10  FORMAT(2X,F8.4)
    END
```

.4663

4. **a.** X = MAX(A(1),A(2),A(3),A(4),A(5))

   b. R = MOD(X,Y)

   c. X = SQRT(REAL(I))

5. **a.** −3   **d.** 4.

   b. 3.   **e.** −6.

   c. 0.   **f.** 1.

6. **a.** 0   **e.** −5.   **i.** −1.0   **m.** 0.14

   b. 1   **f.** −1   **j.** 1.0   **n.** 2.1

   c. −1   **g.** −1   **k.** −3.0   **o.** −3

   d. −1   **h.** 0.0   **l.** 4

7.
```
IMPLICIT INTEGER(A-Z)
READ(*,1)YEAR
A = MOD(YEAR,19)
B = MOD(YEAR,4)
C = MOD(YEAR,7)
D = MOD(19*A+24,30)
E = MOD(2*B+4*C+6*D+5,7)
R = 22 + D + E
IF(R.GT.31)THEN
   R = R-31
   PRINT*,'EASTER SUNDAY IS APRIL',R
ELSE
   PRINT*,'EASTER SUNDAY IS MARCH',R
ENDIF
STOP
```

```
8.    DO 5 I = 5,10000,2          Skip all even numbers.
         K = SQRT(REAL(I))        Determine √I. Argument of SQRT
         DO 4 J = 3,K,2           must be real.
            IF(MOD(I,J).EQ.0)GO TO 5    Check if I is divisible by any integer
    4    CONTINUE                 up to and possibly including √I.
         WRITE(6,31)I             Number is prime; print it.
    5 CONTINUE
      STOP
   31 FORMAT(1X,I6)
      END
```

8.4 PROGRAMMING EXAMPLES

8.4.1 A Function Subprogram

At the beginning of the semester, Professor X agrees with her students on the way in which their final grades will be determined from their 6 weeks' test, 12 weeks' test, and final exam. Their semester score will be either the average of the three test scores or the final exam grade, whichever is higher. A "pass" grade is given if the semester score is greater than 70, otherwise a "fail" grade is given.

Write a program to read student records (name and three test scores) and determine the students' semester scores and letter grades as well as the letter grade of the class based on the average of the students' semester scores. The output report should be similar to the following:

STUDENT NAME	TEST1	TEST2	FINAL	SEMESTER GRADE	LETTER GRADE
DENTON	30	90	80	80.0	PASS
AMAURY	90	80	70	80.0	PASS
MALLORY	100	20	60	60.0	FAIL
MANARIN	80	80	70	76.7	PASS

CLASS LETTER GRADE = PASS

Problem Solution. We will organize our program by dividing it into three modules:

1. The main program, which will coordinate the use of the other two modules (subprograms).

2. A function subprogram called BEST that will determine the student's best score combination.

3. A function subprogram called LETTER that will determine whether a grade is pass or fail.

The hierarchy chart for the problem can be diagrammed as follows:

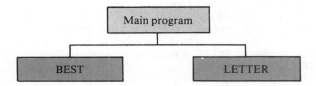

Let us first write the pseudo code to solve the problem.

```
*    Function Subprogram Example
     set class total and student count to 0
     WHILE end of file not encountered DO
          read student name, test1, test2 and final
          add 1 to student count
          semester score = BEST (test1,test2,final)
          add semester score to class total
          letter grade = LETTER (semester score)
          write student name, test1, test2, final, semester score, letter grade
     ENDWHILE
     class letter grade = LETTER (class total/student count)
     write class letter grade
     stop
*    function BEST determines the student's best score combination
```

FUNCTION BEST	arguments are t1, t2 and t3

BEST = (t1 + t2 + t3)/3
IF BEST < t3 THEN
   BEST = t3
ENDIF
end	

```
*    function LETTER determines whether semester score is passing or failing
```

FUNCTION LETTER	argument is score

LETTER = "pass"
IF score ≤ 70 THEN
   LETTER = "fail"
ENDIF
end	

The FORTRAN program is shown in Figure 8.11.

In the main program, the statement SCORE = BEST(TEST1,TEST2,FINAL) at line 19 sets up the internal linkage to communicate (send values) between two distinct areas of memory—one containing the main program and the other containing the BEST subprogram. The arguments T1, T2, and T3 specified in FUNCTION BEST at line 37 refer to the same memory locations as TEST1, TEST2, and FINAL in the main program. Note that if for some reason one of the arguments T1, T2, or T3 is changed in the subprogram, the corresponding argument TEST1, TEST2, or FINAL would also change in the main program.

To understand the return mechanism from the subprogram to the main program, the user should think of BEST as a memory location defined in the main program. The subprogram causes the value of the function (either T3 or (T1 + T2 + T3)/3) to be

```
 1: *** FUNCTION SUBPROGRAM: COMPUTING A SEMESTER SCORE
 2: *** TEST1, TEST2, FINAL: 1ST, 2ND AND FINAL TEST SCORES
 3: *** GRADE: LETTER GRADE FOR SEMESTER (PASS OR FAIL)
 4: *** SCORE: STUDENT'S SEMESTER SCORE (FINAL OR (TEST1+TEST2 + FINAL)/3)
 5: *** CLASS: LETTER GRADE FOR ENTIRE CLASS (AVERAGE OF ALL SEMESTER SCORES)
 6: *** COUNT: TOTAL NUMBER OF STUDENTS
 7: *** NAME:  STUDENT NAME
 8: *** SUM:    ADDS ALL STUDENT FINAL SEMESTER SCORES
 9:        CHARACTER GRADE*4, CLASS*4, NAME*8
10:        INTEGER TEST1, TEST2, FINAL, COUNT
11:        REAL SCORE, SUM
12: * FUNCTIONS USED
13:        CHARACTER*4 LETTER
14:        REAL BEST
15:        DATA SUM, COUNT/0., 0/
16:        WRITE(6,1)
17: 5      READ(5,2,END=88)NAME,TEST1,TEST2,FINAL
18:           COUNT = COUNT + 1
19:           SCORE = BEST(TEST1, TEST2, FINAL)
20:           SUM  = SUM + SCORE
21:           GRADE = LETTER(SCORE)
22:           WRITE(6,3)NAME,TEST1,TEST2,FINAL,SCORE,GRADE
23:        GO TO 5
24: 88     CLASS = LETTER(SUM/COUNT)
25:        WRITE(6,4)CLASS
26:        STOP
27: 2      FORMAT(A8,3I3)
28: 3      FORMAT(1X,A8,2X,I3,4X,I3,4X,I3,5X,F5.1,5X,A4)
29: 4      FORMAT('0','CLASS LETTER GRADE = ',A4)
30: 1      FORMAT(' STUDENT   TEST1  TEST2  FINAL  SEMESTER  LETTER'/
31:        A         ' NAME                            AVERAGE   GRADE'/1X)
32:        END
33: *
34: *** FUNCTION BEST DETERMINES BEST SCORE COMBINATION
35: *** T1, T2, T3: REPRESENT TEST1, TEST2 AND FINAL
36: *** BEST:        EQUALS EITHER T3 OR (T1+T2+T3)/3
37:        REAL FUNCTION BEST(T1, T2, T3)
38:        INTEGER T1, T2, T3
39:        BEST = (T1 + T2 + T3)/3.
40:        IF(BEST .LT. T3) BEST = T3
41:        RETURN
42:        END
43: *
44: *** FUNCTION LETTER DETERMINES STUDENT'S LETTER GRADE
45: *** SCORE:  SEMESTER FINAL SCORE
46: *** LETTER: GETS "PASS" IF SCORE > 70 , "FAIL" OTHERWISE
47:        CHARACTER*4 FUNCTION LETTER(SCORE)
48:        LETTER = 'PASS'
49:        IF(SCORE .LE. 70.0) LETTER = 'FAIL'
50:        RETURN
51:        END
```

COUNT counts the number of students. Find the student's semester final score. Accumulate semester final scores for class score. Find letter score. Function will return either a PASS or a FAIL depending on whether semester grade is greater than 70. Determine PASS or FAIL for entire class. Note that the expression SUM/COUNT is a valid argument.

BEST determines a student's best score combination, either the final score or the average of the three scores. T1, T2, and T3 are the same as TEST1, TEST2, and FINAL; they are just different variable names referring to the same memory locations.
If the average of the scores is less than the final, the final score is passed on to the main program, otherwise the average is passed on. Note how the name of the function BEST is used to communicate the result to the main program.

LETTER returns either 'PASS' or 'FAIL' to the main program.
This function is called from two different locations in the main program, the first time to compute the letter grade for each student and the second time to compute the overall class average.

Input File

Name	T1	T2	Final
DENTON	030	090	080
AMAURY	090	080	070
MALLORY	100	020	060
MANARIN	080	080	070

STUDENT NAME	TEST1	TEST2	FINAL	SEMESTER AVERAGE	LETTER GRADE
DENTON	30	90	80	80.0	PASS
AMAURY	90	80	70	80.0	PASS
MALLORY	100	20	60	60.0	FAIL
MANARIN	80	80	70	76.7	PASS

CLASS LETTER GRADE = PASS

FIGURE 8.11
SEMESTER GRADE COMPUTATION

stored in that memory location (BEST). Note that any reference to BEST in the main program must include arguments, since BEST is a function name.

In Figure 8.11 notice that LETTER is typed as CHARACTER*4, since that function returns a four-character value; similarly, the function BEST has been typed REAL, since BEST returns an average. Also note that the function names are typed in both the function program and in the program that uses them.

Notice how it is possible to avoid duplication of code through the use of functions. Whenever a task is to be performed, a transfer is made to that task; when the task is completed, it returns control to the program that called it. In the program in Figure 8.11 the task of determining the letter grade needs to be done at two different places in the program, once to compute the letter grade for each student and again to compute the overall class letter grade when all records have been read. Instead of writing the code to determine the letter grade every time it is needed, one block of code is written to perform this task, then it can be called any number of times by the main program (or even by other subprograms).

8.4.2 Subroutine Subprogram

Dr. D teaches two FORTRAN classes. Array CLASS1 contains the 10 final scores of class 1, while array CLASS2 contains the 8 final scores of class 2. To ensure fairness, Dr. D assigns final scores as follows:

- If the average of class 1 is less than the average of class 2, all class 1 students get 5% of their class's average added to their scores.

- If the average of class 2 is less than the average of class 1, all class 2 students get 5% of their class's average added to their scores.

- If the difference between the two class averages is less than 5 points, the scores are left unchanged.

Write a program to do the following (in the sequence shown):

1. Read the scores in arrays CLASS1 and CLASS2 and print both sets of scores.

2. Write a subroutine to compute the average scores for CLASS1 and CLASS2 and print the averages.

3. Write a subroutine to compute the 5% bonus, add the bonus to each score, and print the bonus and the adjusted scores.

For example, the following input file should produce the output shown below:

Input File

►class 1 scores

```
060 070 080 090 050 060 070 080 080 065
010 020 030 040 050 060 070 090
```

►class 2 scores

Output

```
CLASS 1 SCORES: 60.0 70.0 80.0 90.0 50.0 60.0 70.0 80.0 80.0 65.0
CLASS 2 SCORES: 10.0 20.0 30.0 40.0 50.0 60.0 70.0 90.0
CLASS 1 AVERAGE = 70.50
CLASS 2 AVERAGE = 46.25
CLASS 2 BONUS   =  2.3
ADJUSTED SCORES: CLASS 2:  12.3 22.3 32.3 42.3 52.3 62.3 72.3 92.3
```

The program to solve this problem is shown in Figure 8.12. The various modules are:

1. The main program (lines 7–29), which coordinates the use of the two subroutines AVRGE and ADJUST.

```
 1:       SUBROUTINE PROBLEM
 2: *** GIVEN CLASS 1 AND CLASS 2 ,ALL STUDENTS IN THE CLASS WITH THE LOWEST
 3: *** CLASS AVERAGE GET 5% OF THEIR CLASS AVERAGE ADDED TO THEIR SCORES.
 4: *** AVG1, AVG2: CLASS 1 & CLASS 2 AVERAGES
 5: *** CLASS1(10): CLASS1 SCORES
 6: *** CLASS2(08): CLASS2 SCORES
 7:       INTEGER SIZE1,SIZE2
 8:       PARAMETER (SIZE1=10,SIZE2=8)
 9:       REAL AVG1, AVG2, SUM
10:       REAL CLASS1(SIZE1), CLASS2(SIZE2)
11:       READ(5,3) CLASS1, CLASS2
12:       WRITE(6,1)CLASS1, CLASS2
13:       CALL AVRGE(CLASS1,AVG1,SIZE1)
14:       CALL AVRGE(CLASS2,AVG2,SIZE2)
15:       WRITE(6,4)AVG1,AVG2
16:       IF(ABS(AVG1-AVG2) .GT. 5.0)THEN
17:         IF(AVG1 .GT. AVG2) THEN
18:             CALL ADJUST(CLASS2,AVG2,SIZE2,2)
19:         ELSE
20:             CALL ADJUST(CLASS1,AVG1,SIZE1,1)
21:         ENDIF
22:       ENDIF
23:       STOP
24: 1     FORMAT(' CLASS 1 SCORES:',   10F5.1/
25:     A         1X,' CLASS 2 SCORES:',10F5.1/)
26: 4     FORMAT(' CLASS 1 AVERAGE = ',F6.2/
27:     A         1X,' CLASS 2 AVERAGE = ',F6.2)
28: 3     FORMAT(10(F3.0,1X))
29:       END
30: *
31: *** THIS SUBROUTINE COMPUTES THE AVERAGE OF THE NUMBERS STORED AN ARRAY
32: *** CLASS CONTAINING N ELEMENTS. THE AVERAGE IS STORED IN AVG.
33:       SUBROUTINE AVRGE(CLASS,AVG,N)
34: ***   ARGUMENT DEFINITIONS
35: ***     INPUT ARGUMENTS
36:           INTEGER N
37:           REAL CLASS(N)
38: ***     OUTPUT ARGUMENTS
39:           REAL AVG
40: ***   LOCAL VARIABLES
41:       REAL SUM
42: *
43:       SUM = 0.0
44:       DO 5 I = 1, N
45:          SUM = SUM + CLASS(I)
46:  5 CONTINUE
47:       AVG = SUM/REAL(N)
48:       END
49: *
```

Call the AVRGE program to compute the average (AVG1) of ten scores stored in array CLASS1. In subroutine AVRGE the array CLASS1 is referred to as CLASS, AVG1 is referred to as AVG, and SIZE is equal to ten. The subroutine stores the result (average) into AVG, which is the same memory location as AVG1.

The AVRGE program is called again, this time to compute the average of eight scores stored in CLASS2. The resulting average is stored in memory location AVG2 (called AVG in subprogram).

Determine which class has lower average. If AVG2 is lower, the 8 scores in CLASS2 and the average of class 2(AVG2) are transmitted to program ADJUST. The argument 2 identifies the class number (NUMBER in subroutine ADJUST).

Program ADJUST adds five percent of AVG1 or AVG2 (BONUS) to each class 1 or class 2 score and stores the resulting adjusted scores in CLASS.

Upon return from ADJUST, the adjusted scores will either be in CLASS1 and CLASS2, and BONUS will be equal to five percent of AVG1 or AVG2.

CLASS refers to either CLASS1 or CLASS2.
AVG refers to either AVG1 or AVG2

FIGURE 8.12
DETERMINING FINAL GRADES (Part 1)

```
50: *** THIS SUBROUTINE ADDS TO EACH ELEMENT OF ARRAY CLASS 5 PERCENT OF AVG
51: *** N REPRESENTS THE NUMBER OF ELEMENTS IN ARRAY CLASS. NUMBER IS
52: *** EITHER 1 OR 2 & IDENTIFIES ON THE OUTPUT WHICH CLASS GETS THE BONUS.
53:      SUBROUTINE ADJUST(CLASS,AVG,N,NUMBER)
54: ***    ARGUMENT DEFINITIONS
55: ***       INPUT ARGUMENTS
56:              INTEGER NUMBER,N
57:              REAL AVG
58:          INPUT & OUTPUT ARGUMENTS
59:              REAL CLASS(N)
60: ***    LOCAL VARIABLES
61:          REAL BONUS
62: *
63:      BONUS = AVG * 0.05
64:      DO 9 I = 1, N
65:         CLASS(I) = CLASS(I) + BONUS
66:    9 CONTINUE
67:      WRITE(6,2)NUMBER,BONUS,NUMBER,
68:    A         (CLASS(I),I=1,N)
69:    2 FORMAT(1X,'CLASS ',I1,' BONUS     =',F5.1/1X
70:      *'ADJUSTED SCORES: CLASS',I2,':',10F5.1)
71:      END
```

Line 59: CLASS refers to CLASS1 if AVG1 ≤ AVG2 or to CLASS2 if AVG2 < AVG1.

Line 63: BONUS is equal to 5% of AVG. AVG refers to either AVG1 or AVG2

Line 67: NUMBER is either 1 or 2 to identify the particular class.

```
CLASS 1 SCORES: 60.0 70.0 80.0 90.0 50.0 60.0 70.0 80.0 80.0 65.0
CLASS 2 SCORES: 10.0 20.0 30.0 40.0 50.0 60.0 70.0 90.0
CLASS 1 AVERAGE =  70.50
CLASS 2 AVERAGE =  46.25
CLASS 2 BONUS   =   2.3
ADJUSTED SCORES: CLASS 2  12.3 22.3 32.3 42.3 52.3 62.3 72.3 92.3
```

Input File

```
060 070 080 090 050 060 070 080 080 065
010 020 030 040 050 060 070 090
```

FIGURE 8.12
DETERMINING FINAL GRADES (Part 2)

2. The AVRGE program (lines 31–48), which computes and returns to the main program the average of N scores stored in array CLASS.

3. The ADJUST program (lines 50–71), which adds a constant (BONUS) to each of the N scores in the array CLASS (line 65) and prints the adjusted scores.

In the ADJUST subroutine, array CLASS is a two-way (input and output) argument: it sends the values to the subroutine, where they are modified and then sent back to the calling program (through the same array!). The AVG argument in subroutine AVRGE is an output argument—it transmits a result from the subroutine back to the main program.

8.4.3 A Statistical Problem

Write a function subprogram to compute and print the median of N numbers stored in an array X.

Problem Solution. Recall that the median of a set of numbers is the number that divides the set into two equal parts, that is, the median is the middle value in a distribution, above and below which lie an equal number of values. Note that the median itself may not be one of the actual numbers in the set, particularly when there are an even number of items. Thus, the median of 1, 2, 3, and 4 is $(2+3)/2 = 2.5$, whereas the median of 1, 2 and 3 is 2.

To find the median we must first sort the numbers in order (ascending or descending). We will sort the numbers in a subroutine (see lines 39–63 in Figure 8.13) using the Shell method (section 6.7.2 ex. 39). The Shell Metzner sort is much more efficient and therefore much faster than the other sort techniques discussed in chapter 6. The code is intriguing and somewhat similar to the bubble sort. Instead of comparing consecutive numbers, it compares numbers that are d positions away from one another, where d takes on successively lower values with each pass. The value of d during the first pass is $(N+1)/2$, and for each successive pass its value is halved ($d=(d+1)/2$ as long as $d>1$). The number of passes is directly related to d, since there are as many passes as there are different values of d generated by the above formula. In Figure 8.13 the variable name for d is POS (lines 50 and 52).

The following table compares the Shell and bubble sorts in terms of the number of passes and the number of comparisons between elements (line 54 in Figure 8.13).

Number of Elements N	Number of Passes		Number of Elements Comparisons (line 54)	
	Shell	Bubble	Shell	Bubble
10	4	9	28	36
50	6	49	246	1,176
100	7	99	535	4,851
1,000	10	999	8,990	498,501

Once the numbers are sorted, the median is either equal to $X(N/2+1)$ if N is odd (line 34) or to $(X(N/2)+X(N/2+1))/2$ if N is even (line 32). The MOD function is used to determine whether N is even or odd (line 31).

8.4.4 A Graph of the TAN Function

Figure 8.14 shows a program that produces a rough graph of the function $y = \tan x$ in the interval $0, 5\pi/2$ for values of x in steps of 0.2 radian. Special precautions must be taken, however, since in that interval $\tan x$ is $\pm \infty$ at $\pi/2$, $3\pi/2$ and $5\pi/2$ as shown:

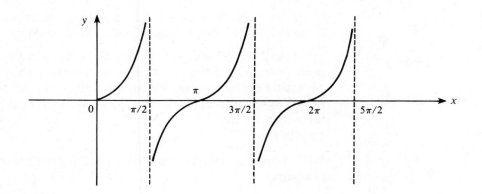

```
 1: ******MAIN PROGRAM FINDING THE MEDIAN FOR A SET OF NUMBERS
 2: ******X:      ARRAY CONTAINING REAL NUMERIC ENTRIES
 3: ******MAXSIZ: MAXIMUM NUMBER OF ARRAY ELEMENTS
 4: ******N:      NUMBER OF ELEMENTS ACTUALLY READ INTO ARRAY X
 5: *
 6: ******PARAMETER NAMES
 7:         PARAMETER(MAXSIZ=100)
 8: ******FUNCTIONS USED
 9:         REAL MEDIAN
10: ******PROGRAM VARIABLES
11:         REAL X(MAXSIZ)
12:         INTEGER N
13: *
14:        OPEN(5,FILE='MEDIAN')
15:        READ(5,6,END=88)(X(N),N=1,MAXSIZ)
16: 88     N = N - 1                              N is the number of items read into array.
17:        WRITE(*,9)MEDIAN(X,N),(X(I),I=1,N)     Print median of the N elements of array X.
18: 6      FORMAT(F5.2)
19:        STOP
20: 9      FORMAT(1X,'MEDIAN = ',F5.2/1X,'SORTED ARRAY:',(10F7.2))
21:        END
22: *
23:        REAL FUNCTION MEDIAN(X,N)
24: ******ARGUMENT DEFINITIONS
25: ******    INPUT ARGUMENT
26:            INTEGER N
27: ******    INPUT/OUTPUT ARGUMENT
28:            REAL X(N)
29: *
30:        CALL SORT(X,N)
31:        IF(MOD(N,2) .EQ. 0)THEN
32:            MEDIAN = (X(N/2) + X(N/2+1))/2.0    if N is even
33:        ELSE
34:            MEDIAN = X(N/2 + 1)                 if N is odd
35:        ENDIF
36:        RETURN
37:        END
38: *
39: ******SUBROUTINE SORT SORTS N NUMBERS IN ARRAY X IN ASCENDING ORDER
40:        SUBROUTINE SORT(X,N)
41: ******ARGUMENT DEFINITIONS                    This subroutine is a Shell sort routine.
42: ******    INPUT ARGUMENT
43:            INTEGER N
44: ******    INPUT/OUTPUT ARGUMENT
45:            REAL X(N)
46: ******LOCAL VARIABLES
47:          REAL TEMP
48:          INTEGER POS
49: *
50:      FLAG = 1
51:      POS = N
52: 5  IF(POS .GT. 1 .OR. FLAG .EQ. 1) THEN
53:        FLAG = 0
54:        POS = (POS + 1)/2
55:        DO 10 I = 1, N-POS
56:           IF(X(I) .GT. X(I+POS))THEN
57:                TEMP     = X(I)
58:                X(I)     = X(I+POS)
59:                X(I+POS) = TEMP
60:                FLAG     = 1
61:           ENDIF
62: 10     CONTINUE
63:        GO TO 5
64:    ENDIF
65:    RETURN
66:    END
```

MEDIAN = 11.67
SORTED ARRAY: -1.90   -.06 23.40 32.80

Input File

-.06
32.8
23.4
-1.9

FIGURE 8.13
FINDING A MEDIAN

We must decide what portion of the graph we want to retain, since we cannot graph all those points close to the asymptotes. We might decide, as we did in the program of Figure 8.14, to graph only those points where y lies between -9 and 9. Then, when writing the program, we must test the values for y and graph only those points falling in the restricted area.

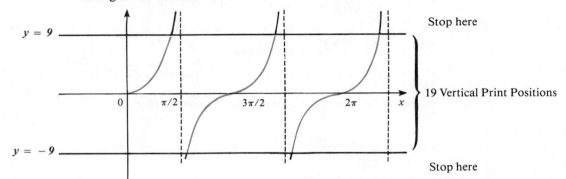

Since graphs are printed on the printer output form with the y axis horizontal and the x axis vertical, $y = \tan x$ could be printed using only 19 print positions (-9 to 9). Recall that to print the graph of a function, an array is used to simulate successive lines where each line consists of blank entries except for one entry containing the graphic symbol *. That symbol is located at LINE (y). Therefore to avoid negative values for y, we add 9 to $\tan x$; the range of $\tan x + 9$ is now 0 to 18. To spread out the graph over more than 19 positions on the line, we multiply the range 0–18 by 4 for example; the expression $4(\tan x + 9)$ gives us a range of 73 print positions (0 through 72) in which to insert the graphic symbol '*'. The graph is then drawn one horizontal line at a time using the array LINE to print a line that is blank except for the graphic character * inserted at position $4(\tan x + 9)$. See the following diagram.

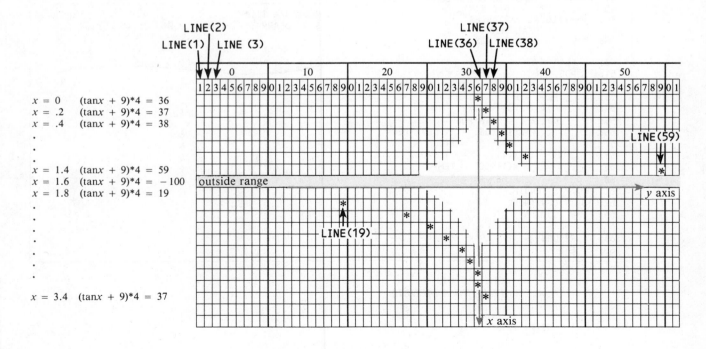

```
C GRAPH OF THE TANGENT FUNCTION
C   LINE: LINE CONTAINING THE GRAPHIC SYMBOLS
C
        CHARACTER LINE(72)
        DATA LINE/72*'.'/                   Initialize LINE array to dots.
        WRITE(6,3)
        X = 0.0
10      IF(X .LE. 8.) THEN                  x varies from 0 to 5π/2
           Y = TAN(X)
           J = (Y + 9.)*4. + .5
           IF(J.LT.1 .OR. J.GT.72) THEN     Check for points that cannot be graphed
              WRITE(6,15) X, Y, J           because they are outside the range 0-72.
           ELSE
              LINE(J) = '*'
              WRITE(6,15) X, Y, J, LINE
              LINE(J) = '.'                 Reset line array to all dots.
           ENDIF
           X = X + .2                       Increment by 0.2 radians
           GO TO 10
        ENDIF
        STOP
3       FORMAT(3X,'X',7X,'Y',5X,'J')
15      FORMAT(1X,F4.1,2X,F6.2,2X,I4,3X,72A1)
        END
```

X	Y	J
.0	.00	36
.2	.20	37
.4	.42	38
.6	.68	39
.8	1.03	40
1.0	1.56	42
1.2	2.57	46
1.4	5.80	59
1.6	-34.23	-100
1.8	4.29	19
2.0	-2.19	27
2.2	-1.37	31
2.4	-.92	32
2.6	-.60	34
2.8	-.36	35
3.0	-.14	35
3.2	.06	36
3.4	.26	37
3.6	.49	38
3.8	.77	39
4.0	1.16	41
4.2	1.78	43
4.4	3.10	48
4.6	8.86	71
4.8	-11.38	-9
5.0	-3.38	22
5.2	1.89	28
5.4	-1.22	31
5.6	-.81	33
5.8	-.52	34
6.0	-.29	35
6.2	-.08	36
6.4	.12	36
6.6	.33	37
6.8	.57	38
7.0	.87	39
7.2	1.30	41
7.4	2.05	44
7.6	3.85	51
7.8	18.51	110
8.0	-6.80	9

FIGURE 8.14
GRAPH OF THE SCALED TANGENT FUNCTION

In Figure 8.14, the variable J is used to place the asterisk at the Jth position in the array LINE (the asterisk will be in LINE(J)). If J is zero or negative or J ≥ 72, the asterisk cannot be graphed, since it is outside the designated interval 1 – 72 for the array LINE.

8.5 YOU MIGHT WANT TO KNOW

1. Why use subroutines?

Answer: A subroutine can be an aid in writing shorter and more compact programs. The programmer can break a program into smaller logical components that are easier to work with, resulting in a more readable program. A subroutine can also result in an economy of code for procedures or tasks that are to be performed repeatedly at different places in a program(s). The code for the procedure is written just once and is not recoded wherever it is needed in the program.

Subroutines that are to be used frequently should be compiled and tested until thoroughly debugged. They can then be stored in object form in a user's library or on the user's diskette, where they can be retrieved by other FORTRAN programs. This saves computer time, since the subroutine need not be recompiled each time it is to be used. Both computer time and programming time can be saved when subroutines are shared by users through "share" libraries. A brief subroutine description and its use (calling sequence) should be included in the listing of the subprogram by means of comment statements.

2. There are no repetitive tasks in most of the programs I write. Are subroutines of any value to me?

Answer: Perhaps, particularly in long or complex problems. It is generally possible to segment the tasks that make up the complete program, write subprograms to perform these tasks, and verify that each subprogram executes properly. The complete program can then be constructed using the already written and debugged subprograms.

3. Can I use the names of existing FORTRAN functions such as SQRT, ABS, and COS as names for my own function subprograms?

Answer: No. These functions are predefined by the FORTRAN compiler and are machine code generated during the compilation process. Hence no linkage will be made to any user-defined function subprograms having such names.

4. What statements can be used in a subroutine?

Answer: Any FORTRAN statements except other SUBROUTINE or FUNCTION declarative statements.

5. Is a STOP statement necessary after the RETURN statement?

Answer: No. The STOP instruction cannot be executed, since RETURN passes control back to the calling program.

6. If an argument in a CALL statement is just used by the subroutine to pass a particular result to the calling program, need that argument be initialized to a specific value in the calling program?

Answer: No. For example:

```
CALL ADD(X,Y,RES)          SUBROUTINE ADD(A,B,RES)
                           RES = A + B
```

There is no need to initialize RES to any value in the calling program.

7. If I use a DATA statement to initialize a variable in a subroutine, will that variable be reinitialized every time the subroutine is called?

Answer: No. For example:

```
CALL TX(Y,3)          SUBROUTINE TX(X,K)
   :                  DATA SUM/0./
   :                  SUM = SUM + K
CALL TX(Y,4)          RETURN
```

As a result of the first call to TX, the value of SUM is 3. The second time through TX, SUM will equal 7, not 4. If you need to reset SUM to 0, use the statement SUM = 0.0.

8. Can a subroutine use a STOP statement?

Answer: Yes. Consider the following example:

```
SUBROUTINE QUAD(A,B,C,X,ROOT1,ROOT2)
   :
   :
DISC = B**2 - 4.*A*C
IF(DISC.LT.0.)THEN
    WRITE(6,*) 'ROOTS ARE IMAGINARY'
    STOP
ELSE
   :
   :
```
Note the STOP statement.

The practice of using the STOP statement in a subroutine is *not* recommended, as many programmers feel it should be the privilege of the main program to stop execution of the complete program. A flag can be used in the subroutine and tested in the main program if there is cause for immediate termination of the job.

9. Can a subroutine or a function call another subroutine or function subprogram?

Answer: Yes, as long as the subroutine does not call itself. Nor can a subroutine call a subroutine that calls the original subroutine. You must avoid calling sequences that result in a closed loop (called a daisychain) such as:

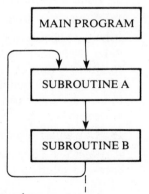

FORTRAN does not allow recursion.

10. Is a subroutine permitted to change the value of any argument?

Answer: Yes. However, care must be exercised to avoid problems such as those shown in the following example:

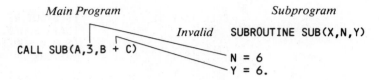

The value of the second argument is changed to 6 by the subroutine; however, the actual argument is a constant 3. This can have an unpredictable effect in the program. Similarly, the value of the third argument is changed by the subroutine, but the actual argument is an expression, not a storage location. Again, unpredictable effects will occur.

11. Functions and subroutines seem to have a lot in common. Can I change the value of an argument in a function subprogram as I can in a subroutine subprogram?

Answer: Yes, you can write a function to perform exactly the same tasks as a subroutine; however, this is contrary to the purpose of a function subprogram. A function is generally used to return a single value to the calling program via the function name. A subroutine should be written when the value of more than one variable is to be changed.

12. Can an argument expression contain a reference to another function?

Answer: Yes. For example:

```
SQRT(ABS(X))
SQRT(SQRT(Y))
```

13. Is it better to use SQRT or **.5 to calculate the square root?

Answer: In general, SQRT is more efficient if not more accurate than exponentiation. In either case the result will be a close approximation to the actual square root. Most systems use logarithms to perform exponentiation, while iterative methods are generally used to evaluate the SQRT function.

14. What other functions are available?

Answer: The lists of functions in Figures 8.9 and 8.10 are by no means exhaustive. Refer to the manufacturer's reference manual for your FORTRAN system for a complete listing. Also, most installations have packages of statistical and other mathematical functions with a wide variety of capabilities. When available, these functions may considerably reduce the amount of effort involved in program development.

15. Can an array element be used as a function argument?

Answer: Yes. For example, if A and XYZ are arrays, the following function references are valid:

```
SQRT(A(4))
ABS(XYZ(L,J))
```

16. Can the MAX/MIN functions return the value of the largest/smallest value contained in an array?

Answer: Yes, but each element of the array must be listed as a separate argument. For example:

```
SMALL = MIN(X(1),X(2),X(3),X(4),X(5),X(6),X(7))
```

It would, of course, be better to write a function subprogram that would accept the array as an argument and return the smallest element.

17. If I dimension an array SIN(10) and I refer to Y = SIN(X) in my program, will the sine function of X be computed?

Answer: No. The compiler will treat any reference to SIN as an array reference.

18. Why would I ever want to write a subroutine without arguments such as CALL SUB?

Answer: Perhaps you might want to write a subroutine just to set up headings for each page of a lengthy computer-generated report or to control the printer for special editing effects.

8.6 EXERCISES

8.6.1 Test Yourself

Exercises Involving Functions

1. Write FORTRAN statements for each of the following:

   a. $a = \sin^2 x - \cos^2 x$ **d.** Find the largest of A, B, C, D, and E.

   b. $z = e^x - e^{-x}$ **e.** Find the smallest of I, J, K, and 3.

   c. $x = \sqrt{|p - q|}$

2. How could INT be used to round to the nearest hundred? To the nearest thousandth?

3. What will be the value of each of the following if A = 100., B = −2.4, C = 81., D = 0 and E = −2.9?

a. SQRT(C)	**i.** MAX(A,B,4.*B,C,D)
b. SQRT(SQRT(C))	**j.** ABS(B) + ABS(C)
c. INT(B)	**k.** LOG10(A)
d. SIGN(A,B)	**l.** SIN(D) + COS(D)
e. SIGN(B,A)	**m.** AINT(E)
f. DIM(A,B)	**n.** ANINT(E)
g. DIM(B,A)	**o.** NINT(E)
h. MIN(A,B,C,D)	**p.** AMOD(E, − 1.3)

4. Determine which of the following calling/called functions are invalid. If invalid, explain why.

Calling Program	Function Subprogram
a. S = COT(A,B,COT(1.,1.,1.))	FUNCTION COT(X,Y,Z)
b. REAL Q(100) T = DAM(Q(1),Q,-4)	FUNCTION DAM(T(1),T,J) REAL T(100)
c. WRITE(6,11)FUNC(1.,2.)	FUNCTION FUNC(X,Y)
d. MIM = SUB(X,2*J,9.8)	INTEGER FUNCTION SUB(X,K,S)
e. SON = OF(A,OF(A,GUN))	FUNCTION OF(A,NON)
f. IF(MAT(2.,X).GT.3.) THEN	INTEGER FUNCTION MAT(X+Y,Z)
g. REAL B(5) X = TIP(B(1),X,B(5))	FUNCTION TIP(A,B,C) REAL A(5)
h. REAL A(5) Z = CAN(T,3,6/L)	FUNCTION CAN(T,J,3)
i. A = PAT(L,M,N)	FUNCTION PAT(N,M,L) DATA N,M,L/1,1,3/ RETURN END
j. S = LARG(2,LARG(3,4))	FUNCTION LARG(I,J)
k. X = COT(X)	FUNCTION COT(X)

5. Which of the following function subprogram declarative statements are incorrect? State the reason in each case.

a. FUNCTION AD(A,B,C+D)   **e.** FUNCTION A(A,B,C)

b. FUNCTION SORT(X,Y,Z)   **f.** FUNCTION B(A,C(1))

c. FUNCTION FUNCTION(X)   **g.** FUNCTION (A,AA,B)

d. FUNCTION SQRT(I)   **h.** FUNCTION C(3,B,B)

6. Are the following statements true or false?

a. The type of a FORTRAN-supplied mathematical function is always determined by its arguments.

b. The argument of the ABS function must be real.

c. If SQRT is dimensioned, Y = SQRT(3) could mean to store the third element of array SQRT into Y.

d. The trigonometric supplied functions are actually function subprograms.

e. The END statement in some cases is not needed in function subprograms.

f. Function subprograms are supposed to return only one value to the calling program.

g. The function reference I = STAN(X,Y) is invalid, since I and STAN are not of the same type.

h. In some cases, function subprograms can be compiled concurrently with the calling program.

i. Since only one value can be returned by a function subprogram, only one RETURN statement is allowed in the subprogram.

j. In the definition of a function subprogram, a dummy argument cannot be a subscripted variable name.

k. Array names are permitted as arguments in a function subprogram.

7. The length of a vector is defined as $\sqrt{A_1^2 + A_2^2 + \ldots + A_N^2}$. A data record contains the N components of the vector as follows:

$$\boxed{N \quad A_1\ A_2 \ldots A_N} \qquad N = \text{number of coordinates}$$

Write a main program to read records of this form (for $N \leq 10$) and a function subprogram to compute the length of the vector associated with the components read.

8. Write a main program to read the coefficients $a_1, a_2, \ldots, a_n$ of the polynomial $P(x) = a_1 x^{n-1} + a_2 x^{n-2} + \ldots + a_{n-1} \cdot + a_n$ ($n \leq 10$) into an array A. Print a table of the values of $P(x)$ for $x = -5., -4.5, -4., \ldots, 4.5, 5.$, using a function to compute the polynomial values. The input data layout is

$$\boxed{N \quad a_1\ a_2\ \ldots\ a_n}$$

9. How would the graph of Figure 8.14 be different if we used $J = TAN(X) + 35$ to determine the position of the graphic character on the line instead of $J = (TAN(X) + 9.)*4$. Why do you think it is necessary to have a magnifying factor such as 4 in this case?

10. What statements would you change in the program of Figure 8.14 to display the graph of the tangent function in 126 print positions instead of 72?

11. Systems analysts at the XYZ Company computed the revenue function associated with the manufacture and marketing of a new company product. A cost function was also projected for that product. The functions are as follows:

Revenue function: $y = 15xe^{-x/3} + 0.5$

Cost function: $y = \dfrac{x^3}{16} - \dfrac{x^2}{2} + \dfrac{7x}{4} + 4$

Write a program to plot both functions to determine the break-even points.

12. As a promotional gimmick, every patron of the Circle L gas station gets a lucky card with three numbers on it ranging from 1 to 1,000. The station manager then draws at random a number from 1 to 1,000. If any of the customer's numbers matches the one drawn by the manager, the customer gets an amount in cents equal to one-tenth of his lucky number. Write a program to read ten lucky cards and determine the dollar amount of any win. For example, if the lucky card contains the numbers 50, 100, and 200 and the manager draws the number 50, the customer wins five cents.

To solve this problem, you will need

1. A function that will simulate a drawing by generating random numbers between two specified integers. If your installation does not have a random number generator, use the function IRAND, which is coded in Figure 5.3.

2. A function called WIN to determine whether the customer has a lucky number and if so, to compute the amount won.

Exercises Involving Subroutines

1. What would happen if you tried to execute a subroutine all by itself?

2. List two distinct differences between function and subroutine subprograms.

3. What advantages are there in using subroutines?

4. Modularization of a program can only be achieved through subroutines.

5. Why can't you write the code equivalent to a subroutine in the main program and branch to it whenever you want to execute that code?

6. Would the statement REAL X(N) be valid in a main program? In a subroutine? In a function subprogram? What restrictions would be placed on X and N?

7. Is it a good idea to use the DATA statement in a subroutine to initialize accumulators and counters that are used in the subroutine?

8. Find the error in each of the following:

Main Program	Subroutine

a. `DIMENSION A(10),B(10)`
`    .`
`CALL SUB(A,B)`
`    .`
	`SUBROUTINE SUB(I,J)`
	`DIMENSION I(10),J(10)`
	`DO 10 K = 1,10`
	`    I(K) = J(K)`
	`10 CONTINUE`
	`RETURN`
	`END`

b. `REAL X(100)`
`    .`
`CALL SUB(X,14.)`
`    .`
	`SUBROUTINE SUB(A,X)`
	`REAL A(100)`
	`X = 0.0`
	`DO 3 I = 1,100`
	`    X = X + A(I)`
	`3  CONTINUE`
	`RETURN`
	`END`

c. `REAL X(10,10),Y(3,4)`
`    .`
`CALL SUBC(X)`
`    .`
`CALL SUBC(Y)`
	`SUBROUTINE SUBC(A)`
	`REAL A(10,10)`
	`    .`
	`RETURN`
	`END`

d. `REAL A(15)`
`    .`
`CALL SUBD(A,B)`
`    .`
	`SUBROUTINE SUBD(P,Q)`
	`REAL Q(15)`
	`DO 10 I = 1,15`
	`    Q(I) = P`
	`10 CONTINUE`
	`RETURN`
	`END`

e. `REAL X(3,4)`
`    .`
`CALL SUBE(X)`
	`SUBROUTINE SUBE(X,N,M)`
	`REAL X(N,M)`
	`    .`

f. `REAL X(3,4)`
`    .`
`CALL SUBF(X,3,4)`
	`SUBROUTINE SUBF(X,A,B)`
	`REAL X(A,B)`
	`INTEGER AB`
	`    .`

```
g.  REAL JSUM(1Ø)                        SUBROUTINE (JSUM,K,R)
       :                                 REAL JSUM(1)
    CALL SUB(JSUM,N,3.1)                    :
       :
```

```
h.  INTEGER C(5Ø)                        SUBROUTINEL(K,S,C)
    CHARACTER B*2                        INTEGER K(5Ø)
       :                                 CHARACTER*2 B
    CALL L(C,3.,B)
```

9. Ms. X. must decide whether to buy a condominium now at a relatively high interest rate or wait one year and buy at what is anticipated to be a lower interest rate. She is looking at a $55,000 condo that she can purchase with 20% down and a 30-year mortgage at 14%. The current rate of inflation for housing is 8–10% per year; thus in one year the condominium is expected to be worth $60,000. However, the interest rate may decline to 11.5% in the next year. Should Mrs. X. buy the condominium now or wait?

Write a subroutine to compute the monthly and total payments for each of the scenarios. Use a main program to test your code. The output produced by the main program should be similar to the following:

```
INTEREST   PRINCIPAL   MONTHLY PAYMENT      TOTAL

Ø.14Ø       55ØØØ.          521.34        198683.66
Ø.115       6ØØØØ.          475.34        183122.31
THE DIFFERENCE IN TOTAL COST IS 15561.35
```

The formula to compute the monthly payment is:

$$\text{monthly payment} = \frac{\text{principal} * \dfrac{\text{interest}}{12}}{1 - \left(\dfrac{1}{1 + \dfrac{\text{interest}}{12}}\right)^{12*\text{years}}}$$

10. An input file consists of grade rosters that contain grades for different classes. Each roster is identified by a header record specifying the course name and number and the number of students for that class. The following records contain one student grade per record. No class is expected to contain more than 100 students. Write a complete program to determine each class's grade average and the number of grades below the average. Print the course name and number, the grades, the average, and the count of grades below the average. The input file must be read in the main program. One subroutine should take care of all output functions, while another subroutine should calculate the class average and the number of grades less than the average. The input and output have the following form: (Don't forget the dotted lines.)

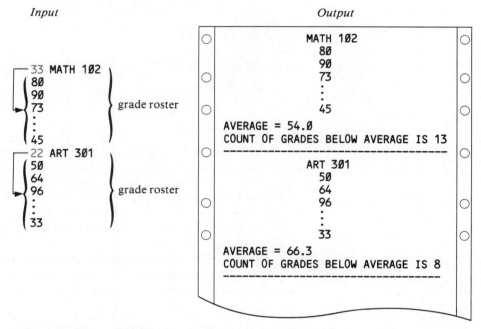

Input   *Output*

11. An input file consists of an unknown number of records, where each record contains the scores obtained by a particular FORTRAN class. The first two digits in each record identify the number of scores for a particular class (record). The department head wants to sort the scores of each FORTRAN class into ascending order, then sort all the combined scores into ascending order. The sorted scores are to be printed 12 per line. Assume there will be no more than 25 students in each class and no more than 500 students in all. A sample input and output are shown below.

Since the code for sorting is fairly long and since the program requires that the sorting procedure be performed several times, use a subroutine to carry out the sort.

Number of Scores Per Record   Scores   *Input File*

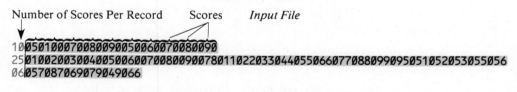

```
10 05010007008009005006007008009
25 010020030040050060070080090078011022033044055066077088099095051052053055056
06 057087069079049066
```

	CLASS 1:	50	50	60	70	70	80	80	90	90	100		
	CLASS 2:	10	11	20	22	30	33	40	44	50	51	52	53
		55	55	56	60	66	70	77	78	80	88	90	95
		99											
	CLASS 3:	49	57	66	69	79	87						
	ALL CLASSES:	10	11	20	22	30	33	40	44	49	50	50	50
		51	52	53	55	55	56	57	60	60	66	66	69
		70	70	70	77	78	79	80	80	80	87	88	90
		90	90	95	99	100							

Functions

1. The coordinates of three ships are accepted as input. Write a program to print the distances between each pair of ships. If x_1 and y_1 and x_2 and y_2 are the coordinates of any two ships, the distance separating them is

$$d = \sqrt{|x_1 - x_2|^2 + |y_1 - y_2|^2}$$

where the symbol $|x_1 - x_2|$ means the absolute value of $x_1 - x_2$

2. You are dealt 13 cards, which are entered on one data record in the following manner: the numbers 01–13 represent the spades from the 2 to the ace; 14–26 represents the hearts from the 2 to the ace; 27–39, diamonds from the 2 to the ace; 40–52, clubs from the 2 to the ace. The 13 numbers are not in order. Write a program to count the number of kings. Use the MOD library function.

3. A salesperson is assigned a commission on the following basis:

Sales	Commission
$0.00–$ 500.00	1%
$500.01–$5000.00	5%
over $5000.00	8%

a. Write a main program to read a name and a sale (both on one record) and a subprogram to compute the commission. Print the name and commission.

b. Same as part (a), except that a name and eight sales recorded on each record.

4. a. Array A contains N elements (N < 100). Write a function subprogram to perform a sequence check on the elements of A. If the array is in sequence (ascending), return a value of 1.

b. Same as part (a), except that it is not known whether the elements of A are in ascending or descending order. The first two entries set the ordering sequence.

5. Each student record of an input file consists of a name and 10 test scores. The student is allowed to drop his or her lowest score before an average is figured. Use one subprogram to find the sum of the scores for each student and another subprogram to find the minimum score. Print the student's name and average. (The subprograms should be general, allowing an array of up to 100 in size.)

6. Write a function subprogram to calculate the difference in absolute value between the largest and smallest elements of an array of variable length.

7. a. Write a function to accept a number between 1 and 10 and return the corresponding word. For example, 3 would yield THREE.

b. Write another function to accept a number between 20 and 99 and return the corresponding words. For example, 25 would yield TWENTY FIVE.

8. Write a function subprogram to return a three-character abbreviation for the name of a month given the month number as an argument. Test your program with appropriate data.

9. On the first record of an input file we have entered the answers (1, 2, 3, or 4) to a multiple choice test of 10 questions. On the second record, we have entered the number of students taking the test. Each following record consists of a student's name and 10 answers to the 10 questions. Write a function to determine the percentage of correct answers for each student and another subprogram to determine the student's grade (90–100 = A, 80–89 = B, 60–79 = C, below 60 = D). (See next page for input and output samples.)

The output should be performed by a subroutine that prints the student's name, the letter grade, and percentage of correct answers. Given the following input, the output should be as follows:

Correct answers to the 10 questions

```
1123142433
3 ← number of students
JONES  1123142433
SATO   1123111324
LAKY   4123142432
```

```
NAME   GRADE   PERCENTAGE
JONES    A        100
SATA     D         50
LAKY     B         80
```

10. A store maintains an inventory data file in the following form: The first record in an input file contains the current date in the form YYDDD, where YY refers to the year and DDD the number of days elapsed since the year started. Each succeeding record contains an item number, the date (same format as above) of the last time an item was sold, the number of items on hand, the cost per item, and the regular selling price. The store plans a sale to try to sell slow-moving items. A program is needed to produce a report showing the recommended sale price using the following guidelines:

If the item has not been sold in last 30 days, the discount is 10%.
If the item has not been sold in last 60 days, the discount is 20%.
If the item has not been sold in last 90 days, the discount is 40%.

However, any item that has been sold in the last 30 days is not to be put on sale, and if there is only one of an item left in stock, it is not to be placed on sale no matter what the last date of sale was. In addition, the sale price may not be lower than the cost. Write a subprogram to return the sale price of a particular item, and use a main program to read the data and produce a report for all the items read. Note that some of the sales may have occurred in a prior year.

A typical output report follows:

```
CURRENT DATE 80:220
```

ITEM NO.	LAST SALE DATE	DAYS ELAPSED	NO. IN STOCK	COST	REG. PRICE	SALE PRICE
302	200	20	20	10.00	15.00	15.00
400	189	31	5	6.50	10.00	9.00
101	159	61	15	3.00	5.00	4.00
100	101	119	50	2.00	3.00	2.00
901	100	120	1	12.00	25.00	25.00
999	180	40	2	6.50	7.15	6.50

11. a. Each record of an input file contains an employee's name, a number of hours worked, and a rate of pay. Write a main program to read the records and call a function subprogram to compute each employee's pay. Hours in excess of 40 are paid at a rate of time and a half. The printout should list the employee's name, number of hours worked, rate of pay, and pay.

b. Same as part (a), except that the input file is recorded on one record:

N   Name1 Hours1 rate1   Name2 hours2 rate2 ...   Name*n* hours*n* rate*n*

↓

number of employee records

c. Same as part (a), except that the input file consists of at most 100 records where each record contains 10 employee records. For example, the input file might be as follows:

Name1   hours1   rate1 ...   Name9   hours9   rate9   Name10 hours10 rate10
Name11 hours11 rate11 ...   Name19 hours19 rate19   Name20 hours20 rate20

10 employee records per record

12. Write a program to read sets of data records with the following form: The first entry on a record is N, which tells how many numbers are to be read from that record. N may not exceed 25. The entire input file must be stored in just one two-dimensional array. Write a program to compute the average of each of the sets of numbers and then the average of all the numbers, using a function subprogram to compute the average of each set of numbers. The input and output have the following forms:

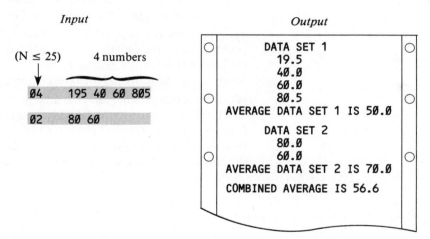

Input

(N ≤ 25)   4 numbers

Ø4   195 4Ø 6Ø 8Ø5

Ø2   8Ø 6Ø

Output

```
DATA SET 1
   19.5
   40.0
   60.0
   80.5
AVERAGE DATA SET 1 IS 50.0
   DATA SET 2
   80.0
   60.0
AVERAGE DATA SET 2 IS 70.0

COMBINED AVERAGE IS 56.6
```

13. You are the personnel director of a large company, and for every person you place in a job you enter the following two entries on a record: sex code (2 = male, 1 = female) and first year's starting salary. Write the code to read all the input data into a two-dimensional array and *then* use different subprograms to determine each of the following:

a. Total number of persons placed in jobs.

b. Total amount of salaries paid the first year.

c. Average salary per person.

d. Maximum salary paid to males.

e. Average salary paid to females.

14. The president of the XSTAR Company realizes that the company's present accounting procedures are too slow, too inefficient, and not sufficiently accurate to deal with the company's increasing annual processing volume. Plans have been made to replace manual accounting operations with a wholly computerized system. The current total manual operating cost in millions of dollars in terms of annual processing volume is given by $y = x + .5$ (where y is the dollar cost and x is the annual processing volume). Projected total computerized cost is given by the formula $y = .75x + 2$. The anticipated annual processing volume will be close to four units. Write a program to:

   a. Determine graphically whether the president's decision to switch to a computerized system is economically sound (graph both lines).

   b. Determine graphically the break-even point (the annual volume of processing that would justify the president's plan for changing methods of operation).

Realizing that an annual volume of processing of four units is not sufficient to warrant such a change in operations, a compromise is effected. The new operational procedures will involve both manual and computer operations. The cost attached to such a new system is given by $y = .445x + 1.5$. Write a program to:

   c. Determine graphically whether such a system would be economically beneficial to the company.

   d. Determine graphically the break-even point for the total computerized system versus the computer manual plan.

15. The Toystar Corporation is marketing a new toy. Expected revenues are approximated by the function $y = 3\sqrt{x}$. Costs associated with the production and the sales of the toy are defined by the function $y = 2 + x^2/4$. Write a program to determine graphically the break-even point for the production of the new toy.

16. Write a program to graph the total profit function of the example in exercise 15. The total profit function is defined as the difference between the cost and revenue function, that is, $T(x) = |R(x) - C(x)|$, where R, C, and T are, respectively, the revenue, the cost, and the total profit functions. Identify on the total profit graph the point at which profit is maximum.

8.6.3 Programming Problems: Mathematical/ Scientific

Functions

1. Write a program to find the square roots of ten positive real numbers read from one record. Remember that there are two roots, a positive and a negative root.

2. Modify the program in question 3, section 8.3.3 to produce a table showing the distance traveled by the ship for angles varying from 1° to 45°. How is the program changed if the ship is two miles offshore?

3. Write a function to compute the square root of 43, using the formula

$$x = \frac{1}{2}(x + \frac{43}{x})$$

Start with $x = 1$ to get a new value for x, then use that new value in the formula to get a newer value. Proceed in this fashion until the refined value is such that

$$|x^2 - 43| < \epsilon \quad \text{where } \epsilon \text{ is a prescribed degree of accuracy } (\epsilon = .01)$$

4. Given an equation of the form $ax^2 + bx + c = 0$, the roots (values for x that make the statement true) are given by $(-b \pm \sqrt{b^2 - 4ac})/(2a)$. Write a main program to read values for a, b, and c. If a is zero, then there is only one real value for x ($x = -c/b$). If $b^2 - 4ac$ is negative, then there are two complex roots for x. If $b^2 - 4ac$ is positive or zero, then there are two real roots, which are given by the formula. Write a subprogram that returns a 1 if $a = 0$, returns a 2 if $b^2 - 4ac$ is negative, and returns a 3 if $b^2 - 4ac$ is positive or zero. Then, depending on the value returned, write an appropriate message or answer.

5. Write a function to calculate the standard deviation of a set of measurements contained in an array of variable length (see section 6.7.3 exercise 3).

6. Iterative methods for solving systems of linear equations in x and y (see Ex. 23 section 3.9.3) can be terminated under either of the following criterions:

a. when $|x_{n+1} - x_n| < \epsilon$ and $|y_{n+1} - y_n| < \epsilon$, where ϵ is a prescribed degree of accuracy and where x_n, x_{n+1}, y_n and y_{n+1} are successive approximations to x and y.

b. when x_n and y_n are substituted back into the equations and the numerical results are within ϵ of the constants on the righthand side of the original system of equations.

Write a program using the above method to solve a system of equations and use programmer-defined functions to terminate the iterative process using both of the above termination criteria. Set $\epsilon = 0.01$. Will criterion a above, require fewer iterations than criterion b to solve the system of equations?

7. It can be shown that:

$$\sin(x) = x - \frac{x^3}{3!} + \frac{x^5}{5!} - \frac{x^7}{7!} + \cdots$$

where x is expressed in radians. Write a function to calculate values of $\sin(x)$ using the first five terms of the formula for values of x ranging from $0°$ to $90°$ in increments of $10°$. Compare your results with the values returned by the FORTRAN function SIN.

8. The number e can be defined as the limit of $\left(\frac{n+1}{n}\right)^n$ as n tends to infinity:

$$e = \lim_{n \to \infty} \left(\frac{n+1}{n}\right)^n$$

Using this definition of e, write a function to determine n such that:

$$\left| e - \left(\frac{n+1}{n}\right)^n \right| < 0.001$$

Use the function EXP for e.

9. Write a program to show that as n gets larger and larger, each of the following expressions converges to a limit. Can you guess the limits from your printouts?

a. $\left(\frac{n^2 + 1}{n + 1}\right)$ **b.** $\frac{\log(n)}{n}$ **c.** $n \cdot \log\left(1 + \frac{1}{n}\right)$

10. Write a program to determine the limits of the following expressions as x approaches 0. (Let x range from 1° to .1° in steps of .1°.)

a. $\dfrac{\sin(x)}{x}$

b. $\dfrac{\tan(x)}{x}$

c. $\dfrac{\tan(2x)}{\sin(7x)}$

d. $\dfrac{x \cdot \sin(x)}{1 - \cos(x)}$

e. $\dfrac{15t}{\tan(6t)}$

Recall that x must be expressed in radians.

11. Using the exponential function EXP(X), compute EXP(1). The value of e to eight places is 2.71828182. Can you obtain a better approximation than EXP(1) by using the following series definition?

$$e^x = 1 + \frac{x}{1!} + \frac{x^2}{2!} + \frac{x^3}{3!} + \ldots + \frac{x^n}{n!} + \ldots$$

How many terms of the series do you need to improve on EXP(1)? Use double precision for the computations.

12. Write a function subprogram to evaluate the determinant of a 3 by 3 matrix. The determinant of a 3 by 3 matrix is

$$\begin{vmatrix} a_{11} & a_{12} & a_{13} \\ a_{21} & a_{22} & a_{23} \\ a_{31} & a_{32} & a_{33} \end{vmatrix} = a_{11} \begin{vmatrix} a_{22} & a_{23} \\ a_{32} & a_{33} \end{vmatrix} - a_{21} \begin{vmatrix} a_{12} & a_{13} \\ a_{32} & a_{33} \end{vmatrix} + a_{31} \begin{vmatrix} a_{12} & a_{13} \\ a_{22} & a_{23} \end{vmatrix}$$

13. Sometimes it is helpful to expand or contract a graph. Scale factors are used for this purpose. Rewrite the break-even analysis program of question 11, section 8.5.1(1), to change both graphs by using the functions:

$$y = n(15xe^{-x/3}) \text{ and } y = n\left(\frac{x^3}{16} - \frac{x^2}{2} + \frac{7x}{4} + 4\right)$$

where n is a scale factor accepted from input. If $n = 1$, the graph should be identical to the one in Figure 8.16. If $n = 10$, the graph should be steeper, and if $n = .5$ the graph should be wider (more flattened). Try various scale factors.

14. Determine graphically the roots of $y = x\sin(x)$ as x varies from 0 to 3π. You may have to use a scale factor. Remember that this does not affect the roots.

15. What scale factors could you use on $y = 1/x$ to get a feel for the shape of that function? Experiment by graphing that function.

16. Write a program to enter a value for a radius and plot the corresponding circle.

[*Hint*: The equation of a circle of radius r centered on the y axis passing through the origin is given by:

$$(y - r)^2 + x^2 = r^2 \quad \text{or} \quad y = \pm \sqrt{r^2 - x^2} + r$$

Plot both branches by adding .5 to the y positive branch and $-.5$ to the y negative branch. Use $r = 4.5$ initially.]

17. A company has 10 delivery trucks. It uses a two-dimensional coordinate scheme to keep track of the location of each truck:

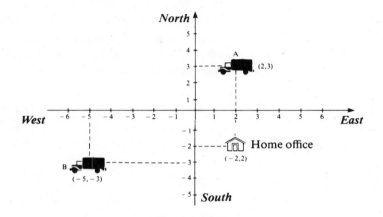

a. Write a program to read 10 truck coordinates and vehicle numbers to determine which truck is closest to the home office. Write a subprogram to compute the distances between each truck and the home office and another subprogram to determine the least distance. The main program should print the location of the closest truck and its vehicle number.

b. In an interactive environment, how would you structure your program to keep accepting new truck coordinates (as some of the trucks move about) and determine which truck is closest to the home office at any given time?

c. Keep the trucks moving along their preset line equations and let user interrupt the program to determine closest truck location to home office.

8.6.4 Programming Problems

Subroutines

1. A toy store sells 20 different toys.

a. Write a main program to read the prices of the toys into a one-dimensional array.

b. Write a subroutine to print all items over $5.00.

c. The store decides to run a sale on all its merchandise; everything is reduced to 60% of its original price. Write a subroutine to output the new prices.

2. Write a subroutine that accepts a one-dimensional array and returns the largest and the smallest elements of that array.

3. Write a subroutine that accepts a one-dimensional array and returns the positions of the largest and the smallest elements.

4. Repeat exercise 3 with a two-dimensional array. Specify the row and column position numbers of the largest and smallest element.

5. Repeat exercise 4 with a three-dimensional array.

6. Write subroutines to perform the following tasks on two-dimensional arrays: a. Set all elements of an array to a constant. b. Add corresponding elements of two arrays, storing results in a third array. c. Multiply each element of an array by a constant.

7. Write a subroutine that accepts a one-dimensional array and reverses the order of the elements of the array.

8. Write a subroutine that accepts any integer and sets a flag to one if the integer is a prime number and sets the flag to zero otherwise.

9. Each record of an input file (no more than 50 records) contains a name and an address. Write a program to read the names and corresponding addresses into a 50 by 2 array with names in column 1 and addresses in column 2, for example:

K(1,1)	MARTIN M	23 SCENIC DR.	K(1,2)
K(2,1)	JONATH L	113 NORTH AVE.	K(2,2)
	⋮	⋮	

Write a subroutine to sort this data on demand either by name or by address in ascending order and let the main program produce a table of names and corresponding addresses.

10. Student X has been asked by two of her teachers to write a program to compute two classes' average grades and the numbers of A's (grades > 90) in each class. Teacher 1's grades are recorded on just one record, 25 grades in all, while teacher 2's grades are recorded one grade per record (number of records is unknown).

Write a main program to read the data. The main program should call one subroutine to compute the average and the number of A's and another subroutine to perform the output functions. The input and output have the following form:

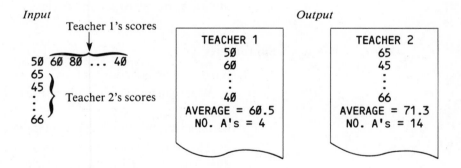

11. Write a subroutine to accept a number from 1 to 10 and return a variable (argument) spelling out the number; for example, 3 yields THREE. Should a function subprogram be used in this case? What would be the difference between a function subprogram and a subroutine?

12. Each record of a file consists of the names of cities and the average daily temperatures for those cities. For example,

```
MOBILE  17MADISON -3PARIS    ØNEW YORK 33
TAMPA   65TUCSON  48WAUSAU  -5SEATTLE   Ø
```

Write a program to produce an output similar to

```
ABOVE ZERO:    MOBILE      NEW YORK      TAMPA
               TUCSON
AT ZERO:       PARIS       SEATTLE
BELOW ZERO:    MADISON     WAUSAU
```

Use a subroutine for the output functions. Note that only three city names are printed per line.

13. Each record of an input file consists of an employee name, a number of hours worked, and a rate of pay. Write a main program to read the input file and a subroutine to compute each employee's pay. Hours over 40 are paid at time-and-a-half the regular rate. The printout should list the employee name, number of hours, rate of pay, and pay.

Use a subroutine to perform input data validation. The rate of pay should not exceed $50.00 per hour, and the hours worked should not exceed 80 hours. The main program should write the error messages, if any; note that there could be two error messages if both the rate and the hours exceed their maximums.

14. The Stayfirm Company accounting system keeps sales records for each salesperson on a day-to-day basis. This data is transcribed on records as follows:

Salesperson	Date of Sale	Amount of Sale
MONISH	011586	100.00
MONISH	011386	50.00
GLEASON	012786	10.00
MONISH	012786	150.00
GLEASON	012686	190.00
HORN	011386	100.00

Note that the transactions are not arranged alphabetically by salesperson name. Also note that the dates are not sorted in ascending order.

Write a program using a sort subroutine to produce a monthly sales report for January 87 summarizing the company's total sales and the total sales for each salesperson. Entries in the report must be listed by salesperson's name in alphabetical order, and these in turn must be sorted by sales date. For example, given the above data, the output should be as follows:

```
SALESPERSON    DATE OF SALES    SALES AMOUNT    TOTAL AMOUNT
   GLEASON        012686           190.00
                  012786            10.00
                                                   200.00
   HORN           011386           100.00
                                                   100.00
   MONISH         011386            50.00
                  011586           100.00
                  012786           150.00
                                                   300.00
                               TOTAL SALES         600.00
```

15. The Department of Management Science has received the final scores obtained by their students in the various sections of Introduction to Management. The input file consists of the various class records, where each record contains the section number and the section's corresponding scores. A negative value terminates the list of scores (there is a maximum of 20 scores per class). An example of an input file is as follows:

```
MNGM 102    30 20 60 -4
MNGM 103    10 40 -4
MNGM 104    10 90 20 80 -4
```

Write a program for the department to sort the scores in ascending order for each class and then produce one list of sorted scores containing all the scores from all the sections.

Use a subroutine for the sorting procedure and write another subroutine for the output functions. The output should be similar to the following:

```
MNGM 102          20  30  60
MNGM 103          10  40
MNGM 104          10  20  80  90
COMBINED SCORES   10  10  20  20  30  40  60  80  90
```

16. There are five sections of a financial management course FI 550. For each of these sections, we have entered on separate records the section number and the number of students who enrolled in that section during preregistration (two entries per record). Following these five records, we have other records for students wishing to add FI 550. These student records contain two entries: a name and the section number the student wants to add. The maximum number of students permitted in sections 1 through 5 is 13, 15, 17, 9, and 8, respectively. Write a program using subroutines to register these "add" students. If a request for a section cannot be filled, print out the student's name and the section requested. At the conclusion of the program, print out each section number and the updated enrollment. For example, the following input would produce the output shown:

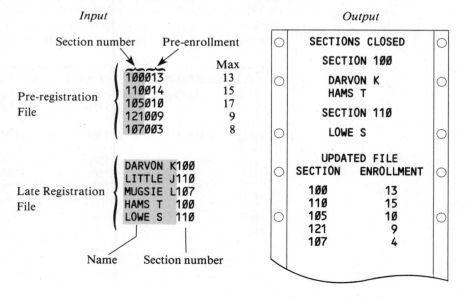

17. Dr. X has unusual grading practices. He assigns random grades (1–100) to his class of N students (where N < 99 is accepted from input). Each student gets three random test scores for three tests. Write a program to assign the grades (use a random number routine, if available) and compute the average grade of each student and the average of the entire class. First read the entire input file into a two-dimensional array, and *then* work from the array. The results should be tabulated in page form as follows:

					PAGE 1
STUDENT NUMBER		SCORE 1	SCORE 2	SCORE 3	AVERAGE
	1	20	30	40	30
	2	20	80	20	40
	⋮	⋮	⋮	⋮	⋮
	15	1	0	98	33

2 blank lines
1 dotted line
----
2 blank lines

					PAGE 2
STUDENT NUMBER		SCORE 1	SCORE 2	SCORE 3	AVERAGE
1 blank line
	16	50	60	70	60
	17				
	⋮	⋮	⋮	⋮	⋮
	30				

2 blank lines
1 dotted line
----
2 blank lines

					PAGE 3
STUDENT NUMBER		SCORE 1	SCORE 2	SCORE 3	AVERAGE
	⋮	⋮	⋮	⋮	⋮

A subroutine should be used to simulate automatic ejection to the top of a new page and provide a page number, headings, and a demarcation line to be used by Dr. X. to cut each page and bind them in booklet form. The average class grade should be printed by itself on a new numbered page. (Assume page = 15 lines.)

18. LUXURMART is an exclusive clothing store where Luxurmart members are required to maintain $1,000 in their accounts at all times. Members charge all purchases on Luxur credit cards. Write a main program to create a master member file (array) consisting of member names with an initial $1,500 credit for all members. See sample input and output file on next page.

There are several types of transactions that require members' accounts to be updated. Some members return merchandise that must be credited to their accounts. Other members purchase items; if a purchase causes a member's credit to fall below $1,000, a message should be printed requesting the member to write a check for an amount to bring his/her credit back to $1,000. If the name listed on a transaction is not on the master file, an appropriate message should be printed.

Write a subroutine to update each customer's account. Transaction records contain member names and dollar amounts for credit or debit. The subroutine tells the main program whether a message is to be printed. The main program performs all output functions and should produce an updated member file after all transaction records have been processed. Sample input and output data are shown below.

Input	*Output*

Master File

```
HOWARD    1500
NIARCO    1500
PELLON    1500
ROCKER    1500
```

Transaction File

```
PELLON    106.00
MOCKER    500.00
NIARCO    -10.00
HOWARD   -600.00
NIARCO     -5.00
```

```
**NO MATCHING NAME FOR MOCKER**
       UPDATED MASTER FILE

       HOWARD     900.00
       NIARCO    1485.00
       PELLON    1606.00
       ROCKER    1500.00
--HOWARD MUST PAY 100.00 NOW--
```

19. Repeat the preceding exercise with the following variation:

To simplify and minimize transcription errors, the transaction records contain tag numbers, instead of dollar amounts, for items purchased or returned. D or C signifies debit or credit, respectively. For example:

```
HOWARD    9 D        means debit Howard's account by whatever item 9 costs.
NIARCO   10 C        means credit Niarco's account by the value of item 10.
```

Create a table of costs for the different items. For example:

Item Tag	Cost
1	44.50
2	100.75
3	94.50
:	:
10	46.00

20. Write a subroutine that will accept an integer number and return via an array all permutations of the digits that make up the number. The subroutine should also compute the number of digits and return this value. For example:

Input

321

Output

```
NUMBER IS 321
NUMBER OF DIGITS   3
PERMUTATIONS
      1 2 3
      1 3 2
      2 1 3
      2 3 1
      3 1 2
      3 2 1
```

21. An interesting method of encoding data is to load a message to be encoded into a two-dimensional array and then interchange rows and interchange columns a number of times. The resulting sequence of characters is the encoded message. In order to decode the message, the sequence of steps used in the encoding process is followed in reverse order. For example, consider the message I HAVE BUT ONE LIFE TO GIVE FOR MY COUNTRY. Let us load the message into a 6 × 7 array:

I		H	A	V	E	
B	U	T		O	N	E
	L	I	F	E		T
O		G	I	V	E	
F	O	R		M	Y	
C	O	U	N	T	R	Y

Now consider the following encoding process:

(1.) Interchange rows 1 and 3   (2). Interchange columns 2 and 5

L	I	F	E		T	
B	U	T		O	N	E
I		H	A	V	E	
O		G	I	V	E	
F	O	R		M	Y	
C	O	U	N	T	R	Y

E	I	F	L		T	
B	O	T		U	N	E
I	V	H	A		E	
O	V	G	I		E	
F	M	R		O	Y	
C	T	U	N	O	R	Y

(3.) Interchange rows 4 and 6   (4.) Interchange columns 1 and 5

E	I	F	L		T	
B	O	T		U	N	E
I	V	H	A		E	
C	T	U	N	O	R	Y
F	M	R		O	Y	
O	V	G	I		E	

L	E	I	F			T
U	O	T		B	N	E
	V	H	A	I	E	
O	T	U	N	C	R	Y
O	M	R		F	Y	
V	G	I	O	E		

The resulting string is LEIF   TUOT BNE VHAIE OTUNCRYOMR FY VGIOE. To decode the message, the encoding process is reversed; i.e., the encoded message would be loaded into a 6 by 7 array and then the following interchanges would be performed:

columns 1 and 5
rows 4 and 6
columns 2 and 5
rows 1 and 3

Write a main program to encode and decode messages, using subroutines to perform the column interchange and row interchange operations.

22. A variation on the encoding technique just described is to include in the encoded message the transformations required to decode the message. These instructions may be embedded into the body of the message using any scheme you desire. Repeat exercise 21 with embedded instructions.

23. Write a subroutine to accept the coordinates of up to 20 ships and determine which two ships are the closest to each other. If (x_1, y_1) are the coordinates of ship 1 and (x_2, y_2) are the coordinates of ship 2, then the distance d separating the two ships is given by:

$$d = \sqrt{(x_1 - x_2)^2 + (y_1 - y_2)^2}$$

24. Grades for a particular class are based on homework, quizzes, and tests. For each student there is a record with his or her name, eight homework scores, four quiz scores, and three test scores. Write a program to print out each student's name, homework average, quiz average, and test average. To do this, write a *general* subprogram to find the average of an array of real numbers. There are at most 100 students.

25. Each record of an input file contains three segment lengths A, B and C. Write a subprogram to determine whether these three segments make up the sides of a triangle (the sum of any two is more than the third). If they do, let K = 1 and find the area of the triangle where area = $\sqrt{S*(S - A)*(S - B)*(S - C)}$ and S = .5 (A + B + C). If the three values do not make up the sides of a triangle, let K = 0 and let the area = 0. Then, if the values do make up the sides of a triangle, write another subprogram to determine whether it is a right triangle. Let RIGHT = 1 if it is; let RIGHT = 0 if it is not. The main program should print out appropriate messages and areas.

26. Each record in a data file contains two forty-digit integer numbers. Write a subprogram to print the two numbers and their sum.

27. Write a subroutine to compute the trace of a matrix (defined in exercise 29, section 7.6.2,) and then use it to compute the inverse of the matrix (see exercise 30 of section 7.6.2).

28. The Furniture Company has stock in three different warehouses. The controller-dispatcher needs to know at any given time the number of a particular furniture item in each of the three warehouses; he may also need to know the number of each particular item at one warehouse. Initially the stock of items in all warehouses is as follows:

	Warehouse 1	Warehouse 2	Warehouse 3
Desks	123	44	76
Chairs	789	234	12
Beds	67	456	90

He has at his fingertips a terminal where he can inquire about a particular item. For example, when he types BEDS the system furnishes him with the number of beds at the three warehouses. He can also type a warehouse number to list all items at that warehouse. Write a program to allow the following communications between the dispatcher and the data base.

```
ENTER REQUEST
BEDS

            WAREHOUSE1   WAREHOUSE2  WAREHOUSE3
BEDS            67          456          90      TOTAL  613

ENTER REQUEST
WAREHOUSE3

             DESKS        CHAIRS       BEDS
WAREHOUSE3     76           12          90      TOTAL  178

ENTER REQUEST
CHAIRS

            WAREHOUSE1   WAREHOUSE2  WAREHOUSE3
CHAIRS         789          234          12      TOTAL 1035

ENTER REQUEST
```

Note that the message ENTER REQUEST is printed after each request has been satisfied. If the dispatcher enters an invalid request, the system should print an appropriate error message to force him to renew his request.

29. If you have access to a conversational computing system, write a program to play tic-tac-toe. The program should allow the user to make the first move, then calculate its next move, and so forth. Can you make the program always win? If not, can you design the program so that it can never lose?

30. If you have access to a conversational computing system, write a program to play blackjack. The program should deal cards from the deck in a randomized fashion. You may choose to start with a new deck for each hand or keep track of all cards dealt until the entire deck has been used. The program should act as the dealer and include routines to evaluate its own hand to determine whether to deal itself more cards or stand pat. It must also evaluate the player's hand to determine the winner of each hand.

31. a. Write separate subroutines to print each of the following geometric symbols:

$$\triangle \quad \square \quad \triangledown \quad \times \quad \square$$

b. Write a main program to generate primitive art artificially (through a random generator routine) by printing the above geometric symbols vertically in random fashion, for example:

$$\square$$
$$\triangle$$
$$\square$$
$$\times$$
$$\triangledown$$
$$\square$$
$$\vdots$$

32. You work for the BCD Polling Company. They want you to write a program that will evaluate data from questionnaires of the following form:

1. There are three groups of questions on each questionnaire. The first group has four questions, the second group has eight questions, and the third group has seven questions.

2. Each question will be answered with a number between one and five inclusively: 1 = strongly disagree; 2 = disagree; 3 = don't care; 4 = agree; 5 = strongly agree.

You are asked to write a program to do the following for each questionnaire, in this order:

    a. Use a subprogram AVE to find the average response for each group of questions (this subprogram must be invoked three times for each questionnaire).

    b. Use a subprogram HIST to draw a histogram (bar graph) showing the average response to each of the three groups of questions.

    c. Use a subprogram OP to write the respondent's (person's) average opinion (in words) for each of the three groups of questions.
You will process an unknown number of questionnaires.

Input: When a person answers the questionnaire, the answers are recorded on a record in the following manner:

Column positions:	
1–3	ID number for the person responding (integer).
5–8	The four responses to the questions in group 1, one column each (each is an integer between 1 and 5, inclusive).
10–17	The eight responses to the questions in group 2, one column each (each is an integer between 1 and 5, inclusive).
19–25	The seven responses to the questions in group 3, one column each (each is an integer between 1 and 5, inclusive).

A sample record might look like:

            218 4213 43145244 4144535

Your main program should read in a record and use the subprograms described for each record.

Write a *general* real function AVE with two arguments, an integer array (the answers to a particular group of questions) and the length (integer) of the array (the number of questions). AVE should compute the average of the numbers in the array. Use this same subprogram three times for each questionnaire to find the average response for each of the three groups of questions. An example of a call to AVE is:

    Y = AVE (*array name, length of array*).

Store the three averages in an array (in the main program).

Write another subroutine HIST with one real argument, the array of average responses to the three groups of questions. An example of a call to this subroutine is:

         CALL HIST (*array name*)

The subroutine HIST should make a histogram of the three averages using the following style:

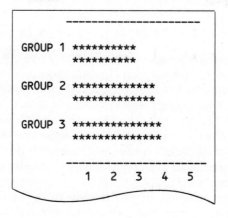

```
          ---------------------

GROUP 1  **********
         **********

GROUP 2  **************
         **************

GROUP 3  ***************
         ***************

          ---------------------
           1   2   3   4   5
```

Start the histogram at the top of a new page. For each 0.25 points an asterisk is printed. For example, if the average response for group 3 is 3.71, then 14 asterisks are used, since there are 14 full 0.25 points in 3.71. Do not round off. Any fraction less than 0.25 is ignored. Note that a double line of asterisks is drawn for each average. The preceding histogram shows what the output would be if the averages were 2.5, 3.3333, and 3.71 for the three groups, respectively (this is only an example). Be sure to have your histogram print the dashed lines (minus signs), the words GROUP 1, GROUP 2, and GROUP 3 in the left-hand columns, and the numbers 1 through 5 on the bottom, as shown.

Write a subroutine OP with two arguments. The first is the respondent's ID number (INTEGER); the second argument is a REAL array containing the averages of the responses to the three groups of questions. This subroutine should print the following:

```
PERSON xxxS VIEW ABOUT GROUP 1 QUESTIONS IS ____
PERSON xxxS VIEW ABOUT GROUP 2 QUESTIONS IS ____
PERSON xxxS VIEW ABOUT GROUP 3 QUESTIONS IS ____
```

The xxx is to be replaced by the person's ID number, and the blank spaces are to be filled with the appropriate capitalized words shown below.

If the average is 1, the person STRONGLY DISAGREES.

If the average is greater than 1 but less than or equal to 2, the person DISAGREES.

If the average is greater than 2 but less than or equal to 3, the person DOES NOT CARE.

If the average is greater than 3 but less than or equal to 4, the person AGREES.

If the average is greater than 4 but less than or equal to 5, the person STRONGLY AGREES.

33. Write a program that will read in a bridge hand for each of four players (West, North, East, and South, in that order). Each hand has 13 cards. There are four data records, each containing one hand. For example, one data record might be

```
02 14 41 12 42 01 49 48 22 21 13 40 24
```

Each two-digit number represents one playing card. The numbers 1–13 represent the spades, 2 through ace (1 represents the 2 of spades, 11 represents the queen of spades, and 13 represents the ace). The numbers 14–26 represent the hearts, 2 through ace (25 represents the king of hearts); the numbers 27–39, the diamonds; and 40–52, the clubs. The 13 numbers of a hand should be stored in an integer array. Call a subroutine SORT to sort the numbers in each hand into ascending order. (Notice that by representing the cards this way, SORT arranges the cards into their separate suits and puts them in ascending order *within* the suits.) Call an integer function ITOTAL to calculate the number of points in the hand (a definition of points follows). Write the name of the hand (West, North, East, or South) in the main program and then call a subroutine SHOW to write out the contents of the hand and the number of points in the hand. Repeat these steps for each hand.

Write a general subroutine SORT that will take any integer array and return an array containing the same elements sorted into ascending order. An example of a call to SORT is:

CALL SORT (*array, length of array*)

where both *array* and *length of array* are integers.

Write a general integer function ITOTAL that calculates the number of points in a given hand. This subprogram has two arguments. An example of the use of ITOTAL is:

IX = ITOTAL (*array, length of array*)

where both *array* and *length of array* are integers.

The points are calculated as follows:

4 points for each ace
3 points for each king
2 points for each queen
1 point for each jack

[*Hint:* the MOD function might help in this routine.]

Write a subroutine SHOW with two arguments. The first argument is an integer array of length 13 containing the sorted cards, and the second argument is an integer variable containing the number of points in the hand. An example of a call to SHOW is:

CALL SHOW (*array, number of points*).

Subroutine SHOW prints the contents of the hand passed to it as an argument and prints the number of points in the hand. It prints out the cards by suit, in ascending order within a suit. The printed order of the suits is spades, hearts, diamonds, and then clubs. Print the information according to the sample shown below. Note: The array will have already been sorted into ascending order of spades, hearts, and so forth, by the subroutine SORT; subroutine SHOW is merely a printing routine. Print an A for an ace, a K for a king, a Q for queen, and a J for jack. Output for the sample data record given above is: (see page 485).

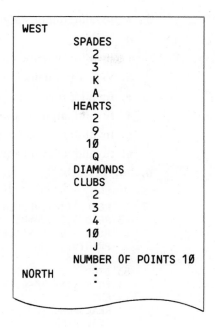

```
WEST
        SPADES
          2
          3
          K
          A
        HEARTS
          2
          9
         10
          Q
        DIAMONDS
        CLUBS
          2
          3
          4
         10
          J
        NUMBER OF POINTS 10
NORTH    :
```

Exercises Involving Functions

1. **a.** A = SIN(X)**2 - COS(X)**2   **d.** ALARG = AMAX1(A,B,C,D,E)

 b. Z = EXP(X) - EXP(-X)   **e.** KSMAL = MIN∅(I,J,K,3)

 c. X = SQRT(ABS(P - Q))

2. To round the value in A to the nearest hundred:

$$A = 100.*INT((A + 50.)/100.)$$

To round the value in A to the nearest thousandth:

$$A=INT((A+.0005)*1000.)/1000.$$

3. **a.** 9.   **e.** 2.4   **i.** 100.   **m.** −2

 b. 3.   **f.** 102.4   **j.** 83.4   **n.** −3.

 c. −2   **g.** 0.   **k.** 2.   **o.** −3

 d. −100.   **h.** −2.4   **l.** 1.   **p.** −.3002

4. **a.** Valid.

 b. Invalid; subscripted variable T(1).

 c. Invalid; function reference cannot occur in I/O statement list.

 d. Invalid; function name type conflict.

 e. Invalid; GUN, NON different types.

 f. Invalid dummy argument X + Y.

 g. Invalid; A is an array but B(1) is not an array.

 h. Dummy argument cannot be a constant.

 i. Invalid; function is not assigned a value.

 j. Valid.

 k. Valid.

5. **a.** Invalid; dummy argument cannot be an expression.

   b. Valid.

   c. Invalid; function name too long.

   d. Valid (user defines own SQRT).

   e. Invalid; function name and argument cannot be the same.

   f. Invalid; argument cannot be subscripted variable.

   g. Invalid; function name is missing.

   h. Invalid, dummy argument cannot be a constant.

6. **a.** F.   **b.** F.   **c.** T.   **d.** T.   **e.** F.   **f.** T.   **g.** F.
   h. T.   **i.** F.   **j.** T.   **k.** T.

7.
```
      REAL A(10),VECLEN
    3 READ(5,1,END=88) N,(A(I),I = 1,N)
      ALEN = VECLEN(A,N)
      PRINT*, ALEN
      GO TO 3
   88 STOP
    1 FORMAT(I2,10F4.1)
      END
      REAL FUNCTION VECLEN(A,N)
      REAL A(N)
      VECLEN = 0.
      DO 9 I = 1,N
         VECLEN = VECLEN + A(I)**2
    9 CONTINUE
      VECLEN = VECLEN**.5
      RETURN
      END
```

8.
```
      REAL A(10),FUNC,PX,X
      READ*,N,(A(I),I = 1,N)
      X = -5.
    6 IF(X.LE.5.) THEN
         PX = FUNC(N,A,X)
         PRINT*,X,PX
         X = X + .5
         GO TO 6
      ENDIF
      STOP
      END
      REAL FUNCTION FUNC(N,A,X)
      REAL A(10)
      FUNC = 0.
      DO 5 I = 1,N N
         FUNC = FUNC + A(I)*X**(N-I)
    5 CONTINUE
      RETURN
      END
```

9. The values for tan x for values of x close to 0, 2π, etc., would appear to fall on a straight line, because the differences between successive values of the function are small in these intervals. The factor 4 is needed to magnify the differences so that they are visible on the graph.

10. INTEGER LINE(126)

$\vdots$

```
J = (Y + 9)*7 + 0.5
IF(J.LT.0 .OR. J.GT.126) THEN
```

11. See Figure 8.15.

12. See Figure 8.16.

```
C GRAPHICAL BREAK-EVEN ANALYSIS
C    LINE(70): ARRAY THAT PRINTS EACH LINE WITH GRAPHIC SYMBOLS
C    R:   VALUE OF THE EXPONENTIAL FUNCTION
C    C:   VALUE OF THE POLYNOMIAL FUNCTION
C    J:   ROUNDED INTEGER VALUE OF THE EXPONENTIAL FUNCTION
C    L:   ROUNDED VALUE OF THE POLYNOMIAL VALUE FUNCTION
C    X:   GRADUATION UNITS FOR THE X AXIS
C
      REAL R, C
      INTEGER J, L, X, LINE(70),BLANK
      DATA LINE/70*' '/,R,C,BLANK/'R','C',' '/
      WRITE(6,10)
      DO 6 I = 1, 13
         C = (((X - 8.)*X + 28.)*X + 64.)/16.
         R = 15.*X*EXP(-X/3.) + .5
         J = R + .5
         L = C + .5
         LINE(J) = R                  Insert graphic symbols in line to be printed.
         LINE(L) = C
         WRITE(6,11)X, R, C, LINE
         LINE(J) = BLANK              Replace graphic symbols by blank characters
         LINE(L) = BLANK              to blank out the LINE array.
6     CONTINUE
      STOP
10    FORMAT(' X   REVENUE   COST'/)
11    FORMAT(I3,4X,F4.1,4X,F4.1,12X,70A1)
      END
```

X	REVENUE	COST
0	.5	4.0
1	11.2	5.0
2	15.9	6.0
3	17.1	6.0
4	16.3	7.0
5	14.7	8.0
6	12.7	10.0
7	10.7	13.0
8	8.8	18.0
9	7.2	24.0
10	5.9	34.0
11	4.7	45.0
12	3.8	61.0

First break-even point

$y = 15xe^{-x/3} + 0.5$

$y = \dfrac{x^3}{16} - \dfrac{x^2}{2} + \dfrac{7x}{4} + 4$

Second break-even point

x axis

FIGURE 8.15
A BREAK-EVEN ANALYSIS

```
C LOTTERY PROBLEM
C    CARD(3): CONTAINS 3 LUCKY NUMBERS
C    IRAND:    RANDOM NUMBER GENERATOR FUNCTION
C    WIN:      DETERMINES A WINNING AMOUNT
C    AMT:      AMOUNT OF LUCKY WIN
C    NAME:     NAME OF CUSTOMER
      INTEGER K,CARD(3)
      REAL AMT
      CHARACTER*5 NAME
C FUNCTION NAMES USED IN PROGRAM ARE:
      INTEGER IRAND
      REAL WIN
C
5     READ(5,1,END=8)NAME, CARD
      K = IRAND(1,1000)
      AMT = WIN(CARD, K)
      WRITE(6,2)NAME, AMT
      GO TO 5
8     STOP
1     FORMAT(A5,3F5.0)
2     FORMAT(1X,A5,' GETS',F10.0,'CENTS')
      END
C
C FUNCTION WIN RETURNS WINNING AMOUNT
      REAL FUNCTION WIN(SLIP, N)
      INTEGER SLIP(3)
      WIN = 0.
      DO 15 I = 1, 3
        IF(SLIP(I).EQ.N)WIN=SLIP(I)/10.
15    CONTINUE
      RETURN
      END
C
C FUNCTION IRAND GENERATES A RANDOM NUMBER
C BETWEEN THE INTEGER VALUES IBEG & ITER
      INTEGER FUNCTION IRAND(IBEG,ITER)
      INTEGER M, B, A
      REAL X
      DATA M, B, A/25211, 32767, 19727/
      A = MOD(M*A, B)
      X = REAL(A)/REAL(B)
      IRAND = X*(ITER - IBEG + 1) + IBEG
      RETURN
      END
```

Read the records one at a time.
Call the function IRAND to choose a random number from 1 to 1,000. The arguments of the random routine are 1 and 1,000. The function WIN computes the amount won. If the customer loses, AMT = 0. The array CARD is transmitted to the function WIN along with the lucky number K, which is the random number returned by the function IRAND.

The array SLIP in the function WIN really refers to the array CARD in the calling program. Similarly, N is just a dummy name for the variable K, defined in the calling program.

If no match exists between the numbers on the card and the number drawn by the manager, the value of the function is WIN = 0. If there is a match, WIN is one-tenth of the lucky number.

Note how the name of the function WIN returns the value of the function to the calling program.

Function IRAND returns any integer value between IBEG and ITER (IBEG < ITER). In this program, IBEG and ITER take on those values passed by the calling program, i.e., IBEG = 1 and ITER = 1,000. The value X, as a result of the computations, is always a real number from 0 to 1. The value IRAND becomes any number from 1 to 1,000. Note how IRAND transmits the function value to the calling program.

FIGURE 8.16
RANDOM NUMBER LUCKY WIN

Exercises Involving Subroutines

1. The dummy variables are not initialized properly and might destroy memory; also the return address is unknown.

2. (1) A function generally returns one value; a subroutine returns many values. (2) A subroutine is invoked by the CALL statement, whereas a function is invoked implicitly by using its name in an expression.

3. Program modularization, utilization of coding segments from program libraries.

4. Yes, along with function subprograms.

5. Return to a variable point (location) is not possible using the simple GO TO statement.

6. A variable as a size declarator is valid only in a subprogram. X and N must be dummy variables.

7. No; they will be initialized *only* on the first call to the subroutine.

8. **a.** Type of real and dummy arguments must match.

b. Value of the constant 14. cannot be changed in the subprogram.

c. Dimension of an array in a subprogram must match dimensions in the calling program (except for one-dimensional arrays). Use variable dimension.

d. P should be declared as an array instead of Q.

e. Number of arguments does not match.

f. The dimensions of X in the REAL statement must be integers.

g. Subroutine name is missing.

h. Dummy argument C should be typed CHARACTER in subroutine.

9. See Figure 8.17.

10. See Figure 8.18.

11. See Figure 8.19.

```
C INVESTMENT DECISION PROGRAM
C  I1,I2:   INTEREST RATES (.14 and .115)
C  P1,P2:   PRINCIPALS    ($55,000 AND $60,000)
C  PAYMT:   MONTHLY PAYMENT
C  TOT1,TOT2:  TOTAL PAYMENTS OVER THE YEARS
C  DIF: DIFFERENCE IN COST(TOT1-TOT2)
      IMPLICIT REAL(A-Z)
      READ(5,6)I1,I2,P1,P2
      WRITE(6,5)
      CALL CALC(I1,P1,PAYMT,TOT1)
      WRITE(6,1)I1,P1,PAYMT,TOT1
      CALL CALC(I2,P2,PAYMT,TOT2)
      WRITE(6,1)I2,P2,PAYMT,TOT2
      DIF = TOT1 - TOT2
      WRITE(6,2)DIF
      STOP
    2 FORMAT('0THE DIFFERENCE IN TOTAL COST IS',F9.2)
    1 FORMAT(T5,F5.3,T19,F6.0,T37,F6.2,T49,F10.2)
    5 FORMAT(T4,'INTEREST',4X,'PRINCIPAL',4X,'MONTHLY PAYMENT',4X,'TOTAL')
    6 FORMAT(2F5.0,2F6.0)
      END
C SUBROUTINE CALC COMPUTES MONTHLY AND TOTAL PAYMENT
C  I:        INTEREST RATE
C  DOWN:    20% DOWN PAYMENT
C  P:        PRINCIPAL
C  PAYMT:   MONTHLY PAYMENT
C  TOT:     TOTAL PAYMENT OVER 30 YEARS
      SUBROUTINE CALC(I,P,PAYMT,TOT)
      IMPLICIT REAL(A-Z)
      DOWN = .2*P
      PAYMT = (P - DOWN)*(I/12.)/(1.-(1.+I/12.)**(-360.))
      TOT = PAYMT*360. + DOWN
      RETURN
      END
```

INTEREST	PRINCIPAL	MONTHLY PAYMENT	TOTAL
0.140	55000.	521.34	198683.66
0.115	60000.	475.34	183122.31

THE DIFFERENCE IN TOTAL COST IS 15561.35

FIGURE 8.17
INVESTMENT DECISION PROGRAM

```
      CHARACTER*11 HEADER
      REAL AVG
      INTEGER GRADE(100),N,BELOW
5     READ(5,6,END=8)N,HEADER,(GRADE(I),I=1,N)
      CALL AVRGE(GRADE,N,AVG,BELOW)
      CALL PRINT(GRADE,N,AVG,BELOW,HEADER)
      GO TO 5
8     STOP
6     FORMAT(I3,4X,A11/(I3))
      END
      SUBROUTINE AVRGE(SCORE,L,AV,BLOW)
      INTEGER SCORE(100),L,BLOW
      REAL AV
      AV = 0.
      BLOW = 0
      DO 1 I = 1, L
         AV = AV + SCORE(I)
1     CONTINUE
      AV = AV/L
      DO 2 I = 1, L
         IF(SCORE(I).LT.AV)BLOW=BLOW+1
2     CONTINUE
      RETURN
      END
      SUBROUTINE PRINT(GRADE,N,AV,BLOW,HDNGS)
      CHARACTER*11 HDNGS
      INTEGER GRADE(100),N,BLOW
      REAL AV
      WRITE(6,5)HDNGS,(GRADE(I),I=1,N)
      WRITE(6,6)AV,BLOW
      RETURN
5     FORMAT('1',15X,A11/(18X,I3))
6     FORMAT(1X,'AVERAGE IS',F5.1/1X,
     *'COUNT OF GRADES BELOW AVERAGE IS',I2)
      END
```

HEADER gives the course name and number.
No more than 100 students per class.

Read the number of grades N, the header, and the grades in a given class. Transfer control to subroutine AVRGE.
GRADE transfers the grades to the subprogram.
N transfers the number of grades.
AVG returns the average from the subprogram.
BELOW returns the number of scores below the average.
Transfer control to subroutine for printout.
HEADER communicates the course name and number to the subroutine.
The subroutine prints the heading, the N grades, the average, and the number of grades below average.
Subroutine AVRGE will compute the average of L grades stored in an array SCORE and store the result in AV. The count of grades below the average is stored in BLOW. Initially, BLOW is set to 0.
The array SCORE is really the array GRADE, which has been read in the main program, and L (or N) is the number of grades to be processed. Note that the subroutine does not change the array SCORE or the variable L, and hence these are not changed in the main program. The average and the count of grades below average are returned to AVG and BELOW in the main program via AV and BLOW.
Subroutine PRINT will print a heading found in HDNGS on a new page, with N grades listed vertically. The average grade AV and the count below average BLOW will also be printed.
Note that none of the arguments are changed in the subroutine (set to any value).
HDNGS is another name for HEADER defined in the main program.

FIGURE 8.18
A PROGRAM CALLING TWO SUBROUTINES

```
C SORT SUBROUTINE
C    CLASS:   COUNTS NO. OF CLASSES
C    J:       COUNTS TOTAL NO. OF SCORES READ
C    TEMP:    ARRAY CONTAINING SCORES OF A CLASS
C    GRADE:   ARRAY CONTAINING ALL SCORES READ
C    N:       NUMBER OF SCORES IN ONE CLASS
C
      INTEGER TEMP(25),GRADE(500),CLASS
      DATA CLASS,J/2*0/
   10 READ(5,6,END=88)N,(TEMP(I),I=1,N)    Read number of scores N and then load N scores in TEMP.
      CALL SORT(TEMP,N)                     Call subroutine SORT to sort the N scores.
      CLASS = CLASS + 1
      WRITE(6,5)CLASS,(TEMP(I),I=1,N)       Print out the class number and the sorted scores.
C MERGE ALL SCORES INTO ARRAY GRADE
      DO 15 I = 1, N
          J = J + 1                         Count all scores
          GRADE(J) = TEMP(I)                and store them in array GRADE.
   15 CONTINUE
      GO TO 10                              Go read another record.
   88 CALL SORT(GRADE,J)                    When all class records have been read, go sort all scores.
      WRITE(6,7) (GRADE(I),I=1,J)
      STOP
    5 FORMAT(1X,'CLASS',I2,':',4X,12I4/(13X,12I4))
    6 FORMAT(I2,(25I3))
    7 FORMAT('0','ALL CLASSES:',12I4/(13X,12I4))
      END
C
      SUBROUTINE SORT(G,N)                  Bubble sort.
      INTEGER G(500),Q
      M = N - 1                             Number of passes = M
      DO 15 I = 1, M
         DO 10 J = 1, N - I
            IF(G(J) .GT. G(J+1))THEN
               Q      = G(J)
               G(J)   = G(J+1)
               G(J+1) = Q
            ENDIF
   10    CONTINUE
   15 CONTINUE
      RETURN
      END
```

Output

```
CLASS 1:       50  50  60  70  70  80  80  90  90 100
CLASS 2:       10  11  20  22  30  33  40  44  50  51  52  53
               55  55  56  60  66  70  77  78  80  88  90  95
               99
CLASS 3:       49  57  66  69  79  87

ALL CLASSES:   10  11  20  22  30  33  40  44  49  50  50  50
               51  52  53  55  55  56  57  60  60  66  66  69
               70  70  70  77  78  79  80  80  80  87  88  90
               90  90  95  99 100
```

FIGURE 8.19
SORT PROGRAM WITH SUBROUTINES

9 File Processing

9.1 INTRODUCTION

9.1.1 File Concepts

Many applications of computers, particularly in business environments, require the storage and processing of large amounts of data. Typically there is too much data to store in memory at one time, so the data is stored externally on such devices as magnetic tape or disks.

Data is organized into *records* containing related data items. Groups of related records compose a *file*. For example, a personnel file might contain one record for each employee in a company. Each record would be composed of such data items as the employee's name, social security number, age, date hired, and so on. For convenience in processing, the data items in each record are stored in the same order.

Records within a file are organized for easy access to process the data they contain. A data item that has a unique value for each record is designated as the *record key* and is used as the basis for the file organization. In the example just given, the employee social security number might be the record key, as shown in the following illustration:

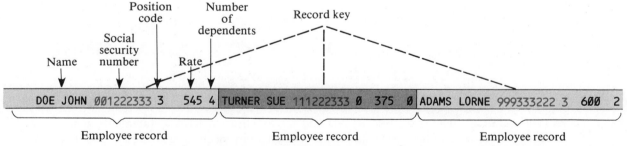

The file might be organized sequentially, randomly, or in any one of a number of other schemes. When sequential organization is used, records are placed in the file in order by record keys; each record has a record key value larger than that of its predecessor. A file that is organized sequentially is usually processed sequentially; a program processes each record in turn, starting with the first record in the file. When random organization is used, records are placed in the external storage device in a location that is calculated from the value of the record key. This organization allows a program to have random access to any specified record in a file without processing other records in the file. This type of file organization is not commonly supported in FORTRAN systems. Direct-access file organization (discussed in section 9.4) offers a compromise between the limitations of sequential and the advantages of random organization.

9.1.2 Programming
Example

Mr. X has just taken inventory, and he wishes to use a computer to maintain data on the number of parts on hand at his store. The part numbers and corresponding quantities are entered into the computer system and retained on a disk file. Later, as parts are sold or as parts are added to the inventory, the parts file is updated. Then, on either a daily or a weekly basis, reports are produced to list the contents of the inventory file to identify those parts that need to be ordered.

Such an information-processing system inevitably leads to the following file-processing considerations: Once the initial file is created, certain procedures must be defined to maintain the file, i.e., to keep the file current. In the case of personnel or payroll files, new employees are hired, others retire, and some may be fired, the marital status and the number of exemptions may change, certain employees may be promoted thereby causing a change in their pay/salary formula, and so forth. Clearly the files must be updated to reflect such changes before paychecks can be written. In any type of information-processing system, one or more of the following tasks will generally need to be performed:

1. Creating files.

2. Merging files, i.e., combining the records of two or more files into one new file.

3. Adding records.

4. Deleting records.

5. Changing individual items within file records.

6. Generating detailed or summary reports.

Such processes are illustrated in Figure 9.1, where a master inventory file is created (step 1) and then run against a transaction file (step 2) to produce a newly updated master file (step 3). In real-life applications, of course, the updated master file becomes the current master file, which continually evolves into new updated master files as a result of continual transactions.

9.2 FILE PROCESSING STATEMENTS

9.2.1 Formatted versus
Binary Files

The formatted READ and the list-directed READ statements generally reads data that has been entered into the system by means of a keyboard. Each keyboarded digit or character is automatically converted into an ASCII or EBCDIC character code. Such numeric data cannot be processed directly by the CPU; another conversion from ASCII or EBCDIC code to internal number representation is necessary before such numeric data can be processed algebraically by the system. Thus the integer 3, encoded as a single ASCII character, must first be translated to its internal form before it can be added, multiplied, and so forth. Likewise, numeric results produced by the CPU cannot be printed directly by a printer—they too must first be converted from internal form to ASCII or EBCDIC code. Printers and keyboards are character-set–sensitive devices that use the ASCII or EBCDIC code to represent characters.

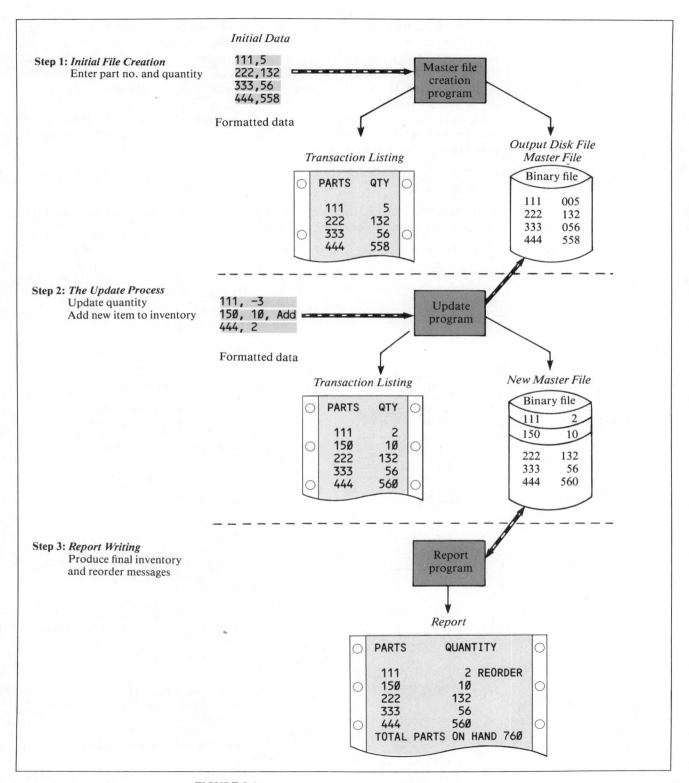

FIGURE 9.1
FILE PROCESSING TASKS

FORMATs are thus used to translate an internal number representation into character form before that number can be printed. Data, however, may be stored on devices such as tapes and disks in either internal (binary form) or character form (see Figure 9.2). The WRITE statement specifying a device number without a format will write the internal form of the numbers on disk or tape. Data that has been written out in the internal form on a storage medium does not need to be retranslated when it is read, and hence the formatless READ statement is used. Using binary data whenever possible may save space on the external storage device being used and speed up the processing of data by the program.

EXAMPLE

```
READ(7)A,B,K
```

Three values will be read from a record on device 7. No conversion will take place; the data will be assumed to be in internal form.

```
WRITE(10)X,Y,LL,KK
```

Four values in internal form will be written on device 10. Carriage control codes do not apply in this context, since we are not trying to control "paper movement" on disk or tape.

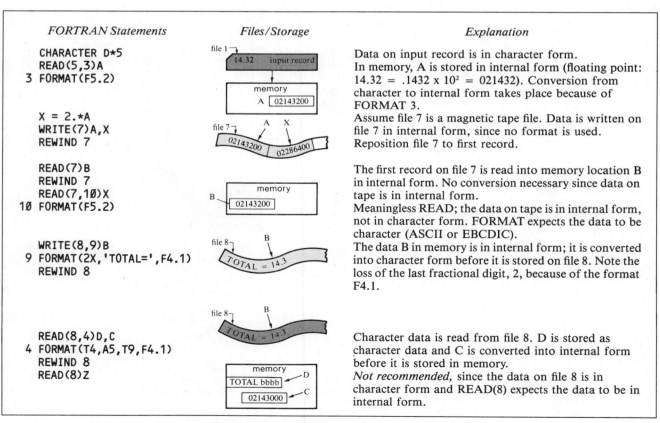

FORTRAN Statements	Files/Storage	Explanation
CHARACTER D*5 READ(5,3)A 3 FORMAT(F5.2)	file 1 ⌐ 14.32 input record memory A 02143200	Data on input record is in character form. In memory, A is stored in internal form (floating point: 14.32 = .1432 x 10² = 021432). Conversion from character to internal form takes place because of FORMAT 3.
X = 2.*A WRITE(7)A,X REWIND 7	file 7 ⌐ A X 02143200 02286400	Assume file 7 is a magnetic tape file. Data is written on file 7 in internal form, since no format is used. Reposition file 7 to first record.
READ(7)B REWIND 7 READ(7,10)X 10 FORMAT(F5.2)	memory B 02143200	The first record on file 7 is read into memory location B in internal form. No conversion necessary since data on tape is in internal form. Meaningless READ; the data on tape is in internal form, not in character form. FORMAT expects the data to be character (ASCII or EBCDIC).
WRITE(8,9)B 9 FORMAT(2X,'TOTAL=',F4.1) REWIND 8	file 8 ⌐ B TOTAL = 14.3	The data B in memory is in internal form; it is converted into character form before it is stored on file 8. Note the loss of the last fractional digit, 2, because of the format F4.1.
READ(8,4)D,C 4 FORMAT(T4,A5,T9,F4.1) REWIND 8 READ(8)Z	file 8 ⌐ B TOTAL = 14.3 memory TOTAL bbbb ← D 02143000 ← C	Character data is read from file 8. D is stored as character data and C is converted into internal form before it is stored in memory. *Not recommended*, since the data on file 8 is in character form and READ(8) expects the data to be in internal form.

FIGURE 9.2
FORMATTED VS. UNFORMATTED READ/WRITE

9.2.2 The OPEN and CLOSE Statements

Recall that a formatted READ or WRITE statement always specifies a device number. The OPEN statement sets up the internal code to link the specified device number to the particular external file that is to be processed by the input/output statement. The general form of the OPEN statement is:

$$\text{OPEN}\ (device\ number,\ \text{FILE} = file\ name\ [,\text{STATUS} = \left\{{\text{'NEW'} \atop \text{'OLD'}}\right\}][,\text{ACCESS} = \left\{{\text{'SEQUENTIAL'} \atop \text{'DIRECT'}}\right\}]$$

$$[,\text{FORM} = \left\{{\text{'FORMATTED'} \atop \text{'UNFORMATTED'} \atop \text{'BINARY'}}\right\}][,\text{RECL} = record\ length])$$

where   *file name*   is either the name of the catalogued data file in quotation marks or a character variable containing the data file name.

STATUS   specifies OLD for reading or writing on existing files and NEW for creating a new file. The default option is OLD.

ACCESS   reflects the file organization. SEQUENTIAL is the default, and DIRECT must be specified for direct-access organization.

FORM   IF access mode is sequential, the default is FORMATTED; if the access mode is direct, the default is UNFORMATTED.

RECL   is used only for direct-access files; it specifies the record length as an integer expression.

The OPEN statement, which is an executable statement, must precede the I/O operation that it affects. It tells the system to make the input or output file ready for processing. Error messages will be printed if the file cannot be found or the disk/tape drive is not ready etc.

As noted above, a file can be opened in either sequential or direct mode. A sequential file contains records whose order is determined when the file is created. You cannot insert records or delete records within a sequential file; insertion and deletion can only be done by copying the existing file to a new file and skipping over records (deletion) and adding records (insertion) during the copying process.

A direct-access file can be read/written in any order. Records are numbered sequentially (the first record is number 1). All records have the same length. Records can be written out randomly, i.e., records 9, 3, and 12 can be written in that order without writing the records in between. Once a record is written, it cannot be deleted—it can, however, be written over with a new value.

All files that are opened should be closed. The general form of the CLOSE statement is:

$$\text{CLOSE}\ (device\ number\ [,\text{STATUS} = \left\{{\text{'KEEP'} \atop \text{'DELETE'}}\right\}])$$

If DELETE is specified, the file is discarded, i.e., a particular application may require a scratch file that is no longer needed at the end of the application. The default option is KEEP.

EXAMPLES

1. OPEN (5, FILE='DEVIATION')

2. OPEN (6, FILE='FLIGHT', STATUS='NEW', FORM='BINARY')

```
3. CHARACTER FNAME*8
   WRITE(*,*) 'SPECIFY FILE NAME'
   READ(*,*) FNAME
   OPEN (7, FILE=FNAME, FORM='BINARY')

4. OPEN (9, FILE='VECTORS', ACCESS='DIRECT', RECL=64)

5. CLOSE (3)

6. CLOSE (7, STATUS='DELETE')
```

9.2.3 The END FILE Statement

The END FILE statement is used to write an end-of-file record when a disk or tape file is being created by a FORTRAN program. The general form of this statement is:

> END FILE *device number*

where   *device number* is the number associated with the disk or tape file.

EXAMPLE

```
 1 READ(5,10,END = 100)A,B,C
      SUM = A + B + C
      WRITE(7)A,B,C,SUM
      GO TO 1
100 END FILE 7
 10 FORMAT(3F5.0)
```

Statement 100 will cause the system end-of-file record to be written on device number 7.

9.2.4 The REWIND Statement

One major advantage of a disk or tape file is that it can be processed repeatedly by a program. The REWIND statement causes the next input operation addressed to a file to return to the first record of the file. When the file is on tape, the tape is physically rewound and repositioned so that the first record of the file is available at the next operation. When the file is on disk, the rewinding is logical rather than physical. The result, however, is the same; the first record of the file is the next one available for processing. The general form of the REWIND statement is:

> REWIND *device number*

where   *device number* is the number associated with the file to be rewound.

EXAMPLE

```
      :
      END FILE 7
      REWIND 7
  2 READ(7,END = 1000)A,B,C,SUM
      WRITE(6,110)A,B,C,SUM
      GO TO 2
1000 STOP
```

After processing of the file on device 7 is terminated, the file is rewound and processed again (statement 2).

9.3 SEQUENTIAL ACCESS PROGRAMMING EXAMPLES

9.3.1 File Creation

In the following programming examples, we shall assume that a file MASTER (device number 7) has been established; it contains payroll data records with identification numbers, names, and hourly wages. The program used to create the file is shown in Figure 9.3. Line 6 opens the formatted input data file 'PAYROLL'. Line 7 opens a new MASTER file (STATUS = 'NEW') onto which data read from the PAYROLL file is to be written in binary form (FORM = 'BINARY'). When all records have been read from the PAYROLL file and transmitted to the MASTER file, an end-of-file record is written on file 7 at line 11. Note that in Figure 9.3 the binary file is listed in character form and not in binary form. This is to make it easier to read since on disk the binary form is unreadable to the human eye!

The program to list the contents of the binary file is shown in Figure 9.4. This time the file is not 'NEW', but 'BINARY' form must be specified at line 7. Note that the user can specify the name of the file to be opened at run time through the character variable FNAME at lines 6 and 7.

```
1: ***** CREATING A MASTER FILE AS A BINARY FILE
2: ***** FILE 7: BINARY FILE WHICH IS TO BE CREATED
3: ***** FILE 5: FORMATTED DATA FILE TO BE COPIED TO FILE 7
4:        REAL RATE
5:        CHARACTER NAME*12,ID*9
6:        OPEN(5,FILE='PAYROLL')
7:        OPEN(7,FILE='MASTER',FORM='BINARY',STATUS='NEW')
8: 20     READ(5,30,END=88)ID,NAME,RATE        Read a record from the data file.
9:        WRITE(7)ID,NAME,RATE                 Write the record onto the
10:       GO TO 20                             binary file and keep repeating
11: 88    ENDFILE 7                            until the end of file is
12:       CLOSE (7)                            encountered on the input file.
13:       STOP
14: 30    FORMAT(A9,A12,F5.2)
15:       END
```

| | *Data File* | | | *Binary File* |
| Input file | *(File 5)* | | Output file | *(File 7)* |

```
123456789DOE MARCEL  05.00          123456789DOE MARCEL  05.00
222222222BROWN JIM   02.50          222222222BROWN JIM   02.50
333333333GREEN ZABETH07.25          333333333GREEN ZABETH07.25
456789000SMITH HILARY04.21          456789000SMITH HILARY04.21
```

FIGURE 9.3
CREATING A MASTER FILE
AS A BINARY FILE

```
 1: ***** PROGRAM TO LIST CONTENTS OF MASTER FILE     123456789DOE MARCEL  05.00
 2: ***** FILE 7: BINARY FILE TO BE LISTED            222222222BROWN JIM    02.50
 3:       REAL RATE                                    333333333GREEN ZABETH07.25
 4:       CHARACTER NAME*12,ID*9,FNAME*8               456789000SMITH HILARY04.21
 5:       WRITE(*,*)'ENTER FILE NAME'
 6:       READ(*,*)FNAME                        Determine name of file to be listed.
 7:       OPEN(7,FILE=FNAME,FORM='BINARY')      Enter name of file to be listed ('MASTER').
 8:       WRITE(*,*)                            Make that file available.
 9: 20    READ(7,END=88)ID,NAME,RATE            Read a record from binary file
10:       WRITE(*,30)ID,NAME,RATE               and print it.
11:       GO TO 20                              Repeat above steps until end of file.
12: 88    CLOSE (7)
13:       STOP
14: 30    FORMAT(1X,A9,A12,F5.2)                ENTER FILE NAME
15:       END                                   MASTER

                                                123456789DOE MARCEL    5.00
                                                222222222BROWN JIM      2.50
                                                333333333GREEN ZABETH   7.25
                                                456789000SMITH HILARY   4.21
```

FIGURE 9.4
LISTING (BINARY FILE)

9.3.2 Merging   As new employees are hired, records must be added to the file MASTER. If there is no ordering in the file MASTER, adding records at the end of the file presents no special difficulties. However, it is usually advantageous to store a file in ascending order by record key. Note that the sample file listed in Figure 9.4 is arranged in ascending sequence by identification number. We will write a program that will accept new items to be added to the file and then merge the new items with the old items in a way that preserves the order of the records in the new file.

Figure 9.5 shows the contents of the binary file MASTER (line 8) and the contents of the transaction file TRAN (line 10), which is to be merged with the MASTER file. Since records cannot be inserted into an existing sequential file, a new binary master file NEWMAST (line 9) is created to receive records from both the MASTER and the TRANsaction files. The contents of the merged file (NEWMAST) are also shown in Figure 9.5. Note two error conditions showing up in the program listing as a result of the merge process: transaction record 222222222 already exists in the master file, and transaction record 111111111 is out of sequence (the out-of-sequence record is not recorded into the new master file). Obviously, if records are to be arranged by ascending id number in the master file, it is critical that the transaction records be in order before the merge takes place.

The logic to solve this problem is shown in flowchart form in Figure 9.6. The flowchart only displays the logic for the merge process and not the code to perform a sequence check or the code to determine whether a transaction record read is already in the master file. Note that when the end of file is encountered on one file, the id key for that file is set to its highest possible value (999999 lines 42 and 44) so that on subsequent key comparisons, the record keys of the remaining file will all be less than 999999999 and hence all corresponding records of the last active file will automatically be written on the new file.

As a result of the merge process, a new file called NEWMAST has been created. The old file MASTER can now be used as a backup file in the event the transaction file is found to contain incorrect data.

```
 1: ***** THIS PROGRAM MERGES A DATA FILE WITH A MASTER FILE
 2: ***** IT ALSO PERFORMS A SEQUENCE CHECK ON THE INPUT FILE
 3: ***** FILE 7: MASTER FILE (ID,NAME,RATE)
 4: ***** FILE 5: INPUT FILE TO BE MERGED (ID,NAME,RATE)
 5: ***** FILE 8: NEWLY CREATED MASTER FILE (ID,NAME,RATE)
 6:       REAL RATE,TRRATE
 7:       CHARACTER NAME*12,ID*9,TRID*9,TRNAME*12,OLDID*9
 8:       OPEN(7,FILE='MASTER',FORM='BINARY')
 9:       OPEN(8,FILE='NEWMAST',FORM='BINARY',STATUS='NEW')
10:       OPEN(5,FILE='TRAN')
11:       READ(7,END=88)ID,NAME,RATE
12:       READ(5,20,END=44)TRID,TRNAME,TRRATE
13:       OLDID = '000000000'
14: 10    IF(ID.NE.'999999999' .OR. TRID.NE.'999999999')THEN
15:          IF(TRID .LT. OLDID)THEN
16:             WRITE(*,*)TRID,' IS OUT OF SEQUENCE'
17:             READ(5,20,END=44)TRID,TRNAME,TRRATE
18:          ELSE
19:             OLDID = TRID
20:             IF(TRID .LT. ID)THEN
21:                WRITE(*,*)TRID,TRNAME,TRRATE
22:                WRITE(8)TRID,TRNAME,TRRATE
23:                READ(5,20,END=44)TRID,TRNAME,TRRATE
24:             ELSE
25:                IF(TRID .EQ. ID)THEN
26:                   WRITE(*,*)TRID,
27:    A                ' ALREADY EXISTS IN MASTER FILE'
28:                   READ(5,20,END=44)TRID,TRNAME,TRRATE
29:                ELSE
30:                   WRITE(*,*)ID,NAME,RATE
31:                   WRITE(8)ID,NAME,RATE
32:                   READ(7,END=88)ID,NAME,RATE
33:                ENDIF
34:             ENDIF
35:          ENDIF
36:          GO TO 10
37:       ENDIF
38:       CLOSE(5)
39:       CLOSE(7)
40:       CLOSE(8)
41:       STOP
42: 88    ID = '999999999'
43:       GO TO 10
44: 44    TRID = '999999999'
45:       GO TO 10
46: 20    FORMAT(A9,A12,F5.2)
47:       END
```

MASTER

```
123456789DOE MARCEL  05.00
222222222BROWN JIM   02.50
333333333GREEN ZABETH07.25
456789000SMITH HILARY04.21
```

```
100000000ABLE BAKER  03.00
222222222BROWN JIM   05.00
555555555JONES MARC  07.50
111111111JACOBS TIM  10.50
```

For sequence check of transaction records

} Take care of sequence check

} Print error message if transaction record exists in master file.

ID = '999999999' End of file encountered on binary master file

TRID = '999999999' End of file encountered on formatted data file

Program Listing

```
100000000ABLE BAKER                3.0000000
123456789DOE MARCEL                5.0000000
222222222 ALREADY EXISTS IN MASTER FILE
222222222BROWN JIM                 2.5000000
333333333GREEN ZABETH              7.2500000
456789000SMITH HILARY              4.2100000
555555555JONES MARC                7.5000000
111111111 IS OUT OF SEQUENCE
```

File 8: New Master File (Merged File)

```
100000000ABLE BAKER  03.00
123456789DOE MARCEL  05.00
222222222BROWN JIM   02.50
333333333GREEN ZABETH07.25
456789000SMITH HILARY04.21
555555555JONES MARC  07.50
```

FIGURE 9.5
MERGING A BINARY FILE WITH A DATA FILE

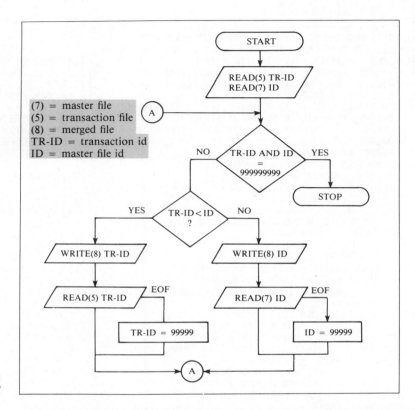

FIGURE 9.6
MERGING TWO FILES

9.3.3 Report Generation

We are now ready to produce a pay report. Given an HOURS data file (see Figure 9.7) where each record contains an id number and a number of hours worked, we are to calculate the pay corresponding to each id number in the HOURS file. Since the hourly rate of pay is missing from that file, it must be looked up in the master file. Figure 9.7 displays the printed pay report; note the error message concerning record 444444444, which has no match in the master file. When the end of file has been encountered in both the HOURS file and the MASTER file the program stops.

The logic to solve this problem is shown in pseudo code in Figure 9.8 and in FORTRAN code in Figure 9.7.

```
read id, name, rate
read transaction id, hours
WHILE both id and transaction id are ≠ 99999 DO
      IF id = transaction id THEN
            compute gross
            write gross
            read transaction id, hours (if end of file set transaction id = 99999)
      ELSE
            IF id < transaction id THEN
                  read id, name, rate (if end of file set id = 99999)
            ELSE
                  write error message
                  read transaction id, hours (if end of file set transaction id = 99999)
            ENDIF
      ENDIF
ENDWHILE
END
```

FIGURE 9.8
PRINTING A PAY REPORT

```
 1: * EACH RECORD OF A MASTER FILE CONTAINS AN ID
 2: * NUMBER,A NAME & A CORRESPONDING HOURLY RATE.
 3: * EACH RECORD OF A TRANSACTION FILE CONTAINS          Master File in Binary Format
 4: * AN ID NUMBER & A CORRESPONDING NUMBER OF
 5: * HOURS WORKED.                                       100000000ABLE BAKER  03.00
 6: * THIS PROGRAM DETERMINES THE PAY FOR EACH            123456789DOE MARCEL   05.00
 7: * ID NUMBER BY LOOKING UP THE RATE OF PAY IN          222222222BROWN JIM    02.50    MASTER
 8: * THE MASTER FILE AND MULTIPLYING THE HOURLY          333333333GREEN ZABETH07.25
 9: * RATE OF EMPLOYEE BY CORRESPONDING NUMBER            456789000SMITH HILARY04.21
10: * OF HOURS WORKED IN TRANSACTION FILE.                555555555JONES MARC   07.50
11: *** FILE 5: INPUT FILE (ID, HOURS WORKED)
12: *** FILE 8: BINARY MASTER FILE (ID,NAME,RATE)         Number of Hours File
13:       REAL RATE,TRHOUR,GROSS
14:       CHARACTER NAME*12,ID*9,TRID*9                   12345678940.00
15:       OPEN(8,FILE='MASTER',FORM='BINARY')             22222222253.00
16:       OPEN(5,FILE='HOURS')                            44444444430.00    HOURS
17:       WRITE(6,40)                                     45678900024.00
18:       READ(8,END=88)ID,NAME,RATE                      55555555550.00
19:       READ(5,20,END=44)TRID,TRHOUR
20: 10    IF(ID.NE.'999999999' .OR. TRID.NE.'999999999')THEN
21:         IF(ID .EQ. TRID)THEN                          If there is an id match
22:            GROSS = TRHOUR*RATE                         between the master and hours file,
23:            WRITE(6,30)ID,NAME,RATE,TRHOUR,GROSS        compute the corresponding pay.
24:            READ(5,20,END=44)TRID,TRHOUR
25:         ELSE
26:           IF(ID .LT. TRID)THEN                         Skip master records that have no
27:              READ(8,END=88)ID,NAME,RATE                corresponding entries in the hours file.
28:           ELSE
29:              WRITE(6,50)TRID                            An entry in the hours file has no
30:              READ(5,20,END=44)TRID,TRHOUR              corresponding entry in the master file.
31:           ENDIF
32:         ENDIF
33:         GO TO 10
34:       ENDIF
35:       CLOSE(5)
36:       CLOSE(8)
37:       STOP
38: 88    ID = '999999999'                                End of file encountered in the master file.
39:       GO TO 10
40: 44    TRID = '999999999'                              End of file encountered in the hours file.
41:       GO TO 10
42: 20    FORMAT(A9,F5.2)
43: 40    FORMAT(1X,'ID NUMBER',4X,'NAME',8X,'HOURLY WAGE'
44:      1       3X,'HOURS',4X,'GROSS'/1X)
45: 30    FORMAT(1X,A9,4X,A12,2X,F5.2,7X,F5.2,3X,F7.2)
46: 50    FORMAT(1X,'NO MATCHING RECORD ',A9,' IN MASTER FILE')
47:       END
```

```
ID NUMBER    NAME          HOURLY WAGE   HOURS    GROSS

123456789    DOE MARCEL        5.00      40.00    200.00
222222222    BROWN JIM         2.50      53.00    132.50
NO MATCHING RECORD 444444444 IN MASTER FILE
456789000    SMITH HILARY      4.21      24.00    101.04
555555555    JONES MARC        7.50      50.00    375.00
```

FIGURE 9.7
A GROSS PAY REPORT

9.4 DIRECT-ACCESS FILES

9.4.1 Sequential versus Direct-Access File Organization

Recall the characteristics of sequential file processing:

1. The records in a sequential file are organized in sequence based on a unique record key.

2. Updating a sequential file requires that all transaction records already be sorted in record key sequence (ascending or descending).

3. A new master file, physically distinct from the old master file, is always created as a result of a sequential update; this is true regardless of the number of transaction records, be it one or one thousand!

Sequential file organization is ideal in many information-processing environments where transactions can be accumulated, sorted in batches, and periodically run against a master sequential file. In other types of situations this approach may be less than ideal, especially in cases where random inquiries or random updates are to be processed on the spot or within a short time interval. In such cases, different file-processing methods must be used: one suitable method involves direct access files. A direct-access file-processing system can be characterized as follows:

1. The user can access and process a particular record either sequentially or directly. Accessing a record directly (randomly) can be achieved by a hash function (section 9.4.2) or by a table look-up procedure based on the record key. When processing records directly (randomly), no search of prior records is necessary. Internally, retrieving a record randomly is somewhat like using a table look-up procedure to retrieve a particular entry from a table. Thus a direct-access file system can enable a bank agent to look up a customer's credit balance almost instantaneously, regardless of whether the record is the first or the last in the file, quite unlike a sequential search.

2. Unlike a sequential file update, which creates a new physical master file, no new master file is created as a result of updating a direct-access file. Records can be added to the file without physical relocation of adjacent records. Changes can be made to a particular record on the same disk area that the record occupies. Similarly, records can be deleted without altering the physical sequence of records in the file. Deleted records are simply flagged as unavailable to the user.

9.4.2 How Direct Access Works

Before a file can be used as a direct-access file, it must be OPENed with the entry ACCESS = DIRECT (see Section 9.2.2). Direct access of records is made possible through the REC= entry in the READ/WRITE statement:

$$\left\{ \begin{array}{l} \text{READ} \\ \text{WRITE} \end{array} \right\} (device\ number, [format\ number], \text{REC} = integer\ expression, \ldots)$$

For example, if the value of REC = 5, then the fifth record of the file is read/written; if REC = 10, then the tenth record is accessed. The access of any record is based on its position in the file, *not* on the recognition of some data value in the record. To read the records sequentially, the following code can be used:

```
    I = 1                                    Set the counter to the first record.
 10 READ(7,2Ø,END=88,REC=I)NAME,HOURS,...
    I = I + 1                                Point to next record.
    :
    :
    GO TO 1Ø
 88 ...
```

If we need to directly access a particular record, say a record with a name key such as 'SIMS', we need to know the record's physical position in the file (1st? 10th? 37th?). To that end we use an array which contains all the names in the file listed in the same order as they appear on the disk file (see Figure 9.9). We then search this index of names for a matching name key. This gives us the relative position of the corresponding record—position 5 for SIMS in our example—and we use that number in the REC= entry of the READ or WRITE statement.

This index of names is created at file-creation time (as each record is written on the direct-access file, the corresponding record key—name in this case—is stored in an array). This name array is then stored on disk as a separate file and loaded back into memory every time the direct-access file is to be processed. Whenever new records are added to the file, the corresponding record keys (names) are added to the name index.

In very large files, this type of look-up procedure is necessary to find the actual position of a particular record; note that the search for record position takes place in memory, *not* on disk—thus it is a very fast process, especially if a binary search is used to locate the record index. The linkage between the index, the corresponding disk file, and the READ/WRITE statement is illustrated in Figure 9.9.

Hashing Technique

In the preceding example, the reader may rightfully argue that a name is not a good choice for a record key, since duplicate names may exist in a given file—a social security number, an account number, or an employee number would be a better choice since it is unique.

If we used a three-digit number instead of the name as the record key in this example, the question could be asked, Why not use the number itself to represent the position of the record? That is, given a file consisting of three employees 032, 105, and 404, could we not create a direct-access file as follows:

```
WRITE(8,1Ø,REC=32)NAME,EMPNO,HOURS, ...
WRITE(8,1Ø,REC=1Ø5)NAME,EMPNO,HOURS, ...
WRITE(8,1Ø,REC=4Ø4)NAME,EMPNO,HOURS, ...
```

and in general

```
WRITE(8,1Ø,REC=EMPNO)NAME,EMPNO,HOURS ...
```

The answer is yes, but the system will create a file consisting of 404 records, of which only three are active. Such an organization is extremely costly in terms of disk storage.

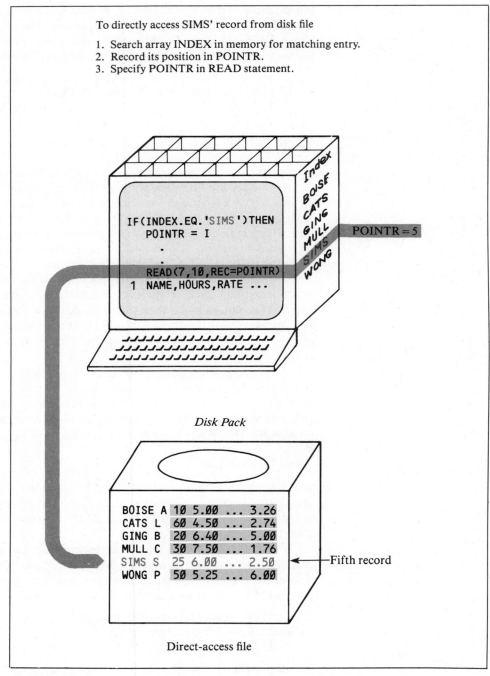

To directly access SIMS' record from disk file

1. Search array INDEX in memory for matching entry.
2. Record its position in POINTR.
3. Specify POINTR in READ statement.

```
IF(INDEX.EQ.'SIMS')THEN
    POINTR = I
       .
       .
    READ(7,10,REC=POINTR)
1   NAME,HOURS,RATE ...
```

POINTR = 5

Disk Pack

```
BOISE A 10 5.00 ... 3.26
CATS L  60 4.50 ... 2.74
GING B  20 6.40 ... 5.00
MULL C  30 7.50 ... 1.76
SIMS S  25 6.00 ... 2.50
WONG P  50 5.25 ... 6.00
```
← Fifth record

Direct-access file

FIGURE 9.9
DIRECT ACCESS OF A RECORD

Of course, if most positions are utilized, this type of organization can be used in which case there is no need for an index search. In general, however, key fields will exceed three digits, which makes this type of scheme unadvisable.

However, a similar approach can be used that still does not require an index search. The position of the record is determined indirectly by the key field itself. A *hash* function is used to assign a physical position to a record whose key field can be a very large number. One unsophisticated hash function is the division/remainder method (modulo arithmetic).

EXAMPLE

Assume employee numbers are in the range 1 to 4000, and assume there are 347 employees. The physical position of each employee record in the file is determined by the following function:

$$\text{position of record} = \text{remainder of}\left(\frac{\text{key field}}{\text{no. records}}\right) + 1 \quad \text{(integer division)}$$

For instance, the position of the employee record with number 4000 is

$$\text{position of record} = \text{remainder of}\left(\frac{4000}{347}\right) + 1 = 183 + 1 = 184$$

In FORTRAN, the code to access the employee record with employee number 4000 is

```
INTEGER EMPNO,POINTR
READ(*,*)EMPNO                4000, for example
POINTR=MOD(EMPNO,347)+1
READ(7,1Ø,REC=POINTR)NAME,EMPNO,HOURS,...
```

Using this approach, only 347 record slots are created for the direct-access file (instead of the 4000 that would be required if we used the employee number as the key field). It is possible that different key fields will yield the same address (position). Such addresses are called *synonyms;* discussion of synonyms and their treatment is beyond the scope of this text.

9.5 DIRECT-ACCESS PROGRAMMING EXAMPLE

9.5.1 Creation of a Direct-Access File

Problem Specification. Each record of an input file consists of an employee name, a number of hours worked, and an hourly rate of pay. Write a program to create a direct-access binary file from this input file. Also record the number of records stored in the direct-access file and its corresponding index array (list of names in the order in which they appear in the binary file) on a disk file (sequential).

Solution. The input file and both output files are displayed in Figure 9.10.

```
 1: ***** CREATION OF A DIRECT-ACCESS FILE WITH BINARY RECORDS
 2: ***** FILE 5: INPUT DATA FILE
 3: ***** FILE 7: DIRECT-ACCESS FILE
 4: ***** FILE 8: SEQUENTIAL FILE CONTAINING THE NAME INDEX
 5: *****          AND THE TOTAL COUNT OF RECORDS
 6: ***** NUMBER: COUNTS THE RECORDS & IS USED BY THE WRITE STATEMENT
 7: *****          TO PLACE THE NEXT RECORD IN THE DIRECT-ACCESS FILE
 8: ***** INDEX: ARRAY CONTAINING ALL RECORD KEYS (NAMES)
 9:        INTEGER NUMBER,HOURS
10:        REAL RATE
11:        CHARACTER*10 NAME,INDEX(100)
12:        OPEN(7,FILE='DIR',STATUS='NEW',ACCESS='DIRECT'
13:       1,FORM='BINARY',RECL=18)
14:        OPEN(8,FILE='INDEX',STATUS='NEW')
15:        OPEN(5,FILE='DATA')
16:        NUMBER = 0
17: 5      READ(5,10,END=88)NAME,HOURS,RATE
18:        NUMBER = NUMBER + 1
19:        INDEX(NUMBER) = NAME
20:        WRITE(7,REC=NUMBER)NAME,HOURS,RATE
21:        GO TO 5
22: 88     WRITE(8,15)NUMBER,(INDEX(J),J=1,NUMBER)
23:        CLOSE (7)
24:        CLOSE (8)
25:        STOP
26: 10     FORMAT(A10,I2,F5.2)
27: 15     FORMAT(I3,100A10)
28:        END
```

Note 'NEW' for file creation.
Each record is 18 bytes long.
File 8 will contain the index of names.
Open data file.
Use NUMBER as a counter and as a pointer for the WRITE at line 20.

Store name in array.
Write a binary record on direct-access file.
Write the total number of records and the name index into a sequential file called INDEX.

Input File

```
ARMSTRON L2020.50
HANNIBAL L4509.50
MASTERS J 6030.00
TIMMONS S 5030.00
VANOCUR T 4050.00
```

Output Files

Sequential File (File 8) INDEX

| 005 | ARMSTRON L | HANNIBAL L | MASTERS J | TIMMONS S | VANOCUR T | |

count of records (5)
index of names stored in file 8

Direct-access file (File 7) DIR

| ARMSTRON L | ...|.... | HANNIBAL L | ...|.... | MASTERS J | ...|.... | TIMMONS S | ...|.... | VANOCUR T | ...|.... |

Binary value for HOURS   Binary value for RATE   Both integer and real values are in internal
        (20)   (9.50)   code and thus are not printable.

FIGURE 9.10
CREATION OF A DIRECT-ACCESS FILE

Program Analysis

- Line 12 opens the direct-access file. Since it is to be created, the entry STATUS = 'NEW' must be specified. The form is 'BINARY' and the length for each record is equal to 18 characters (bytes); 10 bytes are reserved for the name, 4 bytes for the internal form of the integer HOURs, and 4 bytes for the real number RATE.

- Line 14 opens a sequential file into which the count of records (NUMBER) and the index of names is to be stored. Since this file is also to be created, the 'NEW' option is specified.

- Line 20 stores each record read into the direct-access file. Note that the records are written in the order they are read, since NUMBER takes on values 1 through 5.

- Line 22 stores NUMBER and the array of names into file 8.

9.5.2 Listing the Contents of a Direct-Access File

Let us write the code to list the contents of the direct-access file created in Figure 9.10. The program to solve this task is shown in Figure 9.11. Note that in this case the name index is not used since we are reading the records one after the other. See program analysis on next page.

```
 1: *****  LISTING THE CONTENTS OF A DIRECT-ACCESS FILE
 2: *****  FILE 7: DIRECT-ACCESS FILE
 3: *****  NUMBER: TELLS THE READ STATEMENT WHICH RECORDS TO READ
 4:        INTEGER HOURS
 5:        REAL RATE
 6:        CHARACTER*10 NAME
 7:        OPEN(7,FILE='DIR',ACCESS='DIRECT',FORM='BINARY',RECL=18)
 8:        NUMBER = 1
 9: 5      READ(7,END=88,REC=NUMBER)NAME,HOURS,RATE
10:        NUMBER = NUMBER + 1
11:        WRITE(6,10)NAME,HOURS,RATE
12:        GO TO 5
13: 88     CLOSE (7)
14:        STOP
15: 10     FORMAT(1X,A10,2X,I2,2X,F5.2)
16:        END
```

```
ARMSTRON L  20  20.50
HANNIBAL L  45   9.50
MASTERS  J  60  30.00
TIMMONS  S  50  30.00
VANOCUR  T  40  50.00
```

Contents of direct-access file is printed.

FIGURE 9.11
LISTING THE CONTENTS OF A DIRECT-ACCESS FILE

Program Analysis

■ Line 7 opens an already created direct-access file (OLD is the default for the status).

■ Line 9 reads one record at a time from the direct-access file. Note the absence of any format statement number since the records are in binary form.

Caution

If an existing file is opened with STATUS = NEW, the file will be automatically destroyed!

9.5.3 Updating a Direct-Access File

The direct-access file created by the program in Figure 9.10 contains employee names, hours worked, and hourly rates of pay. Write a program to allow management to obtain an interactive report similar to the one shown in Figure 9.13 (see page 513). The user should be able to perform the following five functions:

1. Compute and print the pay for any employee
2. Insert a new record in the file
3. Change the hours, the hourly rate, or both
4. List the current contents of the file
5. Terminate the session

A program to solve this problem is shown in Figure 9.12.

Program Analysis

As in Figures 9.10 and 9.11, the name is used as a record key. Since functions 1 and 3 require that we determine a record's position in the file, a function called LOCATE (lines 82–97) serves that purpose. Note the error message printed by line 93 if a name is misspelled.

The direct-access file (DIR) and its associated name index are opened at lines 13 and 14. The number of records in the file (NUMBER) and the index of names are loaded into memory at line 15. NUMBER is needed only when a new record is to be inserted into the file; the statement WRITE(7,REC = NUMBER)... (line 56) is then used to place the new record as the current last physical record in the file. If NUMBER were not available, we could read the file until the end of file and then write out the record, but that would be time-consuming. NUMBER is also used by the function LOCATE (line 83) to determine a record's position in the file.

When the session is terminated, the current number of records and the index of names are stored back onto disk at line 28. Because of the insert function, NUMBER may have changed and new names may have been added to the index table. Note that file 8 (INDEX) is opened as an input file at line 14 and closed at line 26 so that INDEX can be rewritten as the most current file (line 27).

The DO loop at lines 36–39 prints the contents of the file. A "WHILE end of file not encountered DO" structure could also have been used to print the file instead of the DO statement at line 36. Note that new name inserts are *not* listed in alphabetical sequence but in the order the records have been added to the file. A sort could be carried out on the names to generate an updated relative order of the records so that these records could be accessed alphabetically from the disk file.

```
 1: ***** AN ON-LINE UPDATE & INQUIRY PROGRAM
 2: ***** FILE 7: CONTAINS EMPLOYEE DIRECT-ACCESS FILE
 3: ***** FILE 8: CONTAINS NAME INDEX OF DIRECT ACCESS FILE
 4: ***** INDEX  : ARRAY CONTAINING THE NAME INDEX
 5: ***** NUMBER : CONTAINS THE NUMBER OF RECORDS IN THE FILE
 6: ***** NAME, HOURS, RATE ARE THE 3 ITEMS ON EACH DIRECT RECORD
 7: ***** LOCATE IS A FUNCTION WHICH RETURNS THE ADDRESS OF A RECORD
 8: ***** PAY: IS THE PRODUCT OF HOURS BY RATE
 9: ***** CODE: IS ONE OF 4 POSSIBLE CODES FOR THE VARIOUS FUNCTIONS          File 7: DIR
10:        INTEGER*4 NUMBER,HOURS,CODE,POINTR
11:        REAL RATE                                                      ARMSTRON L2020.50
12:        CHARACTER*10 NAME,INDEX(100)                                   HANNIBAL L4509.50
13:        OPEN(7,FILE='DIR',ACCESS='DIRECT',FORM='BINARY',RECL=18) ───►  MASTERS J 6030.00
14:        OPEN(8,FILE='INDEX')                                          TIMMONS S 5030.00
15:        READ(8,15)NUMBER,(INDEX(J),J=1,NUMBER)                        VANOCUR T 4050.00
16: 10     WRITE(*,*)'TO LOOK UP A PERSON''S PAY      ENTER 1'
17:        WRITE(*,*)'TO INSERT A NEW RECORD          ENTER 2'              File 8: INDEX
18:        WRITE(*,*)'TO CHANGE HOURS AND/OR RATE     ENTER 3'
19:        WRITE(*,*)'TO LIST THE FILE                ENTER 4'   005 ARMSTRON L HANNIBAL L MASTERS J TIMMONS S VANOCUR T
20:        WRITE(*,*)'TO STOP                         ENTER 0'
21:        READ(*,*)CODE
22: * SAVE # OF RECORDS & THE NAME INDEX AT END OF SESSION
23: * FUNCTION CODE IS 0
24:        IF(CODE .EQ. 0)THEN                               Terminate session
25:           CLOSE(7)
26:           CLOSE(8)                                       Make sure the name index and the
27:           OPEN(8,FILE='INDEX',STATUS='NEW')              number of records are stored on
28:           WRITE(8,15)NUMBER,(INDEX(J),J=1,NUMBER)        disk.
29:           CLOSE(8)
30:           STOP
31: * USER ENTERS INVALID CODE
32:        ELSEIF(CODE .GT. 4)THEN                           Code is neither 1, 2, 3, 4, or 0.
33:           WRITE(*,*)'INCORRECT CODE: RETYPE'
34: * LIST THE FILE ON THE PRINTER
35:        ELSEIF(CODE .EQ. 4)THEN
36:           DO 50 I = 1,NUMBER                             Obtain a listing of the file.
37:              READ(7,REC=I)NAME,HOURS,RATE
38:              WRITE(*,55)NAME,HOURS,RATE
39: 50        CONTINUE
40:        ELSE                                              At this point code is either 1, 2, or 3.
41:           WRITE(*,*)'ENTER NAME'
42:           READ(*,20)NAME
43: * COMPUTE AND PRINT THE EMPLOYEE PAY
44:           IF(CODE .EQ. 1)THEN
45:              POINTR = LOCATE(INDEX,NAME,NUMBER)           Compute and print employee pay.
46:              READ(7,REC=POINTR)NAME,HOURS,RATE
47:              PAY = HOURS * RATE
48:              WRITE(*,*)'PAY= ',PAY
49: * INSERT A NEW RECORD
50:           ELSEIF(CODE .EQ. 2)THEN
51:              WRITE(*,*)'ENTER HOURS     (2 DIGIT NUMBER)'
52:              READ(*,21)HOURS
53:              WRITE(*,*)'ENTER RATE      (IN THE FORM dd.dd)'
54:              READ(*,22)RATE                                Insert a new record.
55:              NUMBER = NUMBER + 1
56:              WRITE(7,REC=NUMBER)NAME,HOURS,RATE
57:              INDEX(NUMBER) = NAME
```

FIGURE 9.12
A DIRECT-ACCESS FILE UPDATE AND INQUIRY (Part 1 of 2)

```
58: * CHANGE EITHER THE HOURS OR THE RATE FIELD, OR BOTH
59:         ELSE
60:             POINTR = LOCATE(INDEX,NAME,NUMBER)
61:             READ(7,REC=POINTR)NAME,HOURS,RATE
62:             WRITE(*,30)HOURS,RATE                              Change either the
63:             READ(*,21)HOURS
64:             WRITE(*,*)'ENTER RATE IN THE FORM dd.dd'           HOURS or the RATE field
65:             READ(*,22)RATE
66:             WRITE(7,REC=POINTR)NAME,HOURS,RATE                 or both.
67:         ENDIF
68:      ENDIF
69:      GO TO 10
70:      STOP
71: *
72: 15   FORMAT(I3,100A10)
73: 20   FORMAT(A10)
74: 21   FORMAT(I2)
75: 22   FORMAT(F5.2)
76: 25   FORMAT(A10,I2,F5.2)
77: 30   FORMAT(1X,'CURRENT HOURS= ',I2,' CURRENT RATE= ',F5.2/
78:    1      1X,'ENTER HOURS FIRST (dd)')
79: 55   FORMAT(1X,A10,1X,I2,1X,F5.2)
80:      END
81: *
82: **** THIS FUNCTION RETURNS THE RECORD'S POSITION IN THE FILE
83:      FUNCTION LOCATE(INDEX,NAME,NUMBER)
84:      CHARACTER*10 INDEX(100),NAME
85:      INTEGER*4 NUMBER
86: 20   DO 10 I = 1, NUMBER
87:          IF(INDEX(I) .EQ. NAME)THEN                    Determine the position of the
88:              LOCATE = I                                record within the file.
89:              RETURN
90:          ENDIF
91: 10   CONTINUE
92: * IF NAME DOES NOT EXIST IN THE NAME INDEX GIVE ERROR MESSAGE
93:      WRITE(*,*)'INCORRECT NAME SPELLING; RETYPE'
94:      READ(*,30)NAME
95:      GO TO 20
96: 30   FORMAT(A10)
97:      END
```

FIGURE 9.12
A DIRECT-ACCESS FILE UPDATE AND INQUIRY (Part 2 of 2)

The LOCATE function is used at lines 45 and 60 to produce POINTR, the position of the record corresponding to the name inquiry at line 42. POINTR is then used at line 46 to capture the desired record in the file, enabling us to compute the pay (line 47).

The insertion of a record takes place at lines 51 through 57. Since we are writing out a new record, the corresponding key field for that record (NAME) must be added to the name index (line 57) and the count of records must be updated (line 55).

Changing the contents of an existing record field is accomplished at lines 60 through 66. It is of course possible to change the key field—such an operation, however, would require that the name also be changed in the name index! The statement at line 66 rewrites the updated record "on top of" the old record, i.e., no new record is written.

```
TO LOOK UP A PERSON'S PAY      ENTER 1        4
TO INSERT A NEW RECORD         ENTER 2        ARMSTRON L 20 20.50
TO CHANGE HOURS AND/OR RATE    ENTER 3        HANNIBAL L 45  9.50
TO LIST THE FILE               ENTER 4        MASTERS J  60 30.00
TO STOP                        ENTER 0        TIMMONS S  50 30.00
4                                             VANOCUR T  40 50.00
ARMSTRON L 20 20.50                           DEGAULLE A 60 77.00
HANNIBAL L 45  9.50                           TO LOOK UP A PERSON'S PAY      ENTER 1
MASTERS J  60 30.00                           TO INSERT A NEW RECORD         ENTER 2
TIMMONS S  50 30.00                           TO CHANGE HOURS AND/OR RATE    ENTER 3
VANOCUR T  40 50.00                           TO LIST THE FILE               ENTER 4
TO LOOK UP A PERSON'S PAY      ENTER 1        TO STOP                        ENTER 0
TO INSERT A NEW RECORD         ENTER 2        6
TO CHANGE HOURS AND/OR RATE    ENTER 3        INCORRECT CODE: RETYPE
TO LIST THE FILE               ENTER 4        TO LOOK UP A PERSON'S PAY      ENTER 1
TO STOP                        ENTER 0        TO INSERT A NEW RECORD         ENTER 2
1                                             TO CHANGE HOURS AND/OR RATE    ENTER 3
ENTER NAME                                    TO LIST THE FILE               ENTER 4
MASTERS                                       TO STOP                        ENTER 0
INCORRECT NAME SPELLING; RETYPE               3
MASTERS J                                     ENTER NAME
PAY=      1800.0000000                        HANNIBAL L
TO LOOK UP A PERSON'S PAY      ENTER 1        CURRENT HOURS= 45 CURRENT RATE=  9.50
TO INSERT A NEW RECORD         ENTER 2        ENTER HOURS FIRST (dd)
TO CHANGE HOURS AND/OR RATE    ENTER 3        45
TO LIST THE FILE               ENTER 4        ENTER RATE IN THE FORM dd.dd
TO STOP                        ENTER 0        10.50
2                                             TO LOOK UP A PERSON'S PAY      ENTER 1
ENTER NAME                                    TO INSERT A NEW RECORD         ENTER 2
DEGAULLE A                                    TO CHANGE HOURS AND/OR RATE    ENTER 3
ENTER HOURS    (2 DIGIT NUMBER)               TO LIST THE FILE               ENTER 4
60                                            TO STOP                        ENTER 0
ENTER RATE      (IN THE FORM dd.dd)           4
77.00                                         ARMSTRON L 20 20.50
TO LOOK UP A PERSON'S PAY      ENTER 1        HANNIBAL L 45 10.50
TO INSERT A NEW RECORD         ENTER 2        MASTERS J  60 30.00
TO CHANGE HOURS AND/OR RATE    ENTER 3        TIMMONS S  50 30.00
TO LIST THE FILE               ENTER 4        VANOCUR T  40 50.00
TO STOP                        ENTER 0        DEGAULLE A 60 77.00
1                                             TO LOOK UP A PERSON'S PAY      ENTER 1
ENTER NAME                                    TO INSERT A NEW RECORD         ENTER 2
DEGAULLE A                                    TO CHANGE HOURS AND/OR RATE    ENTER 3
PAY=      4620.0000000                        TO LIST THE FILE               ENTER 4
TO LOOK UP A PERSON'S PAY      ENTER 1        TO STOP                        ENTER 0
TO INSERT A NEW RECORD         ENTER 2        0
TO CHANGE HOURS AND/OR RATE    ENTER 3
TO LIST THE FILE               ENTER 4
TO STOP                        ENTER 0
```

FIGURE 9.13
SAMPLE INQUIRY SESSION WITH TERMINAL

Program Questions

1. If the user enters the code 4 the contents of the file are printed. Change the code so that the listing is always displayed alphabetically—even when new records have been inserted.
2. Replace the current direct access file with an updated direct access file such that all records including inserts are now in ascending order.
3. Validate the user's input code—for example if the user types the character A instead of the digit 1, the program should ask the user to retype the code.

9.6 PROGRAMMING EXERCISES

1. Each record of a sequential file contains a name (key value) and a score. Write the code to do the following:

    a. Add 10% of the class average to each score. No resulting score should exceed 100.

    b. Delete all records with scores below 50.

    c. Print the names of all students whose scores exceed 90, *then* print the names of all students whose scores are between 50 and 70.

2. Dr. Teach keeps her students' grades on diskettes on her own microcomputer system. She has already entered the following information on each student into her master file: name, two test scores, and two blank entries for the final average and the corresponding letter grade. Dr. Teach's input data might be similar to:

Name	Test 1	Test 2	Average	Grade
Doe J	80	90	?	?
Hill K	60	62	?	?
⋮				

A   = 90 or above
B+ = 85–89
B   = 80–84
C+ = 75–79
C   = 60–74
D   = 50–59
F   = below 50

Dr. Teach is now ready to write a program to compute each student's final score and corresponding letter grade. She realizes that in some cases, either or both test scores may have to be changed. Some students have withdrawn from the class and need their names deleted from the master file. Write a program to:

    a. Create a class file arranged alphabetically by student name. Each record should contain a name, two test scores, and two initially blank fields for the final average and the letter grade.

    b. Create a transaction file consisting of change records. Such records can cause deletion of certain records or changes in either one or both test scores. Use change codes of your choice.

    c. Print an updated grade roster file listing the names of the students and their scores and letter grades. Identify transaction names that do not have matches in the master file.

The master file, transaction file, and output have the following form:

Master File	Transaction File	Output

```
Master File                Transaction File                      Output

DOE JOE      050070         DOE JOE     DELETE         ┌─────────────────────────────────┐
LIKE SALLY   080090         LIKE SALLY  CHANGE1070    ○ │ NAME        T1  T2  AVG  GRADE │ ○
TASS MIKE    065070         TASS MIKE   CHANGE1080      │                                 │
TURAN LEO    080070         TURAN LEO   CHANGE2080      │ LIKE SALLY  70  90   80    B    │
                            TURAN LEO   CHANGE1060    ○ │ TASS MIKE   80  70   75    C+   │ ○
                            AMIGO LUIS  CHANGE1060      │ TURAN LEO   60  80   70    C    │
                                                        │ NO MATCH FOR AMIGO              │
```

3. The Furniture Company has stock in three different warehouses. The controller/dispatcher needs to know at any given time the number of particular furniture items at each of the three warehouses. He may also need to know the number of each particular item in one warehouse. Initially, the stock of items in all warehouses is as follows:

	Warehouse 1	Warehouse 2	Warehouse 3
Tables	100	100	50
Desks	123	44	76
Chairs	789	234	12
Beds	67	456	90
Sofas	10	50	20
Lamps	100	200	100

The controller has at his fingertips a terminal where he can inquire about a particular item. For example, when he types "BEDS," the system furnishes him with the number of beds at the three warehouses.

a. Write a program to allow the following communications between the dispatcher and the data base:

```
ENTER REQUEST
BEDS
              WAREHOUSE1    WAREHOUSE2    WAREHOUSE3
                  67           456            90          TOTAL 613

ENTER REQUEST
WAREHOUSE3
              TABLES    DESKS    CHAIRS    BEDS    SOFAS    LAMPS
                50        76        12      90       20      100     TOTAL 348

ENTER REQUEST
CHAIRS
              WAREHOUSE1    WAREHOUSE2    WAREHOUSE3
                 789          234            12          TOTAL 1035

ENTER REQUEST
```

Note that the message ENTER REQUEST is printed after each request has been satisfied. If the dispatcher enters an invalid request, the system should print an appropriate error message to force him to correct his request.

b. How would you design a program to update the master file? Do so.

4. Station WKNE meteorologist has access to a master file containing weather data on most of the cities that lie within a 50-mile radius of the WKNE broadcasting station. Each record contains the name of the city and its record high and low temperatures for each of the past 20 years. The master file records have the following layout:

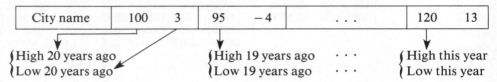

| City name | 100 | 3 | 95 | − 4 | . . . | 120 | 13 |

{High 20 years ago / Low 20 years ago   {High 19 years ago · · · / Low 19 years ago · · ·   {High this year / Low this year

a. Write a program to read a data file where each record contains the name of a city and the corresponding high and low temperatures for the day. These records have the following form:

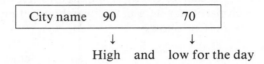

| City name | 90 | 70 |

↓　　↓
High　and　low for the day

The program should list the high and low temperatures of the day for each city and indicate whether any temperature records were broken during the day. A typical listing might be:

```
CITY          HIGH   LOW
ATMORE         98     70
BEULAH         95     68   PREVIOUS RECORD HI WAS 94 IN 1971
CHUMUCKLA      92     65   PREVIOUS RECORD LO WAS 66 IN 1979
MILTON         98     62
MARYESTHER    100     58   PREVIOUS RECORD HI WAS 98 IN 1974
                           PREVIOUS RECORD LO WAS 60 IN 1981
PACE           94     71   PREVIOUS RECORD LO WAS 72 IN 1984
```

Be sure to update the master file when record temperatures are broken; i.e., change the records in the master file to identify new highs or lows.

b. Design an on-line inquiry system to allow the meteorologist to perform the following functions:

　i. Key in a city name and a year and list the high and low for that city and year.

　ii. Key in a city name and identify the year(s) of its record high and low for the last 20 years. Print the city, year(s), and record high and low.

　iii. Key in a year and identify the city (cities) with the record high and low for that year.

　iv. Produce a listing arranged by year, identifying the record high and low for each city during the year. Over the 20-year period the output might be as follows:

```
  YEAR    CITIES        HI    LO

  1966    ATMORE        94    15
          BEULAH        91    21
          CHUMUCKLA     96    16
          MILTON        89    23
          MARYESTHER    90    20
          PACE          94     9

  1967    ATMORE        98    10
          BEULAH        94    16
          CHUMUCKLA     89    14
                   .
                   .
                   .
  1985    ATMORE        91    10
          BEULAH        90    12
                   .
                   .
          PACE          99    20
```

5. Each record of a direct-access file contains the bank account number of a customer, the name of the customer, and a balance amount. Write a program to

   a. Create such a direct-access file.

   b. Subtract from each account a monthly service charge fee of $6.50.

   c. List all records at any given time during the program.

   d. Change the name of a customer.

   e. Delete specified records.

   f. Compute and print the total amount deposited by all customers.

   g. Accept an account number and a deposit (positive number) or a debit (negative number), and update the balance of that account.

   h. Print the account number and customer name for any account in debit. Print the debit, to which is added a $10.00 penalty charge.

   i. Add new account numbers whenever needed.

   j. Provide the bank with a current list of accounts with balances exceeding $100,000.

6. At the end of the semester, students' final grades are recorded in a file called GRADE ROSTER FILE. The file is organized sequentially using students' social security numbers as a key. Identical social security numbers occur in groups, i.e., a group contains a particular student's grades in every course taken by the student, for example

GRADE–ROSTER–FILE

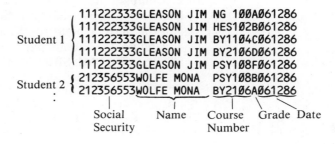

The Registrar's office also has a list of student names organized sequentially by social security key on a disk file called STUDENT ADMISSION FILE. In addition to the student's name and social security number, each disk record contains the student's current cumulative hours (credits), cumulative grade point, major field of study, and classification. An example of STUDENT ADMISSION FILE is:

STUDENT ADMISSION FILE

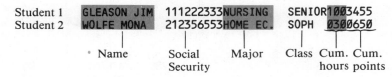

| | | Name | Social Security | Major | Class | Cum. hours | Cum. points |

Accumulation of Hours and Points

3 credits A = 3 × 4 = 12 cum. pts.
2 credits B = 2 × 3 = 6 cum. pts.
4 credits F = 4 × 0 = 0 cum. pts.

Total credits = 9 Cum. pts. = 18

Since the records of the GRADE ROSTER FILE indicate neither the number of credits nor the verbal descriptions of the courses, a file called COURSE CATALOG FILE is used as a course identification directory for looking up the number of credits for each course and the corresponding verbal description. Courses are identified by their three-digit course numbers. An example of such a file is shown below:

COURSE CATALOG FILE

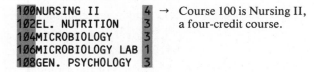

→ Course 100 is Nursing II, a four-credit course.

Write a program that will:

1. Read the GRADE ROSTER FILE and print each student's end-of-semester grade report.
2. Compute the student's grade point average for the semester, as well as his/her cumulative grade point average.
3. Print the total hours for the semester and the total cumulative hours.
4. Update the cumulative points and cumulative hours in file called STUDENT-ADMISSION-FILE.

The student's end-of-semester grade report should have the following form:

```
┌─────────────────────────────────────────────────────────────────────────────┐
│ FIELD STUDY   CLASS    STUDENT NAME        DATE        SS. NUMBER             │
│ NURSING       SENIOR   GLEASON JIM         06 12 86    111222333             │
│ ****************************************************************************** │
│ COURSE        NUMBER   DESCRIPTION        HOURS  GRADE   POINTS   GPA         │
│ **************CUMULATIVE TOTALS           100            345.5                │
│ NG            100      NURSING II          4      A       16.0                │
│ HES           102      EL. NUTRITION       3      B        9.0                │
│ BY1           104      MICROBIOLOGY        3      C        6.0                │
│ BY2           106      MICROBIOLOGY LA     1      D        1.0                │
│ PSY           108      GEN. PSYCHOLOGY     3      F        0.0                │
│ ****************************************************************************** │
│                        SEMESTER TOTALS    14            32.0    2.285        │
│                        CUM.     TOTALS    114           377.5   3.311        │
└─────────────────────────────────────────────────────────────────────────────┘
```

The relationships between the various transaction files and the master file is shown in the following diagram which illustrates the way in which data should be captured from the various files to produce a complete end-of-semester grade report.

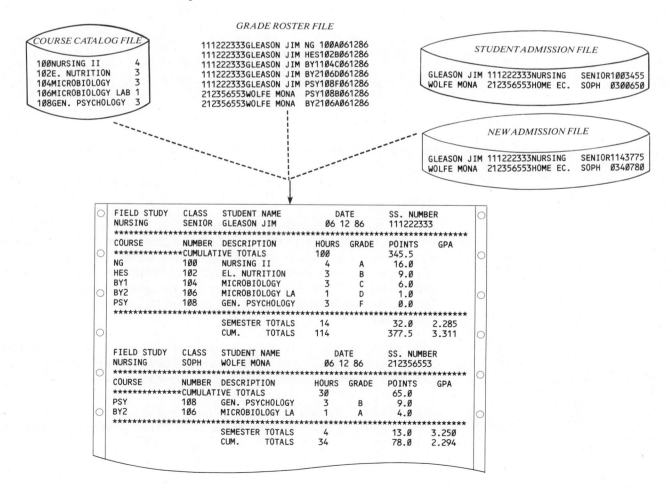

7. A direct-access file PASSENGER FILE is stored on disk and contains the names of passengers and their corresponding seat numbers. The record key for the file is the passenger name. Write a program to allow a counter agent to interact with the file and perform the following functions in any order at any given time from his/her terminal:

1. Assign a seat number to a passenger whose name is accepted from the terminal. Both the name and seat number are then added to the file.

2. Obtain at any given time a passenger list showing each passenger name in alphabetical order and his/her seat number.

3. Cancel passenger reservations: a passenger name is accepted from the terminal and then deleted from the file.

4. Look up the seat number of any given passenger.

5. Change a passenger's seat number to another seat number.

6. Bring the on-line session to a close at any given time.

The initial passenger file might be similar to the following one:

```
ARMONK K    050
SIMMONS S   100      Assume this indexed file
SIMS L      033      is already stored on the disk
SIMS P      077
       .      .
       .      .
       .      .
```

The program should react to possible error situations as follows:

1. Ask the agent to retype the code for a desired function if that code is mistyped.

2. Since the file is organized by name key and since each name must be unique in the file, the program should tell the agent to extend names with a numeric digit if a duplicate name is encountered while the agent is trying to assign a seat number. For example, if JONES M is already present in the file and another JONES M is to be assigned a seat, the agent will enter JONES M 1 for the new name and then assign a seat number; that transaction will then be recorded on disk.

3. In tasks 3, 4, and 5, the agent should be asked to retype any names that have been spelled incorrectly on the terminal. The system will know that such names are incorrect because they will not be present in the file.

A typical session between the agent and the terminal is shown in Figure 9.14. The following inquiry codes are used by the agent to carry out the six functions discussed earlier:

LI: List the passengers in alphabetical order (along with their seat numbers)

RE: Assign seat numbers to passengers (reservation)

CH: Change a passenger seat to another seat

SE: Look up a passenger's seat (search)

CA: Cancel a reservation (delete name of passenger)

TE: Terminate session

8. Modify the airline reservation program of Figure 9.14 so that

a. The agent can print out the number of seats that have been assigned so far.

b. The agent can enter a seat number and determine the name of its occupant.

c. The system will print an error message if the agent assigns a seat number that has already been given to another passenger.

d. The agent can print out a list of all unreserved seats.

e. The agent can print out the seating arrangement of the airplane starting with row 1. Each row contains four seats, and there are 40 rows. Place the name of each passenger in his/her seating position. For example:

Row 1	ADAMS J	SKULLS K	DENNIS M	*****
Row 2	*****	SIMS L	*****	LONG G
Row 3	WONG K	*****	BELL P	BELL M
Row 4	ARTEMIS L	GORDON K	SUWAMI L	JENKINS L

9. A hospital maintains a patient file where each record contains the following information:

a. Patient identification number (record key).

b. Patient name.

c. Date of admission and date of discharge (latter field is initially blank). Express the dates in Julian form and omit the year. For example 033 is February 2nd and 364 is December 30th.

d. Weight in and weight out (the latter is left blank until the patient's discharge).

e. Name of patient's doctor.

f. A maximum of 10 drugs to which the patient is allergic. This particular entry is comprised of one data item specifying the number of allergies, followed by a table containing a maximum of ten drugs, for example

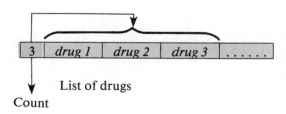

List of drugs

Count

```
LI                                          DOBERMAN J    SEAT 022 CANCELLED
***LIST PASSENGERS                          ............................
NAMES          SEAT                         ENTER SELECTION
                                            CA
ARMONK S       050                          ***CANCELLATION
SIMMONS K      100    Initial indexed file  ENTER NAME
SIMS L         033    stored on disk.       ARMONK K
SIMS P         077                          NO SUCH PASSENGER EXISTS
............................                ENTER NAME
ENTER SELECTION                             ARMONK S
RT                                          ARMONK S      SEAT 050 CANCELLED
INVALID INQUIRY CODE                        ............................
                                            ENTER SELECTION
............................                LI
ENTER SELECTION                             ***LIST PASSENGERS
RE                                          NAMES          SEAT
***RESERVATION
ENTER NAME                                  SIMMONS K      100
DOBERMAN J                                  SIMS L         076
ENTER SEAT                                  SIMS L 1       074
22                                          SIMS P         077
SEAT 022 CONFIRMED FOR DOBERMAN J           ............................
                                            ENTER SELECTION
............................                SE
ENTER SELECTION                             ***SEAT LOOK-UP
SIMS L                                      ENTER NAME
INVALID INQUIRY CODE                        SIMMONS K
                                            SIMMONS K      SEAT NUMBER: 100
............................                ............................
ENTER SELECTION                             ENTER SELECTION
RE                                          SE
***RESERVATION                              ***SEAT LOOK-UP
ENTER NAME                                  ENTER NAME
SIMS L                                      SIMS B
DUPLICATE NAME; USE NAME EXTENSION          NO SUCH PASSENGER EXISTS
ENTER NAME                                  ENTER NAME
SIMS L 1                                    SIMS P
ENTER SEAT                                  SIMS P         SEAT NUMBER:077
55                                          ............................
SEAT 055 CONFIRMED FOR SIMS L 1             ENTER SELECTION
                                            RE
............................                ***RESERVATION
ENTER SELECTION                             ENTER NAME
LI                                          YOUNG F
***LIST PASSENGERS                          ENTER SEAT
NAMES          SEAT                         106
                                            SEAT 106 CONFIRMED FOR YOUNG F
ARMONK S       050                          ............................
DOBERMAN J     022                          ENTER SELECTION
SIMMONS K      100                          RE
SIMS L         033                          ***RESERVATION
SIMS L 1       055                          ENTER NAME
SIMS P         077                          MARRIOTT E
                                            ENTER SEAT
............................                063
ENTER SELECTION                             SEAT 063 CONFIRMED FOR MARRIOTT E
CH                                          ............................
***CHANGE SEATS                             ENTER SELECTION
SIMS L                                      LI
ENTER NEW SEAT NUMBER                       ***LIST PASSENGERS
76                                          NAMES          SEAT
SEAT 076 CONFIRMED FOR SIMS L
                                            MARRIOTT E     063
............................                SIMMONS K      100
ENTER SELECTION                             SIMS L         076
CH                                          SIMS L 1       074
***CHANGE SEATS                             SIMS P         077
ENTER NAME                                  YOUNG F        106
SIMS L1
NO SUCH NAME: RETYPE                        ............................
ENTER NAME                                  ENTER SELECTION
SIMS L 1                                    TE
ENTER NEW SEAT NUMBER
74
SEAT 074 CONFIRMED FOR SIMS L 1

............................
ENTER SELECTION
CA
***CANCELLATION
ENTER NAME
DOBERMAN J
```

Legend

LI: List
RE: Reserve seat
CH: Change seat
SE: Search seat
CA: Cancel
TE: Terminate

to next column

FIGURE 9.14
ON-LINE INQUIRY SYSTEM

g. A table, initially consisting of 10 blank entries, to be used to record drugs administered to the patient and corresponding dosage (expressed in units). The format is as follows:

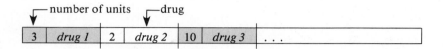

Write a program to create a direct file containing the information in items (a)–(g).

Then write another program to allow the medical staff to ask questions about and to update a particular patient record. For each of the following actions, the patient's I.D. number and a special query code should be entered:

aa. Enter a patient I.D. number and print the name of the patient's doctor.

bb. Print the list of drugs to which the patient is allergic.

cc. Record any drug administered to the patient and the number of units.

dd. Print the list of drugs administered to the patient.

ee. Delete a particular drug from the patient's list of drug allergies.

ff. Add a drug to the patient's list of drug allergies (limited to a maximum of 10).

gg. Accept a particular drug and determine if the patient is allergic to it.

hh. When a patient is discharged from the hospital, fill in his/her discharge date.

ii. Compute the number of days the patient spent at the hospital.

jj. Record the patient's weight on his/her discharge day.

kk. Print the patient's total room cost ($200 per day). Print the patient's total weight gain or loss. Print the total number of days he/she spent at the hospital.

ll. Compute each patient's drug bill. To produce this bill you will need to read a sequential file DRUG, where all drugs and corresponding unit costs have been recorded. Print each of the patient's drugs and its corresponding cost, as well as the total cost.

10. Each record of an input file consists of three entries: a region number, a salesperson number and a sales amount. All salespersons records are grouped by region, and within each region records are grouped by employee numbers.

Write a program to produce a summary report of sales by salesperson and by region. The salesperson's subtotal should appear on the same line as the last sales entry. The printout should indicate the total sales amount for all regions and should skip to the top of a new page whenever a page consists of more than 23 lines (a page includes top-of-page headings). Major and minor headings should appear at the top of each numbered page. A sample output file is shown in Figure 9.15.

```
            SALES REPORT              PAGE 1

            NUMBER     SALES   SUBTOTALS   TOTALS
REGION  9
            10888       9.00       9.00
            REGION TOTALS.................   9.00

REGION 10
            11111      54.78
            11111      60.00
            11111      70.00     184.78

            22222      67.00
            22222      78.90     145.90

            33333      34.00
            33333      56.78      90.78

            REGION TOTALS................. 421.46
```
```
            SALES REPORT              PAGE 2

            NUMBER     SALES   SUBTOTALS   TOTALS
REGION 11
            44444      78.90      78.90

            55555      67.00
            55555      78.00     145.00

            REGION TOTALS................. 223.90

REGION 12
            66666      89.75      89.75

            REGION TOTALS.................  89.75

REGION 13
            77777      87.69
```
```
            SALES REPORT              PAGE 3

            NUMBER     SALES   SUBTOTALS   TOTALS
REGION 13
            77777      78.00
            77777       9.80
            77777      89.00
            77777      45.00     309.49

            REGION TOTALS................. 309.49

REGION 14
            88888       5.60
            88888       9.80
            88888      70.00
            88888      30.00
            88888      20.00
            88888      34.00
```
```
            SALES REPORT              PAGE 4

            NUMBER     SALES   SUBTOTALS   TOTALS
REGION 14
            88888      54.00
            88888      20.00
            88888      50.00     293.40

            REGION TOTALS................. 293.40
        TOTALS                         1347.00
```

page consists of 23 lines

note two blank lines at bottom of page

page consists of 23 lines

note four blank lines at bottom of page

note four blank lines at bottom of page

FIGURE 9.15
A MULTI LEVEL CONTROL
BREAK PROBLEM

11. The Tricity College library staff is thinking about using computers to assist them in dealing with the high volume of book transactions. Four types of transactions must be considered: (1) books checked in, (2) books checked out, (3) new books put into circulation, (4) old books withdrawn from circulation.

Books have an 8-digit numeric code identification, the last two digits of which indicate a multicopy identification number:

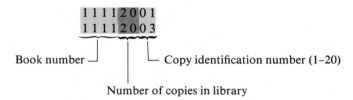

The library clerks deal manually with four types of files:

1. The CHECK IN OUT FILE.

This file consists of a daily list of books that have been checked in or checked out. The record layout for each file is as follows:

Item	Nature
1	Book number identification
2	Disposition code (1 = check in, 2 = check out)
3	Julian date (025 means Jan. 25, 365 is Dec. 31)
4	Patron's identity (1 = faculty, 2 = student)
5	Patron's telephone number

2. The NEW BOOK FILE.

This file consists of books that have been either purchased or donated and do not exist in the master file. The record layout for such file records is:

Item	Nature
1	Book number identification
2	Year of edition
3	Disposition status (1 = available, 2 = reserve)
4	Author
5	Acquisition code (1 = purchased, 2 = donation)

3. The DELETE FILE.

Transaction records in this file allow the librarian to delete books from the master file or to change the status field of a particular book. The record layout for such file records is:

Item	Nature
1	Book number identification
2	Change code

Change code:
- 1 = delete
- 2 = make status available
- 3 = make status reserve

┌─All 1130 books are deleted from the inventory.

```
1 1 3 0 | 1
1 4 0 0 | 2    ← change code
```

└─All 1400 books are now changed to available status (however many there were).

4. The MASTER FILE.

All records in the master file have the following layout:

Item	Nature
1	Book identification number
2	Author
3	Edition Year
4	Status disposition (1 = on loan, 2 = on shelf)
5	Date loaned (0 if book is not loaned)
6	Patron's identity (1 = faculty, 2 = student, 3 = on the shelf)
7	Acquisition code (1 = purchased, 2 = donation)
8	Reserve status (1 = available, 2 = reserve)
9	Patron's telephone number

Write a program to perform the following tasks:

a. Create the four files described above and store them on disk. Assume the records are arranged sequentially according to the 8-digit book identification number.

b. Print the four disk files.

c. i. Assume that all disk file records are in sequence and that all transaction records are valid; i.e., transaction keys all have corresponding keys in the master file. Update MASTER FILE with CHECK IN OUT FILE.

ii. Print a listing of the updated file.

iii. Print a list of telephone numbers of patrons who have overdue books. A book is overdue if it has been kept 30 days or more. A fine of 10 cents a day is charged for each day over 30 days. This report should indicate the telephone number, the number of days overdue, the original checkout day, and the corresponding fine in dollars and cents. No fines are listed for faculty members. Books that have not been returned after a 100-day overdue period are considered stolen. Flag such books on the output to allow the librarian to charge the patron for the cost of the book plus the 100-day fine. (These books will be deleted in part (f) of this exercise by their inclusion in the DELETE FILE.)

iv. List each book identification number of MASTER FILE and summarize for each volume the number of copies in (on the shelf) or out (on loan). The report should be similar to:

```
 ○ | BOOK IDENTIFICATION    IN    OUT | ○
    |                                  |
    |    1111 20 03                    |
    |    1111 20 08                    |
 ○ |    1111 20 17                    | ○
    |                      3     17    |
    |    2000 18 02                    |
    |    2000 18 12                    |
 ○ |            :         2     16    | ○
```

v. Determine the percentage of books currently held by faculty and the percentage of books currently held by the students.

d. i. Update the current MASTER FILE with NEW BOOK FILE; i.e., merge the two files. It is understood that no book in NEW BOOK FILE exists in the current MASTER FILE. (See part (g) for additions of books that currently exist in the master file.) Print an updated inventory listing.

ii. During the update pass (i.e., do not reprocess the master file), keep track of all the identification numbers of books that have been donated, and print a list of such titles at the conclusion of the update process.

e. i. Identify any author who has written two or more different books. Specify the author and corresponding list of books.

ii. Produce a list of books arranged by ascending author order.

f. i. Update MASTER FILE with DELETE FILE.

ii. Print the list of books that have been deleted (all such books are assumed to be currently on the shelf). Remember, there may be more than one of the same title.

iii. Any book that has not been returned 100 days after the checkout date is considered stolen and hence should be deleted and brought to the attention of the librarian by means of an appropriate message.

iv. Print the updated file.

g. On many occasions, the library purchases additional copies of existing books. Design a system to allow the librarian to add these books to the master file. Such purchases of new books can give rise to the following situations: Either the new books purchased need to be added to similar copies already on the shelf, in which case the quantity of existing books on hand needs to be changed; or the books to be added are newer editions, in which case all books with edition years less than that of the new edition must be taken out of circulation, i.e., deleted. If this is the case, the librarian would like to obtain a list of all books that are to be deleted so that these entries can be added to the DELETE file of part (f). Write the code to take care of these possibilities.

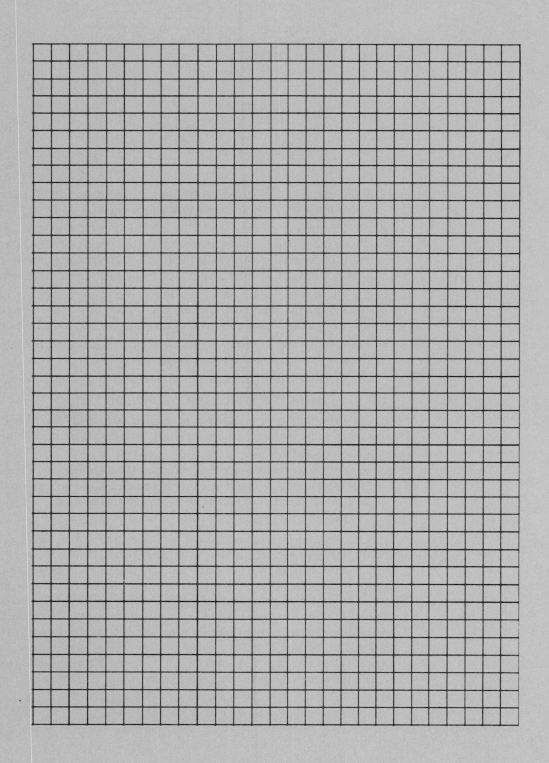

Appendix A
Conditional Statements
The **IMPLICIT** Statement

A.1 THE LOGICAL IF/GO TO STATEMENT

The general form of the IF/GO TO statement is

> IF (*condition*) GO TO *statement number*

If the condition is true, control is transferred to *statement number*. If the condition if false, control is transferred to the statement following the IF.

EXAMPLES

Logical IF Statements	*Meaning*
1 IF(X .EQ. 0.)GO TO 5 A = 4.	If X = 0., transfer to statement 5; otherwise (if X is less than or greater than 0), process the next statement.
IF(CITY .EQ. 'PARIS')GO TO 9 CITY='ROME'	CITY must be declared as CHARACTER data. IF CITY = 'PARIS' transfer to 9, otherwise store 'ROME' in location CITY.
4 IF((X-Y)**2 .LT. Z)GO TO 40 8 IF(Z .GT. 2.)GO TO 60	If $(X - Y)^2 < Z$, process statement 40; otherwise (if $(X - Y)^2 \geq Z$), fall through and execute statement 8.
5 IF(SQRT(X) .GE. 2.)GO TO 50 WRITE(6,11)X	If $\sqrt{X} \geq 2$, go to 50. If $\sqrt{X} < 2$, process the next sequential statement.
2 IF(X+Y .NE. (J-K))GO TO 70 READ(5,5)A	If $X + Y = J - K$, process the next statement; otherwise go to statement 70.

A.2 THE ARITHMETIC IF STATEMENT

The arithmetic IF allows a three-way transfer out of a decision block, as opposed to the two-way transfer of a logical IF. For example, when comparing two numbers, A and B, the decision block can have three exits: one if A is less than B, a second one if

A equals B, and third one if A is greater than B. The flowchart symbol for an arithmetic IF is:

The colon (:) can be interpreted as "compared to."

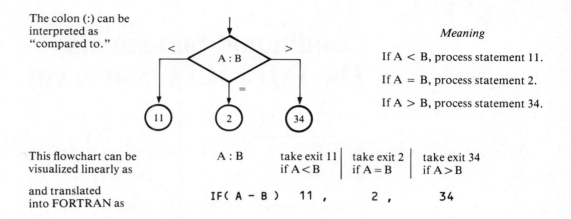

Meaning

If A < B, process statement 11.

If A = B, process statement 2.

If A > B, process statement 34.

This flowchart can be visualized linearly as

A : B	take exit 11 if A < B	take exit 2 if A = B	take exit 34 if A > B

and translated into FORTRAN as

IF(A − B)   11 ,   2 ,   34

The general form of the arithmetic decision statement is:

> IF (*expression*) *statement number 1,statement number 2,statement number 3*

where   *expression* is any FORTRAN expression
statement number 1, 2, and *3* are FORTRAN statement numbers defined in the program.

The IF statement can be interpreted as follows:

1. Evaluate the expression.
2. If the result is negative, transfer to *statement number 1*.
   If the result is equal to zero, transfer to *statement number 2*.
   If the result is positive, transfer to *statement number 3*.

It should be noted that the three statement numbers in the IF statement always correspond to the sequence: less than 0, equal to 0, and greater than 0, in that order. The reader can visualize this sequence as follows:

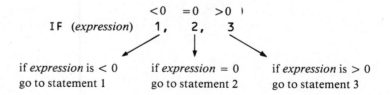

	<0	=0	>0
IF (*expression*)	1,	2,	3

if *expression* is < 0   if *expression* = 0   if *expression* is > 0
go to statement 1   go to statement 2   go to statement 3

Two numbers, A and B, can be compared in an IF statement using the expression A − B as follows:

IF(A−B)11,2,34   means
if A − B < 0 or if A < B, then go to 11
if A − B = 0 or if A = B, then go to 2
if A − B > 0 or if A > B, then go to 34

In some cases a decision may require only a two-way transfer, in which case appropriate IF statement numbers can be combined as follows:

```
IF(A-B)1,5,1      means if A = B, go to 5; otherwise go to 1 (unequal).
IF(A-B)11,11,4    means if A ≤ B, go to 11; otherwise go to 4 (greater).
```

Some valid IF statements and their meanings are:

IF Statements	*Meaning*
IF(X)1,3,5	If X < 0, go to 1; if X = 0, go to 3; if X > 0, go to 5.
IF(X - (-4))1,1,2	These two statements are logically the same and are
IF(X + 4)1,1,2	equivalent to comparing X with −4.
IF(X + Y*Z)3,4,3	If X + Y*Z = 0, go to 4; otherwise go to 3.
IF(2.*X + (Z-4)*X**2)1,2,3	Evaluate the expression and transfer to 1, 2, or 3

A.3 THE COMPUTED GO TO STATEMENT

The computed GO TO statement is a useful and convenient statement that transfers to different points in a program with just one FORTRAN statement. The general form of the computed GO TO is:

> GO TO (*statement number 1, statement number-2,..., statement number-n*), *variable*

where   *variable* must be an *integer* variable name and *statement number 1,2,..., n* are FORTRAN statement numbers defined in the program.

If the value of the integer variable is 1, control is transferred to *statement number 1*. If the value of the integer variable is 2, control is transferred to *statement number 2*. In general, if the value of the variable is *i*, control is passed to the *i*th statement in the list of statement numbers.

EXAMPLE

	Meaning
GO TO (3,57,100,4) N	If N = 1, go to 3
	N = 2, go to 57
Note the comma!	N = 3, go to 100
	N = 4, go to 4

If N is less than 1 or exceeds the number of statement numbers within the parentheses, control is passed to the statement immediately following the computed GO TO.

The reader is cautioned that an integer variable must be used in the computed GO TO; no expressions are allowed, i.e., GO TO(2,3,4),2*I is invalid, since 2*I is not a variable.

Consider, for example, the following problem. We want to write out the meaning associated with a class code read from a data record. The possible codes and meanings are:

Class Code	Meaning
1	Freshman
2	Sophomore
3	Junior
4	Senior
5	Graduate

The program shown in Figure A.1 could be used to solve this problem. The flowchart version of this program is shown in Figure A.2.

```
      CHARACTER CLASS*12
      READ(5,6)KODE
      GO TO(15,20,25,30,35),KODE
      PRINT*, 'INVALID CODE'          If KODE is not equal to 1,2,3,4, or 5, then go to
      STOP                            the next statement and print an error message.
   15 CLASS = 'FRESHMAN'
      GO TO 40
   20 CLASS = 'SOPHOMORE'
      GO TO 40
   25 CLASS = 'JUNIOR'
      GO TO 40
   30 CLASS = 'SENIOR'
      GO TO 40
   35 CLASS = 'GRADUATE'
   40 PRINT*, CLASS
      STOP
      END
```

FIGURE A.1
COMPUTED GO TO
EXAMPLE

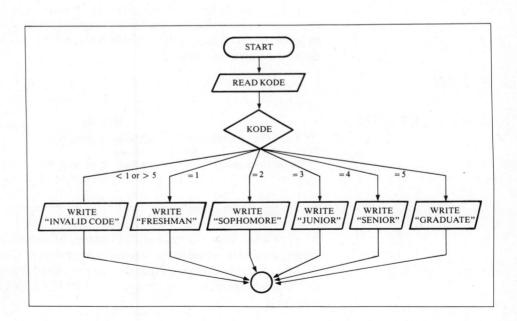

FIGURE A.2
FLOWCHART OF A
COMPUTED GO TO
EXAMPLE

A.4 THE DO STATEMENT

The general form of the DO statement is:

> DO *statement number index = initial, test* [*, increment*]

where   *statement number* is the number of the last statement in the body of the loop, sometimes called the *foot* of the loop.

Restrictions. The increment must not evaluate to 0. The foot of loop cannot be a GO TO, IF THEN ELSE, STOP, END, arithmetic IF, RETURN, or another DO statement.

Except for the fact that *statement number* need not be a CONTINUE statement, this DO loop is identical to the DO structure discussed in chapter 4.

A.5 THE IMPLICIT STATEMENT

In programs that make extensive use of integers and/or real variables, it becomes cumbersome to list all such variables in explicit mode declaration statements. For this reason the IMPLICIT specification statement allows the programmer to formulate his/her own conventions for type declaration. For example, the statement IMPLICIT REAL (I) would cause all variables with names beginning with the character I to be real. It is also possible to specify a range of letters in alphabetical order in the IMPLICIT statement; for example, the statement IMPLICIT INTEGER (A–D) would make any variable beginning with A, B, C, or D an integer variable. The general form of the implicit statement is:

> IMPLICIT *type* (*a*[,*a*] . . .)[,*type*(*a*[,*a*] . . .)] . . .

where   *type* can be INTEGER, REAL, or other mode type,
    a can be a single letter or a range of letters denoted by $l_1 - l_2$, where l_1 and l_2 are single letters of the alphabet.

Implicit typing does not necessarily negate the automatic implicit roles for integer or real variables, i.e., IMPLICIT INTEGER (C–F) does *not* mean that only variables starting with C through F will be integer variables—variables starting with I through N will *also* be integer variables.

Examples

1. IMPLICIT INTEGER(A,C–F),REAL(I–N)
2. IMPLICIT REAL (C), INTEGER (A,B)
3. IMPLICIT CHARACTER (G,I), CHARACTER * 15 (N)
4. IMPLICIT CHARACTER*3 (A–D)

In the first statement variables beginning with A, C, D, E, and F are implicitly integer; all other variables are real. In the second statement, variable names starting with the letter A or B become integer variables, (along with those starting with I–N). REAL (C) does not change the mode of C since it is implicitly real. In the third statement, any variable starting with the letter G or I will be a character variable of length 1, while all variables starting with the letter N will be character variables of length 15. In the fourth statement, all variables starting with A, B, C, or D will be character variables of length 3.

The positioning of the IMPLICIT statement within the FORTRAN program is shown in Figure A.3.

Comment statements	FUNCTION, SUBROUTINE or BLOCK DATA statements		
	FORMAT and ENTRY statements	PARAMETER statements	IMPLICIT statements
			COMMON and other specification statements
		DATA statements	Statement function statements
			Executable statements
End statement			

FIGURE A.3
ORDER OF FORTRAN STATEMENTS

Appendix B
Substrings

B.1 CHARACTER SUBSTRING REFERENCES

Character constants are examples of character strings. The **CHARACTER** specification statement reserves a specific number of character positions for a particular character variable (but it does not generally initialize character variables to blanks). In many programming applications it is important to be able to process one or more characters (substrings) within a given string. FORTRAN allows us to operate on substrings through an index mechanism that identifies the position of a character within a string. The general form of a substring reference is:

> *string variable* (*start position* : *last position*)

where   *string variable* is the name of a **CHARACTER** variable.

        start position identifies the position of the first character of the substring; if omitted, the default position is 1.

        last position identifies the position of the last character in the substring; if omitted, the default position is the position of the last character in the string.

Both start position and last position can be arithmetic expressions.

EXAMPLE 1:
NONSUBSCRIPTED
SUBSTRINGS

```
CHARACTER LINE*20,A*5,B*7,C*4,D*4
```

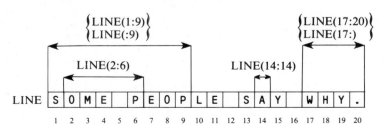

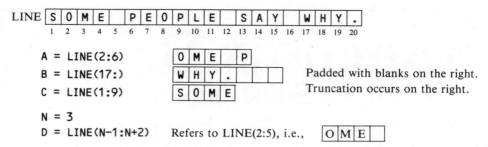

In general, LINE(I:J) where I ≤ J refers to the segment of the string starting at position I up to and including the Jth position. The values of I and J must be such that 1 ≤ I ≤ J ≤ length of LINE as declared in the CHARACTER statement.

LINE(2:6) is just like any other CHARACTER variable and can be used in the same way as other character variables in IF statements, input/output statements, and so forth. It looks different, but it is just another character variable!

EXAMPLE 2: SUBSCRIPTED SUBSTRINGS

Character arrays are conceptually similar to numeric arrays. For example, if TEXT is an array declared as CHARACTER*5 TEXT(6), then TEXT(1), TEXT(2), …, TEXT(6) are the six elements that make up array TEXT. Each array element consists of five characters, for example, array TEXT might have the following configuration:

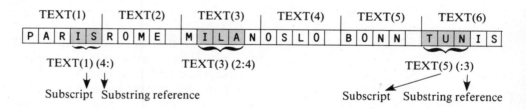

Analyze the following:

Subscript Form	Example	
		L I
		`A B C 1 4 3 + – * T H E D O G` `1`
constant	L(3)	Third element of array (+ – *).
constant/substring	L(3)(1:1)	First character of the third array element (+).
expression	L(2*I)	2*I = 2, so this refers to the second element, i.e., characters 143.
expression/substring	L(2*I)(2:3)	This refers to characters 2 and 3 of the second element, which are 4 and 3.
expression/substring	L(2*I)(I:5*I–3)	This evaluates to L(2)(1:2), so it refers to characters 1 through 2 of the second element (14).

B.2 SUBSTRINGS IN REPLACEMENT STATEMENTS

For assignment purposes, substring variables can appear on the left of the equal sign in a replacement statement. The DATA statement can also be used to assign characters to substrings.

EXAMPLE

```
CHARACTER DAY*9,M*3
DATA M /'NES'/
```

DAY

DAY = 'SUNDAY'	S U N D A Y ▢ ▢ ▢	Trailing blanks provided.
DAY(1:3) = 'WED'	W E D D A Y ▢ ▢ ▢	Replace first 3 characters.
DAY(7:) = 'DAY'	W E D D A Y D A Y	Replace last 3 characters.
DAY(4:6) = M(2:)	W E D E S ▢ D A Y	Replace characters 4, 5, and 6.

No substring may be "equated" to a substring of the same parent string if there is a resulting overlap in position assignments, for example, the following assignment is invalid due to the overlap of characters in positions 3 and 4:

```
DAY(2:4) = DAY(3:5)        Overlapping characters not allowed.
DAY(2:5) = DAY(6:9)        Valid assignment, no overlap.
```

This restriction is necessary because a character string assignment normally takes place in several steps (unlike replacement of numbers), and hence part of a string might be altered before the completion of the assignment. It can be circumvented by using a temporary variable:

```
TEMP = DAY(3:5)        where TEMP is a character variable at least three positions long.
DAY(2:4) = TEMP
```

B.3 SUBSTRINGS IN INPUT/OUTPUT STATEMENTS

Substrings can appear in list-directed and format-controlled input/output statements.

EXAMPLE 1

```
CHARACTER FAMILY*16
FAMILY = 'MARC ANDREW GOOD'
WRITE(6,1) FAMILY(13:)              will print GOOD
PRINT*,FAMILY(:5),FAMILY(13:)       will print MARC GOOD
```

EXAMPLE 2

```
CHARACTER FAMILY*16
DATA FAMILY/16*' '/
READ*,FAMILY(8:),FAMILY(1:6),AGE

PRINT*, FAMILY
PRINT*,FAMILY(8:),FAMILY(1:6),AGE
```

Input Record

'MANSOOR', 'TIM', 17.

TIMbbbbbMANSOORbb
MANSOORbbTIMbbb 17.

Nine characters will be printed   Six characters will be printed

B.4 SUBSTRINGS IN IF STATEMENTS

Substring variables can be used in IF statements in the same way that character variables are used.

EXAMPLE 1

Count the occurrences of the letter E in a word.

```
CHARACTER WORD*8
WORD = 'SENTENCE'
K = 0
DO 5 I = 1,8
    IF(WORD(I:I) .EQ. 'E')K = K+1
5 CONTINUE
PRINT*,K          The value 3 will be printed.
```

EXAMPLE 2

Replace the words MIGUEL and LAURA in an 80 character line of text by the words MICHEL and LAURE.

```
CHARACTER TEXT*80
READ*,TEXT
DO 5 I = 1,73
    IF(TEXT(I:I+7) .EQ. ' MIGUEL ')THEN
        TEXT(I:I+7) = ' MICHEL '
    ELSE
        IF(TEXT(I:I+6) .EQ. ' LAURA ') THEN
            TEXT(I:I+6) = ' LAURE '
        ENDIF
    ENDIF
5 CONTINUE
```

In this case we are searching for strings of seven and eight characters (two blanks plus the name) and replacing it with different strings of the same length.

B.5 CONCATENATION OF STRINGS

To chain or fuse two or more strings into one string, we use the double slash operator // between the strings, i.e., *string 1*//*string 2* fuses *string 1* and *string 2* into one string. No additional spaces are inserted between the strings.

EXAMPLE

```
CHARACTER A*3,TAG1*6,TAG2*7,TAG3*5,B*5,TAG4*8
A = 'XYZ'
B = 'HI'
TAG1 = 'ABC'//'DEF'        TAG1 =  A B C D E F
TAG2 = A//'DEF'            TAG2 =  X Y Z D E F
TAG3 = A//' '//A           TAG3 =  X Y Z   X          Truncation occurs.
TAG4 = B//A(1:2)           TAG4 =  H I     X Y        B has size 5.
PRINT*,A//'CORPORATION'    will print XYZCORPORATION
```

Note that the concatenation operator can be used in IF statements as in:

```
IF(COIN//TEMP .EQ. C(1:K+1))THEN ...
IF(A//B//C .EQ. WORD//CONT)THEN ...
```

The concatenation process can be very convenient when we want to remove one or more characters from a particular string. Suppose, for example, that we wanted to remove the first period encountered in the string TEXT = 'HE SAID TO T. CARSON' in order to obtain 'HE SAID TO T CARSON'. To do this, we need to tie the first 12 characters of TEXT to the character substring in positions 14 through 20. Hence we concatenate the first 12 characters with the last 7 characters, as follows:

```
CHARACTER*20 TEXT, TEMP
TEMP = TEXT(1:12)//TEXT(14:)
TEXT = TEMP
```

TEXT(:12)   TEXT(14:)

HE SAID TO T   ␢CARSON

TEXT was originally 20 characters long; even though we have removed one character, the length of TEXT does *not* shrink by 1—it is still 20 characters long, so there will be a blank in position 20.

The complete code to extract the first period found in a sentence is:

```
    CHARACTER*20 TEXT,TEMP             Assume TEXT contains a complete
    DO 5 I = 1,20                      sentence.
        IF(TEXT(I:I) .EQ. '.')GO TO 6  Locate the position of the period.
  5 CONTINUE
    PRINT*,'NO PERIODS FOUND'
    STOP
  6 IF(I .EQ. 20)THEN                  If the period is in position 20,
        TEMP = TEXT(:19)               retain only the first 19 characters.
    ELSE
        TEMP = TEXT(:I-1)//TEXT(I+1:)  Excise the period. Trailing blanks
    ENDIF                              are provided for TEMP.
    TEXT = TEMP                        Place text back into TEXT.
    PRINT*,TEXT
```

B.6 CHARACTER COLLATING SEQUENCE

There are two codes for the internal representation of characters. ASCII (pronounced ask-ee) and EBCDIC (pronounced ebb-si-dic).

The EBCDIC code (Extended Binary Coded Decimal Interchange code) is a code where each character is represented internally using eight bits; for example, the character A is C1 in hexadecimal or 11000001 in binary. The EBCDIC code is used by such computers as IBM, Digital PDP-11 series, and Amdahl.

The ASCII code (American Standard Code for Information Interchange) is a seven-bit code used by large computers and by most of the microcomputers.

The collating sequence for the two codes is shown in Figure B.1.

ASCII Code			EBCDIC Code		
Character	*Decimal*	*Hex*	*Character*	*Decimal*	*Hex*
space	32	20	space	64	40
!	33	21	.	75	4B
"	34	22	<	76	4C
#	35	23	(	77	4D
$	36	24	+	78	4E
%	37	25	!	79	4F
&	38	26	&	80	50
single quote	39	27	$	91	5B
(	40	28	*	92	5C
)	41	29	)	93	5D
*	42	2A	;	94	5E
+	43	2B	minus −	96	60
comma	44	2C	/	97	61
−	45	2D	comma	107	6B
.	46	2E	%	108	6C
/	47	2F	>	110	6E
0	48	30	?	111	6F
:	:	:	:	122	7A
			#	123	7B
			@	124	7C
9	57	39	single quote	125	7D
:	58	3A	=	126	7E
;	59	3B	"	127	7F
<	60	3C	a	129	81
=	61	3D	b	130	82
>	62	3E	:	:	:
?	63	3F			
@	64	40	z	169	A9
A	65	41	A	193	C1
:	:	:	:	:	:
Z	90	5A	Z	233	E9
a	97	61	0	240	F0
:	:	:	:	:	:
z	122	7A	9	249	F9

FIGURE B.1
*CHARACTER COLLATION
SEQUENCE*

B.7 CHARACTER FUNCTIONS

Four lexical functions allow the user to determine the order relationship between characters according to the collating sequence used by the computing system (see Figure B.1). These four functions are:

Function Name	Meaning	Value	Examples (Using ASCII Code)
LGE (X1,X2)	lexically $\geq$	true if $x_1 \geq x_2$	LGE ('B', 'A') is true
LGT (X1,X2)	lexically $>$	true if $x_1 > x_2$	LGT ('BAT', 'BAY') is false
LLE (X1,X2)	lexically $\leq$	true if $x_1 \leq x_2$	LLE ('a', 'A') is false
LLT (X1,X2)	lexically $<$	true if $x_1 < x_2$	LLT ('5', 'R') is true

There are several other character functions:

■ LEN (*string*) returns the length of the string.

```
M = LEN('THE DOG')        M = 7
M = LEN(LINE)             M = length of string LINE
M = LEN(ST(N-1: N+2) )    M = 4
```

■ ICHAR (*character*) returns the integer value of the internal code representing *character*. See Figure B.1 for internal character codes.

```
J = ICHAR('A')      J = 65  These values depend on the collating
K = ICHAR('D')      K = 68  sequence; ASCII code is used here.
```

■ CHAR (*integer*) returns the character corresponding to the integer value in the collating sequence. See Figure B.1 for collating sequence.

```
CHARACTER M
M = CHAR(65)              M will contain the character A, i.e., M = 'A'
```

Note that CHAR(ICHAR (*character*)) = *character,* while
ICHAR(CHAR (*integer*)) = *integer.*

■ INDEX (*string1, string2*) is used to search for the first occurrence of *string2* in *string1*. The function returns the starting position of substring *string2* within *string1*. If no *string2* is found, the value returned is 0.

```
K = INDEX('THE DOG','DO')      K = 5 DO starts at position 5 in the string.
K = INDEX('THE CAT','DOG')     K = 0 DOG does not exist in the string.
K = INDEX('YOU ARE ALL','A')   K = 5 the first occurrence of A.
K = INDEX(LINE(3:12),' ')      searches characters 3 through 12 of LINE
                               for a blank.
```

B.8 PROGRAMMING EXAMPLES

B.8.1 Word Search

Each record of a text file consists of 80 characters of uppercase text. Write the code to print the occurrence of the word "THE".

Solution. We read each 80-character record into an 82-character string called LINE, with blank spaces in the first and last positions of LINE. We then search the string for the 5-character substring ' THE '. Since LINE starts and ends with a blank space, we can capture a starting "THE" as well as a terminating "THE" in any record. The FORTRAN program is shown in Figure B.2.

```
***** WORD SEARCH PROGRAM FOR ANY WORD LENGTH
***** WORD:    WORD TO BE FOUND
***** LINE:    CONTAINS 1 LINE OF TEXT WITH BLANKS IN POSITIONS 1 AND 82
***** POINTR: IDENTIFIES LINE POSITION WHERE SEARCH IS TO START
***** POSITN: IDENTIFIES SUCCESSIVE POSITIONS OF THE WORD IN LINE
***** COUNT:   COUNTS THE OCCURRENCES OF THE WORD SEARCHED FOR
***** MAXIMN: MAXIMUM NUMBER OF TIMES WORD CAN BE FOUND IN LINE
       INTEGER POINTR, COUNT, POSITN
       CHARACTER WORD*5, LINE*82
*READ THE WORD WHOSE OCCURRENCE IS TO BE FOUND
       READ(*,*)WORD (2:)
*READ THE TEXT RECORD INTO LINE
10     READ(5, 6, END=88) LINE (2:81)
       POINTR = 1
       MAXIMN = 80/(LEN(WORD-2)+1)
       DO 30 I = 1,MAXIMN
*FIND POSITION OF FIRST LETTER OF WORD IN LINE
           POSITN = INDEX (LINE (POINTR:), WORD)
           IF (POSITN .NE. 0) THEN
               COUNT  = COUNT + 1
               POINTR = POINTR + POSITN + LEN (WORD)
           ENDIF
30     CONTINUE
88     WRITE(6,*) WORD, ' OCCURRED ', COUNT, ' TIMES '
       STOP
6      FORMAT(A)
       END
```

FIGURE B.2
A WORD SEARCH

B.8.2 Counting Words

An input file consists of an unknown number of records, where each record consists of a line of text, i.e., 80 characters of information. Write a program to compute the number of characters and words in the entire text file and determine the average word length.

Assume that no word is hyphenated from one line to the next and that punctuation characters are followed by one or more blank spaces to the right and preceded by a nonblank character to the left, i.e., the word DOG could be in any one of the following forms:

DOG. DOG DOG? DOG, DOG; DOG!

In the context of this problem, a word is a sequence of nonblank contiguous characters. If the word terminates with a punctuation symbol, the punctuation symbol is not counted as a character.

Solution. One way to proceed is to analyze each character, one at a time, and ask if that character is a nonblank character. If it is a nonblank character, we determine whether the character that follows it is a blank. If it is blank, then we have found the end of a word. The program to solve this problem is shown in Figure B.3.

```
 1: ***** COUNTING WORDS
 2: ***** LINE:   LINE OF TEXT
 3: ***** CHARS: NUMBER OF CHARACTERS
 4: ***** WORDS: NUMBER OF WORDS
 5: ***** AVE:   AVERAGE NUMBER OF WORDS
 6:        CHARACTER LINE*81, NEXT
 7:        INTEGER I,WORDS,CHARS
 8:        REAL AVE
 9:        CHARS = 0
10:        WORDS = 0
11: *FORCE A BLANK IN POSITION 81 IN CASE WORD TERMINATES AT POSITION 80
12:        LINE(81:81) = ' '
13: 10     READ(5,30,END=88)LINE(:80)
14:        DO 5 I = 1,80
15:          IF(LINE(I:I) .NE. ' ')THEN
16:            NEXT = LINE(I+1:I+1)
17:            IF(.NOT.(NEXT .EQ. '.' .OR. NEXT .EQ. ',' .OR.
18:     1        NEXT .EQ. '?' .OR. NEXT .EQ. ';'))THEN
19:              CHARS = CHARS + 1
20:              IF(NEXT .EQ. ' ')WORDS = WORDS + 1
21:            ENDIF
22:          ENDIF
23: 5      CONTINUE
24:        GO TO 10
25: 88     AVE = 1.*CHARS/WORDS
26:        WRITE(6,20)CHARS,WORDS,AVE
27:        STOP
28: 20     FORMAT(1X,'NO. CHARACTERS=',I5,'NO. WORDS=',I4,
29:     1         'AVERAGE LENGTH=',F5.1)
30: 30     FORMAT(A)
31:        END
```

FIGURE B.3
COUNTING WORDS

B.8.2 Message Encryption

Write a program to read a message and code it in such a way that each letter in the message is replaced by the "next" letter of the alphabet, for example, A will be replaced by B, ..., Y by Z, and Z by A, while all other special characters remain unchanged. Use a function that accepts a character as an argument—if the argument is a letter of the alphabet, the function returns the "next" letter, otherwise the function leaves the argument unchanged. For example, the message I AM 30 YRS. OLD! becomes J BN 30 ZST. PME!

Solution. Many versions of FORTRAN use the ASCII code (see Figure B.1) to represent letters of the alphabet; for example the letter A is coded internally as 65, the letter B as 66, C as 67, .., Y as 89, and Z as 90. Thus, for any letter L of the alphabet, the "next" letter has an internal code value equal to the (internal code of L) + 1. Hence if L is any letter of the alphabet other than Z, the letter following L is

LETTER = CHAR(ICHAR(L) + 1)

For example, if the ASCII code for Y is 89 then the "next" letter after Y is

LETTER = CHAR(ICHAR(Y) + 1) = CHAR(89 + 1) = CHAR(90) = Z

The FORTRAN code to solve this problem is shown in Figure B.4.

```
    1:      CHARACTER LINE*80,C,L
    2: 10   READ(5,6,END=88)LINE              Read a line of text.
    3:      DO 5 I = 1,80
    4:          L = NCRYPT(LINE(I:I))         Convert each character and
    5:          LINE(I:I) = L                 replace it in the text.
    6:  5   CONTINUE
    7:      GO TO 10                          Read more lines.
    8: 88   STOP
    9:  6   FORMAT(A80)
   10:      END
   11:      CHARACTER FUNCTION NCRYPT(L)       L is the character to be encrypted.
   12:      CHARACTER L*1
   13:      IF(L.GE.'A' .AND. L.LE.'Y')THEN    Check whether character L
   14:          NCRYPT = CHAR(ICHAR(L) + 1)    is a letter of the alphabet.
   15:      ELSE IF (L .EQ. 'Z')THEN
   16:              NCRYPT = 'A'               If L is 'Z' change L to 'A'.
   17:      ELSE
   18:              NCRYPT = L                 Don't change character if it is
   19:      ENDIF                              not a letter of the alphabet.
   20:      RETURN
   21:      END
```

FIGURE B.4
MESSAGE ENCRYPTION

B.8.3 Converting Letters to Block Letters

In section 7.1.2 a program was written to display digits in block digit form. Let us write a program to translate a sequence of letters of the alphabet into block letters, where each block letter consists of 7 rows and 5 columns. The program in Figure B.5 translates a string of 15 characters into a corresponding 15 block display.

Program Analysis. To understand the logic in Figure B.5 let us assume that the word "HELLO" is to be converted to block letter form. The 26 letters of the alphabet and the blank character are stored in array BLOCK (7,27) as follows:

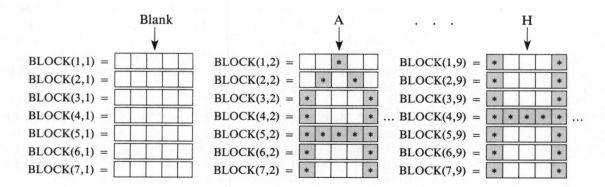

The letter H is in BLOCK (I,9) for values of I ranging from 1 to 7
The letter E is in BLOCK (I,6) for values of I ranging from 1 to 7
The letter L is in BLOCK (I,13) for values of I ranging from 1 to 7
The letter O is in BLOCK (I,16) for values of I ranging from 1 to 7

Continued on page B-12.

```
 1: ***** BLOCK LETTER PROGRAM
 2: ***** MESSGE: EACH LETTER OF THE 15-CHARACTER MESSAGE IS TRANSLATED
 3: *****        INTO CORRESPONDING BLOCK LETTERS
 4: ***** LETTER: ARRAY CONSISTING OF 15 ENTRIES.
 5: *****         LETTER(1)=ALPHABETIC POSITION OF 1ST LETTER OF MESSGE
 6: *****         I.E., IF 1ST LETTER OF MESSGE IS "H" THEN LETTER(1)=9
 7: *****              IF 1ST LETTER OF MESSGE IS "B" THEN LETTER(1)=3
 8: *****         LETTER(15)=ALPHABETIC POSITION OF LAST LETTER IN MESSGE
 9: ***** BLOCK: 7 ROWS BY 27 COLUMNS. REPRESENTS A BLANK AND THE 26 BLOCK LETTERS.
10: *****        BLOCK(1,2), (2,2),...(7,2) DRAWS BLOCK LETTER "A" (7 LINES)
11: *****        BLOCK(1,27),(2,27)...(7,27) DRAWS BLOCK LETTER "Z" (7 LINES)
12: *****        BLOCK(1,LETTER(1)),(2,LETTER(1),...(7,LETTER(1) DRAWS THE
13: *****        BLOCK LETTER CORRESPONDING TO FIRST LETTER IN MESSGE
14: ***** ALFABT: IS A STRING OF A BLANK AND THE 26 LETTERS OF THE ALPHABET;
15: *****         IT IS USED BY THE INDEX FUNCTION TO DETERMINE THE ALPHABETIC
16: *****         POSITION OF THE VARIOUS SUCCESSIVE LETTERS IN THE MESSAGE
17: *
18: * PARAMETERS
19: *
20:         CHARACTER ALFABT*27
21:         PARAMETER(ALFABT=' ABCDEFGHIJKLMNOPQRSTUVWXYZ')
22: *
23: * ARRAYS
24: *
25:         INTEGER LETTER(15)
26:         CHARACTER BLOCK(7,27)
27: *
28: * PROGRAM VARIABLES
29: *
30:         CHARACTER MESSGE*15
31: ***** READ THE 27 BLOCK LETTERS AND THE MESSAGE TO BE CONVERTED
32:         READ(5,10)((BLOCK(I,J),J=1,27),I=1,7)
33:         READ(5,20)MESSGE
34: ***** DETERMINE ALPHABETIC POSITION OF EACH LETTER IN MESSGE
35:         DO 15 I = 1,15
36:             LETTER(I) = INDEX(ALFABT,MESSGE(I:I))
37: 15      CONTINUE
38: ***** WRITE MESSAGE IN BLOCK LETTERS USING 7 LINES FOR ENTIRE MESSAGE
39:         DO 25 LINE = 1,7
40:             WRITE(6,30)(BLOCK(LINE,LETTER(I)),I=1,15)
41: 25      CONTINUE
42:         STOP
43: 10      FORMAT(27A5)
44: 20      FORMAT(A15)
45: 30      FORMAT(1X,15(A5,2X))
46:         END
```

Input File

HELLO ← Message to be converted to block form

Output

FIGURE B.5
PRINTING BLOCK LETTERS

Thus to print the letters HELLO we need to process the 9th, 6th, 13th, 13th and 16th columns of array BLOCK. These column numbers are stored in array LETTER at line 36:

LETTER(1) = 9   since H is the 9th letter of ALFABT (line 21).
LETTER(2) = 6   since E is the 6th letter of ALFABT (line 21).
LETTER(3) = 13   since L is the 13th letter of ALFABT (line 21).
LETTER(4) = 13   since L is the 13th letter of ALFABT (line 21).
LETTER(5) = 16   since O is the 16th letter of ALFABT (line 21).

Note that when LINE = 1 at line 40 we are writing

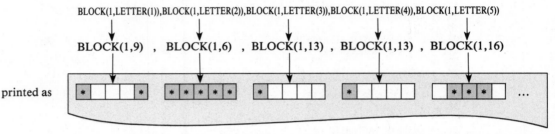

which corresponds to the top line of the block characters HELLO followed by 10 blanks in block form.

B.9 EXERCISES

1. Specify the output for the following:

```
CHARACTER MESSG*6,PLUS*5,ONE*3
MESSG = 'WEAMUS'
```

a. PRINT*,MESSG(:4)   **f.** PRINT*, CHAR(ICHAR'A')

b. PRINT*,MESSG(6:6)   **g.** PRINT*, ICHAR(CHAR(65))

c. PRINT*,MESSG(3:)   **h.** PRINT*, LLT('Z','A')

d. PRINT*,MESSG(3:7)   **i.** PRINT*, LGT('NEWARK','NEW YORK')

e. ONE = '3+'
```
    PLUS = ONE//'4=8'
    PRINT*,PLUS
```

2. Show the contents of each variable as a result of the following codes. Identify any errors.

```
CHARACTER NAME*8,WORD*6, TEMP*6
CHARACTER*5 FIRST,LAST,MIDDLE
WORD = 'SHE IS'
```

a. NAME = 'SALLY MCGOON'   **f.** NAME(2:5) = 'NONO'//NAME(4:7)

b. FIRST = NAME(:6)   **g.** NAME = 'TALLYHO'

c. LAST = NAME(6:)   **h.** TEMP = NAME(1:4)//NAME(3:)

d. MIDDLE = NAME(1:2)//'L'//NAME(4:5)   **i.** TEMP(3:) = WORD(1:2)//WORD(3:)

e. NAME(1:2) = NAME(7:)

3. Show the contents of variable Z. Identify any errors.

```
CHARACTER Z*5,A,B
```

   a. `Z = 'A'//'B'//'  C'`

   b. `A = '542'`
      `Z = A//'542'`

4. Show the contents of each variable. Identify errors, if any.

```
CHARACTER N*5
N = 'MICHEL'
```

   a. `N = N(5:5)//N(4:4)//N(3:3)//N(2:2)//N(1:1)`

   b. `N = '123456'`
      `N = N(1:)//N(2:)//N(3:)//N(4:)//N(5:)`

5. Determine what is stored in Z as a result of the following code:

```
CHARACTER*4 X,Y,Z
X = '.'
Y = X//X
Z = X//Y
```

6. Determine the output produced by the following code (assume LINE contains blanks):

```
CHARACTER LINE*10
```

   a.
```
    DO 5 I = 1,10
        LINE(I:I) = '.'
  5 CONTINUE
    PRINT*,LINE
```

   b.
```
    DO 5 I = 1,7
        LINE(I:I) = '.'
        PRINT*,LINE
  5 CONTINUE
```

   c.
```
    DO 5 K = 1,10
        LINE(K:K) = ' '
        PRINT*,LINE(:K)//'HELLO'
  5 CONTINUE
```

7. What does the following code accomplish? Assume TEXT consists of N characters.

```
    DO 10 I = 1,N/2
        TEMP = TEXT(I:I)
        TEXT(I:I) = TEXT(N-I+1:N-I+1)
        TEXT(N-I+1:N-I+1) = TEMP
 10 CONTINUE
```

8. Specify what the following coding segment does. Assume SEN is not all blanks.

```
    CHARACTER SEN*51,DUP*51
    SEN(51:51) = ' '
    DO 5 I = 50,1,-1
        IF(SEN(I:I) .NE. ' ') GO TO 6
  5 CONTINUE
  6 DUP = SEN(I+1:)//SEN(:I)
```

9.   CHARACTER*4 T(3)

Given the array T: | H E | I S | T O O | M E |

T(1)   T(2)   T(3)

Evaluate each of the following expressions:

    a. T(2)

    b. T(3)(3:)

    c. T(1)//T(3)(2:)

    d. T(2)(3:)//T(3)(1:1)

    e. T(3)//T(2)//T(1)

10. How could you type and store your English term paper, which contains 80-character lines, into a character string of 10000 positions, i.e., CHARACTER TEXT*10000?

Answers

1. a. WEAM   **f.** 65

    b. S   **g.** 4

    c. AMUS   **h.** .FALSE.

    d. Invalid; too many characters   **i.** .FALSE.

    e. 3+ 4=

2. a. | S A L L Y | | M C | **f.** Invalid; overlapping field

    b. | S A L L Y | | **g.** | T A L L Y H O | |

    c. | | M C | | **h.** | T A L L L L |

    d. | S A L L Y | **i.** | T A S H E | |

    e. | M C L L Y | | M C |

3. a. | A B | | | | **b.** | 5 5 4 2 | |

4 a. | E H C I M | **b.** | 1 2 3 4 5 |

5. Z contains | | | | | Remember, X, Y, and Z are each four characters long!

6. a. .... (10 periods)   **c.** HELLO
    HELLO
      HELLO
        · ·   } 10 lines
           HELLO

    b. .
    ..
    ...
    .... } 7 lines
    .....
    ......
    ....

7. Reverses the sentence, for example, WE AM US would become SU MA EW

8. Trailing blanks of sentence now become leading blanks. For example:

| H E | I S | | becomes | | | H E | I S |

9. a. S TO   **d.** TOO

    b. ME   **e.** O MES TOHE I

    c. HE I ME

10. `CHARACTER TEXT*10000,LINE*80`
Read a line of your paper into LINE and concatenate it to TEXT.
READ a second line of text and concatenate it to TEXT(81:), and so forth.

B.10 PROGRAMMING EXERCISES

1. a. Write a program to read a sentence and list each word on a separate line. For example:

`'I HAVE BUT ONE LIFE'`   gives

```
I
HAVE
BUT
ONE
LIFE
```

b. Write the code to extract all blank spaces from a sentence to form one string. Given the above example, we get   `IHAVEBUTONELIFE`

2. To facilitate transmission, words in telegrams are usually separated by slashes (/). Write a program to regenerate the original line of a telegraph message by substituting blanks wherever slashes appear.

3. Do the same problem as in exercise 2, but now compute the cost of the telegram. Each word up to and including the twentieth word costs 15 cents; thereafter, each word costs 12 cents.

4. Addresses in telegrams are transmitted serially. A double slash indicates a new line. Write the code to read five such addresses and recreate them as envelope addresses. For example:

1301/NORTH12TH/AVE//ATLANTA//GEORGIA/75603//

5. Write a program to convert military time to civilian time. For example:

1818 should produce   `THE TIME IS 18 PAST 6 PM`
1545 should produce   `THE TIME IS 15 BEFORE 4 PM`

6. Write a program to convert civilian time to 24-hour time. Civilian time should contain only the key words P.M. and A.M. The format for the input is

hours, minutes, $\begin{Bmatrix} \text{"PM"} \\ \text{"AM"} \end{Bmatrix}$

For example 2 15 PM should produce 1415.

7. Write a program to translate dates expressed numerically into the usual month, day, and year representation. For example:

11/07/87 should produce NOVEMBER 7 1987

8. Write the code to determine the number of syllables in a word and in a sentence.

9. Write the code to determine the number of sentences and words in a paragraph (the end-of-sentence identifiers are .?!).

10. A palindrome is a sequence of characters that is the same read from left to right as from right to left. For example 22, 303, 111, and "level" are examples of palindromes. Write a program to generate all two-digit, three-digit, and four-digit palindromes.

11. Write a program to determine if a number accepted as input is a palindrome.

12. Write a program to determine if a character string accepted as input is a palindrome.

Appendix C
Logical Data

C.1 LOGICAL EXPRESSIONS

A logical expression is an expression that evaluates to either true or false; thus the simple and compound conditions that we have used in decision and WHILE DO structures are examples of logical expressions.

C.2 THE LOGICAL SPECIFICATION STATEMENT

Logical expressions, like arithmetic expressions, can be processed in replacement statements and in IF statements. In either case, the logical expression is first evaluated and the result of this evaluation is one of the logical values .TRUE. or .FALSE. (these values are called *logical constants*), just as the evaluation of 3. + 5. results in the numerical value 8.0. The logical values .TRUE. and .FALSE. can be stored in logical variables in the same way that arithmetic constants can be stored in variables. However, logical variables must be declared in a LOGICAL statement. The LOGICAL statement has the general form:

> LOGICAL   *variable list*

where   *variable list* is a list of variable names.

EXAMPLE
```
LOGICAL X,I,GUESS
```
X, I, and GUESS are now logical variables.

Replacement Statements

Once a variable is declared LOGICAL, it can be assigned the values .TRUE. or .FALSE. through replacement statements, DATA statements, or READ statements.

It cannot, however, be assigned numeric or CHARACTER values. The general form for logical replacement statements is:

$$logical\ variable\ =\ logical\ expression$$

The following code contains valid examples of logical replacement statements:

```
CHARACTER*5 LAST
LOGICAL A,B,C
DATA X,Y,B,LAST/4.,-2.,.TRUE.,'NEWS'/
A = .TRUE.              A is true. (.TRUE. is stored in A)
C = A                   C is true. (.TRUE. is stored in C)
B = X .LT. Y            B is false since    4 ≮ −2.
C = Y .NE. X**.5        C is true since    −2 ≠ 2.
B = (X + Y)**2 .EQ. 4.  B is true since     4 = 4.
C = 2.*Y .GT. X−Y       C is false since   −4 ≯ 6.
A = LAST .LE. 'NEW'     A is false since    S ≮ blank.
```

The following are examples of invalid logical replacement statements:

```
LOGICAL A,B,C
A = 2.1*X               Expression is arithmetic.
B = 2.*C                C is logical, 2. is numeric.
C = A + B               Cannot add two logical variables.
A = B .EQ. .TRUE.       Cannot compare two logical algebraically values.
C = A .LT. X            A is not numeric.
A = IF(X .LT. 4.)       Invalid logical expression, IF key word not allowed.
Z = .FALSE.             Z is not declared logical.
C = X.LT.Y + Z.GT.3.    Cannot add logical values.
```

Compound Logical Expressions

Sometimes it may be practical to create a more complex proposition by combining (*conjuncting*) elementary logical expressions. For example, it might be desirable to know whether "SEX is 1 and STATUS is 4" or "AGE is less than 18 or AGE is greater than 65." Such a combination of elementary logical expressions is called a *compound logical expression*. A compound logical expression can be defined as elementary logical expressions linked to one another by the logical operators .AND., .OR., and .NOT..

The effect of the logical operators on two logical expressions, e_1 and e_2, can be described as follows:

e_1 .AND. e_2	is .TRUE. if and only if e_1 and e_2 are both .TRUE..
e_1 .OR. e_2	is .TRUE. if either e_1 or e_2 (or both) are .TRUE..
.NOT. e_2	is .TRUE. if e_2 is .FALSE. (evaluate e_2 and negate it).

This can be illustrated in table form, as shown in Figure C.1. Note that the .NOT. operator can only be connected to one logical expression.

FIGURE C.1
TRUE TABLES FOR
LOGICAL OPERATORS

e_1	e_2	e_1 .AND. e_2	e_1 .OR. e_2	.NOT. e_1
.TRUE.	.TRUE.	.TRUE.	.TRUE.	.FALSE.
.TRUE.	.FALSE.	.FALSE.	.TRUE.	.FALSE.
.FALSE.	.TRUE.	.FALSE.	.TRUE.	.TRUE.
.FALSE.	.FALSE.	.FALSE.	.FALSE.	.TRUE.

The values of compound logical expressions can be stored in logical variables. Consider the following examples:

```
LOGICAL A,B,C,D,E,F                    Logical Value Outcomes
CHARACTER T*1
DATA X,Y,T/3.,-2.3,'X'/
A = X.LT.Y .OR. T.GE.'Y'       A = .FALSE.   3 ≮ -2.3. and 'X' < 'Y'.
B = Y .LE. 20.                 B = .TRUE.    -2.3 < 20.
C = A .AND. B                  C = .FALSE.   .FALSE. .AND. .TRUE. = .FALSE.
F = .NOT. X .LT. Y             F = .TRUE.    .NOT.X.LT.Y is same as X.GE.Y
D = A .OR. X .LT. 6            D = .TRUE.    since A is .FALSE. but X < 6 is .TRUE.
E = .NOT. C                    E = .TRUE.    since C is .FALSE..
F = A .AND. .NOT. B            F = .FALSE.   Both A and .NOT. B are .FALSE..
G = (.TRUE. .OR. .FALSE.) .AND. .TRUE.  G = .TRUE.  The expression is evaluated as .TRUE.
```

Some examples of invalid compound expressions are:

```
INTEGER X,Y,Z
LOGICAL A,B,C,CA
A = .NOT. X               X is not logical
B = X + 1 .OR. Y + 6      X + 1 and Y + 6 are not logical expressions.
C = X .LT. Y + Z .GT. 3   Logical values cannot be added.
A = CA .OR. 'BUST'        BUST is not a logical value.
```

If more than one logical operator is used in a compound logical expression, parentheses may be used to specify which expression is to be evaluated first. Consider the logical expression e_1 .AND. e_2 .OR. e_3 with e_1 = .FALSE. and $e_2 = e_3$ = .TRUE.. Depending on the placement of parentheses, this logical expression could be interpreted two ways:

e_1 .AND. $(e_2$ .OR. $e_3)$ = .FALSE.
or
$(e_1$ .AND. $e_2)$ .OR. e_3 = .TRUE.

Since all of the arithmetic operations, arithmetic relation operations, and logical operations can appear in one expression, it becomes important to know the relative precedence of the operations (in the absence of parentheses). This precedence or hierarchy of operations is summarized in the following table:

Operation	Comment	Precedence
Grouping (parentheses)	Innermost parentheses first	Highest
Arithmetic operations.	According to usual rules of precedence.	
Arithmetic relations. (.LT.,.LE.,.GT.,.EQ....)	In order from left to right.	
.NOT.	Operates on expression to immediate right.	
.AND.		
.OR.		Lowest
.EQV. .NEQV.		

Parentheses can be used as necessary to change the implied precedence.

The EQV and NEQV Relational Operators

The EQV (equivalent) and NEQV (not equivalent) relational operators are used to test logical expressions for equivalence or nonequivalence. They can also be part of logical expressions. Consider the following examples:

```
LOGICAL VALUE, FLAG, SWITCH, X
VALUE = .TRUE. .EQV. .TRUE.                 VALUE = .TRUE. since true = true
IF (FLAG .EQV. SWITCH) THEN                 If the values in FLAG and SWITCH are
                                            equivalent, carry out the THEN actions.
X = (.NOT. FLAG) .EQV. (NAME .NE. 'SIMS')   Store logical value in X
(X.GT.3.1) .AND. (Y.LE.2.0) .NEQV. ((X+Y)/2.0.GT.-4.6)  has value true or false!
```

The Lexical Functions LGE, LGT, LLE and LLT

The following functions determine the order relationship between characters according to the collating sequence in use by the computing system (ASCII or EBCDIC codes).

Function	Meaning	Action	Arguments	Type	Example
LGE(X1,X2)	Lexically $\geq$	True if $x_1 \geq x_2$	2 character *n	logical	LGE('B','A')=.TRUE.
LGT(X1,X2)	Lexically $>$	True if $x_1 > x_2$	2 character *n	logical	LGT(WORD,'HI')=?
LLE(X1,X2)	Lexically $\leq$	True if $x_1 \leq x_2$	2 character *n	logical	LLE('a','A')=.FALSE. (ASCII CODE)
LLT(X1,X2)	Lexically $<$	True if $x_1 < x_2$	2 character *n	logical	LLT('5','R')=.TRUE (ASCII CODE)

C.3 INPUT/OUTPUT OF LOGICAL VALUES: THE L FORMAT CODE

Logical variables can participate in input/output statements. In order to assign a value to a logical variable via the READ or WRITE statements, the L format code must be used. The general form of the L code is:

$$\boxed{\text{L}w}$$

where w represents the field width.

When reading a logical variable, the system will scan the input field from left to right. If the first nonblank character is T, the value stored for the logical variable is .TRUE.; the value .FALSE. will be stored if no T is present. Any remaining characters in the field are ignored. On output, a T or an F is printed, depending on whether the variable is .TRUE. or .FALSE.. The character T or F is right-justified on the output field with $w - 1$ blanks to the left.

EXAMPLE

```
    LOGICAL X,Y,Z
    READ(5,2)X,Y,Z
    WRITE(6,2)X,Y,Z
    STOP
  2 FORMAT(L3,L1,L5)
    END
```

Data Record

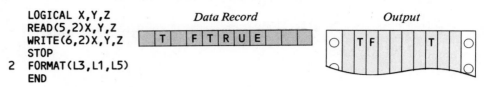

Output

The value of X and Z is .TRUE. and the value of Y is .FALSE..

C.4 A PROGRAMMING EXAMPLE: SWITCHING CIRCUITS

Consider an electrical circuit consisting of a power source and a switch, such as:

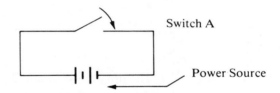

If the switch is up, no current travels through the circuit; if the switch is down, current flows through the circuit. Let us represent the switch A with a logical variable having value .TRUE. if the switch is down and .FALSE. if the switch is up.

Two switches can be arranged in series as:

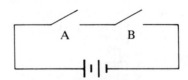

In this case, current travels through the circuit only when both A and B are down. The expression A .AND. B represents the series circuit.

Two switches can also be arranged in parallel:

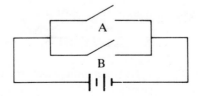

In this case, current travels through the circuit when either A or B (or both) are down. The expression A .OR. B represents the parallel circuit.

It is possible to write logical expressions for any switching circuits:

EXAMPLES

Circuits   *Logical Expressions*

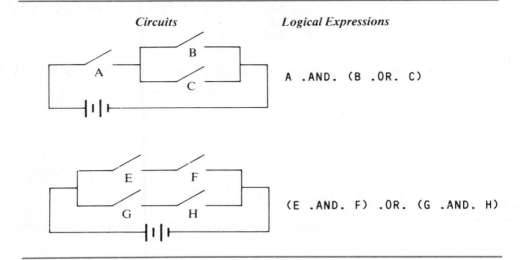

A .AND. (B .OR. C)

(E .AND. F) .OR. (G .AND. H)

The program shown in Figure C.2 can be used to evaluate the above circuits for various values of the switches.

```
      LOGICAL A,B,C,E,F,G,H,X,Y
    2 READ(5,1,END=10)A,B,C,E,F,G,H
      X = A .AND. (B. OR. C)
      Y = (E. AND. F) .OR. (G .AND. H)
      WRITE(6,3)A,B,C,X
      WRITE (6,4)E,F,G,H,Y
      GO TO 2
   10 STOP
    1 FORMAT(7L1)
    3 FORMAT(3X,'CIRCUIT1',3L2,'IS',L2)
    4 FORMAT(3X,'CIRCUIT2',4L2,'IS',L2)
      END
```

FIGURE C.2
EVALUATION OF CIRCUIT EXPRESSIONS

C.5 EXERCISES

1. Determine whether the logical data type is supported by the compiler you are using.

2. A marriage proposal letter will be written when the following logical expression is .TRUE.. Under what conditions will the letter be written?

```
IF(HAIR.EQ.'BLOND' .AND. HEIGHT.GT.5.6 .OR. EARNIN.GT.100000.)THEN...
```

3. Assume X = 30., Y = 40., A = 1., and B = 4. Is the following statement true or false?

```
IF(.NOT. (X + Y .LT. 100 .OR. A .EQ. 1.) .AND. B .GT. 3.0) THEN...
```

4. Assume X = 3, Y = 2, Z = −1. Which of the following statements are valid?

    a. `IF((X + Y)**2 .LT. -1 .AND. Y .GT. Z) THEN...`

    b. `IF(X - Y .EQ. 0.0 .OR. Z .AND. X .EQ. 0) THEN...`

    c. `IF(-3.0 .LT. Z .OR. 1 .EQ. X) THEN...`

    d. `IF( X + 1.0 .OR. Y + Z .GT. 3 ) THEN...`

    e. `IF( X .NOT. .GT. 4. ) THEN...`

    f. `IF( .NOT. (Y .NE. -1)) THEN...`

5. Which of the following statements are correct?

    a. A + B could be a valid logical expression, depending on how A and B are specified.

    b. X + Y.LT.5. is an elementary logical expression.

    c. B.OR.10 is a compound logical expression.

    d. A.NOT.B is an invalid compound logical expression.

    e. The value of A.AND.(.NOT.A) is .FALSE..

    f. Y.AND.X could be a valid logical expression.

    g. 3 .EQV. 3

6. Evaluate each of the following logical expressions if A = 3.0, B = −4., and C = 0.

    a. A .LT. B

    b. .NOT. A .GT. 0.

    c. B .LT. C .OR. A .LT. B

    d. B .LE. C .AND. A .LT. B

    e. C .GT. B .AND. (A .LE. 16.0 .OR. B .EQ. 4.)

    f. .NOT.(A .GT. B .OR. C .EQ. 0.)

    g. .NOT. A .GT. B .OR. C .EQ. 0.

    h. A .EQ. B .AND. B .LT. C .OR. (.NOT. A .LT. B)

    i. A + B .LT. −1 .NEQV. .FALSE.

7. Determine the value of the following expressions, given A = .TRUE., B = .TRUE., C = .FALSE..

    a. A.OR.B

    b. .NOT.C

    c. (A.OR.B).AND.C

    d. .TRUE..OR.C

    e. .TRUE..AND.C (Read it quickly!)

    f. .NOT.C.OR.B

    g. .NOT.(A .OR. B).EQV.(.NOT.A .AND. .NOT. B)

8. Write a LOGICAL expression involving two LOGICAL variables, A and B, which has the value .TRUE. if only A is .TRUE. or if only B is .TRUE. and which has the value .FALSE. if both A and B are .TRUE. or both are .FALSE.. (This expression is called the *exclusive or.*)

9. Write a program to determine whether the following logical equations are always satisfied regardless of the values of A, B, and C.

    a. .NOT. (A .AND. B) = .NOT. A .OR. (.NOT. B)

    b. A .OR. (B .AND. C) = (A .OR. B) .OR. (A .OR. C)

    c. .NOT.(A .AND. B) .OR. A = .TRUE.

    d. A .AND. B .OR.(.NOT. A .AND. C) =
       .NOT. A .AND.(.NOT. B) .AND. C .OR. A .AND. B .AND. (.NOT. C)
       .OR. B .AND. C

10. What output would be produced by each of the following?

    a.

```
    LOGICAL A,B
    READ(5,3)A
    B = .TRUE.
    WRITE(6,4)A,B
  3 FORMAT(L2)
  4 FORMAT(2L3)
```

Data Record

| T | | | | | | | |

    b.

```
    LOGICAL X,Y,Z,W,R
    READ(5,6)X,Y
    Z = X .OR. Y
    W = X .AND. Y
    R = .NOT. X .OR. Z
    WRITE(6,7)X,Y,Z,W,R
  6 FORMAT(2L1)
  7 FORMAT(5L2)
```

Data Record

| T | F | | | |

11. Represent each of the following circuits with a logical expression.

    a.

    b.

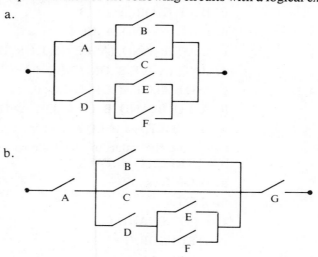

c.
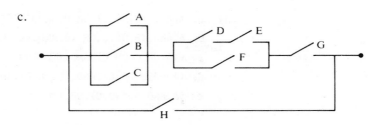

d.
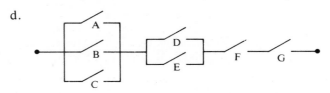

e.
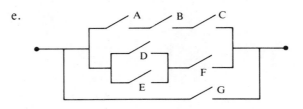

2. A marriage proposal letter will be written under either of the following conditions:

    a. If earning exceeds $100,000

    b. If hair is blond and height is at least 5 foot 6

3. False

4. **a.** Valid

    b. Invalid "Z.AND.X"   (Z or X are not logical values).

    c. Valid

    d. Invalid use of the .OR.

    e. Invalid .NOT. .GT.

    f. valid

5. **a.** F.   **b.** T.   **c.** F.   **d.** T.   **e.** T.   **f.** T.   **g.** F. (EQ not EQV)

6. **a.** F.   **b.** F.   **c.** T.   **d.** F.   **e.** T.   **f.** F.   **g.** T.   **h.** T.   **i.** T.

7. **a.** T.   **b.** T.   **c.** F.   **d.** T.   **e.** F.   **f.** T.   **g.** T.

8.   `(A.AND.(.NOT.B)).OR.((.NOT.A).AND.B)`

10. **a.**
```
        T        T
  |--+--+--+--+--+--+--|
```

    b.
```
  T     F     T     F     T
  |--+--+--+--+--+--+--+--+--|
```

11. a. A.AND.(B.OR.C).OR.D.AND.(E.OR.F)

b. A.AND.(B.OR.C.OR.(D.AND.(E.OR.F))).AND.G

c. ((A.OR.B.OR.C).AND.((D.AND.E).OR.F).AND.G).OR.H

d. (A.OR.B.OR.C).AND.(D.OR.E).AND.F.AND.G

e. (A.AND.B.AND.C).OR.((D.OR.E).AND.F).OR.G

Appendix D
Complex Data

D.1 DEFINITION AND FORM

A complex number is a number of the form:

$$a + bi \qquad \text{where } i = \sqrt{-1} \ (i^2 = -1) \text{ and } a, b \text{ are real numbers.}$$

real part   imaginary part

For example, the following are complex numbers:

$4 + 3i$
$3.2 + (-4)i$
$-.6 + 70 \cdot i$
3 which is $3 + 0 \cdot i$

A FORTRAN complex constant is written as follows:

(a,b) ◄— parentheses required

where a and b are **real constants**, with a representing the real part of the constant and b the imaginary part. Note the enclosing parentheses.

EXAMPLES

FORTRAN Constants	Value
(4.,3.)	$4 + 3i$
(3.2,-4.)	$3.2 + 4i$
(24.3E-2,79.)	$.243 + 79i$
(1.1E+10,.2E-3)	$11000000000 + .0002i$

The following examples are invalid complex constants:

(X,Y)	X and Y are not constants.
(0.,I)	I is not a constant.
1.,1.	No parentheses.
(3115,3.4)	The real part is an integer.
(.004E+4,5.1D10)	Difference in precision specification.

Complex constants can be added, subtracted, multiplied, and divided as follows:

Addition: $(a+bi) + (c+di) = (a+c) + (b+d)i$
Subtraction: $(a+bi) - (c+di) = (a-c) + (b-d)i$
Multiplication: $(a+bi) * (c+di) = (ac-bd) + (ad+bc)i$
Division: $(a+bi) / (c+di) = \dfrac{(ac+bd)}{c^2+d^2} + \dfrac{(bc-ad)}{c^2+d^2}i$

The absolute value of $(a+bi)$ is $\sqrt{a^2+b^2}$

Before a complex variable can be processed, it must be declared in the COMPLEX specification statement, which has the form:

COMPLEX	*list of variable names*

For example, COMPLEX A,B,X(10) specifies that A, B, and array X of size 10 are complex variables.

Internally, each complex variable consists of two memory words, the first for the real part and the second for the imaginary part of the number. Complex expressions can be formed with complex constants in much the same way they are formed with real and integer constants. The result of evaluating an expression with a complex term is always a complex value.

EXAMPLES

```
REAL X
COMPLEX A,B,C
A = (2.,2.) + (Ø.,1.)          A = 2 + 3i
B = (5.,-1.)*2.                B = 10 - 2i
C = A + B - 5.                 C = 7 + i
X = A - B                      X = -8. (X is real, so the imaginary part is discarded.)
C = A*B                        C = 26 + 26i
C = (3.,5.) - A                C = 1 + 2i
C = (A*B)/2.*(Ø.,1.)           C = -13 + 13i
C = A**2 - (2.,3.4)**3         C = 56.36 + 10.504i
C = (X,Z)                      Invalid (X,Z not constants).
C = A + 2.                     C = 4 + 3i
```

It should be noted that the exponent in an exponentiation (**) operation cannot be complex; for example, 3.14**(1.,3.) is invalid. Additionally, complex numbers cannot be raised to a real power. Thus C = A**2.0 is invalid. However, complex numbers (expressions) can be raised to an integer power, i.e., C = A**2 is valid if A is complex.

Most FORTRAN libraries have complex functions available to the user to carry out COMPLEX operations. The following list shows the usually available COMPLEX functions:

Functions	Arguments	Value	Meaning
REAL	1 Complex	Real	REAL $(a,b) = a$ (a,b real constants)
AIMAG	1 Complex	Real	Imaginary $(a,b) = b$
CONJG	1 Complex	Complex	Conjugate $(a,b) = (a,-b)$
CABS	1 Complex	Real	Absolute value $(a,b) = \sqrt{a^2+b^2}$
CSQRT	1 Complex	Complex	Square root of $a+bi$
CLOG	1 Complex	Complex	Logarithm
CSIN	1 Complex	Complex	Sine function
CCOS	1 Complex	Complex	Cosine function
CEXP	1 Complex	Complex	Exponential function
CMPLX	2 Real	Complex	CMPLX (a,b) refers to $a+bi$

A well-documented description of these functions is generally available in the FORTRAN technical reference manual for the particular computer system.

D.2 INPUT/OUTPUT OF COMPLEX VARIABLES

Input/output of complex variables requires two data descriptor format codes for each complex variable. The first format code describes the real part of the number and the second describes the imaginary part.

EXAMPLE

```
      COMPLEX A,B,C
      READ(5,1)    A ,          B
    1 FORMAT(F4.0,  F6.0,  F3.2,  F4.3)
```

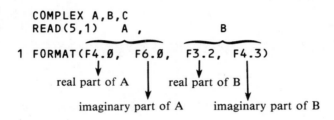

real part of A   real part of B

imaginary part of A   imaginary part of B

```
      C = (6.2,-4.325)
      WRITE(6,3)C
    3 FORMAT(1X,F7.4,1X,F7.4)
```

Output

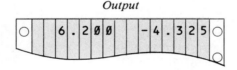

Input

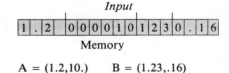

Memory

A = (1.2,10.)   B = (1.23,.16)

D.3 A PROGRAMMING EXAMPLE: COMPLEX ROOTS OF A QUADRATIC

The roots of $ax^2 + bx + c = 0$ are given by

$$x_1 = \frac{-b + \sqrt{b^2 - 4ac}}{2a} \qquad x_2 = \frac{-b - \sqrt{b^2 - 4ac}}{2a}$$

If $b^2 - 4ac \geq 0$, the values of x_1 and x_2 are real; otherwise, they are complex. The program shown in Figure D.1 will determine the roots of the quadratic equation. If the solutions are real, the imaginary part of the roots will be zero (assume A1 $\neq$ 0).

```
***** FINDING ROOTS OF A QUADRATIC
      COMPLEX X1,X2,A1,B1,C1,D
    1 READ(5,2,END=1Ø)A,B,C          Read coefficients
      A1 = A
      B1 = B                          Convert coefficients to COMPLEX type.
      C1 = C
      D = CSQRT(B1**2 - 4.*A1*C1)     CSQRT requires complex arguments.
      X1 = (-B1 + D)/(2.*A1)
      X2 = (-B1 - D)/(2.*A1)
      WRITE(6,3)A,B,C,X1,X2
      GO TO 1
   1Ø STOP
    2 FORMAT(3F4.Ø)
    3 FORMAT(2X,'A=',F5.Ø,'B=',F5.Ø,'C=',F5.Ø,'X1=',2F7.3,'X2=',2F7.3)
      END
```

FIGURE D.1
*COMPLEX ROOTS OF
A QUADRATIC*

D.4 EXERCISES

1. Determine if the complex data type is supported by the compiler you are using.

2. What output would be produced by each of the following?

   a.
   ```
        COMPLEX A,B,C,D
        A = (-2.,3.)
        B = (1.,-2.)
        C = A + B
        D = (4.,2.)*A
        WRITE(6,11)A,B,C,D
     11 FORMAT(1X,8F4.Ø)
   ```

   b.
   ```
        COMPLEX A,B,C,D
        READ(5,12)A,B
        C = CONJG(A)
        E = 4.Ø
        F = 6.Ø
        D = CMPLX(E,F)
        WRITE(6,13)A,B,C,D
     12 FORMAT(4F2.Ø)
     13 FORMAT(1X,8F4.Ø)
   ```

   Data Record

   | - | 1 | | 3 | | 2 | - | 1 | | |

3. Which of the following are valid complex constants:

   a. (0.0)

   b. (6,4)

   c. $(12.3, -1.2E-3)$

   d. (X,Y)

4. Determine the values of the following expressions:

    a. 2.*(1.4, − 3.7)

    b. (0.,1.)**2

    c. C*(1.,0.) + D*(0., + 1.) where C = 2., D = − 3.

    d. A*(1., − 1.) where A = (2., − 3.)

5. Compute the values for each of the following:

```
REAL X
COMPLEX C,Z
A = 3.Ø
B = -2.Ø
```

    a. C = (-7.Ø, -4.Ø)/(2.Ø, 3.Ø)

    b. Z = CMPLX(3.Ø,4.Ø) - CMPLX(A,B)

    c. R = CABS((5.Ø, 12.Ø))

    d. T = CMPLX(5.Ø + 2.Ø, A+B)

    e. X = (-.5, $\sqrt{3.}/2.$)*(-.5, − $\sqrt{3.}/2.$)

Answers

2. a. <u>-2. 3. 1. -2. -1. 1.-14. 8.</u>

   b. <u>-1. 3. 2. -1. -1. -3. 4. 6.</u>

3. a. (− 2.0, 1.0)

   b. (0.,6.)

   c. 13.

   d. (7.0, 1.0)

   e. 1.

4. a. Invalid.   **b.** Invalid.   **c.** Valid.   **d.** Invalid.

5. a. (2.8, − 7.4)   **b.** (− 1.0,0.0)   **c.** (2.0, − 3.0)   **d.** (− 1.0, − 5.0)

Appendix E
Statement Functions

E.1 INTRODUCTION

As we have seen, FORTRAN allows you to define your own functions through function subprograms. The function subprogram, in general, can require several lines of code and can produce several answers, even though only one value can be returned to the calling program. In cases where the function is so simple that it can be expressed in one line of code, the statement function can be used to great advantage. Statement functions are generally used when a particular arithmetic expression needs to be evaluated for different values of the variable at different places in the program. Unlike function subprograms, which are compiled independently, statement functions are defined in the program that uses the statement function. For example, if a second-degree polynomial is to be evaluated several times in a program for different values of the variable, the statement function POLY could be used as follows:

Program without Statement Function
```
X = -5.6
Y = 2.1*X**2 - 3.*X + 1.
X = 2.12347
    .
    .
    .
IF(2.1*X**2 - 3.*X + 1. .GT. 3.)THEN
    .
    .
    .
T = 10.6
SUM = SUM + SQRT(2.1*T**2 - 3.*T + 1.)
```

Program with Statement Function
```
POLY(X) = 2.1*X**2 - 3.*X + 1.
X = -5.6
Y = POLY(X)
    .
    .
    .
IF(POLY(2.12347).GT. 3.) THEN
    .
    .
    .
T = 10.6
SUM = SUM + SQRT(POLY(T))
```

The general form of the statement function definition is:

$$\boxed{\textit{function name} \ (a_1, a_2, a_3, ..., a_n) = \textit{expression}}$$

where   *function name* is the name of the function (any variable name);

$a_1, a_2, a_3, ..., a_n$ are dummy arguments that must be nonsubscripted variable names,

expression is any arithmetic expression that contains $a_1, a_2, a_3, ..., a_n$ and possibly other constants, variables, array elements, or references to function subprograms or previously defined statement functions.

The statement function definition should precede the first executable statement of the program but follow all DIMENSION and specification statements (see order of FORTRAN statements Figure A.3). The following code illustrates the use of a statement function.

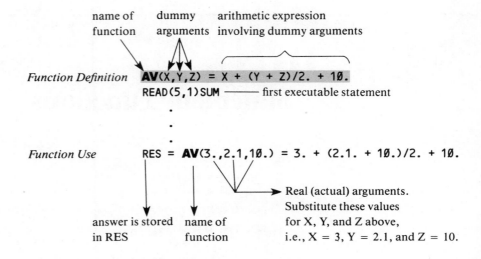

When a statement function is executed, the values of the real (actual) arguments replace the dummy arguments in the expression in the function definition. If variables other than the dummy arguments are used in the expression, then their current values will be used when the function is evaluated. The use of a variable as a dummy argument does not preclude its use as a variable in the program. The only purpose of the dummy argument is to illustrate the way in which the real arguments are manipulated to produce the function value.

In the expression in the function definition, the dummy arguments must be non-subscripted variable names. In the calling statement for the function, the real arguments *can* be subscripted variables or arithmetic expressions. **As with function subprograms, the real arguments must agree in number, order, and type with the dummy arguments in the function definition.** The type of the value returned is determined implicitly by the name of the function but can be changed by appropriate type statements.

EXAMPLE 1

```
F(X) = (X+2.)/(X-2.) + X**2
   .
   .
Y = F(4.0)
Y = F(T)
```

$$F(X) = \frac{X + 2}{X - 2} + X^2$$

The value of Y will be 19.
The value of Y is computed, substituting T for X in the function definition.

EXAMPLE 2

```
BETA(Y) = A*Y**2 + B*Y + C
   .
   .
   READ(5,1)A,B,C
   DO 10 IX = 1,10
      Q = BETA(REAL(IX))
10 CONTINUE
   WRITE(6,2)IX,Q
```

The expression involves variables other than the formal argument Y.
The values of A, B, and C are established. The function will be evaluated for values of IX varying from 1 to 10. Note that the type of the actual argument and the formal argument must be the same.

EXAMPLE 3

```
CHARACTER C
LOGICAL LETTER
LETTER(C) = C.GE.'A' .AND. C.LE.'Z'          LETTER(C) is .TRUE. if C is a letter of
  .                                           the alphabet.
  .
READ(5,2)L
IF(LETTER(L))K = 1                            If L is a letter of the alphabet, set K to 1.
```

The following examples show *invalid* statement function definitions or invalid references to statement functions:

a. `PAY = HRS*RATE`
    `RES = PAY(40,5)`   Arguments needed for PAY.

b. `CONS(X,3) = 3*X + 1`   Dummy argument must be a variable..

c. `DUE(X,A(1),Z) = A(1) + X + Z`   Subscripted variables cannot be used as dummy arguments.

d. `DOG(X,Y,Z) = X + Y*DOG(C,D,F)`   Recursive definition of DOG—a function cannot refer to itself.

e. `TRUE(NCY) = NCY*3/256`
    `DIMENSION A(100)`   Statement functions should follow specification statements.

f. `SIGN(X) = -X`
    `Y = SIGN(3)`   Real and dummy arguments differ in type.

g. `BR(AV,OS) = (AV + OS)**3`
    `Z = BR(3.12*X)`   Arguments differ in number—only one argument in BRA.

E.2 PROGRAMMING EXAMPLE

The program in Figure E.1 illustrates the use of a statement function to solve a set of linear equations of the following form:

$$a_1x + b_1y = c_1$$
$$a_2x + b_2y = c_2$$

The program uses the Gauss-Seidel iteration procedure, which involves starting with an approximation of the solution (y_0) and computing successive approximations for x and y using the following formulas:

$$x_{n+1} = \frac{1}{a_1}(c_1 - b_1y_n) \qquad y_{n+1} = \frac{1}{b_2}(c_2 - a_2x_{n+1})$$

It can be shown that this sequence of approximations x_i, y_i converges towards the solution of the system of linear equations if:

$$|a_1| \cdot |b_2| > |b_1| \cdot |a_2|$$

The program in Figure E.1 accepts as input the values a_1, b_1, c_1, a_2, b_2, c_2 and tests to see if the Gauss-Seidel iteration procedure will converge. If it will not converge, an appropriate message is produced; if it will converge, the first eight terms of the sequence are computed.

```
* GAUSS SEIDEL ITERATIVE METHOD
*   XNEW: FUNCTION TO COMPUTE X VALUES
*   YNEW: FUNCTION TO COMPUTE Y VALUES
*
      IMPLICIT REAL(A-M,O-Z), INTEGER(N)
*
      XNEW(Q) = (1./A1)*(C1 - B1*Q)
      YNEW(Q) = (1./B2)*(C2 - A2*Q)
*
   10 READ(5,6,END=88)A1,B1,C1,A2,B2,C2
      WRITE(6,2) A1,B1,C1,A2,B2,C2
      IF(ABS(A1)*ABS(B2) .GT. ABS(B1)*ABS(A2))THEN
         WRITE(6,3)
         Y = 0.
         DO 20 N = 1, 8
            X = XNEW(Y)
            Y = YNEW(X)
            WRITE(6,4)N, X, Y
   20    CONTINUE
      ELSE
         WRITE(6,5)
      ENDIF
      GO TO 10
   88 STOP
    2 FORMAT(1X/(1X,F4.1,'*X+',F4.1,'*Y=',F4.1))
    3 FORMAT('0',2X,'N',5X,'X',6X,'Y')
    4 FORMAT(2X,I2,2X,F5.2,2X,F5.2)
    5 FORMAT('0',2X,'SYSTEM WILL NOT CONVERGE')
    6 FORMAT(6F4.0)
      END
```

Input File

```
A₁   B₁   C₁   A₂  B₂  C₂

8.002.0018.01.001.003.00
3.00-4.0-1.02.006.008.00
1.003.004.004.002.006.00
```

Output panel:

```
8.0*X+ 2.0*Y=18.0
1.0*X+ 1.0*Y= 3.0

N    X      Y
1   2.25   .75
2   2.06   .94
3   2.02   .98
4   2.00  1.00
5   2.00  1.00
6   2.00  1.00
7   2.00  1.00
8   2.00  1.00

3.0*X+-4.0*Y=-1.0
2.0*X+ 6.0*Y= 8.0

N    X      Y
1  -.33   1.44
2  1.59    .80
3   .74   1.09
4  1.12    .96
5   .95   1.02
6  1.02    .99
7   .99   1.00
8  1.00   1.00

1.0*X+ 3.0*Y= 4.0
4.0*X+ 2.0*Y= 6.0

SYSTEM WILL NOT CONVERGE
```

FIGURE E.1
GAUSS-SEIDEL METHOD

E.3 EXERCISES

1. Write a statement function to compute the determinant of a 2 by 2 matrix.
   (*Note:* Determinant of A = $|A| = \begin{vmatrix} a_{11} & a_{12} \\ a_{21} & a_{22} \end{vmatrix} = a_{11} \cdot a_{22} - a_{21} \cdot a_{12}$)

2. Write statement functions for each of the following:
   a. $V = \pi r^3$
   b. $y = ax^3 + bx^2 + cx + d$

   c. $q = x\sin(x) + x^2 \cos(x)$ where x is to be expressed in degrees

   d. the difference in absolute value between the largest and smallest values in a list of the four values A, B, C and D.

3. Which of the following statement function definition statements are valid? If invalid, explain why.

a. `SOME(A(I),B) = A(I)*2`

b. `SQRT(A,B) = SQRT(A) + SQRT(B)`

c. `T(Y) = Y**2 + 2.`
   `A(X) = T(X) + 1.`

d. `SQRT(X) = X**0.5`

e. `ROOT = -B + SQRT(B*B - 4.*A*D)`
   `C(B) = B**2 + FUN`

f. `LONE(I,J,K) = I*J*K`
   `L = LONE(1,2,3) + I*J*K`

g. `HI(2,B,C) = (B-C)/2.`

h. `A(L) = REAL(L) + AL + SIM`
   `Y = A(K) - AL - SIM`

i. `ADD(X,Y,Z) = X + Y + Z`
   `T = ADD(X*Y,T)`

j. `C(X + 1.,A) = (X + 1.)*3. + A`

k. `MIX(K) = LOG(K + 1.)`
   `S = MIX(3.1) + 3.`

4. Write one statement function that could be used for all statements 5,6,7,8 and show how the function would be used in each case.

```
5 Y = 3.*X**2 + 2.*X -1.
  WRITE(6,1)Y
6 T = I*X**2 + 7.*X - TOT
7 S = 3.*X**2 - K(2)*X + SIN(T)
  SUM = S + T
8 IF(17.*X**2 + MIN (A,B)*X - SQRT(A) .GT. 0.3) THEN
```

5. Same exercise as 4, except that 5 is coded as $Y = 3.*T**2 + 2.*T - 1$.

6. Write statement functions to perform the following:

   a. $C = A^2 + B^2 - 2AB \cos(C)$ Length of one side of a triangle.

   b. $A = P(1 + I/J)^{J \cdot T}$ Compound interest: P is fixed.

   c. $A = P(1 + R)^N$ Simple interest: P is fixed.

   d. $1/R = 1/R1 + 1/R2 + 1/R3$ Compute R: Total resistance.

   e. $Q = .92A(T_1 - T_0)/H$ Heat flow: H is fixed.

   f. $E = 1 + X + X^2/2! + X^3/3!$ Approximation to e^x.

   g. $y = be^{-ax} \cos(\sqrt{b^2 - a^2x - t})$ a is a fixed value.

7. Write a statement function that computes the approximate difference between two dates M1, D1, Y1 and M2, D2, Y2. (M = month, D = day, Y = year; assume 365.25 days per year and 30.4 days per month.) Then compute the number of hours that you have slept since you were born, assuming that you sleep eight hours per day.

8. Write a statement function that rounds a value Q to the nearest hundredth.

9. Write a statement function that computes the remainder after dividing argument X by argument Y, for example, 15/7 has remainder 2.

10. Write a statement function that computes the length of the hypotenuse of a right triangle, given sides A and B. (*Note:* $H^2 = A^2 + B^2$.)

Answers

1. `DET(A1,A2,A3,A4) = A1*A4-A3*A2`

2. **a.** `V(R) = 3.14 * R ** 3`

   b. `Y(X) = A*X*X*X+B*X*X+C*X+D` or
   `Y(A,B,C,D,X) = A*X**3+B*X**2+C*X+D`

   c. `Q(X) = X*SIN(X/57.3)+X**2*COS(X/57.3)`

   d. `DIF(A,B,C,D) = ABS(AMAX1(A,B,C,D)-AMIN1(A,B,C,D))`

3. **a.** Invalid; dimensioned variable cannot be a dummy argument list.

   b. Invalid; function cannot refer to itself.

   c. Valid.

   d. Valid.

   e. Invalid; function definition must precede executable statements.

   f. Valid; dummy variables may be used as actual variables in a program.

   g. Invalid; dummy arguments may not be constants.

   h. Valid.

   i. Invalid; number of arguments in function reference and function definition do not match.

   j. Invalid; expression $(X + 1)$ cannot be used as a dummy argument.

   k. Invalid; type of actual arguments must match type of dummy arguments.

4.
```
REAL L,J,I
FN(L,J,A) = L*X*X + J*X - A
Y = FN(3.,2.,1.)
T = FN(I,7.,TOT)
S = FN(3.,-K(2),-SIN(T))
IF(FN(17.,MIN(A,B),SQRT(A)).GT.0.3) THEN
```

5.
```
REAL L,J,I
FN(L,J,A,Y) = L*Y*Y + J*Y - A
Y = FN(3.,2.,1.,T)
T = FN(I,7.,TOT,X)
S = FN(3.,-K(2),-SIN(T),X)
IF(FN(17.,MIN(A,B),SQRT(A),X) .GT. 0.3) THEN
```

6. **a.** `SIDE(A,B,C) = A*A + B*B - 2.*A*B*COS(C)`

   b. `A(T,AI,J) = P*(1. + AI/J)**(J*T)`

   c. `SINT(R,N) = P*(1. + R)**N`

   d. `R(R1,R2,R3) = (1./R1 + 1./R2 + 1./R3)**(-1)`

   e. `HF(A,TI,TO) = .92*A*(TI - TO)/H`

   f. `E(X) = 1. + X*X + X*X/2. + X**3/6.`

   g. `F(B,ASM,X,T) = B*EXP(-A*X)*COS(SQRT(B*B-A**2*X - T))`

7. `APPROX(M,D,Y) = 365.25*Y + (M-1)*30.4 + D`
   `PROX(M1,D1,Y1,M2,D2,Y2) = ABS(APPROX(M1,D1,Y1)-APPROX(M2,D2, Y2))`

8. `ROUND(Q) = INT((Q + 0.005)*100.)/100.`

9. `REM(X,Y) = X - INT(X/Y)*Y`

10. `HYP(A,B) = SQRT(A**2 + B**2)`

Appendix F
Global Storage; COMMON and BLOCK DATA

F.1 LOCAL VERSUS GLOBAL STORAGE

Local storage consists of those variables or arrays that are defined in a program module and that are not accessible to other program modules. Global storage refers to variables or arrays that can be directly accessible to any number of program modules. In this case, *directly accessible* means that the data does not need to be passed as arguments in a particular calling sequence. Global storage is provided to program modules by means of either blank COMMON or named COMMON blocks.

Whether global or local, storage implies either numeric storage (integer, real, logical, double precision, complex) or character storage.

F.2 BLANK COMMON

One way to pass data from one subprogram to another is to specify each data item (variable) in the argument lists of the CALL and SUBROUTINE statements or in the FUNCTION invocation statement and FUNCTION subprogram. It should be noted that the dummy arguments of the subroutine function do not really have a fixed memory address. When a dummy variable is encountered in the subprogram, the system must look up the address of the corresponding argument in the calling program and process the contents (value) of that memory location or use it for storage (output argument). For example,

Calling Program	*Memory*	*Comments*

```
A = 1.0
B = 2.0
CALL SUB(A)
   .
   .
CALL SUB(B)
   .
   .
```

As a result of the first call to SUB, Z points to the address of A in memory. As a result of the second call to SUB, Z points to the address of B in memory.

```
SUBROUTINE SUB(Z)
```

Another way to pass data from one subprogram to another is to use the COMMON statement. Variables to be shared among subprograms are declared in a COMMON statement. COMMON can be thought of as a block of memory locations that can be accessed (shared) by any program containing a COMMON statement. The names of the variables that refer to the data in the COMMON block may be different in the various subprograms—the ordering and length of the variables in COMMON determines which names in one program will be associated with which names in another program.

The use of COMMON in a subprogram offers immediate access to data in memory; there is no "look-up address" procedure as in the case of dummy variables (subroutine arguments), since each variable in COMMON has a predetermined (fixed) memory address:

EXAMPLE 1

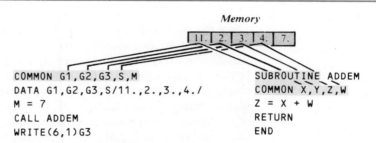

```
COMMON G1,G2,G3,S,M                    SUBROUTINE ADDEM
DATA G1,G2,G3,S/11.,2.,3.,4./          COMMON X,Y,Z,W
M = 7                                  Z = X + W
CALL ADDEM                             RETURN
WRITE(6,1)G3                           END
```

G1 and X identify the first element of the COMMON block, G2 and Y refer to the second element of the COMMON block, and so forth. M refers to the fifth element of the block. It is not used by subroutine ADDEM; it could be used by another subprogram. This subroutine adds the first and fourth elements of the COMMON block and stores the result in the third location. Hence Z = 11. + 4. = 15. In the main program, the name of the third element of the COMMON block is G3, hence G3 = 15. Note that M is not shared by the subroutine ADDEM.

EXAMPLE 2

```
COMMON X(4),A,I,B(2)
      ⋮
CALL XYZ(TOTAL)
WRITE(6,4)TOTAL
```

COMMON block

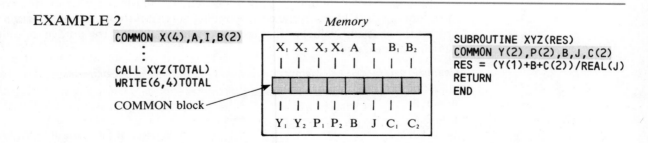

```
SUBROUTINE XYZ(RES)
COMMON Y(2),P(2),B,J,C(2)
RES = (Y(1)+B+C(2))/REAL(J)
RETURN
END
```

The resulting value for TOTAL is $(X(1) + A + B(2))/REAL(I)$

EXAMPLE 3

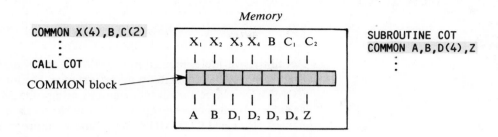

Note the correspondence between the data items in COMMON.

The general form of the COMMON specification statement is:

COMMON *list of variables*

where the *list of variables* can contain either variables or array names.

Dummy arguments specified in a subroutine or function argument list may not be declared in a COMMON statement. Variables listed in COMMON **may not** be initialized through the DATA statement. The COMMON statement can be used instead of a type or DIMENSION statement to declare arrays; the following three coding sequences have same effect:

```
REAL X              or   REAL X(100)   or  COMMON X(100)
COMMON X(100)            COMMON X
```

However, ```REAL X(100)```   is invalid.
          ```COMMON X(100)```

```
          COMMON A,B
Note that  COMMON D(5)   is equivalent to COMMON A,B,D(5),K
          COMMON K
```

Both give rise to the following COMMON block arrangement:

| A | B | D_1 | D_2 | D_3 | D_4 | D_5 | K |

COMMON block arrangement.

The placement of COMMON statement within the FORTRAN program is shown in Figure A.3 in Appendix A. COMMON can be used to great advantage when there is a data base that is needed by several subprograms. It is often more convenient to transmit a lengthy sequence of variables with a COMMON statement than to transmit them as arguments in the calling sequence of a subprogram. A list of COMMON statements can be copied and included in the various subprograms requiring it.
```

F.3 NAMED COMMON BLOCKS

Recall that variables located in COMMON are available to any program containing the COMMON statement. In many instances the number of variables contained in COMMON is large and all subprograms using COMMON do not require access to all variables. In such cases it is possible to construct named blocks of COMMON. These named or labeled COMMON blocks allow subprograms to access only those COMMON blocks that are needed.

EXAMPLE

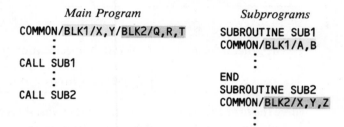

```
        Main Program                    Subprograms
COMMON/BLK1/X,Y/BLK2/Q,R,T      SUBROUTINE SUB1
    .                          COMMON/BLK1/A,B
    .
CALL SUB1                           .
    .                               .
    .                          END
CALL SUB2                      SUBROUTINE SUB2
                               COMMON/BLK2/X,Y,Z
                                    .
                                    .
```

In this example, two blocks of COMMON are defined in the main program. Note that the two subroutines do not share any COMMON area with one another; however, each shares a separate COMMON area with the main program. In BLK1, A refers to X while B refers to Y. In BLK2, X refers to Q, Y refers to R, and Z refers to T.

The general form of the COMMON specification statement is:

> COMMON [/*block name*/] *list of variables* [/*block name*/] *list of variables*...

where   COMMON is a required key word,
          block name is the name of the block COMMON, and
          slashes (/) are a required part of the statement.

If the block name is omitted, the variables are placed in unnamed (sometimes called *blank*) COMMON (see section F.2). The position of the named COMMON blocks within a program is shown in Figure A.3 in Appendix A. Standard FORTRAN requires that all COMMON blocks of the same name must have the same length in all subprograms in which they appear. **Also, if a COMMON block contains any character variables or character arrays, then it cannot contain any variables or arrays of any other type, i.e., integer, real, double precision, logical, or complex data.**

EXAMPLES

```
COMMON/XYZ/X(10),Y(100)/ABC/RR(100)
COMMON A,B,C(10)/BLOCK3/Q,R,S
```

Three blocks of COMMON are named XYZ, ABC, and BLOCK3, while blank COMMON contains the variables A, B, and ten elements of C.

F.4 BLOCK DATA

One way to initialize variables or arrays that appear in named COMMON is through the BLOCK DATA subprogram. Suppose that each element of array R in block BLK2 is to be initialized to 0 and the variable SEX in block BLK1 is to be initialized to "MALE". The following code can be used:

Main Program	*Subprogram*

```
Main Program                          Subprogram
CHARACTER*4 BE,M*1,Y(4)*3             BLOCK DATA
REAL R(10),ITEM                      REAL R(10),ITEM
COMMON /BLK1/M,Y,SEX/BLK2/R,ITEM     CHARACTER*4 NE,L,Z(4)*3
    :                                COMMON /BLK2/R,ITEM
    :                                COMMON /BLK1/L,Z,NE
                                     DATA R/10*0./
                                     DATA CODE/'MALE'/
                                     END
```

Note that the first statement of the subprogram is:

```
BLOCK DATA
```

and the last statement is:

```
END
```

There are no executable statements and no RETURN statement. The only statements allowed besides the COMMON statements are DATA statements and specification statements. If a variable or array is to be initialized, the entire named COMMON block in which it is stored must be specified. All dimensions and type specifications must agree with those in the main program. Standard FORTRAN does not allow blank COMMON in BLOCK data.

CODE, which corresponds to SEX, is declared a CHARACTER*4 variable and is initialized to "MALE" in the DATA statement. Since BLK1 contains character data, no other type of data except character data can be specified in BLK1.

Note how the array R is initialized to zeros in the BLOCK DATA subprogram, while ITEM is not initialized at all.

Appendix G
Multiple Program Entries, EXTERNAL and INTRINSIC Statements, and the EQUIVALENCE Statement

G.1 MULTIPLE ENTRIES IN SUBPROGRAMS

The ENTRY statement allows subroutines or functions to be entered at different points in the subprogram. The general form of this statement, which appears in the subprogram, is:

$$\boxed{\text{ENTRY } name\,(p_1, p_2, p_3, \ldots)}$$

where   *name* is any valid variable name (in a function subprogram, this name returns a value to the calling program);

$p_1, p_2, \ldots$ are dummy arguments used to communicate data to and from the calling program.

Notice that the words SUBROUTINE or FUNCTION do not precede the word ENTRY.

Consider the following example, where subroutine RMAT calculates the sum of the rows of an array and then the sum of the columns of the same array. If you simply want to calculate the sums of the columns of an array, you can enter RMAT at the beginning of the code which computes the column sums, for example:

Main Program

```
     REAL X(2,3),RS(2),CS(3)
     CALL MAT(X,2,3)
   4 READ(5,6,END=40)I,J
     X(I,J) = X(I,J) + 1.
     GO TO 4
  40 CALL RMAT(X,2,3,RS,CS)
       .
       .
     CALL CMAT(X,2,3,CS)
       .
       .
```

Subprogram

```
     SUBROUTINE MAT(A,N,M)
     REAL A(N,M),RSUM(N),CSUM(M)
     DO 10 I = 1,N
        DO 4 J = I,M
   4       A(I,J) = 0.
  10 CONTINUE
     RETURN
     ENTRY RMAT(A,N,M,RSUM,CSUM)
     DO 6 I = 1,N
        RSUM(I) = 0.
        DO 8 J = 1,M
   8       RSUM(I)=RSUM(I)+A(I,J)
   6 CONTINUE
     ENTRY CMAT(A,N,M,CSUM)
     DO 17 J = 1,M
        CSUM(J) = 0.
        DO 19 I = 1,N
  19       CSUM(J)=CSUM(J)+A(I,J)
  17 CONTINUE
     RETURN
     END
```

The first CALL in the main program is to SUBROUTINE MAT, which sets each element of the two-dimensional array X to zero, then control is returned to the main program. (If there had been no RETURN statement after 10 CONTINUE, then the statements after ENTRY RMAT(A,N,M,RSUM,CSUM) and ENTRY CMAT (A,N,M, CSUM) would have been executed also. ENTRY statements are nonexecutable statements and are ignored at execution time.) The second CALL is to RMAT. This call causes execution to start at the first executable statement after ENTRY RMAT. First the row sums are calculated and then the column sums. Finally, the last CALL is to CMAT, and entry occurs at that point in the subroutine. The column sums are calculated and returned to the main program. Notice that all DIMENSION and specification statements are positioned after the SUBROUTINE statement, and *not* after the ENTRY statements.

G.2 MULTIPLE RETURNS FROM SUBROUTINES

When a RETURN is executed in a subroutine, execution in the main program resumes at the statement immediately following the CALL statement. If you want to return to different points in the calling program depending on outcomes in the subroutine, the multiple return can be used.

The general form of the multiple return is:

$$CALL\ name\,(p_1, p_2, * s_1, p_3, * s_2, \ldots)$$

where   *name* is a valid subroutine name;

$p_1, p_2, \ldots$ are arguments used to communicate data to and from the subroutine;

$s_1, s_2, \ldots$ are statement numbers of statements in the main program where control is to be returned (these *must* be preceded by the asterisk or the ampersand (&) symbol in the argument list to differentiate them from constants). The statement numbers can be specified in any order in the CALL argument list.

In the subprogram single asterisks are used to link to the various return points as follows:

```
SUBROUTINE name (p₁, p₂, * , p₃, * ,...)
.
.
RETURN 1      returns to s₁
.
.
RETURN 2      returns to s₂
.
.
RETURN
END
```

where   *name* is a valid subroutine name;

$p_1, p_2, \ldots$ are dummy arguments used to communicate data to and from the calling program;

Asterisks(*) correspond to the $* s_1$, $* s_2$, ... in the calling program's CALL argument list;

RETURN 1 means execution returns to the main program at the statement corresponding to the first * encountered in the CALL argument list;

RETURN 2 means execution returns to the statement corresponding to the second * encountered in the CALL argument list, and so on.

It is also valid to specify RETURN N where N is an integer variable.

EXAMPLE   The following main program and subroutine determine the roots of the equation $ax^2 + bx + c = 0$.

Main Program	Subroutine

```
      Main Program                          Subroutine
60 READ(5,3,END = 80)A,B,C          SUBROUTINE ROOTS(A,*,B,C,*,*)
   CALL ROOTS(A,&5,B,C,&8,&10)      IF (A.EQ.0.0 .AND. B.NE.0.0)RETURN 1
   DI = SQRT(B**2 - 4.*A*C)         DISC = B**2 - 4.*A*C
   R1 = (-B - DI)/(2.*A)            IF (DISC .EQ. 0.0)  RETURN 3
   R2 = (-B + DI)/(2.*A)            IF (DISC .LT. 0.0)  RETURN 2
   WRITE(6,7)R1,R2                  RETURN
   GO TO 60                         END
 5 R = -C/B
   WRITE(6,7)R
   GO TO 60
 8 WRITE(6,81)
   GO TO 60
10 RD = -B/(2.*A)
   WRITE(6,7)RD,RD
   GO TO 60
 3 FORMAT(3F5.1)
 7 FORMAT(1X,2(F10.2,2X))
81 FORMAT(1X,'COMPLEX ROOTS')
80 STOP
   END
```

Meaning
RETURN1 means return to statement 5
RETURN2 means return to statement 8
RETURN3 means return to statement 10

In the subroutine, if A = 0 and B ≠ 0, execution is returned to statement 5 in the main program. If $B^2 - 4AC = 0$, execution returns to statement 10 (the statement that corresponds to the third asterisk). If $B^2 - 4AC < 0$, return is to statement 8. If none of these conditions is true, that is, if $B^2 - 4AC > 0$, control is returned to the statement following the CALL. In each case appropriate messages are printed about the roots.

G.3 THE EXTERNAL AND INTRINSIC STATEMENTS

Suppose we want to determine the maximum value taken on by each of the following functions in the specified intervals:

1. $y = 3x^3 - 2x^2 - 14$ x ranges from 2 to 10 in increments of 3.
2. $y = \sqrt{(x - 4)(x + 6)}$ x ranges from -4 to 5 in increments of 1.
3. $y = \sin(x)$ x ranges from .1 to 1.1 in increments of .1.

We can write two function subprograms, POLY for the first function and SQPOLY for the second function, as shown in Figure G.1. The third function, sin x, does not need to be written since it is a library function.

A subroutine MAXI can be written to calculate the maximum value for any function within a given range. In order for MAXI to know which of the above three functions are to be processed, the name of the function must be one of the arguments transmitted to MAXI. To ensure against the function name arguments POLY, SQPOLY, and SIN being interpreted by MAXI as ordinary variable names in the calling program, the calling program must declare the names of the user-written functions in the EXTERNAL statement and the names of any other compiler-available functions (SIN,SQRT, and so forth) in the INTRINSIC statement. In Figure G.1 the name of the dummy argument representing the particular function to be processed in MAXI is FUNC.

```
EXTERNAL POLY,SQPOLY
INTRINSIC SIN
CALL MAXI(2.,10.,3.,POLY)

CALL MAXI(-4.,5.,1.,SQPOLY)

CALL MAXI(.1,1.1,.1,SIN)
STOP
END


SUBROUTINE MAXI(INIT,TER,INC,FUNC)
REAL INIT,TER,INC,MAX
MAX = FUNC(INIT)
7  IF(INIT .LE. TER)THEN
     IF(FUNC(INIT).GT.MAX)MAX=FUNC(INIT)
     INIT = INIT + INC
     GO TO 7
   ENDIF
8  WRITE(6,3)MAX
3  FORMAT(1X,F10.2)
   RETURN
   END


FUNCTION POLY(X)
POLY = 3.*X**3 - 2.*X**2 - 14.0
RETURN
END


FUNCTION SQPOLY(X)
SQPOLY = SQRT((X - 4.)*(X + 6.))
RETURN
END
```

In the main program POLY, SQPOLY, and SIN are to be construed as function names.
The interval for POLY is [2, 10], and the increment value is 3. Find the maximum value of POLY in that interval.
Go find the maximum value taken on by function SQPOLY in the interval [−4, 5]. Increment is 1.
Find maximum sine value in interval .1 to 1.1. Increment is .1.

The range of the function FUNC is [INIT, TER].

Assume maximum function value is FUNC(INIT).
The first time FUNC is actually POLY, and hence POLY(2), POLY(5), POLY(8) ... will be computed.
Later on, FUNC will be the sine function, and the maximum value for the sine function in the interval .1 to 1.1 will be printed.

FIGURE G.1
USE OF THE EXTERNAL STATEMENT

The general forms of the INTRINSIC and EXTERNAL specification statements are:

> EXTERNAL *name1*, *name2*, ...
> INTRINSIC *name a*, *name b*, ...

where   *name1*, *name2*,... are names for user-written subprograms that are to be passed as arguments to a function or subroutine subprogram.

name *a*, name *b*,... are names of intrinsic functions (functions available to the FORTRAN compiler) that are to be passed as arguments to a function or subroutine subprogram.

The positioning of these two specification statements within the FORTRAN program is shown in Figure A.3 in Appendix A.

G.4 SHARING STORAGE: THE EQUIVALENCE STATEMENT

The EQUIVALENCE specification statement can be used to share storage; it assigns two or more names to the same storage unit. For example, EQUIVALENCE(A,B) causes the variables A and B to have the same address; i.e., any reference to A is equivalent to a reference to B and vice versa. A and B should be thought of as different names for the same memory location. Consider the following example:

```
EQUIVALENCE(A,B)
A = 1.
B = 3.
WRITE(6,11)A        The value written for A will be 3.
```

The general form of the EQUIVALENCE statement is:

> EQUIVALENCE (*list of variables*)...

Each variable in the *list of variables* is thus declared to be equivalent to the others. The variables can be subscripted variable names. Any equivalenced variables should be of the same type.

The positioning of the EQUIVALENCE specification statement within the FORTRAN program is shown in Figure A.3 in Appendix A.

EXAMPLE
```
CHARACTER*5 FIRST,LAST
INTEGER ZZZ,R,STU
REAL X,Y
EQUIVALENCE (X,Y),(ZZZ,R,STU),(FIRST,LAST)
```

The variables X and Y share the same memory locations; ZZZ, R, and STU all refer to the same storage location; and FIRST and LAST occupy the same storage units.

Arrays or parts of arrays can be equivalenced by specifying the starting location at which sequential matching between array elements is desired. Assume arrays A and B are to be equivalenced. The following code could be used:

```
INTEGER A(5),B(5)
EQUIVALENCE (A(1),B(1))
or
EQUIVALENCE (A(5),B(5))          yields the pairing
```
$$\begin{array}{ccccc} A_1 & A_2 & A_3 & A_4 & A_5 \\ B_1 & B_2 & B_3 & B_4 & B_5 \end{array}$$

```
INTEGER A(5),B(5)
EQUIVALENCE (A(1),X),(B(5),Y)    yields the pairing
```
$$\begin{array}{cc} A_1 & B_5 \\ X & Y \end{array}$$

```
REAL A(5),B(4),C(2)
EQUIVALENCE (A(3),B(2),C(1))     yields the pairing
```
$$\begin{array}{ccccc} A_1 & A_2 & A_3 & A_4 & A_5 \\ & B_1 & B_2 & B_3 & B_4 \\ & & C_1 & C_2 & \end{array}$$

Character strings may be equivalenced in an overlapping fashion as shown in the following example.

```
CHARACTER A*7, B*7, C(2)*5       yields
EQUIVALENCE (A(6:7),B),(B(4:),C(2))
```

For two-dimensional arrays, the matching sequence is performed according to the linear memory sequence in which multidimensional arrays are represented.

The EQUIVALENCE statement is sometimes used when two or more programmers working independently on program segments have used different names for the same variable. Rather than rewrite the entire program with the same variable names, the EQUIVALENCE statement can be used. The EQUIVALENCE statement also allows the programmer to reuse arrays that might otherwise be used only once in a program. To reuse the same array for a different purpose and to avoid name confusion, the same array can be given a different name as shown in this example:

EXAMPLE

```
REAL A(10,10),AINVER(10,10),TEMP(10,10)
EQUIVALENCE (AINVER(1,1),TEMP(1,1))
        .
        .
        .
WRITE(6,1)AINVER
        .
        .
READ(5,11)TEMP
```

WRITE(6,1)AINVER — The inverse matrix has now been computed. Write it out. At this point in the program AINVER is no longer needed.

READ(5,11)TEMP — Let us use the storage of AINVER for some temperatures. Calling the array AINVER could be misleading, so we call it TEMP.

Index